HANDBOOK OF MUSIC PSYCHOLOGY

HANDBOOK

OF MUSIC

PSYCHOLOGY

second edition

Donald A. Hodges, editor

MMB
MMB MUSIC, INC.
CONTEMPORARY ARTS BUILDING
3526 WASHINGTON AVENUE
SAINT LOUIS, MISSOURI 63103-1019 USA
314 531-9635; 800 543-3771 (USA/Canada); Fax 314 531-8384
http://www.mmbmusic.com

IMR Press   San Antonio

IMR Press, The University of Texas at San Antonio, San Antonio 78249-0645
© 1996 by The University of Texas at San Antonio
All rights reserved
Manufactured in the United States of America

1999   1998   1997   1996   4   3   2   1

ISBN (paper):   0-9648803-0-X

Preface

This edition of the *Handbook of Music Psychology* appears fifteen years after the first. While much could be written about how the discipline has changed over the years, I will restrict my comments to three general topics—the literature of music psychology, the notion of ecological validity, and the notion of research teams—and to two topics specifically related to this edition of the *Handbook*—redundancies among chapters and the term *nonmusician*.

In chapter 1, Eagle comments on the growth of the literature and, certainly in recent years, many more books and articles have been published. The periodical literature, in particular, appears in a wide array of journals, each reflecting many different disciplines. Electronic databases are providing faster and easier access to this literature.

Whether the literature in music psychology is abundant or not depends on one's perspective. Conducting a literature review on a major topic may seem daunting, as one may be faced with as many as several hundred sources to peruse. However, throughout the *Handbook*, the reader will frequently encounter an author's call for more research on a given topic, because there is insufficient information from which to derive definitive conclusions. This is especially true in comparison to the literature in some other scholarly fields. By way of example, consider the figures I obtained in preparing an article on music reading for the *Handbook of Research on Music Teaching and Learning* (Hodges 1992). Wishing to compare music reading research with research on language reading, I made estimates of fewer than 250 music reading research studies, while more than 12,000 studies in language research were conducted between 1879 and 1972 (Singer 1983). Similarly, more than 400 studies are reviewed in the chapter on neuromusical research (chap. 7), but this must surely be only a small fraction of the studies published on the neurological aspects of language, for example.

Thus, the field of music psychology is developing a rich and ever-expanding research base. At the same time, it must be recognized that the field is in need of a great deal more research before a more secure understanding of the phenomenon of musical behavior can be obtained.

The concept of external or ecological validity—the extent to which the results of a given experiment reflect circumstances as they normally occur outside the research lab—also bears some thought. Those engaged in music psychology research must continue to reflect on whether the experimental results obtained are genuinely moving us toward a greater understanding of the musical experience. For example, consider the auditory stimuli that are frequently used in experiments. Often, these are carefully controlled experiments where only one attribute of sound (e.g., frequency) is varied as the other attributes are held constant. Such rigid laboratory control is necessary to obtain high internal validity—the extent to which independent variables are controlled. But high internal validity often comes at the expense of external validity.

Placing the same stimuli in a more musical context may change the results of the experimental findings entirely. For example, as reported in chapter 5, eliminating the attack transient (the first portion of a sound wave) of a single instrumental tone made it difficult for subjects to identify the instrumental source (Saldanha and Corso 1964). However, when a melody was constructed of similarly prepared tones (i.e., the attack was removed), listeners had no difficulty in identifying the instrumental timbres (Kendall 1986). The point of this brief discussion is not to denigrate or to discourage studies with high internal validity. Obviously, that is one criterion of good research. Rather, the point is simply to encourage researchers to continue to consider whether findings obtained in constrained, perhaps even artificial, situations apply to musical experiences as they occur in the real world.

Even when experiments are conducted with high "musical validity," one must always be aware of the larger picture. For example, one might conduct an experiment in music cognition in which great care has been taken to create a musical context. Imagine that the dependent variable was what subjects heard in the music and that the responses allowed for comments on melody, rhythm, and so on. However, in the real world of music listening, there are a host of sensations that interact with the musical stimulus to create the total human experience.

In the concert hall, for example, one can be aware of many sounds other than the music itself (e.g., the sounds of other audience members coughing or rustling programs). Then, there are visual sensations (e.g., of the performers, of other audience members, of the physical surroundings, etc.), physical sensations (e.g., of being hungry, sleepy, bored, or restless; of an uncomfortable chair; of a choking necktie or tight shoes, etc.). There can even be smell sensations, as one might be seated next to someone with a very strong cologne. One's mental concentration and corresponding affective responses might be focused totally on the music, might be completely distracted, or might be tuned in on the music intermittently.

The point, again, is not to denigrate extant research, but simply to recognize that the comprehensive world of the musical experience is an enormously complicated one. Thus, while we should celebrate the many advances in music psychology that are reflected in the pages of this *Handbook*, we can also be humbled at the enormity of the task of explaining the phenomenon of music that still remains.

The history of music psychology has been a somewhat dichotomous one in terms of the orientation of the researchers involved. To generalize, researchers are generally professional scientists with less formal training in music or professional musicians with less formal training in science. Thus, the research literature often reflects these biases and their corresponding strengths and weaknesses. One obvious solution is to create research teams comprising researchers from different disciplines, and there is some apparent movement in this direction. Perhaps in the future we will see the benefits of such an integrated approach.

With regard to this edition of the *Handbook*, a brief note concerning redundancies might be in order because several topics are discussed in more than one chapter. There are at least two defensible reasons for this: (1) not all readers will read the chapters in order; thus, each chapter must stand alone as much as possible; (2) topics receive different levels of treatment (i.e., cursory or in-depth discussions) and different viewpoints from different authors. Thus, the redundancies are construed to be helpful.

Finally, near the end of chapter 2 there is a brief discussion of the term *nonmusician* that really applies to the entire book. The gist of this discussion is that, while the term is frequently used in the research literature to refer to those individuals who do not display specific musical behaviors (e.g., ability to match pitch or read music), it is not an accurate label. There is no such thing as a nonmusician, because all human beings are capable of some response to the music of their culture. After all, the massive amount of information contained in this book convincingly attests to the fact that we are characterized by our musicality as human beings. That fact alone is justification for a book such as this, for scholars to spend their careers conducting relevant research, for all persons interested in human musical behavior to learn the discipline, and for practitioners to apply it.

viii Preface

Hodges, D. 1992. The acquisition of music reading skills. In *Handbook of research in music teaching and learning*, ed. R. Colwell, 466–71. New York: Schirmer Books.

Kendall, R. 1986. The role of acoustic signal partitions in listener categorization of musical phrases. *Music Perception* 4:185–213.

Saldanha, E., and J. Corso. 1964. Timbre cues and the identification of musical instruments. *Journal of the Acoustical Society of America* 36:2021–26.

Singer, H. 1983. A critique of Jack Holmes's study: The substrate factor theory of reading and its history and conceptual relationship to interaction theory. In *Reading research revisited*, ed. L. Gentile, M. Kamil, and J. Blanchard, 9–25. Columbus: Merrill.

Acknowledgments

As is true with any project of this nature, there are many people to thank for their assistance. Of course, the authors deserve congratulations for committing themselves to paper. Charles Eagle, Julene Johnson, Terry Mikiten, and Ralph Spintge each read one or more chapters and made valuable comments. John Vander Weg served as production editor for this project and edited the manuscript. Sandra Rickett, David Sebald, Brian Harris, and Jim Balentine provided invaluable assistance to the editor, and Jennifer Dielmann turned the manuscript into pages. My grateful appreciation is extended to each of these individuals for his or her contributions to this book.

Contents

1

An Introductory Perspective on Music Psychology

Charles T. Eagle, Jr.

I am excited by the thoughts expressed in this book—what they are and what they say, who says them and how they say them, and why they are said. Those of us who have been working in this field heretofore called "psychology of music" will recognize immediately that this second edition of the *Handbook,* as was the first, has been written, compiled, and edited by professionally trained musicians. These authors are not only trained in the art of music, however, but also are educated in the science of their musical craft. Thus, they have scientifically explored the influence of music on behavior as well as behavioral responses to music. These artistic and scientific explorations have led them to use investigatory strategies incorporated in such disciplines as neurology, physics, physiology, psychology, and socioanthropology. The result has been to provide more *meaningful* applications of findings from these research endeavors to such areas as music composition, music education, music history, music medicine, music performance, music theory, music therapy, and performing arts medicine. The consequence is a quickening awareness of the quintessential importance of music and its function in the life of humankind.

Definition of Music Psychology

The *American Heritage Dictionary* (1982) defines *psychology* as "the emotional and behavioral characteristics of an individual, group, or activity." Psychology, then, may be defined rather broadly as the study of human behavior. As such, this clearly incorporates the various facets of human study through neurology, physiology, and so on. And because music is human behavior, the totality of its study is called Music Psychology.[1] Thus,

---

1. Because the term is a topical, all-encompassing one, as well as being descriptive of the discipline it represents, Music Psychology shall be capitalized throughout the remainder of this chapter.

music describes the action of human endeavors, which we call *psychology*. In this context, *music* and *psychology* are seen as both adjectives and nouns, as both processes and products. I think Carl Seashore,[2] who can be considered the "father of Music Psychology," was alluding to this reasoning when he said that "we may speak of the psychology of musical esthetics, the science of musical esthetics, or possibly, merely musical esthetics" (1938, 375).

But more specifically, what is the subject content of Music Psychology? This question has been a plaguing one during the 27 years I have been developing the Computer-Assisted Information Retrieval Service System (CAIRSS) for Music, an on-line bibliographic database of music research literature. Accordingly, I have had to look in the past, at the present, and into the future for clues as to the composition of what we call Music Psychology. Consider the descriptive molecule model in figure 1 and the following definition.

> Defining music as organized sounds and silences in a flow of time [and in space], several tentative conclusions and questions have arisen: Music→Sound→Vibration (?). And vibration [energy] is the essence of all things [mass]. . . .
>
> But, if music is organized sound, then can we get a better perspective of the essence of music if we study unorganized sound defined as noise? Can we understand music and its influences better if we know the influences of nonmusic (noise)? In what ways do these musical and nonmusical sounds influence behavior, human and infrahuman? What are the biological effects? Physiological? Neurological? Psychological? Sociological? Anthropological? Acoustical? Educational? Therapeutic? (Eagle 1978, vi)

The disciplines I have just enumerated (and others) furnish scientific and artistic approaches in studying the influence of music on behavior and, conversely, behavioral responses to music. Via findings from and methods used by the various sciences, we will make significant strides toward understanding more fully that "music, a form of human behavior, is unique and powerful in its influence" (Gaston 1968a, 7). One of the intriguing aspects of the sciences is that they are not independent of one another. Indeed, they are quite interrelated. For example, we often hear of psychobiology, psychophysics, biochemistry, or neuropsychiatry. But, as a cursory

---

2. During more than 40 years of service to the University of Iowa beginning in 1897, Carl Emil Seashore was Professor of Psychology, Director of the Psychology Laboratory, Dean of the Graduate College, and later Dean Emeritus. A complete bibliography of his published works can be found in Miles 1956.

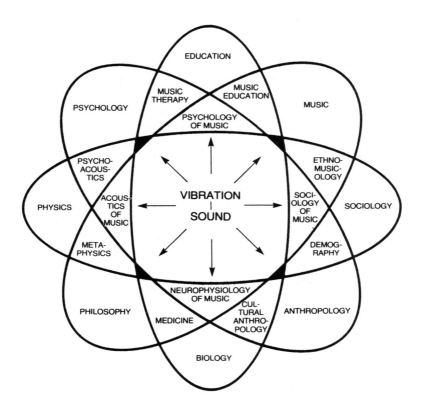

Fig. 1. Descriptive molecule model of the interdisciplinary world of Music Psychology. (Eagle and Miniter 1984. Reprinted by permission.)

review of course offerings in a university department of psychology will show, it is usually left to the psychologist to interpret and apply findings from the various disciplines. As Hargreaves points out, Music Psychology

> includes neurological and physiological investigations of the biological bases of music perception, and hemispheric lateralisation studies; acoustical and psychophysical studies of the mechanisms of auditory perception; cognitive psychological studies . . . ; psychometric analyses of musical ability . . . ; developmental studies of the acquisition of musical skills; social psychological investigations

of the aesthetic and affective aspects of music listening . . . ;
"applied" studies in the fields of therapy, education, and industry;
and so on. (Hargreaves 1986, 3)

The Music Psychologist, then, has to take the "responsibility and
initiative for the work of integration which would otherwise fall for want
of a sponsor" (Seashore 1938, 375).[3] With certainty, Music Psychologists
must be interdisciplinary, even multidisciplinary, in their attempt to
resolve the questions raised in observing the influence of and responses to music. (Similarly, those in other disciplines should be aware
of research in Music Psychology.) I am talking about the necessary merg-
ing of the art and science of music, assimilating the information from
this union, and taking the responsibility for disseminating the outcome
of this merger into educational and clinical practices and curricular plans,
research projects, and theoretical models. Many have harkened to this
clarion call, as you shall see in the following sections of this chapter and
in the chapters that follow in this book.

Review of the Past

Textbooks

To help you gain some perspective of what has been happening in Music Psychology over the past 135 years, I first will present a listed review
and overall commentary of textbooks published in the discipline.[4] This
review does not include all books in Music Psychology, but it does include those landmark texts that were available to me for inclusion in
this chapter. Undoubtedly, there are others of which I am not aware.
These books are listed chronologically by publication date in table 1.

TABLE 1.   Chronological Summary of Textbooks Published in
Music Psychology

Year	Author(s)	Title of Book
1862	Helmholtz	*On the Sensations of Tone*
1883	Stumpf	*Tonpsychologie, Volume 1*

(*continued*)

3. Other authors have written about the interdisciplinary nature of Music Psychology, most notably Farnsworth (1958 and 1969), Franklin (1972), and Phelps (1975).
    4. In the first edition of this book, I presented annotations of texts of Music Psychol-
ogy published up to 1980.

TABLE 1—*Continued*

Year	Author(s)	Title of Book
1890	Stumpf	*Tonpsychologie, Volume 2*
1895	Billroth	*Wer ist Musikalisch?*
1899	Bartholomew	*Relation of Psychology to Music*
1902	Bartholomew	*Relation of Psychology to Music*, 2d ed.
1919	Seashore	*The Psychology of Musical Talent*
1925	Révész	*The Psychology of a Musical Prodigy*
1926	Kries	*Wer is Musikalisch?*
1927	Howes	*The Borderland of Music and Psychology*
1927	Kwalwasser	*Tests and Measurements in Music*
1927	Schoen, ed.	*The Effects of Music*
1927	Swisher	*Psychology for the Music Teacher*
1929	Meyer	*The Musician's Arithmetic*
1930	Farnsworth	*Short Studies in Musical Psychology*
1931	Mursell and Glenn	*The Psychology of School Music Teaching*
1931	Pratt	*The Meaning of Music*
1931	Vidor	*Was ist Musikalität?*
1937	Jeans	*Science and Music*
1937	Mursell	*The Psychology of Music*
1938	Seashore	*Psychology of Music*
1939	Diserens and Fine	*A Psychology of Music*
1940	Schoen	*The Psychology of Music*
1944	Buck	*Psychology for Musicians*
1946	Licht	*Music in Medicine*
1947	Seashore	*In Search of Beauty in Music*
1948	Schullian and Schoen, eds.	*Music and Medicine*
1948	Soibelman	*Therapeutic and Industrial Uses of Music*
1951	Barbour	*Tuning and Temperament*
1952	Gutheil, ed.	*Music and Your Emotions*
1953	Lundin	*An Objective Psychology of Music*
1954	Révész	*Introduction to the Psychology of Music*
1955	Kwalwasser	*Exploring the Musical Mind*
1956	Zuckerkandl	*Sound and Symbol*

(*continued*)

TABLE 1—*Continued*

Year	Author(s)	Title of Book
1958	Farnsworth	*The Social Psychology of Music*
1958	Weber	*The Rational and Social Foundations in Music*
1959	Zuckerkandl	*The Sense of Music*
1962	Valentine	*The Experimental Psychology of Beauty*
1962	Whybrew	*Measurement and Evaluation in Music*
1963	Silbermann	*The Sociology of Music*
1964	Merriam	*The Anthropology of Music*
1964	Noble	*The Psychology of Cornet and Trumpet Playing*
1966	Bentley	*Musical Ability in Children and Its Measurement*
1966	Teplov	*Psychologie des Aptitudes Musicales*
1967	Lundin	*An Objective Psychology of Music*, 2d ed.
1968b	Gaston, ed.	*Music in Therapy*
1968	Lehman	*Tests and Measurements in Music*
1968	Shuter	*The Psychology of Musical Ability*
1969	Farnsworth	*The Social Psychology of Music*, 2d ed.
1969	Phelps	*A Guide to Research in Music Education*
1970	Colwell	*The Evaluation of Music Teaching and Learning*
1970	Madsen and Madsen	*Experimental Research in Music*
1970	McLaughlin	*Music and Communication*
1971	Gordon	*The Psychology of Music Teaching*
1971	Whybrew	*Measurement and Evaluation in Music*, 2d ed.
1972	Franklin	*Music Education*
1973	Bonny and Savary	*Music and Your Mind*
1973	Roederer	*Introduction to the Physics and Psychophysics of Music*
1973	Zuckerkandl	*Man the Musician*
1975	Madsen, Greer, and Madsen, eds.	*Research in Music Behavior*
1975	Roederer	*Introduction to the Physics and Psychophysics of Music*, 2d ed.
1976	Plomp	*Aspects of Tone Sensation*
1977	Critchley and Hensen, eds.	*Music and the Brain*
1977	Shepherd et al., eds.	*Whose Music? A Sociology of Musical Languages*
1978	Davies	*The Psychology of Music*
1979	Radocy and Boyle	*Psychological Foundations of Musical Behavior*
1980	Hodges, ed.	*Handbook of Music Psychology*

(*continued*)

TABLE 1—*Continued*

Year	Author(s)	Title of Book
1980	Phelps	*A Guide to Research in Music Education*, 2d ed.
1981	Shuter-Dyson and Gabriel	*The Psychology of Musical Ability*, 2d ed.
1982	Clynes, ed.	*Music, Mind, and Brain*
1982	Deutsch, ed.	*The Psychology of Music*
1983	Droh and Spintge, eds.	*Angst, Schmerz, Musik in der Anästhesie*
1983	Lerdahl and Jackendoff	*A Generative Theory of Tonal Music*
1984	Cogan	*New Images of Musical Sound*
1985	De la Motte-Haber	*Handbuch der Musikpsychologie*
1985	Howell, Cross, and West, eds.	*Musical Structure and Cognition*
1985	Lundin	*An Objective Psychology of Music*, 3d ed.
1985	Sloboda	*The Musical Mind*
1986	Dowling and Harwood	*Music Cognition*
1986	Hargreaves	*The Developmental Psychology of Music*
1987	Boyle and Radocy	*Measurement and Evaluation of Musical Experiences*
1987	Madsen and Prickett	*Applications of Research in Music Behavior*
1987	Rainbow and Froehlich	*Research in Music Education*
1987	Spintge and Droh, eds.	*Music in Medicine*
1988	Frances	*The Perception of Music*
1988	Radocy and Boyle	*Psychological Foundations of Musical Behavior*, 2d ed.
1988	Roehmann and Wilson, eds.	*The Biology of Music Making*
1988	Serafine	*Music as Cognition*
1988	Sloboda	*Generative Processes in Music*
1988	Swanwick	*Music, Mind, and Education*
1989	Lee, ed.	*Rehabilitation, Music, and Human Well-Being*
1989	McDonald and Simons	*Musical Growth and Development*
1989	Parncutt	*Harmony: A Psychoacoustical Approach*
1990	Fiske	*Music and Mind*
1990	Krumhansl	*Cognitive Foundations of Musical Pitch*
1990	Narmour	*The Analysis and Cognition of Basic Melodic Structures*
1990	Walker	*Musical Beliefs*
1990	Wilson and Roehmann, eds.	*Music and Child Development*
1991	Bamberger	*The Mind Behind the Musical Ear*
1991	Hauptfleisch, ed.	*Music Education: Why? What? How?*

(*continued*)

TABLE 1—*Continued*

Year	Author(s)	Title of Book
1991	Sataloff, Brandfonbrener, and Lederman, eds.	*Textbook of Performing Arts Medicine*
1991	Wallin	*Biomusicology*
1992	Butler	*The Musician's Guide to Perception and Cognition*
1992	Colwell, ed.	*Handbook of Research on Music Teaching and Learning*
1992	Spintge and Droh, eds.	*MusicMedicine*
1994	Aiello and Sloboda, eds.	*Musical Perceptions*
1995	Spintge and Pratt, eds.	*MusicMedicine 2*
1996	Hodges, ed.	*Handbook of Music Psychology*, 2nd ed.

Note: Complete citations are included in the references.

Table 1 lists 108 landmark books published between 1862 and 1995. Over a span of 57 years (1862–1919), there are 7 books. For the remainder of this century up to the time of the publication of this book (1996), analysis of table 1 shows: 1920s = 7 1930s = 8 1940s = 6 1950s = 9 1960s = 13 1970s = 16 1980s = 27, and so far in the 1990s = 15. Of the 108 books, 39 have *psych-* in their titles, 11 deal with measurement and evaluation, and 11 were concerned with music in medicine and therapy. Prior to 1974, 4 books are compiled by editors; in the last 20 years, however, 16 are compilations. During this same 20 years (1975–94), the number of pertinent texts published has been approximately 3 per year versus 2 per year during the previous 20 years (1955–74). Overall, an examination of the titles indicates a breadth of concern of the influence of music by researchers in an increasing number of scientific disciplines—which confirms the philosophy inherent in the molecular configuration presented in figure 1.

Periodicals

Just as no single book contains all the information needed in the the discipline of Music Psychology, so no single periodical series contains all needed information. This becomes readily apparent when one reviews the reference citations in the 108 books listed in table 1 or in article titles included in the reference lists of the chapters in this book. Thus, a long-felt "need for a single, comprehensive index of pertinent periodical literature pertaining to the influence of music on behavior [and responses to music] has been evident for years, particularly by laboratory and clinical researchers and especially by music therapy practitioners" (Eagle 1976, vii). The CAIRSS for Music Project was begun in 1969 to respond to this need. Assistance for the project was received from the National Association for Music Therapy, which awarded five grants from 1970–77, and, in addition, from four institutional grants during the same time from Texas Women's University, and one from Southern Methodist University in 1990.

Pursuant to the goals of the project, sources of pertinent periodical literature were identified, and computer programs were developed specifically for it. Eventually, a word-and-author index was computer-generated and published as the *Music Therapy Index* (MTI) in Eagle 1976. The content of MTI is based on approximately 6,000 keyword descriptors and author names taken from the basic citations of 2,100 articles in 400 periodicals published in 30 countries from 1960–75.

Subsequent and sequential to MTI was the publication of the *Music Psychology Index, Volume 2* (MPI2) in Eagle 1978. The name change from MTI to MPI2 became imperative as the CAIRSS for Music Project continued, which was due mainly to the "change in our collective consciousness as to the primary subject with which we are increasingly concerned" (Eagle 1978, vii), namely, Music Psychology—a term more inclusive than music therapy. Along with figure 1, the subtitle of MPI2 will illustrate the type of literature included in it: *The International Interdisciplinary Index of the Influence of Music on Behavior: References to the Literature from the Natural and Behavioral Sciences and the Fine and Therapeutic Arts for the Years 1976–77*. Music Psychology, then, is used as an umbrella term in the search for periodical literature. Therefore, MPI2 is a "resource for learning what is being done in Music Psychology, who is doing it, and where in the world it is being done" (Eagle 1978, viii). The content of MPI2 is based on approximately 7,000 keyword descriptors and authors taken from the citations of 2,300 articles in 400 journals published in 30 countries during 1976–77.

The last in the series of these indexes was published in 1984 as *Music Psychology Index, Volume 3* (MPI3) (Eagle and Miniter 1984). MPI3 is based on approximately 4,000 keyword descriptors and authors taken from the citations of 2,100 articles in 400 journals published in 25 countries during 1978–80.

Taken in their entirety, the three published indexes contain more than 6,500 citations, which appear under more than 17,000 keyword descriptors and names of authors, and have been published in more than 1,000 journals in some 30 countries during a period of 21 years (1960–80). The continuing compilation of citations through the CAIRSS for Music Project was interrupted in 1984 so that time could be taken for total reassessment.

Purview of the Present

In the Preface to the first edition of this book, Hodges states that "this book is incomplete and out-of-date. It is incomplete because the task of finding every piece of literature related to a particular topic is an impossible one" (Hodges 1980, xv). This impossibility still exists, but the means now exist to increase the probability of the possible.

Beginning in 1988, a concerted effort was begun to redesign the CAIRSS for Music Project. The essential goal that emerged was still (a) to identify relevant bibliography of Music Psychology and (b) to bring this literature into a single and more comprehensive source. This was done through (a) experience gained through the efforts of publishing the three *Indexes*, and (b) developing a computer software program to include 30 fields of expanded information directly from the pertinent articles and not just from the basic citations as had been done previously. An additional goal was to determine a computer program that would allow for immediate accessibility of the resulting database by all users anywhere in the world. This became a reality in 1992 through the Internet.[5] Input continues daily.

In 1996, this unique bibliographic database of music research literature contains articles published in more than 2,000 different journals in 25 languages in 54 countries. Origins of cited publications in the database have been designated primary and secondary. The latter include pertinent citations from such sources as Medline, Embase, lists of references and bibliography, and the aforementioned *Indexes*. Primary sources are those journals in which more than 50 percent of the articles pertain to Music Psychology, and therefore, all articles from each of the following journals are cited in the database.

> *Bulletin of the Council for Research in Music Education*
> *Bulletin of the National Association for Music Therapy*
> *Contributions to Music Education*
> *Hospital Music Newsletter*
> *International Journal of Arts Medicine*
> *Journal of Music Teacher Education*

---

5. For a history of the development of CAIRSS, its present status, and future directions, see Eagle and Hodges 1992.

Journal of Music Therapy
Journal of Research in Music Education
Medical Problems of Performing Artists
Music Perception
Music Therapy
Music Therapy Perspectives
Psychology of Music
Psychomusicology
The Quarterly: Journal of Music Teaching and Learning
Update: Applications of Research in Music Education

To aid the user of the CAIRSS electronic database, the *CAIRSS Thesaurus* (Eagle 1994) has been published. It is a cross-indexed reference of over 21,000 keyword descriptors that have been derived directly from the published articles of a sample of 11,000 bibliographic citations that appear in CAIRSS. Thus, through the miracle of electronics, the probability of identifying past reports of Music Psychology research has been increased and is more immediately available in the present. Therefore, this gives us a more predictable view of the future.

View of the Future

In preparing this section, I am intrigued with the mysteriousness of music as I have experienced it and the science of music as I know it. But in the cosmologically quantum view of existence, it's all one anyhow. Because of its Latin derivation, *science* simply means "to know" and modern science says the way to know is to use the Cartesian scientific method. But the problem seems still to remain in the way to go about knowing how music influences behavior. I agree with Campbell and Heller (1980) when they urge Music Psychologists to look at other methods, and in their case, Humean.[6] As much as I agree with these distinguished colleagues, however, I think there is more. There is some kind of research method that I believe already exists—

---

6. Campbell and Heller contrast a Humean view with a Cartesian view of research. Under a Cartesian view, Truth resides in objective measurements, while in a Humean view, there can be multiple Truths, including not only objective measurements but also individual subjective judgments. Consider a study of intonation, for example. From a Cartesian standpoint, a performer would be considered in or out of tune according to an objective measurement made by a tuner. From a Humean standpoint, the tuner's reading would be considered valid along with subjective judgments made by human observers. The Cartesian view allows for one correct answer; the Humean view allows for multiple correct answers.

not to the exclusion of the deductive-inductive scientific method but in an expanded inclusion of it.

This expanded method includes a combination of factors, both known and as yet unknown. Nevertheless, the combination will spur music researchers to greater heights of knowing. The prime factor is and will continue to be an open mind—open to past knowledges, present researches, and futuristic thinking. This open mind-set will allow us to reinterpret findings from the past, pursuant to a more inclusive analysis of the present, both of which will allow us to move more confidently into the future. All of which entreats me to say: Dream! Because you are only as successful as you allow yourself to be guided by those dreams. But exercise with care, because your dreams might come true! I am reminded that "today's magic is often tomorrow's mundane" (Halpern 1978, 153). As has been shown many times throughout human history, today's science is tomorrow's myths, fables, and legends.

What I see in the future for Music Psychologists is on the cutting edge of science today. Most Music Psychologists have "felt this in their gut" for a long time. This gut feeling is that music is something more. More than manipulating a music variable in an experiment. More than performing music. More than analyzing music in a theory class. More than studying the history of music. More than composing music. More than educating with and therapizing through music. There is just simply more. You know it and I know it. Even the so-called nonmusicians know it. It is this knowing that I will talk about now.

Development of Theory

Theory without practice and research to verify it is impotent. Practice without research based on theory to guide it is blind. Research without theory and resultant practice is inapplicable. "Good theory advances good research and good practice and, in turn, is itself moved ahead by advances in our knowledge (research) and in what we can do (practice)" (Mahrer 1978, 4). The relationship between research findings and practiced applications will help us to emerge with a more general, theoretical comprehension. No one of these in the tripod of theory, practice, and research (fig. 2) can in and of itself help us make significant advances for the betterment of humankind unless there is perceived a significant relationship among all three. If one of the three "legs" is missing, then the tripod does not stand. Each of the three legs makes significant contributions, as each of the three relate significantly to each other. Otherwise, the word *significance* has little substantial meaning and, metaphorically, does not provide a seat upon which we can scientifically sit.

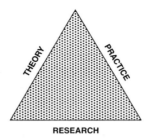

RESEARCH

Fig. 2. A triangular model for music psychology

There is much practice of music: vocal and instrumental, in choruses, orchestras, and wind ensembles, in elementary and secondary schools, colleges and universities, towns and cities, amateur and professional, public and private, home and church, television, movies, and radio, on and on. And there is much research with, in, and of music. For example, witness the several hundreds of references in this book and the thousands of citations in the CAIRSS database. But where are the meaningful theories? Certainly, the most acceptable socioanthropological theory of music is Gaston's, the foundation of which resides in his statement that "all mankind has need for esthetic [musical] expression and experience" (1968a, 21). The psychological theory of music by Sears (1968) remains substantially unchallenged. The basis of his theory resides in his statement that "music demands time-ordered behavior" (Sears 1968, 33), the elaboration of which is presented in *(a)* experiences within musical structure which, in turn, *(b)* provides for experiences in self-organization and *(c)* experiences in relating to others.[7] A physical theory of music has been expressed in my "theory of quantum musichanics" (Eagle 1991a). The foundation for this theory is presented in four of the several principles of quantum physics, namely, those of Einstein (relativity), Bohr (complementarity), Heisenberg (uncertainty), and Bohm (holonomy). Additionally, I compare Newtonian/Cartesian and quantum worldviews and, in my theory, present "quantum givens" and their musical corollaries. Essentially then, the theory of quantum musichanics is a restatement of holonomic physical existencies through musical terminology.

7. An expansion of Sears's theory is made by Cole who names it the Synchronistic Time (S=T) Model of Music Therapy. "It is focused explicitly on the time-orderedness of music and is designed to illustrate that, in providing the three experiences as described by Sears, music induces a time orientation known as Synchronization. At the core of the model is the belief that people in need of therapy are dyssynchronous with their own body rhythms and/or the rhythms of their environment" (Cole 1985, iv–v).

Ultimately, what is called for is a language and a world view that encompass both art and science, especially that of music.

But where is a theory in which a synthesis of past, present, and future practice and research can be fully integrated? Perhaps the theory of quantum musichanics is the first step in this direction. But certainly, a more unified theory will emerge. When this happens, research paradigms will have only the slightest resemblance to our present ones. This done, we will have a more rigorous means of understanding why people make music, how music influences people, and what to do in applying that understanding in practice.

Changes in Music Curricula

One of the reasons Music Psychologists have not developed a more inclusive, acceptable theory in the discipline is that we have not accepted fully (1) that humans make music for people consumption, nor (2) that the fundamental characteristic of nature is periodic functioning in frequency, or musical pitch (Eagle 1991a and 1991b; Eagle and Harsh 1988). When we become consciously aware of either one or both of these two factors, not only will music curricula change but scientific paradigms will as well. These changes will be made because, as we better understand the interaction between people and their music, it will become evident that we musicians must know more about people, how people respond to structured sounds through music, and how people *must* have music for their biological, psychological, sociological, and spiritual well-being. Ultimately, we will have curricula that will help people find *meaning* in life. Out of necessity, then, traditional training programs in music—particularly music education and music therapy—will have to change due to the onslaught of findings from research, consequent practical applications, and formulations of theories.

Interpenetrations of disciplines will take place at an ever-increasing pace, resulting in unique combinations. For example, there now exist programs in psychoneuroimmunology (psychology, neurology, immunology) and biomedical engineering (biology, medicine, engineering). More narrowly cast, perhaps, are programs in psychomusicology (literally the -*ology*—study of—music and psychology) and ethnomusicology (music and anthropology). Consider the possibility of programs in psychoneuromusicology, biomedical musicology, or musimedicology. The pragmatic result will be a new language interrelating the art and science of music with various sciences, a new worldview of how music is made and interpreted, a new *meaning* of life. The applications of this paradigm shift in education and therapy curricula seem obvious.

Research in Music Metaphysics

More research in the future will be based on questions usually relegated to metaphysics or philosophy. Indeed, *metaphysics* is defined as the systematic investigation of "problems of ultimate reality, including the study of being (ontology) and, often, the study of the structure of the universe (cosmology)" (*American Heritage Dictionary* 1982). Research stemming from this definition of metaphysics should not come as a surprise to the musical scholar.

> Practically, metaphysics and philosophy proper are not separated, and they are not marked off in sharp distinction from science, on the one hand, and common sense, on the other. In fact the historical development of any question, such as the nature of musical value, arises as the main question and soon takes on both metaphysical and supernatural interpretations. These are criticized in philosophy and gradually analyzed and clarified by scientific methods; this done, the information tends to be regarded as a matter of common knowledge or common sense. (Seashore 1938, 376)

Metaphysical research will become more of an issue, because we will become more concerned with "the study of being (ontology)" and "the structure of the universe (cosmology)." These issues have continued to be discussed and debated down through the ages. Only within the last several years, however, have scientific methods using modern technology and ideas emanating from that technology been applied to resolving these defined metaphysical issues. For example, research in radionics has shown that humans are sensitive to sounds in ways unheard of until recently. Not only do our ears hear but so do our whole bodies—there are bodily resonances, wholly and in part. The radionic field of inquiry is concerned with these vibratory rates, has catalogued them, and uses the information in diagnosis and treatment (MacIvor and LaForest 1979; Tansley 1975, 1977, and 1984).

The idea that music exercises influences over certain bodily parts as well as the emotions of humans is certainly not new. The writings of Socrates, Plato, Pythagoras, and Confucius—to name a few—allude and, indeed, speak directly to the issue. As humans are resonant beings with vibrating parts giving and receiving energy and force, so tones in certain configurations are musical sounds, and sounds are vibrations produced by energy and force. Much of the music of the future will be composed according to the vibratory nature of musical notes, chords, and instruments as they relate to bodily vibrations of humans. When this happens, such music will be prepared precisely using the physical—in addition to the psychophysiological—attributes of it. Vibratory frequencies (i.e., musical pitches) and intensities (i.e., musical loudnesses), therefore, will be used as prime ingredients in musical compositions and for several specific purposes.

1. To increase mental ability by affecting cerebral function;
2. To sustain physiological well-being by correcting bodily (i.e., vibratory frequency or pitch) disorders;
3. To maintain emotional stability by eliminating fears, habits, and neuroses; or
4. To foster spiritual or holistic awareness by involving aesthetic aspirations.

For composing such "psychosomatic" music (Langdon 1960), electronic synthesizers, MIDI interfaces, and other electronic devices will take on added importance and will be used on a much grander scale. In short, computerization of compositional and music-making functions will become ever more widespread. As a consequence of this activity, more and more emphasis will be on the influence of music on humans as well as their response to it. Logically, music education will be broadened to incorporate audience response and the use of music in leisure time, that is, music education for mental and physical health. Of necessity, music therapy will use music more as a medicament, that is, specific music and musical elements will be used for specific mental and physical illnesses. Perhaps the overall concept here is "stress" that is always present with people in any of their activities. "Whether the stress is joyful or harmful, the body will need to readjust back to a sense of normalcy, or homeostasis, of balance. In other words, the body *seeks to get in 'harmony with itself'*" (Halpern 1978, 49). And music will become more of a prime mode of reducing stress, educationally and therapeutically. Although findings from research show this to be true now, the future says that precise music will be composed and produced for precise stressful, psychophysiological circumstances.

Findings from scientific research also indicate that we are energized, frequencized (i.e., musically pitched) entities, as well as a part of distant stars, and breathing at least one molecule of air that has ever been breathed with every intake of a breath of air (Wolf 1986). Yet, this energy takes shape in a form we call humans. Such findings are reminiscent of Einstein's formula, $E = mc^2$, which means transformation of energy and mass (form) in a (space) time domain. If all things in our own dimensions of existence are contained in that formula, the idea of music through its vibratory → frequency → pitch nature influencing behavior becomes more readily apparent. The concept also indicates that all things are universal and not diversal. Piquing my curiosity at this point are references to "the music of the spheres," a phrase coined by Pythagoras and one that has been embellished upon throughout world literature: Chaucer → Dante → Shakespeare → Milton → Byron → Poe (Flam 1991; Graham 1979; James 1993; Marks 1978; Murchie 1961 and 1967; Walker 1990). I ask you to think critically but newly of music within these concepts and with the interrelationship with musical others, such as those listed in table 2. All of which is to say that

> In the last analysis, magic, religion and science are nothing but theories of thought; and science has supplanted its predecessors, so it may be itself superceded by some more perfect hypothesis, perhaps by some totally different way of looking at the phenomena [of music]. (Albarn and Smith 1977, 133)

TABLE 2.   Music and Related Topics

Topic	Selected Authors
Time	Coveney and Highfield 1990; Davies 1995; Franz 1978; Fraser 1975 and 1987; Morris 1985; Ornstein 1969
Soundscape	Schafer 1977
Sentics	Clynes 1977
Third Wave	Naisbitt and Aburdene 1990; Toffler 1980 and 1990
Body time	Coveney and Highfield 1990; Glass and Mackey 1988; Luce 1971a and 1971b; Reinberg and Ghata 1964
Consciousness	Abraham 1994; Bentov 1977; Berendt 1987; Goswami 1993; Grof 1993; Jaynes 1990; Kafatos and Nadeau 1990; Mishlove 1975; Ornstein 1976
Altered states of consciousness	Anderson and Savary 1972; Bonny and Savary 1973; Zinberg 1977
Spectral sequence	Graham 1979; MacIvor and LaForest 1979
Rhythmic vision	Blair 1975
Synergetics	Fuller 1975 and 1979
Psychic healing	Krippner and Villoldo 1976; Moss 1974; Steiner 1977
Superlearning	Ostrander and Schroeder 1979
Kirlian photography	Davis and Lane 1978; Krippner and Rubin 1974; Moss 1974
Chaos	Abraham 1994; Briggs and Peat 1989; Glass and Mackey 1988; Gleick 1987; Kellert 1993; Schwenk 1978; Stehle 1994

(continued)

TABLE 2—*Continued*

Topic	Selected Authors
Fractals	Glass and Mackey 1988; Gleick 1987
Symmetry	Field and Golubitsky 1992; Zee 1986
Holonomy	Bohm 1980; Bohm and Hiley 1993; Grof 1993; Pribram 1991; Talbot 1991; Wilber 1982
Uncertainty	Cassidy 1992
Relativity	Calder 1979; Lightman 1993
Complementarity[a]	Pais 1991
Primordial music	Jenny 1974
Plants' music	Tompkins and Bird 1973
Chemical music	Andrews 1966
Genetic music	Ohno and Jabara 1986; Ohno and Ohno 1986
Body music	Binkley 1990; Dossey 1991; Gerber 1988; Wolf 1986
Earth music	Eagle 1991a; Johnson 1981
Sun music	Johnson 1981
Galactal music	Cousto 1988; Flam 1991; Kayser 1970; Wilczek and Devine 1988
Hearing motion	Zuckerkandl 1973
Voice toning	Keyes 1973
Music sensing	Zuckerkandl 1959
Music touching	Montagu 1971

Thus, the search for more is our goal as Music Psychologists, the more awareness, the more consciousness, the more understanding, and, hence, the more *meaning*. The ideas expressed here will take on added significance as we re-search "more and more" with intellectual curiosity and emotional intuition. The eventual aim of our endeavors is for synthesis, in reaching inward and outward for our *Self-Aware Universe* (Goswami 1993) and comprehensively toward *The Ultimate Frontier* (Kueshana 1963).

---

[a] The terms *complementarity, relativity, uncertainty,* and *holonomy,* as well as several of the other terms presented in this table, are names of phenomena theorized through the work of quantum physicists. Many authors have presented these concepts in books readable by nonphysicists, among them being Capra (1983), Davies (1980), Davies and Gribbin (1992), Herbert (1985), Wolf (1981), and Zukav (1979). Other authors have made certain theoretical applications of quantum concepts to interpretive designs in such disciplines as *art* (Shlain, 1991), *medicine* (Chopra, 1989; Dossey, 1982, 1984), *music* (Eagle, 1985, 1991a, 1991b; Eagle and Harsh, 1988; Lyden, 1982; Traphagan and Traphagan, 1986), *neurology* (Pietsch, 1981; Pribram, 1991), *philosophy* (Heisenberg, 1958), *physiology* (Wolf, 1986), *psychology* (LeShan and Margenau, 1982; Wilson, 1990; Zohar, 1990), *religion* (Charon, 1983; Davies, 1983, 1992; Dossey, 1989, 1993; Polkinghorne, 1988; Starcke, 1973; Talbot, 1980; Wilber, 1984), and *sociology* (Zohar and Marshall, 1994).

In the preceding sections, I have defined Music Psychology, reviewed its past, purviewed the present, and viewed into its future. Through this overview and in the chapters that follow, the broadening scope of the discipline of Music Psychology becomes apparent. Hopefully, the importance of this subject will be just as apparent to all those who are interested in musical behavior. This book speaks eloquently to the point. As I have reviewed it, I believe it will stand as a landmark for four significant reasons.

1. As with the first edition of this book, this second edition has been written, compiled, and edited by several professionally trained musicians. That we now have views on Music Psychology by musicians in addition to psychologists and other scientists is, in itself, a positive contribution to ArtScience.
2. In each of the chapters, the authors bring together a synthesis of the literature on a particular topic. Heretofore, the literature on many of the topics has been diffuse, making it difficult, if not impossible, to achieve a comprehensive interpretation and holistic viewpoint.
3. In addition to a synthesis of the literature, several of the chapters provide critical commentaries on research and directions for future studies with musical phenomena, by way of models, plans, and suggestions.
4. Finally, the level of scholarship evident in this book stands as a monument to all those who have engaged in the research and practice of Music Psychology—past, present, and future.

REFERENCES

Abraham, R. H. 1994. *Chaos*Gaia*Eros: A chaos pioneer uncovers the three great streams of history*. San Francisco: HarperCollins.
Aiello, R., and J. A. Sloboda, eds. 1994. *Musical perceptions*. Oxford: Oxford University Press.
Albarn, K., and J. M. Smith. 1977. *Diagram: The instrument of thought*. London: Thames and Hudson.
Anderson, M. S., and L. M. Savary. 1972. *Passages: A guide for pilgrims of the mind*. New York: Harper and Row.
Andrews, D. H. 1966. *The symphony of life*. Lee's Summit, MO: Unity Books.
Bamberger, J. 1991. *The mind behind the musical ear*. Cambridge: Harvard University Press.
Barbour, J. M. 1951. *Tuning and temperament: A historical survey*. East Lansing: Michigan State College Press.

Bartholomew, E. F. 1899. *Relation of psychology to music*. Rock Island, RI: New Era Publishing.

Bartholomew, E. F. 1902. *Relation of psychology to music*. 2d ed. Rock Island, RI: New Era Publishing.

Bentley, A. 1966. *Musical ability in children and its measurement*. London: Harrap.

Bentov, I. 1977. *Stalking the wild pendulum: On the mechanics of consciousness*. New York: E. P. Dutton.

Berendt, J. E. 1987. *Nada Brahma: The world is sound: Music and the landscape of consciousness*. Trans. H. Bredigkeit. Rochester, VT: Destiny Books.

Billroth, T. 1895. *Wer ist musikalisch?* Berlin: Gebruder Paetel.

Binkley, S. 1990. *The clockwork sparrow: Time, clocks, and calendars in biological organisms*. Englewood Cliffs, NJ: Prentice-Hall.

Blair, L. 1975. *Rhythms of vision: The changing patterns of belief*. New York: Warner Books.

Bohm, D. 1980. *Wholeness and the implicate order*. London: Routledge and Kegan Paul.

Bohm, D., and B. J. Hiley. 1993. *The undivided universe: An ontological interpretation of quantum theory*. London: Routledge.

Bonny, H. L., and L. M. Savary. 1973. *Music and your mind: Listening with a new consciousness*. New York: Harper and Row.

Boyle, J. D., and R. E. Radocy. 1987. *Measurement and evaluation of musical experiences*. New York: Schirmer Books.

Briggs, J., and F. D. Peat. 1989. *Turbulent mirror: An illustrated guide to chaos theory and the science of wholeness*. New York: Harper and Row.

Buck, P. C. 1944. *Psychology for musicians*. London: Oxford University Press.

Butler, D. 1992. *The musician's guide to perception and cognition*. New York: Schirmer Books.

Calder, N. 1979. *Einstein's universe*. New York: Viking.

Campbell, W., and J. Heller. 1980. An orientation for considering models of musical behavior. In *Handbook of music psychology*, ed. D. Hodges, 29–36. Lawrence, KS: National Association for Music Therapy.

Capra, F. 1983. *The tao of physics: An exploration of the parallels between modern physics and Eastern mysticism*. 2d ed. Boulder, CO: Shambhala.

Cassidy, D. C. 1992. *Uncertainty: The life and science of Werner Heisenberg*. New York: W. H. Freeman.

Charon, J. E. 1983. *The unknown spirit*. London: Coventure.

Chopra, D. 1989. *Quantum healing: Exploring the frontiers of mind/body medicine*. New York: Bantam Books.

Clynes, M. 1977. *Sentics: The touch of emotions*. Garden City, NY: Anchor Press.

Clynes, M., ed. 1982. *Music, mind, and brain: The neuropsychology of music*. New York: Plenum Press.

Cogan, R. 1984. *New images of musical sound*. Cambridge: Harvard University Press.

Cole, C. F. 1985. Synchronistic time in music: A theoretical model of music therapy based on the work of William Sears. Master's thesis, Southern Methodist University.

Colwell, R. 1970. *The evaluation of music teaching and learning*. Englewood Cliffs, NJ: Prentice-Hall.

Colwell, R., ed. 1992. *Handbook of research on music teaching and learning*. New York: Schirmer.

Cousto, H. 1988. *The cosmic octave: Origin of harmony, planets—tones—colors, the power of inherent vibrations*. Trans. C. Baker and J. Harrison. Mendocino, CA: LifeRhythms.

Coveney, P., and R. Highfield. 1990. *The arrow of time: A voyage through science to solve time's greatest mystery*. New York: Fawcett Columbine.

Critchley, M., and R. A. Hensen, eds. 1977. *Music and the brain: Studies in the neurology of music*. Springfield, IL: Charles C. Thomas.

Davies, J. B. 1978. *The psychology of music*. Stanford: Stanford University Press.

Davies, P. 1980. *Other worlds: Space, superspace, and the quantum universe*. New York: Simon and Schuster.

Davies, P. 1983. *God and the new physics*. New York: Simon and Schuster.

Davies, P. 1992. *The mind of God: The scientific basis for a rational world*. New York: Simon and Schuster.

Davies, P. 1995. *About time: Einstein's unfinished revolution*. New York: Simon and Schuster.

Davies, P., and J. Gribbin. 1992. *The matter myth: Dramatic discoveries that challenge our understanding of physical reality*. New York: Simon and Schuster.

Davis, M., and E. Lane. 1978. *Rainbows of life: The promise of Kirlian photography*. New York: Harper and Row.

De la Motte-Haber, H. 1985. *Handbuch der musickpsychologie*. Laaber, Germany: Laaber-Verlag.

Deutsch, D., ed. 1982. *The psychology of music*. New York: Academic Press.

Diserens, C., and H. Fine. 1939. *A psychology of music*. Cincinnati: Authors.

Dossey, L. 1982. *Space, time, and medicine*. Boulder, CO: Shambhala.

Dossey, L. 1984. *Beyond illness: Discovering the experience of health*. Boulder, CO: Shambhala.

Dossey, L. 1989. *Recovering the soul: A scientific and spiritual search*. New York: Bantam Books.

Dossey, L. 1991. *Meaning, and medicine: A doctor's tales of breakthrough and healing*. New York: Bantam Books.

Dossey, L. 1993. *Healing words: The power of prayer and the practice of medicine*. San Francisco: HarperCollins.

Dowling, W. J., and D. Harwood. 1986. *Music cognition*. Orlando, FL: Academic Press.

Droh, R., and R. Spintge, eds. 1983. *Angst, schmerz, musik in der anästhesie*. Basel: Roche.

Eagle, C. T., ed. 1976. *Music therapy index*. Vol. 1, *An international interdisciplinary index to the literature of the psychology, psychophysiology, psychophysics and sociology of music*. Lawrence, KS: National Association for Music Therapy.

Eagle, C. T., ed. 1978. *Music psychology index*. Vol. 2, *The international interdisciplinary index of the influence of music on behavior: References to the literature from the natural and behavioral sciences, and the fine and therapeutic arts for the years 1976–77*. Denton, TX: Institute for Therapeutics Research.

Eagle, C. T. 1985. A quantum interfacing system for music and medicine. In *Music in Medicine*, ed. R. Spintge, and R. Droh, 389–411. Basel: Roche.

Eagle, C. T. 1991a. The quantum reality of music. In *Music education: Why? What? How?*, ed. S. Hauptfleisch, 43–66. Pretoria, South Africa: HSRC Publishers.

Eagle, C. T. 1991b. Steps to a theory of quantum therapy. *Music Therapy Perspectives* 9:56–60.

Eagle, C. T. 1994. *CAIRSS thesaurus: A cross-indexed reference of keyword descriptors in citations of art/science*. San Antonio: Institute for Music Research, University of Texas at San Antonio.

Eagle, C. T., and J. M. Harsh. 1988. Elements of pain and music: The aio connection. *Music Therapy* 7, no. 1:15–27.

Eagle, C. T., and D. A. Hodges. 1992. CAIRSS for Music in arts medicine. *International Journal for Arts Medicine* 1, no. 2:21–25.

Eagle, C. T., and J. J. Miniter, eds. 1984. *Music psychology index*. Vol. 3, *The international interdisciplinary index of the influence of music on behavior: References to the literature from the natural and behavioral sciences, and the fine and therapeutic arts for the years 1978–80*. Denton, TX: Institute for Therapeutics Research and Oryx Press.

Farnsworth, C. H. 1930. *Short studies in musical psychology*. New York: Oxford University Press.

Farnsworth, P. R. 1958. *The social psychology of music*. New York: Holt, Rinehart and Winston.

Farnsworth, P. R. 1969. *The social psychology of music*. 2d ed. Ames: Iowa State University Press.

Field, M., and M. Golubitsky. 1992. *Symmetry in chaos: A search for pattern in mathematics, art, and nature*. Oxford: Oxford University Press.

Fiske, H. E. 1990. *Music and mind: Philosophical essays on the cognition and meaning of music*. Lewiston, NY: Edwin Mellen.

Flam, F. 1991. Listening to the music of the spheres. *Science* 253:1207–1208.

Frances, R. 1988. *The perception of music*. Trans. W. J. Dowling. Hillsdale, NJ: Lawrence Erlbaum Associates.

Franklin, E. 1972. *Music education: Psychology and method*. London: George G. Harrap.

Franz, M-L. von. 1978. *Time: Rhythm and repose*. London: Thames and Hudson.

Fraser, J. T. 1975. *Of time, passion, and knowledge: Reflections on the strategy of existence*. New York: George Braziller.

Fraser, J. T. 1987. *Time: The familiar stranger*. Amherst: University of Massachusetts Press.

Fuller, R. B. 1975. *Synergetics: Explorations in the geometry of thinking*. New York: Macmillan.

Fuller, R. B. 1979. *Synergetics 2: Explorations in the geometry of thinking*. New York: Macmillan.

Gaston, E. T. 1968a. Man and music. In *Music in therapy*, ed. E.T. Gaston, 7–29. New York: Macmillan.

Gaston, E.T., ed. 1968b. *Music in therapy*. New York: Macmillan.

Gerber, R. 1988. *Vibrational medicine: New choices for healing ourselves*. Santa Fe, NM: Bear.

Glass, L., and M. C. Mackey. 1988. *From clocks to chaos: The rhythms of life*. Princeton, NJ: Princeton University Press.

Gleick, J. 1987. *Chaos: Making a new science.* New York: Viking.

Gordon, E. 1971. *The psychology of music teaching.* Englewood Cliffs, NJ: Prentice-Hall.

Goswami, A. 1993. *The self-aware universe: How consciousness creates the material world.* New York: C. P. Putnam's Sons.

Graham, F. L., ed. 1979. *The rainbow book.* Rev. ed. New York: Vintage Books.

Grof, S. 1993. *The holotropic mind: The three levels of human consciousness and how they shape our lives.* San Francisco: HarperCollins.

Gutheil, E. A., ed. 1952. *Music and your emotions: A practical guide to music selections associated with desired emotional responses.* New York: Liveright.

Halpern, S. 1978. *Tuning the human instrument.* Palo Alto: Spectrum Research Institute.

Hargreaves, D. J. 1986. *The developmental psychology of music.* Cambridge: Cambridge University Press.

Hauptfleisch, S., ed. 1991. *Music education: Why? What? How?* Pretoria, South Africa: HSRC Publishers.

Heisenberg, W. 1958. *Physics & philosophy: The revolution in modern science.* New York: Harper and Row.

Helmholtz, H. L. F. von. [1862] 1954. *On the sensations of tone as a physiological basis for the theory of music.* Trans. A. J. Ellis. Reprint, New York: Dover.

Herbert, N. 1985. *Quantum reality: Beyond the new physics.* Garden City, NY: Anchor Press.

Hodges, D. A., ed. 1980. *Handbook of music psychology.* Lawrence, KS: National Association for Music Therapy.

Hodges, D. A., ed. 1996. *Handbook of music psychology.* 2d ed. San Antonio: IMR Press.

Howell, P., I. Cross, and R. West, eds. 1985. *Musical structure and cognition.* London: Academic Press.

Howes, F. 1927. *The borderland of music and psychology.* New York: Oxford University Press.

James, J. 1993. *The music of the spheres: Music, science, and the natural order of the universe.* New York: Grove Press.

Jaynes, J. [1976] 1990. *The origin of consciousness in the breakdown of the bicameral mind.* Reprint, Boston: Houghton Mifflin.

Jeans, J. [1937] 1961. *Science and music.* Reprint, Cambridge: Cambridge University Press.

Jenny, H. 1974. *Cymatics: Wave phenomena, vibrational effects, harmonic oscillations with their structure, kinetics, and dynamics.* Vol. 2. Basel: Basillius.

Johnson, J., ed. 1981. *The rhythms of life.* New York: Crown.

Kafatos, M., and R. Nadeau. 1990. *The conscious universe: Part and whole in modern physical theory.* New York: Springer-Verlag.

Kayser, H. 1970. *Akróasis: The theory of world harmonics.* Trans. R. Lilienfeld. Boston: Plowshare Press.

Kellert, S. H. 1993. *In the wake of chaos: Unpredictable order in dynamical systems.* Chicago: University of Chicago Press.

Keyes, L. E. 1973. *Toning: The creative power of the voice.* Marina del Rey, CA: DeVorss.

Kries, J. von. 1926. *Wer ist musikalisch? Gedanken zur psychologie der tonkunst.* Berlin: Verlag von Julius Springer.

Krippner, S., and D. Rubin, eds. 1974. *The Kirlian aura: Photographing the galaxies of life.* Garden City, NY: Anchor Books.

Krippner, S., and A. Villoldo. 1976. *The realms of healing.* Millbrae, CA: Celestial Arts.

Krumhansl, C. L. 1990. *Cognitive foundations of musical pitch.* New York: Oxford University Press.

Kueshana, E. 1963. *The ultimate frontier.* Chicago: Stelle Group.

Kwalwasser, J. 1927. *Tests and measurements in music.* Boston: C. C. Birchard.

Kwalwasser, J. 1955. *Exploring the musical mind.* New York: Coleman-Ross.

Langdon, A. O. 1960. *Psychosomatic music: Tonal vibrations and their affect on the mind of mankind.* Huntington, WV: Chapman Press.

Lee, M. H. M. 1989. *Rehabilitation, music, and human well-being.* St. Louis: MMB Music.

Lehman, P. R. 1968. *Tests and measurements in music.* Englewood Cliffs, NJ: Prentice-Hall.

Lerdahl, F., and R. Jackendoff. 1983. *A generative theory of tonal music.* Cambridge, MA: MIT Press.

LeShan, L., and H. Margenau. 1982. *Einstein's space and Van Gogh's sky: Physical reality and beyond.* New York: Macmillan.

Licht, S. 1946. *Music in medicine.* Boston: New England Conservatory of Music.

Lightman, A. 1993. *Einstein's dreams.* New York: Pantheon Books.

Luce, G. G. 1971a. *Biological rhythms in human and animal physiology.* New York: Dover.

Luce, G. G. 1971b. *Body time: Physiological rhythms and social stress.* New York: Bantam Books.

Lundin, R. W. 1953. *An objective psychology of music.* New York: Ronald Press.

Lundin, R. W. 1967. *An objective psychology of music.* 2d ed. New York: Ronald Press.

Lundin, R. W. 1985. *An objective psychology of music.* 3d ed. Malabar, FL: Robert E. Krieger.

Lyden, H.F. 1982. Orbital path of electrons using musical principles. *Speculations in Science and Technology* 5, no. 3:289–301.

MacIvor, V., and S. LaForest. 1979. *Vibrations: Healing through color homeopathy and radionics.* New York: Samuel Weiser.

Madsen, C. K., R. D. Greer, and C. H. Madsen, Jr., eds. 1975. *Research in music behavior: Modifying music behavior in the classroom.* New York: Teachers College Press.

Madsen, C. K., and C. H. Madsen, Jr. 1970. *Experimental research in music.* Englewood Cliffs, NJ: Prentice-Hall.

Madsen, C. K., and C. A. Prickett. 1987. *Applications of research in music behavior.* Tuscaloosa, AL: University of Alabama Press.

Mahrer, A. R. 1978. *Experiencing: A humanistic theory of psychology and psychiatry.* New York: Brunner/Mazel.

Marks, L. E. 1978. *The unity of the senses: Interrelations among the modalities.* New York: Academic Press.

McDonald, D. T., and G. M. Simons. 1989. *Musical growth and development: Birth through six.* New York: Schirmer.

McLaughlin, T. 1970. *Music and communication*. London: Faber and Faber.

Merriam, A. P. 1964. *The anthropology of music*. Evanston, IL: Northwestern University Press.

Meyer, M. F. 1929. *The musician's arithmetic: Drill problems for an introduction to the scientific study of musical composition*. Boston: Oliver Ditson.

Miles, W. R. 1956. *Carl Emil Seashore (1866–1949). Biographical memoirs*. Vol. 29. New York: Columbia University Press.

Mishlove, J. 1975. *The roots of consciousness: Psychic liberation through history, science, and experience*. New York: Random House.

Montagu, A. 1971. *Touching: The human significance of the skin*. New York: Columbia University Press.

Morris, R. 1985. *Time's arrows: Scientific attitudes toward time*. New York: Simon and Schuster.

Moss, T. 1974. *The probability of the impossible: Scientific discoveries and explorations in the psychic world*. New York: New American Library.

Murchie, G. 1961. *Music of the spheres*. Boston: Houghton Mifflin.

Murchie, G. 1967. *Music of the spheres*. Rev. ed., vols. 1 and 2. New York: Dover.

Mursell, J. L. [1937] 1971. *The psychology of music*. Reprint, Westport, CT: Greenwood Press.

Mursell, J. L., and M. Glenn. 1931. *The psychology of school music teaching*. New York: Silver Burdett.

Naisbitt, J., and P. Aburdene. 1990. *Megatrends 2000: Ten new directions for the 1990s*. New York: William Morrow.

Narmour, E. 1990. *The analysis and cognition of basic melodic structures*. Chicago: University of Chicago Press.

Noble, C. E. 1964. *The psychology of cornet and trumpet playing: Scientific principles of artistic performance*. Missoula, MT: Mountain Press.

Ohno, S., and M. Jabara. 1986. Repeats of base oligomers $N = 3n \pm 1$ or 2 as immortal coding sequences of the primeval world: Construction of coding sequences is based upon the principle of musical composition. *Chemica Scripta* 26B:41–49.

Ohno, S., and M. Ohno. 1986. The all pervasive principle of repetitious recurrence governs not only coding sequence construction but also human endeavor in musical composition. *Immunogenetics* 1455:1–8.

Ornstein, R. E. 1969. *On the experience of time*. New York: Penguin Books.

Ornstein, R. E. 1976. *The mind field: A personal essay*. New York: Grossman.

Ostrander, S., and L. Schroeder. 1979. *Superlearning*. New York: Delacorte.

Pais, A. 1991. *Neils Bohr's times: In physics, philosophy, and polity*. Oxford: Clarendon Press.

Parncutt, R. 1989. *Harmony: A psychoacoustical approach*. Berlin: Springer-Verlag.

Phelps, R. P. 1969. *A guide to research in music education*. Dubuque, IA: W. C. Brown.

Phelps, R. P. 1975. The psychology of music and its literature. *College Music Symposium* 15:114–25.

Phelps, R. P. 1980. *A guide to research in music education*. 2d ed. Metuchen, NJ: Scarecrow Press.

Pietsch, P. 1981. *Shufflebrain*. Boston: Houghton Mifflin.

Plomp, R. 1976. *Aspects of tone sensation: A psychophysical study*. London: Academic Press.

Polkinghorne, J. 1988. *Science and creation: The search for understanding*. Boston: Shambhala.

Pratt, C. C. 1931. *The meaning of music: A study in psychological aesthetics*. New York: McGraw-Hill.

Pribram, K. H. 1991. *Brain and perception: Holonomy and structure in figural processing*. Hillside, NJ: Lawrence Erlbaum Associates.

Radocy, R. E., and J. D. Boyle. 1979. *Psychological foundations of musical behavior*. Springfield, IL: Charles C. Thomas.

Radocy, R. E., and J. D. Boyle. 1988. *Psychological foundations of musical behavior*. 2d ed. Springfield, IL: Charles C. Thomas.

Rainbow, E. L., and H. C. Froehlich. 1987. *Research in music education: An introduction to systematic inquiry*. New York: Schirmer.

Reinberg, A., and M. D. Ghata. 1964. *Biological rhythms*. Trans. C. J. Cameron. New York: Walker.

Révész, G. 1925. *The psychology of a musical prodigy*. New York: Harcourt, Brace.

Révész, G. 1954. *Introduction to the psychology of music*. Trans. C. I. C. de Courey. Norman: University of Oklahoma Press.

Roederer, J. G. 1973. *Introduction to the physics and psychophysics of music*. New York: Springer-Verlag.

Roederer, J. G. 1975. *Introduction to the physics and psychophysics of music*. 2d ed. New York: Springer-Verlag.

Roehmann, F. L., and F. R. Wilson, eds. 1988. *The biology of music making*. St. Louis: MMB Music.

Sataloff, R. T., A. G. Brandfonbrener, and R. L. Lederman, eds. 1991. *Textbook of performing arts medicine*. New York: Raven Press.

Schafer, R. M. 1977. *The tuning of the world*. New York: Alfred A. Knopf.

Schoen, M., ed. [1927] 1968. *The effects of music*. Reprint, Freeport, NY: Books for Libraries Press.

Schoen, M. 1940. *The psychology of music: A survey for teacher and musician*. New York: Ronald Press.

Schullian, D. M., and M. Schoen, eds. 1948. *Music and medicine*. New York: Henry Schuman.

Schwenk, T. 1978. *Sensitive chaos: The creation of flowing forms in water and air*. Trans. O. Whicher and J. Wrigley. New York: Schocken Books.

Sears, W. W. 1968. Processes in music therapy. In *Music in therapy*, ed. E. T. Gaston, 30–44. New York: Macmillan.

Seashore, C. E. 1919. *The psychology of musical talent*. Boston: Silver Burdett.

Seashore, C. E. 1938. *Psychology of music*. New York: McGraw-Hill.

Seashore, C. E. 1947. *In search of beauty in music: A scientific approach to musical esthetics*. New York: Ronald Press.

Serafine, M. L. 1988. *Music as cognition: The development of thought in sound*. New York: Columbia University Press.

Shepherd, J., P. Virden, G. Vulliamy, and T. Wishart, eds. 1977. *Whose music? A sociology of musical languages*. London: Latimer.

Shlain, L. 1991. *Art, and physics: Parallel visions in space, time, and light.* New York: William Morrow.

Shuter, R. 1968. *The psychology of musical ability.* London: Methuen.

Shuter-Dyson, R., and C. Gabriel. 1981. *The psychology of musical ability.* 2d ed. London: Methuen.

Silbermann, A. 1963. *The sociology of music.* Trans. C. Stewart. London: Routledge and Kegan Paul.

Sloboda, J. A. 1985. *The musical mind: The cognitive psychology of music.* Oxford: Oxford University Press.

Sloboda, J. A. 1988. *Generative processes in music: The psychology of performance, improvisation, and composition.* Oxford: Clarendon Press.

Soibelman, D. 1948. *Therapeutic and industrial uses of music: A review of literature.* New York: Columbia University Press.

Spintge, R., and R. Droh, eds. 1987. *Music in medicine: Neurophysiological basis, clinical applications, aspects in the humanities.* Berlin: Springer-Verlag.

Spintge, R., and R. Droh, eds. 1992. *MusicMedicine.* St. Louis: MMB Music.

Spintge, R., and R. Pratt, eds. 1995. *MusicMedicine 2.* St. Louis: MMB Music.

Starcke, W. 1973. *The gospel of relativity.* New York: Harper and Row.

Stehle, P. 1994. *Order, chaos, order: The transition from classical to quantum physics.* New York: Oxford University Press.

Steiner, L. R. 1977. *Psychic self-healing for psychological problems.* Englewood Cliffs, NJ: Prentice-Hall.

Stumpf, C. 1883. *Tonpsychologie.* Vol. 1. Leipzig: Hirzel.

Stumpf, C. 1890. *Tonpsychologie.* Vol. 2. Leipzig: Hirzel.

Swanwick, K. 1988. *Music, mind, and education.* London: Routledge.

Swisher, W. W. 1927. *Psychology for the music teacher.* Boston: Oliver Ditson.

Talbot, M. 1980. *Mysticism and the new physics.* New York: Bantam Books.

Talbot, M. 1991. *The holographic universe.* New York: HarperCollins.

Tansley, D. V. 1975. *Radionics: Interface with the ether-fields.* Devon, England: Health Science Press.

Tansley, D. V. 1977. *Dimensions of radionics: A Manual of radionic theory and practice for the health-care professional.* Devon, England: Health Science Press.

Tansley, D.V. 1984. *Chakras—Rays and radionics.* Safron Walden, Essex, England: C. W. Daniel.

Teplov, B. M. 1966. *Psychologie des aptitudes musicales.* Paris: Presses Universitaires de France.

Toffler, A. 1980. *The third wave.* New York: William Morrow.

Toffler, A. 1990. *Power shift: Knowledge, wealth, and violence at the edge of the twenty-first century.* New York: Bantam Books.

Tompkins, P., and C. Bird. 1973. *The secret life of plants.* New York: Avon Books.

Traphagan, J. W., and W. Traphagan. 1986. The nature of meaning in music. *Revision* 9, no. 1:99–104.

Valentine, C. W. 1962. *The experimental psychology of beauty.* London: Methuen.

Vidor, M. 1931. *Was ist musikalität?* Munich: Beck.

Walker, R. 1990. *Musical beliefs: Psychoacoustic, mythical, and educational perspectives.* New York: Teachers College Press.

Wallin, N. L. 1991. *Biomusicology: Neurophysiological, neuropsychological, and evolutionary perspectives on the origins and purposes of music.* Stuyvesant, NY: Pendragon Press.

Weber, M. 1958. *The rational and social foundations of music.* Trans. D. Martindale and J. Reidel, ed. G. Neuwirth. Carbondale: Southern Illinois University Press.

Whybrew, W. E. 1962. *Measurement and evaluation in music.* Dubuque, IA: W. C. Brown.

Whybrew, W. E. 1971. *Measurement and evaluation in music.* 2d ed. Dubuque, IA: W. C. Brown.

Wilber, K., ed. 1982. *The holographic paradigm and other paradoxes: Exploring the leading edge of science.* Boulder, CO: Shambhala.

Wilber, K., ed. 1984. *Quantum questions: Mystical writings of the world's great physicists.* Boulder, CO: Shambhala.

Wilczek, F., and B. Devine. 1988. *Longing for the harmonies: Themes and variations from modern physics.* New York: W. W. Norton.

Wilson, F. R., and F. L. Roehmann, eds. 1990. *Music and child development.* St. Louis: MMB Music.

Wilson, R. A. 1990. *Quantum psychology: How brain software programs you and your world.* Phoenix: New Falcon.

Wolf, F. A. 1981. *Taking the quantum leap: The new physics for nonscientists.* San Francisco: Harper and Row.

Wolf, F. A. 1986. *The body quantum: The new physics of body, mind, and health.* New York: Macmillan.

Zee, A. 1986. *Fearful symmetry: The search for beauty in modern physics.* New York: Macmillan.

Zinberg, N. E., ed. 1977. *Alternate states of consciousness.* New York: Free Press.

Zohar, D. 1990. *The quantum self: Human nature and consciousness defined by the new physics.* New York: William Morrow.

Zohar, D., and I. Marshall. 1994. *The quantum society: Mind, physics, and a new social vision.* New York: William Morrow.

Zuckerkandl, V. 1956. *Sound and symbol: Music and the external world.* Trans. W. R. Trask. Princeton, NJ: Princeton University Press.

Zuckerkandl, V. 1959. *The sense of music.* Princeton, NJ: Princeton University Press.

Zuckerkandl, V. 1973. *Man the musician: Sound and symbol.* Vol. 2. Trans. N. Guterman. Princeton, NJ: Princeton University Press.

Zukav, G. 1979. *The dancing Wu Li masters: An overview of the new physics.* New York: William Morrow.

2

Human Musicality

Donald A. Hodges

Music is a universal trait of humankind. Throughout the ages it has played a significant role in the lives of people in every part of the globe. This can be illustrated by imagining an internal soundtrack for each of the following vignettes.

> Fortaleza, Brazil: Nighttime revelers parade down the street by the light of flickering torches. The movements of the *cabocolinhos* (the dancers) are accompanied by drums, *caracaxa* (a scraped gourd), and flutes (Olsen 1980).

> Bayonne, New Jersey: A lonely, confused teenager sits brooding in his room. The headphones he wears are connected to a jambox (tape player), which is playing his favorite rock tapes.

> Barotesland, Ghana: Members of the Frafra tribe play on the *Dagomba* (a one-stringed fiddle) and shake rattles to accompany workers who are cutting grass (Nketia 1974). The workers swing their machetes rhythmically in such a way that the cutting sounds are timed to fall on the main beats of the music.

> Sakaka, Saudi Arabia: As a nervous bride makes last-minute preparations, she can hear the strains of the professional orchestra that has been hired to entertain the wedding guests. The *Nawba*, a suite of pieces, is being played on the *ud* (lute), *nay* (flute), and *duff* (tambourine) (Pacholczyk 1980).

> Madrid, Spain: Thousands of voices roar as the matador strides into the arena, followed by the banderilleros and picadores. Their

Part of this chapter is based on an article that previously appeared in the *Bulletin of the Council for Research in Music Education* 99 (1989): 7–22, and is used here by permission.

measured pace is timed to a pasodoble played by the band. Subsequent phases of the bullfight will be introduced or accompanied by the blaring of trumpets.

Roulers, Belgium: A nun sits in a corner of the convent garden. She is strumming lightly on a guitar and humming softly to herself.

Mazar-e-Sharif, Afghanistan: Mourners gather from all parts of the village at a mass burial for fallen soldiers. Their dirges are accompanied by the sound of a *ritchak,* a two-string lute whose sound box is made of a discarded, rectangular gasoline can (Malm 1967).

Yenyuan, China: Peasant families have been assembled to hear speeches given by visiting political dignitaries. The ceremonies begin with the appropriate, state-approved music played over loudspeakers.

These examples give some indication of the tremendous amount of music there is in the world and the profound and pervasive influences music exerts on human life. But how do we account for the pervasiveness and universality of human musicality? How did we come to be musical creatures? Is musicality indeed universal, and, if so, is it inherited or acquired? The purpose of this chapter is to explore some of these fundamental questions. Many of the issues raised herein will be visited in more detail in subsequent chapters.

For the following discussions, musicality is defined as a responsiveness or sensitivity to musical stimuli. It also includes an appreciation or understanding of music, but does not necessarily include technical proficiency in musical performance (George and Hodges 1980). In this regard, all persons possess some degree of musicality, because everyone responds in some fashion to the music of his or her surrounding culture. Even severely and profoundly retarded individuals respond to music in a rudimentary way. To be totally amusical would require massive, almost total brain damage.

The Musical Significance of Human Nature

What is it about human beings that makes us unique, and how do our musical behaviors fit into this uniqueness? Is music separate from humanness, or is there evidence to support a view of music as an integral part of human nature?

If we attempt to specify the ways in which human beings are unique and different from other animal species, we must quickly conclude that most, if not all, differences are in degree, not in kind. That is, other animals may possess a particular trait similar to humans, but not to the same extent. For example, if we say that a distinctive characteristic of humankind is language, it is possible to point to communication among dolphins or the sign language learned by chimpanzees in certain experiments as rudimentary forms of the same behavior. Or if we say that social organizations are a human trait, a parallel might be found in the behaviors of bees or ants. We have elaborate rituals connected with death, but elephants have been observed engaging in what might be called a burial ceremony. Music may even have its animal counterpart in whale song—to a degree. However, it is the degree of human involvement in such behaviors as language, social organizations, rituals, and music that separates us from other animals.

To say that our humanity arises from the degree of involvement we have in a specific behavior rather than the presence of that behavior implies that, while animals may exhibit rudimentary forms of certain human behaviors, differences between the animal and human versions are so vast as to make us unique. Returning to language, it is true that chimpanzees may, in certain laboratory experiments, learn to communicate via sign language. But it is important to note that they are learning human sign language with the aid of human tutors. Chimpanzees left alone in their natural environment certainly do communicate with each other. However, after millions of years, they still have not developed advanced linguistic skills, and to compare their communication skills with human language is simply to point out the distinctive differences between humans and chimpanzees.[1]

"We" study, write, and talk about "them," but, except in science fiction, "they" don't put "us" in labs or stalk us in our natural habitats to learn more about us and our actions. (Neither do they hunt us to extinction nor undertake major efforts to preserve us.) The Bible refers to ants as a model for improving human behavior—"Go to the ant, you sluggard, watch her ways and get wisdom" (Proverbs 6:6). Do the ants ever refer to humans to improve their behavior? Those animals that do mating "dances" do not choreograph new steps for the next season; whale "songs," for all their haunting lovlinesss, do not equate with the tremendous outpouring of music from all the world's people.

---

1. It must be clearly stated that this entire discussion is focused on the ways in which we are different, not better, than other animals. For example, to say that we are different because we have superior language skills should not imply a value judgment. One only has to witness the human slaughter of baby seals to realize that the question of "better or worse" is not an easy one to answer. Moreover, it is not a question that will be dealt with in these pages.

If human beings are different from animals primarily in degree and not necessarily in kind of behaviors, how then can we be described? What is the nature of human nature? Such a question has engaged philosophers, scientists, and artists for centuries and is not likely to be answered completely in these pages. However, in order to set the stage for subsequent discussions, ten ways in which human beings are unique will be introduced. Following the more general discussion, some brief remarks about the relationship of music to each unique trait will be made. The ten topics are: biological differences, adaptability, cultural evolution, symbolic behaviors, love, religion, play, technology, knowledge, and aesthetic sensitivity.

Biological Differences

As Eagle indicated in chapter 1, we live in a universe, not a diverse, for all living things share certain characteristics. For example, the genetic material for all living things that provides the instructions necessary for reproduction is deoxyribonucleic acid (DNA). Such primates as chimpanzees and apes are our closest relatives, so close that the genetic difference between man and chimpanzees is less than 2 percent and it takes a sophisticated biochemical analysis of our blood and that of a gorilla to tell the difference (Bodmer and McKie 1994). Yet human beings are clearly recognizable as a species.

Anatomically, the human hand is similar to that of a monkey species that lived 25 million years ago. However, even minor differences can have major consequences. For example, a gorilla's hand is long and slender with a short, stubby thumb; our hands are short with long thumbs. Our longer thumb allows for a precision grip with the index finger and makes possible the manipulation of microelectrodes in neurosurgery and other similar feats of dexterity, such as playing the piano. Another example of an anatomical difference that also has profound consequences is found in the larynx. We have a vocal tract that allows us to speak and sing; no other primate can.

Human beings also differ from other animals in the degree to which our behavior is controlled by inborn instructions. In birds, for example, such complex behaviors as nest building, flying south for the winter, and "singing" are largely the product of genetic hardwiring. In terms of behavior, human beings inherit reflexes such as eye blinking and startle responses, basic expressive responses such as blushing and smiling, and life-sustaining actions such as suckling and swallowing. However, more complex behavior patterns are learned, not instinctive. In comparison to birds, we do not build houses, travel, or sing in a genetically predetermined manner.

Anatomical variations and freedom from instincts notwithstanding, the most important difference between humans and other animals is our brain power. Those behaviors that make us distinctively human—language, art, religion, technology, and so on—are all generated from an enormous reservoir of potential. We start life with nearly three-fourths of the brain uncommitted to specific tasks, and there seem to be few limitations on what or how much might be learned (Farb 1978; Springer and Deutsch 1989).

Thus, it is our human biological potential that makes music possible. We are musical creatures because of our physical and mental makeup. Further exploration of this idea will be undertaken in considerable detail in subsequent chapters.

Adaptability

Most animals have a physical specialty. Jaguars are capable of blinding speed, eagles have incredible eyesight, bats fly by means of sophisticated echolocation. Human beings, it might be said, are mental specialists and physical generalists. That is, rather than coming to rely on brute strength, fast running, or a keen sense of smell, we opted for no particular physical specialty. In order to survive, we came to rely on quick wits and an ability to gain an advantage through mental means.

Tremendous intellectual capabilities (including enormous amounts of uncommitted brain power), combined with a lack of predetermined behavior patterns (instincts) and a lack of reliance on a specific physical trait have given us freedoms that no other animals have. We have a freedom to become or to do nearly anything that we can conceive. Said another way, we are enormously plastic creatures. We have survived in every possible climate—from deserts to arctic regions, from the depths of oceans to outer space. While other animals are destined to lead a lifestyle appropriate for their species, we have lived as nomads, nuns, and whalers.

Another way of describing human adaptability is through a term used by Rene Dubos in his book, *Celebrations of Life* (1981). The term he used is *invariants* and he used it to describe how human beings everywhere can be so much the same and yet so very different. As human beings we all have certain invariant needs, but the way in which those needs are satisfied varies tremendously from group to group. The need for food is an invariant, as it is for all animals. But contrast the consistency of diet among members of a particular animal species with the variety in human diets. From vegetables to insects, human beings exhibit an amazing proclivity toward eating nearly anything that is edible. The need for food is an invariant, but particular diets are not. An interesting time can be had by considering the multitudinous ways we realize other invariants—shelter: from igloo to marble palace; clothing: from Scottish kilt to Japanese kimono, and so on through a long list. All these invariants provide illustrations of human adaptability.

Art is another human invariant; people in all times and in all places sing, draw, and dance. Our plasticity has led us to create sand paintings and stained-glass windows, limericks and novels, square dances and grand ballet, the huge stone heads on Easter Island and miniature ivory carvings of the Orient. In music we have the simplicity and immediacy of the African thumb piano as well as the complexity and grandeur of the pipe organ. We have the musical background to 15-second television commercials and four-hour Chinese operas. We are in art, as in all things, highly adaptable creatures.

Cultural Evolution

Another of the clearly distinguishing marks of humanity is the fact that we are the only species engaged in cultural evolution in addition to biological evolution. The general idea behind biological evolution is that organisms possessing an attribute beneficial to survival generally live longer and are thus more likely to confer the same attribute to their descendents. Over hundreds of thousands or even millions of years, that attribute may come to be characteristic of all the members of a species—all elephants have trunks, for example.

Human beings were originally shaped by biological evolution. However, at some point in our history, we began to override the system. We did this by changing our environment rather than having it change us (Dubos 1974; Pfeiffer 1969). Animals trying to exist in arctic climates developed various protective devices, such as heavy fur coats and thick layers of blubber, to combat the frigid temperatures. Humans caught in the same situation did not grow thick coverings of hair (though they did undergo some minor changes, such as the development of a slightly thicker layer of subcutaneous fat). Rather, they modified the environment; they created parkas and igloos and other means of surviving the bitter cold. Even now we continue to evolve primarily through cultural adaptations.

Human culture includes all of our socially transmitted behavior patterns. Thus, our political, social, educational, economic, and religious institutions are a part of culture, as are all other products of human thought. Also included in every culture are ways of enriching the sensory environment. Sights, sounds, tastes, smells, and textures are all manipulated, experimented with, and controlled to a certain degree. This interaction with the sensory environment leads to art, a primary aspect of culture.

Culture also allows each generation to benefit from the accomplishments of the parent generation. Lamarck, a nineteenth century French biologist, believed that children inherited the acquired attributes of their parents. While this is clearly not true, it is true that much of human progress has been the result of a patient accumulation of knowledge over many generations. Even the quantum leaps made by such intellectual giants as Newton or Einstein were possible because of the foundations laid by others. Cooperation is a trait that, while observed in other species, has become a hallmark of human cultural evolution. We have often succeeded because of cooperative efforts. Division of labor is a means of allowing individuals time to devote to a task that may benefit the whole group. Contemporary societies continue to depend heavily on cooperation, perhaps even more than ever before. Cooperation is also a prime requisite for group activities, such as athletic contests and music making.

Culture is important in another way. Human beings are automatically biological members of the human race, but we must learn to behave as other humans do. The stored knowledge of a society allows each individual to become acculturated into that society. Learning to control bodily functions, walk, and talk, all require interactions with other human beings. Music can play an important role in the acculturation process. For example, being aware of the latest top 40 tunes is an important way for a teenager to be accepted by a peer group.

Art has clearly played a major role in cultural evolution. Different groups of people in different times and places can be identified through their art works. Studying a group's art provides unique insights into its character. In fact, it is not possible to know a tribe or nation fully without considering its art.

Symbolic Behaviors

One readily identifiable mark of human uniqueness is our highly developed capacity for symbolic behavior. This is perhaps most evident in our use of language. Language makes it possible for us to communicate a wealth of ideas—from the functionality of the telephone book to the imagery of poetry. But while language is indispensible to human lifestyles, it is, nonetheless, inadequate for expressing the full range of human thought and feeling.

In addition to language, we have developed a broad range of nonverbal symbolic behaviors, including mathematical symbols and computer languages, body language, and art. Symbols such as hair style, body adornments, and mode of dress can communicate an enormous amount of information about an individual or a group of people. Religious tenets are often expressed in a powerful way through symbols—the Star of David or the Crucifix are but two of many familiar examples. Nonverbal forms of communication would be unnecessary if we could express everything with words. However, nonverbal communication not only supplements and extends verbal communication, as in the use of gestures while speaking, but also provides for distinct modes of expression.

Art provides a way of knowing and feeling that is not possible through any other means. What is gained through an art experience can be discussed, analyzed, or shared verbally, but cannot be experienced verbally. Thus, as totem poles, portraits, or national anthems are artistic symbols that give humankind tremendously powerful means of communicating and sharing.

Love

Perhaps more than any other attribute thus far discussed, love demonstrates the truth of an earlier statement: Differences between humankind and other animals are ones more of degree than of kind. Any animal observer can certainly attest to the fact of loving behaviors among animals. Thus, rather than speculate on whether human beings love more than other animals do, suffice it to say that human beings have a tremendous need to love and to be loved.

In fact, love is so important to human beings that without it we suffer severe physical and psychological consequences. Many illnesses might be traced to disabilities in the giving and receiving of love. Because it is so crucial to us, we have developed many ways of sharing and expressing love. We murmur terms of endearment and struggle to articulate inner feelings in poetic verse. The sense of touch is vitally important in our expressions of love. Music, too, is an often-used vehicle.

From the singing of lullabies to the crooning of love ballads, from the use of funeral dirges or wedding songs, music is a powerful means of communicating love from one to another. Alma maters, national anthems, and hymns are examples of ways we use music to express love of school and friends, love of country, and love of God.

Play

Human beings spend enormous amounts of time engaging in activities that do not seem at first glance to be necessary for biological survival.

Even the amount of time we spend daydreaming while supposedly "at work" gives us evidence of that. Beyond daydreaming, there are many other activities we could list under a generic term such as *play:* athletic contests, reading, watching television, even visiting or gossiping with one another.

Celebrations, a formalized style of play, represent another of the human invariants that were discussed previously. All over the world, human beings find almost any excuse to celebrate. Beside obvious celebrations such as birthdays, weddings, and religious holidays, we celebrate the coming of spring, important battles, and the gathering of the harvest. Celebrations are very much a part of human nature; likewise, singing and dancing are integral parts of celebrations. Indeed, it is difficult to think of any celebrations that have no music.

That art and celebrations are interrelated is perhaps supportive of a particular viewpoint of the nature of art. In this view, art is a type of creative play (Pfeiffer 1969). Human beings are quite naturally intrigued by the surprise, adventure, and experimentation that come with the manipulation of objects, ideas, and sensory materials. Our very creativity is born of this sense of adventure and it brings us pleasure. In music, manipulating and experimenting with sounds is at the root of compositional activity.

Humor is a special kind of play. Whether physical comedy, as in slapstick, or mental humor, as in puns, we take great delight in twists and variations on the expected. There are many pieces of music in which the unexpected is likewise intended to elicit a mirthful response. Mozart's *Musical Joke* is but one example.

Religion

Humankind is clearly marked by its spiritual nature. The need to consider a power beyond our own is so universal that it is deeply ingrained in human nature. While each of us must wrestle with the eternal questions—Who put us here? Why are we here? What is the meaning of life?—societies have deemed the issues important enough that certain members of the community are assigned responsibility for such matters. Priest, shaman, rabbi, prophet, monk, muezzin—all are set aside to pursue answers to spiritual questions.

Religious practices have been with us for a long time. The Neanderthals left behind artifacts connected with burial rituals that indicate some sense of concern for the spirits of the dead as long as 60,000 years ago (Constable 1973). Even from the beginnings, as far as we have any knowledge of it, and certainly in all the practices since then, music has been a part of religious worship. This is so because language is inadequate to express fully our spiritual feelings; music can take us beyond the confines of words. Perhaps music and religion are so intertwined because both deal primarily with internal feelings rather than external facts. Whatever the reasons, religious beliefs and the expression of these beliefs through music are a ubiquitous fact of human nature.

Technology

From the time we learned to control and use fire to the time of computerization, humankind has been most conspicuous by our technological inventions. We are a toolmaking species and we seem always to be seeking ways to do a task easier, faster, better. Tools have extended our capabilities far beyond our physical limitations.

It is entirely in keeping with our nature that we extend our toolmaking into areas of life other than work. Consider athletics, for example; we are constantly improving on athletic "tools" that, within the rules, will give us an edge on the competition. The pole used in pole vaulting has changed in recent years from a rigid bamboo pole to a more pliant steel pole and finally to a highly flexible fiberglass pole. Golf balls that will fly farther, tennis rackets with a larger "sweet spot," training devices with more and more gadgets, are all examples. Tools are used in music, too. In fact, all instruments are "tools" used to create sounds beyond the scope of the human voice.

There is another connection between art and tools. Tools have always been made with an eye to something beyond functional design. Spear points and axe handles are created with attention to shape. Jugs— "tools" for carrying water—are shaped in a manner and with a flair that are not necessary for utilitarian purposes, but seem to be necessary for human pleasure. Some anthropologists even consider that the bow was first a musical instrument before it became a weapon. Other technological advances had their genesis in artistic pursuits. Techniques in metallurgy, welding, and ceramics are but three examples. Farb even states explicit that "the great advances in technology would obviously have been impossible without the human urge to explore new directions in artistic creativity" (Farb 1978, 75).

Knowledge

One of the unique traits of humankind is a natural propensity for seeking knowledge. Concepts of the human infant as a tabula rasa or as a passive organism reacting only to the environment are wrong. We are active seekers of knowledge. It is basic to human nature to be curious, to wonder, to explore, to discover.

Knowledge can be gained through all the sense modalities. We can learn about our world by touch; for the blind this becomes an important avenue of information, a substitute way of "seeing." Babies, in particular, explore their world through taste; everything goes immediately into the mouth. Smelling may seem like a less important means of gathering knowledge, but we can "know" something about a stranger based on body odor. Because the olfactory lobes are in close proximity to the site of long-term memory storage, remembrances of past events are often triggered by odors. Vision and hearing are primary means of gathering knowledge.

Some of the first things we know are learned through hearing. Our sense of hearing begins to function in the last few months of fetal development and babies recognize the sounds of their mothers' voices within a few days, if not sooner. Notice that what the baby "knows" about mother is not factual information but feelings—feelings associated with security and pleasure. This is an important concept to remember—that knowledge involves far more than facts.

Music is an important way of knowing. Think, for a moment, of all the things one can learn or know through nursery songs, religious music, popular and commercial music (including music used in advertising, movies, and television shows), folk music, and art music. On a superficial level, one can learn the alphabet through music. At a deeper level, one can learn about foreign cultures through music. Finally, at perhaps the deepest level, one can learn more about oneself and gain insights into the human condition through music.

Aesthetic Sensitivity

In all times and in all places, human beings have sought to create beauty. The variety of ways we have done so is nothing short of staggering. We have decorated our own bodies in nearly every way conceivable (though future generations will find still more ways). We have inserted disks in our lips, scarified and tatooed our arms and trunks, bound our feet, and stretched our necks. No part of our bodies has been immune from this process—we have painted our toenails and twisted, combed, shaped, and colored our hair into innumerable styles.

Lest describing it in this way seems like a description of aboriginies rather than modern, sophisticated Americans, consider that one of the "rages" of recent years has been the tanning parlor. For a sum of money, a person can step into a booth with virtually no clothes on, push some buttons, and toast his skin to just the right shade.

What we have done to our bodies we have done to clothes, food, and dwellings. Beyond the decoration of our surroundings, human beings have always and everywhere explored every mode of sensory experience with an aesthetic sensitivity that is supremely characteristic of our species. The manipulation of sound, sight, space, and movement—the arts—has given us tremendous insights into the human condition and brought us much pleasure in the process. To be human is to have the potential of perceiving and responding to artistic experiences with a depth of feeling. We are as much aesthetic creatures as we are physical, social, intellectual, emotional, and religious beings.

Summary

Human beings differ from other animals primarily in the extent to which we engage in certain behaviors. An overview of these differences has been presented under the following ten topics.

Biological Differences
Human beings are biologically unique in several important ways, including our anatomical differences and freedom from instinctive behaviors. However, the biological potential of our brains is what most separates us from the other animals.

Adaptability
Human beings are unique because of our high degree of adaptability. We have no physical specialty but are mental specialists instead. The concept of invariants is useful in understanding how human beings express common needs in an infinite variety of behaviors. We are not bound to live our lives in a prescribed manner due to genetic programming, but we are free to adapt to many different lifestyles.

Cultural Evolution
We are the only animal species engaged in cultural evolution. Culture is the vehicle by which we continually adapt to our environment. It is also the way we share our accomplishments with each new generation.

Symbolic Behaviors
Verbal language is a very distinctive mark of our humanity. It allows us to communicate and express thought with precision or with imagery.

We also have a broad repertoire of nonverbal symbolic behaviors. These are useful not only for supplementing words but also for expressing ourselves in ways that are impossible through words.

Love
Human beings have a strong need to give and to receive love. The loving process is critical to the development and maintenance of a healthy personality. As is fitting with so important a behavior, we have devised numerous ways of sharing and expressing love.

Play
Play is not only pleasurable, it is an important and necessary part of human life. Play, in the formalized sense of celebrations, occupies a central place in all human cultures. Creative play comes from the manipulation of the sensory environment and contains elements of surprise and adventure. Play as humor is also found everywhere.

Religion
The need human beings have to worship seems to be so ingrained as to be a universal trait. As groups of people and as individuals, all human beings have considered questions of a spiritual nature. So important is our spiritual nature, that certain individuals within each group are set aside to handle matters of religious concern.

Technology
Sometimes we have been called the toolmaker. Our technological achievements have allowed us to make progress in nearly every field of human endeavor.

Knowledge
Human beings are characterized by their thirst for knowledge. We are designed to be curious creatures. Our natural inquisitiveness has driven us to create a wide variety of ways of knowing.

Aesthetic Sensitivity
The human race has always been concerned with the notion of beauty. We are moved by the beauty we experience in our natural world and also by that which we have created. Creating and/or responding to beauty is part and parcel of being human.

These, then, are some of the ways we are unique. While this is but a brief introduction, the significant role that music plays in human nature should already be apparent. Music is not a separate, trivial, side issue of being human; rather, musicality is at the core of what it means to be human. As Thomas has stated:

> I believe fervently in our species and have no patience with the current fashion of running down the human being as a useful part of nature. On the contrary, we are a spectacular, splendid manifestation of life. We have language and can build metaphors as skillfully and precisely as ribosomes make proteins. We have affection. We have genes for usefulness, and usefulness is about as close to a "common goal" for all of nature as I can guess at. And finally, and perhaps best of all, we have music. Any species capable of producing, at this earliest, juvenile stage of its development—almost instantly after emerging on the earth by any evolutionary standard— the music of Johann Sebastian Bach, cannot be all bad. (Thomas 1979, 16–17)

Why Are We Musical? Speculations on the Evolutionary Plausibility of Musical Behavior

In considering the nature of human musicality, one might reasonably wonder why we are musical at all and how did we come to be this way? Oddly enough, there are frequent statements in the literature that make it appear as if there is no known reason for music.[2] "Musical skills are not essential so far as we know" (Brown 1981, 8). "Reactions to music are not obviously of direct biological significance" (Dowling and Harwood 1986, 202). One "might ask why evolution should have provided us with such complex innate machinery, for which there is no evident survival value" (Lerdahl and Jackendoff 1983, 232–33). "Why do we respond emotionally to music, when the messages therein seem to be of no obvious survival value?" (Roederer 1982, 38). "Why do we have music, and let it occupy our lives with no apparent reason?" (Minsky 1982, 12).

These statements are all the more puzzling since it is becoming increasingly clear that every human being has "a biologic guarantee of musicianship" (Wilson 1986, 2). This is so because genetic instructions create a brain and body that are predisposed to be musical. Just as we are born to be linguistic, with the specific language to be learned determined by the culture, so we are born with the means to be responsive to the music of our culture. If music does not confer any survival

---

2. In fairness, several of these statements are somewhat misleading when taken out of context and some of the authors do attempt to provide a rationale for the existence of music.

benefits, why would it be provided for in our neurophysiological structures? Why would it have developed to the point where it is a universal trait of our species?

A place to begin looking for answers is with the central focus of evolutionary theory. Attributes that confer survival benefits upon members of a species, whether arrived at through genetic mutation or adaptation to the environment, are passed on to offspring. Stronger members of a species, by virtue of these attributes, are more likely to live longer and to produce more offspring; thus, the attributes they possess are more likely to be promoted until such time as all members of the species possess the same attributes. In this way did the cheetah get its speed and the giraffe its long neck.

One way of getting at the evolutionary basis for music is to look at the primary element of all music, rhythm. Before proceeding any further, however, a cautionary note must be put forward. While the following discussion is as based on data as possible, much of it is speculative. Because the earliest examples of musical behavior left no fossilized remains, there are no records, no direct vestiges. There are many secondary sources from which to deduce early musical behaviors.[3] But in the final analysis, all one can offer is a best guess based on the scant information available.

Rhythm, a Fundamental Life Process

One of the tenets of quantum physics is that everything that exists is in a state of vibration. Atoms vibrate at rates of a million billion times per second, while the sun vibrates with a period of five minutes (Chen 1983, 392). Helioseismology is the study of the sun's oscillations and astronomers tell us that the galaxies and the entire universe are in states of vibration.

Human beings live in what we perceive to be a rhythmic environment, based on observations of periodicities. Seasons of the year, phases of the moon, and periods of daylight and dark follow in regular, timely patterns. Our bodies, too, operate on rhythmic patterns. Heart and breathing rates are two of the more obvious bodily processes that are periodic. Brain waves, hormonal outputs, and sleeping patterns are examples of the more than 100 complex oscillations monitored by the brain (Farb 1978, 293). Chronobiologists, those who study body rhythms, believe

---

3. Cave paintings are one example of a secondary source from which one might deduce musical behaviors. Some cave paintings as early as 70,000 years ago depict a bow, and many anthropologists believe that the bow may have been as much a musical instrument as it was a weapon (Mumford 1966). (See chap. 12 for more details.)

that rhythm is such an important part of life that a lack of it can indicate illness. For example, complex forms of dysrhythmia may be a symptom of autism, manic depression, or schizophrenia; dysrhythmia can also indicate dyslexia or other learning disabilities (Bohannan 1983; Condon 1982; Wehr 1982).

The impact of rhythmic experiences is widespread. Rhythm is a critical factor in language acquisition. Also, infants who receive stimulation through rocking or other body movements gain weight faster, develop vision and hearing acuity faster, and acquire regularity of sleep cycles at a younger age. Perhaps even more important is the fact that the cerebellum is directly linked to the limbic system, specifically a region of the hypothalamus known as the pleasure center. The result is that body movement brings pleasure. Infants deprived of movement and closeness will fail to develop brain pathways that mediate pleasure (Restak 1979; see also Eccles and Robinson 1985; McCall 1979; Restak 1983). Integration into environmental rhythms begins at birth with the onset of rhythmic breathing and continues as the baby gradually adapts to the rhythmic cycles of the world into which it has been born. Over the next months, the patterns of family life, particularly the parent's cycle of activity and rest, will condition and shape the baby's social rhythms. This is highly important, since nearly all social interactions are rhythmically based.

Researchers have discovered that "persons involved in social interactions unconsciously move 'in space' with one another through a rhythmic coordination of gestures and movements which exhibit all the characteristics of a dance" (Montagu and Matson 1979, 150). Using sophisticated film equipment that allows projection at very slow or very fast speeds, these researchers have filmed such diverse social interactions as two people in conversation and family gatherings. Often the synchronous movements of the participants are so rhythmic they can be coordinated with music as if they had been choreographed. In fact, one researcher, Hall (1976), did exactly that. First, he filmed children on a playground. After extensive study of the four-and-a-half-minute film, he began to see how synchronized the children's movements were. When he later found some music to accompany the film clip, the synchronization between the children's movements and the music was so exact that people could not believe it had not been previously choreographed.

The rhythmic aspects of human behavior are so powerful that entrainment is possible (Hall 1976; see also Brown and Graeber 1982; Davis 1982; Evans and Clynes 1986). Entrainment occurs when two or more persons become attuned to the same rhythm. Nonhuman examples of entrainment include a school of fish or a flying V of migrating birds changing directions suddenly. Human entrainment has been demonstrated experimentally when two people in conversation produced brain wave tracings so identical as to appear to have emanated from the same person. Entrainment may also be operating in riots and other large crowd behaviors. Musical entrainment probably occurs at nearly any concert but is particularly evident in overt audience behaviors such as at rock concerts.

In the midst of all these physiological, environmental, and social rhythms, it is important to consider the fact that human beings are much more time independent than other living things. Plants thrive or wither depending on the time of year. Likewise, many animals, especially the cold-blooded ones, are dependent upon time cycles (light/dark, heat/cold) for their existence. Human beings, instead, rely on homeostasis to provide an internal environment that is relatively constant and somewhat independent of external events. Thus, our internal body temperature varies only one or two degrees above or below 98.6°F, whether it is blazing summer or bone-chilling winter. At the same time, "strategies were acquired by the brain in its fundamental operations of knowing, learning and remembering, which mediate the relationship between the internal environment of mind and the external environment of the world. They supply psychological sameness, as homeostasis provides biological sameness" (Campbell 1986, 55–56).

Hearing is a primary sense through which we create a stable, inner world of time. Millions of years ago, when dinosaurs ruled the earth, mammals, then just small forest creatures, were forced to hunt at night for safety's sake. Hunting at night requires a keen sense of hearing. Sound events occurring across time must be ordered to become meaningful. A rustling of leaves may indicate a predator approaching or prey retreating. Thus, evolution provided us with a remarkable capacity to interpret sounds that are time ordered. "To hear a sequence of rustling noises in dry leaves as a connected pattern of movements in space is a very primitive version of the ability to hear, say, Mozart's *Jupiter* Symphony as a piece of music, entire, rather than as momentary sounds which come and then are no more . . ." (Campbell 1986, 263–64).

This discussion has suggested some of the reasons we are rhythmic creatures and how our ability to deal with time-ordered behavior may have evolved. It does not yet tell us, however, specifically why musical behaviors were necessary. Some aspects of rhythmic and time-ordered behavior are just as true of speech as they are of music. What advantages did music confer on human beings so that it has become a species-specific trait? Because evolution works too stingily to assign only one function to each trait, there are several possible ways music may have conferred survival benefits on humankind. These are organized under four headings: mother-infant bonding, the acquisition of language, a unique mode of knowing, and social organization.

Mother-Infant Bonding

In consideration of the survival benefits music has to offer, the evolutionary advantage of the smile, like music a universally innate human trait, provides a useful analogy. From a more recent, cultural evolutionary standpoint, the smile has taken on many diverse meanings. However, from a biological evolutionary standpoint, the primary survival benefit may have been the bonding of mother and infant (Konner 1987). Likewise, music has many widely diverse cultural meanings today. However, at its roots it may also have had survival benefits in connection with mother-infant bonding. The first step in arriving at this conclusion is to look at the evolutionary history of the brain.

Australopithecus africanus, a small, humanlike primate that evolved nearly five million years ago, had a brain of about 500 cc (Cowan 1979; Feldenkrais 1979; Jastrow 1981; Montagu 1979; Sagan 1977). Within two million years, the brain nearly doubled in size so that Homo erectus had an average brain size of approximately 975 cc. Today, the average adult human brain is about 1450 cc and weighs about three pounds. In the womb, the brain of the fetus grows at the rate of 250,000 brain cells per minute. At birth, the brain is 12 percent of the total body weight, but even then it is incompletely developed. It takes the next six years for the brain to reach 90 percent of its adult size, when it will represent approximately 2 percent of body weight. This is in contrast to rhesus monkeys, for example, who are born with a brain that is already 75 percent of its eventual adult size. If the human fetus were carried "full term" in terms of brain development, the head would be too large to pass through the birth canal and we would be unable to be delivered. The evolutionary solution to this problem was that we are now born with our brains incompletely developed. At birth, the skull bones are not yet knit together, allowing for increase in brain mass.

The result of this postpartum brain development is an increased period of dependency of infants on their parents. Compared with any other animal species, human infants are more helpless and for a far longer time. The fact that human mothers most often give birth to single babies rather than litters means that more time may be devoted to the individual child. While the baby is in this stage, he or she is growing, developing, and learning at a tremendous rate. Nearly 75 percent of a newborn's cerebral cortex is uncommitted to specific behaviors (Farb 1978; Springer and Deutsch 1989). This uncommitted gray matter, called association areas, allows for the integration and synthesis of sensory inputs in novel ways. It is in this way that human ingenuity is possible.

Human behaviors are not instinctive, but acquired, and it is during this period of extended infant dependency that we acquire many important human behaviors.[4] Mothers and newborns confer many important physiological and psychological benefits on each other and perhaps chief among the many behaviors that are first observed at this point are loving behaviors. Babies learn to love almost immediately and in turn are nurtured by love. The importance of these loving interactions cannot be overstated.

In the late nineteenth and early twentieth centuries, records kept in American and European foundling homes indicated that infants under one year of age who were placed in these homes suffered a death rate of nearly 100 percent. This syndrome was so prevalent that many homes would enter "condition hopeless" into the records when the baby was first received because they knew that the child was destined to perish. The condition was even given a name—*marasmus,* a Greek word meaning "wasting away" (Farb 1978; Montagu 1977 and 1978; Montagu and Matson 1979).

For a long time the authorities were unable to trace the cause of the malady; it seemed not to lie in poor diet nor in lack of clothing or shelter. Eventually, the cause of and cure for the problem was discovered in a German foundling home. Soon after the hiring of an elderly woman, the babies began to survive. This old lady merely spent time every day loving each infant. They had been dying from lack of love. (Modern nursing literature recognizes "nonorganic failure-to-thrive" infants as those with acute, life-threatening physical symptoms, as well as potential for long-term psychological and emotional problems. See Beck 1993; Colloton 1989.)

Love and affection are communicated to a baby through a number of ways. Speaking, singing, and touching are three primary modes of communicating with infants. Some psychologists have coined the term *motherese* in reference to the particular kind of speech patterns mothers use with their infants (Birdsong 1984). The musical aspects of motherese are critically important, not only as an aid to language acquisition, but especially in the communication of emotions. Long before youngsters begin to talk, they are adept at deciphering the emotional content of speech, largely due to the musical characteristics of motherese. In motherese speech, it is the pitch, timbral, dynamic, and rhythmic aspects to which

---

4. We do inherit reflexes and many predispositions, such as personality traits, that influence our behaviors. However, instincts, if they are defined as relatively complex patterns of behavior that are essentially unmodifiable over time, are not inherited (Lefrancois 1979).

the baby responds, certainly not the verbal content. "You are an ugly baby" spoken in a soft, sing-song fashion will elicit a far more positive response than "you are a beautiful baby" shouted in an angry tone.

Of course, the communication system is a two-way affair. Babies, too, are learning to give love as well as receive it. Vocalizations are a primary way babies express their feelings (Fridman 1973; Roberts 1987). Even in the first few days, babies begin to establish a relationship with their parents through their cries. In the first few months of life, they develop a wider range of crying styles that form a particular kind of infant language. The development of variations in crying styles is important to emotional development, in providing cues to parents regarding their state, and in practicing for the eventual development of language. Babies learn to cry to gain attention and to express an increasing range of feelings. Because their vocalizations are nonverbal, it is once again the manipulation of pitch, timbre, rhythm, and dynamics that forms the basis of their communications system.

Survival benefits of musical behaviors in terms of mother-infant bonding may be summarized in three steps. (1) As the human brain increased in size over millions of years, it was necessary for birth to occur before the brain reached full development. Likewise, this increased the period of postpartum infant dependency to the point where human infants are totally helpless for an extended length of time. (2) During the period of infant dependency it is critically important for the baby to receive love and affection. Research into the condition identified as marasmus shows that a baby less than one year old will die without enough love. (3) Musical elements are primary means of communicating love and affection to a newborn. These elements include rhythmic behaviors such as rocking, patting, and stroking and the modulation of pitch, timbre, dynamics, and rhythm in both speaking and singing. As the cranial capacity and length of infant dependency increased, there would clearly be survival benefits in building in a responsiveness to nonverbal forms of communication. Even if the earliest examples of these behaviors were what might be called "premusical," cultural evolution could easily have taken advantage of the inherent possibilities once the responsiveness was built in.

Imagine a small tribe of people living many thousands of years ago. A mother sits cradling a newborn baby in her arms. This baby will be totally dependent upon her for all the basic necessities of life—food, clothing, shelter, protection—for nearly two years and somewhat dependent upon her for many years after that. If the baby did not respond to anything related to musical or premusical behaviors, how would the mother communicate love? And if the mother could not communicate love, how would the baby survive? And if the baby could not survive, how could the species survive? Fortunately, the baby has an inborn capacity to respond to a wide range of premusical expressions. A large part of this inborn response mechanism must deal with some notion of pleasure. Warmth, assurance, security, contentedness, even nascent feelings of happiness are all a part of what is being shared with the baby. If these responses to pre-musical activities were wired into the brain, is it not understandable that music still brings us deep pleasure long after cultural evolution has developed these premusical behaviors into bagpipes, grand opera, or gamelan orchestras?

The Acquisition of Language
A second means of conferring survival benefits through music is in the acquisition of language. Acquiring language skills is one of the most important steps to be taken for the survival of the human species and attributes that would assist in this process would thus be selected for their advantages. The musical aspects of language have already been mentioned; melodic contour, timbre variations, and rhythm are of primary importance to speech. One of the outcomes of the mother-infant dyad discussed previously is that the baby becomes motivated to recognize and respond to sound patterns that will later become necessary for speech perception. When parents communicate with their infants, their "baby talk" quite naturally emphasizes the melodic, timbral, and rhythmic aspects used in the native tongue.

Two related experiments demonstrated how alert babies are to sounds (Restak 1983). Three-month-old infants were shown two cartoons simultaneously while the sound track of only one played in the background. The babies stared selectively at the cartoon whose sound was being played. In the second experiment, two cartoons were superimposed, again with the sound track of only one played. As the cartoons were gradually separated, the babies followed the one being accompanied by sound. Clearly, we have inborn mechanisms that orient us toward sound.

Rhythm also plays a crucial role in language acquisition. Newborns move their limbs in rhythm to the speech they hear around them (Bohannan 1983). If they hear a different language, their rhythms will change subtly. Rhythmic activities in the acquisition of language are so important that they form the basis for acquiring cognitive expectancies and for interrelating cognition and affect (Stern 1982). According to Campbell (1986), the ability to interpret microtimed intervals exists only for speech and music and nowhere else.

Simultaneously with the acquisition of the mechanics of listening to and producing speech, infants are learning other useful information through the musical aspects of communication. They are learning that there are important nonverbal messages to be sent and received. Almost any utterance can be spoken with an infinite variety of shadings and resultant meanings. Through such means as body language, context, and primarily through the musical aspects of speech (prosody), one can express the "real" meaning behind the words. In terms of biological evolution, equipping the brain with neural systems that have the ability to produce and interpret both verbal and nonverbal messages was a crucial step in our survival. Considerable data (presented in chap. 7) exist to document that language and music are processed by different neural mechanisms.

One survival benefit of the musical aspects of the brain may be in the acquisition of language. Infants are predisposed to orient toward sounds. Interchanges with adults who use motherese speech motivate the baby to pay attention to the melodic contours, timbres, and rhythms of speech. The baby is also learning to perceive and emit sound with both emotional and cognitive content.

A Unique Mode of Knowing
The preceding discussion of music's role in the acquisition of speech may have seemed to place it in a secondary or supporting role. But remembering that there may be multiple functions for the same attribute, the third survival benefit of music is that it provides a unique mode of knowing: It has immense value in and of itself.

In *Frames of Mind* (1983), Howard Gardner posited his theory of multiple intelligences. In opposition to a single indicator of intelligence, the I.Q. score, Gardner proposed the following seven: linguistic, musical, logical-mathematical, spatial, bodily-kinesthetic, interpersonal, and intrapersonal intelligence. Each of these types of intelligence was included on the basis of eight criteria: potential isolation by brain damage; the existence of prodigies, idiot savants, and other exceptional individuals; an identifiable core operation or set of operations; a distinctive developmental history, along with a definable set of expert "end-state" performances; an evolutionary history and evolutionary plausibility; support from experimental psychological tasks; support from psychometric findings; and susceptibility to encoding in a symbol system.

Each intelligence, or mode of knowing, is uniquely suited to allow human beings to understand the universe in which we live in a unique way. One is not better than another, they are just different. Thus, as powerful as language is, it is limited in what it can communicate. Some of the most important human concepts, such as truth, beauty, justice, love, and faith, can be learned and understood through nonverbal experiences as well as through the use of words. Moreover, it is possible to "think" artistically. The Mozart Requiem and a Lebanese funeral lament represent musical thinking on the subject of death. Why is this important to human survival? The ability of the human race to survive in this world was not dependent upon physical prowess in terms of strength, speed, eyesight, or sense of smell. It depended upon what could be learned. Human beings needed to know about themselves and the world in as many different ways as possible in order to compete successfully.

Much of musical thinking may be placed under a broader heading of play. While this may seem, once again, like a denigration of music, there are, in actuality, significant evolutionary advantages to play. The importance of play is understood more clearly when seen in the fullest sense of exploring, examining, and problem solving (Brown 1994). Curiosity may have killed the cat, but for human beings it has led to discoveries and inventions that have aided survival. Playing with every aspect of the environment has led both to the "invention" of the spear and to the songs and dances that accompany the hunt and the battle. Which is more important? Are not both necessary for survival? There are indeed significant survival premiums in play, generally, and in musical play, specifically. What human beings have learned about themselves and the world through music has been of tremendous benefit.

Perhaps the most important thing human beings have learned through music is how to deal with feelings. Although certain emotional responses may be inborn as a protective mechanism, by and large we have to learn to recognize and express feelings, as the previous discussion of learning to love indicated. One of the hallmarks of humanness is a sensitivity to feelings that allows for many subtle nuances. Being fully human means to experience the infinite shadings that exist between the polar ends of emotional states. Our experience of these finely feathered feelings is essentially nonverbal. Notice how limited our vocabulary is in this area and how often we experience difficulty in telling another exactly how we feel.

Music may provide a means of conferring survival benefits through the socialization of emotions. When group living is mandatory for survival, as it is for human beings, learning to react to others with sensitivity has clear evolutionary advantages. Lions hunt in groups; however, after a kill has been made each individual fights for his or her share. The biggest and strongest get the most to eat. This display of aggression at feeding time necessitates a subsequent period of licking and rubbing—"making up." This is necessary to keep the social bonds of the pride in place (Joubart 1994).

Listening to the daily news is all one needs to do to realize that human beings still have to deal with many aggressive behaviors in our societies. We need to find ways to separate actions from feelings. How does one feel anger without acting on it? How does one avoid giving in to loneliness and despair? These are extreme examples, but at all levels of feeling it is important to learn how to feel deeply without always resorting to action. Music is one of the most powerful outlets for expressing emotions. One can learn to cope with grief, frustration, and anger or to express joy and love through musical experiences.

Each of the seven types of intelligence proposed by Gardner developed because it provides a unique way of knowing about the world. Each type of intelligence may be better suited for providing information about different apects of the inner and outer worlds of human beings. Music, no better and no worse than other types of intelligence, provides it own type of information. Music is particularly useful in providing a medium for dealing with the complex emotional responses that are primary attributes of humanity. Clearly, developing means of controlling and refining emotions would have evolutionary advantages.

Social Organization

A fourth avenue of approach to the possibility of survival benefits being conferred by musical behaviors has to do with social organization (Roederer 1984; Stiller 1987). For prehistoric societies, cooperation was vital for hunting, gathering, protection (from the elements, animals, and enemies), and for the creation of the family unit; a social network was necessary for survival of the human species. Music may have conferred survival benefits in two ways related to social organization: (1) music is a powerful unifying force, and (2) music is a powerful mnemonic device.

Consider, once again, a prehistoric tribe. To the extent that members of the tribe are committed to each other as a group, to that extent survival is possible. If the group scatters at the first sign of danger, the individuals will have a much more difficult time of coping. Behaviors that help promote the notion of group identity would be of immense value. One of music's strongest attributes is that it brings people together for a common purpose. For there to be a feeling of unity, some common ideas, goals, visions, dreams, and beliefs must be shared. What better way to share them than through music and dance?

Members of a tribe are often bonded together by common religious beliefs and these are frequently expressed through music. Members of one tribe must band together to fight off members of another tribe. Music gives courage to those going off to battle and it gives comfort to those who must stay behind. Much of the work of a tribal community requires the coordination of many laborers; music not only provides for synchronous movement but also for relief from tedium. These are but a few of the many ways music may have supplied a unifying force to early communities.

Memory is also of crucial importance to the survival of a society. Not only is memory of a technological nature important—when best to plant? where best to find game? how best to start a fire?—but also the thing that makes the society unique and special. Who are we? Where did we come from? What makes us better than our enemies who live on the other side of the river? Music is one of the most effective mnemonic devices; it enables preliterate societies to retain information, not just facts, but the feelings that accompany the facts as well. Poems, songs, and dances are primary vehicles for the transmission of a heritage.

Summary

As this discussion has shown, the evolutionary process provided human beings with an innate capacity for musical responsiveness. Some of the attributes necessary for musical behaviors came as we developed more sophisticated means of adapting to our rhythmic environment. Our sense of hearing conferred advantages as a means of dealing with time-ordered events. More specifically, music may have provided survival benefits by helping to establish mother-infant bonds, by aiding in the acquisition of language, by providing a unique way of knowing, and by playing important roles in social organization. Speaking only of music may have made it seem more important than it is in the overall scheme of human development. The notion that music is the most important attribute necessary for survival is patently absurd. But the opposite notion—that music is nonessential—is no less misleading. Speaking of an outpourng of artistic expression among human beings 30–35,000 years ago, Pfeiffer said: "It represents activity as basic for the survival of the human species as reproducing, getting food, or keeping predators at bay" (1980, 74).

What has been put forward is an attempt to account for the ubiquitous presence of musical behaviors in human beings. Aside from the fact that this discussion might be interesting to some, it carries a vital message for all. The message is that music is no mere fluke; we are not musical because of a quirk of nature. We are musical because music, like language and all the other forms of intelligence we possess, played (and continues to play) an important role in shaping our humanity. If music is a built-in system, put there because of its importance, it must be important for us still to engage in musical behaviors. Musicians (performers, educators, therapists, et al.) know that music is important through direct experience and involvement; additional support now comes in the form of a plausible theory of music's evolutionary development.

Is Musicality Inherited or Acquired?

If, indeed, there is an evolutionary basis for musicality, obviously some aspects are genetically controlled. The discussion has indicated that we are not controlled by instincts, so, just as obviously, certain aspects of musicality are not genetically controlled, but must be learned.

The extent to which human musicality is inherited or acquired has been and continues to be a subject of controversy. Various individuals have taken positions at either end of the continuum. Seashore expressed the views of those at one end.

> On the basis of our experiments in measuring these sensory capacities, we find that the basic capacities, the sense of pitch, the sense of time, the sense of loudness, and the sense of timbre are elemental, by which we mean that they are largely inborn and function from very early childhood (Seashore 1938, 3).[5]

The opposite viewpoint was expressed by Lundin. Although he recognized that certain biological factors are inherited, he stated quite clearly that "musical behavior is acquired through a long process of individual interaction with musical stimuli" (Lundin 1967, 220). In the next three sections, data supporting each extreme position will be presented, along with a proposed compromise position.

Data in Support of the Inheritance of Musical Attributes

As noted previously, various writers have theorized the inheritance of musical ability (Bentley 1966; Drake 1957; Kwalwasser 1955; Rowley 1988; Scheinfleld 1956; Schoen 1940; Seashore 1919, 1938, 1947; Shuter-Dyson and Gabriel 1981; Wing 1963), while others have attempted to provide data to support such a theory. The following conclusions have been drawn from the available research.

---

5. Seashore has long been associated with the inheritance viewpoint, but may have been somewhat misinterpreted. Some believe that Seashore, when writing about the innateness of sensory capabilities, was referring to biological limitations of the hearing mechanism that cannot be improved through training. Although he does not specifically indicate such, the perception of auditory stimuli can be improved. Moreover, he refers to those basic capabilities as being "elemental" but readily admits that other factors probably contribute to successful achievement as a musician.

1. Genealogical studies have been conducted on musicians' family backgrounds that indicate that the higher the incidence of musical behavior exhibited by the parents, the greater the likelihood the children will be musical (Galton 1869; Mjoen 1926).
2. Correlational studies have yielded data on the degree of relationship existing between standardized test scores (*Seashore Measures of Musical Talents,* for example) of parents and their children. Most of the correlation coefficients are below .50 (Friend 1939; Kwalwasser 1955; Shuter 1964 and 1966; Smith 1914; Stanton 1922).
3. Studies conducted on twins, both fraternal and identical, occasionally yield higher correlations between pairs, but generally support the data cited previously (Coon and Cavey 1989; Kwalwasser 1955; Shields 1962; Shuter 1964; Stafford 1955 and 1970; Vandenberg 1962; Yates and Brash 1941).
4. A relationship between anatomical brain structures and musical abilities has been hypothesized (Blinkov and Glezer 1968; Scheid and Eccles 1975; Schlang et al. 1994 and 1995).

A number of researchers have applied principles of Mendelian genetics to the study of various families' musical backgrounds (Ashman 1952; Drinkwater 1916; Hurst 1912; Kalmus 1949 and 1952; Northrup 1931; Reser 1935). The results are inconclusive and certainly open to subjective interpretation. A brief look at the fundamentals of genetic inheritance may help to explain why this is so.

Each normal human cell contains 46 chromosomes arranged into 23 pairs. Information that determines the presence or absence of specific traits in any individual is encoded in some 3 million genes distributed throughout the 23 pairs of chromosomes (Bodmer and McKie 1994, 223).

Genetic instructions are stored in chemical compounds known as deoxyribonucleicacid (DNA) that are "read" by messenger ribonucleic acid (RNA) (Watson 1968). The genetic influence on any given trait may be determined by the specific chemical content of a given gene pair, in many instances by the interaction of a number of gene pairs, and by the order of the gene pairs. If one person's gene pairs were passed under an electron microscope at the rate of one per second, it would take 200 years to identify the order in which they are lined up for that individual (Fincher 1976, 228).

Given even this limited information about genetics, one may quickly see the enormous complexity of a question such as the inheritance of musical attributes. The Human Genome Project, begun in the 1970s, has a goal of mapping out the molecular composition of all the human genes.

Although scientists have made rapid progress in genetics, few human behaviors or traits have been traced to specific gene pairs. Until specific gene pairs can be linked to specific behavioral traits, any answers to questions such as that posed in this discussion will have to remain, in large part, speculative.

Data in Support of the Acquisition of Musical Attributes

Some would argue that most of the data presented in the previous section can be used in support of environmental factors as well as for inheritance: If a musical person is found to have come from a musical family, could this not be due as much to the musical home environment in which he or she grew up as to his or her genetic makeup? The following conclusions have been drawn from the literature in support of the acquisition of musical attributes.

1. A number of researchers have attempted to establish the degree of relationship that exists between home and social environments and musical attributes (Baumann 1960; Burt 1909; Gilbert 1942; Gordon 1967 and 1968; Graves 1947; Holmstrom 1963; Jamieson 1951; Kirkpatrick 1962; Parker 1961; Rainbow 1965; Rogers 1956; Shelton 1965; Shuter 1964 and 1966; Valentine 1962; Vernon 1960; Whellams 1973; Wing 1936 and 1948). While the results are mixed and somewhat inconclusive, a generalized conclusion might be that moderate, positive support has been given to the influence of home musical environments on musical attributes.

2. Strong support for environmental factors, though again there are mixed results, comes from the effects of practice on various musical attributes. A number of researchers have provided data in support of the hypothesis that pitch discrimination and/or absolute pitch, as an example, can be improved with training (Andrews and Diehl 1970; Baird 1917; Cameron 1917; Capurso 1934; Coffman 1951; Connette 1941; Copp 1916; Henderson 1931; Jersild and Bienstock 1935; Leontiev 1957; Lundin 1963; Lundin and Allen 1962; Mull 1925; Pflederer 1964; Pond and Moorhead 1941–44; Riker 1946; Ross 1914; Seashore 1935; Selzer 1936; Sievers 1931; Skinner 1961; Skornika 1958; Smith 1914; Vance and Grandprey 1931; Whipple 1903; Wolner and Pyle 1933; Wright 1928; Wyatt 1945).

3. There are thousands of private and classroom music teachers who believe that performance skills do improve with training. Fortunately, there are data to support such a hypothesis

(Culpepper 1961; Fieldhouse 1937; Jersild and Beinstock 1931 and 1935; Kalmus 1952; Lawton 1933; Pollock 1950; Smith, 1963; Updegraff, Heileger, and Learned 1938; Williams, Winter, and Wood 1938).

4. Less conclusive are the results of studies in which the effects of training on the scores of standardized music tests were measured. In general, the results from these studies indicate minimal effects of training on test scores (Brennan 1926; Drake 1945 and 1957; Fosha 1960; Gordon 1961 and 1968; Graves 1947; Heller 1962; Holmstrom 1963; Horbulewicz 1963; Kwalwasser 1955; Newton 1959; Seashore and Mount 1918; Shuter 1964; Stanton 1922; Stanton and Koerth 1930; Tarrell 1965; Whittington 1957; Wing 1948; Wyatt 1945). One reason for such a conclusion may be the lack of specific training given between test administrations geared toward the tasks of the test at hand. Another reason may be the relatively brief time between administrations of a given test. Most persons would probably show greater musical gains as a result of training over a period of years than over a period of months. Also, the effects of training will be somewhat different for aptitude than for achievement tests.

Resolution of the Inheritance or Acquisition of Musical Attributes

A commonly accepted solution to the discrepancy between data in support of inheritance or acquisition of musical attributes is the premise that behavior is a function of the organism and the situation. Thus, behavioral traits are subject to modification by genetic as well as environmental factors. No less an authority than the former president of the Human Genome Project, Walter Bodmer, has stated that "musical aptitude . . . is inextricably bound up both with environmental influences and a person's genetic heritage" (Bodmer and McKie 1994, 5).

An analogy may help to illustrate the premise: Corn seeds cannot produce wheat plants. However, environmental factors, such as soil acidity, amounts of rainfall and sunlight, or presence of disease, will determine whether a corn seed produces a tall, healthy plant or a weak, spindly one.

To take the position that either inheritance or the environment is solely responsible for musical attributes does not seem tenable. It is difficult to imagine that a brilliant performer (composer, therapist, etc.) could simply "emerge" without years of study and practice. Conversely, it is equally difficult to accept the notion that a poor performer (composer, therapist, etc.) needs only more practice to become great. Quite clearly, most, if not all, musical attributes are a result of inherited characteristics that have been realized in a particular set of environmental circumstances.

The Relationship of Musical Attributes to Other Human Attributes

Several studies have been conducted for the purpose of determining whether there are any significant and meaningful relationships between musical attributes and other human attributes. Examples of the latter are aural acuity, intelligence, sex, race, and abilities in the other arts. Regardless of the criterion, the results are mixed and, therefore, inconclusive. It should be emphasized that research results are as much a function of the test used as they are of the criterion. Thus, the results may be due to the relative inadequacy of the music tests. Nevertheless, it can probably be assumed, without a specific research base, that persons who are better auditory learners can be successful in learning music, at least as a sophisticated listener. It is also reasonable to assume that persons who achieve well academically will probably achieve well in music. Any differences found between sexes and among races can probably be attributed to cultural and social phenomena. Generalized conclusions are as follows.

1. One researcher concluded that aural acuity is related to musical ability (Farnsworth 1941), while five reached the opposite conclusion (Farnsworth 1938; Fieldhouse 1937; Graf 1952; Lamp and Keys 1935; Sherbon 1975).

2. One group of researchers found a relatively high degree of relationship between musical ability and intelligence (Beinstock 1942; Colwell 1963; Cooley 1961; Edmunds 1960; Lehman 1952; Moore 1966; Phillips 1976; Sergeant and Thatcher 1974). Another group found only moderate or low correlations between the same two factors (Drake 1957; Farnsworth 1931; Gordon 1968; Highsmith 1929; Hollingsworth 1926; Kwalwasser 1955; Lundin 1949; Mursell 1939; Whittington 1957; Wing 1948). (See Robinson 1983 for a review.)

3. Those who have studied the problem agree that the major differences between males and females (beyond early childhood developmental differences such as found by Petzold [1963], Shuter-Dyson [1979], and Whellams [1973]) in terms of musical attributes are the result of socio-cultural influences (Abeles and Porter 1978; Bentley 1966; Gilbert 1942).

4. A similar conclusion has been reached in terms of racial differences in musical attributes: while some differences have been identified, they have, for the most part, been ascribed to differences in cultural backgrounds (Drake 1957; Eels 1933; Farnsworth 1931; Garth and Candor 1937; Garth and Isbell 1929; Gray and Bingham 1929; Johnson 1928; Lenoire 1925; Peacock 1928; Peterson and Lanier 1929; Porter 1931; Robinson and Holmes 1932; Ross 1936; Sanderson 1933; Streep 1931; Sward 1933; Van Alstyne and Osborne 1937; Woods and Martin 1943).
5. Only one researcher found a significant relationship between musical ability and other artistic abilities (Alexander 1954); others found little or no relationship between the two (Carroll 1932; Morrow 1938; Rigg 1937; Strong 1959; Williams, Winter, and Wood 1938).

Musicality is at the core of what it means to be human. For, to be human is to be musical and to be musical is to be human. In fact, music is such a ubiquitous aspect of human behavior that Blacking (1973) calls it a species-specific trait. A species-specific trait has two characteristics. First, all members of the species possess the trait. In this case, anthropologists tell us that all people in all places and in all times have engaged in musical behaviors (see chap. 12). Second, only a particular species possesses the particular trait. Remembering the discussion of differences between human and other animal behaviors (in degree, not kind) at the outset of this chapter, it can also be said that human beings are the only species that engage in musical behaviors.

Commonly, in music research literature, subjects are identified as musicians or nonmusicians. The latter term is a misnomer because there is no such thing as a nonmusician. Certain individuals may suffer from amusia—loss of specific musical skills due to destruction of particular brain tissue (see chap. 7 for more details)—but all human beings are musical by nature. More accurate terminology, though admittedly more awkward, would be "sophisticated and naive musicians" or "formally and informally trained musicians." All persons are able to respond to the music of their culture, just as they can to the language and speech of their culture.

Music psychology will continue to play an increasingly important role, as more data are gathered to support the significance of music. The accumulation of scientific evidence will document the significance and meaning of music in such a way that society's views will recognize more clearly its importance and, indeed, necessity. There is potential for tremendous change in business, religion, education, therapy and medical practice, and all throughout society, and the place of music in these endeavors will become more and more evident.

A final point: The scientific study of human musicality will not detract from the wonder, awe, and appreciation we have for music. The beauty of music and the power it has in our lives can only be enhanced, not diminished, by seeking answers to the hows and whys of music. "Music is not mystical; it is mysterious" (Gaston 1968, 10). If it were magical, there would be no accounting for it. The fact that music is mysterious simply implies that there are many things we do not know about it. Because music is a form of human behavior, it is subject to the same laws and principles that govern all human behaviors. The role of music psychology, then, is to explicate the phenomenon of music.

REFERENCES

Abeles, H. F., and S. Y. Porter. 1978. The sex-stereotyping of musical instruments. *Journal of Research in Music Education* 26:65–75.

Alexander, C. 1954. The longevity of scientists. *Journal of Social Psychology* 39:299–302.

Andrews F., and N. Diehl. 1970. Development of a technique for identifying elementary school children's musical concepts. *Journal of Research in Music Education* 18:214–22.

Ashman, R. 1952. The inheritance of simple musical memory. *Journal of Heredity* 43:51–52.

Baird, J. W. 1917. Memory for absolute pitch. In *Studies in psychology: Titchener commemorative volume*. Worcester, MA: L. H. Wilson.

Baumann, V. H. 1960. Teen-age music preferences. *Journal of Research in Music Education* 8:75–84.

Beck, C. 1993. Commentary on antecendents to nonorganic failure-to-thrive. *Nursing Scan in Research* 6, no. 4:11.

Beinstock, S. A. 1942. A predictive study of musical achievement. *Journal of Genetic Psychology* 61:135–45.

Bentley, A. 1966. *Musical ability in children and its measurement*. New York: October House.

Birdsong, B. 1984. Motherese. In *Science yearbook 1985: New illustrated encyclopedia*, 56–61. New York: Funk and Wagnalls.

Blacking, J. 1973. *How musical is man?* Seattle: University of Washington Press.

Blinkov S. M., and I. I. Glezer. 1968. *The human brain in figures and tables: A quantitative handbook*. Trans. B. Haigh. New York: Basic Books.

Bodmer, W., and R. McKie. 1994. *The book of man*. New York: Scribner.

Bohannan, P. 1983. That sync'ing feeling. *Update: Applications of Research in Music Education*, 2, no. 1:23–24. First published in *Science* 81:25–26.

Brennan, F. 1926. The relation between musical capacity and performance. *Psychological Monographs* 36:190–248.

Brown, F., and R. Graeber, eds. 1982. *Rhythmic aspects of behavior.* Hillsdale, NJ: Lawrence Erlbaum Associates.

Brown, R. 1981. Music and language. In *Documentary report of the Ann Arbor symposium*, 233–265. Reston, VA: Music Educators National Conference.

Brown, S. 1994. Animals at play. *National Geographic* 186, no. 6:2–35.

Burt, C. 1909. Experimental tests of general intelligence. *British Journal of Psychology* 3:94–177.

Cameron, E. H. 1917. Effects of practice in the discrimination and singing of tones. *Psychology Monographs* 23:159–80.

Campbell, J. 1986. *Winston Churchill's afternoon nap.* New York: Simon and Schuster.

Capurso, A. A. 1934. The effect of an associative technique in teaching pitch and interval discrimination. *Journal of Applied Psychology* 18:811–18.

Carroll, H. A. 1932. A preliminary report of a study of the interrelations of certain appreciations. *Journal of Educational Psychology* 23: 505–10.

Chen, A. 1983. Tones of the oscillating sun. *Science News* 123, no. 25:392–95.

Coffman, A. R. 1951. The effect of training on rhythm discrimination and rhythmic action. Ph.D. diss., Northwestern University.

Colloton, M. 1989. Investigating failure to thrive. *Journal of the American Academy of Physician Assistants* 2, no. 5:359–67.

Colwell, R. 1963. An investigation of musical achievement among vocal students, vocal-instrumental students, and instrumental students. *Journal of Research in Music Education* 11:123–30.

Condon, W. 1982. Cultural microrhythms. In *Interaction rhythms: Periodicity in communication behavior*, ed. M. Davis, 53–77. New York: Human Sciences Press.

Connette, E. 1941. The effect of practice with knowledge of results. *Journal of Educational Psychology* 32:523–32.

Constable, G. 1973. *The Neanderthals.* New York: Time-Life Books.

Cooley, J. 1961. A study of the relation between certain mental and personality traits and ratings of musical ability. *Journal of Research in Music Education* 9:108–17.

Coon, H., and G. Cavey. 1989. Genetic and environmental determinants of musical ability in twins. *Behavior Genetics* 19, no. 2:183–93.

Copp, E. F. 1916. Musical ability. *Journal of Heredity* 7:297–305.

Cowan, W. 1979. The development of the brain. *Scientific American* 241, no. 3:113–33.

Culpepper, F. 1961. A study of the hearing impairments in defective singers. Ph.D. diss., George Peabody College for Teachers.

Davis, M., ed. 1982. *Interaction rhythms: Periodicity in communication behavior.* New York: Human Sciences Press.

Dowling, W., and D. Harwood. 1986. *Music cognition.* New York: Academic Press.

Drake, R. 1945. The effect of ear training on musical talent scores. *Journal of Musicology* 4:110–12.

Drake, R. 1957. *Drake musical aptitude tests.* Chicago: Science Research Associates.

Drinkwater, H. 1916. Inheritance of artistic and musical ability. *Journal of Genetics* 5:229–41.

Dubos, R. 1974. *Beast or angel? Choices that make us human.* New York: Scribner.

Dubos, R. 1981. *Celebrations of life.* New York: McGraw-Hill.

Eccles, J., and D. Robinson. 1985. *The wonder of being human.* Boston: New Science Library.

Edmunds, C. B. 1960. Musical ability, intelligence, and attainment of secondary modern and E. S. N. children. Leeds University. Typescript.

Eels, W. 1933. Mechanical, physical, and musical ability of the native races of Alaska. *Journal of Applied Psychology* 17:493–506.

Evans, J., and M. Clynes, eds. 1986. *Rhythm in psychological, linguistic, and musical processes.* Springfield, IL: Charles C. Thomas.

Farb, P. 1978. *Humankind.* New York: Bantam Books.

Farnsworth, P. R. 1931. An historical, critical, and experimental study of the Seashore-Kwalwasser Test Battery. *Journal of Genetic Psychology* 9:291–393.

Farnsworth, P. R. 1938. Auditory acuity and musical ability in the first four grades. *Journal of Psychology* 6:95–98.

Farnsworth, P. R. 1941. Further data on the Adlerian theory of artistry. *Journal of General Psychology* 24:447–50.

Feldenkrais, M. 1979. Man and the world. In *Explorers of humankind*, ed. T. Hanna, 19–29. New York: Harper and Row.

Fieldhouse, A. E. 1937. A study of backwardness in singing among school children. Ph.D. diss., London University.

Fincher, J. 1976. *Human intelligence.* New York: Putnam.

Fosha, L. 1960. A study of the validity of the musical aptitude profile. Ph.D. diss., University of Iowa.

Fridman, R. 1973. The first cry of the newborn: Basis for the child's future musical development. *Journal of Research in Music Education* 21, no. 3:264–69.

Friend, R. 1939. Influence of heredity and musical environment on the scores of kindergarten children on the Seashore measures of musical ability. *Journal of Applied Psychology* 23:347–57.

Galton, F. 1869. *Heredity and genius.* London: Macmillan.

Gardner, H. 1983. *Frames of mind: The theory of multiple intelligences.* New York: Basic Books.

Garth, T. R., and E. Candor. 1937. Musical talent of Mexicans. *American Journal of Psychology* 49:203–7.

Garth, T. R., and S. R. Isbell. 1929. The musical talent of Indians. *Music Supervisors Journal* 15:85–87.

Gaston, E. 1968. Man and music. In *Music in therapy*, ed. E. Gaston, 7–29. New York: Macmillan.

George, W., and D. Hodges. 1980. The nature of musical attributes. In *Handbook of music psychology*, ed. D. Hodges, 401–14. Lawrence, KS: National Association for Music Therapy.

Gilbert, G. M. 1942. Sex differences in musical aptitude and training. *Journal of General Psychology* 26:19–33.

Gordon, E. 1961. A study to determine the effects of practice and training on Drake musical aptitude test scores. *Journal of Research in Music Education* 4:63–74.

Gordon, E. 1967. A comparison of the performance of culturally disadvantaged with that of culturally heterogenous students on the musical aptitude profile. *Psychology in the Schools* 15:260–68.

Gordon, E. 1968. A study of the efficiency of general intelligence and musical aptitude tests in predicting achievement in music. *Bulletin of the Council for Research in Music Education* 13:40–45.

Graf, S. 1952. Measurement of hand length, muscular control, and motibility related to handedness. Master's thesis, Syracuse University.

Graves, W. S. 1947. Factors associated with children's taking music lessons, including some parent-child relationships. *Journal of Genetic Psychology* 7:65–89 and 91–125.

Gray, C. T., and C. W. Bingham. 1929. A comparison of certain phases of musical ability in colored and white school pupils. *Journal of Educational Psychology* 20:501–6.

Hall, E. 1976. *Beyond culture.* New York: Anchor Press.

Heller, J. 1962. The effects of formal training on Wing musical intelligence scores. Ph.D. diss, University of Iowa.

Henderson, M. T. 1931. Remedial measures in motor rhythm as applied to piano performance. Master's thesis, University of Iowa.

Highsmith, J. A. 1929. Selecting musical talent. *Journal of Applied Psychology* 13:486–93.

Hollingsworth, L. 1926. Musical sensitivity of children who score above 135 I. Q. *Journal of Educational Psychology* 17:95–109.

Holmstrom, L. G. 1963. *Musicality and prognosis.* Uppsala: Almqvist and Wilksells.

Horbulewicz, J. 1963. The development of musical memory. Ph.D. diss., Higher School of Education, Danzig.

Hurst, C. C. 1912. Mendelian heredity in man. *Eugenics Review* 4:20–24.

Jamieson, R. P. 1951. An investigation into songs known by Scottish schoolchildren and their musical preferences. *British Journal of Educational Psychology* 22:74–75.

Jastrow, R. 1981. *The enchanted loom: Mind in the universe.* New York: Simon and Schuster.

Jersild, A., and S. Bienstock. 1931. The influence of training on the vocal ability of three year old children. *Child Development* 2:272–90.

Jersild, A., and S. Bienstock. 1935. Development of rhythm in young children. *Child Development Monographs* 22:1–97.

Johnson, G. B. 1928. Musical talent and the American Negro. *Music Supervisors Journal* 81:13–86.

Joubart, D. 1994. Lions of darkness. *National Geographic* 18, no. 2:34–53.

Kalmus, H. 1949. Tune deafness and its inheritance. *Proceedings of the International Congress of Genetics,* Stockholm, 605.

Kalmus, H. 1952. Inherited sense defects. *Scientific American* 186:64–70.

Kirkpatrick, W. C. 1962. Relationships between the singing ability of prekindergarten children and their home musical environment. Ph.D. diss., University of Southern California.

Konner, M. 1987. The enigmatic smile. *Psychology Today* 21, no. 3:42–46.

Kwalwasser, J. 1955. *Exploring the musical mind.* New York: Coleman-Ross.

Lamp, C. J., and N. Keys. 1935. Can aptitude for specific musical instruments be predicted? *Journal of Educational Psychology* 26:587–96.

Lawton, A. 1933. *Foundations of practical ear training.* London: Oxford University Press.

Lefrancois, G. 1979. *Psychology for teaching.* 3d ed. Belmont, CA: Wadsworth.

Lehman, C. F. 1952. A study of musically superior and inferior subjects as selected by the Kwalwasser Dykema music tests. *Journal of Educational Research* 45:517–22.

Lenoire, Z. 1925. Measurement of racial differences in certain mental and educational abilities. Ph.D. diss., University of Iowa.

Leontiev, A. N. 1957. The nature and formation of human psychic properties. In *Psychology in the Soviet Union,* ed. B. Simon, 226–32. London: Routledge and Kegan Paul.

Lerdahl, F., and R. Jackendoff. 1983. *A generative theory of tonal music.* Cambridge, MA: MIT Press.

Lundin, R. W. 1949. The development and validation of a set of musical ability tests. *Psychological Monographs* 63:1–20.

Lundin, R. W. 1963. Can perfect pitch be learned? *Music Educators Journal* 49:459–51.

Lundin, R. W. 1967. *An objective psychology of music.* New York: The Ronald Press.

Lundin, R. W., and J. D. Allen. 1962. A technique for training perfect pitch. *Psychological Records* 12:139–46.

Malm, W. 1967. *Music cultures of the Pacific, the Near East, and Asia.* Englewood Cliffs, NJ: Prentice-Hall.

McCall, R. 1979. *Infants: The new knowledge.* Cambridge: Cambridge University Press.

Minsky, M. 1982. Music, mind, and meaning. In *Music, mind, and brain,* ed. M. Clynes, 1–19. New York: Plenum Press.

Mjoen, J. 1926. Genius as a biological problem. *Eugenics Review* 17:242–57.

Montagu, A. 1977. *Life before birth.* New York: New American Library.

Montagu, A. 1978. *Touching: The human significance of the skin.* New York: Harper and Row.

Montagu, A. 1979. My conception of the nature of human nature. In *Explorers of humankind,* ed. T. Hanna, 90–102. New York: Harper and Row.

Montagu, A., and F. Matson. 1979. *The human connection.* New York: McGraw-Hill.

Moore, R. 1966. The relationship of intelligence to creativity. *Journal of Research in Music Education* 14:243–53.

Morrow. R. S. 1938. An analysis of the relations among tests of musical, artistic, and mechanical abilities. *Journal of Psychology* 5:253–63.

Mull, H. K. 1925. The acquisition of absolute pitch. *American Journal of Psychology* 36:469–93.

Mumford, L. 1966. *The myth of the machine: Technics and human development.* New York: Harcourt Brace Jovanovich.

Mursell, J. L. 1939. Intelligence and musicality. *Education* 59:559–62.

Newton, G. 1959. Selection of junior musicians for Royal Marines School of Music: An evaluation of H. D. Wing's test. Senior Psychologist's Department. Admirality.

Nketia, J. 1974. *The music of Africa.* New York: Norton.

Northrup, W. C. 1931. The inheritance of musical ability, student pedigree studies. *Eugenics News* 16.

Olsen, D. 1980. Folk music of South America. In *Music of many cultures—A musical mosaic,* ed. E. May, 386–425. Berkeley: University of California Press.

Pacholczyk, J. 1980. Secular classical music in the Arabic near east. In *Music of many cultures—A musical mosaic,* ed. E. May, 253–68. Berkeley: University of California Press.

Parker, O. G. 1961. A study of the relationship of aesthetic sensitivity to musical ability, intelligence, and socioeconomic status. Ph.D. diss., University of Kansas.

Peacock, W. 1928. A comparative study of musical talent in whites and negroes and its correlation with intelligence. Ph.D. diss., Emory University.

Peterson, J., and L. Lanier. 1929. Studies in the comparative abilities of whites and Negroes. *Mental Measurement Monographs* 5.

Petzold, R. 1963. The development of auditory perception of music sounds by children in the first six grades. *Journal of Research in Music Education* 11:21–43.

Pfeiffer, J. 1969. *The emergence of man.* New York: Harper and Row.

Pfeiffer, J. 1980. Icons in the shadows. *Science80* 1, no. 4:72–79.

Pflederer, M. 1964. The responses of children to musical tasks embodying Piaget's principle of conservation. *Journal of Research in Music Education* 12:251–68.

Phillips, D. 1976. An investigation of the relationship between musicality and intelligence. *Psychology of Music* 4:16–31.

Pollock, T. 1950. Singing disability in school children. Master's thesis, Durham Universiy.

Pond, D., and G. Moorhead. 1941–44. *Music of young children.* Parts 1–4. Santa Barbara: Pillsbury Foundation for the Advancement of Music Education.

Porter, R. 1931. *A study of the musical talent of the Chinese attending public schools in Chicago.* Chicago: University of Chicago Press.

Rainbow, E. L. 1965. A pilot study to investigate the constructs of musical aptitude. *Journal of Research in Music Education* 13:2–14.

Reser, H. 1935. Inheritance of musical ability: Student pedigree studies. *Eugenics News* 20.

Restak, R. 1979. *The brain: The last frontier.* New York: Warner Books.

Restak, R. 1983. Newborn knowledge. In *Science yearbook 1984: New illustrated encyclopedia,* 48–52. New York: Funk and Wagnalls.

Rigg, M. 1937. The relationship between discrimination in music and discrimination in poetry. *Journal of Educational Psychology* 28:149–52.

Riker, B. L. 1946. The ability to judge pitch. *Journal of Experimental Psychology* 36:331–46.

Roberts, M. 1987. No language but a cry. *Psychology Today* 21, no. 5:41.

Robinson, R. 1983. The relationships between musical ability and intelligence. *Update: Applications of Research in Music Education* 1, no. 4:19–21.

Robinson, V., and M. Holmes. 1932. A comparison of negroes and whites in musical ability. Syracuse University. Typescript.

Roederer, J. 1982. Physical and neuropsychological foundations of music. In *Music, mind, and brain,* ed. M. Clynes, 37–46. New York: Plenum Press.

Roederer, J. 1984. The search for a survival value of music. *Music Perception* 13:350–56.

Rogers, V. R. 1956. Children's expressed musical preferences at selected grade levels. Ph.D. diss., Syracuse University.

Ross, F. B. 1914. The measurement of time sense as an element in the sense of rhythm. *Psychological Monographs* 16:166–72.

Ross, V. 1936. Musical talents of Indian and Japanese children. *Journal of Juvenile Research* 20:133–36.

Rowley, P. 1988. Identifying genetic factors affecting music ability. *Psychomusicology* 7, no. 2:195–200.

Sagan, C. 1977. *The dragons of Eden.* New York: Ballantine Books.

Sanderson, H. 1933. Differences in musical ability in children of different national and racial origins. *Journal of Genetic Psychology* 42:100–120.

Scheid, P., and J. C. Eccles. 1975. Music and speech: Artistic functions of the human brain. *Psychology of Music* 3, no. 2:1–35.

Scheinfield, A. 1956. *The new heredity and you.* London: Chatto and Windus.

Schoen, M. 1940. *The psychology of music.* New York: The Ronald Press.

Schlang, G., L. Jancke, Y. Huang, and H. Steinmetz. 1994. In vivo morphometry of interhemispheric asymmetry and connectivity in musicians. In *Proceedings of the 3d international conference for music perception and cognition*, ed. I. Deliege, 417–18. Liege, Belgium.

Schlang, G., L. Jancke, Y. Huang, and H. Steinmetz. 1995. In vivo evidence of structural brain asymmetry in musicians. *Science* 267, no. 5198:699–701.

Seashore, C. E. 1919. *Seashore measures of musical talent.* New York: Columbia Phonograph Co.

Seashore, C. E. 1938. *Psychology of music.* New York: McGraw-Hill.

Seashore, C. E. 1947. *In search of beauty in music.* New York: The Ronald Press.

Seashore, C. E., and G. Mount. 1918. Correlation of factors in musical talent and training. *Psychological Monographs* 25:47–92.

Seashore, R. H. 1935. Improvability of pitch discrimination. *Psychology Bulletin* 32:546.

Selzer, S. 1936. A measure of the singing and rhythmic development of preschool children. *Journal of Educational Psychology* 27:412–24.

Sergeant, D., and G. Thatcher. 1974. Intelligence, social status, and musical abilities. *Psychology of Music* 2:32–57.

Shelton, J. S. 1965. The influence of home musical environment upon musical response of first-grade children. Ph.D. diss., George Peabody College for Teachers.

Sherbon, J. W. 1975. The association of hearing acuity, diplacusis, and discrimination with music performance. *Journal of Research in Music Education* 23:249–57.

Shields, J. 1962. *Monozygotic twins brought up apart and brought up together.* London: Oxford University Press.

Shuter, R. P. 1964. An investigation of hereditary and environmental factors in musical ability. Ph.D. diss., London University.

Shuter, R. P. 1966. Hereditary and environmental factors in musical ability. *Eugenics Review* 58:149–56.

Shuter-Dyson, R. P. 1979. Unisex or "vive la difference"? *Bulletin of the Council for Research in Music Education* 59:102–6.

Shuter-Dyson, R., and C. Gabriel. 1981. *The psychology of musical ability.* 2d ed. London: Methuen.

Sievers, C. H. 1931. A study of the rhythmic performance with social consideration of the factors involved in the formation of a scale for measuring ability. Ph.D. diss., University of Iowa.

Skinner, B. F. 1961. Teaching machines. *Scientific American* 205:90–102.

Skornika, J. D. 1958. The function of time and rhythm in instrumental music reading competency. Ph.D. diss., Oregon State University.

Smith, F. O. 1914. The effect of training in pitch discrimination. *Psychological Monographs* 17:67–103.

Smith, R. 1963. The effects of group vocal training on the singing ability of nursery school children. *Journal of Research in Music Education* 11:137–41.

Springer, S., and G. Deutsch. 1989. *Left brain, right brain.* 3d ed. New York: W. H. Freeman.

Stafford, R. E. 1955. Nonparametric analysis of twin data with the Mann-Whitney U Test. Research Report no. 10, Louisville Twin Study, Child Development Unit, University of Louisville School of Medicine.

Stafford, R. E. 1970. Estimation of the interaction between heredity and environment for musical aptitude of twins. *Human Heredity* 20:356–60.

Stanton, H. 1922. Inheritance of specific musical capacities. *Psychological Monographs* 31:157–204.

Stanton, H., and W. Koerth. 1930. Musical capacity measures in adults repeated after music. *Studies in the aims and progress of research.* Iowa City: University of Iowa.

Stern, D. 1982. Some interactive functions of rhythm changes between mother and infant. In *Interaction rhythms: Periodicity in communication behavior*, ed. M. Davis, 101–17. New York: Human Sciences Press.

Stiller, A. 1987. Toward a biology of music. *Opus* 35:12–15.

Streep, R. L. 1931. A comparison of white and negro children in rhythm and consonance. *Journal of Applied Psychology* 15:53–71.

Strong, E. K. 1959. *Vocational interest blank for men, vocational interest blank for women.* Stanford, CA: Stanford University Press.

Sward, K. 1933. Jewish musicality in America. *Journal of Applied Psychology* 17:675–712.

Tarrell, V. V. 1965. An investigation of the validity of the musical aptitude profile. *Journal of Research in Music Education* 13:195–206.

Thomas, L. 1979. *The medusa and the snail.* New York: Viking Press.

Updegraff, R., L. Heileger, and J. Learned. 1938. The effect of training upon the singing ability and musical interest of three-, four-, and five-year-old children. *University of Iowa Studies of Child Welfare* 14:83–121.

Valentine, C. W. 1962. *The experimental psychology of beauty.* London: Methuen.

Van Alstyne, D., and E. Osborne. 1937. Rhythm responses of Negro and white children two to six. *Monographs of Social Research in Child Development* 2:4.

Vance, F., and M. Grandprey. 1931. Objective methods of ranking nursery school children on certain aspects of musical capacity. *Journal of Educational Psychology* 22:577–85.

Vandenberg, S. G. 1962. The hereditary abilities study: Hereditary components in a psychological test battery. *American Journal of Human Genetics* 14:220–37.

Vernon, P. E. 1960. *Intelligence and attainment tests.* London: University of London Press.

Watson, J. D. 1968. *The double helix.* New York: Mentor Books.

Wehr, T. 1982. Circadian rhythm disturbances in depression and mania. In *Rhythmic aspects of behavior*, eds. F. Brown and R. Graeber, 399–428. Hillsdale, NJ: Lawrence Erlbaum Associates.

Whellams, F. S. 1973. Musical abilities and sex differences in the analysis of aural-musical capacities. *Journal of Research in Music Education* 21:30–39.

Whipple, G. M. 1903. Studies in pitch discrimination. *American Journal of Psychology* 14:289–309.

Whittington, R. W. 1957. The assessment of potential musical ability in secondary school children. *Journal of Educational Psychology* 48:1–10.

Williams, E. D., C. Winter, and J. M. Wood. 1938. Tests of literary appreciation. *British Journal of Educational Psychology* 8:265–84.

Wilson, F. 1986. *Tone deaf and all thumbs?* New York: Viking Penguin.

Wing, H. D. 1936. Tests of musical ability in school children. Master's thesis, London University.

Wing, H. D. 1948. Tests of musical ability and appreciation. *British Journal of Psychology*, supplement no. 27:88.

Wing, H. D. 1963. Is musical aptitude innate? *Review of Psychology in Music* 1:1–7.

Wolner, M., and W. H. Pyle. 1933. An experiment in individual training in pitch-deficient children. *Journal of Educational Psychology* 24:602–8.

Woods, R., and L. Martin. 1943. Testing in music education. *Education and Psychological Measurement* 3:29–42.

Wright, R. F. 1928. The correlation between achievement and capacity in music. *Journal of Educational Research* 17:50–56.

Wyatt, R. F. 1945. The improvability of pitch discrimination. *Psychological Monographs* 58:1–58.

Yates, N., and H. Brash. 1941. An investigation of physical and mental characteristics of a pair of twins reared apart from infancy. *Annual of Eugenics* 2:89–101.

3

Basic Physical and Psychoacoustical Processes

Wanda B. Lathom-Radocy

and

Rudolf E. Radocy

Introduction

Music is a product of human cognition and affect operating under particular psychological and physiological constraints. The physical processes described in this chapter provide the basic input from which human beings construct music, but in and of themselves they are not music. Neither do the sensations that arise from the basic human perceptual processes that humans apply to the results of physical processes constitute music. Perception introduces certain constraints; for example, not all physically possible sounds lie within the human hearing range. Physical processes present possibilities; the human organism organizes those possibilities in accordance with probabilities. The old riddle regarding whether or not any sound exists if a tree falls in a forest when no one is there to hear it is really fairly simple if one maintains a distinction between a physical and a psychological concept of sound. Physically, there most definitely is sound—massive vibrations resulting in powerful traveling disturbances occur. Psychologically, there is no sound—no human auditory processing occurs. Similarly, physical stimuli with the potential to become music may exist quite independently of any human observer; it takes human information processing to create music from incoming aural stimuli.

This chapter describes the production and propagation of musical sounds and basic aspects of acoustical environments. It also describes rudimentary psychoacoustics, the operation of sensory processes on auditory stimuli to build tonal sensations that may function as musical building blocks. It is based on the authors' experience and study of the literature. Deliberately nonmathematical in scope, the presentation may appear "watered down" to readers who are knowledgable in acoustics

and psychoacoustics. Little concern is shown for any particular performance medium. Readers who wish more detail or depth or wish to learn
about the mechanics of the voice and musical instruments should consult such sources as Backus 1977, Butler 1992, Geerdes 1987, Hall 1991,
Rossing 1990, or Wadhams 1988.

Vibration

The basis of all sound is vibration. Movement of some type characterizes every particle in the universe. Groups of particular particles may
move with their own characteristic group patterns. Of myriad possible
vibrations, some occur at rates and in settings that result in audible sound.

The rate at which a particular vibration occurs is frequency. More
specifically, a vibrating object's frequency is the number of cycles in a
designated amount of time. A cycle is a "complete" journey or excur-
sion of a vibrating object, starting from some given point, moving through
both extremes of displacement, and returning to the same point, moving in the same direction. A vibrating pendulum illustrates a cycle: From
the time it is at a particular point until it returns there, moving in the
same direction, a cycle is occurring. Once the pendulum returns, the
cycle is complete, and a new cycle begins.

For the range of vibration frequencies that produce audible sound,
the second is the most logical amount of time to employ in measurement, so in musical acoustics one usually defines frequency as the number of cycles completed in one second. Cycles per second in turn usually
are referred to as Hertz (Hz), in honor of Heinrich Hertz, an early investigator of electromagnetic phenomena.

Each cycle requires a particular amount of time for its completion.
If one assumes that each cycle lasts as long as any other, which will be
the case if frequency does not change, the time required for one cycle or
period is the reciprocal of the frequency. For example, if the frequency is
100 Hz (100 cycles per second), the period is 1/100 sec (.01 sec); if the
frequency is 500 Hz, the period is 1/500 sec (.002 sec). Conversely, the
frequency is the reciprocal of the period; if the period is 1/200 sec (.005
sec), the frequency is 200 Hz.

Another basic vibration property is amplitude. When one speaks of
amplitude in reference to a vibrating object, one usually is referring to the
distance between an "undisturbed" position and a point of maximal displacement.[1] (In terms of a vibrating pendulum, the displacement ampli-

1. This is displacement amplitude. There is also pressure amplitude, the difference
between a middle pressure value (ambient pressure) and a pressure extreme, and velocity amplitude, the difference in velocity between a middle rate of velocity and a velocity
extreme.

tude is the distance from the middle position to the maximum displacement to either side.) Amplitude, which is independent of frequency in most types of vibratory motion related to music, is related to the strength of vibration, which affects loudness: The more powerful the vibration, the greater the amplitude and the louder the resulting sound.

The vibrations responsible for virtually all music are quite complex, but they may be analyzed into simple components, each of which has its own single characteristic frequency and amplitude. These simple components are called by various terms, including *partials, sine tones, sinusoids,* and *pure tones.* The terms *harmonics, overtones,* and *inharmonics* occasionally are employed when a particular mathematical relationship is of concern.[2] In the simplest case, each component vibration pattern illustrates simple harmonic motion (SHM), a form of motion where the restoring force (a force that directs a displaced object to its original position) is proportional to the displacement.

Propagation

Sound waves, unlike electromagnetic waves, are a series of disturbances following each other through a physical medium. A medium is an intervening physical substance. Sound may travel through air, water, and solid substances; without some medium, it can not travel. For musical purposes, the medium is usually air.[3]

The process by which the disturbance travels is propagation. The moving object responsible for the original vibration—a drumhead, a string, a reed, vocal folds—disturbs particles in the surrounding medium. These in turn disturb other particles: bump, bump, bump. With each bump, the vibration is conveyed to another particle. Each particle moves relatively little, but the vibration moves on for a relatively long distance. The disturbance travels through the medium, outward from the source; particular particles do not travel through the medium. A ball flying through the air does not illustrate the travel of a sound wave well; a row of cascading dominoes is far more accurate. Stacking the

---

2. Any component of a complex tone is a partial. A harmonic is a frequency that is in an integral multiple relationship with the fundamental frequency, which usually is the lowest frequency component. An overtone is a harmonic, excluding the fundamental, that is present in the complex tone under discussion. An inharmonic is a partial that is not also a harmonic.

3. When music is broadcast, it is not in the form of physical sound. The physical disturbances in air that music making creates are converted to an electrical current by microphones and to an electromagnetic disturbance by the broadcasting station's transmitter. The radio receiver and speakers convert the incoming electromagnetic wave back to a sound wave. The broadcast medium is an electromagnetic field, not air.

dominoes at appropriate distances and then pushing on the first to create a ripple effect shows how the ripple travels through the entire domino chain, but no one domino moves from the beginning to the end. Similarly, no one particle of the medium moves from the sound source to a wall, microphone, or listener's ear.

Sound waves may propagate in two basic movement patterns. In transverse waves, the overall disturbance travels perpendicular (at right angles) to the direction of individual particle displacements. In longitudinal waves, the overall disturbance travels parallel with (in the same direction as) the direction of the individual particle displacements. Waves in air are always longitudinal, so the waves that carry musical sounds in a concert hall are longitudinal. Transverse waves also have musical importance because the travel of a disturbance along a string or in a solid surface such as a piano soundboard or drumhead is partly transverse.

Three properties of traveling waves are quite important: speed, frequency, and wavelength. Speed is the rate at which the disturbance travels through the medium.[4] It depends on properties of the medium, such as temperature (each rise or fall of temperature 1°C increases or decreases the speed of a sound wave by 0.6 m/sec), density, and chemical composition; when one speaks of the "speed of sound," one usually means the rate of propagation through a particular medium. Waves in air travel at the speed determined by the air's properties: Waves originating from high frequency sounds travel at the same speed as waves originating from low frequency sounds.

A wave's frequency is the vibration rate of the individual particles that convey the disturbance. A wave's frequency depends on the frequency of the source of vibration; a tuning fork vibrating at 440 Hz will create a traveling wave that has a frequency of 440 Hz.

A wave's speed and frequency are independent of each other in air, but they are related mathematically through the wavelength, which is the distance between a point in one wave (or "wave front") and the corresponding point in the next wave. The relevant equation is

$$S = fw,$$

where S = speed of the wave in some linear unit (usually meters or feet per second), f = frequency of the wave in Hz, and w = wavelength in the linear unit. For example, a vibration source vibrating at 165 Hz

---

4. One could be more complete and speak of velocity, which is the rate of travel in a particular direction. Speed, "directionless velocity," is sufficient when one is not concerned about a particular target for a sound wave.

(frequency), which causes a disturbance in air with properties such that the resulting disturbance travels at 330 meters per second (speed), produces a wavelength of 2 meters ($330 = 165 \times 2$).

In the process of traveling, particular phenomena may alter the wave. Such wave phenomena include interference, reflection, absorption, refraction, and diffraction. Although it has virtually no musical importance, the Doppler effect excites some authors.

Interference is the result of adding two or more waves together. Particular particles in a medium may be displaced in one way or another by each disturbance that meets them; their particular locations at any given time are the net result of all the traveling disturbances acting on them. During a performance in a concert hall, numerous sound waves propagate through the air, including waves coming directly to the audience from the performers, waves reflected from walls, floor, and ceiling, and waves caused by sounds other than the performers, such as audience members' coughing. All of those waves act on the particular particles of the medium; interference creates a highly complex displacement pattern that varies from instant to instant. The combined wave form resulting from interference is a superposition; superpositions abound in the concert hall.

Reflection is a sudden change in the direction of wave travel resulting from a sudden change in properties of the medium. A wave bouncing off a wall illustrates reflection. Surfaces vary in how reflective they are because the amount of energy absorbed varies with particular surfaces: A heavy velvet curtain absorbs a considerable proportion of the energy in a sound wave and reflects very little; a concrete wall absorbs very little and reflects a considerable amount. A room's "liveliness" is a matter of how much sound is reflected versus how much is absorbed. From the perspective of being inside the room, sound that is not reflected may be considered absorbed, but some of the energy in the sound wave may transmit right through the wall: An observer in an adjoining room would hear the sound as coming into that room from next door.

Refraction is a gradual change in the direction of wave travel resulting from a gradual change in properties of the medium. Refraction occasionally results from temperature inversions. Since they take place over relatively long distances, refractions are of little importance for music. They might explain hearing a band outdoors from a long distance, while observers somewhat closer to the band's location hear nothing.

Diffraction is the process whereby a wave passes through a small opening or bends around a corner. If the opening is smaller than the wavelength, the wave will "bubble" through and reform. If the opening is larger, the wave simply will beam ahead without spreading to either side. Similarly, a wave's ability to turn corners is a function of wavelength; because lower frequency waves have longer wavelengths, they turn corners more effectively. Diffraction helps explain why a person with an obstructed view of a performance nevertheless may hear quite well.

The apparent pitch of a rapidly approaching sound source rises; that of a rapidly vanishing sound source lowers. (A passing train's whistle often illustrates this.) The pitch change, called the Doppler effect, is due to the frequency with which corresponding points of the sound wave pass the observer: As a rapidly approaching source comes closer to the observer, the wave fronts come by more frequently. As the source goes away, the fronts come by less frequently. The Doppler effect is of considerable importance in wave mechanics, but its importance to music is nil.

Standing Waves

Waves that propagate throughout a medium until they spend their energy are traveling waves. In the process of propagation, each medium particle has its turn at vibrating, at the wave's frequency, to the maximal amplitude possible. Under special conditions, a wave may reflect back on itself in a small confined medium to form a standing or stationary wave. Standing waves exist in vibrating violin and guitar strings, in a singer's vocal tract, in the air column of a sounding woodwind or brass instrument, and elsewhere. Unlike a traveling wave, a standing wave does not propagate through the medium: Rather, it vibrates in a series of characteristic patterns. Some particles, located at points called nodes, do not vibrate at all. Particles located at antinodes vibrate maximally (i.e., vibrate to the maximum amount of displacement possible in the standing wave). Particles located between nodes and antinodes vibrate to less than the wave's maximum amplitude. The wave formed on a string or in an air column is quite complex; its overall pattern often may be analyzed mathematically into a series of simple patterns, each with its own characteristic frequency and amplitude. The standing wave's vibrations are conveyed to a surrounding medium, in which a traveling wave forms and propagates.

The Auditory Environment

The environment in which one hears music interacts with the physical disturbances to provide the auditory stimuli from which people create music. People often listen in a confined space such as an auditorium, a recital hall, an arena, or a living room. Reflection or lack thereof is especially important. This section reviews some of the basic aspects of a performance space; considerably greater detail is available in acoustics textbooks.

Reverberation time is a vital acoustical characteristic of a room. Defined as the time necessary for a sound to decay to one millionth (.000001) of its original intensity[5] (a 60 dB[6] drop in intensity level), reverberation time is a function of two room properties: volume and absorption. The larger the room, the longer the reverberation time; the smaller the room, the shorter the reverberation time. Sound that is not reflected by a particular surface is absorbed (although some sound may pass through or transmit), and absorption is related inversely to reverberation time. Increases in absorption reduce the reverberation time; decreases in absorption lengthen it. Rooms that are overly "live" have too long a reverberation time. "Dead" rooms have too short a reverberation time. Just what the ideal time is varies with the musical medium and style; reverberation times shorter than about 1.0 sec or longer than about 1.7 sec are rarely satisfactory.

Another important aspect of the auditory environment is sound distribution. Sound should spread evenly throughout a room, with no "dead" or "live" spots. Even distribution is encouraged by rough, irregular surfaces and a lack of an overly symmetrical shape. Rectangular rooms or rooms with a concave wall may focus sound in particular places. In some rooms, such architectural structures as fluted columns, gargoyles, and ornate facades, created for visual aesthetic reasons, may serve a useful acoustical purpose because they help prevent focused reflections.

Freedom from unwanted sounds, internal as well as external, is desirable in a room intended for musical performance. This requires special attention to lighting, climate control systems, windows, doors, and even walls.

Architectural acoustics is a discipline in itself. Anyone contemplating constructing or remodeling a room intended as a performance or rehearsal space should consult with individuals who are knowledgable regarding auditory environments.

---

5. Intensity is the amount of power passing through a unit area, as in .000001 (10^{-6}) watts per square meter. The human ear deals with tiny amounts of power, over about a trillionfold range.

6. Decibels (dB) represent ratio comparisons of particular amounts of a property in question to an arbitrary baseline. The 60 dB value compares 10^{-6} w/m^2 to a baseline of 10^{-12} w/m^2. With intensity level dB, a difference of 10 represents a tenfold change in intensity.

Psychoacoustic Phenomena

Psychoacoustics is an area of psychophysics, which traditionally concerns itself with human sensation in response to physical stimuli. Psychoacoustics concerns itself in particular with tonal sensations arising from sound stimuli; while music is far more than tones, tones are basic sonic structures for most music. This section discusses some basic physical and psychological tonal properties and elementary aspects of auditory processing.

While "dualism" may not always be fashionable, the authors see value in distinguishing between physical aspects of a tone and roughly corresponding psychological aspects. Physical aspects include frequency, intensity, waveform, and time. Psychological aspects include pitch, loudness, timbre, duration, and the more controversial aspects volume and density. The physical aspects exist quite independently of any observer. The psychological aspects require a human observer.

As mentioned earlier, frequency is the rate of cycle completion for a particular vibration. Pitch, the roughly corresponding psychological sensation, is, in its most obvious dimension, a metathetic variable of apparent location on a highness-lowness continuum.[7] In general, the greater the frequency, the higher the pitch, although not every change in frequency will be heard as a pitch change. Also, other physical attributes may have an effect on pitch perception; for example, a change in perceived pitch may occur when the intensity of a tone is altered while maintaining the frequency.

In addition to the obvious highness-lowness dimension, two other pitch dimensions are musically relevant. Some sounds have a clearer pitch sensation than others. The sound of a sustained trumpet tone of good quality has a more definite pitch than the sound of a triangle, which has a more definite pitch than the sound of a cymbal crash, which in turn is more definite than a snare drum tap. This pitch property of "obviousness" is called definity.

The other pitch property, called similarity, circularity, or intimacy, means little in regard to any one tone. Within an established tonal context, a particular tone is more related to some tones than to others. Some of the more seminal work in cognitive music psychology (Krumhansl 1979 and 1983; Shepard 1982) showed a basis for traditions of music theory, at least in Western tonal music. For example, in the key of C

---

7. A metathetic variable is a variable of apparent location. In addition to the highness-lowness dimension of pitch, apparent location in visual space is an example. A prothetic variable, such as loudness or brightness, is a variable of apparent size or magnitude.

major, the tonic C-E-G triad contains especially clearly related tones. The remaining tones of the diatonic scale, D, F, A, and B, are less closely related, and the out-of-scale tones, such as F-sharp and B-flat, are even less related. The apparent relationships among tones are largely a function of musical experience.

Pitch sensation is a function of neural activity. For tones of just one frequency, which are relatively rare, the point of stimulation in the inner ear is the basis for pitch assignment. For complex tones, which contain mixtures of frequencies and are far more common in music, the pattern of stimulation in the inner ear, as "deciphered" by neural processes occurring between the inner ear and the brain, is the basis for pitch assignment. The pitch of a complex tone, often called low pitch or periodicity pitch, is produced by the neural process of fundamental tracking, which employs information about where and how often stimulations occur in the inner ear. (More details are presented in chap. 4.)

Combinations of pitches become simultaneous intervals. Interval phenomena include beating, consonance and dissonance (the apparent "restfulness" or "activity" of the interval), and combination tones (extra tonal sensations beyond those resulting from the two physical stimulations).

Beating is the periodic rise and fall in loudness experienced when two simultaneously sounding tones are not quite in tune.[8] The closer the frequencies, the slower the beat rate (e.g., two tones sounding at 440 Hz and 442 Hz would produce two beats per second). If the frequency distance is increased the beat rate will quicken; with too great a distance, the sensation becomes a roughness rather than beating. If the frequency distance continues to increase until a distance called the critical bandwidth is reached, the sensation becomes one of two clearly different simultaneous sounds.

Consonance and dissonance may refer to interval qualities or overall composition qualities. Various physical theories of consonance and dissonance abound (see Farnsworth 1969 for several); the most contemporary probably is the theory of colliding harmonics (Radocy and Boyle 1988; Roederer 1975). Musical consonance very well may be a matter of training and experience as well as musical context.

Combination tones are extratonal sensations experienced due to distortion in the inner ear; that is, more stimulation occurs than that which may be accounted for by the input sound waves. The most obvious

---

8. Technically, the beating of a mistuned unison is first-order beating. The beating rate is equivalent to the difference between the two frequencies contained in the combined waveform. Second-order beating, resulting from a neural process, is the perceptual "waver" or "clash" experienced from an out-of-tune larger interval, such as a fourth or fifth.

combination tone, often referred to as a difference tone, is one elicited by a frequency equivalent to the difference between two frequencies (e.g., two tones of 1,000 Hz and 750 Hz would produce a difference tone of 250 Hz); other combination tones are theoretically possible. Combination tones may arise from two adjacent, well-tuned violin strings, from two sopranos, or from two organ pipes. In all cases, the frequency eliciting the combination tone sensation is not in the external waveform; the sensation is supplied by the ear. One may imitate true combination tones by sending two electronic inputs into one speaker and thereby cause distortion products that are heard as extra tones, with the frequency equivalent to the difference between the two input frequencies being the most common.

Groups of intervals become chords, and chord movement is a basis for harmony. One unexplained mystery in pitch perception regards why a complex tone, which is a mixture of frequencies in one complex vibration arising from one source, sounds like one sound with one pitch while two tones, even two simple tones of one frequency each, arising from two separate sound sources sound like a simultaneous interval.

Successive frequencies need to be sufficiently far apart in order for listeners to hear the resulting pitches as clearly different. The just noticeable difference (JND) for frequency discrimination (distinguishing between two successive tones) and frequency resolution (distinguishing that a continuously sounding tone of changing frequency has risen or fallen in pitch) varies with the frequency range, the listener, and time. For musical purposes, there is little value in trying to establish a precise JND for pitch discrimination; the literature reports different values as well as criteria for establishing those values. Suffice it to say that the JND is well within most necessary tonal distinctions for music. Having an unusually large JND may cause a person to have difficulty with intonation tasks.

Since not every minute frequency change elicits a change in pitch sensation, and tones of constant frequency but changing intensity may appear to change in pitch, albeit idiosyncratically, the relationship between frequency and pitch is not perfect. Still, it is useful to think of a quasi-parallel relationship between frequency and pitch.

Another quasi-parallel relationship exists between the physical property of intensity and the psychological property of loudness. Intensity is a function of the amount of power in a sound; it is defined as the amount of power passing through a unit area.[9] Loudness, a prothetic

---

9. "Sound power" by itself is the amount of power in a sound, regardless of direction. "Sound intensity," often a quantity that engineers and sound technicians would like to measure, is that power flowing through a designated area, such as a square meter.

variable, is the sound's apparent strength or magnitude. People occasionally substitute the term amplitude, a wave property that describes graphically the degree of displacement from a point of rest, for intensity. Indeed, greater amplitude usually elicits greater loudness, and amplitude is proportional to intensity, but the authors believe that a relationship between power and apparent strength is more clear. Unfortunately, people often use "volume" as a synonym for loudness, which may be misleading because volume also designates another tonal property, to be discussed later.

While the ears are sensitive to roughly a thousandfold frequency range, they are sensitive to roughly a trillionfold intensity range, from the weakest audible sounds to sounds that are virtually painful. Despite the much larger intensity than frequency range, most musicians make far more fuss over small differences in pitch than they do in loudness. Standard musical notation makes rather specific reference to pitch relationships through designated lines and spaces on the musical staff, but far less specific letters and Italian terms indicate loudness levels. An international frequency standard sets A_4 at 440 Hz, but there is no standard for any reference loudness.[10]

The ears are not equally sensitive across all frequencies in the hearing range. Although considerable individual differences exist, in general, a sound of a particular intensity level becomes louder and louder with increasing frequency until somewhere in the 1,500–3,000 Hz area; then it becomes softer with increasing frequency. The effect is more pronounced for lower intensity levels. In more succinct terms, the intensity-loudness relationship is "confounded" by frequency.

Combining the loudnesses of individual sounds into the loudness of a combination of sounds is not simply a matter of addition. For one thing, combined sounds may have less intensity and hence seem softer than the individual components due to the nature of the combined waveform. In destructive interference, the combined wave form (superposition) is smaller than the component wave forms; with totally destructive interference, the combination has zero displacement throughout. In addition, loudnesses add differently with different frequency relationships; in general, sounds further apart in frequency summate to a greater loudness than sounds close together—unless they are "quite a bit" apart.

Prolonged exposure to loud sounds, regardless of their nature, may reduce hearing sensitivity permanently. The tendency to listen to music

---

10. There are designated standards for units employed in measuring loudness level and loudness (see Radocy and Boyle 1988), but these lack the status of the frequency standard.

at sustained high intensities, whether through earphones or speakers, deserves serious concern from people who are interested in hearing conservation.

Waves carrying particular sounds have their own characteristic shape, which may be viewed on an oscilloscope or described mathematically. This shape or waveform is a function of the particular frequencies contained within the complex vibration, the relative strengths of the frequency components, and where each particular component is in its vibration cycle in relation to where the other components are.[11] The waveform changes continually during the history of a tone; in particular, the beginning or onset of a tone contains additional frequencies.

The psychological tonal aspect that is quasi-parallel to waveform is timbre. Timbre is a rather multidimensional property; orchestration texts abound with descriptions of instrumental tone qualities. Human auditory systems learn labels for particular sounds associated with characteristic waveforms; these are timbres. Research, occasionally featuring removing initial segments from recorded tones, shows that the initial portion often is crucial for identifying timbres reliably (Elliott 1975).

Physically, tones last for a particular amount of time, and duration, virtually the same thing, is the apparent amount of time a tone lasts. Rhythm is an extension of the duration relationships of sounds and silences.

Pitch, loudness, timbre, and duration are well-established psychological tonal aspects; each has one quasi-parallel physical aspect. Volume, the apparent size ("extensity") of a sound, and density, the apparent compactness of a sound, are more controversial. Each results from a combination of frequency and intensity. An increase in intensity increases both volume and density. Volume decreases with increasing frequency and increases with decreasing frequency; for example, a piccolo tone is "smaller," or less voluminous, than a tuba tone. Conversely, density increases with increasing frequency and decreases with decreasing frequency; for example, a piccolo tone is more compact than a tuba tone. S. S. Stevens, an extremely influential figure in modern psychophysics, insisted that volume and density were perceptibly real and not simply opposites of each other. In our experience, many people are unable to make judgments of volume and density independently of loudness, and some individuals who do recognize the two properties as different than loudness may judge volume and density to be opposite ends of one continuum.

---

11. The portion of a cycle that has been completed is the phase; when one speaks of where one cycle is in relation to another cycle, one speaks of relative phase.

Things, and the particles that compose those "things," vibrate. They vibrate in particular lawful ways, with particular frequencies or combinations of frequencies and amplitudes. They bump particles of a surrounding medium, often air. Those particles in turn bump other particles, which bump still other particles and set up a disturbance that travels outward as a sound wave. As the wave travels, especially in an enclosed space, things happen. For music, the important "things that happen" or wave phenomena include reflection and diffraction.

People's auditory systems sense the traveling waves that interact with the performance space. The waves eventually stimulate the inner ear, where motions associated with the waves become electrochemical signals from which the auditory system produces sounds. The sounds that are tones have basic psychological properties, including pitch, loudness, timbre, and duration. The tones in turn are the building blocks of sequential patterns that may become music.

REFERENCES

Backus, J. G. 1977. *The acoustical foundations of music.* 2d ed. New York: W. W. Norton.
Butler, D. 1992. *The musician's guide to perception and cognition.* New York: Schirmer Books.
Elliott, C. 1975. Attacks and releases as a factor in instrument identification. *Journal of Research in Music Education* 23, no. 1:35–40.
Farnsworth, P. R. 1969. *The social psychology of music.* 2d ed. Ames: Iowa State University Press.
Geerdes, H. P. 1987. *Music facilities: Building, equipping, and renovating.* Reston, VA: Music Educators National Conference.
Hall, D. E. 1991. *Musical acoustics.* 2d ed. Wadsworth, CA: Brooks/Cole.
Krumhansl, C. L. 1979. The psychological representation of pitch in a musical context. *Cognitive Psychology* 11:346–74.
Krumhansl, C. L. 1983. Perceptual structures for tonal music. *Music Perception* 1:28–62.
Radocy, R. E., and J. D. Boyle. 1988. *Psychological foundations of musical behavior.* 2d ed. Springfield, IL: Charles C. Thomas.
Roederer, J. G. 1975. *The physics and psychophysics of music.* 2d ed. New York: Springer-Verlag.
Rossing, T. D. 1990. *The science of sound.* 2d ed. Reading, MA: Addison Wesley.
Shepard, R. N. 1982. Structural representations of musical pitch. In *The psychology of music,* ed. D. Deutsch, 344–90. New York: Academic Press.
Wadhams, W. 1988. *Dictionary of music production and engineering terminology.* New York: Schirmer Books.

4

Hearing and Music Perception

Scott D. Lipscomb

and

Donald A. Hodges

As mentioned in chapter 3, three elements are needed for the perception of sound to take place—a source of vibrations, a medium of transmission, and a perceiver. The first two elements have been discussed; this chapter includes a discussion of the third element—the perception of sound. A thorough understanding of the physiology of the hearing mechanism is essential to understanding many aspects of musical behavior, because it is the sense of hearing that makes music possible. In the following pages, a sound wave will be traced from outside the ear to the brain and the perception of psychological attributes of sound will be discussed.

Throughout this discussion, the reader is urged to keep in mind the incredible sensitivity of the hearing mechanism and its extreme miniaturization. For instance, one can perceive sound when the eardrum has been deformed as little as one-tenth the diameter of a hydrogen molecule (Everest 1986) and the ratio of the softest sound we can hear to the loudest is more than a trillion to one (Schroeder 1993). One of the bones of the middle ear, the stirrup, is the smallest in the human body at "about half the size of a grain of rice" (Stevens and Warshofsky 1965, 35) and Reissner's membrane in the cochlea is only two cells thick (Gulick, Gesheider, and Frisina 1989). All this marvelous engineering should give musicians and all others who enjoy the sounds they hear a feeling of awe and appreciation.

The Hearing Mechanism

Outer Ear

The hearing process begins as sound pressure waves, traveling through the atmosphere, strike the ears. Ears, as one can readily observe, vary considerably in size and shape from person to person. Some animals have muscular control over their ears and can tilt or rotate them in different directions, an aid to the localization of sound. Humans do not possess this ability and, instead, turn their heads toward a sound to aid in localization.

A commonly supposed function of the outer ear (pinna)[1] is that it catches sound waves. "The sound waves coming towards us from all sides, however, have wave lengths measured in many inches, feet, or even yards, whereas the diameter of the pinna and especially of the inner conch [the ear canal] is not much more than one inch. The sound is, therefore, scattered rather than collected and focused" (Lowenstein 1966, 126). Man's outer ears do help to make sounds originating from in front of the head slightly more intense than those originating from behind and this aids in sound localization. Cupping a hand behind an ear demonstrates how the outer ear makes sounds louder and easier to hear.

Another aid to sound localization is the inner contour of the ear shell. As sound waves reflect off the ridges and folds of the outer ear, they provide localization cues to the brain. Using a dummy head equipped with artificial ears, researchers demonstrated that by gradually smoothing out the inner surface of the outer ears they were able to reduce the ability to localize sounds (Everest 1986; Hood 1977; Moore 1987). Localization of sounds is also greatly aided by timing cues. Sounds arrive at the two ears a microsecond apart (e.g., a sound coming from your left side must go around the head to reach the right ear) and the brain uses these minute discrepancies in arrival time to locate the direction of the sound.

The connecting passageway from the outer ear to the middle ear is the ear canal (external auditory meatus). This air-filled cavity has two protective devices to keep unwanted dust particles or other foreign bodies from entering the ear; the outermost edge is lined with hairs and the surface of the ear canal is lubricated with a sticky wax. The primary function of the ear canal is to channel air pressure waves to the eardrum. It also acts as a resonator and amplifies sounds in the range of 2,000–4,000 Hz as much as 15 dB, precisely the frequencies most important for music and speech (Handel 1989). Finally, the ear canal has the function of controlling the temperature and humidity of the eardrum (tympanum), which lies at the far end of the canal.

The eardrum receives air pressure waves from the atmosphere via the ear canal and vibrates in accordance with the frequency and intensity

---

1. Throughout this chapter, Latin and medical terms are included so that those readers who pursue related topics in more extensive scientific literature will have a point of reference.

of the waves. It is an extremely sensitive membrane. Responding to the movement of molecules of air, the eardrum transmits a wide variety of vibrations, from the faintest whisper to the loudest explosion. Evidence of the eardrum's sensitivity is the fact that its thinnest portion is only 0.055 mm thick (Donaldson and Duckert 1991).

Middle Ear

Between the eardrum and the cochlea in the inner ear is the air-filled cavity called the middle ear. This cavity is not completely closed, but has an opening into the oral cavity, the Eustachian tube. The eardrum connects with the inner ear by means of three small bones. Known collectively as the ossicles and separately as the hammer (malleus), anvil (incus), and stirrup (stapes), these bones are among the smallest in the human body. The ossicles serve as a link between the outer ear and inner ear. At one end, the hammer is attached to the eardrum, and, at the other end, the stirrup is connected to the cochlea at the oval window (see fig. 1).

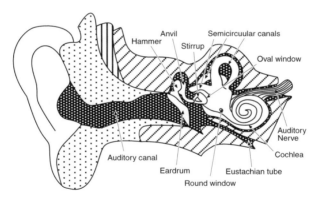

Fig. 1. Detail of the hearing mechanism

A sound wave traveling in the atmosphere reaches the ear and is channeled through the ear canal to the eardrum. The eardrum, in sympathetic vibration with the sound wave, vibrates back and forth, moving the hammer, anvil, and stirrup. These bones not only transfer the vibration to the oval window, but, due to their specific motions and the disparity in size between the eardrum and oval window, also amplify the vibrations. As they travel through the air, sound waves meet with very little resistance, especially when compared to the resistance found in the dense fluid (perilymph) of the cochlea. In fact, the impedance of cochlear fluid is approximately 3,750 times greater than that of air (Everest 1986). If a sound wave traveling through the air struck the oval window directly, without receiving amplification from the auditory canal, the eardrum, and the ossicles, only 1/1000 of the energy would be transmitted to the fluid-filled cochlea (Handel 1989). Actually, the motions of the middle ear are quite complex, but the important fact is this increase in energy from the eardrum to the oval window.

The increase in energy from that found at the eardrum to that necessary at the oval window as it pushes against the perilymph is created in three ways. First, the eardrum is much larger than the oval window, which causes an increase in pressure of 35 times. Second, the eardrum buckles in the middle, which doubles the pressure at the oval window. Third, the ossicles, acting as levers, increase the pressure by a factor of 1.15. Taking these three factors into account gives an overall increase of pressure at the oval window of 80.5 times ($35 \times 2 \times 1.15 \times 80.5$) (Handel 1989).

Three muscle actions, combining to form the acoustic (or stapedius) reflex, play an important role in protecting the ear against loud noises. First, the muscles that control the eardrum can contract and draw the drum into a conical shape. This stiffens the membrane so that it cannot vibrate so much. Second, the muscles of the ossicles can twist the bones so that they are somewhat rotated and lose a little of their amplifying efficiency. Third, the muscle attached to the stirrup can alter it in relation to the oval window, again causing a loss of amplification. Also, the Eustachian tube, normally closed, can be opened by opening the mouth or swallowing. This allows air pressure to be equalized on both sides of the eardrum. Unfortunately, even with all these protective devices, the ear has no way of protecting itself against sudden, loud noises. Each of the muscle actions can take place only after a realization that a sound is too loud and, even though the reaction is very quick, it is not quick enough to protect against a sudden, unexpected, loud noise (Bluestone 1991; Pickles 1988).

Inner Ear

The oval window separates the air-filled middle ear cavity from the fluid-filled inner ear. The inner ear consists of the semicircular canals and the cochlea. The semicircular canals serve an important function in determining body position, but they are not involved in the process of hearing. The cochlea has another surface membrane besides the oval window. This is the round window, which serves to release pressure built up in the cochlea.

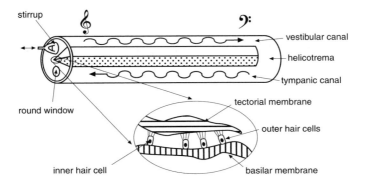

Fig. 2.   Diagram of the cochlea as if it were unrolled

The cochlea is a spiral-shaped body of two and one half turns, "no bigger than the tip of the little finger" (Stevens and Warshofsky 1965, 43). "It is about 1-1/3 inches long and perhaps 1/8 inch wide at its broadest point" (Pierce and David 1958, 136). Along most of its length it is divided by the cochlear duct into two parts: the vestibular canal (scala vestibuli) and the tympanic canal (scala tympani) (see fig. 2). These two canals are connected at the tip of the cochlear spiral by the helicotrema and are filled with perilymph. The cochlear duct is filled with endolymph and is bound on one side by Reissner's membrane (next to the scala vestibuli) and on the other side by the basilar membrane (next to the scala tympani).

> The system of vestibular and tympanic canals, with the cochlear duct, is so tiny that it takes only a fraction of a drop of perilymph— a liquid almost identical with spinal fluid—to fill the canals, and even less endolymph—similar to the fluid within cells—to fill the duct. (Stevens and Warshofsky 1965, 43)

Reissner's membrane, only two cells thick, is the thinnest in the human body. The basilar membrane is made of relatively stiff fibers and, from the oval window to the apex, widens to six times its original size (Gulick, Gesheider, and Frisina 1989). One side of the basilar membrane is attached to a bony shelf; the other side is attached to ligaments and is free to vibrate.

Resting on the basilar membrane is the organ of Corti. The organ of Corti contains the arches of Corti, which support one inner and three (four or five near the apex) outer rows of sensory hair cells. There are about 3,500 inner hair cells and 20,000 outer hair cells (Donaldson and Duckert 1991). Outer hair cells can shorten their length up to two microns as many as 30,000 times per second. This is 100 times faster than anything else in biology (Miller 1993). The conjecture is that this fast length change may enhance the auditory signal, improving sensitivity and fine tuning.

Overlapping the organ of Corti is the tectorial membrane (see fig. 2). About 100 microscopic, threadlike filaments, called stereocilia, emerge from each outer hair cell and are imbedded in the tectorial membrane. About 50 stereocilia emerge from each inner hair cell but these are not imbedded in the tectorial membrane.

Linking the inner ear to the brain is the auditory nerve which allows for two-way communication. For each cochlea, there are about 50,000 fibers that carry information from the cochlea to the brain along ascending (afferent) pathways and 1,800 fibers that carry signals from the brain to the cochlea along descending (efferent) pathways (Gulick, Gescheider, and Frisina 1989). About 93 percent of the fibers of the auditory nerve supply the inner hair cells (Hackney 1987), which represent only 20 percent of the total number of hair cells. While many outer hair cells may converge on a single auditory nerve, each inner hair cell may stimulate up to 20 auditory nerve fibers, most of which are afferent. Because of this arrangement, inner hair cells provide more acoustic information. Efferent nerves, bringing information from the brain to the inner ear, may have to do with increasing the frequency resolution of the inner hair cells (Handel 1989; Hood 1977; Russell 1987; Wallin 1991).

As the stirrup pushes on the oval window, causing it to move in and out, waves are propogated through the perilymph and passed along the vestibular canal to the helicotrema, making the return trip through the tympanic canal. At the end of this two-way trip through the spirals of the cochlea, the waves push against the round window. When the oval window is pushed in by the action of the stirrup, the round window is pushed out by the pressure of the waves traveling through the perilymph. The energy transmitted by the movements of the round window is released into the air cavity of the middle ear, where it returns to the atmosphere via the Eustachian tube.

On its journey through the vestibular and tympanic canals, the pressure wave transmits some of its energy to the membranes of the cochlear duct and the endolymph contained in it. As the membranes and the endolymph vibrate, the arches of Corti are also vibrated. "When the basilar membrane is deformed in vibration, the reticular lamina, tectorial membrane and organ of Corti slide with respect to each other, bending the hairs" (Pierce and David 1958, 140).

It is this "shearing" action—caused by the membranes traveling in opposite directions—that excites the hair cells. Hair cells can be stimulated when they are deformed as little as 100 picometers, or one-trillionth of a meter (Hudspeth 1983). An analogous experience can be felt if the hairs on the arm are lightly stimulated; as the hairs are bent, they propagate signals to the brain transmitting information about the touch sensation. The hair cells act as transducers, and it is at this point that the mechanical energy of the waves in the cochlear fluid is converted to electrochemical energy.

The hair cells are arranged along the length of the basilar membrane in such a way that those nearest the oval window respond to higher frequencies and those nearest the helicotrema at the far end respond to lower frequencies. It is interesting to note that "the musically most important range of frequencies (approximately 20–4,000 Hz) covers roughly two-thirds of the extension of the basilar membrane (12–35 mm from the base)" (Roederer 1975, 21).

From Ear to Brain

Auditory information does not travel from the inner ear to the primary auditory cortex along a simple, straight-line route. Rather, information is transmitted along a very diffuse and intricate pathway. Since even the brief overview that follows is fairly complicated, it may be more important to remember these general points: (1) Analysis of auditory information takes place in many localized processing centers scattered along a diffuse pathway between the inner ear and the auditory cortex; (2) each of these processing centers analyzes the auditory information for a particular feature, such as location of the source of the sound; and (3) all these bits and pieces of information are put back together to create a coherent sound experience with meaning (e.g., music) in the primary auditory cortex and the surrounding association areas.

Frequency representation of the basilar membrane is retained along the auditory nerve. Fibers carrying midrange frequency information form the center of the cable with fibers from the far end of the cochlea (representing low frequencies) twisting around it in one direction and fibers from the near end (representing high frequencies) twisting around the center cable in the other direction (Fletcher 1971; Martin 1975). Maintenance of frequency information in a spatial representation or map is called tonotopicity or tonotopical organization. The first portion of the auditory nerve is sometimes referred to as the "bottle neck" of auditory sensation because at this point all the information relayed between the ear and the brain is carried in a single bundle of fibers, unlike the more diffuse pathways higher in the brain.

The auditory nerve, as part of the VIIIth cranial nerve, divides as it enters the brainstem and sends fibers to both the upper (dorsal) and lower (ventral) cochlear nuclei (see fig. 3). More fibers go to the larger ventral cochlear nucleus than to the smaller dorsal cochlear nucleus. Beginning at this level, the auditory pathway rapidly increases in diversity and complexity. Tonotopic organization is retained, with higher frequencies represented in the dorsal cochlear nucleus and lower frequencies in the ventral cochlear nucleus. Different neurons in the cochlear nuclei respond to different aspects of the acoustic information, such as stimulus onset or offset. The cochlear nuclei not only relay information but also sort, enhance, and encode information to be sent to higher auditory nuclei (Gulick, Gescheider, and Frisina 1989).

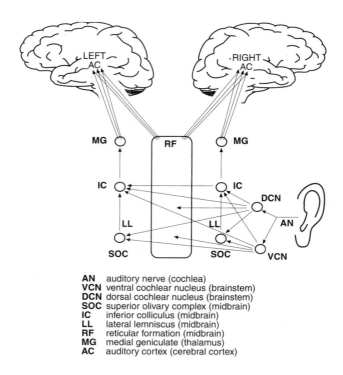

AN   auditory nerve (cochlea)
VCN ventral cochlear nucleus (brainstem)
DCN dorsal cochlear nucleus (brainstem)
SOC superior olivary complex (midbrain)
IC   inferior colliculus (midbrain)
LL   lateral lemniscus (midbrain)
RF   reticular formation (midbrain)
MG   medial geniculate (thalamus)
AC   auditory cortex (cerebral cortex)

Fig. 3.   Schematic drawing of the ascending auditory pathway

As fibers leave the cochlear nuclei, the first crossovers (decussations) in the auditory pathway occur and some fibers are sent to the superior olivary complex and inferior colliculus on the opposite (contralateral) side. This is the beginning of bilateral representation of sound. Other fibers that leave the cochlear nuclei extend to the superior olivary complex and inferior colliculus on the same (ipsilateral) side and to the reticular formation (Martin 1975).

The superior olivary complex is tonotopically organized in some portions. The portions not so organized are believed to be involved in processing binaural time and intensity disparity cues for sound localization (Milner 1970). Also, at the superior olivary complex there are already individual cells that receive incoming signals from both ears (Gacek 1967) as well as from the eyes (Shepherd 1994).

Some of the fibers from the ventral cochlear nucleus extend to the reticular formation. The reticular formation communicates with virtually all areas of the brain, including the cortex and spinal cord. There is a parallel pathway in the reticular formation (not shown in fig. 3) that connects with descending tracts in the spinal cord to allow for reflex-type responses to sound stimuli. The descending or efferent pathway emanating from the reticular formation also serves to inhibit lower auditory centers and elevate thresholds of hearing. The ascending pathway from the reticular formation serves to alert the cortex of important upcoming signals (Martin 1975). Animals whose classical auditory pathways have been cut regain their ability to respond to sounds using this alternate auditory pathway through the reticular formation (Fletcher 1971).

Cells in the medial olivary complex respond to temporal delays and are tuned to specific tonal frequencies. Because there are more cells tuned to lower frequencies, these nuclei may have a significant role in locating the source of lower frequencies (Hackney 1987). Cells in the lateral superior olive specialize in detecting intensity differences in the two ears and provide localization of higher frequency tones (Gulick, Gescheider, and Frisina 1989). As sound waves travel through the air, the head casts a "shadow" such that there is a slight time differential in the arrival of the sound wave at the two ears. Since lower frequencies have longer waves, this shadow effect has more consequences for higher frequency tones. One role of the olivary complex, then, is to create a "spatial map" (Handel 1989).

The last point for fibers from one ear to cross over to the opposite side is at the inferior colliculus, which receives its fibers from the superior olivary complex via the lateral lamniscus and from the cochlear nuclei. The descussations, which extend to the contralateral inferior colliculus, are probably responsible for certain forms of sound

integration, since up to 80 percent of the cells can be stimulated binau-
rally (Handel 1989; Moore 1987). There is considerable tonotopical organization with low frequencies at the sides and higher frequencies in
the center (Milner 1970).

The final relay station before the auditory pathway reaches the cortex is the medial geniculate body, located in the thalamus. Frequency-
specific fibers leaving the medial geniculate body fan out in ascending
auditory radiations and provide frequency information to the auditory
cortex. For a detailed examination of all the auditory way stations between the inner ear and the auditory cortex, see Altschuler et al. 1991;
Brugge 1991; Gulick, Gescheider, and Frisina 1989; Haggard and Evans
1987; Handel 1989; and Wallin 1991.

It is important to note that approximately 70 percent of the fibers
in the auditory pathway cross over to the contralateral side. Conduction is faster and stronger for the crossed pathway (Handel 1989). Thus,
while both ears send all information to both sides, each hemisphere
listens more carefully to the ear on the opposite side and will suppress
information from the ipsilateral side if there is any conflict (Calder
1970). (See also Kimura 1961 and 1967; Milner 1970; and Robinson and
Solomon 1974).

The Auditory Cortex

The final connection for the auditory pathway is in the temporal region
of the cerebral cortex (see fig. 4). The primary auditory projection areas
lie in the superior temporal gyrus (area 41) and occupy a surface only
one-half to one-third the size of the optic cortex. This represents 0.3 to
1.0 percent of the surface of the entire cerebral cortex (Blinkov and Glezer
1968). According to Weinberger, "the primary auditory cortex lies in
Heschel's gyrus which is within the Sylvian fissure. The surface of the
primary auditory cortex thus extends more or less perpendicular to the
surface of the temporal bone, in depth within the fissure" (1994, 21).

Various neural units within the auditory cortex respond to different types of sound stimuli. For instance, approximately 40 percent of
these neurons can be stimulated only by a complex tone or by a tone of
steady frequency (Lindsay and Norman 1972). Other neural units respond to stimulus onset, termination of a stimulus, or to "on-off"
(Deutsch and Deutsch 1973; Pickles 1988). The primary auditory cortex
is further organized in that tonotopicity is retained and, for pure tones,
cells are systematically arranged according to their characteristic frequencies (that is, the frequencies to which they best respond). Also, cells
are arranged so that those excited by one ear are separated from those

inhibited by the other ear. In other words, ear dominance is anatomically represented (Gulick, Gescheider, and Frisina 1989).

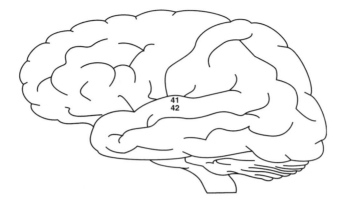

Fig. 4.   Primary auditory projection areas. Area 41 = primary auditory cortex; area 42 = associative auditory cortex.

Recent research is challenging old concepts. One new idea is that the receptive fields of certain individual auditory cortex neurons are capable of being retuned to respond more favorably to a different frequency (Weinberger 1992; Weinberger, Ashe, and Edeline 1993). This is an indication that learning can cause modifications in sensory processing. Another idea is that place information (tonotopic organization) in the auditory cortex is based on frequency for pure tones only. For complex tones, the auditory cortex is tonotopically arranged to reflect pitch, not frequency (Pantev et al. 1989). This indicates that considerable frequency analysis has taken place at the subcortical way stations. Using a superconducting quantum interference device (SQUID), researchers have documented that there is a common mapping in the primary auditory cortex with the pitch for complex tones superimposed onto the same areas as frequency for pure tones. Thus, one group of cells responds to middle C, another to C-sharp, and so on (Berger 1992; Lu, Williamson, and Kaufman 1992). "This kind of tone map shows that each octave (factor of 2 in frequency) of the frequency scale spans equal distance across the cortex, much like the arrangement of keys on a piano keyboard" (Williamson and Kaufman 1988, 503–04). Higher tones are mapped deeper in the fold and lower tones are nearer the surface (Hari 1990).

Infants have more neural connections in the auditory cortex than adults. This seems to be due to the fact that environmental circumstances cause certain pathways to be retained and others discarded. The marvelous plasticity of the brain allows for normal individuals to learn the music or speech of virtually any culture. Having learned the sounds of our culture, other acoustic patterns may be more difficult to acquire (Handel 1989; Wallin 1991).

There may be significant anatomical variations in different portions of the auditory cortex between hemispheres. For instance, one area (commonly labeled Area 42) is frequently larger in the left hemisphere (Chusid 1985; Schlang et al. 1995), while another portion (the polar area of the superior temporal region) is usually larger in the right hemisphere. Wide variability also exists between subjects, some of whom have a larger middle temporal subregion, a larger basal temporal subregion, or a larger superior temporal subregion. "Evidently this type of variability is associated with individual differences in the development of certain auditory functions (for example, those connected with music)" (Blinkov and Glezer 1968, 233). (For a full discussion of anatomical variations in the cerebral hemispheres, see Geschwind 1974).

The primary auditory zone is surrounded by association areas. These areas serve interpretive functions. Damage to these or other portions may cause amusia (loss of musical skills; discussed in chap. 7). For instance, damage to one area produces an inability to understand or interpret sounds, while primary sensory discriminations are not impaired (Grossman 1967). Other areas are concerned with frequency or temporal aspects, with the association of sound and past experiences, or with the retention of aural memories.

The roles of the subcortical areas, the primary auditory cortex, and the association areas are not completely understood. Research with animals indicates, for instance, that the auditory cortex may not be necessary for certain aspects of hearing and that many auditory discriminations may be mediated at subcortical levels (Martin 1975; Moore 1987; Pickles 1988). In general, however, it appears that the subcortical levels provide basic auditory discriminations, the auditory cortex makes more sophisticated discriminations, and the association areas provide integration, interpretation, and understanding. Also, a sound stimulus perceived in one ear is better processed by the hemisphere on the opposite side. Finally, there are anatomical variations in various areas of the auditory cortex and surrounding association areas that may account for some of the variations in the abilities shown by individuals.

Having traced a sound wave from outside the body to the brain, it is time to consider the cognitive processes that transform raw information into something meaningful, such as the elements that make up music. The study of these processes is organized under the term *perception*.

The Perception of Pitch, Loudness, Timbre, and Duration

In human perception, the acoustical and physiological phenomena previously discussed sometimes coalesce into a culturally recognized form referred to by members of the society as music. What are the specific processes that transform these minute molecular vibrations and electrochemical variations into an organized structure of sounds? These questions provide a foundation for the following discussion.

It is possible to discuss musical sound from any number of frames of reference. For example, a music theorist frequently considers music from a notational frame of reference, while an ethnomusicologist discusses music from a cultural frame of reference. The field of music psychology has focused largely on the interrelationship between the physical and the perceptual frames of reference. These basic concepts were introduced initially in the discussion of rudimentary psychoacoustics presented in chapter 3 and will serve as a point of departure for the consideration of the processes involved in music perception.

Carl E. Seashore (1938) proposed a model of music perception delineating the relationships between physical and perceptual variables involved in the process of perceiving musical sound (see table 1).

TABLE 1.   Seashore's Model of Music Perception

Physical	Perceptual	Trunklines of Musicality
Frequency	Pitch	Tonal
Amplitude	Loudness	Dynamic
Signal shape	Timbre	Qualitative
Time	Duration	Temporal

His earlier work (1919) suggested that musical aptitude could be measured by testing an individual's sensitivity (i.e., "elemental capacity") to each of the physical aspects of sound (i.e., frequency, amplitude, signal shape,[2] and temporal interval). Therefore, he considered these the

---

2. Seashore used the term *waveform* to describe the physical correlate of musical timbre. In his discussions, he frequently referred to signal graphs (two-dimensional graphs of amplitude by time) as sound waves. In actuality, a sound wave involves the three-dimensional propogation of energy through an elastic medium (e.g., air or water). Therefore, throughout this chapter, the more accurate term *signal shape* will be used in lieu of the commonly misused waveform. The term *signal* will be reserved for a graph of amplitude by time; e.g., the well-known visual representation of a sine function.

tonal, dynamic, qualitative, and temporal "trunklines of musicality." In the discussion to follow, each of the perceptual variables will be considered in turn, its role in music perception, and the results of scientific research relevant to that aspect of musical sound.

Each of the physical attributes of sound—frequency, intensity, signal shape, and time—has a primary perceptual correlate—pitch, loudness, timbre, and duration. Perceptions are the subjective sensations that arise from the presence of particular physical stimuli. Pitch, for example, is the place a tone is perceived to occupy in a relatively fixed region of the musical scale. Tones with a higher frequency are generally perceived to be higher in pitch than tones with a lower frequency. Pitch is primarily a function of frequency, but it can also be influenced by amplitude, signal shape, and time. Since the ancient Greeks, many persons have tried to explain how we perceive these psychological attributes of sound. Current explanations involve an understanding of the critical band.

The Critical Band

When a sound stimulus strikes the ear, the acoustic information in the wave is transmitted via the eardrum, ossicles, and cochlear fluid to the basilar membrane. The hair cells along the undulating basilar membrane are stimulated at a particular point determined by the frequency. Moreover, the hair cells a certain distance on either side of the point of maximum excitation are also stimulated. This region of hair cells, whose width is determined by the intensity of the sound stimulus, is called the resonance region.

If two tones of differing frequencies are sounded, two resonance regions that correspond to the stimulus frequencies will be formed on the basilar membrane. If these two resonance regions are separated, because the frequency difference of the two tones is great enough, two tones will be heard. If the frequency difference is small and the resonance regions overlap, roughness or beating can occur.

Imagine that two pure tones with identical frequencies are sounded; no beats will be perceived. If one tone remains constant and the frequency of the other is gradually raised, beating will occur. As the two tones are moved farther apart, the beating will get more and more pronounced until a sensation of roughness occurs. If the tones continue to move still farther apart, two separate tones will eventually be perceived and the roughness will then gradually give way to a feeling of smoothness. The approximate point at which the transition from roughness to smoothness occurs is called the critical band. At about 2,000 Hz, for example, two tones must be at least 200 Hz apart to be discriminated as separate tones and more than 300 Hz apart to sound "smoothly" (Roederer 1975). Although the frequency range of the critical bandwith increases as the frequency of the stimulus tone rises, the relative width of the critical band stays fairly constant. The role of the critical band is important to the understanding of aural perception and will be referred to in the ensuing discussions.

The Perception of Pitch

For pure tones, the sense of pitch is related to the frequency, that is, the greater the frequency, the higher the corresponding pitch. However, in more complex sounds (i.e., any real acoustic musical instrument), pitch is usually related to the fundamental frequency of vibration. If a pianist plays a low A (110 Hz) on the piano, the resulting vibration does not consist of only a single, periodic vibration at the rate of 110 times per second. Rather, the string vibrates as a whole (110 Hz) as well as at each of its integral divisions: in halves (220 Hz), in thirds (330 Hz), in fourths (440 Hz), and so on. Therefore, there is vibrational energy not only at the fundamental frequency of 110 Hz but also at each of these integer multiples (i.e., 220 Hz, 330 Hz, 440 Hz, etc.; see fig. 5).

Fig. 5.   The fundamental frequency and the first seven overtones

Frequencies that are integer multiples of the fundamental are called overtones. They are sometimes referred to as partials or harmonics, though these terms include both the fundamental and the overtones. Usually, the amount of vibrational energy present in an overtone decreases in proportion to the difference in frequency between it and the fundamental frequency (i.e., higher partials generally have less energy than lower partials). Vibrational energy is represented graphically in a spectrum as shown in figure 6. In this example, the greatest amount of energy is contained in the fundamental and each consecutive overtone has a smaller amount of energy. Spectra will be discussed in more detail in the section on timbre perception.

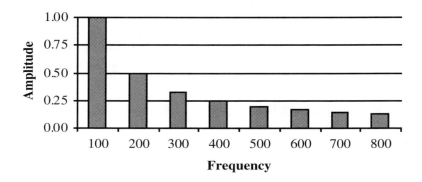

Fig. 6.   Spectrum of a sawtooth signal

The difference between sounds that have a definite pitch (e.g., a note played by a flute) and those that do not (e.g., a snare drum) is that the former consist of periodic vibration patterns, while the latter do not. Periodic vibrations are those that repeat a similar pattern of motion over and over.

The ear can perceive pitches over a frequency range of approximately 20 to 20,000 Hz. Sounds of primary importance for music fall within a general range of 20 to 4,000 Hz, or approximately the range of the piano (Backus 1977). Sounds below the range of the piano are more felt than heard. The upper limit of hearing is defined as the highest tone that can be perceived at an intensity level below the threshold of pain. Both the lower and upper limits of hearing vary greatly from person to person, and, as part of the normal aging process, the upper range of hearing begins to decline, a process called presbycousis. In middle age, the highest tones perceived may be about 15,000 Hz. Since the timbre of most musical instruments is not affected by cutting off all frequencies above 10,000 Hz, presbycousis has little effect on music listening (Backus 1977).

The first significant "modern" theory of hearing was proposed by Helmholtz in 1863 (1954). Helmholtz called his theory the resonance theory (also known as the place theory) because he was struck by the resemblance of the basilar membrane to the strings of a piano or harp. Just as each string on the piano or harp sounds a particular pitch, Helmholtz theorized that a given place on the basilar membrane is responsible for a particular pitch; overtones stimulate specific fibers spaced down the membrane.

According to the place theory of pitch perception (Helmholtz 1954; von Békésy 1960), such periodic vibration patterns allow the inner ear to separate complex vibrations into a series of consistent peaks of maximal stimulation along the basilar membrane. From this perspective, the ear is considered to be a frequency analyzer that merely accepts incoming vibrations and breaks them down into their simple components. In most cases, the location of these points of maximal stimulation are closely related to the perceived pitch. The points nearest to the oval window respond to higher frequencies, while those nearest to the helicotrema respond to lower frequencies. As the resonance region moves in one direction or another along the basilar membrane, our sensation of pitch generally moves up or down accordingly.

Although the hair cells within the resonance region are spread along a certain length of the basilar membrane, the tonal sensation is one of a single pitch. This single pitch perception is due to a "sharpening mechanism" (Pickles 1988). By means of neural inhibition, the nerves on either side of the point of maximum excitation may be firing in the inhibitory rather than excitatory mode (Roederer 1975). (See chap. 7 for more information on inhibitory and excitatory modes of firing.)

The place theory of pitch perception appeared to be quite reliable until von Békésy (1960), reporting on his research in the 1920s, discovered that at frequencies below 100 Hz the basilar membrane vibrates as a whole, so that stable peaks of stimulation no longer exist along its length. However, we can still perceive frequencies as low as 20 Hz. How can this be possible according to the place theory of pitch? Simply stated, if the place theory explained the process completely, it should be impossible for us to clearly distinguish pitches below about 200 Hz (Dowling and Harwood 1986, 28). Therefore, additional explanations are necessary.

An alternative theory of pitch perception emphasizes the periodicity of an incoming vibration. Seebeck's famous experiments in 1833 (cited in Helmholtz 1954, 11) demonstrated that, by controlling the number of energy pulsations per second, it was possible to alter the perceived pitch of a tone. Using a simple siren created by rotating a disk with equally spaced holes in front of an air flow, he showed that the faster the disk was rotated (i.e., the more puffs of air emitted per second) the higher the resulting pitch was perceived to be. The importance of this discovery was confirmed by von Békésy (1960) when he proposed that, since the basilar membrane vibrates as a whole below 100 Hz, response of the auditory system below approximately 200 Hz must be based on neural transmission of the periodicity of the acoustic vibrations via the firing rate of nerves attached to the hair cells.

A simplified way of thinking of this process is shown in figure 7, representing a sine signal. If the compressed portion of the energy wave (i.e., the point marked with an x in the figure) arrives at the ear 440 times per second, then the resulting periodicity pitch would usually be A above middle C. Therefore, the higher the number of repetitions of the signal within a specified period of time, the higher the perceived pitch. This explanation works reliably until the realization is made that the upper threshold for direct neural transmission of auditory frequencies is approximately 1,000 Hz due to the refractory (i.e., recovery) period. Single cells cannot fire at a rate substantially greater than 1,000 times per second. As a result, though neither place theory nor periodicity pitch alone appears to be sufficient to provide a complete explanation of the process of pitch perception, both appear to be necessary to fully understand the decoding of physical vibration into musical sound.

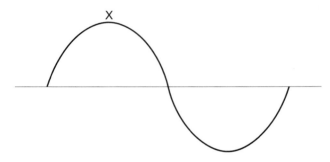

Fig. 7. Sine signal as an example of periodicity pitch

It is quite probable that both mechanisms are at work simultaneously in this coding process: the periodicity pitch mechanism operating at frequencies between 20–2,000 Hz and the place mechanism operating at frequencies from 200–20,000 Hz. Dowling and Harwood point out that "it is perhaps not surprising that our best performance in discriminating one frequency from another is in the frequency range where the two mechanisms overlap: 200–2,000 Hz" (1986, 29).

The volley theory of pitch perception was proposed by Wever (1949) and Lindsay and Norman (1972). According to this theory, at frequencies above 1,000 Hz, the brain combines signals from a large number of nerve fibers, allowing an internal "clock" mechanism to monitor the total number of energy spikes per second—taking into account all fibers in the bundle. Therefore, the volley theory allows for resolution of higher frequencies than the periodicity pitch theory. However, neither volley theory nor a combination of the place and periodicity coding mechanisms can provide a complete and accurate account of how acoustical vibrations are translated into perceived pitches. At present, the elusive black box of human perception has not yet yielded completely to scientific investigation.

Dimensions of Pitch

Pitch perception has often been considered to consist of only a single dimension (i.e., high-low). Many investigators now believe, however, that pitch is actually complex and multidimensional (Carterette and Kendall 1989). One of the earliest researchers to demonstrate more than one dimension of pitch was Roger Shepard (1964). Experiments using his "Shepard scale" demonstrate the independence of two pitch dimensions. He created a special stimulus set consisting of 10 sine components spaced an octave apart. Imposed upon these frequency components was an overall intensity envelope centered on a constant frequency (see fig. 8).

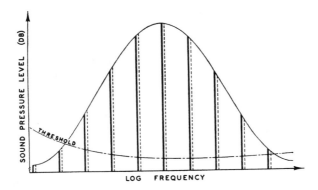

Fig. 8.   Spectrum representing the intensity envelope used by Shepard (1964). Sound-pressure levels (in dB) of 10 simultaneously sounded sinusoidal components spaced at octave intervals. (The dotted lines correspond to an upward shift in the frequencies of all components.)

This simply means that there was a central point in the range of frequencies at which the tones were always loudest and the farther away from this central point that a frequency lies (either higher or lower) the lower is the corresponding amplitude, such that the lowest and highest tones would have been barely audible if played alone. As a result, absolute pitch height (i.e., the highness or lowness) of the tone never changed.

In figure 8, the solid lines represent the starting frequency complex, and the dashed lines represent the second chromatic frequency complex.

In his experiment, Shepard played a rising chromatic scale (e.g., all the white and black notes on the piano keyboard between two notes spaced an octave apart) for his subjects, repeating it over and over. Amazingly, because the amplitude envelope was kept constant, the subjects did not hear a repeating chromatic scale as shown in the upper system of musical notation in figure 9a. Instead, they heard a constantly rising chromatic scale that continued upward until an arbitrary point at which the pitch appeared to leap downward before resuming its upward progression (see fig. 9b). The point at which the pitch appeared to leap downward varied among subjects. Another striking example of a similar phenomenon is Deutch's "tritone paradox" (Deutsch 1987; Deutsch, Kuyper, and Fisher 1987). Using octave-related components and an overall intensity envelope similar to Shepard's, she played tritone intervals for her subjects. Some subjects heard the interval ascending while others heard it descend. These experiments illustrate that there are at least two dimensions of pitch: pitch height and chroma (or pitch class).

Fig. 9. (*a*) **The repeating pitch pattern utilized in Shepard 1964.** (*b*) **One possible subject interpretation of the Shepard scale provided in fig. 9a.**

The concept of pitch height is familiar to most listeners as the highness or lowness of a pitch. Pitch chroma is simply the aspect of a pitch that all C's (or all D's or all F sharps, etc.) share in common. For example, if you play middle C on a piano, then the octave above, then the octave below, you can immediately sense that the height of these three pitches changes, yet there is some aspect of the perceived pitch that remains unchanged—this is the pitch chroma.

To a great degree, pitch height and chroma can be considered independent of one another. This was illustrated elaborately by the Shepard scale, as described above. However, the same effect may be easily illustrated at any piano by playing the series of tones presented in figure 10. Listen carefully as the series progresses. Most people hear the height of the pitches continue to descend from beginning to end. However, do you also hear an ascending major scale as well? In this example, the independence of pitch height and chroma is illustrated clearly, because pitch height descends while pitch chroma ascends.

Fig. 10.   Simple illustration of the independence of pitch height and chroma

Later work by Krumhansl and Shepard (1979) and Krumhansl (1979) has provided a model of pitch perception frequently referred to as the pitch spiral. Rather than considering pitch on a single dimension from high to low, their experiments suggest that a helix (or spiral) may provide a more accurate representation of the relationship between pitches from the Western chromatic scale. The helical model resembles a coiled spring, such that each consecutive pitch of the chromatic scale is equally spaced around the circumference of a single coil (see fig. 11). If we were to follow the coil for one complete rotation (e.g., from middle C to the C above middle C), our point of arrival would be on the next coil directly above where middle C is located. Therefore, this model encapsulates both pitch height (i.e., tones close together around the circumference of the spiral) and chroma (i.e., tones close along the vertical dimension). Shepard later extended this model into what he called the "double helix of musical pitch in three dimensions" (1982, 362). To the dimensions of pitch height and chroma incorporated into Krumhansl and Shepard's (1979) helical model, the double helix model adds the following: the cycle of fifths, semitone relationships, whole tone relationships, diatonic major scales, chromatic scales, and whole tone scales (Shepard 1982, 375).

Pitch Discrimination
As mentioned previously, the human ear is capable of perceiving a broad range of frequencies. Of particular interest has been the issue of

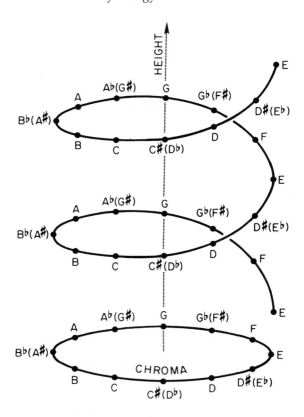

Fig. 11. Shepard's (1982) pitch spiral with pitch height as the vertical dimension and the chroma circle as the projection onto the horizontal plane.

the smallest detectable differences. In his *Elemente der Psychophysik* (1860), Gustav Fechner proposed that it is possible to measure psychological magnitudes by determining an individual's ability to discriminate between two nearly equal sounds. The smallest change in a stimulus that an observer can detect 50 percent of the time is referred to as the just noticeable difference (JND) or difference limen (DL). It is possible to determine a discrimination measure for any of the musical parameters we have discussed thus far: frequency, amplitude, signal shape, and duration.

Most listeners can discriminate between two tones separated by only 0.5 to 2.0 Hz at low and mid-range frequencies; that is, most people will hear a pitch difference between a 400 Hz tone and a 402 Hz tone—assuming that amplitude, signal shape, and duration are kept constant (Handel 1989). A general rule of thumb states that the frequency discrimination threshold may be approximated by multiplying a given frequency by 1 percent (e.g., the frequency discrimination threshold of a 250 Hz tone is approximately 2.5 Hz).

A number of factors can influence pitch discrimination (Hedden 1980). The type of measurement used can vary from judging successive tones (one tone sounded after another), judging simultaneously sounding tones, or judging a single tone that is fluctuating up and down. The smallest changes can usually be detected with the latter method, particularly if the fluctuations are sudden rather than continuous. The results of experiments with other factors lead to the following conclusions: (*a*) more refined discriminations can be made with complex tones than pure tones, at least below 4,000 Hz; (*b*) presenting stimuli under standardized free field conditions (i.e., subjects sit in the same place in a room) lead to smaller DLs than group testing in a free field or using headphones; (*c*) more refined discriminations can be made at an optimum loudness level (*d*) more refined discriminations can be made in the 500–1,000 Hz range than above or below; and (*e*) smaller DLs are obtained with binaural presentation of stimuli than with monaural.

Pitch matching—asking a subject to match one tone exactly to another—is a different task altogether. Although pitch matching is an often-used skill in the real musical world (e.g., when instruments in an ensemble must play in tune with each other), it has not been thoroughly studied experimentally. One such study, however, indicates the degree of refinement capable by accomplished musicians. During a concert in 1963, 106 musicians of the Boston Symphony Orchestra were performing Britten's *War Requiem* in the outdoor Shed at Tanglewood (Pottle 1970). With a high temperature that was raised further by television cameras and lights, the orchestra was faced with the prospect of trying to play in tune with a pipe organ tuned at A-447.5, a portative organ at A-446.5, pretuned percussion instruments at A-444, and a piano at A-442. The orchestra started right in the middle at A-444.6, and, in fifteen measurements made throughout the performance, the maximum discrepancy recorded within the orchestra was an incredibly minimal 19 cents (there are 100 cents in a semitone).

Psychophysical Pitch Scales

Providing an alternative to the commonly held mathematical (i.e., logarithmic) relationship between frequency and pitch, Stevens proposed that the relationship was instead a power function (Stevens and Volkmann 1940).[3] Stevens and his colleagues arrived at this conclusion utilizing a method called magnitude estimation. In this procedure, subjects were required to provide a number as a means of expressing the relationship between two pitches. For instance, if a 100 Hz tone and a 200 Hz tone are presented, the subject might say that the second tone is "2 times as high" as the first tone. Theoretically, a pitch perceived as "twice as high" should receive a number twice as large. Stevens referred to this measurement of pitch as the mel scale. Such psychophysical scales have not proven as reliable as the logarithmic (or octave) relationship. As Dowling and Harwood point out, "people are very precise at making octave judgments and very imprecise at the kinds of judgments required by magnitude estimation" (1986, 105).

Consonance and Dissonance

Up to now, we have only considered consecutively sounding tones. What happens when two or more notes are played simultaneously? As stated in chapter 3, the vibration patterns of each tone will interfere, both constructively and destructively, resulting in a composite signal shape. Some frequency combinations sound pleasing or restful, while others seem rough and, within some cultural contexts, cause the listener to desire resolution to a more stable combination.

A combination of tones that sounds pleasant and stable is referred to as consonant, and a tonal combination that sounds discordant or rough is said to be dissonant. These concepts do not form a simple dichotomy; instead, they anchor the poles of a perceptual continuum. In other words, the level of consonance can extend from total consonance through many varieties of consonance or dissonance to utter dissonance (i.e., cacophony).

Two types of consonance are commonly recognized: tonal and musical. In Western music, musical consonance is exemplified in a full cadence (see fig. 12) and is strongly influenced by the rules of music theory. The contextual tension built up by the initial chord (V^7) is brought to resolution with the arrival of the tonic (I). Tonal consonance (Plomp and Levelt 1965) or sensory consonance (Terhardt 1974), on the other hand, usually refers to the level of consonance between simple sine components (as opposed to complex vibration patterns), removed from a musical context. Dowling and Harwood provide a lucid discussion of musical

---

3. A logarithmic function correlates additive perceptual units (pitch) with physical ratios (frequency), while the power function describes the relationship between pitch ratios and frequency ratios (Dowling and Harwood 1986).

consonance (1986, 14–18) and the topics are covered frequently in texts devoted to music theory, so this discussion will focus primarily on tonal consonance.

Fig. 12.   Musical consonance illustrated with a full cadence

Tonal consonance appears to be directly dependent upon the frequency difference between tones. If the frequency difference is either small enough that the tones do not interfere with each other or large enough that the peaks of stimulation on the basilar membrane are beyond the critical bandwidth, the tones are judged to be perceptually consonant. The highest level of tonal dissonance results from a frequency separation of about 1/4 of a critical band (i.e., approximately 20 Hz in the low-frequency range or about 4 percent—slightly less than a semitone—in the the higher regions; see Rasch and Plomp 1982).

The range of tonal consonance can be easily illustrated using two sine-tone generators. When both oscillators are set to 100 Hz, the two tones fuse into a single pitch creating a perfect consonance. As the frequency of one oscillator is slowly raised, the two tones begin to cause a beating effect (i.e., a periodic increase and decrease in amplitude, similar to the tremolo of a flute). This beating results from the interference of energy emanating from the two oscillators. The number of beats per second is equal to the frequency difference between the two tones. For example, when the second oscillator reaches a frequency of 104 Hz, the beating will occur 4 times per second (i.e., 104 - 100 = 4). Perceptual dissonance reaches its maximum as the frequency difference equals approximately 1/4 of a critical bandwidth. At this point, most listeners perceive an extremely high level of roughness. This roughness begins to decline as the frequency of the second oscillator continues to rise until, at a frequency difference corresponding to the critical bandwidth, the two tones separate perceptually into two distinct pitches. The level of consonance continues to rise steadily from this point (approximately the musical interval of a minor third) until the tones are an octave apart (Plomp and Levelt 1965). Since consonance and dissonance are inversely related, the point of maximal dissonance is equivalent to the point of minimal consonance.

Kameoka and Kuriyagawa (1969a and 1969b) extended the concept of tonal consonance to complex tones consisting of six partials with a fundamental frequency of 250 Hz. Results of their study confirmed that consonance ratings are related to interference between neighboring partials (see Hutchinson and Knopoff 1978). Basically, any two partials (other than a unison) that fall within a critical bandwidth add to the total dissonance. This is significant, because it suggests that roughness occurs not only as a result of interference between fundamental frequencies, but can occur between any (or all) of the harmonics of a complex tone (Rossing 1990, 157). Therefore, the first interval (perfect fifth) shown in figure 13 is perceived as less dissonant than the second interval (tritone) due to the lower number of partials interacting within a critical bandwidth. In figure 13, partials in the harmonic series above the upper pitch that fall within a critical band of pitches in the lower pitch are represented by diamond-shaped noteheads. As indicated, the second interval exhibits many more neighboring partials within a range of a minor third (i.e., three semitones).

Fig. 13. **Interaction of partials in two complex tones, each consisting of six harmonics. The lower staff represents the interval formed by the fundamental frequencies of the complex tones and the upper staff provides an illustration of all partials concurrently present. All partials in the upper tone that interact within a critical band with partials in the lower tone are represented by a diamond-shaped notehead.**

Absolute Pitch

Another ability associated with the process of pitch perception is labeled absolute (or perfect) pitch. In contrast to relative pitch (i.e., the ability to identify musical intervals by name), perfect pitch involves the capacity to identify a specific tone by frequency or pitch name without the assistance of a comparison tone. Absolute pitch (AP) also often includes the ability to accurately produce a specific pitch on demand. Ward and Burns (1982) discuss the major theories concerning the acquisition of this ability. The heredity viewpoint (Bachem 1937; Révész 1913) holds that AP is an innate ability. The learning theory of AP asserts that heredity is irrelevant and that the ability develops as a result of early reinforcement following an individual's attempt to assign pitch names to musical sounds. Abraham's (1901) and Watt's (1917) unlearning theory of AP requires an individual to unlearn the commonly held belief that transposed melodies (i.e., an identical series of musical intervals played in several different keys) are inherently similar. Proponents of the unlearning theory of AP also claim that it is extremely difficult for an individual to develop absolute recognition of a particular frequency, when middle C on one piano may vary by as much as 10 to 20 Hz from middle C on another piano. Another theory of AP acquisition (Copp 1916) is closely related to the concept of imprinting in the learning theory literature, suggesting that AP—like developing accent-free speech in a foreign language—can be learned only by children.

Research into whether this ability can be acquired later in life is inconclusive. Wellek (1938) discovered a correlation of .80 between the age at which AP ability was recognized and the number of errors on a pitch identification task (see also Sergeant 1969). Though some studies have claimed to result in the acquisition of AP (Brady 1970; Cuddy 1968 and 1970), it appears that, when the ability is learned later in life, accuracy of absolute pitch identification declines rapidly when a strict practice regimen is discontinued (Gough 1922; Meyer 1899; Mull 1925; Weddell 1934).

The Perception of Loudness

Loudness is the perceptual variable related primarily to the physical characteristic amplitude (or intensity). The term *volume* is often used erroneously in discussions of loudness; for example, stereo equipment often has a "volume knob" that actually controls loudness. However, the two are not synonymous. Loudness is related to increasing intensity, while volume involves a complex interaction between intensity, density, and area of the auditory experience (Stevens 1934). Volume is the psychological perception of how much space a sound seems to occupy. For example, low frequency sounds at high intensity seem to be "larger" than high frequency sounds at low intensity.

Loudness is usually expressed as sound pressure level (i.e., dB_{SPL}).[4] This unit of measurement serves to quantify the amplitude of physical vibration using a logarithmic scale. Because this scale is logarithmic, the amplitude difference between the lower threshold of hearing (0 dB_{SPL}, i.e., an intensity level of 10^{-12} watts/meter^2) and the upper threshold of hearing (120 dB_{SPL}, i.e., 1 watt/meter^2), the threshold of pain, is about a trillionfold (Roederer 1975). The softest sounds that can be heard, at the threshold of hearing, are incredibly faint. At 3,000 Hz, a sensation of tone can occur when the eardrum is displaced as little as one-tenth the diameter of a hydrogen molecule (Schiffman 1976). If the ear were any more sensitive, the brain would be constantly bothered by the sounds of internal bodily processes, such as blood flowing through veins. At the other end of the continuum, the upper limit of loudness perception is marked by pain.

Measurements of actual music performance tend to range from 40 dB_{SPL} (a quiet pianissimo) to about 90 dB_{SPL} for a full orchestra fortissimo (Winckel 1962). In fact, research has shown that the average dynamic range of performers on most musical instruments varies from only a 5 dB range for the English horn to a 45 dB range for the clarinet (Clark and Luce 1965; Patterson 1974). Though this does not include the entire range of human hearing, the intensities in musical performance from pianissimo to fortissimo represent an intensity increase of about one million-to-one (Backus 1977). Naturally, significantly higher levels of amplitude can be reached by utilizing electronic amplification. Table 2 provides a list of common sounds and their approximate dB ratings in order to provide the reader with a point of reference for various dB levels.

TABLE 2.   Sample Decibel Levels

Sound	dB_{SPL}	Qualitative Level
Threshold of hearing	0	Barely audible
Rustling leaves	10	
Broadcast studio	20	
Bedroom at night	30	Quiet
Living room	40	

(continued)

---

4. The formula for calculating sound pressure level in decibels is: $dB_{SPL} = 20 \times \log_{10}(SPL_x/SPL_{REF})$, where SPL_x is the measure of sound pressure and SPL_{REF} is the reference value of .0002 dynes/cm^2. This is in contrast to another common decibel measurement: intensity level. The latter is calculated as follows: $dB_{IL} = 10 \times \log10 (I_x/I_{REF})$, where I_x is the intensity level being measured and I_{REF} is the reference value of 10^{-12} watts/meter^2.

TABLE 2—*Continued*

Sound	dB$_{SPL}$	Qualitative Level
Office/classroom	50	Moderate
Normal conversation	60	
Auto interior	70	Noisy
Urban street	80	
Heavy truck (at 15 feet)	90	Very noisy
Shout (at 5 feet)	100	
Construction site	110	Intolerable
Jet taking off	120	Pain

There is a growing notion in our society that many of us are losing our hearing and that a primary cause may be exposure to loud sounds (Elias 1991). The *Journal of the American Medical Association* (American Medical Association 1990) reports that, of 28 million Americans who experience a hearing loss, approximately 10 million obtained the loss from exposure to loud sounds. Harmful effects are measured in dB$_{SPL}$ across time and any sound over 85 decibels is considered potentially harmful. Thus, the OSHA standards for the legally allowed level of exposure without harmful effects is 90 dB$_{SPL}$ for 8 hours daily (Occupational Safety and Health Administration 1981). However, for each increase of 5 dB$_{SPL}$ above 90 dB$_{SPL}$, it takes only half as much time for damage to occur. Damage can occur under the following representative conditions: 95 dB$_{SPL}$ for 4 hours, 100 dB$_{SPL}$ for 2 hours, 110 dB$_{SPL}$ in a half hour (Melnick 1994; Williams 1992).

Of particular concern are teenagers and others who listen to popular music styles; the contention is that many are listening to rock music at loudness levels that can damage hearing. When the rock group Metallica was measured as putting out 113 dB$_{SPL}$ in live performance (Koss 1993), the damage risk for certain musical experiences should be readily apparent. The effects of high loudness levels may be exacerbated with the use of headphones, especially smaller ones that are inserted into the ear canal (Feldman and Grimes 1991; Goldstein and Newman 1994).

While the notion of teenagers listening to rock music at ear-shattering levels fits the popular notion, what research data is available to confirm this stereotype? One of the earliest studies was done by an audiologist, David Lipscomb, who tested the hearing of entering college freshmen in 1969 and found that 60 percent had a significant hearing loss (Williams 1992). When this figure was compared to less than 4 percent of sixth graders who had similar hearing losses, it was evident that something happened in the intervening years to cause hearing damage.

Based on interviews, Lipscomb suspected the primary culprit was listening to rock music through headphones.

Kuras and Finday (1974) asked 25 college students to set most-comfortable-loudness (MCL) levels for rock music samples. They found that 75 percent of the MCL levels fell between 70–100 dB and that more than half the subjects exceeded national damage risk criteria. Barrett and Hodges (1995) found that middle school and college students had music loudness preferences (MLP) for heavy metal and jazz samples that were significantly louder than classical, country, chant, or rap selections. Furthermore, these two styles were the only ones that exceeded the OSHA safety levels of 85 dB (heavy metal MLPs ranged from 84.48–96.60 dB and jazz from 77.17–88.80 dB). College music students and middle school band students exceeded 85 dB with MLPs for jazz of 85.05 and 86.75 dB, respectively. All three groups approached or exceeded this level for heavy metal music (college nonmusic majors = 84.48 dB, college music majors = 91.55 dB, and middle school band students = 92.88 dB). It should also be noted that 12 of the 40 middle school students had an MLP over 100 dB. The highest registered MLP was 120 dB; at that level it would take repeated exposures of only seven and one-half minutes for permanent damage to occur.

Damage occurs because overly loud sounds cause hair cells in the cochlea to vibrate so violently that they are damaged (Henderson et al. 1994; Nielsen and Slepecky 1986). Prolonged exposure flattens outer and inner hair cells and they lose their resilience and die. Once these hair cells are destroyed, they can never be replaced, and associated hearing loss is permanent. Persons who listen to music at just under "damage limits" may experience a temporary threshold shift (TTS), which is a temporary loss of hearing acuity (Alberti 1991; Kryter 1984; Melnick 1994). Their hearing sensitivity may be dampened for a few hours but generally will be recovered. When teenagers were given a hearing test at a live rock-music concert, 19 of 20 experienced significant average threshold shifts (Danenberg, Loos-Cosgrove, and LoVerde 1987). Of more concern is the fact that 4 of 6 subjects who were retested three days later had only partially recovered to pre-exposure thresholds.

Loudness Discrimination
In addition to physical measurements of intensity, several investigators have tried to quantify the perceptual loudness of sounds (i.e., a psychological measure). An early attempt at a purely psychophysical loudness scale was Stevens' (1936) sone scale in which the loudness of a 1,000 Hz sine tone at 40 dB_{SPL} was arbitrarily assigned a value of 1 sone. Stevens utilized a method of magnitude estimation in which listeners assign a

value to a tone based on its perceived loudness; for example, a tone considered twice as loud as the reference was rated at 2 sones, and so on. However, subjects appear to be uncertain about what is meant by "two times louder" or "three times louder," so the sone scale has not proven to be a particularly reliable metric. The phon scale (Fletcher and Munson 1933) provides a psychophysical measurement derived from comparative judgments of equal loudness. In deriving this metric, subjects were required to listen to a 1,000 Hz reference tone and adjust tones of varying frequencies until they were equally as loud as the reference. Many levels of intensity were utilized in this comparison task. The resulting equal loudness contour is shown in figure 14. Loudness of a tone in phons is referred to in decibels as loudness level (dB$_{LL}$). Finally, the sensation level (dB$_{SL}$) scale is defined as the sound pressure level at the auditory threshold (i.e., the level at which a tone of a given frequency can just be perceived). This measure varies not only as a function of frequency but also from subject to subject (Rasch and Plomp 1982). The concept of equal loudness—and its implications concerning Seashore's model of music perception—will be discussed subsequently.

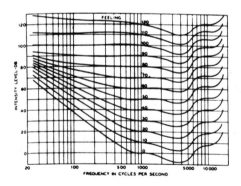

Fig. 14. Equal loudness contour (after Fletcher and Munson 1933)

Significance of the Critical Bandwidth
Loudness is coded and transmitted by the firing rate of the hair cells within the resonance region of the basilar membrane. When the intensity of a tone is increased, the nerves fire at a faster rate—up to a point. If the tone continues to increase in intensity, the hair cells quickly reach their maximum firing rate with the result that the resonance region spreads wider along the basilar membrane including more and more

hair cells that join in the firing. Thus, the perception of loudness is a result of the total number of neural impulses—a combination of the firing rate of individual neurons and the number of neurons within the resonance region.

The critical band is important in the perception of loudness for a tone complex. If all the tones of the complex are within a critical bandwith, loudness depends solely on the overall sound pressure level. However, when tones of a complex lie within different critical bands, loudness is "equal to the sum of the loudness contributions of successive adjacent critical bands covering the excitation pattern of the stimulus" (Plomp 1976, 84).

It might seem reasonable to assume that the relationship between sound pressure level in decibels and perceptual loudness is simply additive, that is, the loudness of two flutes at 40 dB_{SPL} would be perceptually equivalent to a single flute at 80 dB_{SPL}. However, this is not the case for two reasons. First, the decibel scale is logarithmic (not linear), meaning that the relationship between 40 dB_{SPL} and 80 dB_{SPL} is about a 10,000-fold increase (i.e., 10^4) rather than a mere doubling (see Rossing 1990, 89–90, for a detailed explanation of this relationship). A common "rule of thumb" suggests that an increase of 6 dB_{SPL} is a good estimate of the level at which the sound pressure is doubled. Since the relationship between intensity (i.e., vibrational energy) and sound pressure is exponential (Intensity = SPL^2), the "rule of thumb" for intensity level (dB_{IL}) requires an increase of 3 dB_{IL} to approximate a doubling of the energy.

Secondly, the relationship between physical intensity levels and perceived loudness is not isomorphic. One reason for this difference is that the perceived loudness of complex tones is dependent upon the distance between frequency components. If a listener is presented with two sine tones having the same sound pressure level, perceived loudness does not increase until the frequency separation of the two tones exceeds the critical bandwidth. In fact, manipulating the frequency spacing of four sine components, Zwicker, Flottorp, and Stevens (1957) found that, if the tones are within the same critical bandwidth, perceived loudness actually diminishes.

Masking

Another intriguing characteristic of loudness perception is the ability of one sound to hide (or mask) another sound. This phenomenon occurs to a varying degree whether using pure tones, complex sounds, or noise. In fact, masking can occur even if the masking sound occurs as much as 20–30 milliseconds before (forward masking) or a few milliseconds after (backward masking) the masked sound. Rossing (1990) provides the following conclusions based on the results of experimental research. First, if the pure tones are close together in frequency, masking is more likely to occur. Second, a pure tone will more effectively mask another tone of higher frequency than a tone of lower frequency. Third, the range of masked frequencies is dependent upon the intensity of the masking tone, such that higher intensities result in a wider range of effected frequencies. Fourth, two tones that are widely separated in frequency will show little effect of masking.

These conclusions may be explained by reconsidering the way that the basilar membrane is excited by pure tone stimulation. Remember that high frequencies excite the region of the basilar membrane nearest to the oval window, while low-frequency tones reach their point of maximal displacement at the opposite end, near the helicotrema. Excitation along the basilar membrane is not symmetrical in its pattern of displacement, resulting in a "tail" that extends toward the oval window (see fig. 15). Therefore, due to the presence of this extension, it is quite logical that higher frequency tones are more easily masked than low-frequency tones. Also, as the intensity of a masking tone is increased, the amplitude of a greater proportion of its tail is sufficient to mask higher frequency tones.

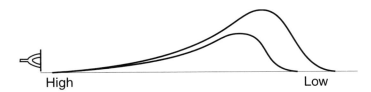

High   Low

Fig. 15. An illustration of masking, using two pure tone components (after Rossing 1990, 103)

Amplitude Envelope
The intensity, and hence the resulting loudness, of musical sound rarely remains constant. When you hear a musical instrument—even a single note—the loudness level usually changes from beginning to end. This amplitude envelope (i.e., the way that a musical note starts, sustains, and stops) is a characteristic property that assists in distinguishing one instrument from another. Every amplitude envelope of a musical tone consists of at least three specific components: onset, steady state, and offset (Handel 1989, 23). The onset portion of an amplitude envelope consists of the time interval required to begin the note, for example, from the time a violinist sets his or her string into vibration until the

amplitude reaches a percentage of its steady-state amplitude. This percentage is arbitrarily defined, but many studies have used a value of 90 percent of the steady state to define the end of the onset transient (Kendall 1986).

The steady state is so named due to its relative stability, though the steady-state portion of any acoustic instrument never remains completely "steady." The offset is simply the time interval between when the musicians stops applying energy (i.e., stops blowing air or pulling a bow) and when the sound dies away. Length of the offset varies due to the specific resonance properties of the musical instrument. Perhaps a few examples will assist in clarifying these concepts. Notes played by an oboe have a very short onset and offset, while the steady state portion lasts as long as the player blows into the reed. A violin tone has a relatively slow onset because it takes a finite period of time to set the string into motion. Its steady-state period lasts as long as the bow is drawn, and then there is a fairly long offset as the violin body continues to vibrate. In contrast, a single note on the timpani exhibits an extremely short onset, no steady state (i.e., the sound begins to die away immediately), and a relatively long offset.

The onset and offset are often called transients, because the intensity level changes dramatically during these portions of the sound. Considering single tones in isolation, Saldanha and Corso (1964) and Elliot (1975) have suggested that onset transient patterns appear to be the most important cues to instrument identification, because, when they are eliminated from the sound, even experienced musicians have considerable difficulty in identifying common orchestral instruments. Using similarly modified tones within a musical context (i.e., as part of a melody), however, Kendall (1986) found that there was little difficulty in identifying the instruments. When one note of a melody leads smoothly into the next, Kendall suggests that the transition from one note to another should be referred to as a legato transient to distinguish this phenomenon from the onset and offset of isolated tones.

The Perception of Timbre

Musical timbre (or tone quality) is a difficult property to explain in words, as evident by past attempts to provide a clear and concise definition. The American Standards Association (ASA) suggests that timbre is "that attribute of auditory sensation of [sic] which a listener can judge that two steady-state tones having the same pitch and loudness are dissimilar" (cited in Carterette and Kendall 1989, 134). This simply assumes that if two sounds are different, but pitch and loudness are identical, then the differentiation must be based on timbre. The ASA definition suggests two things (i.e., pitch and loudness) that timbre is not. However, it makes very little headway toward determining what timbre actually is. What is it that allows us to distinguish between a cello and a trumpet playing the same pitch at the same loudness level? More interestingly, what differentiates the violin tone of Isaac Stern from that of Itzhak Perlman or either one of these performers from the jazz violin quality of Stephane Grappelli?

In his *Harmonielehre* (1978), Arnold Schoenberg suggested that it was possible to create complete musical compositions based on timbre change. *Klangfarbenmelodie,* as he referred to this technique, is exemplified by a composition in which "instruments maintaining constant pitches drop in and out of an orchestral texture, creating a melody of tone colors" (Grout and Palisca 1988, 767). *Farben,* one of Schoenberg's *Five Orchestra Pieces* (op. 16) from 1900, is based on this compositional device. Though *Klangfarbenmelodie* is certainly an intriguing theoretical position, research indicates that it is extremely difficult for listeners to reliably detect rapid timbre shifts. Using only four different sounds (beep, hiss, eeh, and buzz), Warren et al. (1969) found that subjects identified the correct order of occurrence only at the level of chance when sounds were presented at a rate of five per second. If a series of pitches were presented at this rate, most listeners would have no difficulty identifying the order of presentation.

Unlike loudness, timbre cannot be considered on a single scale. Rather, it is a multidimensional attribute of musical sound. Recall the previous discussion of partials in a complex tone. Each partial has its own associated frequency and amplitude. The relationship of these frequencies and their respective intensities form the foundation of our understanding of timbre perception. The physical attributes associated with timbre may be represented in a spectrum, that is, a graph of frequency components by amplitude.

Figure 16 presents the spectra of three different synthetically generated tones. The first (fig. 16a) is a sine tone, distinguished by a large amount of energy in the fundamental and no overtones. There is no acoustical instrument that can recreate this energy spectrum. The second spectrum (fig. 16b) represents the components of a sawtooth signal shape. Though the spectrum in the figure is idealized, violins and trumpets exhibit spectral relationships similar to this example, having a "buzzy" quality. Figure 16c shows the spectrum of a square signal shape, similar to the spectral components of a clarinet (i.e., a "round," "hollow" tone, emphasizing the odd-numbered partials). Therefore, it can clearly be seen that the number of partials, along with their respective

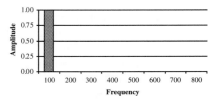

(*a*) Spectrum for Sine Signal Shape

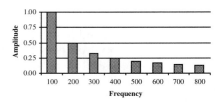

(*b*) Spectrum for Sawtooth Signal Shape

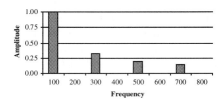

(*c*) Spectrum for Square Signal Shape

Fig. 16.   Spectra representing different signal forms

frequencies and amplitudes, determines the timbre that is perceived (Plomp 1976; Slawson 1968). It is important to note, however, that actual clarinets and real trumpets do not have a single spectrum that remains consistent from the lowest note to the highest note of their range. Lehman (1962) created a synthesized tone using a spectral analysis of a bassoon tone in the high register as a model. He then played a three-octave scale, so that the frequency of the partials changed, but the spectral amplitude relationships remained constant. He found that no tone other than the model sounded like a bassoon. In actual instrumental performance, the spectrum changes not only from note to note, but also during steady-state portions of the same pitch as well as from performer to performer and instrument to instrument.

Researchers have demonstrated that timbre depends upon the "absolute frequency position of the spectral envelope rather than upon its position relative to the fundamental frequency" (Plomp 1976, 110). In other words, the energy distributed among the critical bands, as a result of the fundamental and its overtones, gives rise to timbre sensation, not the energy of the overtones relative to the fundamental. "This is easily verified by listening to a record or magnetic tape played at the wrong speed. This procedure leaves the relative spectra unchanged, merely shifting all frequencies up or down; yet a clear change in timbre of all instruments is perceived" (Roederer 1975, 136).

Several experimental studies have attempted to determine strategies that listeners use to discriminate between sounds varying in timbre. Some timbre studies have utilized verbal scales such as the semantic differential scale (e.g., von Bismarck 1974) or verbal attribute magnitude estimation (Kendall and Carterette 1993a and 1993b). Another technique that has shown promising results is multidimensional scaling. In this procedure, each subject listens to pairs of sounds and judges how "similar" the second sound is to the first. Plomp (1976) asked his subjects to judge the similarity of synthesized tones representing the brass, woodwind, and string families. He then compared the subject responses to energy distribution in the spectra for these same signals and found that the similarity judgments and the spectral analyses were very closely related. Using a similar procedure, Miller and Carterette (1975) determined that similarity ratings gathered from their subjects appeared to be based on the number of partials present in a complex tone and characteristics of the amplitude envelope. Grey and Gordon (1978) found that their subjects seemed to make judgments based on three parameters: spectral energy of the steady state, the onset and offset of these spectral components, and the noisiness of attack (e.g., the "blat" at the beginning of a trumpet tone). Therefore, timbral judgments seem to be based primarily on the configuration of partials and their respective amplitudes, though onset and offset characteristics are also influential.

The Perception of Duration

Music consists of sounds organized in time. In fact, it is impossible to imagine musical sound apart from its temporal dimension. This is one quality of music that separates it from most of the visual arts. As John Booth Davies suggests,

> If we look at a painting we can build up an impression of its wholeness in a very short space of time. Although we perhaps cannot direct our attention to every aspect of it simultaneously, our field of

vision is such that we can take it all in in an instant. We can see its boundaries, and its extent, and make judgments about its various qualities. Further, we can scan and rescan particular elements of the painting before us. Finally, if we leave the room for a while, we can return at leisure to examine the picture further, and can indeed find it exactly as it was before. . . . None of this is possible with music, however. Nobody has ever seen (perceived) a symphony in its entirety, since as soon as a note is played it is gone, vanished, and all we have left is its memory. We can only make judgments about music by comparing recent memories with less recent memories, all concerning events that have taken place in the past. (Davies 1978, 47)

Time is such a significant aspect of music that, in the vocabulary of the music theorist, there are a number of important musical concepts related to this single physical variable. For the sake of clarification, several definitions for common terms will be provided (after Monahan and Carterette 1985, 4): Duration is simply the psychological variable that is associated with time. Beats divide a temporal period into equal units of duration. The rate at which these beats occur is referred to as tempo. Meter arises when the musical pulse is organized into a regularly occurring pattern of accented and unaccented beats. Finally, rhythm results when a sequence of sounds of either equal or varying durations is perceived by a listener.

Psychological Present

Before pursuing the perception of duration and rhythm, perhaps it will prove helpful to consider a couple of questions that are much more general. How do we perceive the passing of time? Is it a continuous flow, as intuition would suggest, or a series of discrete "windows" of time? William James (1950) proposed that temporal perception results from a series of "psychological moments" each having its own temporal span. We shall refer to any current "window of time" as the psychological present. Abraham Moles (1968) based his definition of the present on a person's ability to differentiate between successive events. If two events occur so close together in time that they cannot be distinguished as separate, then he believed that they must be perceptually simultaneous and, therefore, fall within the same "present" (also see Massaro 1972; Stroud 1955). Motion picture perception provides an excellent example of how a series of finite "moments" can be processed perceptually to create a continuous stream of apparent motion. Usually, each frame of the film is exposed for a period of approximately 42 ms—that is, 24 frames per second or .0042 seconds per frame. We do not see the images as a series of still pictures, but fuse them perceptually into continuous motion. Later work by Fraisse (1978 and 1982) suggests that, at a more general level, the psychological present typically extends from 2 to 5 seconds.

Virtual Time
There can be differences in the psychological perception of duration and the physical length of the stimulus, in other words, a difference between time as we experience it ("felt" time) and time as measured by a clock. For example, Vierordt's law (Woodrow 1951) states that short time intervals (usually less than one second) are overestimated, while longer ones are underestimated. Furthermore, there is evidence that different perceptual processes are in operation in the discrimination of time intervals above and below 600 milliseconds (Divenyi 1971). The experience of duration is influenced both by subject variables (age, physical condition, and drugs) and stimulus variables (complexity and spacing).

A unique aspect of time within a musical context is its apparent elasticity. Most people have noticed how time flies when totally absorbed in listening to a favorite musical piece or how interminably long an uninteresting concert can seem to last. Once again according to James, "in general, a time filled with varied and interesting experiences seems short in passing, but long as we look back. On the other hand, a tract of time empty of experiences seems long in passing, but in retrospect short" (1950, 624). This characteristic of temporal flow has been referred to as virtual time (Langer 1953, 109), in contrast to ontological time (i.e., clock time). Igor Stravinsky (1956, 32) claimed that each piece of music establishes its own temporal world. He suggested that some pieces exist in the "normal flow of time" while others are dissociated from this normal flow.

Investigations into the Temporal Element of Musical Sound
The temporal dimension is an extremely important aspect of musical sound. In fact, it is possible for individuals to identify melodies by simply tapping the rhythm alone (James 1950). Povel (1981) asked his subjects to listen to a rhythm and then recreate it by tapping. His analysis suggests that there are two steps involved in the perceptual encoding of rhythmic patterns. First, the listener attempts to find a regular beat pattern, such that the beat is rarely slower than 40 beats per minute. Secondly, the listener tries to subdivide this beat rate into equal divisions, preferring a ratio of 2:1.

Using a multidimensional scaling procedure, Gabrielsson (1973a and 1973b) asked his subjects to rate the similarity of a variety of rhythmic patterns. He found that rhythmic discrimination appeared to be made on the basis of meter, tempo, accentuation of the first beat, the pattern of accents, and absolute durations. In a study of the interaction between pitch and time in a melodic context, Monahan (1984) found that the two most conspicuous dimensions resulting from her subjects' similarity ratings were tempo and rhythmic contour, a pattern of long and short note durations across time. Confirming the importance of music's temporal element, she found that the two most prominent dimensions used to distinguish between these short melodies were both rhythmically oriented rather than pitch oriented.

Anomalies and Secondary Relationships in Seashore's Model

Now that we have discussed all of the primary relationships in Seashore's auditory mapping model, let us return for a moment and see how reliably this model can explain the process of music perception. Remember that, according to Seashore (1938), each physical variable has a psychological correlate, that is, frequency relates to pitch, amplitude relates to loudness, signal shape relates to timbre, and time relates to duration. If Seashore had presented a truly isomorphic model, then frequency would only affect pitch and pitch would likewise only be affected by frequency. In fact, this relationship would hold true for all primary relationships in the model. Unfortunately—or fortunately, as the case may be—the interaction does not stop there. In addition to these primary relationships, research has shown that there are a large number of cross-relationships as well. Beginning with frequency, several, though not all, anomalies of the model will be highlighted.

Frequency
Recall that partial frequencies of a complex, periodic tone are integer multiples of a fundamental frequency. Rather than perceiving several simultaneous pure tones, however, in perception these sine components are fused into a single sound, the timbre of which is determined by the number and intensity of these partials. If frequency correlated isomorphically to pitch, we should hear each of the sine components as a distinct pitch, essentially making timbre perception, as we experience it, impossible.

There are other occasions when perceived pitch maps to a frequency that does not actually exist in the physical domain. This phenomenon is known as the missing fundamental, a special case of the difference tone phenomenon. Research by Schouten (1938 and 1940) confirmed the existence of the missing fundamental and brought into question the reliability of the place theory of perception. If a 1,000 Hz pure tone occurs simultaneously with a pure tone of 800 Hz (both at least 50–60 dB, according to Plomp 1966), most listeners will perceive a pitch that is normally associated with 200 Hz. This "missing fundamental" can be explained in terms of the constructive and destructive interference occurring between the two sine components.

Recall in an earlier example that, as the difference in frequency between two pure tones is increased, the number of beats per second between sine components increases. The number of beats per second is exactly equivalent to the mathematical difference between the upper frequency and the lower frequency (in this case: 1,000 - 800 = 200). Therefore, amplitude modulation (i.e., periodic increase and decrease in amplitude) occurs 200 times per second, resulting in a periodic amplitude fluctuation at a rate of 200 Hz. The missing fundamental occurs at beat rates from 50–2,000 Hz. At lower frequencies the interference results in a roughness, and at higher frequencies the nerve cells cannot fire fast enough to lead to a pitch sensation (Dowling and Harwood 1986, 36). Houtsma and Goldstein (1972) found that, even with remote harmonics (the 10th and 11th partials), subjects were able to perceive the missing fundamental when these tones were placed in a musical context. This phenomenon occurred even if one partial was presented to the left ear and the other partial to the right ear, suggesting the presence of a central processor for pitch perception.

There are also situations in which frequency affects loudness as well as pitch. Fletcher and Munson's (1933) equal loudness contour illustrates that sensitivity of the human ear is not consistent across its entire frequency range (refer to fig. 14). Therefore, when played at the same physical amplitude, frequencies around 4 KHz and 13 KHz (the first and second resonance frequencies of the outer ear canal) appear to be louder, while frequencies lower than about 1,000 Hz or higher than about 8 KHz gradually appear softer. (KHz is an abbreviation for kilohertz and simply means 1,000 Hz).

Amplitude
In addition to its affect on loudness, amplitude has been shown to influence pitch perception. Stevens (1935) presented his subjects with pairs of pure tones. He found that, even when the frequency of both tones was held constant, perceived pitch was altered in some subjects by increasing intensity to between 80 and 90 dB. If the frequency was above 2 KHz, the louder tone appeared to be slightly higher in pitch than the softer tone. If the frequency was below 1 KHz, the pitch shift was downward. Using 40 ms bursts of frequencies from 200–3,200 Hz, Rossing and Houtsma (1986) confirmed a decrease in pitch with intensity. Terhardt (1974), however,

found that the pitch-shifting effect of intensity varies greatly from individual to individual and, though the perception was significant for some subjects, the change was considered insignificant when averaged over his entire group of subjects. Also, von Békésy (1960) demonstrated that periodicity pitch was not affected by intensity increase.

Duration

Temporal duration affects both pitch and loudness. As the duration is increased gradually from 0 ms, clicks take on a sense of pitch. Moles (1968) determined that approximately 50 ms of a signal is required before pitch can be reliably assigned. Shorter signals are perceived as merely a pop or click. Zwislocki (1969) found that both pure tones and broadband noise increase in loudness when duration is increased from 0 to 100 ms. Broadband noise is more strongly dependent on stimulus duration.

Signal Shape

Signal shape affects not only timbre perception, but it also has a clear influence on perceived loudness. Comparing the loudness of broadband noise and a 1,000 Hz sine tone, Scharf and Houtsma (1986) found that white noise was judged by subjects to be twice as loud when presented at 55 dB, but at higher and lower levels the difference was substantially less. This suggests a complex interaction between frequency, intensity, and signal shape. Also, in Zwislocki's (1969) study mentioned previously, perceived duration was affected differentially when using pure tones and broadband noise.

As can be seen from the examples cited above, there is certainly not an isomorphic relationship between the physical and perceptual variables in Seashore's model. This, however, need not lead to despair. Thus far, we have discussed only low-level perceptual processing. In the next chapter, the discussion will turn to higher level cognitive functioning and, in the words of John Booth Davies, attempt to explain "how people can organize this auditory material and extract form and meaning from an array of sounds which, according to scientific evidence, should be cacophonous to a high degree" (1978, 46).

Of all our senses, hearing is the most pervasive. Although the other senses can be regulated somewhat, we can never escape from sound. With eyes closed, one cannot see; with nose held shut, one cannot smell. As long as skin and tongue do not come into contact with anything, there is no sensation of touch or taste. But no amount of putting hands over ears will shut out the world of sound. Even during sleep, the body responds to sounds that are not consciously perceived (Raloff 1983).

This pervasiveness of hearing has had important consequences for human beings and the music we produce. Music may have been invented, in part, because people were surrounded by a sound world from which they could not escape. Musical sound may result from the human need to organize and elaborate sensory input.

The important point here, as stated in the first paragraph of this chapter, is that the sense of hearing makes music possible. Understanding musical behavior presupposes an understanding of the hearing process. Knowledge about the way the hearing mechanism works influences our understanding of general musical behavior.

Beyond simply knowing about the hearing process, understanding musical behavior requires comprehension of the relationships among the physical (frequency, amplitude, signal shape, and time) and perceptual (pitch, loudness, timbre, and duration) attributes of sound. First, there are the primary relationships between a physical attribute and its perceptual correlate (e.g., our sense of pitch is primarily determined by the frequency of a sound). Then, there are secondary relationships between the physical and perceptual frames of reference, as discussed in this chapter (e.g., intensity, signal shape, and time also influence our perception of pitch).

A considerable amount of psychoacoustical research has been devoted to describing the relationships among physical and perceptual attributes. One might appropriately wonder, however, how much these studies have to do with the perception of music. It may be interesting to know, for example, that the pitch of a pure tone with a frequency of 3,000 Hz will appear to rise as intensity is increased, but what does that have to do with the experience of listening to a Mozart symphony?

It is at this point that Seashore's trunklines of musicality become relevant (review table 1). Physical vibrations are transmitted through the air and are perceived as elements to be organized in the human mind, resulting in a musical experience. Thus, frequencies are perceived as pitches (influenced secondarily by other physical attributes), providing a basis for the tonal aspects of music (e.g., scales, melodies, etc.). Likewise, sound intensities lead to perceptions of loudness that create dynamic experiences in music (e.g., *forte, piano, crescendo,* etc.). Signal shapes are perceived as timbres and thus give rise to qualitative aspects of music (e.g., flute, string quartet, jazz combo, etc.). Finally, all sounds have a time element, perceived as durations and organized cognitively into temporal aspects of music (e.g., tempo, meter, rhythm, etc.).

The process of organizing auditory perceptions into melodies, rhythms, and other aspects of the musical experience forms the basis for chapter 5. Knowing about the hearing mechanism and the relationship between physical and perceptual attributes of musical sound is a prerequisite for a thorough understanding of music cognition.

REFERENCES

Abraham, O. 1901. Das absolute Tonbewußtsein. *Sammelbände Internationalen Musikgesellschaft* 3:1–86.
Alberti, P. 1991. Occupational hearing loss. In *Diseases of the nose, throat, ear, hand, and neck.* 14th ed. Ed. J. Ballenger, 1053–68. Philadelphia: Lea and Febiger.
Altschuler, R. A., R. P. Bobbin, B. M. Clopton, and D. W. Hoffman. 1991. *Neurobiology of hearing: The central auditory system.* New York: Raven Press.
American Medical Association. 1990. Noise and hearing loss. *Journal of the American Medical Association* 263, no. 23:3185–90.
Bachem, A. 1937. Various types of absolute pitch. *Journal of the Acoustical Society of America* 9:146–51.
Backus, J. 1977. *The acoustical foundations of music.* 2d ed. New York: Norton.
Barrett, D., and D. Hodges. 1995. Music loudness preferences of middle school and college students. *Texas Music Education Research,* 1–6.
Békésy, G. von. 1960. *Experiments in hearing.* New York: McGraw-Hill.
Berger, B. 1992. Mapping the mindfields. *Omni* 14, no. 4:56–58.
Bismarck, G. von. 1974. Timbre of steady sounds: A factorial investigation of its verbal attributes. *Acustica* 30, no. 3:146–59.
Blinkov, S. M., and I. I. Glezer. 1968. *The human brain in figures and tables: A quantitative handbook.* Trans. B. Haigh. New York: Basic Books.
Bluestone, C. 1991. Physiology of the Middle Ear and Eustachian Tube. In *Otolaryngology.* Vol. 1, *Basic Sciences and Related Principles.* 3d ed. Ed. M. Paparella, D. Shumrick, J. Gluckman, and W. Meyerhoff, 163–97. Philadelphia: Saunders.
Brady, P. T. 1970. Fixed-scale mechanism of absolute pitch. *Journal of the Acoustical Society of America* 48:883–87.
Brugge, J. 1991. Neurophysiology of the Central Auditory and Vestibular Systems. In *Otolaryngology.* Vol. 1 *Basic Sciences and Related Principles.* 3d ed. Ed. M. Paparella, D. Shumrick, J. Gluckman, and W. Meyerhoff, 281–314. Philadelphia: Saunders.
Calder, N. 1970. *The mind of man.* New York: Viking.
Carterette, E. C., and R. A. Kendall. 1989. Human music perception. In *The comparative psychology of audition: Perceiving complex sounds,* ed. R. J. Dooling and S. H. Hulse, 131–72. Hillsdale, NJ: Lawrence Erlbaum Associates.
Chusid, J. 1985. *Correlative neuroanatomy and functional neurology.* 19th ed. Los Altos, CA: Lange Medical Publications.
Clark, M., and D. Luce. 1965. Intensities of orchestral instrument scales played at prescribed dynamic markings. *Journal of the Audio Engineering Society* 1, no. 3:151.
Copp, E. F. 1916. Musical ability. *Journal of Heredity* 7:297–305.
Cuddy, L. L. 1968. Practice effects in the absolute judgment of pitch. *Journal of the Acoustical Society of America* 43:1069–76.

Cuddy, L. L. 1970. Training the absolute identification of pitch. *Perception and Psychophysics* 8:265–69.

Danenberg, M., M. Loos-Cosgrove, and M. LoVerde. 1987. Temporary hearing loss and rock music. *Language, Speech and Hearing Services in the Schools* 18, no. 3: 267–74.

Davies, J. B. 1978. *The psychology of music*. Stanford, CA: Stanford University Press.

Deutsch, D. 1987. The tritone paradox: Effects of spectral variables. *Perception and Psychophysics* 41:563–75.

Deutsch, D., W. L. Kuyper, and Y. Fisher. 1987. The tritone paradox: Its presence and form of distribution in a general population. *Music Perception* 5, no. 1:79–92.

Deutsch, J. A., and D. Deutsch. 1973. *Physiological psychology*. 2d ed. Homewood, IL: Dorsey Press.

Divenyi, P. L. 1971. The rhythmic perception of micro-melodies: Detectability by human observers of a time increment between sinusoidal pulses of two different, successive frequencies. Rev. A. Gabrielsson. *Bulletin of the Council for Research in Music Education* 53:49–56.

Donaldson, J., and L. Duckert. 1991. Anatomy of the Ear. In *Otolaryngology*. Vol. 1, *Basic Sciences and Related Principles*. 3d ed. Ed. M. Paparella, D. Shumrick, J. Gluckman, and W. Meyerhoff, 23–58. Philadelphia: Saunders.

Dowling, W. J., and D. L. Harwood. 1986. *Music cognition*. New York: Academic Press.

Elias, M. 1991. Loud music beats away at kids' eardrums. *USA Today*, March 22.

Elliot, C. 1975. Attacks and releases as factors in instrumental identification. *Journal of Research in Music Education* 23, no. 1:35–40.

Everest, F. A. 1986. *Auditory perception: An audio training course*. Berkeley, CA: Mix Bookshelf.

Fechner, G. T. [1860] 1966. *Elements of psychophysics*. Trans. H. E. Adler, ed. D. H. Howes and E. G. Boring. New York: Holt, Rinehart, and Winston.

Feldman, A., and J. Grimes. 1991. Audiology. In *Diseases of the nose, throat, ear, hand, and neck*. 14th ed. Ed. J. Ballenger, 1029–52. Philadelphia: Lea and Febiger.

Fletcher, H., and W. A. Munson. 1933. Loudness, its definition, measurement, and calculation. *Journal of the Acoustical Society of America* 5:82.

Fletcher, S. G. 1971. Anatomy and physiology of the auditory system. In *Audiological assessment*, ed. D. E. Rose. Englewood Cliffs, NJ: Prentice-Hall.

Fraisse, P. 1978. Time and rhythm perception. In *Handbook of perception*, ed. E. C. Carterette and M. P. Friedman, 8:203–54. New York: Academic Press.

Fraisse, P. 1982. Rhythm and tempo. In *The psychology of music*, ed. D. Deutsch, 149–80. New York: Academic Press.

Gabrielsson, A. 1973a. Similarity ratings and dimension analyses of auditory rhythm patterns: I. *Scandinavian Journal of Psychology* 14:138–60.

Gabrielsson, A. 1973b. Similarity ratings and dimension analyses of auditory rhythm patterns: II. *Scandinavian Journal of Psychology* 14:161–76.

Gacek, R. R. 1967. Afferent auditory neural system. In *Sensorineural hearing processes and disorders*, ed. A. B. Graham, 49–60. Boston: Little, Brown.

Geschwind, N. 1974. The anatomical basis of hemispheric differentiation. In *Hemisphere function in the human brain*, ed. S. J. Diamond and J. G. Beaumont, 7–24. New York: Halstead Press.

Goldstein, B., and C. Newman. 1994. Clinical masking. A decision-making process. In *Handbook of clinical audiology*. 4th ed. Ed. J. Katz, 109–31. Baltimore: Williams and Wilkins.

Gough, E. 1922. The effects of practice on judgments of absolute pitch. *Archive of Psychology* (New York) 7, no. 47:93.

Grey, J. M., and J. W. Gordon. 1978. Perceptual effects of spectral modifications on musical timbres. *Journal of the Acoustical Society of America* 63:1493–1500.

Grossman, S. P. 1967. *A textbook of physiological psychology*. New York: Wiley and Sons.

Grout, D. J., and C. V. Palisca. 1988. *A history of Western music*. 4th ed. New York: Norton.

Gulick, W. L., G. A. Gescheider, and R. D. Frisina. 1989. *Hearing: Physiological acoustics, neural coding, and psychoacoustics*. New York: Oxford University Press.

Hackney, C. M. 1987. Anatomical features of the auditory pathway from cochlea to cortex. *British Medical Journal* 43, no. 4:780–801.

Haggard, M. P., and E. F. Evans, eds. 1987. Hearing. *British Medical Journal* 43:4.

Handel, S. 1989. *Listening: An introduction to the perception of auditory events*. Cambridge, MA: MIT Press.

Hari, R. 1990. The neuromagnetic method in the study of the human auditory cortex. In *Auditory evoked magnetic fields and electric potentials. Advances in audiology*, ed. F. Grandori, M. Hoke, and G. Romani. 6, no. 1:222–82.

Hedden, S. 1980. Psychoacoustical parameters of music. In *Handbook of music psychology*, ed. D. Hodges, 63–92. Lawrence, KS: National Association for Music Therapy.

Helmholtz, H. L. F. von. [1863] 1954. *On the sensations of tone as a physiological basis for the theory of music*. 2d ed. Trans. A. J. Ellis. New York: Dover.

Henderson, D., R. Salvi, F. Boettcher, and A. Clock. 1994. Neurophysiologic correlates of sensory-neural hearing loss. In *Handbook of clinical audiology*. 4th ed. Ed. J. Katz, 37–55. Baltimore: Williams and Wilkins.

Hood, J. D. 1977. Psychological and physiological apects of hearing. In *Music and the brain: Studies in the neurology of music*, ed. M. Critchley and R. A. Henson, 32–47. Springfield, IL: C. C. Thomas.

Houtsma, A. J. M., and J. L. Goldstein. 1972. The central origin of the pitch of complex tones: Evidence from musical interval recognition. *Journal of the Acoustical Society of America* 51:520–29.

Hudspeth, A. J. 1983. The hair cells of the inner ear. *Scientific American*, 248:54–64.

Hutchinson, W., and L. Knopoff. 1978. The acoustic component of Western consonance. *Interface* 7:1–29.

James, W. [1890] 1950. *The principles of psychology*. New York: Dover.

Kameoka, A., and M. Kuriyagawa. 1969a. Consonance theory part I: Consonance of dyads. *Journal of the Acoustical Society of America* 45:1451–59.

Kameoka, A., and M. Kuriyagawa. 1969b. Consonance theory part II: Consonance of complex tones and its calculation method. *Journal of the Acoustical Society of America* 45:1460–71.

Kendall, R. A. 1986. The role of acoustic signal partitions in listener categorization of musical phrases. *Music Perception* 4:185–213.

Kendall, R. A., and E. C. Carterette. 1993a. Verbal attributes of simultaneous wind instrument timbres: I. von Bismarck's adjectives. *Music Perception* 10, no. 4:445–67.

Kendall, R. A., and E. C Carterette. 1993b. Verbal attributes of simultaneous wind instrument timbres: II. Adjectives induced from Piston's Orchestration. *Music Perception* 10, no. 4:469–501.

Kimura, D. 1961. Some effects of temporal lobe damage on auditory perception. *Canadian Journal of Psychology* 15:156–65.

Kimura, D. 1967. Functional asymmetry of the brain in dichotic listening. *Cortex* 3:163–78.

Koss, M. 1993. Why noisy fun is no laughing matter. *Nation's Business* 81, no. 2:57.

Krumhansl, C. L. 1979. The psychological representation of pitch in a tonal context. *Cognitive Psychology* 11:346–74.

Krumhansl, C. L., and R. N. Shepard. 1979. Quantification of the hierarchy of tonal functions within a diatonic context. *Journal of Experimental Psychology: Human Perception and Performance* 5:579–94.

Kryter, K. 1984. *Physiological, psychological, and social effects of noise.* Washington, DC: National Aeronautics and Space Administration.

Kuras, J., and R. Finday. 1974. Listening patterns of self-identified rock music listeners to rock music presented via earphones. *Journal of Auditory Research* 14:51–56.

Langer, S. K. 1953. *Feeling and form: A theory of art.* New York: Scribner.

Lehman, P. R. 1962. The harmonic structure of the tone of the bassoon. Ph.D. diss., University of Michigan.

Lindsay, P. H., and D. A. Norman. 1972. *Human information processing.* New York: Academic Press.

Lowenstein, O. 1966. *The senses.* Baltimore: Penguin.

Lu, Z. L., S. Williamson, and L. Kaufman. 1992. Behavioral lifetime of human auditory sensory memory predicted by physiological measures. *Science* 258:1668–70.

Martin, F. N. 1975. *Introduction to audiology.* Englewood Cliffs, NJ: Prentice-Hall.

Massaro, D. 1972. Perceptual images, processing time, and perceptual units in auditory perception. *Psychological Review* 79, no. 2:124–45.

Melnick, W. 1994. Industrial hearing conservation. In *Handbook of clinical audiology.* 4th ed. Ed. J. Katz, 534–52. Baltimore: Williams and Wilkins.

Meyer, M. 1899. Is the memory of absolute pitch capable of development by training? *Psychological Review* 6:514–16.

Miller, J. 1993. Quick as a hair cell. *Bioscience* 43, no. 2:83–84.

Miller, J. R., and E. C. Carterette. 1975. Perceptual space for musical structures. *Journal of the Acoustical Society of America* 58:711–20.

Milner, P. 1970. *Physiological psychology.* New York: Holt, Rinehart, and Winston.

Moles, A. 1968. *Information theory and esthetic perception.* Urabana, IL: University of Illinois Press.

Monahan, C. B. 1984. Parallels between pitch and time: The determinants of musical space. Ph.D. diss., University of California, Los Angeles.

Monahan, C. B., and E. C. Carterette. 1985. Pitch and duration as determinants of musical space. *Music Perception* 3, no. 1:1–32.

Moore, D. R. 1987. Physiology of the higher auditory system. *British Medical Journal* 43, no. 4:856–70.

Mull, H. K. 1925. The acquisition of absolute pitch. *American Journal of Psychology* 36:469–93.

Nielsen, D., and N. Slepecky. 1986. Stereocillia. In *Neurobiology of hearing: The cochlea*, ed. R. Altschuler, R. Bobbin, and D. Hoffman, 23–46. New York: Raven Press.

Occupational Safety and Health Administration. 1981. Occupational noise exposure. Hearing conservation ammendment. *Federal Register*, Part 3. Department of Labor 39:37773–78.

Pantev, C., M. Hoke, B. Lutkenhoner, and K. Lehnertz. 1989. Tonotopic organization of the auditory cortex: Pitch versus frequency representation. *Science* 246, no. 4929:486–88.

Patterson, B. 1974. Musical dynamics. *Scientific American* 231, no. 5:78.

Pickles, J. 1988. *An introduction to the physiology of hearing.* 2d ed. New York: Academic Press.

Pierce, J. P., and E. E. David, Jr. 1958. *Man's world of sound.* Garden City, NY: Doubleday.

Plomp, R. 1966. *Experiments on tone perception.* Soesterberg: Institute for Perception, RVO-TNO.

Plomp, R. 1976. *Aspects of tone sensation.* New York: Academic Press.

Plomp, R., and W. J. M. Levelt. 1965. Tonal consonance and critical bandwidth. *Journal of the Acoustical Society of America* 38:548–60.

Pottle, R. 1970. How a great orchestra resolves an intonation dilemma. *Selmer Band Wagon* 59:28–29.

Povel, D. J. 1981. The internal representation of simple temporal patterns. *Journal of Experimental Psychology: Human Perception and Performance* 7:3–18.

Raloff, J. 1983. Noise: The subtle pollutant. In *Science yearbook: New illustrated encyclopedia*, 194–99. New York: Funk and Wagnalls.

Rasch, R. A., and R. Plomp. 1982. The perception of musical tones. In *The psychology of music*, ed. D. Deutsch, 1–24. New York: Academic Press.

Révész, G. 1913. *Zur Grundlegung der Tonpsychologie.* Leipzig: Veit.

Robinson, G. M., and D. Solomon. 1974. Rhythm is processed by the speech hemisphere. *Journal of Experimental Psychology* 102:508–11.

Roederer, J. G. 1975. *Introduction to the physics and psychophysics of music.* 2d ed. New York: Springer-Verlag.

Rossing, T. D. 1990. *The science of sound.* 2d ed. New York: Addison-Wesley.

Rossing, T. D., and A. J. M. Houtsma. 1986. Effects of signal envelope on the pitch of short sinusoidal tones. *Journal of the Acoustical Society of America* 79:1926.

Russell, I. J. 1987. The physiology of the organ of Corti. *British Medical Journal* 43, no. 4:802–20.

Saldanha, E., and J. F. Corso. 1964. Timbre cues and the identification of musical instruments. *Journal of the Acoustical Society of America* 36:2021–26.

Scharf, B., and A. J. M. Houtsma. 1986. Audition II: Loudness, pitch, localization, aural distortion, pathology. In *Handbook of perception and human performance*, ed. K. R. Boff, L. Kaufman, and J. P. Thomas, 15/1–15/60. New York: J. Wiley.

Schiffman, H. R. 1976. *Sensation and perception: An integrated approach.* New York: Wiley.

Schlang, G., L. Jancke, Y. Huang, and H. Steinmetz. 1995. In vivo evidence of structural brain asymmetry in musicians. *Science* 267, no. 5198:699–701.

Schoenberg, A. [1911] 1978. *Theory of harmony*. Trans. R. E. Carter. Berkeley: University of California Press.

Schouten, J. F. 1938. The perception of subjective tones. *Proceedings Koninklijke Nederlandse Akademie van Wetenschappen* 41:1086–93.

Schouten, J. F. 1940. The perception of pitch. *Philips Technical Review* 5:286–94.

Schroeder, M. 1993. Listening with two ears. *Music Perception* 10, no. 3:255–80.

Seashore, C. E. 1919. *Manual of instructions and interpretations of measures of musical talent*. Chicago: Stoeltig.

Seashore, C. E. 1938. *The psychology of music*. New York: Dover.

Sergeant, D. 1969. Experimental investigation of absolute pitch. *Journal of Research in Music Education* 17:135–43.

Shepard, R. N. 1964. Circularity in judgments of relative pitch. *Journal of the Acoustical Society of America* 36:2346–53.

Shepard, R. N. 1982. Structural representations of musical pitch. In *The Psychology of Music*, ed. D. Deutsch, 343–90. New York: Academic Press.

Shepherd, G. 1994. *Neurobiology*. 3d ed. New York: Oxford University Press.

Slawson, A. W. 1968. Vowel quality and musical timbre as functions of spectrum envelope and fundamental frequency. *Journal of the Acoustical Society of America* 43:87–101.

Stevens, S. S. 1934. The volume and intensity of tones. *American Journal of Psychology* 46:397–408.

Stevens, S. S. 1935. The relation of pitch to intensity. *Journal of the Acoustical Society of America* 6:150–54.

Stevens, S. S. 1936. A scale for the measurement of psychological magnitude. *Psychological Review* 43:405–16.

Stevens, S., and J. Volkmann. 1940. The relation of pitch to frequency: A revised scale. *American Journal of Psychology* 53:329–53.

Stevens, S. S., and F. Warshofsky. 1965. *Sound and hearing*. New York: Life Science Library.

Stravinsky, I. 1956. *Poetics of music*. New York: Vintage.

Stroud, J. 1955. The fine structure of psychological time. In *Information theory in psychology*, ed. H. Quastler, 174–207. New York: Free Press.

Terhardt, E. 1974. Pitch, consonance, and harmony. *Journal of Acoustical Society of America* 55:1061–69.

Wallin, N. L. 1991. *Biomusicology: Neurophysiolgical, neuropsychological, and evolutionary perspectives on the origins and purposes of music*. Stuyvesent, NY: Pendragon Press.

Ward, E. M., and W. D. Burns. 1982. Absolute pitch. In *The psychology of music*, ed. D. Deutsch, 431–51. New York: Academic Press.

Warren, R. M., C. J. Obusek, R. M. Farmer, and R. P. Warren. 1969. Auditory sequence: Confusion of patterns other than speech or music. *Science* 164:586–87.

Watt, H. J. 1917. *The psychology of sound*. New York: Cambridge University Press.

Weddell, C. H. 1934. The nature of the absolute judgment of pitch. *Journal of Experimental Psychology* 17:485–503.

Weinberger, N. M. 1992. Neocortical plasticity: Auditory cortex. In *Encyclopedia of learning and memory,* ed. L. Squire. New York: Macmillan. In press.

Weinberger, N. 1994. Music and the auditory system. In *The psychology of music.* 2d ed. Ed. D. Deutsch. New York: Academic Press. In press.

Weinberger, N. M., J. Ashe, and J. Edeline. 1993. Learning-induced receptive field plasticity in the auditory cortex: Specificity of information storage. In *Neural bases of learning and memory*, ed. J. Delacour. Singapore: World Scientific. In press.

Wellek, A. 1938. Das absolute Gehör und seine Typen. *Zeitschrift für Angewandte Psychologie and Charakterkunde Beihefte* 83:1–368.

Wever, E. G. 1949. *Theory of hearing.* New York: Wiley.

Williams, R. 1992. On the teen scene: Enjoy, protect the best ears of your life. *FDA Consumer* 26, no. 4:25–27.

Williamson, S., and L. Kaufman. 1988. Auditory evoked magnetic fields. In *Physiology of the ear*, ed. A. Jahn and J. Santos-Sacchi, 497–505. New York: Raven Press.

Winckel, F. 1962. Optimum acoustic criteria of concert halls for the performance of classical music. *Journal of the Acoustical Society of America* 34:81–86.

Woodrow, H. 1951. Time perception. In *Handbook of experimental psychology*, ed. S. S. Stevens, 1224–36. New York: Wiley.

Zwicker, E., G. Flottorp, and S. S. Stevens. 1957. Critical bandwidth in loudness summation. *Journal of the Acoustical Society of America* 29:548–57.

Zwislocki, J. J. 1969. Temporal summation of loudness: An analysis. *Journal of the Acoustical Society of America* 46:431.

5

The Cognitive Organization of Musical Sound

Scott D. Lipscomb

During the past quarter century, music perception research has been increasingly influenced by the field of cognitive psychology. Theories proposed by cognitive psychologists are based on mental structures and processes (Craik 1991; Matlin 1994). Other contemporary psychological orientations include behaviorism (emphasizing observable behaviors), psychoanalysis (focused on unconscious emotions), and humanism (emphasizing personal growth and interpersonal relationships). Within a musical context, research questions generated by the cognitive approach include such inquiries as: What knowledge do listeners have about musical structure? How does this knowledge affect the way individuals listen to and remember music? Thus, music cognition involves more than simply registering pitch, loudness, timbral, and durational characteristics of musical sound. Rather, these sonic events are "recoded, organized, and stored in memory in a form different from sensory codes" (Krumhansl 1990, 281). An individual's past musical experience plays a key role in this interpretive process.

Sensation, Perception, and Cognition

Throughout the history of cognitive psychology, definitional boundaries between sensation, perception, and cognition have been decidedly blurred. There seems to be a determined hesitance to state clearly where each of these processes begins and at what point the next stage takes over. It is possible, however, to derive a general sequential ordering of these stages of human experience. Sensory information is required for perception to occur and cognitive processes act upon knowledge gained from perception. We can determine, therefore, that these stages generally occur in the following sequential order: sensation, perception, then cognition.

Sensation involves the transformation of energy that impinges upon any of our sensory receptors (e.g., hair cells of the cochlea, retina of the eye, etc.) into neural information. This process is described in detail for the hearing mechanism in chapter 4. In essence, sensation serves as a catalyst for the interaction between an organism and its environment (Kendall 1980). Roederer states that "a given sensation is related to neural activity, evoked by sensory input signals, and 'displayed' on the cortical area to which the stimulated sense organ is wired (primary auditory cortex receiving area, visual cortex, etc.)" (1979, 9). This information is retained, albeit briefly, in sensory memories (Anderson 1985). Sensory memories include an echoic memory for auditory information and an iconic memory for visual information.

Perception utilizes sensory information to make further sense of the world. During this stage of processing, important elements of the incoming data stream are filtered out for further processing, while less important elements are ignored (data reduction; see Davies 1978). Attention plays an important role at this level. Automatic registration of features (preattentive processing) and focused attention result in the recognition of objects (visual and/or auditory) and patterns that will eventually be integrated into the perceiver's ordered interpretation of the environment (Treisman 1988; Treisman and Gelade 1980).[1] So important are these perceptual processes in developing knowledge of the world around us that McAdams and Bigand claim emphatically that "no knowledge can be acquired in the absence of perceiving" (1993, 1).

Finally, cognition involves the acquisition, storage, retrieval, and use of knowledge obtained through the sensory and perceptual systems. This assimilation and interpretation of new ideas based on past experience is referred to as apperception. The view taken in this chapter considers the musical listener as a "gatherer and interpreter of information from the environment" (Dowling and Harwood 1986, ix). The listener is not believed to be an automaton—in a behaviorist sense (i.e., a simple stimulus-response object)—but rather an active participant in the musical experience, constantly generating expectations based on past experience and interpreting auditory information on the basis of immediately preceding sounds. As a result, the following discussion will focus on mental activities involved in listening to music.

Music as Communication

Though ubiquitous, music follows specific, culture-dependent rule systems. In his investigations of music indigenous to Central Africa, Arom (1985 and 1988) reported that African listeners perceive rhythmic passages

---

1. Attention will be discussed at length in a later section of this chapter.

differently than American listeners. Variation of perception due to a person's past experience is a natural consequence of social acculturation. One common example of this phenomenon is the fact that speech sounds are categorized differently throughout the world (*Sprachgefühl;* see Bruner, Goodnow, and Austin 1986). If exposed to a multilingual environment at a young age, it is quite possible to distinguish the subtle differences between speech sounds and speak each language without a "foreign" accent. However, attempts to learn another language later in life can be difficult because of the firmly established phoneme categories derived from one's own native language.

Similar difficulties arise in listening to music of other cultures, both at low levels (e.g., tuning systems, pitch patterns) and high levels (e.g., overall organization of musical sounds within a piece) of processing. As stated by Campbell and Heller (1980), music involves a process of communication among composers, performers, and listeners (also see Kendall and Carterette 1990; Lipscomb and Kendall 1996; Meyer 1956). Figure 1 provides a representation of Kendall and Carterette's (1990) model of music communication. In the Western tradition, musical information is often communicated from composer to performer by notational symbols (or verbally, if the tradition is oral). These symbols are then interpreted by a

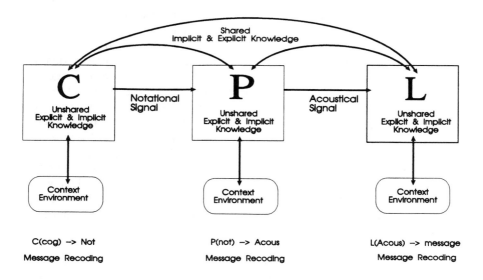

Fig. 1. Graphic representation of the music communication model (after Kendall and Carterette 1990). C = composer; P = performer; L = listener.

performer, reaching the listener via the acoustical signal generated by the musical instrument(s). Therefore, each of these individuals actively recodes the musical message. The composer translates his or her cognitive musical ideas to notational symbols, the performer translates the perceived notation into an acoustical signal, and the listener recodes the acoustical message into musical structures in the mind.

In order for reliable communication to take place, the composer, performer, and listener must share certain common knowledge. This knowledge may be either implicit or explicit. Explicit knowledge is that which can be put into words. For example, it is possible to tell someone how many sharps are in the key of D major or to describe the pitches that form the *Tristan* chord. Beyond such basic explanations, however, it is clear that one of the difficulties in studying music results from the fact that musical expression consists primarily of implicit (i.e., nonverbal) procedures (Kendall and Carterette 1990). It is not simply by chance that instruction in musical performance continues to be given one to one (teacher to pupil). A great deal of the information passed along in such sessions is nonverbal. For instance, the first time a student is told to perform a musical passage with a "warmer" tone, the instructor is bound to get a look of consternation in return. However, if the instructor plays a tone similar to that produced by the student followed by a more pleasing sound (demonstrated as "warmer"), the student gains understanding. Music performance, to a great degree, is passed on by means of this type of teacher emulation (i.e., modeling). Very often, such information is inexpressible in words. Training and education frequently involve a process of transforming implicit knowledge into explicit knowledge.

The model of music communication begs two fundamental questions: "*How* is a musical message communicated?" and "*What* is the message?" Chapter 4 has given us the tools to answer the initial question. A musical message is transmitted from performer to listener by adding expressive deviations to the pitch, loudness, timbral, and durational parameters of musical sound. Kendall and Carterette (1990) found that, when musicians were asked to emulate varying levels of expression (i.e., without expression, with expression, and with exaggerated expression) as performed by a world-renowned concert pianist, the primary distinguishing physical characteristics were timing and amplitude (see also Shaffer and Todd 1994; Todd 1985).

The second question—*What* is communicated?—is less understood. Some authors have suggested an analogy between musical organization and verbal discourse. In essence, these authors assume that music operates in a manner similar to the lexical breakdown of language into sections, paragraphs, sentences, words, syllables, and phonemes

(Aiello 1994b). In this comparison, the communicative property of musical sound derives from a similar breakdown of a piece into movements, sections, themes, phrases, notes, and, finally, specific characteristics of the amplitude envelope. This analogy was taken to the extreme by Leonard Bernstein (1976) in his series of Harvard lectures. Rather than pursue this reductionist approach to musical communication, I consider the process of musical communication to be one of coding and decoding messages between and among the various participants in Campbell and Heller's model (Kendall and Carterette 1990; Lipscomb and Kendall 1996). This model fits nicely with the stated belief that the listener is a gatherer and interpreter of information. As a result, our discussion must take into account not only the physical characteristics of sound, but also the culture, experience, and expertise of the individual listener.

Stages of Auditory Processing

Processes involved in listening to music include sensory transduction, auditory grouping, analysis of auditory properties and features, and matching immediate sonic events with an auditory lexicon of previously experienced sounds (McAdams 1993). Sensory transduction was addressed thoroughly in chapter 4. The later stages of processing will be discussed subsequently.

Two observations are worth noting at the outset. First, most of the studies cited here utilize subjects acculturated into the Western musical tradition. Cross-cultural musical research is still in its infancy. As a larger body of research appears, this type of investigation will undoubtedly provide significant advances in our knowledge of general musical principles. Second, the complexity of the actual musical experience makes it inherently difficult to study empirically. Therefore, in an attempt to increase the reliability of experimental results, many of the investigators cited here are admittedly reductionist in their method. For example, studies of melody perception often incorporate monophonic pitch sequences played by a computer-controlled synthesizer. In terms of ecological validity,[2] this experimental situation certainly does not represent the reality of

---

2. One of the major difficulties in carrying out music perception research is balancing internal validity with ecological (external) validity. Internal validity has to do with the degree of control the experimenter has over independent variables. External validity has to do with the degree to which the results of a given experiment can be generalized to the real (external) world. Ecologically valid experimental procedures incorporate methods that provide a representative musical context for studying musical sound. This is in contrast to many psychophysical studies that utilize vastly oversimplified ("beep boop") pitch sequences in an effort to study music perception.

attending a symphony concert in an auditorium specially designed for such an acoustical performance—not to mention the fact that listening to musical sound in a laboratory is quite different from listening in surroundings more conducive to an aesthetic experience (Aiello 1994a). Past research has provided a significant number of conclusions about the process of music cognition. However, the field of music psychology (as practiced today) is relatively young, having begun in earnest with the work of Hermann von Helmholtz (1954).[3] Therefore, while a great deal has been learned over the past century, these results must be considered within the context of a new science.

Pattern Recognition

As we begin to consider specific experiments and their derived theories, it will be beneficial to contrast two general model types that have been proposed in the cognitive literature: bottom-up and top-down processing. Bottom-up processing stresses the important role played by the stimulus in pattern recognition. According to this model, information arrives at the sensory receptors (the lowest level of processing), setting the pattern recognition process into motion. Whole patterns of great complexity are derived from the combination of simple, low-level features. Therefore, the bottom-up model proposes that an incoming stimulus is analyzed upon reaching the sensory system, salient sound objects are segregated from extraneous sounds, these objects are integrated into groups, and then meaning is assigned.

In contrast, top-down processing emphasizes the fact that an individual's concepts and higher level processes influence the recognition of patterns. Knowledge about the world and how it is organized (i.e., past experience and associated expectations) assist in this process (see Bharucha 1994; Carlsen 1981; Carlsen, Divenyi, and Taylor 1970; Deutsch and Feroe 1981; Jones 1981a and 1981b; Meyer 1956; Narmour 1977 and 1990; Schmuckler 1989). Such knowledge is largely implicit. Most cognitive psychologists currently believe that it is necessary to incorporate both bottom-up and top-down models into any complete theory of the complexities involved in pattern recognition (Matlin 1994).

Descriptions of sensory stimulation—tracing the energy transduction process from the eardrum to electrochemical activity in the brain to

---

3. A discussion of the methods utilized in typical psychophysical investigations is beyond the scope of this chapter. For specific information on Fechner's (1966) psychophysical scales (e.g., constant stimuli, limits, and adjustment) as well as more contemporary methods (e.g., multidimensional scaling and signal detection theory), the reader is referred to Gescheider 1985 and Schiffman, Reynolds, and Young 1981.

structures in the mind—are illustrative of bottom-up processing. These processes have been dealt with in earlier chapters of this text. The remainder of this chapter will deal almost exclusively with top-down (i.e., holistic or global) processing.

Schemata

When we listen to music, we actively select salient moments from the stream of musical sound, focusing our attention one minute on one part of our sound environment, the next moment on another. Attentional focus is guided by knowledge structures, or schemata, developed through past experience (Bartlett 1932; Dowling and Harwood 1986; Neisser 1967). Guidance provided by these schemata leads to expectations of what will happen next, influencing which elements are attended to and remembered.[4]

Using interleaved melodies, Dowling (1973) discovered that listener expectation assists in the identification of melodies. Interleaving is accomplished by simply alternating back and forth between consecutive notes of two different melodies. Without knowing what either of the melodies are ahead of time, many listeners perceive only a jumble of notes when presented with the interleaved melodies shown in figure 2.

Fig. 2.   Interleaved version of "Frère Jacques" and "Twinkle, Twinkle Little Star" (after Dowling 1973)

To verify this hypothesis, Dowling provided his subjects with either a "true label" (i.e., the label was the title of one of the interleaved melodies) or a "false label" (i.e., the song referred to in the label was not one of the interleaved melodies). With the true labels, subjects were almost always able to hear the target tune. With the false labels, subjects almost never reported hearing the target tune—after all, it was not present. Most significantly, however, neither did they report hearing either of

---

4. Bharucha distinguishes two kinds of musical expectation: schematic and veridical. He states that "schematic expectations are . . . automatic, culturally generic expectations. . . . They must be generated by a system that has learned to expect the events that are the most likely. Veridical expectations are for the actual next event in a familiar piece, even though this next event may be schematically unexpected" (Bharucha 1994, 216).

the melodies that were actually present. This confirms that expectation and the presence of schemata play an important role in melodic identification.[5]

What are the constituents of a melodic schema? A number of investigations have shown that pitch contour (i.e., the pattern of ups and downs) is the first aspect of melody that is stored upon hearing a new melody. Dowling and Fujitani (1971) presented subjects with pairs of melodies: a five-note atonal melody and a second melody that was either an exact transposition, a preserved-contour imitation (same pattern of ups and downs, but the size of the intervals were not identical), or a contour-violated imitation (see fig. 3). The investigators found that subjects could easily distinguish between melodies that have different contours (i.e., between fig. 3d and figs. 3a, 3b, or 3c). The level of accuracy was from 85 to 90 percent. However, the distinction between figures 3b and 3c was at the chance level (i.e., an accuracy level of 50 percent). Since melodies with different contours are clearly distinguishable while melodies with the same contour are easily confused, contour appears to be an important cue in short-term melodic memory.

Fig. 3. Example of (*a*) an atonal melody, (*b*) an exact transposition, (*c*) a contour-preserved imitation, and (*d*) a contour-violated imitation. Notes that are altered are marked with an asterisk.

Additional confirmation for the importance of contour in melodic memory was provided by Deutsch (1972). She created a set of stimuli by moving the pitches of her melodies to different octaves, so that the pitch chroma of the melody remained the same as the original but the melodic contour was altered (fig. 4). Her subjects found these octave-scrambled melodies very difficult to recognize (see also Dowling and Hollombe 1977; Idson and Massaro 1978; Kallman and Massaro 1979).

---

5. Neisser (1967, 1979) discusses an analogous visual situation, where subjects found it easy to follow the action in one set of images when the images from two videotapes were superimposed. Their accuracy in performing the experimental task seemed to be affected very little by the presence of the second set of images. An interesting point concerns these superimposed visual images and interleaved musical sounds: though the observer may attend to *either* of the two melodies (or images), it is impossible to attend to both simultaneously.

Further support comes from neuropsychological investigations. Peretz has determined that contour extraction is "a preliminary and indispensable step to the precise encoding of intervals" (1993, 219).

Fig. 4. An octave-scrambled melody

Dowling (1978) performed a variation of his earlier work with Fujitani (Dowling and Fujitani 1971) by incorporating tonal melodies rather than atonal pitch sequences. The presence of a key center allowed subjects to distinguish between exact transpositions and contour-preserved imitations at better than chance level. As a result, Dowling concludes that "the pitch information in melodies might be stored in a schema consisting of the contour . . . plus an indication of where that contour should be hung on a tonal scale" (Dowling and Harwood 1986, 128). In contrast to this reliance on melodic contour in the immediate recognition of melodies (i.e., short-term memory), Dowling proposes that schematic representations of familiar tunes in long-term memory consist of rhythmically organized sets of relative pitch chromas (Dowling 1994).

Recent research into the way brainlike systems learn (Rumelhart and McClelland 1986) may provide important clues concerning the formation of musical schemata. Many theories of cognitive organization (see Lerdahl and Jackendoff 1983, discussed subsequently) consist of sets of rules with little concern for how such implicit rules are acquired in the mind of the listener. However, associative models of brainlike systems consist of nodes that represent objects or features of the world. These nodes are linked together, forming a network, encapsulating all of the complex interrelationships between individual nodes. Associative models representing brain functions are often referred to as neural nets. For example, a neural net of music cognition might consist of nodes representing such musical elements as tones and chords. In a reliable model, connections between nodal points will mirror the perceptual relationships determined to exist between these same tones and chords. Connections between nodes (associations) become stronger in proportion to the number of times they are activated simultaneously. The state of activation (i.e., degree to which any single node is being attended) at any moment in time is determined by the number of connections currently active in response to a given musical stimulus. Such activation can occur directly or indirectly. In the former case, a node is directly set into activity when the tone or chord represented is present in the musical sound. A node may be set into an active state indirectly if the network of nodes associated with it are active (even though it is not directly activated), possibly resulting in an implied tone or an expectation for a certain future event.

Bharucha (1994) proposes several arguments in favor of considering associative networks as a means of understanding music cognition. Neural nets accomodate ambiguities well, because the model takes into account the fact that different nodes may be active simultaneously and to varying degrees, mirroring the manner in which tones, chords, or keys may be suggested to various degrees. Second, they provide a means of explaining the "filling in" process for elements in perception that do not exist in the physical world. In the case of the missing fundamental, for instance, stimulation of the nodes representing various components of the complex tone will suggest the fundamental pitch even though physical vibration at that frequency does not exist. At a higher level of cognitive organization, if a dominant seventh chord follows a subdominant chord, the representational unit for the tonic chord of the key will be strongly activated, exemplifying a strong expectation for a harmonic progression to the tonic. Perhaps the most important argument in favor of neural net models is the fact that they can "learn" (Bharucha 1994, 232). Formation of associations through past experience causes certain connections to be strengthened while others remain relatively weak. This arrangement seems to represent accurately the processes occurring in the human mind.

Lexicon of Schemata

Rhythmic-melodic configurations that occur frequently within a cultural context are stored in long-term memory, resulting in a schematic lexicon. Based on a theory proposed by Meyer (1973) and further developed by Narmour (1983 and 1990), Bigand (1993) describes two of the most common characteristics of musical schemata inherent in many tonal melodies. The first is called gap-fill melody and consists of two parts: a disjunct interval (gap) followed by a series of conjunct intervals serving to fill the gap. The gap rarely exceeds the interval of an octave. Examples of this compositional technique abound in Western tonal music. Figure 5, the third theme from the first movement of Beethoven's Symphony no. 1, provides an example of gap-fill melody. As can be seen, the initial ascending perfect fourth is followed by a series of descending scalar tones. This group of five notes is followed by an ascending minor seventh and three more descending scalar tones.

Fig. 5.   Gap-fill melody

The second type of common schema is the changing-note pattern revolving around the tonic scale degree (or sometimes the third). In the key of C major, this pattern would occur as illustrated in figure 6a. It is also permissible to invert the order of the upper and lower neighbor tones, as shown in figure 6b.

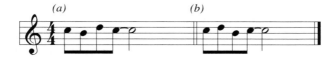

Fig. 6.   Illustration of (*a*) the changing-note pattern, and (*b*) its inversion.

In addition to local pattern schemata, listeners possess knowledge structures[6] of typical formal schemata making up the "temporal macro-structure" for pieces of tonal music (e.g. the exposition, development, and recapitulation of single-movement sonata form or the refrains and episodes of a typical rondo; see Bigand 1993, 243).[7] Because all musical listening occurs in individuals who have developed both shared and unshared knowledge structures, it is quite possible that two people listening to the same musical passage will hear it quite differently (see Arom 1985 and 1988). As McAdams and Bigand have suggested, "our perception of the sound world thus greatly surpasses the quality of the sensory information available at each instant" (1993, 3). Therefore, we may say that a person listening to musical sound not only gathers and interprets but actively synthesizes a cognitive interpretation based on incoming sensory data, influenced by the individual's common (i.e., shared with other members of the culture) and individual-specific (i.e., unshared) knowledge structures formed from past experience with similar sounds and in similar listening environments.

6. These knowledge structures may be either implicit or explicit, heavily influenced by the level of formal musical training.

7. These macrostructures, or what Lerdahl and Jackendoff refer to as "normative prolongational structures," provide abstract frames of reference for the temporal organization of musical events (see Lerdahl and Jackendoff 1983, 196–201).

This interpretive process may sometimes result in "mistaken" perceptions. For example, have you ever been sitting in a room, unaware of the extraneous noises that surround you, when suddenly—very clearly—you hear your name (or another familiar word) spoken? Chalikia and Warren (1990) suggest that such perceptions are based on erroneous segregation of combinatory spectral content. In such circumstances, recognized sounds are matched to their related schemata (what Chalikia and Warren refer to as "templates") and "the remaining spectral components of the stimulus are either perceived as an extraneous nonlinguistic noise, or matched to a second linguistic template" (Warren 1993, 58). Sometimes this second schema is close enough to the schematic representation of a familiar word stored in memory that an erroneous perceptual event is triggered.

Auditory Stream Segregation

What are the processes involved in separating the plethora of sounds surrounding us into individually recognized sound "objects?" Bregman (1990 and 1993) has proposed a theory for parsing auditory information into perceptual "streams" (i.e., cognition of simultaneously occurring sound events). He refers to the process of perceiving a complex sonic environment as auditory scene analysis. Analogous to research into the visual interpretation of complex scenes (e.g., Guzman 1969), it is the "process whereby all the auditory evidence that comes, over time, from a single environmental source is put together as a perceptual unit" (Bregman 1993, 11). His research identifies perceptual and cognitive strategies for parsing auditory information.

Bregman suggests that there are three processes occurring in the listener in order to decompose an auditory scene. The automatic activation of learned schemata (primitive auditory scene analysis) involves perceptual grouping believed to occur preattentively (Neisser 1967). Specifics of this grouping process will be discussed below in relation to the Gestalt psychologists. The second process (schema-based auditory scene analysis) incorporates the voluntary use of learned schemata and can be exemplified in the act of listening for the recurrence of a musical theme. The act of "trying" to listen for a specific series of sounds involves voluntary attention, which distinguishes this process from automatic activation. Finally, Bregman delineates general methods for partitioning an incoming auditory mixture into separate acoustic sources, including determination of the number of sound sources and sound localization. Bregman (1993) identifies several "regularity rules" exploited by the auditory system in the process of analysis, as shown in table 1 (for a detailed discussion, see Bregman 1993, 17–30).

TABLE 1.   Bregman's Regularity Rules

Rule	Description
1. Onset/offset	Unrelated sounds seldom start or stop at exactly the same time.
2. Gradualness of change	A single sound tends to change its properties smoothly and slowly over time.
3. Grouping partials in a spectrum	When a body vibrates with a repetitive period, its vibrations give rise to an acoustic pattern in which the frequency components are multiples of a common fundamental.
4. Synchronous patterns of change	Many changes that take place in an acoustic event will affect all of the components of the resulting sound in the same way and at the same time.

Source: Bregman 1993.

Auditory Gestalts

The capability of organizing individual musical sounds into a coherent structure is an ability required of every listener. This process of organization consists of nothing more than recognizing patterns in a series of separate tonal events (i.e., auditory scene analysis). Organizing discrete elements into "a whole" (or Gestalt) is one of the central tenets of the Gestalt psychologists (Köhler 1929; Wertheimer 1923). Another basic tenet of Gestalt psychology is that the whole is greater than the sum of its parts. In other words, human perception is not a simple input-output system (i.e., stimulus-response), but a complex process requiring cognitive interpretation of events within an immediate environmental context. Koffka (1935) proposed the law of *Prägnanz*, stating that psychological organization will always be as good as prevailing conditions allow. This organizational principle holds that an individual, when confronted with a disorganized state of affairs, will begin to impose order according to a set of subsidiary principles: proximity, similarity, common direction, simplicity, and closure. These principles assist in the process of recognizing the most important events and abstracting them perceptually from a less significant background of activity. This is often referred to as a figure-ground relationship, an ability essential to musical listening. How would it be possible to understand the intricacies of sonata form if we were incapable of abstracting the primary theme (figure) from its accompaniment (ground)?

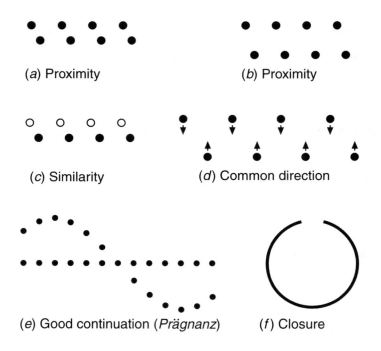

Fig. 7. Visual examples of the Gestalt principles of organization: (*a*) and (*b*) proximity, (*c*) similarity, (*d*) common direction, (*e*) simplicity or good continuation, and (*f*) closure (after Dowling and Harwood 1986).

Psychologists of the Gestalt school formulated visual examples of these principles (see fig. 7). Because similar cognitive processes are at work whether perceiving sounds or images, it is possible to create musical analogies of these Gestalt principles (see fig. 8). The principle of proximity states that objects that are close to one another tend to be grouped together. Similarity involves the grouping of objects that share common attributes. Common fate results when either visual or sonic objects appear to have the same motion trajectory. Simplicity (or good continuation) is an extension of *Prägnanz*, as described previously, and closure involves the perceptual completion of an object that is physically incomplete.

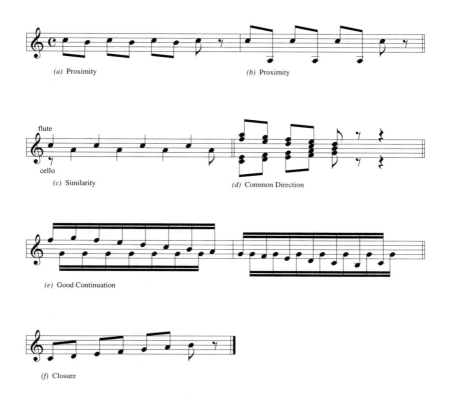

Fig. 8. Simple musical analogies of the Gestalt principles

The principle of proximity is validated musically by the fact that, in most musical styles, small intervallic distances between consecutive notes of a melody occur more frequently than large intervals. Lundin refers to this attribute of melody as propinquity, claiming that a melody progressing from note to note by small intervals provides a greater sense of unity and coherence than a melody full of large skips (1985, 78). In fact, even when large skips do occur, they are usually followed by a small interval in the opposite direction (e.g., gap-fill melody).

Violations of the law of proximity sometimes cause the listener to hear an organizational structure different than the one that actually exists in the physical stimulus. Deutsch (1975) created an auditory illusion by presenting subjects with musical stimuli through a pair of headphones (see fig. 9). Notes in the figure with their stems down were presented to the left ear, while notes with stems up were presented to the right ear.

However, 99 percent of the subjects perceived the low tone as always occurring in one ear and the high tone in the other ear.[8] Interestingly, when the earphones were reversed (stereo channels switched), subjects heard the high and low tone in the same ear as before. Deutsch suggested that the perceptual localization of high and low pitch was related to right- or left-handedness (i.e., dominant hemisphere).

Fig. 9. Aural stimuli from Deutsch 1975 illustrating the robustness of the principle of proximity: (*a*) pitches as presented (notes with the stems down presented to the left ear, stems up to the right ear), and (*b*) resulting subject perception.

The phenomenon of organizing musical events into streams based on pitch proximity is sometimes referred to as auditory streaming. When two pitches are far enough apart, fission (a perceptual splitting apart) occurs. Likewise, when two pitches are close together, they tend to fuse.[9] Miller and Heise (1950) found that fission occurs, in most cases, at about an intervallic distance of three semitones, referred to as the trill threshold (see fig. 10).[10] Perceptual fission is a function of both intervallic distance and tempo. At slower rates of presentation, listeners are more tolerant of large intervallic leaps.

Fig. 10. Illustration of musical fusion and fission

Composers have often exploited the principle of proximity in musical compositions. Examples of musical fission can be found in almost

---

8. Butler (1979a) replicated this experiment in a variety of musical situations, including a free sound-field environment (i.e., through spatially separated loudspeakers). Musically trained subjects were asked to transcribe what they heard. Almost all of the responses exhibited grouping by frequency proximity rather than exact representation of the physically alternating octaves.

9. Deutsch (1982) and Schouten (1962) refer to this phenomenon as temporal coherence.

10. Also see Schouten 1962 and Van Noorden 1975.

any solo instrument work (e.g., the Gigue from J. S. Bach's Suite no. 2 for Unaccompanied Cello) or in the vocal gymnastics of singer Bobby McFerrin (e.g., "Mañana Iguana"). In each of these cases, a single instrument (or voice) is capable of creating the illusion that multiple parts (i.e., a melody, bass line, and harmonic accompaniment) are present simultaneously. One of the most striking examples of the principle of proximity in classical music (Butler 1979b) is the opening phrase of the fourth movement of Tchaikovsky's Sixth Symphony (see fig. 11a). Though the melodies played by the first and second violins consist almost exclusively of large melodic intervals, listeners hear this section as if it were written as shown in figure 11b. It is practically impossible to hear the parts as written in the score due to the robust character of perceptual grouping based on pitch proximity.

Fig. 11.   Excerpt from the opening measures of the fourth movement of Tchaikovsky's Sixth Symphony: (*a*) as written in the musical score, and (*b*) as perceived by listeners.

Since the principle of proximity has proven to be such an important factor in music perception, I have dealt with it in some detail. The musical relevance of the other Gestalt principles will be mentioned briefly (for more exhaustive accounts, see Deutsch 1982; Dowling and Harwood 1986; or Franklin 1972).

Musical sounds of similar timbre tend to be grouped on the basis of the principle of similarity (Erikson 1975). The principle of similarity also applies to musical tones that share a common amplitude. For instance, Dowling (1973) found that subjects were able to discern his interleaved melodies more easily when amplitude differences between the melodies were introduced.

Grouping by simplicity (i.e., *Prägnanz* or good continuation) is exemplified in an experiment performed by Bregman and Dannenbring (1973). As in the trill threshold experiments discussed earlier, they found that a repeating passage alternating a high tone with a low tone segregated into two separate auditory streams. However, when a frequency glide was introduced from one pitch to the other, the fission tendency was reduced. It would seem that the glide assisted in joining the two pitches into a single perceptual stream, whereas the interval between discrete pitches in the initial version (i.e., with no glide) caused the high tones to fuse only with other high tones and low tones only with other low tones on the basis of frequency proximity.

A musical passage exhibiting several consecutive ascending chords would be grouped together according to the principle of common direction. This perceptual group would further be considered distinct from a group of instruments simultaneously performing a series of consecutive descending chords.

Finally, numerous examples of closure may be found in the literature. In these instances, past experience causes the mind to synthesize (i.e., fill in) sounds that are not present in the physical stimulus. The missing fundamental, as discussed in chapter 4, provides an impressive illustration of this process. In a more complex context, several studies have shown that, presented with two alternating sounds of different amplitudes, a listener often hears a fainter sound continue underneath an intermittent louder one (Miller and Licklider 1950; Thurlow 1957; Vicario 1960). Numerous experiments in speech perception have confirmed that if a phoneme is replaced in a sentence by a loud noise, the listener will synthesize the missing phoneme to complete the expected sound sequence (Warren 1970; Warren, Obusek, and Ackroff 1972). Applying this phenomenon to pitched sound, Dannenbring (1976) presented subjects with a sine signal that continuously glided up and down in frequency. Substituting a loud noise burst for a portion of the pitched sound, he discovered that subjects still reported hearing the pitch glide through the noise. Perhaps the best (and most obvious) example of musical closure is the cadence, bringing a musical idea to completion.

As I have shown, grouping mechanisms in operation during musical listening can be identified and delineated. However, when considering actual musical contexts, the grouping process is considerably more complex, due to multiple interactions between the various Gestalt principles.

The Spotlight of Attention

Due to limitations of our perceptual system, it is impossible to pay attention to everything going on in our immediate environment. A necessary part of the cognitive process is selecting elements around us that warrant attention. Jones and Yee (1993) elaborate on the various definitions of attention that have been suggested within the field of psychology.

For the purpose of the present chapter, however, a general definition will suffice. We shall consider attention to be simply "a concentration of mental activity" (Matlin 1994, 43). It will be helpful to distinguish between two common uses of attending: selective attention and divided attention. Selective attention requires the observer to focus on one aspect of the environment to the exclusion of all others. An example of this process is listening to a conversation in the midst of a cocktail party (Cherry 1953). In this context, the listener effortlessly "tunes out" the multitude of simultaneously occurring conversations and extraneous noises in order to follow the output from a single source. Divided attention requires that focus be spread among several stimuli occurring simultaneously. Using divided attention at the same cocktail party, it is often possible to follow two simultaneously occurring conversations by alternately focusing the spotlight of attention on one sound stream and then the other (shadowing). As might be expected, this task is much more difficult than selective attention, because the structured flow of information inherent in the perception of events from one source can be disrupted by another, unrelated source of information (Neisser and Becklen 1975).[11] Both selective attention and divided attention rely heavily on schemata for guiding our expectations of what will happen next, what we attend to, and what is retained in memory.

It is quite possible to experience music listening as either a divided attention task or a selective attention task. Intensely active listening situations (e.g., symphonic score reading) require attention to be focused on multiple streams of sound, frequently shifting back-and-forth from one to another (i.e., divided attention). However, when experiencing a musical performance in a more relaxed setting, the listener is likely to invoke a selective attention strategy, following one of several concurrent melodic lines in a complex composition then shifting to another. Both divided attention and selective attention require that the listener be actively involved in the "listening" experience, rather than passively "hearing" the sound. One may also focus on various aspects of the musical structure (e.g., specific instrumental sections of the orchestra, rhythmic or harmonic content, etc.). Research has shown that selective attention is facilitated by specific instructions given to the subject, increased pitch distance between target and distracter, metrically relating subparts temporally, and fulfillment of pitch and temporal expectations (Jones and Yee 1993).

---

11. For the interested reader, Matlin (1994) provides an excellent general overview of theories of attention. Jones and Yee (1993) present a review of research investigating attention focusing on audition.

Memory

Music is a transitory art form consisting of sounds organized in time. No sooner has a musical tone been perceived than others are impinging upon the sensory system. Since it is impossible to consider music cognition apart from this temporal element, memory must play a significant role. As discussed previously, schemata in memory are not the musical sounds themselves, but rather an abstracted schematic representation that can be accessed either as a source for comparing present sounds to those heard in the past or in mentally recreating (i.e., imaging) previously experienced sounds.[12] Dowling (1994) concludes that memory approximates the original melody, coding only the most significant features on initial hearing and filling in more details, given the opportunity of repeated listening.

Current theories often divide human memory storage into two broad types: short term and long term (Atkinson and Shiffrin 1968; Tulving 1983).[13] Short-term (or episodic) memory (STM) is limited in both its duration and capacity. Items stored in STM can begin to fade after about 30 seconds unless they are repeated within that time period. A series of often-cited studies by Miller (1956) concluded that the capacity of short-term memory is limited to approximately seven discrete items—what he refers to as "the magical number seven, plus or minus two." In contrast, long-term (or semantic) memory (LTM) has a virtually unlimited capacity and contains memories of events that occurred decades ago, as well as memories formed only a few minutes before.

Directly applicable to musical situations, STM actively participates in the storing of novel melodies (i.e., those that have never been heard before), while LTM stores the schema for the melodies with which we have become familiar over our lifetime. Research by Dowling and his colleagues has shown that specific melodic information (e.g., chroma and interval) is more important for LTM, where a melody must be differentiated from a large number of similar alternatives, than in STM, where the few alternatives are readily available. In the latter situation, contour dominates over other aspects of a melody (Bartlett and Dowling 1980; Dowling 1978; Dowling and Bartlett 1981; Dowling and Fujitani 1971). Dowling and Bartlett (1981) found that accuracy of interval or chroma information that listeners have for familiar melodies does, however, begin to develop during the first few times that these melodies are entered into LTM.

---

12. Musical imaging is a fascinating area of study. For more information, see Seashore 1938 or Halpern 1988 and 1992.

13. Matlin (1994) discusses both of these models in great detail.

Modularity in Memory

Results of many investigations into human memory have concluded that different parts of the brain are used to process various aspects of incoming sensory information. Such modularity has been proposed by music psychologists as well as neuropsychologists studying the physiology of brain-damaged individuals. Deutsch (1970 and 1975) showed that introducing distracter words into a pitch-matching experiment caused no degradation in performance. Likewise, introducing tonal distracters into a word task did not interfere. When two processes (e.g., word and pitch processing) are determined to be noninterfering (i.e., processed by different systems), they are said to be dissociated from one another. Semal and Demany (1991) extended Deutsch's work to show that the properties of pitch and timbre are dissociated in experiments utilizing single tones. A paper by Pechmann and Mohr (1992) suggests that the results obtained by Deutsch (1970 and 1975) are reliably characteristic of formally trained musicians. However, results of their study showed that there was, in fact, interference between the tones and speech sounds in the responses gathered from a group of subjects without formal musical training. This suggests that individual subject factors (e.g., musical training) figure prominently into musical listening tasks, even in such simple procedures as pure-tone pitch comparisons (Crowder 1993).

Additional support for modularity comes from the field of neuropsychology. This field of study examines the relationship between cerebral organization and mental functioning. Much of the scientific research in this area has been carried out using individuals who have sustained localized brain damage. By comparing the performance and behavior of these individuals to the "normal" (i.e., undamaged) population, differences can be identified and functions of specific regions of the brain may be postulated. Acquired clinical disorders of music perception or performance (including reading music notation) are identified by the generic term *amusia* (see Benton 1977; Jellinek 1956; Marin 1982; Wertheim 1963, 1969, and 1977; see also chap. 7). Many studies relate these musical disorders to disturbances in speech and language (aphasias), hoping to identify areas of the brain responsible for verbal and/or nonverbal processes. Clinical cases of each of the following disorders have been identified: (1) amusia with aphasia, (2) aphasia without amusia, and (3) amusia without aphasia (for a complete review, see Marin 1982).

Peretz (1993) provides data supporting the claim that linguistic and nonlinguistic (e.g., musical) aspects of auditory perception are often dissociated in stroke patients (see Assal 1973; Brust 1980; Dorgeuille 1966; Mavlov 1980). In contrast, Serafine, Crowder, and their colleagues claim to have found an integration effect when presenting music and words concurrently to normal subjects (Crowder, Serafine, and Repp 1990; Serafine, Crowder, and Repp 1984; Serafine et al. 1986). Initially, each subject heard a series of 24 short (i.e., six- second), unfamiliar folk melody excerpts—some paired with words, others not. This presentation was followed immediately by a recognition task in which subjects were asked to identify melodies that had been among the initial group of 24. Sometimes the melodies in the recognition task were accompanied by companion words and other times with the music alone. In the companion word conditions, the text might be identical to that presented with the melody or new text. Identical combinations (i.e., the same music-text pair) were responded to more accurately than the other conditions, suggesting that verbal and musical information is stored together in memory. Therefore, the investigators concluded that "a song heard some minutes previously is stored as 'those particular words' in conjunction with 'that particular melody'" (Crowder 1993, 133). Future research must resolve the conflict between this conclusion and the dissociation exhibited in the results of Peretz (1993) outlined previously.

Memory for Music

Having just completed a brief introduction to attention and general memory issues, we can now focus our discussion on how these processes affect the perception and cognition of musical sound. Since music essentially involves an interaction between pitch and time, the next section will deal explicitly with the tonal and temporal parameters of music.

Musical Scales

Music cognition always occurs within a cultural context. Significant factors in a culture's music are the tuning system and pitch collections considered appropriate for use in music performance. Acculturated into a social milieu that has come to recognize the equal-tempered scale as "correct," Western listeners may find the sound of the pelog scale of the Javanese gamelan or the Indian raga quite unusual. The perception may even be that of instruments playing slightly out of tune. In addition, the familiar hierarchical relationships implicitly learned by Western listeners and the expectations generated for future musical events can no longer be made, due to a lack of previous experience with Javanese or Indian music. Only those individuals familiar with the music rule system (either implicitly or explicitly) are able to make such musical predictions accurately.

One of the most important psychological constructs in the musical reduction process is the musical scale. Scales provide a finite set of pitches that may be used as a psychological standard by which a listener can measure melodic motion and pitch-interval size (Dowling and Harwood 1986; Helmholtz 1954). Restriction of available pitches simplifies a listener's task immensely. For example, if a solo performer plays a middle C at 254 Hz instead of the "correct" frequency of 256 Hz (when A = 440 Hz), the listener will probably not hear the tone as a different pitch—in fact, in this case the difference may not be noticed at all. Instead, the listener considers this frequency within the range of "acceptable C's." Even when the frequency is significantly larger (e.g., if the player had played a tone of 250 Hz), the listener tends to "nudge" the frequency perceptually so that it remains a C in perception, though perhaps it is considered slightly flat. Limiting the number of note choices significantly reduces the workload imposed upon memory processing.

Dowling and Harwood (1986) propose four primary psychological constraints that should be satisfied by a musical scale: (1) Listeners must be able to discriminate between the discrete pitches of a scale; (2) octaves (i.e., notes of the same pitch class) are considered equivalent; (3) a scale may consist of only a moderate number of pitches (usually seven; see Miller 1956); and (4) there should be a "uniform modular pitch unit" from which all other pitch intervals may be built. In Western music, this modular unit is the semitone. With few exceptions, these psychological constraints are supported by cross-cultural studies.

Tonality

Almost all art music produced between the beginning of the seventeenth century and the end of the nineteenth century, as well as a significant amount of music continuing to the present day, can be classified as tonal compositions. Tonality requires that the individual notes and chords of a piece of music be organized hierarchically in relation to a tonic pitch, that is, the most important tone. This tonal hierarchy distinguishes relative differences in stability of the various pitches within a key. As Bharucha points out, "when the key of C major has been strongly established during a piece of music, the diatonic tones (C, D, E, F, G, A, B) are more stable than the nondiatonic tones" (1994, 222). When a new key is established, the stable diatonic set will shift to a different set of tones.

Krumhansl (1979) confirmed the importance of tonal context to musical memory using a probe tone technique. This procedure consists of presenting subjects with a standard tone lasting 500 ms, followed immediately by a series of seven pitches (interference tones), a pause for 1.5 sec, and finally a comparison tone that is either the same as the standard or one semitone away. She varied the interference tones to form the following conditions: interference tones from the same key as the standard tone, interference tones from a different key than that of the standard tone, and interference tones that formed atonal pitch sequences (i.e., not from any major or minor key). When the standard and the interference tones were from the same key, subjects responded correctly 95 percent of the time. With atonal sequences of interference tones, performance accuracy fell to 80 percent. However, when the standard tone was outside the tonality of the interference tones, subjects responded more accurately after atonal interference than after tonal interference from a different key, suggesting that memory for pitch is affected by tonal context. If the context is tonal, pitches related to that tonality are remembered well, while pitches that do not belong are disruptively influenced. However, atonal interference was less disruptive when the target pitch was outside the tonality of the tonal interference tones.

The presence of a tonal context appears to result in a perceptual shift of the listener's internal (tonal) frame of reference (Blackburn, cited in Dowling and Harwood 1986, 13; Cuddy, Cohen, and Miller 1979; Dewar, Cuddy, and Mewhort 1977; Guilford and Hilton 1933; Guilford and Nelson 1936 and 1937). In essence, if the subject attempts to remember a pitch that is outside the current tonal context, emphasizing the tonality is disruptive to this memory task while atonal interference is not. If, however, the target pitch is within the tonality, tonal interference tones confirm the subject's memory for the target pitch while an atonal series of pitches denigrates performance. The context in which a pitch is heard affects memory for that pitch. Tonal scale contexts can aid in memory for context-compatible pitches and in the detection of those that are incompatible, while contexts that include pitches outside the scale schema of an inferred tonal scale can interfere with accurate memory and cause systematic errors of judgment.

Brown and Butler (1981) required listeners to identify the key center following presentation of a three-note pitch sequence. They found that sequences containing a "rare interval" (e.g., the tritone interval between F and B in the key of C major) resulted in much higher agreement between subjects. In contrast, "common-interval combinations" elicited responses from subjects that were spread among several appropriate alternatives. The three-tone common-interval combination C-F-G, for example, could have been derived from any of the following major keys: C, F, B-flat, E-flat, or A-flat. They also found that varying the presentation order of the three tones of a sequence containing a "rare interval" altered the accuracy level of the responses. The most reliable sense of key center arises when the seventh degree of the major scale (the leading tone) was heard following the fourth degree. When the presentation order of these two tones is reversed, response accuracy and confidence levels both fell (Butler and Brown 1994). Results of such investigations will add validity to the conclusions derived from more reductionist procedures, such as the probe tone technique described previously.

Key Relationships
While discussing the concept of tonality, it is important to realize that some keys are more closely related than others. This is commonly referred to as key distance and is mainly based on the number of pitches the two keys share in common (Carterette and Kendall 1989). For example, the keys of C major and F major are closely related because they share all but one pitch (i.e., B-natural vs. B-flat). In contrast, the keys of C major and F-sharp major are maximally distant because they share only one pitch in common (i.e., B-natural). In a study of key distance, Bartlett and Dowling (1980) asked subjects to compare two melodies and determine whether they were the same or different. The investigators manipulated the test melodies so that sometimes the standard and the comparison were in the same key, sometimes in closely related keys, and other times in distant keys. Interestingly, judgments were more accurate as key distance increased. In other words, the fewer tones that the two keys had in common, the easier it was to correctly reject imitations. Bartlett and Dowling explained this result by suggesting that if the keys of a pair of melodies are closely related, they share both contour and chroma (i.e. a number of same-chroma pitches), making it more difficult to reject an imitation. However, if the keys of a pair are distantly related (i.e., sharing few tones in common) the melodies exhibit the same contour, but chroma is not shared to the same degree as in closely related keys, reducing the chance of confusion.

Rhythmic Organization

Though a commonsense view may suppose that the perception of music is determined by its pitch content to a large extent, temporal aspects of music have been shown to be even more salient. Rhythmic alteration, for example, transforms a simple descending major scale into "Joy to the World" (see fig. 12a) or the opening tones of Schubert's Symphony no. 8 ("Unfinished") into the familiar theme from the television series

"Dragnet" (Monahan and Carterette 1985; see fig. 12b). It has long been suggested that familiar tunes can be recognized from their rhythmic patterns alone (James 1950; White 1960). In fact, similarity judgments provided by subjects in response to pairs of brief melodies suggest that rhythmic aspects of these brief melodies actually dominate the pitch dimension (Carterette et al. 1982; Monahan 1984; Monahan and Carterette 1985).

Fig. 12. The influence of rhythm on the perception of a pitch sequence: (*a*) descending major scale and "Joy to the World"; (*b*) opening tones of Schubert's "Unfinished" Symphony and the theme from "Dragnet."

Data reduction influences rhythmic perception as well as pitch perception. When asked to tap along with complex rhythmic patterns, subjects tend to migrate toward a 2:1 ratio. Povel (1981) has suggested that there are two steps involved in the process of encoding rhythms. First, the listener attempts to identify a beat framework (i.e., a regular beat pattern) with interbeat intervals of not much more than 1.5 seconds. Then, this pattern of beats is divided further into an equal number of subdivisions. Once again, the preference is for a 2:1 ratio. Fraisse (1982) points out that this preference is well justified, since there is a prevalence of such subdivisions (80–90 percent) in Western music composed in the period from Beethoven to Bartok. Metrical organization (i.e., the search for underlying regularity) with a preference for nested hierarchical relationships constitutes a cognitive framework for the temporal dimension of music perception, similar to the framework that the scale provides for the pitch dimension. Beyond providing a framework, meter assists in the generation of expectations for future events, resulting in feelings of musical tension and relaxation.

In another tapping procedure, Handel and Lawson (1983) created complex rhythmic patterns utilizing two to three tones at different pitch levels. Listeners were simply asked to tap along with the complex rhythm in any way they wished. At slow tempos (i.e., approximately 3.0 seconds per measure), subjects tended to tap the polyrhythm. As tempo increased to between 1.2 to 1.6 seconds per measure, listeners began to tap along with one of the component beat patterns (i.e., the rhythm of one of the pitches). Handel and Lawson noted that their subjects rarely followed beat patterns when notes were separated by more than 0.8 seconds.

One technique that has been particularly useful in psychological investigations of music perception is multidimensional scaling (MDS). In such investigations, the researcher obtains similarity ratings from subjects (i.e., how similar is one musical example to another?). These similarity ratings are assumed to be "a measure of proximity in a psychological space" (Dowling and Harwood 1986, 190). A complex mathematical procedure then converts these similarities into virtual distances between the various musical examples, placing them in a reasonably small number of spatial dimensions. When considering the resulting graphic output, the investigator's task involves interpreting the dimensions into psychologically meaningful characteristics of the stimuli.

In a series of such experiments, Gabrielsson (1973a, 1973b, and 1973c) asked subjects to rate the similarity between monophonic and polyphonic percussion rhythm patterns as well as piano melodies utilizing these same rhythms. The MDS solution suggests that the main dimensions used by subjects to differentiate between rhythms included perceived meter and tempo. In addition, two other factors were considered to be important in the subject ratings: (1) whether the first beat of the example was accented or not, and (2) the composite pattern of note durations and accents.

In another study, Monahan (1984) presented subjects with pairs of rhythmic patterns at various tempos. She discovered that pairs preserving the durational relationships (i.e., identical rhythms at different tempos) were judged more similar than those with different rhythmic patterns. Tempo interacted with the type of comparison such that, as the tempo of the comparison stimulus diverged from that of the initial stimulus, pairs with the same relative (but different absolute) rhythms were judged more similar. Monahan concluded that this shift of tempo allowed listeners to place less reliance on the absolute durations of the rhythmic pattern and pay more attention to the relative durational information in the rhythmic contour.[14]

----

14. It is quite possible to discuss rhythm, like pitch, in terms of its contour (i.e., longer or shorter note durations).

As illustrated in the previous discussion, both pitch and temporal duration are important in the perception of musical sound, providing a means of cognitive organization based on principles of pattern recognition. Monahan, Kendall, and Carterette conclude that "composers who ignore the Gestalt principles of grouping, in the domain either of frequency (pitch) or of time, run the risk of writing music that is difficult to code or to remember easily in the short term" (1987, 600–601). This psychological explanation may provide insight into specific reasons for the failure of twentieth-century art music to gain acceptance by the general listening public. Its high level of complexity and frequent violations of listener expectations often provide a challenge for even the most sophisticated listener.

Musical Timbre

In chapter 4, the concept of musical timbre and its associated dimensions was introduced. Orchestration (i.e., the composer's decision concerning which instruments will perform the various parts of a composition) is an important factor in the musical experience. Instrumental voicings assist in creating contrasts between thematic elements of a piece, providing variety and interest. Ravel's *Bolero* is an excellent example of how a composer, using artful orchestration, can maintain listeners' interest for more than 15 minutes, even though only a single thematic idea is presented.

Research has shown that important characteristics of instrumental timbres include—in hierarchical order of importance—characteristics of the attack portion of the amplitude envelope, the spectral envelope and the time-variant nature of its sustain portion,[15] and tiny variations in component frequencies (McAdams 1993). The importance of these dimensions has been borne out in studies requiring subjects to discriminate between musical instrument tones (Charbonneau 1981; Elliott 1975; Grey and Moorer 1977) and studies utilizing the multidimensional scaling technique (Grey 1977; Grey and Gordon 1978; Krumhansl 1989; Miller and Carterette 1975).

Results of identification studies, in which the subject is asked to determine what instrument is being heard, exhibit a strong inverse correlation with results from similarity scaling studies (McAdams 1993). In other words, the more similar two instruments are determined to be in the latter task, the more likely they are to be confused in the former. It is

---

15. Amplitude, precise frequency, and phase of the sine components of a complex instrumental tone change continually during the so-called steady-state portion of the amplitude envelope. This characteristic of musical sound is referred to as time variance.

important to note that there is a danger in generalizing the results of these studies to real musical situations because all of the procedures used single tones in isolation, performed with the same frequency, amplitude, and duration—a situation that never occurs in actual musical contexts. For example, the importance of the attack portion in identifying musical instruments was taken for granted following the pioneering work of Saldanha and Corso (1964). However, when Kendall (1986) removed the attack portion of the amplitude envelope and placed these tones within a musical context (i.e., sequentially to form a melody), listeners had little difficulty in accurately identifying the musical instrument. This directly contradicts the findings of studies using isolated tones and confirms the importance of musical context (ecological validity). In addition, almost without exception, earlier studies of timbre used synthesized timbres rather than natural instrument sounds. With the advent of the multimedia personal computer and its capability for digital sampling, future investigations will provide more ecologically valid results.[16]

Melody

Listening to music is not simply a passive process of sensory reception. The ear is responsible for responding physiologically to mechanical vibrations that enter the ear canal, but it is up to the human mind to construct a melody. Aiello defines melody as "a sequence of single pitches organized as an aesthetic musical whole" (1994b, 173). According to Davies, "a tune is not a tune simply by virtue of its physical properties, but only when it is perceived as such by a person" (1978, 82). Active participation in the perceptual process is what distinguishes the art of *listening* to music from merely *hearing* it.

In the music listening experience, melody is often the most perceptually salient aspect of musical sound. As a result, it is the component of music that is easiest to recognize, remember, and reproduce. Four features of melody are delineated by Dowling: contour, interval size, key (or tonality), and rhythm (1994). Melodic contour is simply the pattern of ups and downs when considering pitch relationships within the melody. Coding of interval size involves the process of keeping track of the distances between each consecutive pair of tones within the melodic context. As defined previously, the key of a melody sets up certain

---

16. More recent investigations are beginning to look into the perception of simultaneously sounding instrument timbres and their resulting blend using both synthesized timbres (Sandell 1989a and 1989b) and digitized versions of natural instrument tones (Kendall and Carterette 1991).

expectations for the relationship of one tone to another with primary significance given to the tonic pitch. The pattern of accents and note durations inherent in a melody's rhythm (also referenced in terms of contour) is the final feature proposed by Dowling. Following 20 years of significant contributions to the literature about melody perception, Dowling concludes that "melodies are remembered as ordered sets of pitches . . . [with] dynamic tendencies to gravitate toward points of stability in a tonal context" (1994, 191).

Recognition and Identification

A fertile domain for research within the field of music psychology is melody recognition.[17] Recognition requires that the listener retain musical sounds of the present in STM long enough to compare them with schema formed in the past (LTM). In studies of musical memory, recognition is often operationally defined as the proportion of times a subject correctly judges whether a given melody has been played before. In addition to this basic "familiar/unfamiliar" procedure, it is also possible to ask the subject for a quantitative rating on a scale of familiarity or a rating of the degree of confidence in the judgment made (McAdams 1993). Identification, on the other hand, requires that the listener provide a label (e.g., an instrument name, a song title, or a number to represent some aspect of the sound) in response to a stimulus. Identification may be considered a focused recognition task requiring that the subject not only correctly match the auditory stimulus to a formed schema, but that he or she be able to access a lexicon of names and retrieve the appropriate label for a given stimulus.

Temporal constraints have been found to exist in the process of melody recognition.[18] Warren et al. (1991) presented subjects with a single phrase (7–9 notes) from eight different familiar melodies, altering the note durations from 40 ms to 3.6 seconds. There were temporal limits below and above which melody recognition did not occur. For durations below the recognition limit (extremely fast tempos), distinctive patterns were perceived but were not recognized as a familiar melody. Likewise, at durations above the recognition limit (extremely slow tempos), notes of the melodies appeared to be a string of individual pitches

---

17. Only specifically musical aspects of the incoming stimulus have been considered, to the exclusion of lyrics (i.e., verbal cues) that might be a part of the musical sound. For a discussion of the complexities inherent in considering both textual and musical aspects, see Crowder, Serafine, and Repp 1990; Peretz 1993; Serafine, Crowder, and Repp 1984; and Serafine et al. 1986.

18. For a thorough review of these constraints, see Warren 1993.

lacking melodic organization (Warren 1993). The overall recognition limits (i.e., the grand median across all eight melodies) were 160 ms for the lower limit and 1280 ms for the upper limit.[19]

Melody Research

A significant number of studies have tested melody recognition using a discrimination paradigm. In this method, subjects hear two melodies. Their task is to simply determine whether the melodies are the same or different (sometimes confidence scores are provided). Dowling (1994) provides a lucid description of the method that he (and other investigators) have utilized to manipulate comparison melodies. These altered melodies are typically of three types: exact transpositions, same-contour imitations, and contour-violated imitations (see fig. 3). Exact transpositions involve shifting all of the pitches of a melody up or down by the same number of semitones, retaining the same intervallic relationships between consecutive notes. Same-contour imitations retain the same pattern of ups and downs, although the precise interval relationships between consecutive tones is altered.[20] In contour-violated imitations, however, one or more ascending intervals are replaced by descending intervals, or vice versa.

Experimental evidence has shown that subjects find it easy to identify exact transpositions and to discriminate contour-violated imitations. However, it is much more difficult to reject same-contour imitations correctly. These results have been confirmed with both atonal (Dowling and Fujitani 1971) and tonal (Dowling 1978) melodies. Confusion of same-contour imitations with exact transpositions becomes especially likely when the two melodies are played in closely related keys (Bartlett and Dowling 1980). Summarizing results of his research, Dowling concludes,

> . . . the evidence suggests that contour similarity is especially important for recently encountered novel melodic phrases that are

---

19. Fraisse (1982, 156) has identified temporal limits for the perceptual grouping of sound events. The lower limit (approximately 120 ms apart) corresponds closely to the separation at which psychophysiological conditions no longer allow the two events to be perceived as distinct. The upper limit (1,500–2,000 ms) represents the temporal separation at which two groups of stimuli are no longer perceptually linked (Bolton 1894; MacDougall 1903). Fraisse suggests a value of 600 ms as the optimum for both perceptual organization and precision.

20. Diatonic displacement is a special case of the same-contour imitation. In this particular instance, a melody is shifted up or down within a diatonic key. For example, a melody starting on the tonic in C major, when moved up two semitones, would become a melody in D dorian.

about five notes long. Contour is less important as melodies are remembered for longer periods of time, as they become more familiar, and when they are longer than five notes. (1994, 190)

On initial hearing, contour dominates melodic perception. However, after 30–40 seconds, the importance of contour declines and interval size between consecutive notes becomes more important (DeWitt and Crowder 1986; Dowling and Bartlett 1981). This shift of emphasis is necessary due to the difficulty of discriminating between the large number of similar melodic schemata stored in LTM.

Familiar versus Unfamiliar Melodies

In processing familiar melodies, intervallic relationships are primary (Bartlett and Dowling 1980). Wrong-note deviations from the expected tonal progression are easily recognized (Attneave and Olson 1971). In contrast, contour dominates in the perception of unfamiliar (i.e., novel) melodies. Listeners are unable to distinguish between exact transpositions and contour-preserved imitations (Dowling and Fujitani 1971). Introducing a delay following presentation causes increasing reliance on stored interval information (Dowling and Bartlett 1981).

Global Organization

Identification of large-scale musical form requires the use of low-level sensory information (i.e., pitch, loudness, timbre, and duration) in order to identify local patterns (i.e., Gestalten) and incorporate them into a larger macrostructure. Many music majors have vivid recollections of sitting through listening exams, struggling to determine whether the piece they are hearing falls under the heading of sonata form or rondo. Making this distinction requires the use of melodic and harmonic memory as well as the ability to identify musical repetitions and variations. The role of musical memory must include specific traces of important musical phrases as well as less-specific motivic patterns. Integrating these memory traces into a coherent musical structure is a complex cognitive task.

Generative Theory of Tonal Music

Perhaps the most-cited theory of global organization is that proposed by Lerdahl and Jackendoff (1983) in their generative theory of tonal music (GTTM). They consider the goal of music theory to be "a formal description of the musical intuitions of a listener who is experienced in a musical idiom" (Lerdahl and Jackendoff 1983, 1). This "music theory as psychology" approach to analysis is a valuable contribution to the domain of music theory. Based heavily on Chomsky's (1957) theory of grammatical syntax, GTTM incorporates rhythmic structure, grouping structure (closely related to Gestalt principles), and metrical structure into a comprehensive analysis based on well-formedness rules and preference rules, a list of which are provided in the appendix to their text. In addition to identifying these various grouping strategies, they also perform a reduction of the surface structure (i.e., every note of the piece) to a deep structure consisting of the most significant tones of the composition. Obviously, there are varying levels of structural depth. Carrying this construct to its logical extreme, Heinrich Schenker (1979) theorized that all Western tonal music could eventually be reduced to a deep structure consisting of three basic musical events: establishment of a tonic, prolongation of the dominant, and a return to the tonic. In a sense, the analytical process of GTTM mirrors the perceptual organization that occurs while listening to music. Initially, local patterns (e.g., motives and themes) are identified, then they are placed hierarchically within the context of the entire composition.

Information Theory

Another important aspect of organizing musical sounds is based on listener expectations. These expectations are not innate, but are derived from a person's cultural and social milieu and past musical experience. At Bell Laboratories, Shannon and Weaver (1949) developed a mathematical theory of communication. Their theory, called information theory, is based on the concept of uncertainty.[21] Uncertainty may be generally defined in terms of the probability of different events taking place. If you were to hear a sequence of tones comprising the first seven notes of an ascending major scale, there is a high probability that the next pitch will be the tonic. In this case, there is a low level of uncertainty. However, if seven pitches are played at random, there is a much higher level of uncertainty concerning what note may follow. Uncertainty is greatest when there is a large number of possible outcomes and these outcomes are each equally likely to occur. Musical examples illustrating two levels of uncertainty are provided in figure 13. Notice the level of certainty when trying to predict what the final tone will be in

---

21. The theory of musical meaning proposed by Leonard B. Meyer (1956, 1967, and 1973) derives a great deal from information theory.

the example shown in figure 13a in comparison to the uncertainty of the continuation of the example shown in figure 13b.

Fig. 13.   Examples of two levels of uncertainty: (*a*) "Joy to the World," and (*b*) Schoenberg, Piano Concerto, op. 42, first movement.

Central to Shannon and Weaver's theory is the concept of information. Simply stated, the role of information is to reduce uncertainty. The amount of information in a given event is related to the number of choices required to define the message unambiguously (Davies 1978, 86). Moles (1968) applied this mathematical formula to the various parameters of musical sound (e.g., note durations, pitch intervals, etc.), calculating the amount of information in a typical melody of the classical period. Essentially, this process involves two steps: (1) determining how frequently all possible note durations and pitch intervals occur in a "typical" piece, and (2) comparing these probabilities to an actual piece of music in order to determine how many "likely" notes and how many "unlikely" notes occur. In practice, the higher the number of occurrences of "unlikely" notes, the more complex the piece is considered to be (Davies 1978; Knopoff and Hutchinson 1983; Lipscomb 1988). However, if an entire piece consisted only of "likely" notes, a listening audience would almost certainly find the piece extremely uninteresting. Therefore, the composer walks a tightrope, balancing innovation with familiarity.

With their higher level analyses, theories of global organization begin to address issues of emotional response and assignment of musical meaning. Meyer proposed that emotional response occurs "when an expectation—a tendency to respond—activated by the musical stimulus situation, is temporarily inhibited or permanently blocked" (1956, 31; see also Meyer 1967 and 1973; Narmour 1990).[22] To confirm this theory, play the first seven notes of the C major scale, stopping on the leading tone (B-natural). Notice that the generated melodic expectation causes listeners acculturated in the Western tradition to desire resolution

---

22. Meyer's theory of emotion in music is greatly influenced by John Dewey's (1894 and 1895) conflict theory of emotion.

upward to the tonic pitch (C). The same phenomenon can be illustrated harmonically by playing the following major key chord progression: I–vi–ii–V^7. In this case, there is a strong tendency for the listener to desire resolution to the tonic triad (C-E-G)—so strong, in fact, that a great deal of psychological tension can be produced by refusing to play the tonic chord. After a short period of time, play the submediant chord (A-C-E) instead of the tonic, and observe the listener's response. A complete discussion of emotional response to music is beyond the scope of this present chapter. For the interested reader, however, Dowling and Harwood (1986) provide an excellent discussion of various theories of emotion and meaning as applied to music (also see chap. 7 and 8).

The cognitive branch of music psychology is still in its infancy. A majority of the studies falling in this category continue to be overly reductionist in their methods, trading validity for reliability and control. Cook discusses this weakness, stating that many investigations "use test materials which are so impoverished that they do not really provide a context for musical perception at all" (1994, 67). It will be important in the future to incorporate musical contexts that more closely represent actual musical situations. Technological advances in recent years—particularly the advent of the multimedia personal computer—have provided a tool that will allow investigators to increase the validity of stimulus materials significantly, using digitally sampled sound files to enhance ecological validity (Lipscomb 1993 and 1996).

Another important methodological shift is underway. Until now, a typical empirical investigation has consisted of formulating a research question, determining the most reliable method for conducting an experiment, gathering subject data, and interpreting the responses as a means of reaching a valid conclusion. It is now possible—and practical, with current technology—to use multiple methods (e.g., similarity scaling, categorization, etc.) to converge on the answer to a given research question. Use of multiple methods significantly increases the reliability of resulting conclusions and, in addition, allows a comparative means for analyzing various research methods (Kendall and Carterette 1992). It would also be advantageous to approach research questions from multiple philosophical perspectives. The process of musical investigation will be greatly enhanced by cross-disciplinary, collaborative research among musicians, psychologists, neurologists, and theorists.

In the time since Helmholtz's pioneering work in 1863, a significant amount of knowledge has been acquired about how the human mind processes music—but there is still a great deal to learn. As long as issues remain unresolved, there will be music psychologists anxious to tackle them in an effort to bring us closer to a true understanding of the processes involved in the cognitive organization of musical sound. This realization will, in turn, advance our knowledge of general functions of the human mind.

REFERENCES

Aiello, R. 1994a. Can listening to music be experimentally studied? In *Music perceptions*, ed. R. Aiello, 273–82. New York: Oxford University Press.

Aiello, R. 1994b. Music and language: Parallels and contrasts. In *Music perceptions*, ed. R. Aiello, 40–63. New York: Oxford University Press.

Anderson, J. R. 1985. *Cognitive psychology and its implications*. 2d ed. New York: Freeman.

Arom, S. 1985. De lí Écoute ‡ lí analyse des musiques Centrafricaines. *Analyse Musicale* 1:35–39.

Arom, S. 1988. Du pied ‡ la main: Les fondements mètriques des musiques traditionnelles dí Afrique Centrale. *Analyse Musicale* 10:16–23.

Assal, G. 1973. Aphasie de Wernicke sans amusie chez un pianiste. *Revue Neurologique* 129:251–55.

Atkinson, R. C., and R. M. Shiffrin. 1968. Human memory: A proposed system and its control processes. In *The psychology of learning and motivation: Advances in research and theory*, Vol. 2, ed. K. W. Spence and J. T. Spence, 89–195. New York: Academic Press.

Attneave, F., and R. K. Olson. 1971. Pitch as medium: A new approach to psychophysical scaling. *American Journal of Psychology* 84:147–66.

Bartlett, F. C. 1932. *Remembering*. Cambridge: Cambridge University Press.

Bartlett, J. C., and W. J. Dowling. 1980. The recognition of transposed melodies: A key-distance effect in developmental perspective. *Journal of Experimental Psychology: Human Perception and Performance* 6:501–15.

Benton, A. L. 1977. The amusias. In *Music and the brain*, ed. M. Critchley and R. A. Henson, 378–97. Springfield, IL: Charles C. Thomas.

Bernstein, L. 1976. *The unanswered question: Six talks at Harvard*. Cambridge, MA: Harvard University Press.

Bharucha, J. J. 1994. Tonality and expectation. In *Music perceptions*, ed. R. Aiello, 213–39. New York: Oxford University Press.

Bigand, E. 1993. Contributions of music to research on human auditory cognition. In *Thinking in Sound*, trans. D. Dusinberre, ed. S. McAdams and E. Bigand, 231–77. Oxford: Clarendon Press.

Bolton, T. L. 1894. Rhythm. *American Journal of Psychology*, 6:145–238.

Bregman, A. S. 1990. *Auditory scene analysis*. Cambridge, MA: MIT Press.

Bregman, A. S. 1993. Auditory scene analysis: Hearing in complex environments. In *Thinking in sound*, ed. S. McAdams and E. Bigand, 10–36. Oxford: Clarendon Press.

Bregman, A. S., and Dannenbring, G.L. 1973. Auditory continuity and amplitude edges. *Canadian Journal of Psychology*, 31:151–159.

Brown, H., and Butler, D. 1981. Diatonic trichords as minimal tonal cue-cells. *In Theory Only*, 5, nos. 6 and 7:39–55.

Bruner, J. S., J. J. Goodnow, and G. A. Austin. 1986. *A study of thinking*. New Brunswick, NJ: Transaction.

Brust, J. 1980. Music and language: Musical alexia and agraphia. *Brain*, 103:367–92.

Butler, D. 1979a. A further study of melodic channeling. *Perception and Psychophysics*, 25:264–68.

Butler, D. 1979b. Melodic channeling in a musical environment. In *Research Symposium on the Psychology and Acoustics of Music*, ed. W. May, 101–18. Lawrence, KS: University of Kansas.

Butler, D., and H. Brown. 1994. Describing the mental representation of tonality in music. In *Music perceptions*, ed. R. Aiello, 191–212. New York: Oxford University Press.

Campbell, W. C. , and J. Heller. 1980. An orientation for considering models of musical behavior. In *Handbook of music psychololgy*, ed. D. Hodges, 29–36. Lawrence, KS: National Association for Music Therapy.

Carlsen, J. C. 1981. Some factors which influence melodic expectancy. *Psychomusicology* 1:12–29.

Carlsen, J. C., P. L. Divenyi, and J. A. Taylor. 1970. A preliminary study of perceptual expectancy in melodic configurations. *Bulletin of the Council of Research in Music Education* 22:4–12.

Carterette, E. C., and R. A. Kendall. 1989. Human music perception. In *The comparative psychology of audition: Perceiving complex sounds*, ed. R. J. Dooling and S. H. Hulse, 131–72. Hillsdale, NJ: Lawrence Erlbaum Associates.

Carterette, E. C., C. B. Monahan, E. Holman, T. S. Bell, and R. A. Fiske. 1982. Rhythmic and melodic structures in perceptual space. *Journal of the Acoustical Society of America* 72,S1:S11A.

Chalikia, M. H., and R. M. Warren. 1990. Spectral factors in the organization of vowel sequences into words. *Journal of the Acoustical Society of America* 88,S1: S54A.

Charbonneau, G. R. 1981. Timbre and the perceptual effects of three types of data reduction. *Computer Music Journal* 5:10–19.

Cherry, E. C. 1953. Some experiments on the recognition of speech, with one and two ears. *Journal of the Acoustical Society of America* 25:975–79.

Chomsky, N. 1957. *Syntactic structures*. The Hague: Mouton.

Cook, N. 1994. Perception: A perspective from music theory. In *Music perceptions*, ed. R. Aiello, 64–95. New York: Oxford University Press.

Craik, F. I. M. 1991. Will cognitivism bury experimental psychology? *Canadian Psychology/Psychologie Canadienne* 32:440–44.

Crowder, R. G. 1993. Auditory memory. In *Thinking in sound*, ed. S. McAdams and E. Bigand, 113–45. Oxford: Clarendon Press.

Crowder, R. G., M. L. Serafine, and B. Repp. 1990. Physical interaction and association by contiguity in memory for the words and melodies of songs. *Memory and Cognition* 18:469–76

Cuddy, L., A. J. Cohen, and J. Miller. 1979. Melody recognition: The experimental application of musical rules. *Canadian Journal of Psychology* 33:148–57.

Dannenbring, G. L. 1976. Perceived auditory continuity with alternately rising and falling frequency transitions. *Canadian Journal of Psychology* 30:99–114.

Davies, J. B. 1978. *The psychology of music*. Stanford, CA: Stanford University Press.

Deutsch, D. 1970. Tones and numbers: Specificity of interference in short-term memory. *Science* 168:1604–5.

Deutsch, D. 1972. Octave generalization and tune recognition. *Perception and Psychophysics* 31:596–98.

Deutsch, D. 1975. The organization of short-term memory for a single acoustic attribute. In *Short-term memory*, ed. D. Deutsch and J. A. Deutsch, 107–51. New York: Academic Press.

Deutsch, D. 1982. Grouping mechanisms in music. In *The psychology of music*, ed. D. Deutsch, 99–134. New York: Academic Press.

Deutsch, D., and J. Feroe. 1981. The internal representation of pitch sequences in tonal music. *Psychological Review* 886:503–22.

Dewar, K. M., L. L. Cuddy, and D. J. K. Mewhort. 1977. Recognition memory for single tones with and without context. *Journal of Experimental Psychology: Human Learning and Memory* 3:60–67.

Dewey, J. 1894. The theory of emotion. *Psychological Review* 1:553–69.

Dewey, J. 1895. The theory of emotion. *Psychological Review* 2:13–32.

DeWitt, L. A., and R. G. Crowder. 1986. Recognition of novel melodies after brief delays. *Music Perception* 3:259–74.

Dorgeuille, C. 1966. Introduction ‡ lí Ètude des amusies. Ph.D. diss., Sorbonne, Paris.

Dowling, W. J. 1973. The perception of interleaved melodies. *Cognitive Psychology* 5:322–37.

Dowling, W. J. 1978. Scale and contour: Two components of a theory of memory for melodies. *Psychological Review* 85:341–54.

Dowling, W. J. 1994. Melodic contour in hearing and remembering melodies. In *Music perceptions*, ed. R. Aiello, 173–90. New York: Oxford University Press.

Dowling, W. J., and J. C. Bartlett. 1981. The importance of interval information in long-term memory for melodies. *Psychomusicology* 1:30–49.

Dowling, W. J., and D. S. Fujitani. 1971. Contour, interval, and pitch recognition in memory for melodies. *Journal of the Acoustical Society of America* 49:524–31.

Dowling, W. J., and D. W. Harwood. 1986. *Music cognition*. New York: Academic Press.

Dowling, W. J., and A. W. Hollombe. 1977. The perception of melodies distorted by splitting into several octaves: Effects of increasing proximity and melodic contour. *Perception and Psychophysics* 21:61–64.

Elliott, C. 1975. Attacks and releases as factors in instrument identification. *Journal of Research in Music Education* 23, no. 1:35–40.

Erikson, R. 1975. *Sound structure in music*. Berkeley, CA: University of California Press.

Fechner, G. T. [1860] 1966. *Elements of psychophysics*. Trans. H. E. Adler, ed. D. H. Howes and E. G. Boring. New York: Holt, Rinehart, and Winston.

Fraisse, P. 1982. Rhythm and tempo. In *The psychology of music*, ed. D. Deutsch, 149–80. New York: Academic Press.

Franklin, E. 1972. *Music education: Psychology and method.* Trans. E. Franklin. London: Harrap.

Gabrielsson, A. 1973a. Similarity ratings and dimension analyses of auditory rhythm patterns: I. *Scandinavian Journal of Psychology* 14:138–60.

Gabrielsson, A. 1973b. Similarity ratings and dimension analyses of auditory rhythm patterns: II. *Scandinavian Journal of Psychology* 14:161–76.

Gabrielsson, A. 1973c. Studies in rhythm. *Acta Universitatits Upsaliensis* 7:3–19.

Gescheider, G. A. 1985. *Psychophysics: Method, theory, and application.* 2d ed. Hillsdale, NJ: Lawrence Erlbaum Associates.

Grey, J. M. 1977. Multidimensional perceptual scaling of musical timbres. *Journal of the Acoustical Society of America* 61:1270–77.

Grey, J. M., and J. W. Gordon. 1978. Perceptual effects of spectral modifications on musical timbres. *Journal of the Acoustical Society of America* 63:1493–1500.

Grey, J. M., and J. A. Moorer. 1977. Perceptual evaluations of synthesized musical instrument tones. *Journal of the Acoustical Society of America* 62:454–62.

Guilford, J. P., and R. A. Hilton. 1933. Some configurational properties of short musical melodies. *Journal of Experimental Psychology* 16:32–54.

Guilford, J. P., and H. M. Nelson. 1936. Changes in pitch of tones when melodies are repeated. *Journal of Experimental Psychology* 19:193–202.

Guilford, J. P., and H. M. Nelson. 1937. The pitch of tones in melodies as compared with single tones. *Journal of Experimental Psychology* 20:309–35.

Guzman, A. 1969. Decomposition of a visual scene into three-dimensional bodies. In *Automatic interpretation and classification of images,* ed. A. Grasselli, 243–76. New York: Academic Press.

Halpern, A. R. 1988. Mental scanning in auditory imagery for songs. *Journal of Experimental Psychology: Learning, Memory, and Cognition* 14:434–43.

Halpern, A. R. 1992. Musical aspects of auditory imagery. In *Auditory imagery,* ed. D. Reisberg, 1–27. Hillsdale, NJ: Lawrence Erlbaum Associates.

Handel, S., and G. R. Lawson. 1983. The contextual nature of rhythmic interpretation. *Perception and Psychophysics* 34:103–20.

Helmholtz, H. L. F. von. [1863] 1954. *On the sensations of tone as a physiological basis for the theory of music.* Trans. A. J. Ellis. New York: Dover.

Idson, W. L., and D. W. Massaro. 1978. A bidimensional model of pitch in the recognition of melodies. *Perception and Psychophysics* 24:554–65.

James, W. [1890] 1950. *The principles of psychology.* New York: Dover Publications.

Jellinek, A. 1956. Amusia. *Folia Phonetica* 8:124–49.

Jones, M. R. 1981a. Music as a stimulus for psychological motion: Part 1, Some determinates of expectancies. *Psychomusicology* 2:34–51.

Jones, M. R. 1981b. Music as a stimulus for psychological motion: Part 2, An expectancy model. *Psychomusicology* 2:1–13.

Jones, M. R., and W. Yee. 1993. Attending to auditory events: The role of temporal organization. In *Thinking in sound,* ed. S. McAdams and E. Bigand, 69–112. Oxford: Clarendon Press.

Kallman, H. J., and D. W. Massaro. 1979. Tone chroma is functional in melody recognition. *Perception and Psychophysics* 26:32–36.

Kendall, R. A. 1980. Difference thresholds for timbre related to amplitude spectra of complex sounds. Master's thesis, University of Kansas.

Kendall, R. A. 1986. The role of acoustic signal partitions in listener categorization of musical phrases. *Music Perception* 4:185–213.

Kendall, R. A., and E. C. Carterette. 1990. The communication of musical expression. *Music Perception* 82:129–64.

Kendall, R. A., and E. C. Carterette. 1991. Perceptual scaling of simultaneous wind instrument timbres. *Music Perception* 84:369–404.

Kendall, R. A., and E. C. Carterette. 1992. Convergent methods in psychomusical research based on integrated, interactive computer control. *Behavior Research Methods, Instruments and Computers* 24, no. 2:116–31.

Knopoff, L., and W. Hutchinson. 1983. Entropy as a measure of style: The influence of sample length. *Journal of Music Theory* 27:75–97.

Koffka, K. 1935. *The principles of Gestalt psychology*. New York: Harcourt, Brace.

Köhler, W. 1929. *Gestalt psychology*. New York: Liveright.

Krumhansl, C. L. 1979. The psychological representation of pitch in a tonal context. *Cognitive Psychology* 11:346–74.

Krumhansl, C. L. 1989. Why is musical timbre so hard to understand? In *Structure and perception of electroacoustic sound and music: Excerpta Medica*, ed. S. Nielzen and O. Olsson, 43–53. Amsterdam: Elsevier.

Krumhansl, C. L. 1990. *Cognitive foundations of musical pitch*. New York: Oxford University Press.

Lerdahl, F., and R. Jackendoff. 1983. *A generative grammar of tonal music*. Cambridge, MA: MIT Press.

Lipscomb, S. D. 1988. Information theory: A valid analytical tool for determining stylistic variation? Typescript.

Lipscomb, S. D. 1993. Advances in music technology: The effect of multimedia on musical learning and musicological investigation. In *Proceedings of the Conference on Technological Directions in Music Education*, ed. D. Sebald, 77–97. San Antonio: Institute for Music Research, University of Texas at San Antonio.

Lipscomb, S. D. 1995. The personal computer as research tool and music educator. In *Proceedings of the Second Conference on Technological Directions in Music Education*, ed. K. Walls, 169–73. San Antonio: Institute for Music Research, University of Texas at San Antonio.

Lipscomb, S. D., and R. A. Kendall. 1996. Perceptual judgment of the relationship between musical and visual components in film. *Psychomusicology* 13, no. 1:122–60.

Lundin, R. W. 1985. *An objective psychology of music*. 3d ed. Malabar, FL: Robert E. Krieger.

MacDougall, R. 1903. The structure of simple rhythm forms. *Psychological Review, Monograph Supplements* 4:309–416.

Marin, O. 1982. Neurological aspects of music perception and performance. In *The psychology of music*, ed. D. Deutsch, 453–77. Orlando, FL: Academic Press.

Matlin, M. W. 1994. *Cognition*. 3d ed. New York: Harcourt Brace Jovanovich.

Mavlov, L. 1980. Amusia due to rhythm agnosia in a musician with left hemisphere damage: A nonauditory supramodal defect. *Cortex* 16:321–38.

McAdams, S. 1993. Recognition of sound sources and events. In *Thinking in sound*, ed. S. McAdams and E. Bigand, 146–98. Oxford: Clarendon Press.

McAdams, S., and E. Bigand. 1993. Introduction to auditory cognition. In *Thinking in sound*, ed. S. McAdams and E. Bigand, 1–9. Oxford: Clarendon Press.

Meyer, L. B. 1956. *Emotion and meaning in music.* Chicago: University of Chicago Press.

Meyer, L. B. 1967. *Music, the arts, and ideas: Patterns and predictions in twentieth-century culture.* Chicago: University of Chicago Press.

Meyer, L. B. 1973. *Explaining music: Essays and explorations.* Berkeley, CA: University of California Press.

Miller, G. 1956. The magical number seven, plus or minus two: Some limits of our capacity for processing information. *Psychological Review* 63:81–97.

Miller, G. A., and G. Heise. 1950. The trill threshold. *Journal of the Acoustical Society of America* 22:637–38.

Miller, G. A., and J. C. R. Licklider. 1950. The intelligibility of interrupted speech. *Journal of the Acoustical Society of America* 22:167–73.

Miller, J. R., and E. C. Carterette. 1975. Perceptual space for musical structures. *Journal of the Acoustical Society of America* 58:711–20.

Moles, A. 1968. *Information theory and esthetic perception.* Urabana, IL: University of Illinois Press.

Monahan, C. B. 1984. Parallels between pitch and time: The determinants of musical space. Ph.D. diss., University of California, Los Angeles.

Monahan, C. B., and E. C. Carterette. 1985. Pitch and duration as determinants of musical space. *Music Perception* 31:1–32.

Monahan, C. B., R. A. Kendall, and E. C. Carterette, 1987. The effect of melodic and temporal contour on recognition memory for pitch change. *Perception and Psychophysics* 416:576–600.

Narmour, E. 1977. *Beyond Schenkerianism: The need for alternatives in music analysis.* Chicago: University of Chicago Press.

Narmour, E. 1983. Some major theoretical problems concerning the concept of hierarchy in the analysis of tonal music. *Music Perception* 1:129–99.

Narmour, E. 1990. *The analysis and cognition of basic melodic structures: The implication-realization model.* Chicago: University of Chicago Press.

Neisser, U. 1967. *Cognitive psychology.* New York: Appleton-Century-Crofts.

Neisser, U. 1979. The control of information pickup in selective looking. In *Perception and its development*, ed. A. D. Pick, 210–19. Hillsdale, NJ: Lawrence Erlbaum Associates.

Neisser, U., and R. Becklen. 1975. Selective looking: Attending to visually significant events. *Cognitive Psychology* 7:480–94.

Pechmann, T., and G. Mohr. 1992. Interference in memory for tonal pitch: Implications for a working memory model. *Memory and Cognition* 20:314–20.

Peretz, I. 1993. Auditory agnosia: A functional analysis. In *Thinking in sound*, ed. S. McAdams and E. Bigand, 199–230. Oxford: Clarendon Press.

Povel, D. J. 1981. The internal representation of simple temporal patterns. *Journal of Experimental Psychology: Human Perception and Performance* 7:3–18.

Roederer, J. G. 1979. *Introduction to the physics and psychophysics of music.* 2d ed. New York: Springer-Verlag.

Rumelhart, D. E., and J. L. McClelland. 1986. *Parallel distributed processing: Explorations in the microstructure of cognition.* 2 vols. Cambridge, MA: MIT Press.

Saldanha, E., and J. F. Corso. 1964. Timbre cues and the identification of musical instruments. *Journal of the Acoustical Society of America* 36:2021–26.

Sandell, G. 1989a. Effect of spectrum and attack properties on the evaluation of concurrently sounding timbres. *Journal of the Acoustical Society of America* 86:S:S59A.

Sandell, G. 1989b. Perception of concurrent timbres and implications for orchestration. *Proceedings, International Computer Music Conference*, 268–72. Columbus, OH.

Schenker, H. [1935] 1979. *Free composition [Der freie satz].* Trans. E. Oster. New York: Longman.

Schiffman, S. S., M. L. Reynolds, and F. W. Young. 1981. *Introduction to multidimensional scaling.* New York: Academic Press.

Schmuckler, M. A. 1989. Expectation in music: Investigation of melodic and harmonic processes. *Music Perception* 7:109–50.

Schouten, J. F. 1962. On the perception of sound and speech: Subjective time analysis. Fourth International Congress on Acoustics, Copenhagen Congress Report 2:201–3.

Seashore, C. E. 1938. *The psychology of music.* New York: Dover.

Semal, C., and L. Demany. 1991. Dissociation of pitch from timbre in auditory short-term memory. *Journal of the Acoustical Society of America* 89:2404–10.

Serafine, M. L., R. G. Crowder, and B. Repp. 1984. Integration of melody and text in memory for song. *Cognition* 16:285–303.

Serafine, M. L., J. Davidson, R. G. Crowder, and B. Repp. 1986. On the nature of melody-text integration in memory for songs. *Journal of Memory and Language* 25:123–35.

Shaffer, L. H., and N. P. Todd. 1994. The interpretive component in musical performance. In *Music perceptions*, ed. R. Aiello, 258–70. New York: Oxford University Press.

Shannon, C. E., and W. Weaver. 1949. *The mathematical theory of communication.* Urbana, IL: University of Illinois Press.

Thurlow, W. 1957. An auditory figure-ground effect. *American Journal of Psychology* 70:653–54.

Todd, N. P. 1985. A model of expressive timing in tonal music. *Music Perception* 3:33–58.

Treisman, A. M. 1988. Features and objects: The fourteenth Bartlett Memorial Lecture. *Quarterly Journal of Experimental Psychology* 40A:201–37.

Treisman, A. M., and G. Gelade. 1980. A feature-integration theory of attention: Cognitive postion. In *Thinking in sound*, trans. D. Dusinberre, ed. S. McAdams and E. Bigand, 231–77. Oxford: Clarendon Press.

Tulving, E. 1983. *Elements of episodic memory.* New York: Oxford University Press.

Van Noorden, L. P. A. S. 1975. Temporal coherence in the perception of tone sequences. Ph.D. diss., Technische Hogeschoel Eindhoven, The Netherlands.

Vicario, G. 1960. Lí effetto tunnel acustico. *Revista di Psycologia* 54:41–52.

Warren, R. M. 1970. Perceptual restoration of missing speech sounds. *Science*

167:392–93.

Warren, R. M. 1993. Perception of acoustic sequences: Global integration versus temporal resolution. In *Thinking in sound*, ed. S. McAdams and E. Bigand, 37–68. Oxford: Clarendon Press.

Warren, R. M., D. A. Gardner, B. S. Brubaker, and J. A. Bashford, Jr. 1991. Melodic and nonmelodic sequences of tones: Effects of duration on perception. *Music Perception* 8:277–90.

Warren, R. M., C. J. Obusek, and J. M. Ackroff. 1972. Auditory induction: Perceptual synthesis of absent sounds. *Science* 176:1149–51.

Wertheim, N. 1963. Disturbances of the musical functions. In *Problems of dynamic neurology*, ed. L. Halpern, 162–80. Jerusalem: Jerusalem Press.

Wertheim, N. 1969. The amusias. In *Handbook of clinical neurology*, vol. 4, ed. P. J. Vinken and G. W. Bruyn, 195–206. Amsterdam: North-Holland.

Wertheim, N. 1977. Is there an anatomical localization for musical faculties? In *Music and the brain*, ed. M. Critchley and R.A. Henson, 282–300. Springfield, IL: Thomas.

Wertheimer, N. 1923. Untersuchung zur Lehre von der Gestalt II. *Psychologische Forschung* 4:301–50.

White, B. W. 1960. Recognition of distorted melodies. American Journal of Psychology 73:100–7.

6

Tonal And Musical Memory

Dale L. Bartlett

Insofar as it is known, the ability to recall, or have memory of, the auditory sensation of music is not unlike the memory process for any other sensory experience. This memory process may be described rather generally: sensory perception (stimulus input), establishment of a memory trace, manipulation of trace information through some rehearsal strategy, storage of information into levels or states of retention, storage retrieval, and performance of retained information (output).

Possessing a good memory is an important attribute for persons who desire to be musicians, and the demands that different musical behaviors (listening, performing, composing, conducting) place on the memory system are complex, exacting, and may require different types of "memory behavior." For example, consider the ways in which stored musical information may be recalled and displayed behaviorally. One kind of memory involves hearing and comprehending musical sounds internally without the physical presence of the sound stimulus or what Gordon calls audiation (1977). Gordon differentiates mere memorization, a process that is ". . . primarily related to learning [instrumental] fingerings and other technical matters, . . ." (1993, 17) from audiation, a process of giving meaning to music through the hearing and comprehension of the musical syntax.

In audiation, memory is involved because one must mentally store the various qualities of music in order to have an internal resource to refer to and to participate in the communication of music, either as a listener, for example, or as a performer. Possessing an internal resource might be considered similar to possessing an auditory image or internal representation of the various musical qualities leading to musical communication. Bergan defined an auditory image as "an auditory experience of realistic dimensions for which there is no apparent physical stimulus" (1965, 15), and asserted that pitch as a sound experience requires the utilization of mental processes that rely on a mental representation or tonal image of the sound itself, that is, a tonal image that closely approximates the actual experience of hearing against which one compares actual pitch. Although not associating their findings directly with the concept of audiation, Davies and Yelland (1977) interpreted their finding—subjects were able to demonstrate the ability to draw melodic contours of well-known tunes when given a period of silent rehearsal of the tunes as compared to listening to the tunes prior to drawing—as an indication of the presence of stored tonal representations.

Another kind of memory involves the external display by exact recall of a learned or "memorized" sequence of musical notes, a task perhaps more important to a concert pianist than to a composer who may rely more on audiation, although both aspects of the memory process are essential to both types of musicians. Also, it should be recognized there is not always an obvious relationship between a good memory and musical behavior. A pianist, again, will experience the need for a high degree of physical dexterity. Dexterity, however, does not assure remembering; that is, one may possess exceptional physical skills but lack the artistic expression necessary for achieving a high-quality performance. Of course, the reverse condition is just as plausible; all the notes may be recalled in proper sequence and with some degree of artistic ability, but a lack of adequate physical skills would certainly decrease the musical outcome of the performance.

There are many differences in individuals' abilities to remember. Such differences cover a variety of factors, not the least of which is that stimuli compete for attention and persons are known to have some difficulty maintaining attention to the memory task. For performers, the actual stress of the concert situation is often sufficient to cause a breakdown in memory. In such conditions, the storage retrieval task is in competition with stimuli produced internally as a result of an involuntary autonomic nervous system that often does not cooperate under performance stress situations. This example is a rather obvious one. Contemporary researchers are more interested in examining voluntary cognitive activity that will reveal reasons for memory limitations and for understanding at what stage, or under what conditions, memory breaks down or is enhanced.

The terms *tonal memory* and *musical memory*, as used in this chapter, are perhaps best defined operationally. Tonal memory tasks require the subject to determine whether a test tone is the same as or different than a standard tone. There may be stimulus items such as tones of different pitches that are situated between the test and standard tones, thus forming a sequence or string. These tones are normally presented by electronic instruments and are not necessarily based on musical parameters. Musical memory tasks (of which there are few in the literature) more often use melodic or harmonic material that is more familiar in structure; such stimuli are normally presented by acoustic (musical) instruments. In both cases, however, subjects are asked to interact with the stimulus and then make various kinds of judgments that focus on accuracy of recall.

Early Research on Tonal and Musical Memory

Interest in memory of tonal stimuli emerged in the very early 1900s. In one of the earliest published studies, Whipple (1901) asked six subjects to judge whether two tones, separated from each other by time intervals from 2 to 60 seconds, were the same, higher (+8 Hz), or lower (-8 Hz). Trial tones involved both clang tones (those produced by vibrating reeds) and tones produced by a blown-bottle apparatus. Though a relatively unsophisticated effort compared to present standards, Whipple did set forth what was to become a fundamental principle in our understanding of memory: An increase in the time interval between a test tone and a comparison tone causes a general decrease in accuracy of recall of the test tone. Such a finding can be applied easily to our experience with more complex recall situations in which it is found that the longer the period between input and output, the greater the likelihood of forgetting the input material.

Foremost among early research efforts on musical memory is a series of studies by Rubin-Rabson (1937, 1939, 1940a, 1940b, 1941a, 1941b, 1941c, and 1941d) on the memorization of piano music. Her interest was in determining whether learning could be enhanced through selected music practice methods, methods with established theoretical bases as promulgated by contemporary psychologists.

An example of this type of research is one in which she tested the theory that a difference in learning efficiency and retention of the material might be accomplished depending on whether one practiced the music using a whole method approach rather than a part method approach (1940b). Nine persons from 19 to 24 years of age were the subjects, the mean number of years of piano instruction being 11.4. The test music included nine, eight-measure unfamiliar musical phrases practiced in three different units: (1) as a whole, (2) in two parts, and (3) in four parts. The test for memorization was accomplished by having the subjects transcribe the learned score on paper. With this type of memory task, no differences were found among subjects using the three practice methods.

R. W. Brown (1928) researched the whole and part methods of learning many years earlier, adding a "combination" approach, and found

the whole method of learning piano music to give generally better results, with the part method producing the least efficiency. In Brown's
study, the memorization task was to perform the music on the piano
without error. O'Brien (1943), in contrast, concluded the part method
was a more economical way of memorizing music.

If one examines the findings of the various studies related to those
of Rubin-Rabson, Brown, and O'Brien, it is apparent that experimental
designs representing the kinds of conclusions described above may tend
to favor one method of practice over another depending, at least, on the
length or complexity of the music (both Brown and O'Brien used up to
32-measure pieces; Rubin-Rabson used mostly 8-measure pieces). The
use of subjects with highly advanced piano skills would, also, tend to
distort the findings because of their well-established practice strategies
that, individually, likely would not succumb easily to contrived practice
techniques. Whether subjects actually performed the music or transcribed
it on paper could further confound the results. Additionally, measuring
behavior that supposedly is based on Gestalt experience (the whole
method approach) is subject to imprecise operational definition necessary for experimental control.

Standardized Measures of Tonal Memory

Seashore emphasized the importance of tonal memory research by incorporating a subtest for this behavior in his renowned *Seashore Measures of Musical Talents* (Seashore, Lewis, and Saetveit 1939). Practically
every standardized test of musical aptitude and achievement to follow
his initial attempt has some type of test for tonal or musical memory (a
major exception, of course, is Gordon's *Musical Aptitude Profile*, first
published in 1965, which measures tonal imagery, for example, in contrast to tonal memory). Although Seashore was not convinced that
memory was an all-encompassing attribute for musicianship, he at least
placed its importance in the "serviceable" category. "While retentive and
serviceable memory is a very great asset to a musical person, it is not at
all an essential condition for musical-mindedness." He further stated,
"The musical mind that can reproduce many repertories with precision
is, however, a different mind from one which has neither large scope
nor fidelity in retention nor reproduction. But both may be musical"
(Seashore 1967, 7).

The Seashore test includes a tonal memory test of thirty pairs of
tonal sequences played by an electronic organ. These sequences are divided into ten pairs of three notes each, ten pairs of four notes each, and
ten pairs of five notes each. The first sequence of each pair is played,

followed by the second presentation of the sequence, in which one tone is altered. The listener's task is to remember by numerical association which tone was altered; for example, whether the first, second, or third tone in a three-tone sequence was different in the second presentation.

To the psychologist studying memory, Seashore's measurement format might appear a little simplistic and relatively superficial as an indicator of even a "serviceable" memory; interestingly, Vispoel (1993) demonstrated through computerized adaptive testing that Seashore's 30-item memory test could be reduced to 5–12 items and still retain reliability levels of .80–.90. In addition, both Ortmann (1926) and Heinlein (1928) discussed the seeming impossibility of anyone altering a tone of a melodic sequence without such alteration affecting the psychological status of other tones (also see Taylor and Pembrook 1984 for a follow-up of Ortmann's work in identifying such determinants or variables as note repetition and conjunct-disjunct motion as they relate to immediate recall of short melodies). And, perhaps more objectively, there should be as much concern for Seashore's short span of tones (three to five) and his lack of discussion related to the degree of difficulty associated with the particular tones altered for recognition (a matter of serial position).

Wing (1970) constructed the *Standardized Tests of Musical Intelligence* and, like Seashore, included a subtest for memory. Wing incorporated some changes from Seashore's test. He claimed to have made the tonal items more musical (it seems apparent this was achieved in that both melodic and rhythmic components comprise the tonal sequences); also, he allowed the tones to be played on the piano and extended the sequences to ten tones. Wing believed these changes would improve the test by creating test items that more closely approximate melodies and by providing more interest for those with high musical capacity.

Drake published a musical memory test in 1934 that was incorporated in 1954 into the *Drake Musical Aptitude Tests*. Reference to musical memory should be noted because most other measures of this nature are labeled tonal memory. Accounting for musical memory is, for Drake, the task of remembering changes, if any, in key, time, and note. The test includes two equivalent forms, twelve standard melodies in each form. The respondent is required to listen to the melody and then hear the melody again to determine whether it is the same or whether there is a key change, a time change, or a note change.

The twelve test items require from two to seven repetitions. After the melody is played in its original form, it may not be in this form again throughout the repetitions, although those test items with many repetitions usually include a "same" response, thus reinforcing one's identification of the original melody. The Drake test format is a bit complicated on the surface; however, it does provide for an interesting discussion of short-term memory capability in reference to interference and the need for one to establish rehearsal strategies in order to make meaningful comparisons between the standard melody and its repetitions.

The last music test to be mentioned here is one by Bentley (1966a). His *Measures of Musical Ability* contains a subtest for tonal memory. Of special interest, as a chronological reference, is his concern for "serial position," that is, the placement of a particular note in a tonal sequence. His tonal memory test contains ten items of paired comparisons, each item of the pair containing five tones. The second sequence of the pair is either the same or different. If different, the listener must indicate the specific note altered. Bentley's ten items are divided into serial position changes "equally but randomly distributed between the first and the fifth [tones]" (1966a, 61). Also, for each note change in the sequence, five are of a semitone and five of a whole tone, one for each change in serial position. Thus, it can be seen that Bentley has systematically considered the importance of serial position and degree of test-tone change (research deals with these factors quite extensively as possible inducers of memory failure). Based on his findings regarding serial position of altered tones, Bentley made the following statement.

> The last note was clearly the one most easily remembered, and the first was the most difficult to recall. There is not much difference in difficulty between the first and the third, nor again between the second and the fourth. In fact, apart from the last note, there is insufficient evidence for conclusions concerning the relative difficulty of the first four sounds. (1966b, 113)

These findings conflict slightly with Ortmann's (1926), who reported the first and last notes in a sequence were more easily recalled than the note(s) between (perhaps only because Ortmann chose not to examine more closely slight differences in recall between the first and last tones in a melodic sequence). Bentley's findings showed 41.6 percent errors when recalling the first tone and only 19.5 percent errors when recalling the last. As he points out, this difference hardly appears to place equal difficulty on the two serial positions in question.

Theories of Memory

Psychologists have produced an abundance of information in the field of memory with the majority of such research studies dealing with visual and verbal stimuli. From such research has come theoretical models describing the memory process as basically a two-phase system; that is, short-term and long-term memory (Adams 1967; Norman 1970; Spear and Riccio 1994; Underwood 1976). There appears to be sufficient evidence to suggest a three-phase system, adding an intermediate retention level to the more thoroughly developed short- and long-term levels (Tallarico 1974; Wickelgren 1970) or, as neither a stage-specific storage system but, rather, a system that accommodates a continuous storage process lasting different periods of time (Arnold 1984). Additionally, to further complicate our understanding of memory storage systems, and to illustrate that memory includes more than just the ability to recall, Russell (1979) has posed several "varieties" of memory experience: episodic, factual, semantic, sensory, skills, instinctive, collective, and past-life.

The greatest research interest has been demonstrated for short-term (STM) or immediate memory (and practically all the research on tonal and musical memory is of this type). Short-term memory is more easily researched because testing requires relatively brief time periods for subject response and because there are, at this level, fewer complicating processes (associative processes) that are found in the higher, central-processing systems more directly related to long-term memory

The research literature is oriented toward an explanation of "forgetting." Once stimuli are perceived and memory traces are established (a very rapid neural process), the question arises as to what factors seem most influential in disrupting or enabling the recall process.[1] The kinds of factors studied in research on music-related stimuli have included disruptive effects of intervening stimuli, serial position of stimulus items to be recalled, period of time between stimulus perception and subject report, length of stimulus sequence or amount of information that can be retained, and effects of melodic contour, tonality, and musical structure.

Research on Tonal and Musical Memory Since 1953

One of the most prolific researchers of memory for tonal stimuli is Deutsch.[2] Through a series of articles, she has demonstrated rather clearly that, in short-term memory (STM), there are systematic disruptive or facilitatory effects on recall of a standard tone due to intervening tones of prescribed intervallic relationship to the standard tone or due to selected verbal

---

1. For early discussion of trace decay theory, see Broadbent 1958.
2. For more complete discussions of auditory memory for musical stimuli, see Deutsch 1975a and 1977.

stimuli unrelated to the standard tone. Her research designs have been similar in format: A standard tone is presented, followed by the intervening stimuli and then the test tone. Subjects must determine whether the test tone is the same as, or different than, the standard tone.

In one of her early studies, Deutsch (1970) utilized four conditions. In condition 1, six tones of equal loudness composed the intervening stimuli; the subjects were instructed to ignore these stimuli and judge whether the test tone was the same or different than the standard tone. The total sequence of eight tones lasted two seconds. Condition 2 utilized six spoken numbers of equal loudness with subjects instructed to ignore the numbers; other variables were the same. In condition 3, subjects were instructed to recall the six numbers in their correct order after having judged the test tone same or different than the standard. Condition 4 was similar to condition 2, except the test tone was always the same as the standard (as the subjects were told); subjects were to write "same" followed by the numbers in correct order. Twelve judgments were made in each condition. Deutsch concluded: "Considerable interference was produced by the intervening tones, even though they could be ignored. . . . However, the intervening spoken numbers caused only a minimum decrement" (Deutsch 1970, 1604). As might be expected, similar findings tended to generalize across octaves (Deutsch 1973b).

According to Wang and Sogin (1990), although listeners were able to recall melodic fragments of tonal sequences in the presence of interfering stimuli, spoken numbers can interfere in the tonal recognition task when the tones are of sequential nature and perceptual grouping is activated. Apparently, memory decay is related to specific interactive effects with certain types of information stored in memory (e.g., acoustic as compared to semantic encoding; see Gruneberg and Morris 1978) and not "merely as a limitation in general short-term memory capacity, or distraction of attention" (Deutsch 1970, 1604; also see Massaro 1970).

Deutsch further demonstrated systematic interactive effects by including a tone (or tones) identical to either of the standard and comparison tones in the intervening sequence. Errors in judgments were reduced significantly when an interpolated tone was identical to the standard tone and increased significantly when the interpolated tone was identical to the comparison (test) tone. Other conditions investigated also continued to indicate "that tonal pitch deteriorates rapidly in the presence of other tones" (Deutsch 1972b, 162). A similar study (1973a), in which inclusion of an intervening tone that was a semitone higher or lower than the standard tone, produced an increase in errors and an even greater increase in errors when incorporating two such tones in the intervening sequence. In a later study, Deutsch (1975b) corroborated these findings by inserting a tone in the second serial position of the intervening sequence that was the same pitch as the standard tone and then comparing this condition with one in which the inserted tone, at standard-tone pitch, was located in the fifth serial position. Recall of the standard tone was significantly greater in the second serial position condition.

Elliot (1970) also measured pitch memory in the presence of an interpolated tone of different frequency between standard and comparison tones. In this study, one interpolated tone was placed either just after the standard tone or just prior to the comparison tone. Judgments of the comparison tone were in the form of higher or lower; each standard and comparison tone was 300 ms in length with an eight-second interval between them. Results demonstrated greater interference is caused by the interpolated tone when it follows the standard tone than when it is placed before the comparison tone. Interference effects were clearly shown by the fact that when no interpolated tone was present (an unfilled, eight-second interval), constant errors were, in comparison, not produced, nor was the time span determined to be unduly detrimental. In like manner, Aiken and Lau (1966) found no significant variation in correct judgments of pitch recall whether tones were separated by 0.95, 4.50, or 8.90 seconds.

Based on previous findings suggesting that pitch memory decay is a function of interactive effects and not merely STM capacity, Deutsch (1972a) researched the possible orderly process that takes place in pitch memory with interactions between critical tonal relationships and serial position. Applying the intervening tonal sequence format in eight conditions, she varied the intervallic relationship between the pitch of the first test tone (standard) and the pitch of the tone in the second serial position of the intervening sequence of six tones. This relationship varied from unison to one whole tone. Using frequency relationships of the equal-tempered scale, the critical tones in the different conditions consisted of equal intervals of 1/6 tone and included interval relationships of a unison, 1/6 of a whole tone, 1/3, 1/2, 2/3, 5/6, and a whole tone. The eighth condition did not contain a second tone of critical relationship, serving only as a null baseline for comparison.

Deutsch found a significant decrease in errors, that is, judging the comparison tone as same or different than the standard tone, when the critical tone was identical to the standard. In addition, as the difference in pitch between the critical and standard tones increased, errors increased systematically and peaked at 2/3 tone, approaching null at one whole tone.

Interestingly, Deutsch and Feroe (1975) showed that a mutual inhibitory interaction (in this case, a reverse inhibitory effect causing a decrease in the original inhibition) occurs when the peak disruptive tone of 2/3 intervallic relationship to the standard tone is placed in the second serial position of the interpolated sequence and another tone of critical relationship to the disruptive tone is interpolated in the fourth serial position. The more the second critical tone bore a 2/3 tone relationship to the disruptive tone, the more a substantial return in recognition of the standard tone resulted.

Serial position is, of course, not an isolated factor in determining successful recall of tones in sequence. Williams (1975) designed an experiment to measure the main effects and interactions of sequence length (three, five, and seven tones), tone positions (primary/first pitch, center/middle pitch, and recency/last pitch), and delay times between stimulus termination and subject response (immediate response to 15-second delay). His findings concurred with previous research on STM in that information loss is influenced significantly by each of the three variables measured. In addition, the results regarding the interaction of the three variables showed significantly that retention of a pitch sequence is not strictly a function of these individual variables but "is confounded by their combined effects . . . item decay for pitch is a selective function of time decay depending upon the pitch position within a sequence" (Williams 1975, 62).

Williams (1975) suggested that loss of memory for pitch is more a function of melody length than of time decay (also see Norman 1966). Immediate recall of the last tone, regardless of sequence length, produced approximately the same degree of accuracy (95 percent). For the three-, five-, and seven-tone sequences, recall of the first tone resulted in accuracy of 95, 85, and 77 percent, respectively. After a two-second delay report, the accuracy figures for the first tone resulted in 93, 79, and 65 percent for three-, five-, and seven-tone sequences, respectively, and a 7.5-second delay produced first tone accuracy of 91, 74, and 54 percent. Recall accuracy from the center of the sequence was approximately the same whether the time delay for reporting was immediate, 2.0 seconds, or 7.5 seconds; that is, recall of the middle pitch of the three-tone sequence was 92 percent regardless of delay time. Thus, loss of information from the middle of the melody seems entirely dependent upon the melody length and not upon time delay in reporting.

The recency effect shown in the results of Williams's study,[3] and typically found when one is asked to recall the last item or items of a series, has been analyzed by Crowder and Morton (1969); accordingly,

---

3. See Russell 1979 for reference to the standard serial position curve or U-curve in relation to primacy and recency effects of recalled events.

the last item receives the benefit of sensory traces established by prior items in the series and is described as precategorical acoustic storage (PAS). Leshowitz and Hanzi (1974) and Foreit (1976) adopted the PAS model to nonlinguistic material (tonal sequences) and their results seem to support that concept, providing at least some theoretical explanation of the effect. Roberts's (1986) investigation of recency and suffix effects for written music reportedly refutes the PAS model, supporting more general sensory or STM theories.

Another factor that has been shown to play a part in memory for melodic material is contour. According to Dowling and Fujitani (1971) and Dowling and Bartlett (1981), the pattern of relationships (contour) is a greater facilitator of STM for brief melodies than specific interval recognition, especially for transposed melodies; Edworthy (1982) demonstrated, also, that contour of short melodies played a significant role in recall tasks involving short melodies. However, for familiar melodies, exact interval size, and not just contour characteristics, was concluded to play a more important role in long-term memory, a finding that Davies (1979) argues may not necessarily hold in respect to melodic configuration and interval manipulation of the stimulus material. White (1960) found that both relative interval size and contour were important factors in recognition of distortion of familiar melodies. Balch (1984) reported that abstraction of contour information was demonstrated more efficiently with visual stimuli, rather than melodic stimuli, and suggested recall may well depend on the form of stimulus input.

In testing children for their ability to remember tonal sequences, Huntsinger and Jose (1991) found all the children waited to hear the entire melody before accepting or rejecting it and considered this outcome associated with the importance of the contour factor. Interestingly, Huntsinger and Jose found these same children reported their use of the first and last digits in recalling digit sequences to be a sufficient clue to the correct response—there was no apparent reliance on the relationship of one digit to the next or to whether the digits formed any sense of contour. Though the concept is difficult to explain, M-shaped melodies appear easier to remember than V-shaped melodies (Long 1977).

The influence of musical structure and components of structure on memory has been demonstrated by various authors. Bergan (1966) found the ability of subjects to match a variable tone to a standard using headphones was greater when the dB level was of moderate intensity (50 dB) in comparison to either a 25 dB or 75 dB level. Haack (1975), using a free-field listening format, reported that tonal memory test items from the *Seashore Measures of Musical Talents* were not significantly influenced by various loudness presentation levels (45 dB to 110 dB).

In other studies investigating influence of musical structure, Halpern (1984) found songs similar to each other were less accurately recalled than were distantly related songs. Memory for both pitch and rhythm was significantly greater when placed in a tonal-rhythmic context (Schellenberg and Moore 1985). Tones embedded in sequences constructed according to conventional rules of musical tonality were more easily recognized than tones from randomly constructed sequences (Dewar, Cuddy, and Mewhort 1977). Tonal melodies were easier to recall than atonal ones (Zenatti 1975); and, though this finding is confirmed by Pembrook (1986), he noted an interesting interaction effect with melody length in that as length increases, the ability to remember tones decreases regardless of the differences in tonal systems. On the other hand, subjects with little musical training showed no effective differences in recall of pitch whether from tonal or atonal melodies (Mikumo 1992). Long (1977) found music majors made fewer errors in recalling tones embedded in brief melodies that were tonal rather than atonal. Long attributed these results to the musicians' training and to the structure of the tonal melodies.

Long's conclusion that perception is dependent on learned systems reinforces the idea that memory processing can be facilitated by reordering or regrouping items. Miller (1956), for example, states that to increase the capacity for processing information, some technique is necessary to organize "bits" of information into familiar units or chunks. Dowling (1973) found this concept useful in demonstrating the effects of rhythmic grouping on chunking and memory for melodies. Madsen and Staum (1983) found relatively unsophisticated musicians significantly able to recall identical melodies when extremely similar melodies were interpolated between test and recall melodies, suggesting that melodies may function similarly to chunking of verbal material if one considers a melody to be a comprehensible unit in which the formation is less vulnerable to interference than unrelated single items.

Channel capacity for immediate memory is described by Miller as the "limit with which we can identify absolutely the magnitude of a unidimensional stimulus variable . . . [and] is usually somewhere in the neighborhood of seven" (1956, 90). O'Brien's (1953) study seemed to be confirmed by Miller's description of channel capacity in that only 18 of 110 subjects showed a memory span of more than 6 notes, and no subject succeeded in recalling more than 11 or 12 "nonmelodic" tones after a single hearing. Long (1977) found no significant differences between the effects of 7-pitch melodies and 11-pitch melodies and indicated the likelihood that Miller's allowance may be too limited. Pembrook (1986) appears to have confirmed Long's conclusion about limits by finding a large drop off in accuracy between 10 and 16 notes, suggesting the short-term memory limit for tones to fall somewhere between 10 and 16.

Consideration should be given, also, to the notion that tones in a melodic sequence are quite likely not "unidimensional units" as Miller might describe; rather, they contain such "multidimensional units" as pitch level, intervallic relationships of different character (for example, the perfect fifth and major third), chordal progressions, and cadence. These multiple dimensions found in tonal sequences likely provide recall cues, thereby extending the channel capacity for these types of short-term memory tasks.

Effects of Music on Memory

Though not in the same category as those discussed previously, it seems appropriate to draw the reader's attention to those studies that have focused on the effects of the music-listening experience prior to, and during, a memory task with the intention of enhancing memory for non-musical material. These studies demonstrated successfully that recall of verbal material (e.g., words or digits) in conjunction with songs was greater than recall of spoken words alone (Balch, Bowman, and Mohler 1992; Isern 1959; Jellison 1976; Myers 1979; Prickett and Moore 1991; Wallace 1994), and that other factors such as tempo were important elements associated with recall of lyrics (Smith 1991). Morton, Kershner, and Siegel (1990) found male subjects in a dichotic listening format recalling an increased number of monosyllabic digits after listening to music than following a no-music condition; they suggested that music may serve to increase bilateral cerebral arousal levels. Others found music as background during the encoding process appeared to influence greater recall of information (Balch, Bowman, and Mohler 1992; Thaut and de L'Etoile 1993), with vocal music demonstrating greater disruption of short-term memory performance than instrumental music, which was not significantly worse than the silent control condition (Salamé and Baddeley 1989).

In the opening paragraphs of this chapter, reference was made to the different kinds of memory and to the importance of a good memory system for persons who strive to be musical. Determining whether one has a good memory for music performance would seem easily determined: on the recital stage, "truth will out," so to speak. A memorized performance is primarily an occasion of information retrieved from long-term memory storage, however, and the short-term processes leading up to that stage, including basic music perception (Williams 1978) have been the processes of most interest to contemporary researchers.

Understanding short-term memory and its limitations makes one more cognizant of some of the problems one faces when trying to memorize music, that is, trying to circuit information accurately from one storage level to another without significant interference from competing stimuli. For example, the necessity to attach meaning to units or chunks of information to extend the physical capacity of STM is a very common experience and one that is used to accommodate more information bits. The strain to recall the following ten unidimensional stimulus variables—5175552613—becomes an easier task when grouped into 517-555-2613 (as one tends to do when memorizing telephone numbers). A melodic sequence of limited length can be stored for a brief period and recalled quite accurately, given certain parameters. Accordingly, a longer sequence can be processed if melodic elements are grouped in some meaningful way. Both Wheatley (1992) and Wallace (1994) proposed that music memory or performance can be enhanced through greater ability to chunk musical patterns when such patterns are derived from a rich musical context, and Delis, Fleer, and Kerr (1978) found, similarly, that interpreting patterns of notes into comprehensible themes provides organization for more effective encoding of, and memory for, music. Kauffman and Carlsen (1989) offer the possibility that outer limits of short-term memory for music are not consistent with data reported in psychological literature with nonmusic stimuli. They refer to the inherent structure and meaning in music as possible contributors to such inconsistency; further, as a result of their findings, they suggest a reevaluation of the distinction between short-term and long-term memory and that the memory factors of encoding and retrieval are still far from being well understood.

Some of the other research findings described in this chapter suggest further limitations for tonal and musical memory: that particular melodic features, such as contour, and tonal systems influence the ability to remember tones; that time delay in the recall task is somewhat important in remembering certain portions of a melody, but even more critical for memory is the length of the melody; that remembering tones in a melody may be more difficult depending on the interaction with other tones of prescribed intervallic relationship and upon the particular position of critical tones in the melody. Williams (1982), in a discussion regarding auditory cognition and some similarities in the memory processing of musical tones and spoken words, draws attention to certain factors that remain "hauntingly" unanswered in existing research: questions concerning visual versus auditory imagery, strategy differences in processing of novel and familiar tunes, and differences between recalling a melody by performing it as compared to simply recognizing it are among those that demand more extensive investigation.

Research findings described in this chapter in a somewhat cursory manner do not do justice to the quality of the research behind them. Also, however, they do little to explain the difference in memory capabilities at a neurological level between the average musician and a musical genius. Davies (1981) points out that neurological models proposing to explain memory processing of "meaningless" sensory units may not help us to understand the memory processing of perceptual wholes, and he deferred to Uttal (1973), who suggested that the explanation of complex perceptual phenomena may lie at a level of complexity that current (at least in 1973) neurophysiology was unable to reveal.

It should be said that data obtained from the use of electronically generated tones devoid of musical nuance (a technique used quite extensively in tonal memory research) may not seem directly applicable to the experience of hearing "real" music. In defense of research that may be categorized as "investigations of the processing of meaningless sensory units," it must be recognized that the neural process is sensitive to slight changes in stimulus variables and electronically generated tone sources contain capabilities for greater control of frequency, intensity, waveform, and duration, all of which influence auditory perception. Regardless, researchers have different objectives and use different styles of investigation to reach their objectives. It can only be to our advantage to open our minds to all styles.

REFERENCES

Adams, J. A. 1967. *Human memory*. New York: McGraw-Hill.
Aiken, E. G., and W. Lau. 1966. Memory for the pitch of a tone. *Perception and Psychophysics* 1:231–33.
Arnold, M. B. 1984. *Memory and the brain*. Hillsdale, NJ: Lawrence Erlbaum Associates.
Balch, W. R. 1984. The effects of auditory and visual interference on the immediate recall of melody. *Memory and Cognition* 12, no. 6:581–89.
Balch, W. R., K. Bowman, and L. A. Mohler. 1992. Music-dependent memory in immediate and delayed word recall. *Memory and Cognition* 20, no. 1:21–28.
Bentley, A. 1966a. *Measures of musical ability*. London: George G. Harrap.
Bentley, A. 1966b. *Musical ability in children and its measurement*. London: George G. Harrap.
Bergan, J. R. 1965. Pitch perception, imagery, and regression in the service of the ego. *Journal of Research in Music Education* 13, no. 1:15–32.
Bergan, J. R. 1966. Factors affecting pitch discrimination. *Bulletin of the Council for Research in Music Education* 8:15–21.

Broadbent, D. E. 1958. *Perception and communication*. New York: Macmillan.

Brown, R. W. 1928. A comparison of the "whole," "part," and "combination" methods of learning piano music. *Journal of Experimental Psychology* 11:235–47.

Crowder, R. G., and J. Morton. 1969. Precategorical acoustic storage (PAS). *Perception and Psychophysics* 5:365–441.

Davies, J. 1979. Memory for melodies and tonal sequences: A theoretical note. *British Journal of Psychology* 70:205–10.

Davies, J. B. 1981. Memory for melodies and tonal sequences: A brief note. *Bulletin of the Council for Research in Music Education* 66–67:9–14.

Davies, J. B., and A. Yelland. 1977. Effects of two training procedures on the production of melodic contour, in short-term memory for tonal sequences. *Psychology of Music* 5, no. 2:3–9.

Delis, D., J. Fleer, and N. H. Kerr. 1978. Memory for music. *Perception and Psychophysics* 23, no. 3:215–18.

Deutsch, D. 1970. Tones and numbers: Specificity of interference in immediate memory. *Science* 168:1604–5.

Deutsch, D. 1972a. Effect of repetition of standard and comparison tones on recognition memory for pitch. *Journal of Experimental Psychology* 93:156–62.

Deutsch, D. 1972b. Mapping of interactions in the pitch memory store. *Science* 175:1020–22.

Deutsch, D. 1973a. Interference in memory between tones adjacent in the musical scale. *Journal of Experimental Psychology* 100:228–31.

Deutsch, D. 1973b. Octave generalizations of specific interference effects in memory for tonal pitch. *Perception and Psychophysics* 13:271–75.

Deutsch, D. 1975a. Auditory memory. *Canadian Journal of Psychology* 29:87–105.

Deutsch, D. 1975b. Facilitation by repetition in recognition memory for tonal pitch. *Memory and Cognition* 3:263–66.

Deutsch, D. 1977. Memory and attention in music. In *Music and the Brain*, ed. M. Critchley and R. A. Henson, 95–130. Springfield, IL: Charles C. Thomas.

Deutsch, D., and J. Feroe. 1975. Disinhibition in pitch memory. *Perception and Psychophysics* 17:320–24.

Dewar, K. M., L. L. Cuddy, and D. J. K. Mewhort. 1977. Recognition memory for single tones with and without context. *Journal of Experimental Psychology: Human Learning and Memory* 3, no. 1:60–67.

Dowling, W. J. 1973. Rhythmic groups and subjective chunks in memory for melodies. *Perception and Psychophysics* 14:37–40.

Dowling, W. J., and J. C. Bartlett. 1981. The importance of interval information in long-term memory for melodies. *Psychomusicology* 1, no. 1: 30–49.

Dowling, W. J., and D. S. Fujitani. 1971. Contour, interval, and pitch recognition in memory for melodies. *Journal of the Acoustical Society of America* 49:524–31.

Drake, R. M. 1954. *Drake musical aptitude tests*. Chicago: Science Research Associates.

Edworthy, J. 1982. Pitch and contour in music processing. *Psychomusicology* 2, no. 1:44–46.

Elliot, L. L. 1970. Pitch memory for short tones. *Perception and Psychophysics* 8:379–84.

Foreit, K. G. 1976. Short-lived auditory memory for pitches. *Perception and Psychophysics* 19:368–70.

Gordon, E. E. 1965. *Musical aptitude profile.* Boston: Houghton Mifflin.

Gordon, E. E. 1977. *Learning sequence and patterns in music.* Chicago: GIA Publications.

Gordon, E. E. 1993. *A music learning theory.* Chicago: GIA Publications.

Gruneberg, M. M., and P. Morris. 1978. *Aspects of memory.* London: Methuen.

Haack, P. A. 1975. The influence of loudness on the discrimination of musical sound factors. *Journal of Research in Music Education* 23, no. 1:67–77.

Halpern, A. R. 1984. Organization in memory for familiar songs. *Journal of Experimental Psychology: Learning, Memory and Cognition* 10, no. 3:496–512.

Heinlein, C. P. 1928. A brief discussion of the nature and function of melodies and selected factors. *Journal of Genetic Psychology* 35:45–61.

Huntsinger, C. S., and P. E. Jose. 1991. A test of Gardner's modularity theory: A comparison of short-term memory for digits and tones. *Psychomusicology* 10, no. 1: 3–18.

Isern, B. 1959. The influence of music upon the memory of mentally retarded children. In *Music Therapy,* ed. E. H. Schneider, 162–65. Lawrence, KS: Allen Press.

Jellison, J. A. 1976. Accuracy of temporal order recall for verbal and song digit-spans presented to right and left ears. *Journal of Music Therapy* 13, no. 3:114–29.

Kauffman, E. H., and J. C. Carlsen. 1989. Memory for intact music works: The importance of music expertise and retention interval. *Psychomusicology* 8:3–17.

Leshowitz, B., and R. Hanzi. 1974. Serial position effects for tonal stimuli. *Memory and Cognition* 2, no. 1A:112–16.

Long, P. A. 1977. Relationships between pitch memory in short melodies and selected factors. *Journal of Research in Music Education* 25:273–82.

Madsen, C. K., and M. J. Staum. 1983. Discrimination and interference in the recall of melodic stimuli. *Journal of Research in Music Education* 31, no. 1:15–31.

Massaro, D. W. 1970. Retroactive interference in short-term recognition memory for pitch. *Journal of Experimental Psychology* 83:32–39.

Mikumo, M. 1992. Encoding strategies for tonal and atonal melodies. *Music Perception* 10, no. 1: 73–82.

Miller, G. A. 1956. The magical number seven, plus or minus two: Some limits on our capacity for processing information. *Psychological Review* 63:81–97.

Morton, L. L., J. R. Kershner, and L. S. Siegel. 1990. The potential for therapeutic applications of music on problems related to memory and attention. *Journal of Music Therapy* 27, no. 4:195–208.

Myers, E. G. 1979. The effect of music on retention in a paired-associate task with EMR children. *Journal of Music Therapy* 16, no. 4:190–98.

Norman, D. A. 1966. Acquisition and retention in short-term memory. *Journal of Experimental Psychology* 72, no. 3:369–81.

Norman, D. A., ed. 1970. *Models of Human Memory.* New York: Academic Press.

O'Brien, C. E. 1943. Part and whole methods in memorization of piano music. *Journal of Educational Psychology* 34:552–60.

O'Brien, C. C. 1953. Atypical tonal memory. *Journal of Psychology* 35:267–70.

Ortmann, O. 1926. On the melodic relativity of tones. *Psychological Monographs* 35:1–47.

Pembrook, D. G. 1986. Interference of the transcription process and other selected variables on perception and memory during melodic dictation. *Journal of Research in Music Education* 34, no. 4:238–61.

Prickett, C. A., and R. S. Moore. 1991. The use of music to aid memory of Alzheimer's patients. *Journal of Music Therapy* 28, no. 2:101–10.

Roberts, L. A. 1986. Modality and suffix effects in memory for melodic and harmonic musical materials. *Cognitive Psychology* 18:123–57.

Rubin-Rabson, G. 1937. The influence of analytical prestudy in memorizing piano music. *Archives of Psychology* 31:1–53.

Rubin-Rabson, G. 1939. Studies in the psychology of memorizing piano music: I. A comparison of the unilateral and coordinated approaches. *Journal of Educational Psychology* 30:321–45.

Rubin-Rabson, G. 1940a. Studies in the psychology of memorizing piano music: II. A comparison of massed and distributed practice. *Journal of Educational Psychology* 31:270–84.

Rubin-Rabson, G. 1940b. Studies in the psychology of memorizing piano music: III. A comparison of whole and part approaches. *Journal of Educational Psychology* 31:460–76.

Rubin-Rabson, G. 1941a. Studies in the psychology of memorizing piano music: IV. The effect of incentive. *Journal of Educational Psychology* 32:45–54.

Rubin-Rabson, G. 1941b. Studies in the psychology of memorizing piano music: V. A comparison of prestudy periods of varied length. *Journal of Educational Psychology* 32:101–12.

Rubin-Rabson, G. 1941c. Studies in the psychology of memorizing piano music: VI. A comparison of two forms of mental rehearsal and keyboard overlearning. *Journal of Educational Psychology* 32:593–602.

Rubin-Rabson, G. 1941d. Studies in the psychology of memorizing piano music: VII. A comparison of three degrees of overlearning. *Journal of Educational Psychology* 32:688–98.

Russell, P. 1979. *The Brain Book*. New York: Dutton.

Salamé, P., and A. Baddeley. 1989. Effects of background music on phonological short-term memory. *Quarterly Journal of Experimental Psychology: Human Experimental Psychology* 41, no. 1A:107–22.

Seashore, C. E. [1938] 1967. *Psychology of music*. Reprint. New York: Dover.

Seashore, C. E., D. Lewis, and J. G. Saetveit. 1939. *Measures of musical talents*. New York: Psychological Corporation.

Schellenberg, S., and R. S. Moore. 1985. The effect of tonal-rhythmic context on short-term memory of rhythmic and melodic sequences. *Bulletin of the Council for Research in Music Education* 85:207–17.

Smith, D. 1991. A comparison of group performance and song familiarity on cued recall tasks with older adults. *Journal of Music Therapy* 28, no. 1:2–13.

Spear, N. E., and D. C. Riccio. 1994. *Memory: Phenomena and principles*. Boston: Allyn and Bacon.

Tallarico, P. T. 1974. A study of the three-phase concept of memory: Its musical implications. *Bulletin of the Council for Research in Music Education* 39:1–15.

Taylor, J. A., and R. G. Pembrook. 1984. Strategies in memory for short melodies: An extension of Otto Ortmann's 1933 study. *Psychomusicology* 3, no. 1:16–35.

Thaut, M. H., and S. K. de L'Etoile. 1993. The effects of music on mood state-dependent recall. *Journal of Music Therapy* 30, no. 2:70–80.

Underwood, G. 1976. *Attention and memory.* New York: Pergamon Press.

Uttal, W. R. 1973. *The Psychology of Sensory Coding.* New York: Harper and Row.

Vispoel, W. P. 1993. The development and evaluation of a computerized adaptive test of tonal memory. *Journal of Research in Music Education* 41, no. 2:111–36.

Wallace, W. T. 1994. Memory for music: Effect of melody on recall of text. *Journal of Experimental Psychology: Learning, Memory, and Cognition* 20, no. 6:1471–85.

Wang, C. C., and D. W. Sogin. 1990. The recognition of melodic fragments as components of tonal patterns. *Psychology of Music* 18:140–49.

Wheatley, S. E. 1992. An application of chunking to the memory and performance of melodic patterns. Ph.D. diss., University of Michigan.

Whipple, G. M. 1901. An analytic study of the memory image and the process of judgment in the discrimination of clangs and tones. *American Journal of Psychology* 12:409–57.

White, B. 1960. Recognition of distorted melodies. *American Journal of Psychology* 73:100–107.

Wickelgren, W. A. 1970. Multitrace strength theory. In *Models of Human Memory*, ed. D. A. Norman, 65–102. New York:Academic Press.

Williams, D. B. 1975. Short-term retention of pitch sequence. *Journal of Research in Music Education* 23:53–66.

Williams, D. B. 1978. The nature of listening and music learning. Paper presented at the Music Educators National Conference, April, Chicago.

Williams, D. B. 1982. Auditory cognition: A study of the similarities in memory processing for music tones and spoken words. *Bulletin of the Council for Research in Music Education* 71:30–44.

Wing, H. [1939] 1970. *Standardized tests of musical intelligence.* Reprint. Windsor, England: NFER Publishing.

Zenatti, A. 1975. Melodic memory tests: A comparison of normal children and mental defectives. *Journal of Research in Music Education* 23:41–52.

7

Neuromusical Research:
A Review of the Literature

Donald A. Hodges

Perhaps no other area of music psychology has seen as much advancement since the first edition of the *Handbook of Music Psychology* in 1980 as neuromusical research. Evidence of this may be seen in such publications as: *Music, Mind, and Brain: The Neuropsychology of Music* (Clynes 1982); "Neurological Aspects of Music Perception and Performance" (Marin 1982); *Music and the Mind* (Storr 1992); and *Biomusicology: Neurophysiological, Neuropsychological, and Evolutionary Perspectives on the Origins and Purposes of Music* (Wallin 1991). A number of conferences have also been held, including three Biology of Music Making conferences (in Denver in 1984 and 1987 and in Rochester in 1991) as well as Music and the Brain (in Chicago in 1992) and Setting an Agenda for Neuromusical Research (in San Antonio in 1993). Added to this is a significant amount of research published in a wide variety of journals. Searches on current holdings of CAIRSS (Computer-Assisted Information Retrieval Service System) for Music, an on-line, bibliographic database of music research literature, gave the following results for these truncated terms: *percep* (for perception, perceptual, etc.) = 762 citations; *brain* = 559; *cogni* (cognition, cognitive) = 193; *hemis* (hemisphere, hemispheric) = 164; *neuro* (neurology, neurological) = 107; and cereb (cerebral, cerebellum) = 80. (These totals include the possibility that some articles may be identified under more than one search term.)

Notwithstanding duplications in the CAIRSS searches or articles not included in the system, the sheer volume of relevant research literature is such that an exhaustive treatment is beyond the scope of a single chapter. Rather, the purpose of this chapter is to review and synthesize the research to provide an overview of the field as well as a general understanding of specific topics. First, a brief introduction to cognitive neuroscience is presented, followed by sections on animal research and evolutionary possibilities for musical behaviors, the effects of brain damage on musical behaviors, dichotic listening tasks and hemispheric asymmetry, EEG research, auditory event-related potentials, brain-imaging techniques, emotional responses to music, and neuromotor aspects of music making. The closing section moves toward a musical brain model.

Brief Introduction to Cognitive Neuroscience

The purpose of this section is to make it possible to read the ensuing reviews of neuromusical research with some degree of understanding. Because the brain is incredibly complex, and because thorough explanations of neuroanatomy and neurophysiology are beyond the scope of this chapter, what follows is only a grossly simplified and greatly generalized introduction. Readers wishing to acquire more detailed knowledge are encouraged to consult the sources listed as references.

Neuroanatomy

The human central nervous system consists of the brain, brain stem, and spinal cord as well as the peripheral nerves and the autonomic nervous system. The cerebral cortex—the center for most of the special attributes that separate human beings from other animals—is identified by the layer of gray matter that covers the outer surface of the brain. In contrast to other animals that have no cortex at all (e.g., birds) or that possess a smooth one (e.g., rats), "the human cortex has grown so large that, stretched out flat, it would form a sheet about an eighth of an inch thick, a yard long, and two feet wide. In order to fit within the confines of the skull, it folds in upon itself—a trick that triples the surface area" (Bailey 1975, 13).

Seen from above, the cortex looks to be bilaterally symmetrical; that is, the left and right hemispheres appear to be identical. Actually, there can be substantial anatomical variations between the two halves (Blinkov and Glezer 1968; Geschwind 1979; Springer and Deutsch 1989); but while there is general agreement that the hemispheres may process infomation in various ways, these differences are not so simple or contrasting as was once thought. Further explanation will be presented in the literature review on hemispheric asymmetry.

Each hemisphere is commonly divided into four lobes based on general functions (see fig. 1): the occipital lobes (vision), parietal lobes (sensory processing), temporal lobes (hearing), and frontal lobes (long-term planning, movement control, and speech production). Within each lobe are sensory, motor, and association zones. Sensory zones receive information from the senses, motor zones are concerned with control and coordination of muscle movements, and association zones deal with the more cognitive aspects of human behavior, such as interpretation and understanding. Other important brain sites include the sensory cortex (which provides a map of the body surface), the motor cortex (which initializes movement), the limbic sytem (site of complex chemical processes and emotions), the brain stem (which controls such automatic body functions as breathing), and the cerebellum (which governs muscle coordination and the learning of rote movements) (Begley et al. 1992; Chusid 1985; Shepherd 1994).

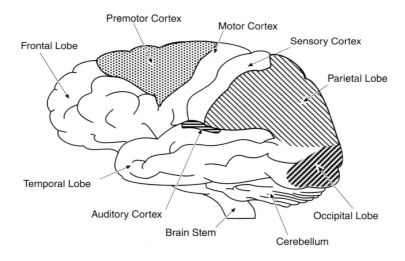

Fig. 1. Diagram of major areas of the brain

Neurophysiology

The adult brain weighs about three pounds and consists of more than 100 billion neurons or brain cells (Aoki and Siekevitz 1988; Shatz 1992a). Neurons are so small that 100 million of them can fit into one cubic inch. They are so richly interconnected that one neuron may connect with as many as a thousand other neurons and there may be as many as 100 million billion connections in the cerebral cortex alone (Nash 1992). This close proximity between neurons and the vast number of interconnections are important in the rapid transfer of information. In the first few years of life, neurons grow in size and in the number of connections. It is believed that a rich sensory environment stimulates these connections, while an impoverished one inhibits cognitive growth (Bloom, Lazerson, and Hofstadter 1985).

Neurons possess four distinctive features: a cell body, an axon, multiple dendrites, and synapses. Dendrites bring messages to the cell body and the axon carries messages away from it. Synapses are connecting points between the axon of one neuron and the dendrites or cell body of another neuron. A single neuron can receive as many as 100,000–200,000 signals on a dendritic tree (Alkon 1989).

A nerve impulse is governed by an "all-or-none" principle. A nerve either fires or it does not. Although the strength at which a nerve fires does not change, the rate at which it fires varies. The more intense the stimulus, the faster the firing rate—up to a point. While there is no lower limit to the rate at which a nerve fires, there is an upper limit determined by a refractory (recovery) period.

The arrival of an electrical signal, called a nerve impulse, to the end of the axon releases a chemical transmitter that transports the message across the synaptic cleft. Chemical transmitters can be either excitatory or inhibitory. Excitatory transmitters allow the message to be continued on the other side of the synaptic cleft by causing the postsynaptic neuron to fire. Inhibitory transmitters have the effect of slowing down or stopping the flow of information by preventing the neuron they reach from firing, even if chemicals at another synapse are trying to fire it. More than 50 chemical compounds have been identified as neurotransmitters, including acetylcholine, serotonin, dopamine, and norepinephrine. Other chemicals, such as cholinesterase, are present in the postsynaptic cell to reduce the neurotransmitters into their original compounds.

Several features of synapses give important clues to understanding behavior. At the time neurotransmitters are diffusing across the synaptic cleft, they are highly vulnerable to the presence of other chemicals. Many harmful substances cannot reach the brain because of the blood-brain barrier, a protective encapsulation of blood vessels in the brain that inhibits many substances in the blood from passing through to the brain cells. But, if and when they do reach the brain, such substances can have a catastrophic effect. Drugs such as nicotine, marijuana, and LSD may have the effects they do by disturbing the normal functioning of the neurotransmitters (Russell 1975).

Another important feature of synapses is that they are modifiable. "Many synapses are altered by their prior experience" (Teyler 1977, 22). Synapses are modified by becoming larger, by adding new synapses, or by regressing (Eccles 1973) and these modifications are very important to the understanding of learning and memory.

Many neuroscientists are guided in their research by a reductionist approach arising from the notion that there is a logical connection from the "top" layer of observable behavior all the way down to the "bottom" layer of neuronal activity. From top to bottom, these layers might include mind, behavior, brain (CNS), systems, maps, networks, neurons, synapses, and molecules (Churchland and Sejnowski 1988). Some researchers work from the bottom up, focusing on the inner workings of single cells. For example, by means of a specialized procedure called a patch clamp technique, researchers can study the molecular details of ion channels involved in the transmission of signals between and within cells (Neher and Sakmann 1992). Nearer the top, researchers might be concerned with how the brain redraws motor maps based on experience (Gazzaniga 1988). Cognitive neuroscientists are interested in explaining behavior (e.g., language) based on neurophysiological data. Because any single research study is, of necessity, focused on a very small area of the top-to-bottom continuum, models of the brain become very important. Models are a way of conceptualizing the working brain so that minute details can be packaged into a more cohesive whole.

Models of Brain Functioning

Triune Brain Model
One model is called the triune brain (MacLean 1973). According to this model, the human brain consists of three components—the reptilian brain, paleomammalian brain, and neomammalian brain. The reptilian brain, the oldest and innermost part of the brain (consisting of the upper brain stem and much of the reticular system, midbrain, and basal ganglia), is largely responsible for homeostasis, the regulation of such routine body functions as blood pressure, body temperature, and blood sugar levels, and with stereotypical aspects of behavior.

The paleomammalian brain (or old mammal brain), the next oldest part of the brain, is frequently referred to as the limbic system. It includes the hippocampus (which integrates incoming sensory information and consolidates recently acquired information, turning short-term memory into long-term memory), the amygdala (which generates emotions from perceptions and thoughts, especially identified with aggression and fear), the hypothalamus (which has widespread connections with many other brain sites and is intimately connected with the pituitary; its main task is the regulation of the autonomic nervous system in the maintenance of homeostasis or body stability), the pituitary (which is the "master gland" that controls the release of hormones into the blood stream), and the thalamus (which is the major relay between sensory

input and cortex; involved in arousal and activation of cortical association areas) (Begley et al. 1992; Bloom, Lazerson, and Hofstadter 1985).
Taken as a whole, the limbic system is a complex system and is deeply
involved in the emotional aspects of human behavior.

The newest part of the brain, from an evolutionary standpoint, is
the neomammalian (new mammal) brain. Also known as the cerebral
cortex or neocortex, it is the center for most of the special cognitive activities that are distinctively human. The cortex has already been described, but it is important to note that MacLean's model, while identifying three components, recognizes their integration into one unified
brain system. Our internal bodily processes (reptilian brain) continue
involuntarily while our affective (paleomammalian brain) and cognitive (neomammalian brain) lives are inextricably intertwined. Sagan sum-
marizes the concept of the triune brain nicely.

> It seems a useful approximation to consider the ritualistic and hierar-
> chical aspects of our lives to be influenced strongly by the R-complex
> [reptilian brain] and shared with our reptilian forebears; the altruis-
> tic, emotional and religious aspects of our lives to be localized to a
> significant extent in the limbic system and shared with our nonprimate
> mammalian forebears (and perhaps the birds); and reason to be a
> function of the neocortex, shared to some extent with the higher pri-
> mates and such cetaceans as dolphins and whales. (Sagan 1977, 81)

All three parts of the triune brain may have a role to play in musical
behavior. The reptilian brain contributes the ritual often associated with
musical performances, the paleomammalian brain provides the emotional responses to music, and the neomammalian brain "masterminds"
the whole affair, making possible all the unique understandings that
come from music. The extent to which this model is supported by existing research may be seen in the literature review sections.

Split-Brain Model

Another model is identified by a variety of labels, including split brain,
cerebral dominance, and hemispheric asymmetry. Although more popular in the lay press, it is highly controversial among neuroscientists, some
of whom would not consider it a viable model. The remainder of this
brief section will present the views of proponents; the literature review
devoted to this topic will present some of the criticisms of this model
and the resulting research.

As indicated previously, the brain consists of two hemispheres. It
has been common knowledge for a long time that the left hemisphere

primarily controls motor functioning of the right side of the body, while the right hemisphere primarily controls the left side. More recently, however, and especially since the 1960s, discoveries have led to the notion that the hemispheres also have different, and somewhat independent, functions. While sensory input feeds into both halves, it is processed in distinctly different ways and for different purposes by the two hemispheres. The left hemisphere processes information in a primarily verbal, sequential, logical, and analytic manner. The right hemisphere functions in a more nonverbal, holistic, intuitive, and synthesizing fashion. This assignment of functions to hemispheres is true for slightly more than 90 percent of persons who are right-handed English speakers and for 60 percent of left-handed persons. For the remainder of the population, the roles of the hemispheres are reversed or an individual may show mixed dominance (Robinson and Solomon 1974).

In a normal, healthy brain, the two hemispheres communicate with each other primarily, but not exclusively, via the corpus callosum at the rate of four billion impulses per second (Eccles 1973). This bundle of nerves, 3 inches long and a quarter-inch thick, contains most of the 200 million fibers that connect the two halves of the brain (Pines 1973). Information can be transferred from one hemisphere to the other at the time of learning or can be supplied later upon demand (Sperry 1966). Thus, the two hemispheres function integratively as a whole and not as two separate and independent processors.

The term cerebral dominance is used to indicate that one hemisphere or the other may be primarily responsible for certain behaviors. Evidence to support this concept comes from several sources. (For a general review of the topic, see Beaton 1985; Benson and Zaidel 1985; Springer and Deutsch 1989; older reviews include Gazzaniga 1967, 1972, and 1977; and Sperry 1966, 1967, 1970, and 1973). Individuals who suffer strokes in the left hemisphere often lose the ability to speak or write. A stroke on the right side often causes a loss of pattern recognition and discrimination of spatial relationships. Patients who have had one hemisphere or the other removed for various medical reasons experience similar losses (Nebes 1977; Pines 1973).

A particular treatment for severe forms of epilepsy also provides evidence in support of cerebral dominance. This treatment involves severing the corpus callosum. In effect, the patient is left with a "split" brain, each half of which possesses different functions. In studying these patients, researchers showed that "the left hemisphere, as would have been predicted from earlier clinical reports, excelled in verbal processing of information of all kinds. The right hemisphere, however, proved superior in managing visual-spatial tasks such as drawing cubes and arranging blocks to match a design" (Gazzaniga 1977, 92–93). A large amount of data has also been derived from experiments that involved dichotic listening tasks. Research on hemispheric asymmetry in relation to music will be critically evaluated in the literature review.

Neural Network Model
Models built on computer simulations have been attractive to many neuroscientists because both the brain and the computer are marvelous pattern detectors (Alkon 1989). However, initially the computer was at a tremendous disadvantage because it worked on an exact-match system, while the brain used an almost-match system. That is, the brain can fill in missing gaps and complete patterns using contextual information. Fill in the missing letter to complete a person's name: John _mith. You probably arrived at "Smith" almost instantaneously, without going through all 26 letters of the alphabet to see that none of the others fits logically. Older computers could not do this simple task, or could do so only with great difficulty.

More recently, computer scientists have provided a more useful model called neural nets or neural networks (Alkon 1989; Barinaga 1990; Roberts 1989; Rolls 1989; for an application of neural nets to music, see Bharucha and Olney 1989; Smoliar 1992). Neural nets consist of a number of processors connected together in three layers—an input layer, an output layer, and a "hidden" or middle layer. Each processor or unit has excitatory and inhibitory inputs (like a neuron). If the combined strength from a number of inputs is above a certain threshold value, the unit sends a signal to other units. Properties emerge from the overall pattern of activation among units and memories are stored in the weighted connections among units. Back-propogation of errors (or back-prop for short) allows the net to "learn" over repeated trials by making slight adjustments in the weighting of connections. This process is repeated until the correct response is achieved.

Neural nets are controversial because some neuroscientists claim they still do not model actual neurons accurately enough (Crick 1989; Searle 1990; Shepherd 1990). For example, neurons in the cortex are arranged in six layers (Shatz 1992b), not three, and do not utilize back-propogation; information flows only one way along axons (to the cell body) and dendrites (from the cell body). Nevertheless, as many as 50–100 different algorithms (algebraic equations) have been formulated to describe synapses (Brown, Kairiss, and Keenan 1990). Considerable debates are encountered concerning the sense in which the brain is or is not computational, that is, whether or not the algorithms used by mathematicians and computer scientists accurately reflect the way biology works. Ideally, the most effective modeling might come when neurobiological data informs and places constraints on computational theories (Churchland and Sejnowski 1988).

Learning and Memory

Biologically, learning and memory seem to work something like the following. As information comes into the brain from the senses, it is analyzed and parceled out into many smaller bits. Most experiences are multimodal, so that watching a pianist perform, for example, involves hearing (not only the pianist but such other sounds as the rustle of programs or coughing), seeing (again, not only the pianist, but other visual aspects of the environment), and physical sensations (such as the temperature, hunger pangs, drowsiness, or the pressure of pinching shoes). It might even involve smell, if, for example, a person seated nearby is wearing a particularly strong perfume.

As the brain is bombarded by all these sensations, the incoming signals are immediately analyzed and broken into smaller bits of information. The colors and shapes of visual information, the pitch, loudness, and timbre of the sounds—all these fragments are processed in different parts of the brain. There may be as many as 60 million neuronal groups set up for this kind of processing (Sanders 1989). Weaving all these disparate bits into a cohesive whole may take place in convergence zones, where fragments from a variety of sensory inputs are reactivated and integrated (Kinoshita 1992).

Another idea is that the individual neuron groups, each encoding one of the fragments—color, pitch, and so on—fires short bursts of action potentials from 40–70 Hz in what is called a binding frequency (Economist 1993). As all the neurons oscillate or fire in synchrony—forming and disappearing within 50–100 milliseconds—the idea or perception is brought together as a unified experience. As each image is formed in a tenth of a second, it is bound together with others (like individual frames in a motion picture) to create a whole.

For a while, all this information circulates in the neuronal circuitry as short-term memory or working memory. For example, using magnetoencephalography (MEG) data, researchers established that neuronal activation in response to a tone lasted several seconds longer in the association cortex than in the primary auditory cortex (Lu, Williamson, and Kaufman 1992). They also confirmed that short-term memory traces are modality specific.

As long as something is kept "in mind," it remains active in the neural networks; the prefrontal cortex is particularly involved in working memory. To be transferred to long-term memory or permanent storage, the information must be passed onto the hippocampus, located in the limbic system. Filtered out by the reticular activating system, unimportant aspects of the experience are discarded before they are placed into long-term storage. For example, while listening to a recital you may be perceptually aware that someone across the auditorium just coughed, but it is unlikely that that bit of information is significant enough for you to encode it into a permanent memory.

In the hippocampus a process known as long-term potentiation (LTP) begins the transfer of working memory into long-term memory (Madison et al. 1991). LTP occurs when an axon releases the neurotransmitter glutamate that is picked up on the dendrite side of the synaptic cleft by an N-methyl–D-aspartate (NMDA) receptor. This reaction between glutamate and NMDA receptors enhances the transfer of action potentials by opening up the channels that allow ions to pass through cell membranes. Unusual confirmation of the rhythmic nature of LTP came when mice were exposed to constant, arrythmic drumbeats for eight weeks. They had difficulty learning and there was evidence of neural structural changes. The hypothesis was that the drumbeats disrupted the rhythms in the hippocampus (Lipkin 1988).

NMDA receptors are responsive to glutamate only if the dendrite is already being stimulated by sufficient action potentials. In other words, an individual synapse is affected by other synapses in the neural network and the message transmission is a group effort. The combination of all the excitatory and inhibitory connections produces a particular "weighting" or value for that bit of information. This process is repeated over and over. Individual neurons can be involved in more than one memory as neural networks are superimposed on one another (Crick 1989). By analogy, one person could be involved in a number of different relationships, each characterized by an identifying label, such as father, son, uncle, grandson, husband, and friend. In a similar way, an individual neuron may play different roles in different memories. Long-term storage comes when neural networks have been modified through experience (repeated firings of the same pattern of weightings). Thus, a memory is not stored in a place as an entity but can be retrieved by any sensation, thought, or emotion that reactivates the neural network with its distributed patterns of weights among the many synaptic connections.

The discussion of learning and memory has thus far been at the molecular or reductionist level. At a more functional level, there are at least three stages of memory: acquisition, storage, and recall (Shepherd 1994). Furthermore, information may be stored as declarative ("knowing that") and procedural ("knowing how"). Beyond that there are many subprocesses, including at least "memory encoding and retrieval, working memory and reference memory, automatic memory encoding, behavioral and memorial priming, motor learning, the associative linkage of contextual stimuli to the neural mechanisms for stimulus selection and response priming, the long-term storage of information, and so forth" (Gabriel, Sparenborg, and Stoler 1986, 230).

Obviously, a full discussion of all these topics is beyond the scope of this chapter. Additional information relevant to the understanding of neuromusical research is given in each of the following sections.

Animal Research and Evolutionary Possibilities for Musical Behaviors

Researching how animals process sound has many benefits for our understanding of human musical processing. When humans listen to a Mozart symphony, they utilize many of the same mechanisms as animals do when they respond to sounds. Imagine a dog behind a fence. As he hears various sounds—a garbage truck, the mailman, a jogger, other dogs, a cat, and so on—he is able to do a number of things. He can localize the sound and he can detect familiar from unfamiliar sounds. Many of these sounds have meaning and his behavior is driven accordingly; he will respond differently to a stray cat than he will to the neighbor dog across the fence. The meaning a dog attaches to sounds is based on physical attributes of frequency, intensity, signal shape, and time, as well as on memory, instincts, and learned behaviors (Wertheim 1977).

Although many aspects of auditory processing may be the same, listening to Mozart is different for a human being than it is for a dog. For the sake of simplicity, assume that listening to Mozart with meaning involves attention, perception, cognition, and affect. People and animals pay attention to sounds that have meaning. Human beings may selectively pay attention to Mozart. While a dog may be conditioned to attend to Mozart, normally it will not do so. Thus, it is unlikely to have meaning under normal circumstances. Listening to Mozart with meaning for a human being involves perceptions of melody, rhythm, harmony, form, and so on. While a dog could be trained to discriminate between the sound of an oboe and a trumpet, for example, it cannot perceive "melody" independent of the absolute pitches involved (see subsequent discussion). A host of cognitive structures seem likewise to be out of reach of a dog's capabilities. Listening to Mozart with meaning might involve such cognitive structures as knowledge of style period (eighteenth-century Viennese classicism), musical form (sonata form as the norm for the first movement of a symphony), and on and on. Finally, human beings are capable of responding to the music of Mozart with a wide range of feelings and emotions involving training and experience, past listening experiences, and so on. It is unlikely that a dog might be thinking to itself: "This piece of Mozart's is one of my favorites. I remember so well the first time I heard that haunting second theme; it reminded me so much of the time . . ." Without belaboring the point, humans are able to bring a number of cognitive and affective processes to bear that the dog cannot; but the rudimentary structures may be much the same. Thus, the value of animal research is in providing us with knowledge of these basic structures.

Birds form an especially inviting population because their vocalizations seem to resemble what we humans call music. About half of the 9,000 species of birds are able to produce songs without access to external models (Marler 1991); apparently, in these cases birdsong is genetically encoded and these species produce mature songs from the outset. Birds who must learn to sing start with unrelated songs, progress gradually into subsong, move through "plastic" song, and eventually mature into a crystallized version of adult song. Most song learning is "memory" based, in that birds refer to song models located in long-term memory. However, during certain stages of development, an "action-based" learning strategy is employed. This type of learning is influenced by social experience; for example, reactions from females may help determine which song patterns are retained and which are discarded (Marler 1991).

Auditory feedback is a critical component of song-learning behavior in birds (Marler 1991). Birds deafened at birth never mature beyond the earliest stages of producing random noises. Birds with normal hearing, but raised in isolation and without the opportunity to hear appropriate song models, produce tuneful songs that are flawed in terms of matching appropriate adult song. Auditory feedback of song models and of the learner's own voice is important for complete development.

What a bird hears in auditory feedback has been of interest. During critical stages for song learning, sparrows presented with a choice of listening to songs of their own species or those of alien species will choose their own (Miller and Jusczyk 1989). Some birds pay attention to phonology (the sounds), while others pay attention to both phonology and syntax (the arrangement or organization of sounds). Swamp sparrows can discriminate songs of their own species well before their own attempts at singing are made. While some have cited this as an example of template matching, it appears that birds utilize absolute pitch cues rather than tonal patterns.

In a study that initially began with cebus monkeys and rats, D'Amato (1988) discovered that all of his animal species utilized absolute frequency discrimination as a means of discriminating tonal patterns. He concluded that none of the animals studied so far—rats, monkeys, great apes, songbirds, pigeons—are able to discriminate frequency contours. At first, this finding was puzzling, because it has been demonstrated that birds can make distinctions between the music of various composers (e.g., Bach and Stravinsky) and even between various styles (e.g., Baroque and twentieth century) (Gillis 1990; Hulse 1990).

This caused researchers to look into the extent to which animals are capable of perceptual invariance, that is, the extent to which one acoustic dimension remained recognizable while other dimensions were varied. For example, to what extent is a melody still recognizable if it is transposed to a different pitch level, played at a different speed, or rhythmically altered? Researchers discovered that, while "perceptual invariance holds at all levels of development and for all species throughout the acoustic dimensions surveyed" (Hulse, Takeuchi, and Braaten 1992, 151), the lone exception was that animals fail to show perceptual invariance for "melodies." They contend that both humans and nonhumans use a hierarchy of perceptual strategies that begins with absolute pitch perception and then moves to relative pitch perception. Nonhuman animals prefer to rely on absolute pitch capabilities. Human beings start by using absolute pitch cues; however, as they learn to use relative pitch cues, absolute pitch is gradually weakened.

To return to the issue of what the differences would be between a dog and a human being listening to Mozart; one difference is that a dog is incapable of hearing and discriminating frequency contours (melodies). To a human listener, a "melody" is a series of pitches whose meaning is derived from the intervallic relationships within an overall contour, not the individual notes. As such, a melody can be transposed to higher or lower pitch levels and still be recognized. Also, various abstractions—motives or fragments; augmentation or diminution; variations in harmony, rhythm, or timbre; and so on—can be recognized as referring to the original melody.

While it is tempting to anthropomorphize animal sounds and call them "music," what are these sounds to the animals? Whatever else they may be, they are most certainly involved in social communication and in courtship and mating rituals (Brody 1991). When vervet monkeys hear a "snake call," they stand up and look at the surrounding ground; a "leopard call" causes them to take to the trees, and an "eagle call" produces skyward scanning (Miller and Jusczyk 1989). Japanese macaques have up to 80 distinctive calls. Honeybees use sound in combination with dance movements to communicate information about the location of food sources (Kirchner and Towne 1994). As indicated previously, song learning in male birds can be influenced by female responses. Among whales, only males "sing" and then primarily during breeding season; the purpose of these vocalizations is mostly to attract females (Economist 1989). Elephants communicate over distances of several miles using infrasound (frequencies below the range of human hearing) (Payne 1989).

Although many authors seem to find no biological imperative for human musical behavior (that is, they could identify no survival value), perhaps these animal studies may provide some clues. Darwin (1871) felt that music arose from sounds connected with mating activities. Diamond (1991) drew inferences from animal "artistic" activities and contended that art has biological functions for human beings in that a male who produces art products (songs, sculptures, etc.) displays such desirable attributes as mental acuity, organizational skills, ingenuity (creativity), sensitivity, and so on. Roederer (1982) believed that music was a way of giving the brain practice to prepare for enhanced speech perception, especially for prosody aspects (pitch, rhythm, timbre, and dynamic inflections). Stiller (1987) combined neurological and anthropological evidence, and Hodges (1989) speculated that music could provide survival value in terms of mother-infant bonding, acquisition of language, socialization of emotions, and solidifying individual and corporate identity (see chap. 2). Some ethnomusicologists contend that the ubiquity of musical behaviors in human cultures argues for a genetic base. Blacking (1973) gave the example of the Venda tribe in South Africa, where every member of the group is expected to engage in socially appropriate musical behaviors. This would not be possible (i.e., some would be excluded) if every person were not biologically equipped to participate in the culture's shared musical experiences. (See chap. 12 for further discussions of ethnomusicological research.)

Linked to anthropological evidence of the ubiquity of music may be fetal and infant research. There is abundant evidence showing that the human fetus is aware of and responsive to sounds, including music (Annis 1978; Eccles and Robinson 1985; Friedrich 1983; Restak 1983; Shetler 1985 and 1989; Verny with Kelly 1981; Youcha 1982). Moments after birth, a baby may turn in the direction of a voice, searching for the source. By the end of the first week, babies can select their mother's voice from among a group of female voices. Babies move their arms and legs in synchrony with the rhythms of human speech. In an experiment of early music perception, 36 eight-week-old infants were presented with lullabies played on the piano, the Copland piano sonata, or electronic music (Tims 1981). The music was turned on and off contingent upon visual fixation. The different types of music had an effect on the attending behavior of these infants, as they showed clear preferences for the lullabies.

In a demonstration of how alert babies are to sounds, an experiment was conducted with three-month-old babies (Restak 1983). They were simultaneously shown two cartoons with the sound track to only one playing in the background. The babies stared selectively at the cartoon whose sound was being played. In a similar experiment, two cartoons were superimposed, again with the sound track to only one playing. As the cartoons were gradually separated, the babies followed the one being accompanied by sound. Five-month-old infants can discriminate differences in frequency less than one half step (Olsho 1984), and, by the age of 8–11 months, they rely on melodic contour to make pitch discriminations (Trehub, Bull, and Thorpe 1984).

Continued exploration of animals and their sound producing and analyzing capabilities will give additional evidence on which to build a case for the evolutionary basis of human musical behavior. Equally important is anthropological and fetal-infant research. To this may be added the study of brain-damaged individuals, which is reviewed in the next section.

The Effects of Brain Damage on Musical Behaviors

Neuroscientists have found it very revealing to study brain-damaged patients as a means of understanding cognitive functioning. A large body of research may be classified under the heading "amusia." Following a review of this literature, brief sections will be presented on musical prodigies and savants, Alzheimer's disease, and musicogenic epilepsy.

Amusia

Amusia refers to loss of musical skills due to brain damage. It may be considered parallel to the term *aphasia*, referring to a loss of language skills, about which much more is known. In both amusia and aphasia, losses may be global or specific. For example, a person may suffer a stroke and thereafter lose the ability to read music, to sing or play an instrument, or to understand music.

Because of each individual's unique circumstances, both in terms of musical skills acquired prior to suffering brain damage and in terms of the specific damage, and because of the rarity of amusia being diagnosed, most of the literature reports case studies. Before presenting some examples, it is important to note several organizing variables, so that one can determine whether there is a larger pattern to be made from these individual cases. Studies can be organized according to left (LH) or right hemispheric (RH) damage. Within that large dichotomy, more specific localization of damage may or may not be noted. The presence or absence of aphasia along with amusia may be noted. Finally, the loss of specific musical skills may be detailed. Generally, these losses are divided into receptive amusia (loss of the ability to perceive or undertand music; e.g., the person may no longer be able to track rhythms or follow pitch direction) and expressive amusia (loss of the ability to express oneself musically; e.g., the person may no longer be able to sing or play an instrument). Table 1 lists representative studies reported in the literature.

TABLE 1.   The Effects of Brain Damage on Musical Behaviors

Study	Description and Findings
	Subjects with Left-Hemisphere Damage
Wertheim and Botez 1961	A right-handed man with superior musical aptitude and training had receptive amusia and severe mixed aphasia. He was still able to play the violin.
Basso and Capitani 1985	A conductor suffered damage in the left temporo-parieto-occipital lobes with a resulting aphasia and apraxia (inability to write). Many of his musical skills were spared; however, his music writing was affected (musical apraxia). Although he could not read words, he could still read musical notation.
Levin and Rose 1979	A 58-year-old professor of music had a left parieto-occipital craniotomy. He could not read either words or music; however, he could read musical symbols other than notes. His speech and verbal comprehension were normal. His expressive abilities and appreciation of rhythm were spared, but his judgments of pitch, duration, loudness, timbre, and tonal memory were affected. He could still play the drums.
Signoret et al. 1987	A 77-year-old organist, who had been blind since age 2, suffered from damage to the temporal and inferior parietal lobes. He experienced verbal alexia and agraphia (an inability to read or write) in Braille, but retained all his musical skills. He was

(continued)

TABLE 1—*Continued*

Study	Description and Findings
	able to play the organ, compose, and read musical Braille.
Mavlov 1980	A 61-year-old musician suffered from a LH stroke. He experienced speech disorders and motor difficulties on the right side. He could recognize and produce tones and tone sequences, but he was unable to recognize or produce rhythms, whether presented or perceived auditorily, visually, or tactilely. This rhythmic disorder caused a severe amusia despite his intact pitch skills. The author posits a supramodal time processor not limited to the auditory, visual, or tactile mode.
Brust 1980	Two right-handed, professional musicians, both with LH lesions, retained their musical skills except for an inability to read or write music.
Judd, Gardner, and Geschwind 1983	A 77-year-old composer with left occipital lobe damage had severe alexia (reading disturbance) but no aphasia or writing problems. He could still read music and compose.

	Subjects with Right-Hemisphere Damage
Mazzucchi et al. 1982	A 58-year-old male suffered from a right temporal lesion that caused a loss of timbre perception (including nonmusical timbres) but no loss of pitch or rhythm perception. He also experienced a loss of musical appreciation or pleasure.
Botez and Wertheim 1959	A right-handed male experienced expressive aphasia and amusia following a right-frontal lesion. He was no longer able to play or sing.
McFarland and Fortin 1982	An organist, suffering from damage to the right superior temporal and supramarginal gyri, consequently lost the ability to play familiar melodies.

(*continued*)

TABLE 1—*Continued*

Study	Description and Findings
Mackworth-Young 1983	A professional trumpeter with a RH lesion and encephalitis complained of disturbances of rhythm, pitch, timbre, and loudness.
Gott 1973	Removal of the RH eliminates the ability to sing, while speech is not affected.
Bartholomeus 1974; Borod and Goodglass 1980; Brookshire 1975; Bryden 1986; Mazzucchi, Parma, and Cattelani 1981; Shankweiler 1966	Right-hemisphere dominance for the perception of melodies has been demonstrated by studying patients with RH damage.
Sidtis and Volpe 1988	Patients with RH lesions were impaired in complex pitch perception.
Gordon 1974; Milner 1969	Removal of the RH impairs performance on the *Seashore Measures of Musical Talents*; the Timbre and Tonal Memory sections are most affected, followed by Loudness and Time.

	Subjects with Right- and/or Left-Hemisphere Damage
Shapiro, Grossman, and Gardner 1981	Of 28 right-handed patients with left- or right-hemisphere damage, those with LH damage performed quite well on music processing tasks; those with RH damage did poorly.
Shankweiler 1966	Twenty-one patients with left temporal lobe damage and 24 with right temporal lobe damage performed dichotic tasks with digits and melodies. RH-damaged subjects showed impaired performance on the dichotic melodies test, while LH-damaged subjects showed impaired performance on the digits test.
Samson and Zatorre 1988	Seventy-seven patients who had undergone unilateral temporal, frontal, or frontotemporal lobectomy were compared with 20 normal subjects. Subjects with RH excisions, both temporal and frontotemporal,

(*continued*)

TABLE 1—*Continued*

Study	Description and Findings
	and those with left temporal lobe excisions had a significant deficit in the melodic task. Melodic discrimination apparently depends on the right temporal lobe and the left Heschl's gyri (auditory cortex). No significant differences were found between brain-damaged patients and normal controls on harmonic discrimination.
Mostafa et al. 1989	In a group of 80 patients, those with RH lesions showed deterioration of musical abilities; those with LH lesions demonstrated normal musical abilities.
Samson 1994	Subjects with the right temporal lobe removed performed significantly poorer on timbre perception tasks than those with the left temporal lobe removed or normals. While the RH was primarily involved, the LH was also involved in subtle aspects of timbre discrimination.
Kinsella, Prior, and Murray 1988	In an investigation of the singing abilities of 15 LH-damaged, 15 RH-damaged, and 15 normal subjects, no significant differences in pitch, rhythm, or overall singing were found between the two groups of brain-damaged subjects; normals sang better.
Zatorre 1985	Sixty-eight patients with unilateral brain damage were studied along with 20 normals. RH-damaged patients did poorly on a melodic discrimination task, and both RH- and LH-damaged patients did poorly on a melodic recognition task.
Grossman, Shapiro, and Gardner 1981	Subjects with Broca's aphasia (LH damage causing an inability to articulate speech) and those with RH damage did poorer than normals on a melodic recognition task. Subjects with LH damage other than Broca's area performed as well as normals.
Efron, Bogen, and Yund 1977	Surgical disconnection of the hemispheres (commisurotomy or cutting of the corpus

(*continued*)

TABLE 1—*Continued*

Study	Description and Findings
	callosum) had no effect on the perception of chords but did affect speech.
Brookshire 1975	Subjects with RH damage did poorer on recognition of more complex tonal patterns than did aphasics (LH damage) or normals.

What conclusive patterns can be drawn from these few examples? First, are aphasia and amusia coupled? There are reports in the literature of all three combinations: amusia without aphasia, aphasia without amusia, and aphasia with amusia. Marin (1982) reported that aphasia and amusia coexisted in 33 of 87 clinical cases. He also found 19 cases of amusia without aphasia and 12 cases of aphasia without amusia in professional or amateur musicians. In another review, 21 of 24 patients with Broca's aphasia were still able to sing (Yamadori et al. 1977; see also Benton 1977). Given this variation in linking the two dysfunctions, it is apparent that they are not automatically linked, but that they may be frequently so.

Sergent (1993b) reviewed the cases of several composers who suffered from brain damage. Russian composer Shebalin and French composer Langlais, as well as Britten and Gershwin, were able to continue composing in spite of considerable brain damage. A more detailed examination of Ravel's neurological condition indicated that, as a result of considerable brain damage, he was not able to continue composing or playing the piano but was able to listen to and appreciate music. Based on this and other research on healthy brains (reviewed in the subsequent section on Brain Imaging Techniques), Sergent (1993a and 1993b; Sergent et al. 1992) argued for a widely distributed, locally specialized, neural network for music processing. Receptive and expressive musical behaviors involve visual, auditory, motor, cognitive, and affective processing. The neural substrates subserving music lie in proximity to the verbal areas but remain distinct from them. This may explain the widely divergent relationships between aphasia and amusia. Depending on the precise location and size of a cerebral accident, language, music, or both systems may be disturbed.

Several researchers are beginning to use their data to support the notion of widely distributed, locally specialized musical systems. Steinke, Cuddy, and Peretz (1994) demonstrated that, for 100 normal subjects, the ability to abstract tonality was not associated with general, nonmusical abstraction. This was confirmed with a subject who had amusia following temporal lobe surgery. Her nonmusical abstraction was normal, but her ability to abstract tonality was impaired. These results led the researchers to conclude that there was evidence for functional specificity for musical abilities. Following her study of three subjects with cortical damage, Peretz (1994) also argued for specific neural circuitries devoted to music. The language skills of her subjects were normal (including the ability to identify familiar and unfamiliar song titles and spoken lyrics), but they had auditory agnosia specific to recognizing familiar tunes. Following four related studies of brain-damaged and normal subjects, each linking the right temporal lobe with music perception tasks, Zatorre (1994) echoed recognition for specialized neural systems for music.

For some aspects, language and music may share a common processor. Patel and Peretz (1994) studied two female patients who had undergone bilateral temporal lobe surgeries; both were amusic but not aphasic. No significant differences were found on analogous linguistic (prosody) and musical tasks, suggesting a common location for linguistic prosody and musical melodic/rhythmic processing.

Does the specific type of amusia, when coupled with anatomical localization, support right- or left-hemispheric dominance for musical behaviors? Some have used the clinical data from a given case study to claim support for the notion of right-hemispheric dominance for music (see McFarland and Fortin 1982; Signoret et al. 1987). But clearly there are exceptions to so simplistic a dichotomy, as noted even in the few examples given in this section. Brust (1980) contended that the localization of left- or right-sided damage does not allow for the accurate prediction of the presence, type, or severity of amusia. Other authors agreed with Sergent's position, contending that clinical data from brain-damaged subjects supports the notion that musical behaviors engage many brain areas, with specific areas making contributions to overall abilities (Judd 1988; Judd, Gardner, and Geschwind 1983; Wertheim and Botez 1961).

Zatorre's (1989) view was that the simplest acoustical processing (e.g., pitch extraction) takes place subcortically (in regions of the brain below the cortex), that the next level of processing takes place primarily in the association areas of the RH, and that other tasks may involve the auditory cortex of the LH as well. Marin (1989) contended that language is well-lateralized to the LH, but that music is not so well lateralized. He felt that the processing of acoustical aspects of music (e.g., pitch or rhythm) is well localized, but that an understanding of the internal organization of music requires a more widely distributed, diffuse neural network. The lack of localization in amusia is thus due to the nature of music itself, as it depends not just on separate acoustical events but more on the processing of complex, often abstract, relationships.

Finally, one of the difficulties associated with the study of amusia is an accurate clinical diagnosis. It may be supposed that many physicians might not even think to test for the loss of musical skills. Even when one does propose such a test, there is a problem with assuming previous musical skills (that is, musical skills prior to brain damage). Where one can generally assume that an adult patient had prior possession of reading and writing skills and production and reception of spoken language, no such assumption can be made about specific musical skills (Benton 1977; Marin 1982). However, suppose that a family member or the patient himself or herself indicates the degree of musical background. The following outline lists a battery of tests that can be used to substantiate the loss of specific musical skills (adapted from Botez and Wertheim 1959; Wertheim and Botez 1961).

I. Receptive and mnesic component
    A. Tonal, melodic, and harmonic elements
        1. Appreciation of the pitch of sounds (pitch discrimination)
        2. Naming of pitch
        3. Reproduction of vocal or instrumental sounds (pitch matching)
        4. Recognition of well-known melodies
        5. Recognition of intentional faults in well-known melodies (error detection)
        6. Identification of instruments by timbre
        7. Recognition of intervals
        8. Differentiation of major and minor chords
        9. Numeric decomposition of chords (how many tones in a chord?)
     10. Musical dictation
    B. Rhythmic element
        1. Identification of meter
        2. Imitation (reproduction) of rhythm
        3. Reproduction of a "sounded" (single-pitched) rhythm
        4. Reproduction of the rhythm of a melody played on the piano
    C. Agogic and dynamic elements
        1. Description of time (tempo)
        2. Perception of tempo variations
        3. Perception of dynamic variations
    D. Lexical elements
        1. Knowledge of clefs
        2. Note naming
        3. Identification of time values of notes and rests
        4. Solfège
        5. Naming of clefs, accidentals, and musical signs

6. Interpretation of auxillary musical notation (e.g., *piu forte, allegro assai*)

II. Productive component

A. Singing and whistling tests

1.Tonal, melodic, and harmonic elements

a) Spontaneous singing of well-known melodies

b) Spontaneous whistling of well-known melodies

c) Spontaneous singing with accompaniment

d) Repeated singing (singing back) of familiar melodies

e) Repeated singing of unfamiliar melodies

f) Repeated whistling of familiar melodies

g) Repeated whistling of unfamiliar melodies

h) Vocal reproduction of ascending and descending scales

2. Agogic and dynamic elements

a) Spontaneous singing of crescendo and decrescendo

b) Spontaneous singing of accelerando and ritardando

B. Instrumental tests

1. Appropriate posture and playing position

2. Naming parts of the instrument

3. Spontaneous playing with and without a score

4. Repeated playing (playing back) of melodies

5. Playing an instrument while singing

C. Musical writing

1. Copying of a musical text

2. Transcription of well-known melodies

D. Theory

1. Solfège

2. Musical dictation

3. Transcription

4. Interval and chord identification

5. Conducting patterns

Continued study of brain-damaged subjects is important in the ongoing effort to explicate the phenomenon of music. It would be ideal, however, if a uniform mode of neuromusical assessment, such as the one presented here, were adopted and utilized consistently in dealing with these patients.

Musical Prodigies and Savants

Throughout music history, there have been a number of child prodigies; among the most famous are Mozart, Schubert, and Mendelssohn. Révész (1925) studied a musical prodigy by the name of Erwin Nyiregyhazy from the age of 6 to 12. While Révész thoroughly documented the child's musical skills, he was unable to account for these gifts. Gardner (1983) used these examples and those of musical savants as support for his contention that music represents an autonomous intelligence represented by behavior-specific neural networks in the brain. Although learning is obviously present—each prodigy learned the music of his culture—it is difficult to account for such rapid skill acquisition unless one posits highly receptive brain mechanisms. How was it possible for Mozart to be composing and performing at such an astonishingly high level at the age of five unless he possessed a brain capable of learning these skills at a rate and to a degree far beyond the ordinary?

A musical savant is similar to a prodigy in that both possess highly advanced skills; however, the savant usually is advanced in only one or two areas and is otherwise cognitively limited. Formerly, these individuals were refered to as idiot savants. The term *idiot,* an unfortunate, stigmatizing label, refers to the fact that most of these individuals have IQs of 70 or lower. The term *savant* is from the French word for genius; however, this is misleading in that even their advanced skills are of a restricted nature.

Savants may display extraordinary performance skills or phenomenal feats of memory. Although the range of specialized skills is quite broad, some of the more common feats displayed by savants are in the areas of mathematics, calendar calculations, art, and music. One set of twins, for example, had IQs in the 60–70 range and were incapable of doing the simplest arithmetic problems (Saghal 1981). However, their skill at identifying calendar dates was quite amazing. Given a date, say March 13, they could say on which day of the week it would fall in any year from thousands of years B.C. to thousands of years A.D. Another mathematical savant could calculate the cube root of a six-digit figure within six seconds.

Many examples of savants with musical abilities have been cited (Bergman and DePue 1986; Howle 1993; Miller 1989; Sacks 1987). One blind, imbecile girl was reportedly able to play a piano composition perfectly after hearing it only once. Another young man, though blind as well as retarded, gave piano recitals to high critical acclaim. A young lady, known as Harriet, was studied extensively by a psychologist. She was extremely advanced in a wide variety of musical skills, yet she was diagnosed as both retarded and psychotic. Miller (1989) has provided the most detailed look at a particular musical savant and at musical savant syndrome in general. Continued study of prodigies and musical savants with more sophisticated techniques and cognitive theories will be important in understanding music-brain relationships.

Alzheimer's Disease

Music therapy is used frequently in geriatric situations. Related, but distinct from music therapy per se, is the study of musical behaviors in Alzheimer's patients. Persons with previously learned musical skills often demonstrate resilient procedural memories (e.g., singing or playing the piano) even in the presence of severe cognitive impairment. One 82-year-old male showed a preserved ability to play the piano from memory, even though he could not identify the composer or the title (Crystal, Grober, and Masur 1989). It was felt that this type of procedural memory was stored in the neostriatum, an area of the brain spared until the final stages of Alzheimer's disease. Johnson and Ulatowska (1995) studied an Alzheimer's patient for two years, documenting the progress of deterioration in music (tune) and language (text). In this case, song text persisted after speech was severely disturbed and song production was possible even when the patient could no longer sing the words.

Musicogenic Epilepsy and
Auditory Hallucinations

Musicogenic epilepsy is a form of reflexive epilepsy triggered by a variety of musical experiences. The stimulus may be a popular tune (Newman and Saunders 1980), a variety of classical compositions (Berman 1981), or even the patient's own music making. In one case, a 67-year-old organist induced seizures in himself by playing a specific hymn (Sutherling et al. 1980), and a 2-year-old boy experienced seizures induced by his own singing (Herskowitz, Rosman, and Geschwind 1984). Brainwave abnormalities occur during the music-induced seizures, usually in the temporal lobes and equally as often in the left or right hemispheres (Critchley 1977; Scott 1977). Frequently the cause is unknown, although musicogenic epilepsy has been associated with head injury in some cases (Fujinawa and Kawai 1978).

Some persons experience auditory hallucinations of a musical type. The sensation seems to be one of a sudden onset of a particular piece of music. Patients seem not to have any control over the onset and often it is highly disturbing; it is as if a radio that cannot be turned off were playing inside one's head (Colquhoun 1987; Hammeke, McQuillen, and Cohen 1983; Sacks 1987; Wengel et al. 1989). In personal communications, Morris Lampert, a clinical neurologist, and William Donovan, a psychiatrist, discussed a reverse case of auditory hallucination. A patient of theirs suffered from hearing inner voices that yelled obscenities inside his head; these voices could be stopped only by playing certain

Mozart concerti. As with musicogenic epilepsy, auditory hallucinations are normally accompanied by brainwave disturbances in the temporal lobes; however, this is twice as likely to occur in the left hemisphere as in the right (Scott 1977).

The study of brain-damaged populations is an important area of research. Obviously, it is vital to study musical behaviors in the "normal" population and dichotic listening tasks occupy a major place in this literature.

Dichotic Listening Tasks and Hemispheric Asymmetry

By far the most common means of determining the roles of the two hemispheres in music processing has been through the use of dichotic listening tasks. In these experiments, the subject hears two conflicting aural stimuli, one in each ear, through a set of headphones. For instance, melody A might be presented to the left ear at the same time melody B is presented to the right ear. The subject then hears four melodies—A, B, C, and D—presented to both ears sequentially and is asked to identify which one was heard previously.

If melody A, heard in the left ear, is recognized, then the right hemisphere is dominant in processing the two conflicting melodies. This is because, while each ear sends fibers to the auditory cortex of both sides of the brain, approximately 70 percent of the auditory nerve fibers are contralateral. The contralateral pathways (from one inner ear to the temporal lobe in the opposite hemisphere) are stronger than the ipsilateral pathways (from one inner ear to the temporal lobe on the same side; Kimura 1961b and 1967; Robinson and Solomon 1974). Majkowski et al. (1971) found that the contralateral response time was faster than the ipsilateral response time. Also, "contralateral pathways are capable of occluding impulses arriving along the ipsilateral pathways" (Kimura 1967, 171). Table 2 lists literature that focuses on dichotic listening tasks but includes other relevant strategies.

TABLE 2.   Dichotic Research

Study	Description and Findings
	Attentional Processes
Haydon and Spellacy 1973	The LH appears to have an advantage for attentional processes. If subjects do

(continued)

TABLE 2—*Continued*

Study	Description and Findings
	not know what kind of sound is coming, they prefer to attend with the right ear (LH) until the sound can be identified.
Peretz and Morais 1987; Provins and Jeeves 1975	Shorter reaction times to musical tasks were demonstrated with the LH.
Emmerich et al. 1981	Significantly later responses to offset times of tones were found in the LH than in the RH; there were no significant differences to onset.

Verbal vs. Nonverbal Stimuli

Study	Description and Findings
Bryden 1963; Goldstein 1961; Kimura 1961a, 1961b, 1964, and 1967	There is abundant evidence that the LH is dominant for the perception of verbal stimuli.
Bakker 1967; Curry 1967; Furst 1976; Goodglass and Calderon 1977; Surwillo 1976	Nonverbal stimuli, such as clicks and enviromental noises, are better processed by the RH.
Sidtis and Bryden 1978	Researchers found an initial RH advantage for words and LH for tones; however, following repeated experience, the expected RH advantage for tones was found.
Blumstein, Goodglass, and Tartter 1975	Assignment to hemispheres is not random. Subjects tend to remain in the same categorical dominance upon test-retest; this is especially true when the variable is music.

Singing

Study	Description and Findings
Bogen and Gordon 1971; Gordon 1974	Research data support the hypothesis that the RH is actively involved in singing. When the RH is functionally depressed with the drug sodium amobarbital, singing is severely impaired.
Borchgrevink 1982	When the LH is depressed, both speaking and singing are lost, although singing is regained more quickly than

(*continued*)

TABLE 2—*Continued*

Study	Description and Findings
	speech. A similar experiment provided conflicting information when Borchgrevnik concluded that the LH controls speech perception and production, speech prosody, musical rhythm, and the act of singing, and the RH controls pitch and tonality in singing.
	Handedness
Robinson and Solomon 1974	The pattern of LH advantage for verbal and RH advantage for nonverbal processing is true for approximately 90 percent of persons who are right-handed and 60 percent of persons who are left-handed.
Dee 1971	RH superiority for melodies was demonstrated for 75 percent of right-handed subjects, 93 percent of left-handed subjects, and 79 percent of moderately left-handed subjects.
Byrne and Sinclair 1979	The presence of left-handedness in a subject's family history may be a sign of a low degree of hemispheric specialization for language and superior memory for timbre and tonal patterns.
Kellar and Bever 1980	Family handedness affected musicians but did not affect nonmusician's ear preferences.[a]
	Pitch Discrimination
Doehring 1972; Milner 1969	No significant differences were found between the hemispheres in their ability to discriminate pitches.

(*continued*)

[a] In keeping with the discussion in chap. 2, I believe that there are no "nonmusicians." All human beings are musical in the sense of being able to respond, in some fashion, to the music of the surrounding culture. However, the term *nonmusician* is used frequently in the literature and generally refers to people who do not have formal musical training. Due to its frequency of use, it will be retained here.

TABLE 2—*Continued*

Study	Description and Findings
Martin 1975; Neff 1967	Simple pitch discriminations may be made at subcortical levels.
Sidtis 1982	A RH advantage was found for nonmusicians.
Shannon 1981	Nonmusicians showed no hemispheric advantage; musicians showed a LH advantage.
Deutsch 1975; Efron and Yund 1974	Some evidence indicates that subjects perceive higher pitches better with the right ear (LH).
Deutsch 1983; Gordon 1980	Right-handed subjects heard higher tones in the right ear, but this was not so pronounced for left-handed or ambidextrous subjects.
Deutsch 1978	These results are somewhat contradicted by a study in which there was a strong tendency to lateralize fused tonal perceptions (400 Hz to one ear, 800 Hz to the other ear) to the ear with the 800 Hz signal, even if it was weaker.
Shannon 1984	Musicians preferred higher voices to the left ear (RH).
Yund and Efron 1975	These researchers obtained less than overwhelming confirmation of which hemisphere dominates in higher pitch perception; in their experiment, 31 percent were LH dominant, 33 percent RH dominant, and 36 percent showed no dominance.
Murray and Rushford 1977	The LH appears to be better at identifying minute changes in frequency (2–30 cents, where 100 cents equal one half-step of a musical scale) as being either up or down.
Efron, Koss, and Yund 1983; Murray 1986	Ear dominance for dichotically presented tones showed RH advantage when the frequency difference was small and a shift toward LH dominance with increasing complexity.
Murray 1980	The LH was better for ascending and RH better for descending patterns.

(continued)

TABLE 2—*Continued*

Study	Description and Findings
	Loudness Discrimination
Doehring 1972	The RH demonstrated greater accuracy for loudness discriminations.
Efron and Yund 1974, 1975, and 1976	Ear dominance was not affected by loudness.
Wexler and Halwes 1981	The LH has an advantage for assessing loudness.
	Harmony
Gordon 1970, 1978a, 1978b, and 1980; Molfese, Freeman, and Palermo 1975; Peretz and Morais 1979; San Martini, DePascalis, Montirosso, and Surian 1989; Yund and Efron 1976	The RH appears to be dominant for the perception of musical chords.
Morais, Peretz, and Gudanski 1982	A RH advantage was found for nonmusicians, but not for musicians.
	Rhythm
Borchgrevink 1982; Gordon 1978b; Natale 1977; Robinson and Solomon 1974	These studies indicate that rhythm is processed in the LH.
Craig 1980; Gregory, Harriman, and Roberts 1972	These studies indicate that rhythm is processed in the RH.
Prior and Troup 1988	This study found no significant differences between the two hemispheres.
Ibbotson and Morton 1981	Subjects tapped a steady beat with one hand and a rhythm pattern in the other. Subjects found the task easy when the right hand tapped the rhythm and the left hand kept the steady beat, but almost impossible the other way around.
	Timbre
Prior and Troup 1988	These authors found no significant difference in timbre perception between the hemispheres.

(continued)

TABLE 2—*Continued*

Study	Description and Findings
	Attack and Decay Transients
Rushford-Murray 1977	Legato transients are processed more efficiently by the LH, attack transients by the RH, and steady states equally well by either hemisphere.
	Melody
Baumgarte and Franklin 1981; Cook 1973; Kimura 1964 and 1967; King and Kimura 1972; McCarthy 1969; O'Boyle and Sanford 1988; Rainbow and Herrick 1982; Spreen, Spellacy, and Reid 1970; Zatorre 1978 and 1979	RH dominance has been demonstrated for the perception of melodies.
Goodglass and Calderon 1977	RH dominance for melodic perception is maintained even with the presentation of complex stimuli, such as words superimposed over piano notes or digits sung in tonal patterns.
Kubovy, Cutting, and McGuire 1974	A melody that is unrecognizable to either ear alone (due to incompleteness) can be recognized when the input of both ears is combined.
LaBarba, Kingsberg, and Martin 1992	The results of studies dealing with more complex or analytical tasks are mixed. In a dual-task paradigm, subjects tapped with the right or left index finger as rapidly as possible alone and while listening to make judgments about unfamiliar music. Right-hand tapping was slower in the presence of music, suggesting LH processing of the music.
Pechstedt, Kershner, and Kinbourne 1989; Shannon 1980	LH advantages were found.
Wagner and Hannon 1981	A LH advantage was found for musicians and a RH advantage for nonmusicians.

(*continued*)

TABLE 2—*Continued*

Study	Description and Findings
Halperin, Nachson, and Carmon 1973	With increasing complexity of temporal pattern, subjects tended to shift from RH to LH. As the person was better able to do the task, LH superiority increased for melodic, but not chordal, stimuli.
Peretz, Morais, and Bertelson 1987	Shifting the task to a more analytical one produced a shift toward LH advantage, but shifting to overall contour did not produce a RH advantage.
Sidtis 1980	A RH advantage emerged with increasing item complexity.
Peretz 1987; Piro 1989	A LH advantage was demonstrated for nontransposed melodies (local melodic features) and a RH advantage for transposed melodies (global, contour feature).
Radocy 1979	The LH was better for holistic processing, and no significant differences were demonstrated for analytic processing.

	Musicians vs. Nonmusicians
Bever 1975; Bever and Chiarello 1974; Johnson et al. 1977	Some research indicates that musicians have a right ear (LH) preference for melody recognition and melody fragment identification, while nonmusicians have a RH preference.
Selby et al. 1982	Researchers found the expected RH advantage for nonmusicians, but found no significant differences for musicians.
Aiello 1978	Using arpeggiated triads, a LH superiority was found for nonmusicians and no significant difference in hemispheric preference for musicians.
Peretz and Morais 1980	No significant differences were found in musicians, but nonmusicians who were asked to concentrate on specific constituents of tonal patterns were more likely to show a LH advantage.

(*continued*)

TABLE 2—*Continued*

Study	Description and Findings
Oscar-Berman, Goodglass, and Donnenfeld 1974	It may be that storage mechanisms are more sensitive to laterality than perceiving and reporting mechanisms, as a RH advantage was demonstrated for pitch contours.
Baumgarte and Franklin 1981; Gordon 1978a; Johnson 1977; Morais, Peretz, and Gudanski 1982; Shannon 1981; Wagner and Hannon 1981; Zatorre 1978 and 1979	These studies indicate differences between musicians and nonmusicians; however, these differences vary and are sometimes contradictory.
Gaede, Parsons, and Bertera 1978	Subjects with low musical aptitude had greater ear differences for chords and melodic memory than those with high aptitude; musical experience had no effect.
Franklin and Baumgarte 1978; Gates and Bradshaw 1977a; Gollnick 1978; Gordon 1978b; Pechstedt, Kershner, and Kinbourne 1989; Prior and Troup 1988	No significant differences between musicians and nonmusicians in cerebral dominance for musical tasks.

	Age
Best, Hoffman, and Glanville 1982	Infants (2–4 months) showed RH advantage for music versus speech.
Anderson 1994	Infants (8–9 months) and adults showed a RH advantage for contour-violated melodies.
Johnson et al. 1983	Adults showed a LH advantage for contour-preserved melodies, but infants did not. On dichotic tests, subjects older than 50 showed a RH decline in association with age, but LH performances showed no decline.

	Gender
Borod et al. 1983	Males had a LH superiority for a pure tone audiometric test, but females showed no significant differences between hemispheres.

(*continued*)

TABLE 2—*Continued*

Study	Description and Findings
Dawe and Corballis 1986	Males had a RH advantage for melodies, and, again, no differences were found for females.
Piazza 1980	Males had a nonsignificant RH advantage for tonal sequences and females had a significant RH advantage.
Deutsch 1983; Gates and Bradshaw 1977a; Gollnick 1978; Gordon 1978b; Mazzucchi, Parma, and Cattelani 1981; Pechstedt, Kershner, and Kinbourne 1989	No gender differences were found.

	Emotional Tone
Bryden, Ley, and Sugarman 1982; Corballis 1983	A RH advantage for identifying the emotional content of tonal sequences was found.
Joseph 1988	A review of the literature on normals, neurosurgical, and brain-injured subjects indicated a RH advantage for emotional displays.

	Eye Movements
Bakan 1969	An eye movement to the right at the onset of problem solving indicates activation of the LH and vice versa.
Blakeslee 1980; Krashen 1977	Individuals with a preponderance of eye movements to the right tend to major in science and do better on standardized tests of verbal and mathematical skills, while "left movers" tend to major more often in the humanities and social sciences and consider themselves more musical and artistic.
Williams and Hodges 1980	Using eye positions rather than eye movements, data were obtained that led to the formulation of a hypothesis that individuals who were successful

(continued)

TABLE 2—*Continued*

Study	Description and Findings
	at a selected musical task (determining whether a single tone was part of a previously heard melody) used a balanced processing style, while those unable to do the task used a predominantly analytic or holistic processing style. Perhaps musicians in certain, if not most, musical behaviors utilize a combination of processing styles (also see Rainbow and Herrick 1982).

Critique of Dichotic Listening Tasks

The variety of results reported in the literature has led several authors to take a cautious approach in interpretation. Gates and Bradshaw (1977b) reviewed more than 200 studies concerned with the role of the cerebral hemispheres in music perception. (For a review of several additional non-American sources, see Damasio and Damasio 1977). They concluded that the left hemisphere may take a greater role in sequential and analytical aspects of music, while the right hemisphere may be more important for a sound gestalt. However, they are careful to point out that music perception is extremely complex, and categorical dominance for music perception has not yet been established. This position was echoed by Franklin and Franklin (1978), Hodges (1978 and 1979), Levy (1985), and Luria and Simernitskaya (1977). Bradshaw and Nettleton (1981) stress the notion of a continuum of functions rather than a rigid dichotomy of function between left and right hemispheres. They placed an emphasis on quantitative rather than on qualitative differences and on degree of processing rather than kind.

Corballis, too, sounded a note of caution. "In the more complex tasks, such as the perception of music or of faces, or even in reading, lateral asymmetries may even change direction depending on quite subtle aspects of the task. In most cases, then, we can suppose that both cerebral hemispheres are involved, and the interhemispheric differences are slight compared with the cooperation that exists between them" (Corballis 1983, 56).

Several authors stress that other things going on in the brain affect lateralization; that is, it is not just a function of anatomy (Morais and

Landercy 1977; Reinke 1981; Schweiger and Maltzman 1985). Perhaps laterality effects in audition are due not only to the type of sound being processed (verbal or nonverbal) but also by the task required of the subjects and by subject attributes (e.g., training; see Bartholomeus 1974; Bradshaw, Nettleton, and Geffen 1972; Commandy 1974; LaBarba, Kingsberg, and Martin 1992; Mazzucchi, Parma, and Cattelani, 1981; Mazziotta et al. 1982). Finally, Sergent (1993a) believed that there were enough criticisms of dichotic listening task research to throw any applications to music processing into serious question.

Electroencephalogram Research

Due to the activity of neurons, the brain exhibits a constant state of electrical activity. The nature of this activity varies according to the current state of the organism. To study overall brain responses, neuroscientists monitor the brain's electrical activity by means of an electroencephalogram (EEG). An EEG involves the attachment of several electrodes to the scalp over the frontal, parietal, occipital, and temporal areas, as well as to the ears (Chusid 1985; Gur and Gur 1994). An EEG measures the summed activity of millions of neurons lying under the skull.

An EEG tracing can be analyzed according to frequency (cps or Hz), amplitude (microvolts), form, and distribution. Most often reported are the frequency components of the EEG. These components and their associated states of arousal are: delta rhythm (0.5–4.0 Hz), deep sleep; theta rhythm (4.5–8.0 Hz), periods of dreaming; alpha rhythm (8.5–12.0 Hz) inward directed consciousness or relaxed awareness; beta rhythm (12.5–32.0 Hz), full alertness; beta is sometimes further divided into beta I (12.5–16.0 Hz), beta II (16.5–20.0 Hz), beta III (20.5–24.0 Hz), beta IV (24.5–28.0 Hz), and beta V (28.5–32.0 Hz) (Flohr and Miller 1993).

An EEG is not as useful for determining specific brain functions as it is for discerning general states of arousal. Given the enormous variety of variables in EEG research on music—such as differences in the musical backgrounds of subjects, in the kind of music stimuli used, or in the musical tasks involved—it is not surprising that the results have been less than consistent.

EEG Comparisons Between Music and Other Tasks

Several EEG studies have made comparisons between language and music. Giannitrapani (1970) found that there was a smaller change in EEG amplitude moving from a resting condition to music listening than from resting to listening to speech. Osborne and Gale (1976) found the left hemisphere more activated for words and arithmetic and the right hemisphere for music. Molfese, Freeman, and Palermo (1975) demonstrated that subjects had larger auditory evoked responses for nonspeech sounds (including music) in the right hemisphere. Konovalov and Otmakhova (1984) found that verbal information processing was accompanied by marked depression of the alpha rhythm in the left hemisphere (a hypothesized indicator of attention), but the analysis of music, especially by persons with no special training, affected the left and right hemispheres equally. Davidson and Schwartz (1977) found that nonmusicians had more right hemispheric activation while whistling versus talking, but musicians showed no differences in the two activities; neither group showed differences between singing and talking in the amount of EEG activation.

EEG Studies of Music Tasks

EEG patterns have been examined while subjects engaged in a variety of musical activities. Wang's (1977) subjects had decreases in EEG amplitude in the temporal region when a pitch discrimination task involved intervals of a quarter-step or less. Rogers and Walter (1981) found alpha waves to be in synchrony with strongly rhythmic portions of a Mozart symphony; they called this process "auditory driving." Osaka and Osaka (1992) also found that peak alpha frequency of EEG changed as the tempo of music changed. In contrast, Borling (1981) found no significant differences in alpha production between stimulative (faster) and sedative (slower) music.

Creutzfeldt and Ojemann (1989) recorded neuronal activity in the temporal lobes as they played three kinds of music to patients who were undergoing open brain surgery. Classical music and folk songs caused a decrease in discharge rate, while rock music caused an increase. There were no significant differences among the superior, middle, or inferior temporal gyri or between left and right hemispheres. Some neurons showed a slight entrainment (that is, they fired in synchrony to the musical rhythm), while other neurons showed a change of activity related to musical phrases.

Wieser and Mazzola (1986) demonstrated that EEG recordings made from depth electrodes implanted in the left hippocampus reflected a musical consonance/dissonance dichotomy; the left hippocampus, but not the right, was affected by previous sequences of dissonance in responding to a single consonance. In one study, researchers implanted depth electrodes in the left and right hippocampi (Cornett et al. 1992).

An analysis of beta activity indicated increased activation in the left anterior hippocampal gyrus to dissonant dyads. The right anterior hippocampal gyrus showed greater activation to diminished than to minor triads and to major than to augmented triads. San Martini and Rossi (1988) found a moderate degree of EEG power asymmetry favoring the left hemisphere during a chord recognition task. They were unable to support the hypothesis that individual differences of ear advantage in a dichotic chord test would significantly affect EEG frequencies.

In a study of neuromotor control, subjects tapped out simple and complex rhythm patterns (Lang et al. 1990). In the simple patterns, both left and right primary motor cortices were activated. In the complex patterns, not only were the motor cortices activated, but there was also very large activation of the medial, central cortex. This latter area, which has the function of controlling very precise timing plans, was activated four seconds prior to the performance of the difficult task.

For a music listening task, no significant differences were found in EEG readings between males and females (Hirshkowitz, Earle, and Paley 1978). Right hemispheric activation accompanied music listening for nonmusicians but not for musicians. In another music-listening task, the greatest change in EEG readings was found in the right hemisphere (Duffy, McAnalty, and Schachter 1984). Researchers obtained data showing bilateral involvement, with the left hemisphere predominant, for notes and scales but bilateral involvement, with the right hemisphere predominant, for melody (Breitling, Guenther, and Rondot 1987). Again, given the number of variables, it is difficult to find many significant patterns in this body of research.

Alpha Brainwaves in Music Tasks

The role of alpha production during music and other conditions has received some attention. Because alpha waves are associated with a resting state, a decrease in alpha waves may be associated with an increase in attention. A number of researchers have found that alpha production decreases during music listening conditions (Duffy, Bartels, and Burchfield 1981; Flohr and Miller 1993; Furman 1978; Inglis 1980; Taub, Tanguay, and Clarkson 1976).

Whether musicians and nonmusicians differ in this regard is somewhat debatable. Several earlier studies found that musicians produced more alpha activity than nonmusicians in music listening conditions (Wagner 1975a and 1975b; Wagner and Mentzel 1977) and that musicians increased their alpha output during music while nonmusicians decreased in alpha (McElwain 1979; Wagner and Mentzel 1977). These results would seem to contradict the expectation that musicians would show greater levels of concentration when listening to music and thus produce less alpha. Wagner (1975b) notes this discrepancy and tries to account for it; since his subjects did not show a difference in alpha activity between silence and music conditions, perhaps they were attending to something else during the silence. Walker (1980) concluded that the incidence of alpha waves may vary according to a positive or negative reaction to the music, and Inglis (1980) concluded further that individual differences in musical responses may be as great within a select group of music students as between music and nonmusic students.

Researchers have looked at the differences between musicians and nonmusicians in terms of the amount of alpha present in the left and right hemispheres. Some found no overall difference in alpha between musicians and nonmusicians, but that alpha was significantly higher in the left temporal lobe than the right for musicians, with the reverse pattern for nonmusicians (McElwain 1979; McKee, Humphrey, and McAdam 1973). Others obtained the opposite data for nonmusicians; that is, alpha decreased over the right temporal region during music listening (Duffy, McAnalty, and Schachter 1981; Taub et al. 1976). In the most recent and most sophisticated of these studies (Petsche et al. 1988), researchers found that, for musicians, alpha decreased over a much larger region, with a stronger decrease in the left hemisphere involving the temporal region and invading the precentral, frontal, and parietal areas. Nonmusicians exhibited a decrease in alpha restricted to the left midtemporal area (auditory cortex).

Brainwaves Other Than Alpha

Only a small amount of research has analyzed components other than the alpha bandwidth in relation to music. Wachhaus (1973) was not able to help college students perform better on a standardized music test by training them to register more beta waves (hypothetically, an indication of greater attention). Janata and Petsche (1993) demonstrated that context violation (when a chord progression did not follow the expected resolution) was indicated primarily by changes in delta amplitude at right temporal sites lying above the primary auditory cortex. Context ambiguity evoked increases in delta and theta at central locations (and in alpha at right parietotemporal sites). Identification of individual resolutions occurred in the frontal cortex, mainly on the right side, in all bandwidths except alpha. These data confirmed that a form of expectancy operates in musical contexts and can be observed by changes in EEG readings.

Flohr and Miller (1993) monitored EEG as it changed from a baseline condition (sitting quietly) to one involving tapping a rhythm to music. In this circumstance, beta II decreased as theta increased from baseline to music in the sensory motor cortex, right temporal lobe, and left anterior, but not posterior, temporal lobe. Two years later, the same subjects were monitored again (Flohr and Miller 1995). There were no significant developmental differences across the frequency bands in response to Vivaldi but many differences in response to an Irish folk song; specifically, there was a significant increase in alpha production in the Irish folk song but not Vivaldi.

A tendency toward analyzing more components of the EEG spectrum, along with more detailed localization, is reflected in a study of musicians and nonmusicians (Petsche et al. 1988). For these subjects, alpha and theta decreased in the left temporal region and extended to the precentral, frontal, and parietal areas. This change was more pronounced for musicians.

EEG Coherence Patterns

EEG coherence refers to two brain sites linked in patterns of activation, which may involve connections within or between hemispheres. In the study just mentioned (Petsche et al. 1988), only musicians showed zones of locally increased coherence (two adjacent areas on the same side) and interhemispheric coherence (linking similar regions on the two sides), mainly involving beta II in the temporoposterior, parietal, and occipital regions. In general, the left temporal region was activated for both musicians and nonmusicians, but the right hemisphere was activated only in the musicians. These results corroborated an earlier study (Petsche, Pochberger, and Rappelsberger 1985).

Petsche (1992; Petsche et al. 1993) found that general brain strategies for various mental tasks (including music listening) were revealed by EEG brain mapping. Differences were found between subjects with the best and poorest performances during a creative task. Hemispheric engagement was not the same for every EEG band, and laterality may change with a shift in musical style. He found increased coherence in the alpha band when subjects were engaged in musical tasks. Musical imagination tasks were accompanied by more increases in coherence than music listening and more differences in lateralization across more frequency bands. The difficulty of the task was parallel with the number of coherence changes in upper beta frequencies.

Researchers examined spontaneous EEG (i.e., at rest) and found significant differences between subjects with and without musical training

(Johnson et al. 1995). Musically trained subjects exhibited significantly higher coherence values both within and between hemispheres. These differences, found mainly in the upper and lower frequency bands and less so in alpha, may indicate specialized brain reorganization enhancing the ability to process ordered acoustical patterns (i.e., music).

Whether musical training brings about a reorganization of the brain or the presence of a particular brain organization leads certain individuals into musical studies is presently unknown. However, evidence is gathering for the effect of training. Significantly higher coherence values, particularly between hemispheres, was found for female musicians. These findings are supported by anatomical evidence of more fibers in the corpus callosum of females connecting the parietal and temporal areas of the two hemispheres (Steinmetz et al. 1992). The notion of training effects was further corroborated by research using magnetic resonance imaging to show that the planum temporale (PT, an area of the primary auditory cortex) was more lateralized to the left in musicians than nonmusicians (Schlang et al. 1994). Musicians who began their training before the age of 7 or who had perfect pitch had a larger left PT than other musicians or nonmusicians. In finding a larger corpus callosum (involved in transferring information from one hemisphere to the other) among musicians, again especially for those who started their training early, researchers concluded that these differences were linked to early bimanual training. Corroborating evidence came from Elbert and others (1995) who found that string players differed from non-string players in that an area in the right primary somatosensory cortex, corresponding to control of the fingers of the left hand, was larger and total neuronal activity was greater for the string players. The younger the age at which the string player began studying, the greater the changes.

As with the previously presented general EEG research, it is difficult to discern patterns in the research involving specific EEG bandwidths. Results may be affected by the amount of music training, gender, or the nature of the musical stimuli (Steinberg et al. 1992). Music listening affects broad areas of the brain with specific regions or "nodes" activated. No experiment has yielded strictly lateralized results. Both hemispheres are activated by music, though the level and specific location of activity varies as parameters vary (Petsche et al. 1988; Steinberg et al. 1992).

Auditory Event-Related Potentials

An important line of research involves the measurement of event-related potentials (ERPs), which are transient aspects of the EEG that occur immediately after an internal or external event. A computer is used to average EEG readings of a short period (e.g., 1 second) following multiple presentations of a stimulus. This process allows random aspects of the electrical activity to be cancelled out, while the electrical activity occuring in time-locked response to the stimulus is revealed (Brown, Marsh, and Ponsford 1985).

ERPs have three characteristics: (1) there is a positive or negative change in the direction of the wave pattern, (2) there is an intensity level (or amplitude) to the wave, and (3) there is an onset latency or time lapse (roughly 200–600 milliseconds); this is the time the brain takes to process information. Different components of the ERP are identified by letter and number. For example, P3 (or P300) is a positive wave whose maximum amplitude occurs approximately 300 ms after the stimulus.

ERPs arise as a result of cognitive processes and are generated either in preparation for response or as a result of sensory perception (Arnadottis 1990). Variations in the ERP may vary with the psychological significance of the stimulus situation. For example, N1 has been related to attention, N4 to a more generalized function perhaps reflecting higher levels of perceptual processing, and P3 to cognitive information processing. One of the main advantages of ERP is that it is time-locked to a stimulus (Brown, Marsh, and Ponsford 1985) and provides a means for studying the timing of different mental processes (Hoffman 1986). The order of different ERP components can be observed, and the order of different stages of the processing task can thus be determined. Research on auditory event-related potentials specifically related to music has focused on the following components: N1 (or peak-to-peak N1–P2), N4, and P3.

N1 Event-Related Potentials

The N1 wave (a negative wave occurring 100–200 ms after the onset of a stimulus) is interpreted as indicating selective attention to an initial stimulus; an increase in amplitude is related to the degree of attention being paid to a stimulus (Benson and Zaidel 1985). In one experiment, subjects were presented with a task requiring them to detect changes in a series of tone pips (Schwent, Snyder, and Hillyard 1976). When the differences were pitch changes only, N1 was larger for higher and lower frequencies but not for middle frequencies. For differences in localization cues (left, right, and midline), large N1 amplitude changes were found for both left and right tones but not for the midline. When differences involved both pitch and localization cues, a large N1 was found for left, right, and midline. Others found a smaller and delayed N1 in the presence of music (Dalbokova, Kolev, and Kristeva 1988). Paulus (1992) found no difference in N1–P2 ERPs between consonant or dissonant chords or between hemispheres. In another study involving N1–P2 ERPs, subjects demonstrated greater LH advantange for identifying deviant tones; this effect was enhanced in the presence of music (Dalbokova and Kolev 1992).

N1 is also associated with a mismatch between a stored trace and a novel stimulus and is sometimes referred to as mismatch negativity (MMN). In one study, subjects were divided into high, medium, and low groups based on their scores on the Seashore *Pitch-Discrimination Test* (Lang et al. 1990). For "good" subjects, an MMN was elicited with a difference of only 19 Hz, while, for "poor" subjects, it took a difference of 99 Hz. Another experiment involved the use of an "oddball" paradigm in which subjects were presented with a series of 1,000 Hz tones (Tervaniemi et al. 1993). Tones of 1,016 Hz were interspersed at random intervals, and the MMN was monitored each time they occurred. No differences were found between left and right hemispheres, and no differences were found between subjects with absolute pitch and those without. MMN was larger and earlier with piano tones than with pure tones and for half-steps more than quarter-steps. The data from these two studies are in contrast to an earlier study in which a negative component (N2 at 154 ms) was larger to mismatched tones than to standard tones, regardless of the size of the pitch disparity (Ford, Roth, and Kopell 1976). An N210 wave was identified as a type of mismatch negativity when it was elicited by breaks in the temporal order of a pitch pattern (Nordby, Roth, and Pfefferbaum 1988).

The results of these five studies are not sufficient to lead to broad conclusions about the nature of musical perception. However, they do indicate that continued study of N1 may be of value.

N4 Event-Related Potentials

N4 (N400) is an ERP that reflects violated expectations and has been elicited by linguistic incongruities. However, N4 was not elicited by musical incongruities in two studies (Besson and Macar 1987; Paller, McCarthy, and Wood 1992). This may be one indication of differences between linguistic and musical neural-processing strategies. It has also been pointed out that perhaps Besson and Macar did not find N4 because they used nonmusicians as subjects (Walton et al. 1988). Whereas musicians might be expected to possess the necessary analytical rules for music processing, nonmusicians may not.

A number of studies involving late positive components (LPC) have demonstrated differences between musicians and nonmusicians. Besson and Faita (1994) found that LPCs of musicians had larger amplitudes and shorter onset latencies than nonmusicians for familiar melodies compared to unfamiliar melodies and for nondiatonic rather than diatonic incongruities. They also found that LPC amplitudes decreased with repetitions of incongruous endings of familiar melodies (Faita and Besson 1994). Similarly, LPCs were larger in amplitude and shorter in latency for musicians compared to nonmusicians, for harmonic compared melodic incongruencies, and for the ends of familiar compared to unfamiliar excerpts. Presumably, larger amplitudes are associated with better performance on the task (and/or more confidence in doing the task) and shorter latencies are associated with faster processing times. The LPC may also be an indication of musical expectancy.

P3 Event-Related Potentials

Research involving P3 has been much more extensive than that of N1 and N4. P3 is hypothesized to be an indicator of "working" memory, the comparison of incoming stimuli to long-term memory traces, and has been linked to the detection of musical events (Cohen and Erez 1991; Frisina, Walton, and Crummer 1988; Hantz and Crummer 1988; Paller, McCarthy, and Wood 1992; Paulus 1988; Schwent, Snyder, and Hillyard 1976). It has also been found that the more difficult the discrimination task (i.e., the closer together the pitches were in a pitch discrimination task), the larger the latency of P3 (Ford, Roth, and Kopell 1976; Walton et al. 1988). Musicians showed an inverse relationship between accuracy and P3 latency (Chuang et al. 1988). Presumably, these results indicate the fact that the brain takes longer to make a more difficult discrimination decision. This was confirmed by Levett and Martin (1992), who found that musicians had a larger P300L (a later component of P3) than nonmusicians in identifying harmonic errors; this was presumably due to the additional processing time. They also contended that greater P300L amplitudes for different music perception tasks indicated context updating for rare events.

P3 amplitude was larger when subjects were accurate in their identification of timbral differences (Walton et al. 1988), and P3 was greatly reduced (smaller amplitude and shorter latency) or absent altogether in subjects with absolute pitch (Hantz et al. 1992; Klein, Coles, and Donchin 1984). P3 was not different for musicians and nonmusicians for easier timbre discriminations (between viola and cello or between silver or wooden flutes), but musicians had shorter latencies than nonmusicians for a more difficult timbre discrimination (between B-flat and F tubas) (Crummer et al. 1994). Also, in keeping with the previous research, P3 was smaller in amplitude and shorter in latency for subjects with absolute pitch. Apparently, the possession of absolute pitch reduces or eliminates the need for "working" memory strategies.

No significant differences in P3 amplitudes or latencies were found between musicians and nonmusicians on a timbre or chord discrimination task, except for the most difficult of four tasks (Crummer et al. 1988). Researchers who studied infants (10 wks, 6 days–13 wks, 2 days), found that, for both verbal and musical conditions, females had a higher P3 amplitude in the left than the right hemisphere and males had the reverse pattern (Shucard et al. 1981). Others found no significant differences in P3 responses to a chord stimulus between right and left hemispheres for either autistic children or matched normal subjects (Dawson et al. 1988). P3 was found to be a useful technique for studying neural and cognitive responses to music in patients with senile dementia of the Alzheimer's type (SDAT). SDAT subjects performed poorer and had a longer P3 latency than healthy subjects on a variety of music perception tasks (Swartz et al. 1992).

Using auditory event-related potentials (AERP) without reference to specific wave components, researchers identified responses to music intervals indicating that these intervals may have individual significance, even out of context (Cohen et al. 1993). One group of researchers found a right hemispheric dominance for chords (Taub et al. 1976), and another found a greater AERP amplitude for music in the right hemisphere (Shucard, Shucard, and Thomas 1977). Thomas and Shucard (1983) identified differing patterns of left and right hemispheric AERPs, depending on the task required. Peak amplitudes were smaller in the right hemisphere than left among nonmusicians during a music condition (DePascalis, Marucci, and Penna 1987); this indicated more activation in the right hemisphere. In an experiment comparing sophisticated to unsophisticated musicians, more right hemispheric engagement was found for the unsophisticated subjects and no significant hemispheric differences for sophisticates on a music task (DePascalis et al. 1987).

Because this research has taken place since 1970 and the sophistication of ERP recording techniques is rapidly advancing, this line of research holds promise of significant findings in the future.

Brain-Imaging Techniques

In recent years, neuroscientists have developed new techniques that allow them to produce images related to biological activity in the brain.

Most of these techniques have been applied to the study of music in only limited ways.

MEG and SQUID

The brain's electrical activity produces a magnetic field in the space surrounding the head, and measurements of these magnetic fields can be used to locate neural activity (Williamson and Kaufman 1988). Using magnetoencephalography (MEG), researchers observed the magnetic field over the parietal scalp starting about 300 ms after a novel stimulus (Beisteiner et al. 1994). They called this P300m and linked it to the P300 wave discussed in the preceding section. P300m was found in the right temporoparietal lobe for 7 of 12 subjects performing a harmonic discrimination task. Also using MEG, researchers found that the auditory cortex contributed to the suppression of alpha rhythms while subjects scanned memory for musical tones (Kaufman et al. 1991).

The superconducting quantum interference device (SQUID) is a newer and more sensitive version of MEG; based on the synchronous activity of large cellular groups, SQUID provides spatial information in millimeters and temporal information in milliseconds (Hari 1990). As reported in chapter 4, SQUID data has been used to determine that the auditory cortex is mapped for the frequency of pure tones and the pitch of complex tones (Williamson and Kaufman 1988). Furthermore, the arrangement of the tonotopic map in the auditory cortex is much like that of a piano keyboard, with equal distance between octaves.

MRI

Magnetic Resonance Imaging (MRI) is an imaging technique in which the subject is placed inside a large magnet (Ackerman 1992; Gur and Gur 1994). MRI distinguishes structures with great detail but cannot provide information about functions. As indicated in the section on EEG studies, researchers used MRI data to document that the left planum temporale and corpus callosum of musicians were larger than those of nonmusicians (Schlang et al. 1994). This difference was exaggerated for those musicians who started their training before age 7. Researchers concluded that these results gave evidence of musical training affecting brain organization. A subsequent study of 30 musicians and 30 nonmusicians, matched for age, sex, and handedness (all right-handed), revealed that the planum temporale was more strongly lateralized (i.e., larger) in the left hemisphere for musicians than nonmusicians. Those musicians who possessed perfect pitch were more strongly lateralized to the left than musicians without perfect pitch (Schlang et al. 1995).

PET

Positron emission tomography (PET) requires that a radioactive sub-stance, such as water, glucose, or oxygen, be inhaled or injected into the bloodstream. Depending on the technique used, PET scans show the brain's metabolic activity or its blood flow (*regional cerebral blood flow* or rCBF) (Herscovitch 1994). In constructing a picture of the brain, areas with greater concentrations of the radioactively tagged substance can be identified. Using these procedures while a subject is engaged in a particular task (e.g., reading a book or listening to music), provides in-dications of which parts of the brain are most actively involved (Raichle 1994). Paired-image subtraction is a commonly used technique in which the PET image of one task (e.g., control) is subtracted from another (e.g., experiment). This procedure allows the identification of areas of the brain that are most active during the second task (Posner and Raichle 1994).

Regional cerebral blood flow was measured in 12 adults as they took the Rhythm section of the *Seashore Measures of Musical Talents* (Roland, Skinhoj, and Lassen 1981). The results indicated greater activa-tion of the right temporal and parietal lobe along with the right pos-terior, inferior frontal area. PET data also showed the right temporal cortex to be active in perceptual analyses of melodies (Zatorre 1994; Zatorre, Evans, and Meyer 1994).

Bilateral activation of the temporal lobes was found for a real and imagined performance of a musical task (judging the pitch of selected words in a song), indicating that imaginal and perceptual processes share an underlying neural substrate (Zatorre 1994). However, a comparison of the pitch of a pair of syllables during a speech perception task prefer-entially activated the right inferior frontal cortex (Zatorre et al. 1992). Stimulation with chords also elicited bilateral pariotemporal activations and diffuse right-greater-than-left frontotemporal asymmetries (Mazziotta et al. 1982). These results were corroborated by Mazziota (1988), who used PET scans to demonstrate greater right hemispheric activation on the harmony and tonal memory portions of the Seashore test. In another experiment, Mazziota's subjects showed greater left hemi-spheric activation while listening to speech and greater right hemispheric activation while listening to music. In both conditions, the frontal cortex was also involved.

Twelve subjects were imaged while undergoing four tasks: (1) lis-tening to a sequence of noise bursts, (2) listening to unfamiliar tonal melodies, (3) comparing the pitch of the first two notes of a pair of melodies, and (4) comparing the pitch of the first and last notes of melodies (Zatorre 1994). Melodic processing compared to noise bursts activated right superior temporal and occipital cortices; pitch judgments related to passive listening activated the right frontal lobe and deactivated the left primary auditory cortex. Thus, perceptual analysis and short-term retention of pitch information preferentially activates the right frontal and temporal lobes. However, these tasks activated a widely distributed system in both hemispheres. Mazziotta stresses the fact that localizations in these experiments are areas of maximal activity and that many additional regions are also involved in these different tasks. "In fact, I would be hard pressed to name areas of the brain that did not respond" (Mazziotta 1988, 108).

In a different study, ten accomplished pianists underwent a PET scan while engaged in a variety of musical tasks (Sergent et al. 1992). Subjects listened to scales played on a piano, played scales on a keyboard with the right hand, read a musical score, and read a musical score while hearing it performed. All of these were components of the main task, playing an unfamiliar Bach partita with the right hand. PET scans were coordinated with MRI data about anatomical structures, and data generated by one component of the main task were subtracted from another component. The result allowed the researchers to link specific regions of the brain with specific task components. In each case, there was a broad distribution of neural activity in both hemispheres. For example, when activation from reading the score alone was subtracted from reading the score and listening to it, greater activity was found in both left and right secondary auditory regions, both left and right superior temporal regions, and the left supramarginal gyrus. These data indicate that sight-reading and playing the piano engages broadly distributed neural areas, with locally specialized regions, that are adjacent to, but distinct from, the neural substrates of verbal processing. Furthermore, evidence points to specific, music-processing regions of the brain.

Five professional pianists participated in a PET study involving three conditions: (a) rest, (b) scales, in which they performed scales with both hands up and down on an electronic keyboard suspended above them, and (c) Bach, in which they performed the third movement of Bach's Italian Concerto from memory (Fox et al. 1995). Task-induced changes in regional blood flow were measured by PET imaging and confirmed with MRI data. The subjects' eyes were closed and covered during all three conditions. Despite the similar demands of dexterity and bimanual coordination, the scale condition preferentially activated left somatic sensory and motor systems, while the Bach condition activated supplementary motor areas bilaterally, along with right superior premotor and right superior parietal cortex. Primary motor cortex and cerebellum were symmetrically activated by both tasks. The Bach condition activated extraprimary auditory cortex bilaterally, while scales did not.

Clearly, the use of brain-imaging techniques offers the possibility of major advances in neuromusical research.

Emotional Responses to Music

Emotional responses are obviously a major facet of many musical experiences. Although neuroscientists have studied cognition to a far greater degree than emotion, enough is known about the latter to provide at least a starting point. Included in this section is a brief review of the neurobiology of emotion, a speculative application to music, and a review of the scant research done in this area. To begin with, consider a brief review of the major components involved in emotion (Bloom, Lazerson, and Hofstadter 1985; LeDoux 1986 and 1994).

- The Autonomic Nervous System (ANS) contains both the sympathetic division (prepares the body for fight or flight) and the parasympathetic division (works to conserve energy). The sympathetic division energizes the body by speeding up the heart rate, stimulating the secretion of adrenalin and a variety of neurotransmitters, and stimulating the conversion of glycogen for energy. The parasympathetic division slows down the heart rate and stimulates peristalsis (digestion) and the secretion of saliva. Although the two divisions seem to be contradictory, they work in tandem as the ANS regulates a complicated series of chemical reactions. The historical view of the ANS was one of "mass discharge"; however, recent evidence indicates that the ANS can respond with a wide variety of patterns of peripheral activity.
- The reticular formation in the brain stem receives input from all the sensory organs. It has fibers that connect with the cortex, the limbic system, and motor systems. Within the reticular formation, the locus coeruleus regulates the secretion of the neurotransmitter norepinephrine, triggering emotional arousal, and the substantia nigra regulates the secretion of dopamine, facilitating some pleasurable sensations. The reticular activating system (RAS) monitors incoming sensory signals and acts as a filtering device. Signals that are weak or unchanging are ignored; for example, a person who wears glasses constantly may be unaware of them unless they

begin to rub uncomfortably. Strong or changing signals are sent on to other parts of the brain for further analysis and/or action.

- The limbic system consists of the thalamus (a major relay between sensory input and the cortex; it is also involved in the arousal and activation of the association areas of the cortex), hypothalamus (regulates the autonomic nervous system), pituitary (the "master gland" that controls the release of hormones into the bloodstream), amygdala (involved with agressive behaviors and fear reactions), hippocampus (integrates incoming sensory information and involved in memory storage), and other subcortical structures. There are rich interconnections among the various components of the limbic system and between the limbic system and other parts of the brain. The limbic system receives messages about external events directly from sensory organs and from the primary and association cortex. Because many hormonal reactions take place here, the limbic system is highly involved in emotional experiences.

- Various parts of the cortex are also involved in emotional responses, particularly in cognitive assessment. Of particular importance may be the inferior parietal lobule (IPL). The IPL receives highly processed information directly from the association areas of the sensory modalities (e.g., auditory association area) as well as direct input from the limbic system and reticular activating system. The IPL, thus, serves to integrate information from all these inputs. "Such a pattern of inputs seems ideal for the mediation of conscious feelings" (Ledoux 1986, 352).

    Interestingly enough, experiments have demonstrated that the cortex is not necessary for certain types of emotional experience and that many emotional experiences take place without conscious awareness (Ledoux 1994). For example, auditory fear conditioning can cause a fear reaction in a rat, even if the auditory cortex is removed. This is evidence of an emotional response occurring independent of conscious awareness.

Before looking at music, consider first a nonmusical example of how sounds are linked to emotional responses. Imagine you are walking along the street at night. Suddenly you hear the snarling and growling of an angry dog. Immediately your heart rate increases and you are prepared to run away. Seconds later, however, you realize that the dog is behind a fence and, although your heart is still pounding, you begin to relax as you become aware that you are not in danger. On subsequent nights, you anticipate the dog's barking as you approach his yard and it does not cause the same reaction.

This vignette illustrates several important points that are useful in an understanding of emotional responses to music. First, there are subcortical pathways that give us a "quick-and-dirty" reaction mechanism. This allows us to react immediately to sounds, an important survival benefit. Second, there are cortical pathways that take slightly longer but give us a more complete cognitive assessment of the situation. Finally, expectations, based on memories of past occurrences, shape behaviors in anticipation of events.

The same system is in operation in a music listening situation. Music occurs in real time and we are able to respond immediately to sounds as they happen in the flow of the musical moment. We are especially aroused by sudden changes—in tempo, dynamics, timbre, or even a wrong note. Likewise, cognitive assessment can attach meaning to these sounds. Recognition of relationships between parts takes place over a longer time scale than note-to-note. Familiarity with the music, or even the style of music, can create expectations that influence responses to the music.

It may be helpful to think of emotion in three ways (Buck 1986): Emotion I involves homeostasis (maintenance of body stability) and adaptation and can be measured by monitoring physiological changes. Emotion II involves spontaneous expressive tendencies and can be measured by direct observation of external displays, such as postures and facial expressions. Emotion III involves the subjective experiences of a person and is often monitored by self-report.

Emotion I: Homeostasis and Adaptation

From an evolutionary standpoint, Emotion I provides animals and human beings with a means of maintaining body stability and adapting to environmental circumstances. The effects of Emotion I can be monitored by observing changes in the autonomic nervous system, immune system, and hormonal output. More and more scientific attention is being paid to the effect emotions can have on the body and it is generally accepted that what goes on in the mind/brain can affect the body (Gazzaniga 1988; Hall 1989).

A significant amount of research on physiological responses to music is reviewed in chapter 9. Specific relationships linking particular musical parameters (e.g., increasing tempo) and corresponding physiological responses (e.g., increasing heart rate) have not yet been determined and may not, in fact, exist, due to the idiosyncratic nature of musical responses. However, it is abundantly clear that musical experiences can elicit a wide variety of physiological responses, including changes in heart rate, blood pressure, brain waves, and muscle contractions.

Also reviewed in chapter 9 is research concerning music's effect on the immune system. While the results of music in psychoneuroimmunology are somewhat mixed (as is to be expected in any complicated interaction), there is a growing notion that music can elicit changes in such biochemicals as endorphins, cortisol, ACTH (adrenocorticotropic hormone), interleukin-1, and secretory immunoglobin A. For additional discussions of the effects of music on the immune system, see Aldridge 1993, Maranto and Scartelli 1992, and Scartelli 1992.

Practical applications of these findings are being made, and the International Society for Music in Medicine has been founded with the intent of researching and applying the effects of music in medical/clinical settings. For nearly twenty years, physicians in Germany have been using anxiolytic music to alleviate pain and anxiety (Spintge and Droh 1992 and 1995). They report significant effects of music on the neurovegetative systems based on a study of more than 90,000 patients. Actually, the complete program involves four types of emotional measures: (a) cognitive-behavioral, using psychological tests of state and trait anxiety, (b) physiological, including pulse rate, blood pressure beat-to-beat, EKG, GSR (galvanic skin response), respiratory rate, skin temperature, EMG (electromyograms; measurements of the electrical activity of muscles), surface or deep-brain EEG, EEG brain mapping, blood levels of beta-endorphins, ACTH, cortisol, and, lately, rhythmic variability of neurovegetative functions (here, neurovegetative refers to systems governed by the autonomic nervous system and acting on inner organs and organ systems; Spintge and Droh 1992), (c) nonverbal psychomotor behavior, described by analyzing facial expressions and other behaviors (e.g., nail biting, pacing, etc.), and (d) situational subjective feelings evaluated by patient interviews and questionnaires (Spintge 1992). In each case, regardless of whether the treatment was short term (as in a spinal tap procedure) or long term (as in extended labor of 24 hours or more), there were significant differences between the music and nonmusic groups in all four types of measurement. In addition to reducing stress and anxiety, the music program had the practical effect of reducing drug dosages as much as 50 percent and shortening the recovery period significantly (Spintge 1992).

Goldstein (1980) studied the effects of music listening on emotions in a nonclinical setting. The study was designed to measure endorphins, naturally occuring substances in the brain that have a chemical structure similar to morphine. A release of endorphins can be triggered by a number of experiences and there is growing evidence that music is one of them. Subjects listened to their favorite music and marked their "thrill" scores. After being injected with naxolene, a drug that blocks the effects of endorphins, the thrill scores and the accompanying tingling sensations decreased.

The limbic system contains a large number of opiate receptors, or nerve endings that are highly sensitive to the presence of such chemicals as endorphins. Because the limbic system is that portion of the brain most closely involved in feelingful responses, perhaps a partial explanation for why music affects us so deeply has been found. Music listening, may, under certain conditions, stimulate an increase in the release of endorphins that, in turn, elicit emotional responses in the limbic system. While the specific relationships between music and endorphins are not yet clear, this is obviously a fruitful area of research.

Emotion II: Spontaneous Expressive Tendencies

Emotional experiences tend to elicit spontaneous expressions; these can often be seen in facial expressions, body movements, posture, and so on. In the observation of overt emotional expressions, it is important that they be spontaneous. When the subject under observation is aware of being observed, the expressions can be altered to suit socially learned rules. Chapter 8 contains a review of behavioral measures, such as the operant music listening recorder (OMLR), as they relate to music. Recently, others have adopted the OMLR to indicate aesthetic responses to music (Madsen, Brittin, and Capperella-Sheldon 1993).

A different approach has been concerned with observable expressions of specific emotional states. To study how the brain might represent emotions internally, Clynes (1961, 1969, 1970, 1973, and 1977; Clynes and Nettheim 1982; Clynes, Jurisevic, and Rynn 1990) invented an instrument known as the sentograph. The sentograph is a strain gauge housed in a small box with an actuator that is hooked to a computer. As a subject presses on the actuator, the sentograph measures transient finger pressure in vertical and horizontal movements. In a typical experiment, a subject is asked to express a series of seven emotions—love, hate, grief, joy, reverence, anger, and sex—through finger pressure. Each emotion is expressed from 30 to 50 times by pressing on the button in coordination with a series of clicks presented a few seconds apart. The readings for each expressive act are averaged by the computer, resulting in a visual tracing that represents the expression of an emotion. These sentograms have been correlated with EMG and EEG tracings (Clynes 1973). Spintge (1992) reported results of an experiment in which subjects were trained with Clynes's sentics cycle (creating and experiencing seven emotions in a consistent, systematized manner). Grief, love, and anger were significantly discriminated on the basis of ACTH and beta-endorphin measurements.

Through the use of the sentograph, Clynes has demonstrated that specific emotions have characteristic expressive shapes. Moreover, these expressions of emotions seem to be genetically programmed and consistent across cultures. Throughout his research, no significant differences in sentograms have been found between males and females or among a variety of ethnic and cultural groups. Clynes proposes that there are brain patterns for different emotions in all of us and that music has the powerful effect it does because it acts as a key to unlock these emotional experiences.

Nearly all individuals can modulate the voice in terms of pitch, tone, and rhythm to express emotions. In fact, an inability to do so normally indicates a pathological condition. Music is an extended version of the expression of emotion via sound across time. Traditionally, the question of how music communicates—how it changes our states and provides us insights—has mainly been the concern of aesthetics or music criticism. Langer expressed the idea philosophically when she said, "Music is the tonal analog of the emotive life" (Langer 1953, 27).

But the language of music may also be studied experimentally, in terms of essentic forms. A good composer who intends a particular portion of music to communicate joy can do just that. The performer who understands the composer's intention can transduce joy, and a listener can be sensitive to the performance and perceive joy, a reflection of the vision of joy the composer created perhaps hundreds of years before—all this is possible through the function and stability of essentic form.

A series of experiments have been conducted to document the relationship between music and essentic form. In one experiment (Clynes 1977), several professional musicians were asked to "think" a specific piece of music with no audible sound while producing sentograms. Two primary conclusions were drawn.

1.   Each of several major composers—Bach, Beethoven, Chopin, Debussy, Haydn, Mozart, Ravel, Schubert, Tchaikovsky, Virgil Thompson, and Wagner—had a distinctive essentic form. A Bach essentic form was clearly identifiable from a Beethoven one, for example. Moreover, even within similar styles, such as Haydn and Mozart or Debussy and Ravel, there were clearly unique personal signatures.
2.   The essentic forms produced by internationally famous musicians, such as Pablo Casals, Rudolf Serkin, and Murray Perahia, were consistent within each composer's music. Thus, all created essentic forms for Mozart in a similar manner.

Musicians would say "of course" to both of these propositions. Every composer does have an identifiable personal style and one of the major points of a musician's extended education is to learn to play Mozart as Mozart and Bach as Bach. But here there is experimental evidence that these musical concepts are biologically rooted. More recently, Clynes has developed computer algorithms for the pulse microstructures of various composers (Clynes 1983, 1984–85, 1985, 1986, 1987, and 1990). Using a principle called Predictive Amplitude Shaping, Clynes recreated the expressive shapes that make Mozart's music sound like Mozart, Bach's like Bach, Beethoven's like Beethoven, and so on.

Two studies have provided data that partially corroborate Clynes's findings. De Vries (1991) constructed a sentograph according to Clynes's description. Thirty subjects produced sentograms while listening to 11 pieces of music. An analysis indicated that the sentograms for the same pieces of music were similar for different subjects. The shapes of the sentograms were not dependent upon the subjects' appreciation of or familiarity with the music, and the sentograms produced resembled those that Clynes found for various emotions. Hodges (1992) played a tape of Clynes's aural patterns of emotion (sonic versions of the visual patterns) for 441 subjects. They were able to recognize the aural essentic forms for anger, joy, and reverence. The remaining emotions were either moderately recognized (grief) or poorly recognized (love and sex). Subjects' ability to indentify aural essentic forms correctly was not dependent upon gender, race, or musical training. These replications give indications that more extensive experimentation with sentics is warranted.

Emotion III: Subjective Experiences

Emotion III concerns subjective experiences and is studied by means of self-report (reviewed in chap. 8). Subjective experiences arise from cognitive assessment of events and from feedback via adaptive/homeostatic responses (Emotion I) and from expressive behaviors (Emotion II) (Buck 1986). Presently, the study of Emotion III falls more in the domain of psychology than neuroscience. Nevertheless, in order to provide some completeness to this discussion, selected portions of Fridja's (1988) laws of emotion are presented. For brevity's sake, only a short musical example is given for each law; the reader may supply many additional interpretations and applications.

- *The Law of Situational Meaning.* Emotions arise in response to the meaning structures of a given situation; different emotions arise in response to different meaning structures. Music at a funeral is likely to aid in the expression of grief, while music at a wedding expresses joy.

- *The Law of Concern.* Emotions arise in response to events that are important to the individual's goals, motives, or concerns. Music at the funeral of a loved one is likely to have stronger emotional impact than music at the funeral of a stranger.
- *The Law of Apparent Reality.* Emotions are elicited by events appraised as real, and their intensity corresponds to the degree to which this is the case. Modes of action readiness are biological predispositions that need sensory stimuli; sensory stimulations have the proper input format for the emotion process. Hearing one's favorite musician perform live is a more powerful experience than listening to a recorded performance.
- *The Law of Change.* Emotions are elicited not so much by the presence of favorable or unfavorable conditions but by actual or expected changes in favorable or unfavorable conditions. Music is full of changes, both gradual and sudden.
- *The Law of Habituation.* Continued pleasures wear off; continued hardships lose their poignancy. Popular songs are often listened to with a high degree of frequency for relatively brief periods of time. After a few weeks, the novelty of the latest "hit" tune has worn off to be replaced by a new one.
- *The Law of Comparative Feeling.* The intensity of emotion depends on the relationship between an event and some frame of reference against which the event is evaluated. Frequently, hearing a piece of music is compared (favorably or unfavorably) with previous hearings; often, favorite pieces of music are stored in memory along with "benchmark" performances.
- *The Law of Conservation of Emotional Momentum.* Emotional events retain their power to elicit emotions indefinitely, unless counteracted by repetitive exposures that permit extinction or habituation, to the extent that these are possible. Favorite pieces of music may continue to be enjoyable over long periods of time.
- *The Law of Closure.* Emotions tend to be closed to judgments of relativity of impact and to the requirements of goals other than their own. A person who is passionate about a certain piece or certain type of music does not need to justify that feeling; for example, no amount of discussion on the part of a parent or teacher is likely to convince a teenager that his or her style of music is not "good."

For additional discussions of cognitive theories of emotions and music, see Bever 1988, Dowling and Harwood 1986, Harrer and Harrer 1977, and Sloboda 1992.

Neuromotor Aspects of Music Making

The act of making music is so connected with physical actions that one neurologist calls musicians small-muscle athletes (Wilson 1986). Likewise, a common feature of music listening is a motoric response (tapping the toes, nodding the head, etc.). A complete discussion of this topic would move beyond the scope of this chapter and into related areas such as the biomechanics of movement, the ergonomics of instruments, and performing arts medicine. This section, then, will focus more narrowly on what is known about how the brain controls motor movements in music making and clinical applications of music to affect motor movements.

There are a number of parts of the central nervous system that play active roles in motor movements. Although many different areas are involved, the principal components include the following (Chusid 1985; Freund and Hefter 1990; Wilson 1986 and 1988).

- Each hemisphere has sensory-motor areas. The body is represented in the sensory-motor cortex as a map (known as the homunculus). Those parts over which we have more control are given more space in the cortex. Sensory and motor areas are arranged topographically as mirror images. The left side of the body is represented in the right hemisphere and vice versa.

  The motor cortex is involved in conscious decisions to contract specific muscles. If you wanted to crook your left index finger, the right motor cortex would give the command that the finger obeys. Considerably more space in the motor cortex is devoted to the face, especially the mouth and throat, and to the hands than to other parts of the body. This means that we have much greater control over our lips, tongue, and fingers than we do over our toes or back muscles. It is no accident, then, that our music making involves primarily the hands, mouth, and throat. In front of the motor cortex is the premotor cortex, an area involved in setting up some of the programs run by the motor cortex.

  An interesting feature of sensory and motor maps is that they can be reorganized based on experience (Kaas 1991). The more a body part (e.g., a finger) is stimulated or used, the more extensively it is represented in the brain's map. It may be that extensive training, such as that undertaken by musicians, causes the maps to be redrawn.
- The basal ganglia are large clusters of cells that facilitate the cooperative efforts of groups of muscles. They send messages to the spinal cord and muscles through the neurons in the motor cortex.

The basal ganglia are involved in coordinating muscle actions so that the commands sent by the motor cortex will be carried out most effectively.

- The cerebellum carries out a number of important roles in motor control. Some of these important roles are maintaining balance, coordinating the timing of intricate movements, monitoring feedback on how well the actions are being carried out, and storing habituated motor patterns.

Motor Aspects of Music Making

Musicians frequently rely on the rapid execution of intricate patterns. According to Wilson (1986), the motor cortex acting alone is far too slow to allow for the necessary speed of these movements to be carried out in the tempo required. Accomplishing this feat demands the cooperation of the cerebellum. When a particular sequence of muscle movements is repeated frequently, the pattern of those movements is stored as a unit or program. Thus, when an adult signs his signature, the motor cortex is not directing each of the required muscle movements individually. Rather, the cerebellum has stored a program called "signature." Likewise, musicians may store patterns for nearly everything they do that is repetitive—how to hold an instrument, the finger pattern for a three-octave D minor scale, and so on.

At the time the cerebellum is learning the sequence of movements to a given program, it accepts information whether right or wrong. This is why it is important that early attempts at new motor patterns be practiced slowly and correctly. Once a program is learned, the cerebellum allows for speed of movement because it has figured out all the required movements in advance. When the command is given to run a specific program, the entire sequence of movements is run automatically. Speed is also attained through ballistic movements. Just as a bullet runs its course with no more force applied after the initial explosion, so a muscle completes its specified range of movement following an initial burst of energy. The motor cortex, basal ganglia, and cerebellum work in concert to provide for smooth, facile, musical performances.

Significant work has been done in athletics to demonstrate that motor systems in the brain receive training through mental rehearsal; while the applications should transfer to music making, little research has been done (Coffman 1988). However, in one intriguing experiment, researchers (Pascual-Leone et al. 1995) divided subjects who had never previously played the piano into three groups. One group learned and practiced a specific five-finger pattern on the piano. Cortical motor mapping for finger control was reflected by transcranial magnetic stimulation. The area of the motor cortex controlling the fingers tripled in size, as indicated by a significant increase in peak amplitude and in size of scalp positions from which signals were received. Another group played random finger patterns on the piano for the same length of time; the size of the motor cortex representing their fingers did not change. Finally, a third group mentally rehearsed the same five-finger pattern as the first group, but did not physically play on the piano. The area in the motor cortex representing the fingers tripled in size, just as it had for those who physically practiced the pattern. Apparently, mental rehearsal had the same effect as actual physical rehearsal.

In a related experiment, five subjects in a control group pushed buttons in random order in response to numbers flashed on a computer screen (Pascual-Leone, Grafman, and Hallett 1994). Their reaction times and cortical motor output maps did not change. Five subjects in an experimental group pushed buttons without knowing that there was an embedded pattern. As they gradually became aware that a pattern existed, their reaction times decreased and their cortical output maps became progressively larger. When they had learned the sequence, indicated by a shift in strategy from one of reaction to one of anticipation, the cortical maps returned to baseline conditions. This experiment demonstrated the rapid plasticity of motor cortex associated with learning. Also, the return of the motor cortex to baseline measurements may indicate that the motor cortex was operating more efficiently once the task was learned.

Finally, results of another study (Elbert et al. 1995) indicated that early musical training has long-term effects on brain organization. Cortical representation of left-hand fingers was larger in the right primary somatosensory cortex of string players than it was for non-string players. Also, the total neuronal activity (called a dipole moment) in this area was greater for string players than for controls. There was a correlation ($r = 0.79$) between the age string players began studying and the magnitude of neuronal activity. The earlier the subjects started playing a stringed instrument, the greater the effect. Those who started playing between five and seven years of age showed the greatest changes; those who started as teenagers showed little change over controls. Thus, it is apparent that playing a stringed instrument from an early age on causes long-term changes in the organization of the brain.

Obviously, advanced music performances require enormously complicated timing sequences and muscle movements. While one can ponder how the brain and body make these intricate movements possible, researchers are only at the beginning stages of unraveling these mysteries. Although some researchers are beginning to be concerned about the location of music-related timing mechanisms in the brain (Freund and Hefter 1990; Miller, Thaut, and Aunon 1995; Moore 1992; Thaut et al. 1995; Wilson 1991), most of the research carried out in this area has concentrated on the recording of muscle movements by electromyography (EMG), by using transducers to convert movements into electrical signals, and, more recently, by using MIDI devices (Musical Instrument Digital Interface) to record precise details of muscle movements. A variety of experiments have been conducted with cellists to monitor arm movements in bowing and vibrato and finger movements in trills (Moore 1988; Moore, Hary, and Naill 1988; Winhold 1988; Winhold and Thelen 1988). Other studies have involved pianists (Moore 1984 and 1992; Wilson 1989, 1992, and 1993).

Most measurements of brain activity, such as EEG, cannot be used while a musician is performing, because physical movement on the part of the subject disturbs the readings. Mazziotta (1988) used PET scans to study movements that were similar to, but were not specifically, musical motions; these involved a novel task, tapping the fingers in a prescribed sequence, and an overlearned task, signing one's name. In both tasks, primary and premotor cortex were activated. The basal ganglia were activated only during the overlearned task, not during the novel task. Mazziotta hypothesized that this was because the motor cortex had to take on more of the burden for the novel task, but the basal ganglia took over some of this burden for the overlearned task.

When pianists performed with the right hand, PET data indicated activation in the left premotor cortex, left motor cortex, and right cerebellum, corresponding to motor representation of the right hand (Sergent et al. 1992). PET data for pianists performing scales and Bach with both hands indicated bilateral activation of primary motor cortex and cerebellum, left lateralized activation of supplementary motor cortex for scales, and right lateral activation of supplementary motor cortex for Bach (Fox et al. 1995). Activation in motor areas predominated over other cortical areas; one might hypothesize that other aspects of musical performance (e.g., associated thoughts or feelings) were encoded in muscle movements.

In clinical settings, researchers have been concerned with occupational cramp, or focal dystonia, and what can be learned about brain-hand connections (Wilson 1988 and 1992; Wilson and Roehmann 1992; Wilson et al. 1991). Focal dystonia is loss of control of a specific skill of manual dexterity, such as playing the piano. Currently, it is not clear whether this is a neurological problem or a condition arising from improper learning or faulty practice habits.

The Effects of Music on Motor Activity

Music elicits strong motor responses from listeners. Dance illustrates one aspect of this, and anyone who has tapped a toe as a band marches by has experienced the energizing effect of music. Sacks writes eloquently about the power of music to "awaken" catatonic patients.

> This power of music to integrate and cure, to liberate the Parkinsonian and give him freedom while it lasts ("You are the music / while the music lasts," T. S. Eliot), is quite fundamental, and seen in every patient. This was shown beautifully, and discussed with great insight, by Edith T., a former music teacher. She said that she had become "graceless" with the onset of Parkinsonism, that her movements had become "wooden, mechanical—like a robot or doll," that she had lost her former "naturalness" and "musicalness" of movement, that—in a word—she had been "unmusicked." Fortunately, she added, the disease was "accompanied by its own cure." We raised an eyebrow: "Music," she said, "as I am unmusicked, I must be remusicked." Often, she said, she would find herself "frozen," utterly motionless, deprived of the power, the impulse, the *thought,* of any motion; she felt at such times "like a still photo, a frozen frame"—a mere optical flat, without substance or life. In this state, this statelessness, this timeless irreality, she would remain, motionless-helpless, *until music came*: "Songs, tunes I knew from years ago, catchy tunes, rhythmic tunes the sort I loved to dance to."
>
> With this sudden imagining of music, this coming of spontaneous inner music, the power of motion, action, would suddenly return, and the sense of substance and restored personality and reality; now, as she put it, she could "dance out of the frame," the flat frozen visualness in which she was trapped, and move freely and gracefully: "It was like suddenly remembering myself, my own living tune." But then, just as suddenly, the inner music would cease, and with this all motion and actuality would vanish, and she would fall instantly, once more, into a Parkinsonian abyss. (Sacks 1983, 294–95)

Researchers are using music, particularly its rhythmic and tempo aspects, in a neurologic rehabilitation program. Rhythmic auditory stimulation has facilitated walking in stroke and Parkinson's patients (Thaut et al. 1993; Thaut, McIntosh, and Rice 1995).

Research on the neuromotor aspects of music making offers potential benefits in several areas. Such research will be important in the area of performing arts medicine, not only for treating those performers with motor problems, but also for educating performers in ways to avoid problems. Also, the use of music as a rhythmic organizer of motor behaviors will be important for stroke and Parkinson's patients.

Toward A Musical Brain Model

In the introductory section of this chapter, a number of models were presented that attempt to package certain ideas of brain functioning into coherent theories. Models are typically hybrids based on acquired data and informed speculation. Although neuroscientists are just in the beginning stages of studying the phenomenon of music, it is possible to begin sketching out a musical brain model. The first draft of this model is based on the review of literature presented in this chapter along with informed speculation, and it has the following features.

1. *All human beings are born with a musical brain.* This is not a guarantee that all of us have the potential to be great performers, rather that we all have neurological and bodily mechanisms that allow us to be aware of and responsive to the music of the surrounding culture. Certainly at least, components of the musical brain that serve a variety of musical and nonmusical functions, such as auditory and motor systems, are biologically based.

    As with any form of human behavior, there are wide variations in individual abilities to engage in different kinds of musical experiences. In American society, for example, we do not have the expectation that everyone will learn certain musical behaviors (e.g., to sing or play an instrument) and so we may encounter people who seem "unmusical." Some, then, suppose this to be an indication that musicality has no biological roots. Research, however, indicates that limited performance skills are more likely a problem of poor training or lack of learning opportunity than a biological one (Apfelstadt 1988; Atterbury 1984; Saunders 1988), and that, given proper instruction and reinforcement, nearly everyone can improve musical skills. Even those who do not sing well or who claim to be "tone deaf" can surely recognize and respond to music when they hear it. In societies where everyone is expected to learn to sing or dance, inability to do so is extremely rare or nonexistent (Blacking 1973).

    The notion that all human beings are musical is supported by a wide variety of evidence, including studies of animal sound processing, of fetal and infant responses, of brain-damaged patients, and of prodigies and savants. Anthropologists and ethnomusicologists have documented that all human groups in all times and in all places engage in artistic behaviors generally and musical behaviors specifically. Based on a lifetime of ethnomusical research, Blacking said: "There is so much music in the world that it is reasonable to suppose that music, like language and possibly religion, is a species-specific trait of man" (Blacking 1973, 7).

While Sergent (1993a) made a case for studying the musician's brain because of well-developed musical skills, Peretz and Zatorre emphasize the opposite, claiming that music is widely represented in the population. Following a review of recent neuromusical research, they state:

> In conclusion, studying the nonmusician's brain provides important insight about how music is neurally implemented. By being musically experienced, but not educated, the nonmusician provides a good model of (*a*) how a biological system learns sophisticated abilities by mere exposure to samples, (*b*) how such abilities are sustained by a fixed neural architecture which is, at least in part, specifically dedicated to music, and thus (*c*) how music is probably not an epiphenomenon but a biologically determined function. (Peretz and Zatorre 1994, 36)

2. *The human musical brain is different from other animal brains.* Animal research has been extremely useful in providing details of basic neural systems, such as the auditory system. This line of research has also been useful in drawing distinctions beween the human musical brain and other animal brains. One major distinction is that animals are apparently unable to make frequency contour discriminations. Thus, the musical meanings that derive from recognition of melodies in their original and various guises are unavailable to nonhuman listeners.

3. *The musical brain is in operation in infancy, and perhaps even in the later fetal stages of development.* Immediately following birth, and to a limited extent in the last trimester prior to birth, human beings are responsive to sounds in general and to music specifically. The ubiquity of lullabies and the use of "motherese" speech speaks to the responsiveness that babies have to music. Such early sensitivity to musical sounds argues for the inheritance of neural structures devoted to sound processing, including some

perhaps specifically for musical processing. Continuing research on fetal and infant responsiveness to music is providing more details about the sophistication of the listening skills they possess.

4. *The musical brain consists of an extensive neural system (or systems) involving widely distributed, but locally specialized, regions of the brain*. This musical system is adjacent to, but distinct from, systems subserving language. Musical experiences are multimodal, involving auditory, visual, cognitive, affective, and motor systems. While many of these components subserve nonmusical as well as musical functions, "the realization of musical functions involves unique mental processes that must rely on cerebral structures specifically endowed with the ability to implement these operations exclusively dedicated to the musical domain" (Sergent 1993b, 168).

    Examples of separate musical processors in a modular system may include the encoding of pitch information in a tonal scale (Peretz and Morais 1989), pitch discrimination in the perception of melodic contour (Zatorre 1994), recognition of familiar tunes (Peretz 1994), and ability to abstract tonality in a musical context (Steinke, Cuddy, and Peretz 1994). In reviewing papers presented at the 3d International Conference for Music Perception and Cognition, Peretz and Zatorre stated that

    > We intend to demonstrate that such [musical] processes are the result of computations carried out by self-organizing neural networks, that they may be dissociated from other cognitive domains, that they have very specific neural substrates, and that although they may be modified by explicit training, they are present in the majority of the population. (Peretz and Zatorre 1994, 35)

5. *The musical brain has cognitive components.* Sophisticated listeners recognize a theme when it is repeated, they may attribute musical examples on first hearing to the appropriate style period or even to a particular composer, they can successfully "track" a melody through a series of variations, and on and on. Even naive listeners can engage in a number of relatively sophisticated cognitive processes.

    Neuromusical research strategies focus on both structure (location) and function (process), as neuroscientists have begun to identify various areas of the brain that are involved in music cognition and to provide information about processing. For various reasons, many of necessity, the bulk of the research has used musical fragments as stimuli—excerpts that are very brief or stimuli that constrain all the parameters except one (e.g., pitch). While much has been learned, there are still concerns over the ecological validity of such studies (i.e., the degree to which the experimental situation approximates the real world). For example, measuring event-related potentials in response to an incongruent tone pip does not represent the richness with which a sophisticated musician listens to an entire Brahms symphony.

This is not to denigrate the existing body of research but to recognize the inherent difficulties and the limitations of current technology. Just now, neuroscientists are developing methods that allow for more natural investigations of musical behaviors. All the while, cognitive psychologists are providing better theories of music cognition, and, in time, better tools and better theories will merge into more sophisticated strategies for explicating music cognition.

6. *The musical brain has affective components.* One of the hallmarks of humanity is the richness of feelings and emotions we experience. Anthropological and sociological evidence documents the fact that human responsiveness to music is worldwide (see chap. 12). Extensive study has been made of physiological responses to music, but very little of this research has been linked with particular emotional states. If, for example, a study shows that heart rate increased in a music condition, that increase cannot be attributed to a specific affect; heart rate could have increased due to displeasure as much as to pleasure.

Recent advances in psychoneuroimmunology are providing new tools to study this issue. Already different emotional states have been linked to specific biochemical analyses of blood (Spintge 1992) and the field of music medicine is learning more about the effects of music on sensitivity to pain and feelings of anxiety.

The Clynes sentograph is another tool for studying relationships between music and emotions. According to Clynes (1977 and 1982), different emotions, such as joy and grief, are represented through essentic forms that are stable across gender, race, culture, and time. Essentic forms generated in response to music are likewise consistent. As intriguing as these data are, considerably more research is needed to corroborate and extend these findings.

7. *The musical brain has motor components.* The connection between music and movement holds for both expressive and receptive

modes. In the expressive mode, Wilson's (1986) description of musicians as small-muscle athletes is particularly apt. Recent PET studies (Fox et al. 1995; Sergent et al. 1992) have highlighted the extraordinary amount of activity in primary motor cortex, supplementary motor cortex, premotor cortex, and cerebellum involved in playing the piano.

In the receptive mode, music listeners often respond with motor activity. Researchers are now trying to harness this "power of music" so that it can be used with stroke and Parkinsonian patients in systematic, intentionalized ways (Thaut et al. 1993; Thaut, McIntosh, and Rice 1995). There may also be some interesting connections between movements generated by music and feelings of pleasure. According to Restak (1979), there are two-way connections between pleasure centers in the brain and the cerebellum. Some of the pleasures of music may come from this linkage, although specifically musical investigations have yet to be made.

8. *The degree to which the musical brain is lateralized is still debated.* A considerable amount of research of nearly every type (e.g., studies of brain-damaged subjects, dichotic listening tasks, EEG, etc.) has shown differences in right- and left-hemispheric processing for music. However, no consensus on lateralization for particular tasks has been obtained. Many who have reviewed this literature contend that laterality may depend on particular attributes of the subject (e.g., amount of training), the type of stimulus used (e.g., pitch patterns, rhythm patterns, etc.), and the tasks involved (e.g., listening for global or local features). Some consensus has been achieved on the notion that the left hemisphere may be more involved in sequential and analytic processing, the right hemisphere in holistic and intuitive processing, and that many musical experiences are complex combinations requiring the "whole" brain rather than one side or the other.

9. *The musical brain is a very resilient system.* Any music therapist could testify to the persistence of music in people who are blind, deaf, emotionally disturbed, profoundly retarded, or afflicted with any number of disabilities or diseases (e.g., Alzheimer's disease, Parkinson's disease, savant syndrome, etc.). Indeed, it is difficult to identify a situation in which every vestige of musical responsiveness has been eradicated. As indicated in the review of amusia, patients typically lose only selected aspects of their musical nature. Someone who became totally amusical—a condition that has not been reported in the literature—would surely have suffered from massive, almost total brain damage.

10. *Early and ongoing musical training affects the organization of the musical brain.* A variety of studies support this notion. Musically-trained subjects exhibit significantly higher EEG coherence values when compared to controls with limited musical training (Johnson et al. 1995). The left planum temporale is larger in musically-trained subjects than in untrained subjects; this is especially true for those who started studying music before the age of 7 or who have perfect pitch (Schlang et al. 1994). Motor cortex controlling the fingers increased in response to piano exercises, both actual and imagined (Pascual-Leone et al. 1995). Finally, string players have greater neuronal activity and a larger area in the right primary somatosensory cortex that controls the fingers of the left hand than controls (Elbert at al. 1995). Again, these effects were greater for those who started playing at a young age.

Ultimately, a musical brain model will need to dovetail with cognitive theories. In fact, neuromusical research will progress much faster when there is a comprehensive cognitive theory of music that can be tested with neuroscientific protocols and research tools (e.g., EEG brain mapping, PET scans, hormonal assays, etc.). Neurobiological aspects of music can restrain cognitive theories and cognitive theories can provide focal points for neuromusical research.

In January 1993, the Institute for Music Research at the University of Texas at San Antonio sponsored a conference entitled "Setting an Agenda for Neuromusical Research." Participants in the conference were eight neuroscientists and six musicians who spent three days in a think-tank environment. Their deliberations were focused on theoretical and philosophical issues of neuromusical research, affective issues, cognitive issues, psychomotor issues, applied/clinical issues, and interdisciplinary education issues. One outcome was a summarizing statement.

Neuromusical research, the study of the interrelationships among music, the brain, feelings, and behavior, may lead to:

- A better understanding of and appreciation for the role music plays in the lives of all human beings;
- Greater recognition that music, more than being just a pleasant diversion, has a significant impact on human physiology (e.g., heart rate, brain waves, or blood chemistry) and psychology (e.g., enhancing or creating emotional responses such as joy, grief, and love);
- An awareness that music, in certain circumstances and in combination with other factors (e.g., personality types, presence of drugs,

and peer influences), can have significant effect, positive or negative, on human behavior;

- Increased effectiveness in educating people musically;
- Increased effectiveness in preparing performing musicians and in dealing with performance-related injuries;
- Better use of music in enabling handicapped individuals to have a higher quality of life; and
- Wider use of music in medical/clinical conditions as disparate as childbirth, brain injury, or chronic pain.

The overriding goal of neuromusical research is to better understand the phenomenon of music.

REFERENCES

Ackerman, S. 1992. *Discovering the brain.* Washington, DC: National Academy Press.
Aiello, R. 1978. Cerebral dominance for the perception of arpeggiated triads. *Journal of Research in Music Education* 26:470–78.
Aldridge, D. 1993. The music of the body: Music therapy in medical settings. *Advances: The Journal of Mind-Body Health* 9, no. 1:17–35.
Alkon, D. 1989. Memory storage and neural systems. *Scientific American* 261, no. 1:42–50.
Anderson, L. 1994. Adults and infants show a left-ear advantage for recognition of contour-violated melodies. In *Proceedings of the 3d international conference for music perception and cognition,* ed. I. Deliege, 423–24. Liege, Belgium.
Aoki, C., and P. Siekevita. 1988. Plasticity in brain development. *Scientific American* 259, no. 6:56–64.
Apfelstadt, H. 1988. What makes children sing well? *Update: The Applications of Research in Music Education* 7, no. 1:27–32.
Annis, L. 1978. *The child before birth.* Ithaca, NY: Cornell University Press.
Arnadottis, G. 1990. *The brain and behavior.* St. Louis: C. V. Mosby.
Atterbury, B. 1984. Children's singing voices: A review of selected research. *Bulletin of the Council for Research in Music Education* 80:51–62.
Bailey, R. 1975. *The role of the brain.* New York: Time-Life Books.
Bakan, P. 1969. Hypnotizability, laterality of eye movement, and functional asymmetry. *Perception and Motor Skills* 28:927–32.
Bakker, D. 1967. Left-right differences in auditory perception of verbal and nonverbal material by children. *Quarterly Journal of Experimental Psychology* 19:334–36.
Barinaga, M. 1992. The brain remaps its own contours. *Science* 258, no. 5080:216–18.
Bartholomeus, B. 1974. Effects of task requirements on ear superiority for sung speech. *Cortex* 10:215–23.
Basso, A., and E. Capitani. 1985. Spared musical abilities in a conductor with global aphasia and ideomotor apraxia. *Journal of Neurology, Neurosurgery, and Psychiatry* 485:407–12.

Baumgarte, R., and E. Franklin. 1981. Lateralization of components of melodic stimuli: Musicians versus nonmusicians. *Journal of Research in Music Education* 29:199–208.

Beaton, A. 1985. *Left side, right side*. New Haven: Yale University Press.

Begley, S., L. Wright, V. Church, and M. Hager. 1992. Mapping the brain. *Newsweek*, 20 April, 66–70.

Beisteiner, R., A. Menze, M. Erdler, D. Huter, and L. Deecke. 1994. Objective testing of harmonic processing capabilities by magnetoencephalography (MEG). In *Proceedings of the 3d international conference for music perception and cognition*, ed. I. Deliege, 437–38. Liege, Belgium.

Benson, D., and E. Zaidel. 1985. *The dual brain*. New York: Guilford Press.

Benton, A. 1977. The amusias. In *Music and the brain*, ed. M. Critchley and R. Henson, 378–97. Springfield, IL: C. C. Thomas.

Bergman, J., and W. DePue. 1986. Musical idiot savants. *Music Educators Journal* 72, no. 5:37–40.

Berman, I. 1981. Musicogenic epilepsy. *South African Medical Journal* 59, no. 2:49–52.

Besson, M., and F. Faita. 1994. Electrophysiological studies of musical incongruities: Comparison between musicians and nonmusicians. In *Proceedings of the 3rd international conference for music perception and cognition*, ed. I. Deliege, 41–43. Liege, Belgium.

Besson, M., and F. Macar. 1987. An event-related potential analysis of incongruity in music and other nonlinguistic contexts. *Psychophysiology* 24:14–25.

Best, C., H. Hoffman, and B. Glanville. 1982. Development of infant ear asymmetries for speech and music. *Perception and Psychophysics* 31, no. 1:75–85.

Bever, T. 1975. Cerebral asymmetries in humans are due to the differentiation of two incompatible processes: Holistic and analytic. *Annals of the New York Academy of Science* 263:251–62.

Bever, T. 1988. A cognitive theory of emotion and aesthetics in music. *Psychomusicology* 7, no.2:165–75.

Bever, T., and R. Chiarello. 1974. Cerebral dominance in musicians and nonmusicians. *Science* 185, no. 150:537–39.

Bharucha, J., and K. Olney. 1989. Tonal cognition, artificial intelligence, and neural nets. *Contemporary Music Review* 4:341–56.

Blacking, J. 1973. *How musical is man?* Seattle: University of Washington Press.

Blakeslee, T. 1980. *The right brain: A new understanding of the unconcious mind and its creative powers*. Garden City, NY: Doubleday.

Blinkov, S., and I. Glezer. 1968. *The human brain in figures and tables: A quantitative handbook*. Trans. B. Haigh. New York: Basic Books.

Bloom, F., A. Lazerson, and L. Hofstadter. 1985. *Brain, mind, and behavior*. New York: Freeman.

Blumstein, S., H. Goodglass, and V. Tartter. 1975. The reliability of ear advantage in dichotic listening. *Brain and Language* 2:226–36.

Bogen, J., and H. Gordon. 1971. Musical tests for functional lateralization with intercardial amobarbital. *Nature* 230:524–25.

Borchgrevink, H. 1982. Prosody and musical rhythm are controlled by the speech hemisphere. In *Music, mind, and brain: The neuropsychology of music*, ed. M. Clynes, 151–58. New York: Plenum Press.

Borling, J. 1981. The effects of sedative music on alpha rhythms and focused attention in high-creative and low-creative subjects. *Journal of Music Therapy* 18, no. 2:101–8.

Borod, J., and H. Goodglass. 1980. Lateralization of linguistic and melodic processing with age. *Neuropsychologia* 18:79–83.

Borod, J., L. Obler, M. Albert, and S. Stiefel. 1983. Lateralization for pure tone perception as a function of age and sex. *Cortex* 19:281–85.

Botez, M., and N. Wertheim. 1959. Expressive aphasia and amusia following right frontal lesion in a right-handed man. *Brain* 82:186–202.

Bradshaw, J., and N. Nettleton. 1981. The nature of hemispheric specialization in man. *Behavioral and Brain Sciences* 4, no. 1:51–63.

Bradshaw, J., N. Nettleton, and G. Geffen. 1972. Ear asymmetry and delayed auditory feedback: Effect of task requirements and competitive stimulation. *Journal of Experimental Psychology* 94:269–75.

Breitling, D., W. Guenther, and P. Rondot. 1987. Auditory perception of music measured by brain electrical activity mapping. *Neuropsychologia* 25:765–74.

Brody, J. 1991. Not just music, bird song is a means of courtship and defense. *New York Times*, 9 April.

Brookshire, R. 1975. Recognition of auditory sequences by aphasic, right-hemisphere-damaged and non-brain-damaged subjects. *Journal of Communication Disorders* 8:51–59.

Brown, T., E. Kairiss, and C. Keenan. 1990. Hebbian synapses: Biophysical mechanisms and algorithms. *Annual Review of Neuroscience* 13:475–571.

Brown, W., J. Marsh, and R. Ponsford. 1985. Hemispheric differences in event-related potentials. In *The dual brain: Hemispheric specialization in humans*, ed. D. Benson and E. Zaidel, 163–80. New York: Guildford Press.

Brust, J. 1980. Music and language: Musical alexia and agraphia. *Brain*, 103:367–92.

Bryden, M. 1963. Ear preferences in auditory perception. *Journal of Experimental Psychology* 65:103–5.

Bryden, M. 1986. Dichotic listening performance, cognitive ability, and cerebral organization. *Canadian Journal of Psychology* 40, no. 4:45–46.

Bryden, M., R. Ley, and J. Sugarman. 1982. A left-ear advantage for identifying the emotional quality of tonal sequences. *Neuropsychologia* 20:83–87.

Buck, R. 1986. The psychology of emotion. In *Mind and brain*, ed. J. LeDoux and W. Hirst, 275–300. Cambridge: Cambridge University Press.

Byrne, B., and J. Sinclair. 1979. Memory for tonal sequence and timbre: A correlation with familial handedness. *Neuropsychologia* 17:539–42.

Chuang, S., R. Frisina, G. Crummer, and J. Walton. 1988. Effects of varying chord progressions on P3 event-related potentials in musicians and nonmusicians. *Journal of the Acoustical Society of America* 83, suppl. 1:S13.

Churchland, P., and T. Sejnowski. 1988. Perspectives on cognitive neuroscience. *Science* 242, no. 4879:741–45.

Chusid, J. 1985. *Correlative neuroanatomy and functional neurology*. 19th ed. Los Altos, CA: Lange Medical Publications.

Clynes, M. 1961. Unidirectional rate sensitivity: A biocybernetic law of reflex and humoral systems as physiologic channels of control and communication. *Annals of the New York Academy of Sciences* 92:946–69.

Clynes, M. 1969. Cybernetic implications of rein control in perceptual and conceptual organization. *Annals of the New York Academy of Sciences* 156:629–70.

Clynes, M. 1970. On being in order. *Zygon* 5, no. 1:63–84.

Clynes, M. 1973. Sentography: Dynamic forms of communication of emotion and qualities. *Computing Biological Medicine* 3:119–30.

Clynes, M. 1977. *Sentics: The touch of emotions.* New York: Doubleday.

Clynes, M., ed. 1982. *Music, mind, and brain: The neuropsychology of music.* New York: Plenum Press.

Clynes, M. 1983. Expressive microstructure in music, linked to living qualities. In *Studies of music performance*, ed. J. Sandberg, 76–181. Publications issued by the Royal Swedish Academy of Music, no. 39.

Clynes, M. 1984-85. Music beyond the score. *Somatics* 5, no. 1:4–14.

Clynes, M. 1985. *Secrets of life.* Publications issued by the Royal Swedish Academy of Music, no. 47.

Clynes, M. 1986. Generative principles of musical thought: Integration of microstructure with structure. *Journal for the Integrated Study of Artificial Inteligence, Cognitive Science, and Applied Epistemology* 3, no. 3:185–223.

Clynes, M. 1987. What can a musician learn about music performance from newly discovered miscrostructure principles PM and PAS? In *Action and perception in rhythm and music*, ed. A. Gabrielsson, 201–33. Publications issued by the Royal Swedish Academy of Music, no. 55.

Clynes, M. 1990. Mind-body windows and music. *Musikpadagogische Forschung* 11:19–42.

Clynes, M., S. Jurisevic, and M. Rynn. 1990. Inherent cognitive substrates of specific emotions: Love is blocked by lying but not by anger. *Perceptual and Motor Skills* 70:195–206.

Clynes, M., and N. Nettheim. 1982. The living quality of music: neurobiologic patterns of communication, feeling. In *Music, mind, and brain: The neuropsychology of music*, ed. M. Clynes, 47–82. New York: Plenum Press.

Coffman, D. 1988. Rehearsing in your mind: Review of the mental practice literature with implications for musicians. *Update: The Applications of Research in Music Education* 6, no. 2:5–8.

Cohen, D., and A. Erez. 1991. Event-related-potential measurements of cognitive components in response to pitch patterns. *Music Perception* 8, no. 4:405–30.

Cohen, D., R. Granot, H. Pratt, and A. Barneah. 1993. Cognitive meanings of musical elements as disclosed by event-related potential ERP and verbal experiments. *Music Perception* 11, no. 2:153–84.

Colquhoun, J. 1987. Musical epilepsy: A neurological oddity. *Australian Family Physician* 16, no. 9:1305.

Commandy, R. 1974. Sophisticated or not, we need both ears. *San Francisco Examiner*, 22 December.

Cook, R. 1973. Left-right differences in the perception of dichotically presented musical stimuli. *Journal of Music Therapy* 10, no. 2:59–63.

Corballis, M. 1983. *Human laterality*. New York: Academic Press.

Cornett, G., R. Kendall, J. Engel, and E. Carterett. 1992. Depth-EEG recordings of human medial temporal-lobe responses to dyads and triads. Paper presented at 2d International Conference On Music Perception and Cognition, February, University of California at Los Angeles.

Craig, J. 1980. A dichotic rhythm task: Advantage for the left-handed. *Cortex* 16:613–20.

Crick, F. 1989. The recent excitement about networks. *Nature* 337:129–32.

Critchley, M. 1977. Musicogenic epilepsy. In *Music and the brain: Studies in the neurology of music*, ed. M. Critchley and R. Hensen, 344–53. Springfield, IL: C. C. Thomas.

Cruetzfeldt, O., and G. Ojemann. 1989. Neuronal activity in the human lateral temporal lobe, III: Activity changes during music. *Experimental Brain Research* 77, no. 3:490–98.

Crummer, G., E. Hantz, S. Cherang, J. Walton, and R. Frisina. 1988. Neural basis for music cognition: Initial experimental findings. *Psychomusicology* 7, no. 2:117–26.

Crummer, G., J. Walton, J. Wayman, and E. Hantz. 1994. Neural processing of musical timbre by musicians, nonmusicians, and musicians possessing absolute pitch. *Journal of the Acoustical Society of America* 95, no. 5, pt. 1:2720–27.

Crystal, H., E. Grober, and D. Masur. 1989. Preservation of musical memory in Alzheimer's disease. *Journal of Neurology, Neurosurgery, and Psychiatry* 52:1415–16.

Curry, F. 1967. A comparison of left-handed and right-handed subjects on verbal and nonverbal dichotic listening tasks. *Cortex* 3:343–52.

Dalbokova, D., and P. Kolev. 1992. Cognitive and affective relations in perception of auditory stimuli in the presence of music. *Psychomusicology* 11:141–51.

Dalbokova, D., P. Kolev, and R. Kristeva. 1988. Selective attention in the presence of music: An event-related potentials ERP study. *Biological Psychology* 26, nos. 1–3:307–19.

Damasio, A., and H. Damasio. 1977. Music faculty and cerebral dominance. In *Music and the brain: Studies in the neurology of music*, ed. M. Critchley and R. Hensen, 141–55. Springfield, IL: C. C. Thomas.

D'Amato, M. 1988. A search for tonal pattern perception in cebus monkeys: Why monkeys can't hum a tune. *Music Perception* 5, no. 4:453–80.

Darwin, C. [1859] 1871. *The origin of species* and *The descent of man*. New York: Modern Library.

Davidson, R., and G. Schwartz. 1977. The influence of musical training on patterns of EEG asymmetry during musical and nonmusical self-generation tasks. *Psychophysiology* 14:58–63.

Dawe, S., and M. Corballis. 1986. The influence of gender, handedness, and head-turn on auditory asymmetries. *Neuropsychologia* 24:857–62.

Dawson, G., C. Finley, S. Phillips, L. Galpert, and A. Lewy. 1988. Reduced P3 amplitude of the event-related brain potential: Its relationship to language ability in autism. *Journal of Autism and Developmental Disorders* 18, no. 4:493–504.

Dee, H. 1971. Auditory asymmetry and strength of manual preference. *Cortex* 7:236–45.

DePascalis, V., F. Marucci, and P. Penna. 1987. Event-related potentials as asymmetry indices of lateralized cognitive processes during music and verbal tasks. *Biological Psychology* 24:141–51.

DePascalis, V., F. Marucci, M. Penna, and D. Labbrozzi. 1987. Event-related potentials in musically sophisticated and unsophisticated subjects: A study on hemispheric specialization. *Neuropsychologia* 25:947–55.

Deutsch, D. 1975. Musical illusions. *Scientific American* 233:92–104.

Deutsch, D. 1978. Lateralization by frequency for repeating sequences of dichotic 400- and 800-Hz tones. *Journal of the Acoustical Society of America* 63:184–86.

Deutsch, D. 1983. The octave illusion in relation to handedness and familial handedness background. *Neuropsychologia* 21:289–93.

de Vries, B. 1991. Assessment of the affective response to music with Clynes's sentograph. *Psychology of Music* 19:46–64.

Diamond, J. 1991. Art of the wild. *Discover* 12, no. 2:79–85.

Doerhing, D. 1972. Ear asymmetry in the discrimination of monaural tonal sequences. *Canadian Journal of Psychology* 26:106–10.

Dowling, W., and D. Harwood. 1986. *Music cognition.* New York: Academic Press.

Duffy, F., P. Bartels, and J. Burchfield. 1981. Significance probability mapping: An aid in the topographic analysis of brain electrical activity. *Electroencephalography and Clinical Neurophysiology* 51, no. 5:455–62.

Duffy, F., G. McAnalty, and S. Schachter. 1984. Brain electrical mapping. In *Cerebral dominance: The biological foundations,* ed. N. Geschwind and A. Galaburda, 53–74. Cambridge, MA: Harvard University Press.

Eccles, J. 1973. *The understanding of the brain.* New York: McGraw-Hill.

Eccles, J., and D. Robinson. 1985. *The wonder of being human.* Boston: New Science Library.

Economist. 1989. Four whale tales. *Economist* 311, no. 7597:95–96.

Economist. 1993. The human mind: Touching the intangible. *Economist,* 8 January, 115–20.

Efron, R., J. Bogen, and W. Yund. 1977. Perception of dichotic chords by normal and commisurotomized human subjects. *Cortex* 13:137–49.

Efron, R., B. Koss, and E. Yund. 1983. Central auditory processing, IV: Ear dominance–spatial and temporal complexity. *Brain and Language* 19:264–82.

Efron, R., and E. Yund. 1974. Dichotic competition of simultaneous tone bursts of different frequency. *Neuropsychologia* 12:249–56.

Efron, R., and E. Yund. 1975. Dichotic competition of simultaneous tone bursts of different frequencies, III: The effect of stimulus parameters on suppression and ear dominance functions. *Neuropsychologia* 13:151–61.

Efron, R., and E. Yund. 1976. Ear dominance and intensity independence in the perception of dichotic chords. *Journal of the Acoustical Society of America* 59:889–98.

Elbert, T., C. Pantev, C. Wienbruch, B. Rockstrub, and E. Taub. 1995. Increased cortical representation of the fingers of the left hand in string players. *Science* 270, no. 5234:305–07.

Emmerich, D., L. Pitchford, C. Joyce., and S. Koppell. 1981. Laterality effects in response to offsets of tonal stimuli. *Neuropsychologia* 19:227–34.

Faita, F., and M. Besson. 1994. Electrophysiological index of musical expectancy: Is there a repetition effect on the event-related potentials associated with musical incongruities? In *Proceedings of the 3d international conference for music perception and cognition*, ed. I. Deliege, 433–35. Liege, Belgium.

Flohr, J., and D. Miller. 1993. Quantitative EEG differences between baseline and psychomotor response to music. *Texas Music Education Research*, 1–7.

Flohr, J., and D. Miller. 1995. Developmental quantitative EGG differences during psychomotor response to music. Paper presented at the Texas Music Educators Association convention, February, San Antonio.

Ford, J., W. Roth, and B. Kopell. 1976. Auditory evoked potentials to unpredictable shifts in pitch. *Psychophysiology* 13, no. 1:32–39.

Fox, P., J. Sergent, D. Hodges, C. Martin, T. Jerabek, T. Glass, H. Downs, and J. Lancaster. 1995. Piano performance from memory: A PET study. Paper presented at the Human Brain Mapping Conference, June, Paris.

Franklin, E., and R. Baumgarte. 1978. Auditory laterality effects for melodic stimuli among musicians and nonmusicians. *Journal of Research in Music Education* 26:48–56.

Franklin, E., and A. Franklin. 1978. The brain research bandwagon: Proceed with caution. *Music Educators Journal* 65, no. 3:38–43.

Freund, H., and H. Hefter. 1990. Timing mechanisms in skilled hand movements. In *Music and child development*, ed. F. Wilson and F. Roehmann, 179–90. St. Louis: MMB Music.

Fridja, N. 1988. The laws of emotion. *American Psychologist* 43, no. 5:349–58.

Friedrich, O. 1983. What do they know? *Time Magazine*, 15 August, 52–59.

Frisina, R., J. Walton, and G. Crummer. 1988. Neural basis for music cognition: Neurophysiological foundations. *Psychomusicology* 7, no. 2:99–107.

Fujinawa, A., and I. Kawai. 1978. About musicogenic epilepsy. *Psychiatria Clinica* 11, no. 1:47–59.

Furman, C. 1978. The effect of musical stimuli of the brainwave production of children. *Journal of Music Therapy* 15, no. 3:108–17.

Furst, C. 1976. EEG asymmetry and visuospatial performance. *Nature* 260:254–55.

Gabriel, M., S. Sparenborg, and N. Stolar. 1986. The neurobiology of memory. In *Mind and brain*, ed. J. LeDoux and W. Hirst, 215–54. Cambridge: Cambridge University Press.

Gaede, S., O. Parsons, and J. Bertera. 1978. Hemispheric differences in music perception: Aptitude versus experience. *Neuropsychologia* 16:369–73.

Gardner, H. 1983. *Frames of mind: The theory of multiple intelligences*. New York: Basic Books.

Gates, A., and J. Bradshaw. 1977a. Music perception and cerebral asymmetries. *Cortex* 13:390–401.

Gates, A., and J. Bradshaw. 1977b. The role of the cerebral hemispheres in music. *Brain and Language* 4:403–31.

Gazzaniga, M. 1967. The split brain in man. *Scientific American* 217:24–29.

Gazzaniga, M. 1972. One brain—two minds. *American Scientist* 60:311–17.

Gazzaniga, M. 1977. Review of the split-brain. *The human brain*, ed. M. Wittrock, 89–96. Englewood Cliffs, NJ: Prentice-Hall.

Gazzaniga, M. 1988. *Mind matters*. Boston: Houghton Mifflin.

Geschwind, N. 1979. Specializations of the human brain. *Scientific American* 241, no. 3:180–99.

Giannitrapani, D. 1970. EEG changes under differing auditory stimulations. *Archives of General Psychiatry* 23:445–53.

Gillis, A. 1990. What are birds hearing? *Bioscience* 40, no. 11:810–16.

Goldstein, A. 1980. Thrills in response to music and other stimuli. *Physiological Psychology* 8, no. 1:126–29.

Goldstein, R. 1961. Hearing and speech in follow-up of left hemispherectomy. *Journal of Speech and Hearing Disorders* 26:126–28.

Gollnick, D. 1978. Testing music hearing in right and left ears of children ages ten, eleven, and twelve. *Journal of Research in Music Education* 26, no. 1:16–21.

Goodglass, H., and M. Calderon. 1977. Parallel processing of verbal and musical stimuli in right hemispheres. *Neuropsychologia* 15, no. 3:397–407.

Gordon, H. 1970. Hemispheric asymmetries in the perception of musical chords. *Cortex* 6, no. 4:387–98.

Gordon, H. 1974. Auditory specializations of the right and left hemispheres. In *Hemispheric disconnection and cerebral function*, ed. M. Kinsbourne and W. Smith, 126–36. Springfield, IL: C. C. Thomas.

Gordon, H. 1978a. Hemispheric asymmetry for dichotically presented chords in musicians and nonmusicians, males and females. *Acta Psychologia* 42:383–95.

Gordon, H. 1978b. Left hemisphere dominance for rhythmic elements in dichotically presented melodies. *Cortex* 14:68–70.

Gordon, H. 1980. Degree of ear asymmetries for perception of dichotic chords and for illusory chord localization in musicians of different levels of competence. *Journal of Experimental Psychology: Human Perception and Performance* 6:516–27.

Gott, P. 1973. Cognitive abilities following right and left hemispherectomy. *Cortex* 9:266–74.

Gregory, A., J. Harriman, and L. Roberts. 1972. Cerebral dominance for the recognition of rhythm. *Psychomonic Science* 28:75–76.

Grossman, M., B. Shapiro, and H. Gardner. 1981. Dissociable musical processing strategies after localized brain damage. *Neuropsychologia* 19, no. 3:425–33.

Gur, R., and R. Gur. 1994. Methods for the study of brain-behavior relationships. In *Biological bases of brain function and disease*, ed. A. Frazer, P. Malinoff, and A. Winokur, 261–80. New York: Raven Press.

Hall, S. 1989. A molecular code links emotions, mind, and health. *Smithsonian*, June, 62–71.

Halperin, Y., I. Nachson., and A. Carmon. 1973. Shift of ear superiority in dichotic listening to temporally patterned nonverbal stimuli. *Journal of the Acoustical Society of America* 53:46–50.

Hammeke, T., M. McQuillen, and B. Cohen. 1983. Musical hallucinations associated with acquired deafness. *Journal of Neurology, Neurosurgery, and Psychiatry* 46, no. 6:570–72.

Hantz, E., and C. Crummer. 1988. Neural basis for music cognition: Psychophysical foundations. *Psychomusicology* 7, no. 2:109–15.

Hantz, E., G. Crummer, J. Wayman, J. Walton, and R. Frisina. 1992. Effects of musical training and absolute pitch on the nueral processing of melodic intervals: A P3 event-related potential study. *Music Perception* 10, no. 1:25–42.

Harrer, G., and H. Harrer. 1977. Music emotion and autonomic function. In *Music and the brain: Studies in the neurology of music*, ed. M. Critchley and R. Henson, 233–54. Springfield, IL: C. C. Thomas.

Hari, R. 1990. The neuromagnetic method in the study of the human auditory cortex. *Advances in Audiology* 6, no. 1:222–82.

Haydon, S., and F. Spellacy. 1973. Monaural reaction time asymmetries for speech and nonspeech sounds. *Cortex* 9:288–94.

Herscovitch, P. 1994. Positron emission tomography—basic principles and applications to the study of auditory and language processing. Paper presented at the 45th annual American Speech-Language Hearing Association Research Conference, 15–16 November, New Orleans.

Herskowitz, J., N. Rosman, and N. Geschwind. 1984. Seizures induced by singing and recitation: A unique form of reflex epilepsy in childhood. *Archives of Neurology* 41:1102–3.

Hirshkowitz, M., J. Earle, and B. Paley. 1978. EEG alpha asymmetry in musicians and non-musicians: A study of hemispheric specialization. *Neuropsychologia* 16:125–28.

Hodges, D. 1978. A house divided: Implications of split-brain research for music educators. In *Midwest symposium on music education*, ed. M. Raiman, 107–19. Tulsa, OK: U.S. Jaycees.

Hodges, D. 1979. Split-brain research: A new frontier. In *Proceedings of the University of Kansas research symposium on the psychology and acoustics of music*, ed. E. Asmus, 71–93. Lawrence, KS: University of Kansas Printing Division.

Hodges, D. 1989. Why are we musical? Speculations on the evolutionary plausibility of musical behavior. *Bulletin of the Council for Research in Music Education* 99:7–22.

Hodges, D. 1992. Recognition of aural patterns of emotion: A partial replication of the work of Manfred Clynes. *Texas Music Education Research*, 30–37.

Hoffman, J. 1986. A psychological view of the neurobiology of perception. In *Mind and brain: Dialogues in cognitive neuroscience*, ed. J. LeDoux and W. Hirst, 91–100. Cambridge: Cambridge University Press.

Howle, M. 1993. Musical savants. *Update* 11, no. 1:5–7.

Hulse, S. 1990. The acquisition of pitch and rhythm in songbirds. In *Music and child development*, ed. F. Wilson and F. Roehmann, 139–56. St. Louis: MMB Music.

Hulse, S., A. Takeuchi, and R. Braaten. 1992. Perceptual invariances in the comparative psychology of music. *Music Perception* 10, no. 2:151–84.

Ibbotson, N. R., and J. Morton. 1981. Rhythm and dominance. *Cognition* 9, no. 2:125–38.

Inglis, T. 1980. The effects of music on the electroencephalograms of secondary school music students and nonmusic students. *Bulletin of the Council for Research in Music Education* 62:45–47.

Janata, P., and H. Petsche. 1993. Spectral analysis of the EEG as a tool for evaluating expectancy violations of musical contexts. *Music Perception* 10, no. 3:281–304.

Johnson, J., H. Petsche, P. Richter, A. von Stein, and O. Filz. 1995. Coherence estimates of EEG at rest document differences between subjects with and without music training. In *MusicMedicine 2*, ed. R. Pratt and R. Spintge. St. Louis: MMB Music. In press.

Johnson, J., and H. Ulatowska. 1995. The nature of the tune and text in the production of songs. In *MusicMedicine 2*, ed. R. Pratt and R. Spintge. St. Louis: MMB Music. In press.

Johnson, P. 1977. Dichotically stimulated ear differences in musicians and nonmusicians. *Cortex* 13:385–89.

Johnson, R., P. Green, F. Ahern, and R. Cole. 1983. Cognitive correlates of hemispheric performances on dichotic tasks. *International Journal of Aging and Human Development* 18, no. 3:185–95.

Johnson, R., J. Bowers, M. Gamble, F. Lyons, T. Preshrey, and R. Vetter. 1977. Ability to transcribe music and ear superiority for tone sequences. *Cortex* 3:295–99.

Joseph, R. 1988. The right cerebral hemisphere: Emotion, music, visual-spatial skills, body-image, dreams, and awareness. *Journal of Clinical Psychology* 44, no. 5:630–73.

Judd, T. 1988. A neuropsychologist looks at musical behavior. In *The biology of music making*, ed. F. Roehmann and F. Wilson, 57–76. St. Louis: MMB Music.

Judd, T., H. Gardner, and N. Geschwind. 1983. Alexia without agraphia in a composer. *Brain* 106:435–57.

Kaas, J. 1991. Plasticity of sensory and motor maps in adult mammals. *Annual Review of Neuroscience* 14:137–67.

Kaufman, L., S. Curtis, J. Wang, and S. Williamson. 1991. Changes in cortical activity when subjects scan memory for tones. *Electroencephalography and Clinical Neurophysiology* 82:266–84.

Kellar, L., and T. Bever. 1980. Hemispheric asymmetries in the perception of musical intervals as a function of musical experience and family handedness. *Brain and Language* 10:24–38.

Kimura, D. 1961a. Cerebral dominance and the perception of verbal stimuli. *Canadian Journal of Psychology* 15:166–71.

Kimura, D. 1961b. Some effects of temporal-lobe damage on auditory perception. *Canadian Journal of Psychology* 15:156–65.

Kimura, D. 1964. Left-right differences in the perception of melodies. *Quarterly Journal of Experimental Psychology* 16:355–58.

Kimura, D. 1967. Functional asymmetry of the brain in dichotic listening. *Cortex* 3:163–78.

King, F., and D. Kimura. 1972. Left-ear superiority in dichotic perception of vocal nonverbal sounds. *Canadian Journal of Psychology* 26, no. 2:111–15

Kinoshita, J. 1992. Mapping the mind. *New York Times Magazine*, 18 October, 44.

Kinsella, G., M. Prior, and G. Murray. 1988. Singing ability after right- and left-sided brain damage: A research note. *Cortex* 24, no. 1:165–69.

Kirchner, W., and W. Towne. 1994. The sensory basis of the honeybee's dance language. *Scientific American* 270, no. 6:74–80.

Klein, M., M. Coles, and E. Donchin. 1984. People with absolute pitch process tones without producing a P300. *Science* 223:1306–9.

Konovalov, V., and N. Otmakhova. 1984. EEG manifestations of functional asymmetry of the human cerebral cortex during perception of words and music. *Human Physiology* 9, no. 4:250–55.

Krashen, S. 1977. The left hemisphere. In *The human brain*, ed. M. Wittrock, 107–30. Englewood Cliffs, NJ: Prentice-Hall.

Kubovy, M., J. Cutting, and R. McGuire. 1974. Hearing with the 3d ear: Dichotic perception of a melody without monaural familiarity cues. *Science* 186:272–74.

LaBarba, R., S. Kingsberg, and P. Martin. 1992. Cerebral lateralization of unfamiliar music perception in nonmusicians. *Psychomusicology* 11:119–24.

Lampert, M., and W. Donovan. 1993. Personal communication.

Lang, W., H. Obrig, G. Lindringer, D. Cheyre, and L. Deecke. 1990. Supplementary motor area activation while tapping bimanually different rhythms in musicians. *Experimental Brain Research* 79, no. 3:504–14.

Langer, S. 1953. *Feeling and form*. New York: Scribner.

LeDoux, J. 1986. The neurobiology of emotion. In *Mind and brain*, ed. J. LeDoux and W. Hirst, 301–54. Cambridge: Cambridge University Press.

LeDoux, J. 1994. Emotion, memory, and the brain. *Scientific American* 270, no. 6:50–57.

Levett, C., and F. Martin. 1992. The relationship between complex music stimuli and the late components of the event-related potential. *Psychomusicology* 11:125–40.

Levin, H., and J. Rose. 1979. Alexia without agraphia in a musician after transcallocal removal of the left intraventricular meningioma. *Neurosurgery* 4:168–74.

Levy, J. 1985. Right brain, left brain: Fact and fiction. *Psychology Today*, May, 41–44.

Lipkin, R. 1988. Jarring music takes toll on mice. *Insight*, 4 April, 58.

Lu, Z., L. Williamson, and L. Kaufman. 1992. Behavioral lifetime of human auditory sensory memory predicted by physiological measures. *Science* 258:1668–70.

Luria, A., and E. Simernitskaya. 1977. Interhemispheric relations and the functions of the minor hemisphere. *Neuropsychologia* 15:175–78.

Mackworth-Young, C. 1983. Sequential musical symptoms in a professional musician with presumed encephalitis. *Cortex* 19:413–19.

MacLean, P. 1973. *A triune concept of the brain and behavior*. Toronto: University of Toronto Press.

Madison, D., R. Malenka, and R. Nicoll. Mechanisms underlying long-term potentiation of synaptic transmission. *Annual Review of Neuroscience* 14:379–97.

Madsen, C., R. Brittin, and D. Capperella-Sheldon. 1993. An empirical method for measuring the aesthetic experience to music. *Journal of Research in Music Education* 41, no. 1:57–69.

Majkowski, J., Z. Bochenek, W. Bochenek, D. Knapik-Fijalkowska, and J. Kopec. 1971. Latency of averaged evoked potentials to contralateral and ipsilateral auditory stimulation in normal subjects. *Brain Research* 25:416–19.

Maranto, C., and J. Scartelli. 1992. Music in the treatment of immune-related disorders. In *MusicMedicine*, ed. R. Spintge and R. Droh, 142–54. St. Louis: MMB Music.

Marin, O. 1982. Neurological aspects of music perception and performance. In *The psychology of music*, ed. D. Deutsch, 453–77. Orlando, FL: Academic Press.

Marin, O. 1989. Neuropsychology, mental cognitive models, and music processing. *Contemporary Music Review* 4:255–63.

Marler, P. 1991. Song-learning behavior: The interface with neuroethology. *Trends in Neuroscience* 14, no. 5:199–211.

Martin, F. 1975. *Introduction to audiology*. Englewood Cliffs, NJ: Prentice-Hall.

Mavlov, L. 1980. Amusia due to rhythm agnosia in a musician with left hemisphere damage: A nonauditory supramodal defect. *Cortex* 16, no. 2:331–38.

Mazziotta, J. 1988. Brain metabolism in auditory perception: The PET study. In *The biology of music making*, ed. F. Roehmann and F. Wilson, 106–11. St. Louis: MMB Music.

Mazziotta, J., M. Phelps, R. Carson, and D. Kuhl. 1982. Tomographic mapping of human cerebral metabolism: Auditory stimulation. *Neurology* 32, no. 9:921–37.

Mazzucchi, A., C. Marchini, R. Bulai, and M. Parma. 1982. A case of receptive amusia with prominant timbre perception defect. *Journal of Neurology, Neurosurgery, and Psychiatry* 45:644–47.

Mazzucchi, A., M. Parma, and R. Cattelani. 1981. Hemispheric dominance in the perception of tonal sequences in relation to sex, musical competence and handedness. *Cortex* 17:291–302.

McCarthy, J. 1969. Accuracy of recognition for verbal and tonal stimuli presented to the left and right ears. *Bulletin of the Council for Research in Music Education* 16:18–21.

McElwain, J. 1979. The effect of spontaneous and analytical listening on the evoked cortical activity in the left and right hemispheres of musicians and nonmusicians. *Journal of Music Therapy* 16, no. 4:180–89.

McFarland, H., and D. Fortin. 1982. Amusia due to right temporoparietal infarct. *Archives of Neurology* 39:725–27.

McKee, G., B. Humphrey, and D. McAdam. 1973. Scaled lateralization of alpha activity during linguistic and musical tasks. *Psychophysiology* 10, no. 4:441–43.

Miller, J., and P. Jusczyk. 1989. Seeking the neurobiological bases of speech perception. *Cognition* 33:111–37.

Miller, L. 1989. *Musical savants: Exceptional skill and mental retardation*. Hillsdale, NJ: Laurence Erlbaum.

Miller, R., M. Thaut, and J. Aunon. 1995. Event-related brain wave potentials in an auditory-motor synchronization task. In *MusicMedicine 2*, ed. R. Pratt and R. Spintge. St. Louis: MMB Music. In press.

Milner, B. 1969. Laterality effects in audition. In *Brain and behavior 2: Perception and action*, ed. K. Pribram, 319–20. New York: Penguin Books.

Molfese, D., R. Freeman Jr., and D. Palermo. 1975. The ontegeny of brain lateralization for speech and nonspeech stimuli. *Brain and Language* 2:356–68.

Moore, G. 1984. A computer-based portable keyboard monitor for studying timing performance in pianists. *Annals of the New York Academy of Sciences* 423:651–52.

Moore, G. 1988. The study of skilled performance in musicians. In *The biology of music making*, ed. F. Rochmann and F. Wilson, 77–91. St. Louis: MMB Music.

Moore, G. 1992. Piano trills. *Music Perception* 9:351–60.

Moore, G., D. Hary, and R. Naill. 1988. Trills: Some initial observations. *Psychomusicology* 7, no. 2:153–62.

Morais, J., and M. Landercy. 1977. Listening to speech while retaining music: What happens to the right-ear advantage? *Brain and Language* 4:295–308.

Morais, J., I. Peretz, and M. Gudanski. 1982. Ear asymmetry for chord recognition in musicians and nonmusicians. *Neuropsychologia* 20:351–54.

Mostafa, M., M. Kotby, M. Barakah, S. El-Sady, T. Allosh, A. Elshobary, and M. Saleh. 1989. Dominant function of right versus the left hemisphere. *Acta Oto-laryngologica* 107, nos. 5–6:479–84.

Murray, D., and K. Rushford. 1977. Hemispheric asymmetry in the discrimination and identification of small frequency changes: A dichotic listening experiment. University of Illinois. Typescript.

Murray, J. 1986. The role of spatial complexity in the perception of speech and pure tones in dichotic listening. *Brain and Cognition* 5:452–64.

Murray, K. 1980. Hemisphere and directional asymmetry of pitch discrimination. *Journal of Research in Music Education* 28, no. 4:225–28.

Nash, J. 1992. The frontier within. *Time Magazine* 28 December, 81–82.

Natale, M. 1977. Perception of nonlinguistic auditory rhythms by the speech hemisphere. *Brain and Language* 4:32–44.

Nebes, R. 1977. Man's so-called minor hemisphere. In *The human brain*, ed. M. Wittrock, 97–106. Englewood Cliffs, NJ: Prentice-Hall.

Neff, W. 1967. Auditory discriminations affected by cortical ablations. In *Sensorineural hearing processes and disorders*, ed. A. Graham, 201–6. Boston: Little, Brown.

Neher, E., and B. Sakmann. 1992. The patch clamp technique. *Scientific American* 266, no. 3:44–51.

Newman, P., and M. Saunders. 1980. A unique case of musicogenic epilepsy. *Archives of Neurology* 37, no. 4:244–5.

Nielson, H., and J. Sørensen. 1976. Hemispheric dominance, dichotic listening, and lateral eye movement behavior. *Scandinavian Journal of Psychology* 17:129–32.

Nordby, H., W. Roth, and A. Pfefferbaum. 1988. Event-related potentials to breaks in sequences of alternating pitches or interstimulus intervals. *Psychophysiology* 25:262–68.

O'Boyle, M., and M. Sanford. 1988. Hemispheric asymmetry in the matching of melodies to rhythm sequences tapped in the right and left palms. *Cortex* 24, no. 2:211–21.

Olsho, L. 1984. Infant frequency discrimination. *Infant Behavior and Development* 7:27–35.

Osaka, M., and N. Osaka. 1992. Effect of musical tempo upon reading performance. Paper presented at the 2d International Conference on Music Perception and Cognition, February, University of California at Los Angeles.

Osborne, K., and A. Gale. 1976. Bilateral EEG differentiation of stimuli. *Biological Psychology* 4, no. 3:184–96.

Oscar-Berman, M., H. Goodglass, and H. Donnenfeld. 1974. Dichotic ear-order effects with nonverbal stimuli. *Cortex* 10:270–77.

Paller, K., G. McCarthy, and C. Wood. 1992. Event-related potentials elicited by deviant endings to melodies. *Psychophysiology* 29, no. 2:202–6.

Pascual-Leone, A., J. Grafman, and M. Hallett. 1994. Modulation of cortical motor output maps during development of implicit and explicit knowledge. *Science* 263, no. 5151:1287–89.

Pascual-Leone, A., N. Dang, L. Cohen, J. Brasil-Neto, A. Cammarota, and M. Hallett. 1995. Modulation of muscle responses evoked by transcranial magnetic stimulation during the acquisition of new fine motor skills. *Journal of Neurophysiology* 74, no. 3:1037–1045.

Patel, A., and I. Peretz. 1994. Perception of linguistic prosody in amusic subjects. In *Proceedings of the 3d international conference for music perception and cognition*, ed. I. Deliege, 427–28. Liege, Belgium.

Paulus, W. 1988. Effect of musical modelling on late auditory evoked potentials. *European Archives of Psychiatry and Neurological Sciences* 237, no. 5:307–11.

Paulus, W. 1992. Event-related potentials evoked by music lack a dissonance correlate. *Psychomusicology* 11:152–56.

Payne, K. 1989. Elephant talk. *National Geographic* 176, no. 2:264–77.

Pechstedt, P., J. Kershner, and M. Kinbourne. 1989. Musical training improves processing of tonality in the left hemisphere. *Music Perception* 6, no. 3:275–98.

Peretz, I. 1987. Shifting ear differences in melody comparison through transposition. *Cortex* 23:317–23.

Peretz, I. 1994. Amusia: Specificity and multiplicity. In *Proceedings of the 3d international conference for music perception and cognition*, ed. I. Deliege, 37–38. Liege, Belgium.

Peretz, I., and J. Morais. 1979. A left ear advantage for chords in nonmusicians. *Perceptual and Motor Skills* 3:957–58.

Peretz, I., and J. Morais. 1980. Modes of processing melodies and ear asymmetry in nonmusicians. *Neuropsychologia* 18:477–89.

Peretz, I., and J. Morais. 1987. Analytic processing in the classification of melodies as same or different. *Neuropsychologia* 25:645–52.

Peretz, I., and J. Morais. 1989. Music and modularity. *Contemporary Music Review* 4:279–93.

Peretz, I., J. Morais, and P. Bertelson. 1987. Shifting ear differences in melody recognition through strategy inducement. *Brain and Cognition* 6, no. 2:202–15.

Peretz, I., and R. Zatorre. 1994. Symposium: Music in the brain. In *Proceedings of the 3d international conference for music perception and cognition*, ed. I. Deliege, 35–36. Liege, Belgium.

Petsche, H. 1992. EEG and musical thinking. Paper presented at the 2d International Conference on Music Perception and Cognition, February, University of California at Los Angeles.

Petsche, H., K. Linder, P. Rappelsberger, and C. Gruber. 1988. The EEG: An adequate method to concretize brain processes elicited by music. *Music Perception* 6, no. 2:133–59.

Petsche, H., H. Pochberger, and P. Rappelsberger. 1985. Music perception, EEG, and musical training. *EEG-EMG* 16, no. 4:183–90.

Petsche, H., P. Richter, A. von Stein, S. Etlinger, and O. Filz. 1993. EEG coherence and musical thinking. *Music Perception* 11, no. 2:117–51.

Piazza, D. 1980. The influence of sex and handedness in the hemisphere specialization of verbal and nonverbal tasks. *Neuropsychologia* 18:163–76.

Pines, M. 1973. *The brain changers: Scientists and the new mind control.* New York: Signet.

Piro, J. 1993. Laterality effects for music perception among differentially talented adolescents. *Perceptual and Motor Skills* 76, no. 2:499–514.

Posner, M., and M. Raichle. 1994. *Images of mind.* New York: Scientific American Library.

Pratt, R., and Spintge, R. 1995. *MusicMedicine 2.* St. Louis: MMB Music. In press.

Prior, M., and G. Troup. 1988. Processing of timbre and rhythm in musicians and nonmusicians. *Cortex* 24, no. 3:451–56.

Provins, K., and M. Jeeves. 1975. Hemisphere differences in response time to simple auditory stimuli. *Neuropsychologia* 13:207–11.

Radocy, R. 1979. Hemispheric specialization for a holistic and an analytic musical task: A preliminary report. University of Kansas. Typescript.

Raichle, M. 1994. Visualizing the mind. *Scientific American* 270, no. 4:58–64.

Rainbow, E., and C. Herrick. 1982. An investigation of hemispheric specialization for the pitch and rhythmic aspects of melody. *Psychology of Music*, special issue, 96–100.

Reinke, T. 1981. Simultaneous processing of music and speech. *Psychomusicology* 1:58–77.

Restak, R. 1979. *The brain: The last frontier.* New York: Warner Books.

Restak, R. 1983. Newborn knowledge. In *Science yearbook 1984: New illustrated encyclopedia*, ed. L. Blum, 48–52. New York: Funk and Wagnalls.

Révész, G. 1925. *The psychology of a musical prodigy.* New York: Harcourt, Brace.

Roberts, L. 1989. Are neural nets like the human brain? *Science* 243, no. 4890:481–82.

Robinson, G., and D. Solomon. 1974. Rhythm is processed by the speech hemisphere. *Journal of Experimental Psychology* 102, no. 3:508–11.

Roederer, J. 1982. Physical and neuropsychological foundations of music: The basic questions. In *Music, mind, and brain: The neuropsychology of music*, ed. M. Clynes, 37–46. New York: Plenum Press.

Rogers, L., and D. Walter. 1981. Methods for finding single generators, with application to auditory driving of the human EEG by complex stimuli. *Journal of Neuroscience Methods* 4, no. 3:257–65.

Roland, P., E. Skinhoj, and N. Lassen. 1981. Focal activiations of human cerebral cortex during auditory discrimination. *Journal of Neuropsychology* 45:1139–51.

Rolls, E. 1989. The representation and storage of information in neuronal networks in the primate cerebral cortex and hippocampus. In *The computing neuron*, ed. R. Durbin, C. Miall, and G. Mitchison, 125–59. New York: Addison-Wesley.

Rushford-Murray, K. 1977. Left-right ear differences in the processing of instrument tone segments. *Bulletin of the Council for Research in Music Education* 52:1–6.

Russell, W., with A. Dewar. 1975. *Explaining the brain.* London: Oxford University Press.

Sacks, O. 1983. *Awakenings.* New York: Dutton.

Sacks, O. 1987. *The man who mistook his wife for a hat*. New York: Harper and Row.

Sagan, C. 1977. *The dragons of Eden: Speculations on the evolution of human intelligence*. New York: Ballantine Books.

Saghal, 1981. Idiot geniuses. *Science Digest 89*, nos. 12–13:113.

Samson, S. 1994. Multidimensional scaling analysis of timbre perception after unilateral temporal lobe lesion. In *Proceedings of the 3d international conference for music perception and cognition*, ed. I. Deliege, 419–20. Liege, Belgium.

Samson, S., and R. Zatorre. 1988. Melodic and harmonic discrimination following unilateral cerebral excision. *Brain and Cognition 7*, no. 3:348–60.

Sanders, R. 1989. Highways of the mind. *University of California at San Francisco Magazine 11*, no. 2:36–45.

San Martini, P., V. De Pascalis, R. Montirosso, and R. Surian. 1989. Deutsch's frequency anisotropy and ear advantage in a dichotic test of musical chords. *Neuropsychologia 27*, no. 8:1109–13.

San Martini, P., and R. Rossi. 1988. Hemispheric asymmetry in the perception of musical chords. In *The EEG of mental activities*, ed. D. Giannitrapani and L. Murri, 94–105. Basel: Karger.

Saunders, T. 1988. Why do young children sing out of tune? Providing a proper foundation for children to sing. *Update 6*, no. 2:19–21.

Scartelli, J. 1992. Music therapy and psychoneuroimmunology. In *MusicMedicine*, ed. R. Spintge and R. Droh, 137–41. St. Louis: MMB Music.

Schlang, G., L. Jancke, Y. Huang, and H. Steinmetz. 1994. In vivo morphometry of interhemispheric asymmetry and connectivity in musicians. In *Proceedings of the 3d international conference for music perception and cognition*, ed. I. Deliege, 417–18. Liege, Belgium.

Schlang, G., L. Jancke, Y. Huang, and H. Steinmetz. 1995. In vivo evidence of structural brain asymmetry in musicians. *Science 267*, no. 5198:699–701.

Schweiger, A., and I. Maltzman. 1985. Behavioral and electrodermal measures of lateralization for music perception in musicians and nonmusicians. *Biological Psychology 20*:129–45.

Schwent, V., E. Snyder, and S. Hillyard. 1976. Auditory evoked potentials during multichannel selective listening: Role of pitch and localization cues. *Journal of Experimental Psychology: Human Perception and Performance 2*, no. 3:313–25.

Scott, D. 1977. Musicogenic epilepsy. In *Music and the brain: Studies in the neurology of music*, ed. M. Critchley and R. Henson, 354–64. Springfield, IL: C. C. Thomas.

Searle, J. 1990. Is the brain's mind a computer program? *Scientific American 262*, no. 1:26–31.

Selby, B., J. Rosenfeld, E. Styles, and J. Westcott. 1982. Which hemisphere is trained? The need for a new strategy for interpreting hemispheric asymmetries in music perception. *Psychology of Music*, special issue, 101–3.

Sergent, J. 1993a. Mapping the musician brain. *Human Brain Mapping 1*, no. 1:20–38.

Sergent, J. 1993b. Music, the brain, and Ravel. *Trends in Neuroscience 16*, no. 5:168–71.

Sergent, J., E. Zuck, S. Tenial, and B. MacDonall. 1992. Distributed neural network underlying musical sight reading and keyboard performance. *Science 257*:106–9.

Shankweiler, D. 1966. Effects of temporal lobe damage on the perception of dichotically presented melodies. *Journal of Comparative Physiological Psychology* 62:115–19.

Shannon, B. 1980. Lateralization effects in musical decision tasks. *Neuropsychologia*
18:21–31.

Shannon, B. 1981. Classification of musical information presented to the right
and left ear. *Cortex* 17:583–96.

Shannon, B. 1984. Asymmetries in musical aesthetic judgments. *Cortex* 20:567–73.

Shapiro, B., M. Grossman, and H. Gardner. 1981. Selective musical processing
deficits in brain damaged patients. *Neuropsychologia* 19, no. 2:161–69.

Shatz, C. 1992a. The developing brain. *Scientific American* 267, no. 3:60–67.

Shatz, C. 1992b. Dividing up the neocortex. *Science* 258, no. 5080:237–38.

Shepherd, G. 1990. The significance of real neuron architectures for neural network simulations. In *Computational neuroscience*, ed. E. L. Schwartz, 82–96.
Cambridge, MA: MIT Press.

Shepherd, G. 1994. *Neurobiology.* 3d ed. New York: Oxford University Press.

Shetler, D. 1985. Prenatal music experiences. *Music Educators Journal* 71, no. 7:26–27.

Shetler, D. 1989. The inquiry into prenatal musical experience: A report of the
Eastman project 1980–1987. *Pre- and Peri-Natal Psychology* 3, no. 3:171–89.

Shucard, D., J. Shucard, and D. Thomas. 1977. Auditory evoked potentials as probes
of hemispheric differences in cognitive processing. *Science* 197:1295–98.

Shucard, J., D. Shucard, K. Cummins, and J. Campos. 1981. Auditory evoked potentials and sex-related differences in brain development. *Brain and Language*
13, no. 1:91–102.

Sidtis, J. 1980. On the nature of the cortical function underlying right hemisphere
auditory perception. *Neuropsychologia* 18:321–30.

Sidtis, J. 1982. Predicting brain organization from dichotic listening performance:
Cortical and subcortical functional asymmetries contribute to perceptual
asymmeties. *Brain and Language* 17:287–300.

Sidtis, J., and M. Bryden. 1978. Asymmetrical perception of language and music:
Evidence for independent processing strategies. *Neuropsychologia* 16:627–32.

Sidtis, J., and B. Volpe. 1988. Selective loss of complex-pitch or speech discrimination after unilateral lesion. *Brain and Language* 34:235–45.

Signoret, J., P. Van Beckhout, M. Poncet, and P. Castaigne. 1987. Aphasia without
amusia in a blind organist and composer: Verbal alexia and agraphia without
musical alexia and agraphia in Braille. *Revue Neurologique* 143, no. 3:172–81.

Sloboda, J. 1992. Empirical studies of emotional response to music. In *Cognitive
bases of musical communication*, ed. M. Jones and S. Holleran, 33–50. Washington, DC: American Psychological Association.

Smoliar, S. 1992. Elements of a neuronal model of listening to music. In *Theory
Only* 12, nos. 3–4:29–46.

Sperry, R. 1966. The great cerebral commisure. In *Psychobiology, the biological bases
of behavior*, eds. J. McGaugh, N. Weinberger, and R. Whalen, 240–50. San
Francisco: Freeman.

Sperry, R. 1967. Split-brain approach to learning problems. In *The neurosciences:
A study program*, eds. G. Quarton, T. Melnechuk, and F. Schmitt, 714–22.
New York: Rockefeller University Press.

Sperry, R. 1970. Cerebral dominance in perception. In *Early experience and visual information processing in perceptual and reading disorders*, ed. F. Young and D. Lindsley, 167–77. Washington, DC: National Academy of Sciences.

Sperry, R. 1973. Lateral specialization of cerebral function in the surgically separated hemispheres. In *Psychophysiology of thinking*, eds. F. McGuigan and R. Shoonover, 209–29. New York: Academic Press.

Spingte, R. 1992. The neurophysiology of emotion and its therapeutic applications in music therapy and music medicine. In *Applications of music in medicine*, ed. C. Maranto, 59–72. Washington, DC: National Association for Music Therapy.

Spingte, R., and R. Droh, eds. 1992. *MusicMedicine*. St. Louis: MMB Music.

Spreen, O., F. Spellacy, and J. Reid. 1970. The effect of interstimulus interval and intensity on ear asymmetry for nonverbal stimuli in dichotic listening. *Neuropsychologia* 8:245–50.

Springer, S., and G. Deutsch. 1989. *Left brain, right brain*. 3d ed. New York: Freeman.

Steinberg, R., W. Gunther, I. Stilz, and P. Rondot. 1992. EEG mapping during music stimulation. *Psychomusicology* 11:159–70.

Steinke, W., L. Cuddy, and I. Peretz. 1994. Dissociation of music and cognitive abstraction abilities in normal and neurologically impaired subjects. In *Proceedings of the 3d international conference for music perception and cognition*, ed. I. Deliege, 425–26. Liege, Belgium.

Steinmetz, H., L. Jancke, A. Kleinschmidt, G. Schlaung, J. Volkmann, and Y. Huang. 1992. Sex but not hand differences in the isthmus of the corpus callosum. *Neurology* 42:749–52.

Stiller, A. 1987. Toward a biology of music. *Opus* 3, no. 5:12–15.

Storr, A. 1992. *Music and the mind*. New York: Ballantine Books.

Surwillo, W. 1976. Analysis of interval histograms of periods of the electroencephalogram from homologous left and right derivations in verbal and nonverbal tasks. *Physiological Psychology* 4:307–10.

Sutherling, W., L. Hershman, J. Miller, and S. Lee. 1980. Seizures induced by playing music. *Neurology* 30, no. 9:1001–04.

Swartz, K., J. Walton, G. Crummer, E. Hantz, and R. Frisina. 1992. P3 event-related potentials and performance of healthy older and Alzheimer's dementia subjects for music perception tasks. *Psychomusicology* 11:96–118.

Taub, J., P. Tanguay, and D. Clarkson. 1976. Electoencephalographic and reaction time asymmetries to musical chord stimuli. *Physiology and Behavior* 17, no. 6:925–29.

Taub, J., P. Tanguay, D. Doubleday, D. Clarkson, and R. Remington. 1976. Hemisphere and ear asymmetry in the auditory evoked response to musical chord stimuli. *Physiological Psychology* 4, no. 1:11–17.

Tervaniemi, M., K. Alho, P. Paavilainen, M. Sams, and R. Naatanen. 1993. Absolute pitch and event-related brain potentials. *Music Perception* 10, no. 3:305–16.

Teyler, T. 1977. An introduction to the neurosciences. In *The human brain*, ed. M. Wittrock, 3–38. Englewood Cliffs, NJ: Prentice-Hall.

Thaut, M., S. Brown, J. Benjamin, and J. Cooke. 1995. Rhythmic facilitation of movement sequencing: Effects on spatio-temporal control and sensory modality dependence. In *MusicMedicine 2*, ed. R. Pratt and R. Spintge. St. Louis: MMB Music. In press.

Thaut, M., G. McIntosh, S. Prassas, and R. Rice. 1993. Effect of rhythmic cuing on temporal stride parameters and EMG patterns in hemiparetic gait of stroke patients. *Journal of Neurologic Rehabilitation* 7:9–16.

Thaut, M., G. McIntosh, and R. Rice. 1995. Rhythmic auditory stimulation as an entrainment and therapy technique in gait of stroke and Parkinson's patients. In *MusicMedicine 2*, ed. R. Pratt and R. Spintge. St. Louis: MMB Music. In press.

Thomas, D., and D. Shucard. 1983. Changes in patterns of hemispheric electrophysiological activity as a function of instructional set. *International Journal of Neuroscience* 18, nos. 1–2:11–19.

Tims, F. 1981. Contrasting music conditions, visual attending behavior and state in eight-week-old infants. Rev. A. Gabrielsson. *Bulletin of the Council for Research in Music Education* 66/67:164–68.

Trehub, S., D. Bull, and L. Thorpe. 1984. Infants' perception of melodies: The role of melodic contour. *Child Development* 55:821–30.

Verny, T., with J. Kelly. 1981. *The secret life of the unborn child*. New York: Summit Books.

Wachhaus, G. 1973. Effects of brainwave training on music achievement. Ph.D. Diss. Teachers College, Columbia University.

Wagner, M. 1975a. Brainwaves and biofeedback: A brief history—implications for music research. *Journal of Music Therapy* 12, no. 2:46–58.

Wagner, M. 1975b. Effect of music and biofeedback on alpha brainwave rhythms and attentiveness. *Journal of Research in Music Education* 23, no. 1:3–13.

Wagner, M., and R. Hannon. 1981. Hemispheric asymmetries in faculty and student musicians and nonmusicians during melody recognition tasks. *Brain and Language* 13:379–88.

Wagner, M., and M. Mentzel. 1977. The effect of music listening and attentiveness training on the EEG's of musicians and nonmusicians. *Journal of Music Therapy* 14:151–64.

Walker, J. 1980. Alpha EEG correlates of performance on a music recognition task. *Physiological Psychology* 8, no. 3:417–20.

Wallin, N. 1991. *Biomusicology: Neurophysiological, neuropsychological, and evolutionary perspectives on the origins and purposes of music*. Stuyvesant, NY: Pendragon Press.

Walton, J., R. Frisina, K. Swartz, E. Hantz, and G. Crummer. 1988. Neural basis for music cognition: Future directions and biomedical implications. *Psychomusicology* 7, no. 2:127–38.

Wang, C. 1977. The effects of pitch interval on brain wave amplitudes. *Journal of Research in Music Education* 25, no. 2:150–64.

Wang, C., H. Marple, and R. Carlson. 1975. Increased difficulty of pitch identification and electroencephalographic desynchronization. *Journal of Research in Music Education* 23:197–202.

Wengel, S., W. Burke, and D. Holemon. 1989. Musical hallucinations: The sounds of silence? *Journal of the American Geriatrics Society* 37, no. 2:163–66.

Wertheim, N. 1969. The amusias. In *Handbook of clinical neurology*, vol. 4, eds. P. Vinken and G. Bruyn, 195–206. Amsterdam: North-Holland.

Wertheim, N. 1977. Is there an anatomical localization for musical faculties? In *Music and the brain: Studies in the neurology of music*, ed. M. Critchley and R. Henson, 282–300. Springfield, IL: C. C. Thomas.

Wertheim, N., and M. Botez. 1961. Receptive amusia: A clinical analysis. *Brain* 84:19–30.

Wexler, B., and T. Halwes. 1981. Right ear bias in the perception of loudness of pure tones. *Neuropsychologia* 19:147–50.

Wieser, H., and G. Mazzola. 1986. Musical consonances and dissonances: Are they distinguished independently by the right and left hippocampi? *Neuropsychologia* 24, no. 6:805–12.

Williams, J., and D. Hodges. 1980. Nonmusic major differences in eye positions while performing music tasks. Southern Methodist University. Typescript.

Williamson, S., and L. Kaufman. 1988. Auditory evoked magnetic fields. In *Physiology of the ear*, ed. A. Jahn and J. Santos-Sacchi, 497–505. New York: Raven Press.

Wilson, F. 1986. *Tone deaf and all thumbs?* New York: Viking.

Wilson, F. 1988. Brain mechanisms in highly skilled movements. In *The biology of music making*, eds. F. Roehmann and F. Wilson, 92–99. St. Louis: MMB Music.

Wilson, F. 1989. Acquisition and loss of skilled movement in musicians. *Seminars in Neurology* 9, no. 2: 146–51.

Wilson, F. 1991. Music and the neurology of time. *Music Educators Journal* 77, no. 5:26–30.

Wilson, F. 1992. Digitizing digital dexterity: A novel application for MIDI recordings of keyboard performance. *Psychomusicology* 11:79–95.

Wilson, F. 1993. MIDI Technology: A new window on the structure and stability of motor performance. *Medical Problems of Performing Artists*. In press.

Wilson, F., and F. Roehmann. 1992. The study of biomechanical and physiological processes in relation to musical performance. In *Handbook of research on music teaching and learning*, ed. R. Colwell, 509–24. New York: Schirmer Books.

Wilson, F., C. Wagner, V. Homberg, and J. Noth. 1991. Interaction of biomechanical and training factors in musicians with occupational cramp/focal dystonia. *Neurology* 4, no. 3 suppl. 1:291–92.

Winhold, H. 1988. High speed photography of cello playing. In *Biology of music making*, ed. F. Wilson and F. Roehmann, 180–82. St. Louis: MMB Music.

Winhold, H., and E. Thelen. 1988. Study in perceptual, cognitive, and motor aspects of highly skilled cellists. *Psychomusicology* 7, no. 2:163–64.

Yamadori, A., Y. Osumi, S. Masuhara, and M. Okubo. 1977. Preservation of singing in Broca's aphasia. *Journal of Neurology, Neurosurgery, and Psychiatry* 40, no. 3:221–24.

Youcha, G. 1982. Life before birth. *Science Digest* 90, no. 12:46–53.

Yund, E., and R. Efron. 1975. Dichotic competition of simultaneous tone bursts of different frequency II: Suppression and ear dominance functions. *Neuropsychologia* 13:137–50.

Yund, E., and R. Efron. 1976. Dichotic competition of simultaneous tone bursts of different frequency IV: Correlation with dichotic competition of speech signals. *Brain and Language* 3:246–54.

Zatorre, R. 1978. Recognition of dichotic melodies by musicians and nonmusicians. *Journal of the Acoustical Society of America* 63:S51.

Zatorre, R. 1979. Recognition of dichotic melodies by musicians and nonmusicians. *Neuropsychologia* 17:607–17.

Zatorre, R. 1985. Discrimination and recognition of tonal melodies after unilateral cerebral excisions. *Neuropsychologia* 23, no. 1:31–41.

Zatorre, R. 1989. Effects of temporal neocortical excisions on musical processing. *Contemporary Music Review* 4:265–77.

Zatorre, R. 1994. Musical processing in the nonmusician's brain: Evidence for specialized neural networks. In *Proceedings of the 3d international conference for music perception and cognition*, ed. I. Deliege, 39–40. Liege, Belgium.

Zatorre, R., A. Evans, and E. Meyer. 1994. Neural mechanisms underlying melodic perception and memory for pitch. *Journal of Neuroscience* 14, no. 4:1908–19.

Zatorre, R., A. Evans, E. Meyer, and A. Gjedda. 1992. Lateralization of phonetic and pitch processing in speech perception. *Science* 256:846–49.

8

Responses to Music

Harold F. Abeles and Jin Won Chung

When examining the literature on responses to music, it becomes apparent that the terms often used at the conceptual level to categorize these responses are not employed, or are used inconsistently, at the empirical level. Some writers in this area have chosen to conceptualize aesthetic and affective responses as distinct (e.g., Lundin 1967), while others have not. Those authors who have focused on the differences and similarities between aesthetic and affective responses to music at the conceptual level seem to concur (Hanslick 1891; Hevner 1937; Meyer 1956; Reimer 1989; Schoen 1940; Seashore 1938). They describe the aesthetic experience as an intense, subjective, personal experience that provides insight into the nature of human life. The aesthetic experience is thought to include some mood, emotional, or "feelingful aspect," that is, an affective component. The affective response is generally conceived of as a more superficial response than the aesthetic experience. But other terminology—preference, attitude, or taste—has been used inconsistently.

It is likely that the inconsistent use of terminology has contributed to difficulty in communication among researchers in this field. During the Music Educators National Conference (MENC) National Convention in March 1984, this "terminology issue" was discussed. A representative sample of pertinent books and journals was surveyed and a glossary of terminology developed (Price 1986). Preference was defined as an act of choosing, esteeming, or giving advantage to one thing over another, and differences between behavioral preference and verbal preference were also distinguished. Attitude can be thought of as a learned predisposition reflecting the way one feels about a subject while not in the presence of that subject, which is not directly observable. Taste involves a person's long-term commitment to musical preferences, a social matter that tends to change with different groups of people, places, and times.

Although the aesthetic experience and the affective response to music have been distinguished at the conceptual level, the empirical literature on these responses to music does not reflect this distinction. Researchers have had difficulty operationalizing (defining so that they can be measured) these two constructs. They have tended to employ the same measurement techniques (e.g., verbal reports) to define responses to music that have been labeled as both aesthetic and affective. In some studies, one technique (e.g., semantic differential)[1] may be used as a measure of the aesthetic experience, while in another study the technique is identified as a measure of an affective response. Many researchers simply avoid the terms, employing instead terms such as *preference, mood, or taste.* Other researchers circumvent the problem by choosing to conceptualize the response to music on which they are focusing as being unidimensional, thus simplifying the measurement strategies required. The few researchers who have made a serious attempt to explore the aesthetic experience have tended not to be satisfied with a single measure but have included a battery of measures, as the aesthetic experience is generally conceived of as multidimensional (see chap. 10).

The review of the literature of responses to music that follows does not employ the conceptual distinction between aesthetic and affective responses we have just described, since researchers have generally seemed to ignore this organizational strategy. The organizational strategy that has been employed instead is based on Krathwohl, Bloom, and Masia 1964. Krawthowal and his colleagues presented a five-level hierarchy of the affective domain. The purpose of the taxonomy was initially to provide a scheme to aid educators in organizing and evaluating curricula relating to affective objectives. The continuum upon which the taxonomy is organized is labeled *internalization,* that is, an increasing acceptance and application by the individual of attitudes and values when making judgments.

The five levels into which this continuum are divided have been labeled from lowest to highest: receiving, responding, valuing, organization, and characterization. Receiving is a willingness to attend. Responding refers to active participation. Valuing occurs when value is attached to an object. Organization involves the integration of values into a system, and characterization suggests the development of a characteristic lifestyle based on a value system (for a more detailed review of the taxonomy, see Krawthowal, Bloom, and Masia 1964).

---

1. In a semantic differential scale, subjects are asked to rate an object, subject, or event by selecting a point along a continuum between two bipolar adjectives. Osgood and his associates preferred a seven-point continuum as follows: good +3 +2 +1 0 -1 -2 -3 bad.

The responses to music reviewed in the chapter are organized into the following sections: Measuring Affective Responses to Music, Mood/Emotional Responses to Music, Preference Responses to Music, and Musical Taste. The first section deals with methodological questions, while the last three focus on factors relating to the different categories of responses to music. Mood/Emotional responses to music are thought to be at the lower end of the Krawthowal taxonomy, probably in the responding category. Music preferences responses fall midway on the continuum, representing more than a simple reaction to music but less than a long-term commitment. The term *music taste* as used in this chapter refers to a longer term commitment, as evidenced by behaviors such as record-buying habits, and might be classified on the Krawthowal continuum in either the organization or characterization areas.

Lewy (1971) reported on an attempt to test the applicability of the affective domain taxonomy for musical behaviors. He had "measurement experts" independently classify items, which were collected from available tests of music affective behavior (e.g., Hevner 1937), in accordance with the Krawthowal taxonomy. The judges' classification schemes showed a high level ($r = .71–.82$)[2] of agreement. The items were then administered to 800 high school students and college freshmen. It was expected that the students' responses would decrease for items classified at the higher levels of the taxonomy because of its hierarchical nature. The results of the study confirmed this expectation, suggesting that the taxonomy can be employed appropriately with musical behaviors.

Before examining the empirical literature on responses to music, several theoretical models of the aesthetic and affective response to music will be examined. These have been organized into theories that focus on philosophical issues and theories that seem to lend themselves more readily to empirical validation.

An overview of the major philosophical/theoretical positions with regard to emotion and music will help to organize the several theorists' proposals reviewed in later sections. Historically, two main positions have emerged concerning the association of meaning with music. Absolutists suggest that musical meaning lies exclusively within the content of the work itself, in the perception of the relationship set forth within the musical work of art (Meyer 1956). Referentialists support the position that, in addition to these abstract meanings, music makes references

---

2. A correlation coefficient (r) expresses the degree of relationship between two or more variables. Coefficients range from +1.00 to -1.00, with values approaching 0.00 indicating a lesser degree of relationship and values approaching ±1.00 indicating a greater degree of relationship.

to the world of behaviors, actions, and emotions. A particular work may be selected to support either position, but there seems to be some consensus that certain works (e.g., program music) more easily support one position (referentialists) than the other.

A second distinction is made between two aesthetic theoretical positions. Formalists and expressionists argue that the meaning in music is primarily intellectual or emotional, respectively. A given theorist's position may be a combination of these dichotomies, such as an absolute expressionist who would argue that music is capable of producing emotional reactions from the perception and understanding of the musical relations in a work. Meyer's position is representative of this combination.

Two books (as well as several articles) written by Leonard Meyer (1956 and 1967) have had a major impact on the philosophical, theoretical, and empirical work on aesthetic/affective responses to music in the last 30 years. The major thrust of Meyer's work was to provide an answer to the question, "What makes music great?" Meyer suggested that musical value is related to the goal tendencies of musical units. He then applied information theory to the assignment of value in music, stating that if a musical unit is so well organized that what follows is highly probable (expected), then little value is attached to the music. If the musical consequences are less predictable, then the information contained in the music increases and so does the musical unit's value. It should be pointed out that this theory applies to a given general musical framework (e.g., a musical style), thus complete musical randomness is not a condition under which Meyer's position is applicable. Meyer's theory suggests that an emotional response to music is aroused when an expectation is temporarily delayed by an unanticipated musical consequence. The music first arouses expectations, then builds suspense, and finally provides the resolution.

In Meyer's initial presentation of this position (1956), he supported these propositions by analyzing several compositions, identifying the parallels between his theory and evaluations of the musical examples. Reimer suggested that Meyer's analytical techniques "depend on judgments which are of necessity subjective" (1962, 95), thus not completely validating, in an objective empirical sense, the expectancy theory. Vermazen (1971) suggested that Meyer's theory, because of a lack of precise definitions and formulas, may be more of a philosophy than a theory. This generalness has provided wider bounds under which empiricists have labeled their efforts as tests of Meyer's proposals. Several empirical researchers (e.g., Berlyne 1974; Colwell 1965; McMullen 1974a and 1974b; Standifer 1970; Vitz 1966), whose work is cited in this chapter, have attempted to test Meyer's proposals. Although the methods employed and the results obtained by these studies vary, it is helpful to integrate them with the aid of expectancy theory.

No other philosopher/theorist has had the same impact on thought and research on responses to music as Meyer. Some other contemporary positions actually tend to be refinements of Meyer's initial statements, such as Martin's presentation of Whitehead's theory of perception (1967).

A second category of theories will be examined in this section. They are distinguished from the preceding section because they more readily lend themselves to empirical validation. The proponents of these positions tend to come from different backgrounds than those discussed under the philosophical/theorist heading. The empirical theorists are often experimenters who seem to have felt the necessity of developing theory and often have training in disciplines such as psychology or physics, two sciences in which experimentation is an integral part of the field.

Pinchas Noy presented a series of articles in the *Journal of Music Therapy* that describe attempts at psychoanalytic theories of the meaning in music (1966, 1967a, 1967b, 1967c, and 1967d). He reviewed the extensive literature in the area, highlighting similarities and differences in psychoanalytic theories of music meaning during the past 80 years. Recently, psychoanalytic theory has attempted to focus on the traditional division of content versus form in music, suggesting that a more fruitful perspective would be one that viewed content and form as interrelated. Noy made a distinction between psychoanalytic theory and aesthetic theory by suggesting that the former focuses on the ability of music to serve as "the symbolic expression of unconscious contexts" (1967a, 9), while in aesthetic theory, music is viewed as a "symbolic language expressing overt feeling and contents" (1967a, 9). He elaborated his point by suggesting that some aestheticians think of the emotions evoked by music as an unwanted by-product, a hindrance to the aesthetic experience.

Psychoanalytic theory suggests that the connection between music and emotions is complex and depends on several processes, including the unconscious significance of the music, its impact on impulsive forces, and the transformation of music through ego functions. These functions serve to develop several directions or schools of theory under the psychoanalytic label. These include: libido theory, theorists who "view music as an activity which stems from instinctual energy" (Noy 1967a, 22); dream theory, those who view music as being comprised of two layers, the first organizational, the second functioning "towards change and transformation of deep contents and wishes, according to super-ego and social demands" (Noy 1967b, 47); as well as other theoretical positions that Noy organizes by the extent to which the theory views the interaction of music and the psychic as passive or active. He summarized his extensive investigation of responses to music. These include the methodological weaknesses of much of the empirical research, the tendency to focus on the theoretical and speculative, and the insufficient focus on the specific attributes of the music stimulus. Several of these areas will be elaborated upon subsequently.

Roederer (1974) proposed two possible neurophysiological explanations for the ways in which music evokes meaningful and emotional responses in listeners. The first position is somewhat similar to Meyer's, although Roederer relies on neurological studies to support his propositions. Roederer suggested that because the neural system attempts to process information based on minimum input, it relies heavily on predictions based on past experiences. When an unanticipated musical event occurs, considerably more neural activity is required for processing the information, thus producing the sensations labeled by Roederer as "musical tension." He further suggested that this additional processing occurs involuntarily, thus listeners quite familiar with a composition would continue to experience the sensation upon rehearing a work.

Roederer also suggested that emotional responses to music may likely be due to the engagement of the limbic system (described in chap. 7) during music processing. As the limbic system's primary function is to help ensure self-preservation, it rewards or punishes given environmental events. Thus, the rewards or punishment dispensed by the system during the listening to (or during the recall of) music may provide some understanding of music's emotional content.

A final empirical theoretical position, that of Berlyne, is reviewed in chapter 10. The remainder of this chapter includes reviews of selected research on affective and aesthetic responses to music. It is important that the numerous empirical studies reported be viewed in the context of the organizational strategies and theoretical positions described in this introductory section.

Measuring Affective Responses to Music

Many of the studies described below appear to arrive at conflicting conclusions. Some of the opposing results reported may be due to the different ways in which musical preference and mood/emotion responses to music were operationalized. Was the investigator concerned with a long-range estimate of preference without any music reference, or was he or she focusing on the discriminating preference response between an original and altered melody? Both researchers may have claimed to be measuring musical taste. One investigator may ask subjects to evaluate a variety of excerpts from Honegger to Barry Manilow, while another may only offer a Haydn-Brahms continuum from which respondents are to indicate preferences, yet both may again be looking for indications of taste. Some studies have employed only behavioral assessments, others only verbal reports, while still others only physiological measurements. In many cases, the investigators are asking different questions, thus necessitating different approaches, but they often claim to be examining the same trait (e.g., emotional reactions).

A major concern of all of these investigators is the validity of their results. This question is not easily answered in the case of either preference measures or mood/emotion assessments. Affective responses are complex and may have different independent determinants. Fishbein (1967) suggested that particular affective behaviors result from an affective set (a relatively stable attribute) and environmental factors that may serve as restraints or catalysts on affective behavior. The researcher is often concerned with attempting to strip away or neutralize extraneous environmental factors in order to gain insight on the affective set. The relatively unstable characteristics of mood/emotion responses make this task difficult.

In addition to the different ways of defining affective responses and the instability of some affective responses, a third factor, the relationship between words used to describe affective behavior and actual affective behavior, must be considered an additional threat to the validity of investigations in this area. Investigators who rely solely on verbal reports of affective set must be sensitive to the additional imprecision due to the positive but not perfect relationship between behavioral indicators and behaviors (Fishbein 1967).

The studies reported below are organized by measurement strategies employed (e.g., paired comparisons) as well as by their focus on mood/emotion assessments, preference, or taste. The results of some of these investigations will be also reviewed in later sections, but the studies are discussed here for a closer examination of the measurement techniques employed in the studies.

Measuring Mood/Emotional Responses to Music

Although somewhat varied, approaches to assessing the mood/emotional responses to music seem to differ less than the techniques used to measure preference and taste. These include verbal reports and physiological measures of responses to music.

Verbal Reports

Lifton (1961) used a sorting procedure to assess the amount of aesthetic sensitivity (feelings, ideas, and desires) of college-age respondents. Four classical selections were played. Students were asked to write their reactions and their particular emotional responses to each of the selections. Judges were asked to sort the responses into three categories according to the amount of aesthetic sensitivity displayed by the responses. Lifton reported interjudge agreement was high (interjudge reliability = .94). The test also demonstrated a moderately high (r = .63) relationship with a measure of empathy.

Pike (1972), in a phenomenological analysis of affective responses to music, also asked a college appreciation class to describe their feelings when listening to instrumental symphonic music chosen for its emotional content. Pike emphasized that he was assessing emotional, not aesthetic experience, which to him presupposes a greater degree of training and knowledge. Pike analyzed the content of the respondents' descriptions, categorizing the results into factors of feeling of pleasure, feeling of movement, oneness with music, perception of transient emotional states, and perception of stable moods.

Efforts to quantify responses similar to those used by Lifton and Pike have employed both the checklist (Farnsworth 1954; Hevner 1936) and, more recently, the semantic differential (SD) approaches (Crozier 1973; McMullen 1974a and 1974b).

Hevner, and later Farnsworth, provided respondents with a list of adjectives in an effort to find clusters of adjectives that might be used to describe mood reactions to musical stimuli. Hevner's pioneering work, which is widely reported, produced an 8-cluster structure, 67-adjective scale that could be used to determine the effects of certain characteristics of the musical stimuli (e.g., tempo). Farnsworth updated Hevner's procedures by employing factor analysis and included only 50 of the original 67 adjectives in his revision.

Crozier and McMullen, both representatives of the Berlyne school of experimental aesthetics, have employed semantic differential scales in their efforts to describe aural stimuli and music respectively. A study particularly relevant to the current question was an examination of similarities of the Hevner checklist approach and the dimensions of the semantic differential reported by McMullen (1974b). College art students were asked to indicate on seven-option Osgood-type scales their description of eight classical and pop musical examples. Adjective scales employed in the study were ones that had either previously been shown to be important in SD research or representative of each of the eight

Hevner clusters. The results suggested that the Hevner checklist adjectives are describing two subfactors of the evaluative dimension produced by most SD research. In addition, the data hinted at the presence of an activity dimension. This study has produced some preliminary information regarding the integration of the checklist and the SD approach, but additional study is needed before any firm conclusions can be drawn.

Crickmore (1968a) employed a syndrome or profile test to measure affective responses to music. British college students listened to 22 selections of popular and serious music, indicated on a seven-point scale how much they liked each selection, and indicated on three-option scales their interest, mood, tenseness, desire to talk, satisfaction, and the presence of mental images. Crickmore contended that a pattern of high liking, a sustained interest, a positive mood, relaxation, a desire to remain quiet, high satisfaction, and no mental images indicated positive affect toward music. Factor analysis confirmation of these dimensions was reported by Crickmore as well as the relationship with the measures of musical intelligence and personality. The author presented some evidence that the test may be a useful tool to measure the growth of music appreciation.

Sloboda (1991) undertook a unique survey that examined the relationship between specific characteristics of music and emotional responses that cause physical reactions. He argues that the nature and intensity of felt emotion can vary from moment to moment according to the precise nature of the musical events. Eighty-three adult music listeners completed a questionnaire that provided information about the occurrence of a range of physical reactions while listening to music. Shivers down the spine, laughter, tears, and lump in the throat were the most often reported. Usually shivers or tingles related to pleasant emotions, tears and weeping were associated with sedative emotion. Respondents were asked to locate specific musical passages that evoked such responses. Analysis of these musical passages showed that tears were mostly evoked by sequences and appogiaturas, while shivers were evoked by new or unexpected harmonies. The data generally support theoretical approaches to emotion based on confirmation and violation. Sloboda argues that the emotional response to music should be examined based upon a listener's expectancy, which is due to a listener's musical knowledge and the specific character of musical stimuli.

Physiological Measures

In addition to the various measures of responses to music previously discussed, other researchers have focused on physiological measures in an effort to assess the effects of music. These have included, most frequently, measures of heart rate, respiration rate, and skin response, but researchers have also occasionally employed such other measures of physiological processes as brain waves, muscle tension, or blood pressure.

As with other studies focusing on responses to music, difficulties arise in making generalizations based on the results of different studies, because researchers who have used physiological measures have tended to employ a variety of musics as stimulus material. Particular problems associated with physiological studies are the difficulties inherent in obtaining consistent measures from individuals because environmental conditions other than the music heard (e.g., fatigue or experimental anxiety) often vary.

The results of studies employing physiological measures of responses to music tend to reflect these problems. Although in several cases there are a majority of studies that seem to suggest that a relationship of some type exists, there consistently tend to be studies that suggest the opposite. Heart rate data are especially exemplary of this problem. Several studies show an increase in heart rate when "stimulative" music is heard, while almost an equal number indicate no relationship exists.

Studies employing physiological measures have tended to center on three types of manipulations: stimulative versus sedative music, music versus no music, and the relationship between physiological and other measures of responses to music. With few exceptions, the results of almost a century of these types of investigations show marked inconsistency. The obvious causes for such differences include problems in classifying the music stimuli employed, inconsistency of nonmusic environmental conditions, and the standardization of physiological measures. With few exceptions (tempo), little of this work has focused on particular characteristics of the musical stimulus, thus the classification schemes employed by most researchers tend to be difficult to operationalize.

Periodic reviews of the literature on physiological responses have appeared (Dainow 1977; Diserens 1923; Hodges 1980; Weld 1912; Zimny and Weidenfeller 1962; also see chap. 9). Consistently, those summarizing work in this area have suggested that the studies conducted should be classified as exploratory. Until methodological questions can be resolved and a series of systematic studies undertaken, it appears that few generalizations based on results of research on physiological responses to music can be made.

This brief review of measurement strategies employed by investigators of affective aesthetic responses to music has attempted to illustrate the various techniques, contrast their applications, highlight their diversity, and identify problem areas. Their various implementations are further illustrated by the studies reviewed in subsequent sections.

Measuring Musical Preferences and Tastes

A variety of strategies have been employed to measure musical preferences and taste. To some extent, different strategies can be paired with different research objectives, while, in other cases, several different assessment procedures provide different perspectives on the same objective. Measurement strategies to be included in this section are assessing general attitudes, paired-comparisons, rating scales, and behavioral measures.

Assessing General Attitudes

Both Edwards and Edwards (1971) and the National Assessment on Educational Progress (1974) attempted to measure a general attitude toward music by employing survey instruments. Edwards and Edwards first generated statements, then asked judges to place the statements along a continuum. Items on which the judges agreed and that showed good discrimination power were employed in two, 33-item parallel form scales. The statements were arranged in Likert format.[3] These tests proved to be internally consistent (r = .81–.93) and relatively equivalent (r = .86). The data reported appeared to suggest that the scale is appropriate for measuring group differences in the general affective set toward music.

  The National Assessment of Educational Progress (NAEP) also attempted to measure a general set toward music. The NAEP survey focused on the interest in, or attitude toward, music of 9-, 13-, 17-year-olds, and adults in the United States. The question formats were both structured (multiple choice) and unstructured (open ended). The survey covered a variety of attitude-interest-preference areas in music, including preference for kind of music and interest in participation in musical performance. Results indicated a broadening of taste with increasing age, while interest in musical performing declined with age, possibly due to the lack of opportunities available to adult performers. The report highlighted regional differences that show that people in the Southeast seem to listen to more music, enjoy more music, and sing more music, although they lag behind the nation in interest and participation

---

3. In a Likert scale, subjects respond to a number of positive and negative statements or items by choosing one of the following responses: strongly agree or like, agree or like, undecided or neutral, disagree or dislike, or strongly disagree or dislike.

in instrumental music. The results also indicated women and blacks had more interest in and enjoyed participating in music more than did men and whites, respectively. The results of this study provide a foundation for making some data-based decisions regarding the quality of music education programs across the country but also necessitate followup assessments and periodic monitoring. A second NAEP assessment in music was made in 1979 and another NAEP assessment in music is scheduled for the mid 1990s.

These types of measures are typically employed to measure longer term, relatively stable traits, which we have labeled *musical taste.* The general survey type of music preference measure does not employ musical examples for the respondent but relies on memory and idiosyncratic categorization of music into different types (e.g., jazz, rock and roll). In contrast, the paired-comparison approach provides two musical stimuli from which the respondent is to choose.

Paired Comparisons

The paired-comparison approach is thought to measure short-term, less stable affective responses, which we will label *music preferences.* In a series of experiments, Koh investigated the scalability, that is, the continuum of the categorical nature of musical preference judgments.

In a 1962 study, Koh examined the effect of order and a background excerpt, intervening between pairs, on musical preference judgments. The subjects heard pairs of previously rated musical excerpts (performed on piano or sung) in both orders (AB, BA) and were asked to designate their preference in each pair. The results indicated that if both excerpts had been previously rated pleasant, the second excerpt was most often selected as the most preferred. The first excerpt was selected when the excerpts had been previously rated as unpleasant. In a second experiment, 10 medium-pleasant pairs of excerpts were intervened by a low-pleasant (5 pairs) or high-pleasant (5 pairs) excerpt. The results indicated that the second excerpt in the pair was preferred when the pair was intervened with a low-pleasant excerpt, while the first was preferred when the intervening excerpt had been previously rated as pleasant. A third study indicated that when an intervening excerpt was opposite in pleasantness to the excerpts in the pair, the second excerpt was preferred. The results of these three studies, which relate to the measurement of affective responses and parallel similar studies in psychophysics, suggest that the rating of musical preference is on an intensity continuum and not categorical in nature.

In a second report, Koh (1967) reinforced the continuum nature of affective judgments. One group of subjects rated vocal and piano pieces on a nine-point pleasant scale (categorical judgments). A second group rated the pleasantness of the same piece by comparing each to a standard or model excerpt (magnitude estimation). The relationship of the results of the two rating procedures was logarithmic, again supporting the continuum nature of affective judgments.

Hevner (1935), Long (1972), and Kyme (1967) all employed modified paired comparison procedures in attempts to measure the preference for original versus altered musical excerpts. Hevner's *Oregon Music Discrimination Test* employed 48 "classical" piano excerpts, each paired with an altered version. Respondents were to first designate correctness (or preference) and then to identify whether the alteration was one of rhythm, harmony, or melody. Long revised the test in 1965 by updating some of the examples and adding items from organ, string quartet, and woodwind literatures. Different forms of the test (ranging from 30 to 43 items) produced internal consistency reliability coefficients from .45 to .88. The Kyme *Test of Aesthetic Judgments in Music* also employs items from the Hevner test plus some additional items. The author suggested he was measuring sensitivity to "musical appropriateness" in this instrument, which was designed for junior high school students.

A question of particular interest to readers of this chapter may be: What do these three tests measure? Is it a simple affective response or mere preference, is it a trained skill in discriminating "correctness," or is it aesthetic judgment? (Long suggested that his test might be used as part of a college entrance battery for music majors.) All three positions may be supported by various arguments, thus once more highlighting the problems of operationalizing affective responses to music.

Rating Scales

Ratings of pleasantness or preference on an option Likert scale is a relatively common verbal report technique for measuring the affective response to music. Variations of this approach have been developed by Klemish (1970), Forsythe (1974), and Kuhn (1976), all three of whom reported employing faces displaying different degrees of happiness as response measures of musical affect in young children. Kuhn focused on the effectiveness of these response modes in measuring affective responses. His study employed 11 musical examples ranging from "Country Roads" through *Peter and the Wolf* that first through third graders responded to. He reported internal consistency correlation coefficients ranging from .73 to .85, while test-retest reliabilities for periods of one week to six months were .93 to .43, respectively. Kuhn suggested that a problem in the measurement of preference still exists with regard to choosing between behavioral definitions of preference and preference scales, particularly when the results of the different techniques are contradictory.

Behavioral Measures

There are few studies that employ behavioral measures of musical preference. The more laborious task of data collection has served to limit the number of such studies although some authors (e.g., Abeles 1974) have argued for the increased use of such measures. Studies by Cotter and Toombs (1966), Greer and associates (1973, 1974, and 1975), Clarke (1970), and Palmquist (1990) provide examples of such measures. Geringer (1982) compared verbal measures and behavioral measures.

Cotter and Toombs, in an effort to measure the music preferences of mental retardates, developed a device that would provide nonverbal assessments of preference. Respondents were able to choose, by means of switching channels, auditory stimuli that included children's music, adult background music, a Stockhausen selection, and three noise channels. The experimental sessions lasted 25 minutes, with the time listened to each channel serving as the dependent variable. Results indicated that the mental retardates preferred music over noise, and, within music, preferred children's over adult's background music, which in turn was preferred over Stockhausen.

Greer and associates have employed a similar device, which they have labeled in several studies an Operant Music Listening Recorder (OMLR), to examine preferences for both popular and classical music as well as white noise. Results of both of these studies are detailed elsewhere in this chapter. The OMLR, which can provide several options for music listening (typically four), records the time listened to each channel and contains a "control for key location device" that requires the listener to search the different channels if he or she has listened to any one channel for a continuous period of two minutes. The OMLR has been used with children from nursery school through sixth grade and appears to be a reliable tool for obtaining behavioral measures of musical preference.

Clarke (1970), in examining children's information seeking and social interactions regarding a symphony concert, also employed behavioral measures of musical affect. Sixth-, eighth-, and tenth-grade students were involved in his investigation. A postconcert questionnaire gathered information on (1) the children's enjoyment in watching the musicians and hearing the music, (2) whether they had discussed the concert with others (including peers, teachers, or parents), and (3) offered to mail each student a booklet about symphonies and a photograph of the orchestra they had heard if the students would return a previously stamped postcard included with the questionnaire. Receipt of the postcard constituted the measure of information seeking. Differences were observed in the proportion of students' information-seeking behavior by grade (sixth = 28 percent, eighth = 20 percent, tenth = 16 percent). Correlations between this behavioral measure of information seeking and social interaction (measured by verbal reports) about the symphony concert were generally low. This may be due to the independence of the two variables, for the relationship may be artificially constrained by the difference in the data collection strategies.

Palmquist (1990) investigated the relationship between apparent time duration of music stimuli and music preference among university music and nonmusic majors. Subjects were requested to indicate the ending of an estimated 25-second interval while listening to music examples and also asked to indicate their liking for each example. Statistical analysis indicated no significant correlation between apparent time passage and music preference measures. However, there was a small negative correlation between apparent time passage and music preference, suggesting a slight tendency for apparent time passage responses to increase as dislike increases. Palmquist stressed the importance of time perception in music listening, suggesting that the investigation of time passage in music behaviors should be regarded as a new area of study associated with the measurement of music responses.

Geringer (1982) emphasized free operant selection behavior as a means of assessing and predicting the reinforcement value of music. He conducted verbal and operant music-listening preference tests and compared the results. Subjects were randomly selected elementary students, college nonmusic majors, and college music majors. He required subjects to fill out a survey that asked students to list favorite composers, rank each in order of preference, write the number of live concerts attended where at least one of the composers' pieces had been performed, and indicate the number of the composer's recordings they owned. Subjects listened to music examples presented through earphones. Subjects could choose any of four channels by alteration of button positions of an operant music listening recorder (OMLR). Agreement between the verbal and operant measures of music listening was approximately .50. Clearly, with so few examples to cite, additional development of behavioral measures of preference and additional investigations of the relationship between behavioral measures and verbal reports are warranted.

Mood/Emotional Responses to Music

A major variable that colors the interpretation of studies on mood/emotional responses to music is the perceived stability of the mood or emotion; that is, how long does that state last? Is an individual's emotional state affected only during the listening experience? Do the effects of the listening experience linger? For how long? How do more stable personality traits affect the listener's emotional response? Do shorter term listener feeling-states interact with the music to elicit emotional responses? These are some of the questions that researchers have focused upon and that will serve to organize this section.

This more theoretical consideration has been of interest to only a few researchers, but can provide a context in which the more applied research can be reviewed. The first two areas reviewed here deal with both long- and short-term characteristics of the listener. A third section will examine the different types of mood/emotion reactions to music that have been studied.

Long-Term Characteristics of Listeners

Training

When examining the effects of training on the mood/emotion response of listeners to music, it is necessary to determine the amount and type of training being focused on by a particular study. Some researchers have defined trained listeners as those majoring in music at the college level, while others have classified subjects as trained based on responses to questionnaires. This has resulted in subjects with considerably different amounts of exposure to music all being called "trained." In addition to the multiple definitions of training employed, a variety of measures of emotional responses have been used. Although there are differences in the studies reported herein, they seem generally to support the presence of training effects on mood/emotion responses to music.

Brennis (1970) examined the effects of musical training (having formalized group or private music instruction) and other variables on verbal mood responses to music. Subjects listened to 16 musical excerpts representative of three general categories of music: eighteenth/nineteenth century, twentieth century, and contemporary/popular. Formal musical training, as defined, was found to have a significant effect on both the mood intensity and consequent mood level responses.

Employing an adjective checklist, Sopchack (1955) explored the effects of training, as defined by respondents' reports of past experiences, on the mood/emotion responses to music of college students. The 15 selections to which the students were to respond represented classical, popular, and folk music. Sopchack also reported training effects. He found that respondents with training gave more responses (i.e., checked more adjectives) than respondents without training. Subjects with training were also more responsive to classical music and least responsive to popular selections.

In a more focused study, Trolio (1975) examined the relationship of verbal reports of tension and toleration to distorted melodies and the music background of college-age subjects. The melodies used in the study were variations of "Go Tell Aunt Rhody," written to produce different degrees of expectancy. Subjects rated the examples on tension (seven-point scale) and toleration (which three would you most [least] like developed into a ten-minute melody). Musical background was determined by employing a questionnaire. The subjects with a more extensive musical background (high music) tended to have overall lower tension scores (suggesting more expectations were being met). The high music subjects, while differing significantly from low music subjects on tension responses to diatonic melodies, did not differ on chromatic melodies, suggesting a more limited set of expectations may exist for such melodies. While toleration and tension seemed to be negatively related for both groups, the low music subjects did select more chromatic melodies as most tolerable than the high music group did.

Winold (1963) employed both physiological measures, galvanic skin response (GSR), and verbal reports while examining the effects of changes in harmonic tension. In two separate investigations, listeners were exposed either to isolated chords or to short musical selections that also differed in harmonic tension. GSR or the Hevner adjective circle were employed to assess the response of college undergraduates or graduates. The results of the investigations indicated that both trained (music majors) and untrained (nonmusic majors) listeners' responses to changes in harmonic tension as measured by these two techniques tend to be similar.

While the results of the Brennis, Sopchack, and Trolio studies suggest that differences in the mood/emotional responses of trained and untrained listeners may exist, the Winold study suggests the opposite. It must be noted, though, that Winold's classification of trained and untrained likely differs more than the others and may explain the contradictory results. In addition, Winold chose to focus on the manipulation of a specific aspect of the music (harmonic tension), while the Brennis and Sopchack studies examined less articulated musical stimuli and Trolio focused on melody. Additional research in the area is needed, assessing the effects of different, clearly defined levels of training and specific characteristics on the musical stimuli on mood/emotional responses.

Gender
The effect of gender on mood/emotional responses to music has also been examined in several studies, although most often to search for interactions with other variables (e.g., training). The studies reported again provide a mixed picture regarding the effects of gender on the mood/emotional response to music. Although at least with this variable there is little problem with deciding on an appropriate operational definition, the measures of mood/emotions, while generally focusing on verbal descriptors (except Winold 1963), do vary, and the type of stimulus music listened to has varied. Further research examining the interaction of well-defined music stimuli and characteristics generally associated with females (one may well be advised to employ femininity or androgyny scales instead of relying on more traditional definitions of gender) on mood/emotion responses seems warranted. Two of the studies just cited include an assessment of gender on listeners' responses in their analysis.

Sopchack (1955), in the study described earlier, reported that men and women were equally responsive (i.e., checked a similar number of adjectives) when reporting emotions that they felt were expressed by music, while Winold (1963) reported differences in GSR between male and female subjects when listening to chords of different harmonic tension. Females tended to have greater responses than male listeners. The influence of gender and familiarity on emotional responses to classical music of college age listeners was the focus of an investigation by Hart and Cogan (1976). The subjects were asked to classify four selections in emotional mood categories (e.g., stimulating, joyous). Women tended to report more positive emotional responses to the selections than men. The results also suggest that familiarity with classical selections and the gender of the listener may interact to produce unique mood/emotion responses.

Wheeler (1985) also reported that female subjects responded more positively to music than male subjects. In her study of the relationship of personal characteristics to mood and enjoyment after hearing music, she compared the mood of subjects prior to music listening and after listening. The enjoyment of music was highly correlated to the mood after listening to music, but female subjects showed improvement of mood regardless of whether they enjoyed the music or not.

Fisher and Greenberg further explored the possible effects of gender, but employed only female subjects. In the first study (Greenberg and Fisher 1966), students took both structured and unstructured tests (e.g., *Thematic Apperception Test*) while listening to calm or exciting music. The results suggested that music listening may produce a temporary mood that can effect test performance, with greater effects being observed on projective than structured measuring instruments. In the second study (Fisher and Greenberg 1972), college-age females took several personality scales, including a measure of femininity, while listening to either exciting, calm, or no music. Ten minutes after the onset of music, listeners indicated their mood (on a checklist measuring device) and then rated the music on a semantic differential scale. Those having heard exciting music received significantly higher anxiety and aggression personality variables. Several significant differences were also observed on semantic differential responses as a function of the type of music heard. Of interest here were the results related to femininity scores. While the other personality measures failed to serve as predictors for the effect of the type of music on mood change, femininity was inversely related to the amount of change observed.

Socioeconomic Class
Very few studies have examined the effect of socioeconomic class on mood/emotional responses to music. In a study reported earlier, Brennis (1970) investigated the effects of socioeconomic class as well as formal music training and the type of music heard on the verbal mood response of secondary school students. Brennis reported that the low socioeconomic group (socioeconomic groups were determined by the school's Title I ESEA eligibility and the students' parental occupation) generally did not differ from the high group on mood intensity response, but, when the results were analyzed by the type of music, they differed significantly on the responses to the excerpts by twentieth-century composers. The results also suggested that economic status and training may interact in a way that suggests that formal music training may have a greater impact on the affective mood responses of low socioeconomic class children than of high socioeconomic class children.

Short-Term Characteristics of Listeners

Mood
Several researchers have been interested in examining the existing mood of the listener as a variable which may affect the manner in which the listener responds to music. The mood of the listener has been the focus of several studies and has been examined in others where the primary focus may have been on other factors affecting the mood/emotional responses to music by listeners.

The studies reported all suggest that the existing mood of the listener is likely to affect his or her mood/emotion response to music. All of the studies reported employ verbal response measures, although the specific scales employed differ, as does the way of assessing the existing mood of the listener. A major question for researchers to focus on in this area would seem to be the transient aspects of mood state and mood/emotional responses. Questions such as how long must a musical excerpt be before it affects mood state and how stable are such produced changes in mood, are areas on which future research should center.

Eagle (1971) first measured the present mood of listeners employing a ten-statement *Test for Existing Mood* (TEM). Twenty musical excerpts, both vocal and instrumental, were then played for 274 college music majors who recorded their mood responses to the selections on a five-option semantic differential scale. The results of the study indicated that: (1) the existing mood of the listener as measured by the TEM affected the mood/emotional responses to music, (2) the order of the music presented did not affect the mood/emotional responses to music, and (3) the listener's mood/emotional responses to music differed for vocal and instrumental selections.

Shatin (1970) was interested in examining the ability of music to alter the mood of "normal" subjects. He based his investigation of the isomoodic principle employed in music therapy, which first matches the music played to the mood of the client and then gradually changes the music in hopes of changing the client's mood in the desired direction. College-age male subjects were asked to rate how they felt emotionally during the playing of ten, two-minute excerpts that were selected based on the isoprinciple. The listeners reported their mood/emotions on four verbal scales. An analysis of these responses indicated that significant changes in verbal reports of mood/emotion occurred on all four scales.

Fisher and Greenberg, in a study previously described in detail (1972), suggested that existing mood and mood/emotional responses to music as measured by SD scales may interact to affect listeners' performances on certain tests.

The study by Sopchack (1955) also examined the effects of the existing mood of the listener, as measured on a three-point scale (cheerful-neutral-gloomy), on their mood/emotional responses to music. His results generally support the notion that respondents who have similar existing moods respond to music on mood/emotional scales similarly, but also suggests that results may vary with some musical excerpts and with the sex of the respondent.

Wheeler (1985), in her study of relationship of personality characteristics to mood and enjoyment after hearing music, investigated the influence of listeners' moods before hearing the music on changing moods after hearing. It appears that music can be influential in changing moods, depending upon the moods people have prior to listening and whether they enjoy the music. Mood was improved for people who began in a sad mood and heard music they liked, while moods became worse for those who began in a happy mood and heard music they did not like. People who began in a sad mood and heard music they did not like remained in a sad mood, while those who began in a happy mood and heard music they liked remained happy. The mood prior to music was a negative predictor of enjoyment: subjects who were in good moods before hearing the music did not enjoy the music deeply while those who were in bad moods prior to the music tended to enjoy it deeply.

Familiarity

Although familiarity was a variable of particular interest to several researchers of musical preference, it has been the focus of few studies examining mood/emotion responses to music. One study by Hart and Cogan (1976) examined the effects of familiarity and gender on the verbal reports of college-age listeners to classical music. The students indicated how familiar they were with classical music and then responded on mood/emotion verbal scales for each of four musical selections. The results indicated that females in the sample tended to be more familiar with classical music than the males, but also suggested that mood/emotion affective responses may be affected by a gender and familiarity interaction (e.g., men with low familiarity responded more positively than other men). Additional research is warranted so that more secure conclusions can be made regarding these relationships.

Other Factors

Stratton and Zalanowski (1989) suggest that mood is primarily a cognitive response and music affects mood to the extent that it leads to or enhances "cognitive appraisal." In their study, 72 college students were instructed to tell a happy, sad, or "whatever came to mind (neutral)" story about a painting. Some of the paintings were accompanied by background music and others were not. The musical excerpts were classified as pleasant, depressing, or neutral. Mood changes were recorded on the *Multiple Affect Adjective Checklist.* The sad story instructions were most effective, leading to increased depression and decreased positive affect in all three musical conditions. With neutral story instructions, music appeared to be the determining factor in mood change. Both the happy and sad story instructions superseded any music effect.

Specific Mood-Emotion Responses

Anxiety

The effect of music on anxiety has been the focus of several research projects. Researchers have measured or induced anxiety in subjects in a variety of ways and have employed a range of types of music in their investigations. It is clear from the several studies reported that music does affect anxiety, as measured both by verbal reports and physiological measures. The data are somewhat less consistent on what type of music will produce what specific effect (e.g., Jellison 1975), but they suggest that stimulative music tends to increase anxiety while sedative music tends to decrease anxiety states. Major questions in this area that still appear to be unanswered are related to the duration of the effects on anxiety observed and the classification of music into categories such as stimulative-sedative, calm, exciting, or happy-sad. Other questions still unanswered concern the specific characteristics of the music that produce the observed effects.

In one study on the effects of music on anxiety, Biller, Olson, and Breen (1974) examined the effects of both listening and participation in music on anxiety traits (long-term stable condition) and anxiety states (more transient). The musical stimuli employed in this investigation were two folk songs, one classified as happy, the other sad (as judged by independent raters). College-age students either passively or actively (played tambourine) listened to one of the two songs or heard no music. The results showed no differences among the subjects in different conditions of anxiety traits but showed significantly low anxiety-state results in those subjects exposed to the sad song. Participation had no observable effect.

In two studies previously described, Greenberg and Fisher (1966) and Fisher and Greenberg (1972) noted that exciting music produces more anxiety and aggression than calm music. Smith and Morris (1970) also attempted to assess the effects of stimulative or sedative music (both popular and classical) on anxiety produced by taking an examination in a college course. Students were assigned to either the no music, stimulative music, or sedative music group. Before taking the examination, they responded to a three-item anxiety questionnaire that was administered again after each section of the test. During the examination period, the students were exposed to one of the three conditions (no music, etc.). The results of the study demonstrated that stimulative music significantly increased anxiety (actually defined as worry and emotionality), while sedative music and the no-music condition did not. Test performance of the subjects was not affected.

Jellison (1975) examined the effects of music on both physiological and verbal responses of college-age males in a stress situation. The researcher played either exciting or calm music, white noise, or no sound (control) for students who were put in a stress situation by being administered electrical shocks. Four physiological measures were recorded continuously during the duration of the study. A state-trait verbal anxiety measure was also administered. Jellison found that while no differences in physiological measures were observed between the four groups of subjects, the verbal report data showed that both music groups (calm and exciting) demonstrated significantly less anxiety than the white noise group. In contrast to other studies, there was no difference in verbally reported anxiety between the calm and exciting music conditions.

Elam (1971) also investigated the effects of music employing the threat of shock to produce anxiety. Elam focused on the effects of changes in dynamic (loudness) levels on the emotional responses (as measured by GSR) of subjects put in a state of anxiety. Either stimulative or sedative music was played for subjects at different dynamic levels. He found that, under a stress situation, stimulative music will elicit emotional responses that vary as dynamic levels are manipulated.

Arousal

The effects of music on other states, such as arousal and tension, have also been examined but have not generated as much interest as anxiety. Cantor and Zillman (1973), Neher (1962), and Wallach and Greenberg (1960) reported studies on music and arousal. The results of the three exploratory studies suggest relationships between music and the state of arousal, but provide only tentative directions for future investigations rather than firm foundations on which to base generalizations.

Cantor and Zillman (1973) were interested in examining more closely the effects of current affective state and emotional arousal on both the evaluative and excitation responses to music. The investigators created various levels of evaluative (positive-negative) and excitatory (high-low) responses by showing college-age students film segments representing these conditions. After having viewed one of the four film segments, a subject evaluated three musical selections— one immediately after viewing the film segment, another 2 minutes 15 seconds later, and a third 4 minutes 45 seconds after viewing the film. Their results showed that prior stimulation can affect evaluative and excitatory responses to music. An evaluative contrast effect (e.g., positive prior state-negative evaluation) was noted for the song rated immediately after viewing the film, while an excitation-transfer effect was observed for the song rated second. The rating of the third song did not seem to be affected by prior affective state.

Neher (1962), an anthropologist, explored what he labeled unusual behavior in ceremonies involving drums. Specifically, he was interested in testing the hypothesis that this behavior (which included trance states, hallucinations, and, in one extreme case, convulsions) was the result of the effects of drumming on the central nervous system. Neher employed two approaches to examining this question. Experimentally, he demonstrated in a laboratory setting that rhythmic drumming, as well as rhythmic light stimulation, can produce muscle twitching and unusual perception reports. He then reviewed anthropological reports that tend to reinforce the laboratory finding, specifically that drum rhythms of about 8 to 13 beats per second in a variety of cultures are at least associated with, if not the cause of, unusual behavior.

Wallach and Greenberg (1960) focused on a particular type of arousal, symbolic sexual arousal, to music. The researchers adopted the theoretical position that one of the functions of listening to music may be to permit the symbolic expression of sexual impulses and that subjects with a high anxiety level who are also socially introverted are most likely to demonstrate this symbolic expression. Female college-age subjects were asked to listen to three jazz pieces and then write a story on each that was suggested by the music. The students were told that their "creative imagination" was being tested. The stories were later subjected to content analysis to determine the amount of symbolic sexual arousal they contained. The students were also administered a personality inventory and independently rated other preferences for the selections on which they had written stories. The results of the study tended to confirm the theoretical positions described. A significant interaction was observed in the amount of symbolic sexual arousal contained in the stories inspired by three music selections between listeners classified by anxiety and introversion-extroversion in the predicted direction.

Other Types of Responses
Krevelen (1963) focused on personality characteristics other than anxiety and arousal. Female college students were required to fill out a questionnaire dealing with hypothetical frustrating situations while listening to very dissonant music, harmonically conventional music, or no music. The items on the questionnaire allowed the student to choose a self-punitive, a nonpunitive, or an extropunitive response. The results of the investigation demonstrated that subjects that were exposed to music while completing the questionnaire gave significantly fewer impunitive responses. No music differences were found. Krevelen

suggested that this result may have been due to the presence of music acting as an irritant to subjects filling out the questions, and thus frustrated subjects more than if they had had no music exposure.

A study dealing with music as symbolic of another behavior, social interaction, was reported by sociologist Cecilia Ridgeway (1976). Ridgeway was interested in the relationship between the level of absorption of music listeners (high or low) and their use of musical listening as an aid in dealing with interpersonal interactions. College-age students were first classified as high or low listeners by employing several measures, including self-reports. One group of subjects was then exposed to a difficult affective interpersonal interaction experience, and their level of listening absorption was then reassessed. The results of the data collection supported Ridgeway's hypothesis, suggested that exposure to an affective interaction situation increases high music listeners' absorption in music, and that high listeners are likely to describe music effects in terms of symbolic participation in group processes.

In a more applied investigation, Allen and White (1966) examined the effects of music as a psychotherapeutic agent for improving self-concept. The investigators divided 60 mentally retarded teenagers into three groups. Group 1 was exposed to psychodramatics, group 2 to a folk-song chorus experience, and group 3 acted as a control. Self-concept was measured both by an inventory and behavioral rating scale. The results indicated that both the psychodramatic and choral singing group improved markedly on both measures of self-concept, while the control group showed little change.

As reported previously (Fisher and Greenberg 1972; Greenberg and Fisher 1966), music has been shown to affect performance on tests, particularly personality measures. This effect was likely a secondary effect, with music directly affecting the mood of the subject with this mood (e.g., anxiety) affecting test performance. Hooper and Powell (1970) examined the influence of several categories of music on figural elaboration (total number of different details) in picture-drawing tasks. Employing both graduate students and first graders as subjects, Hooper and Powell had the students listen passively or actively (play rhythm instruments) to either program or absolute music selections. The listeners either drew while listening or after hearing the selection. Both live and taped performances were heard. The results showed live performances produced significantly more elaboration than taped performances for all subjects. The graduate students produced more elaboration with absolute music than program music, while more elaboration was produced in both groups by active listeners than passive listeners.

As can be seen from the studies reported in this section, music can affect a variety of behaviors, including anxiety, symbolic sexual arousal, interpersonal interactions, self-concept, and test performance. The research on anxiety can be set apart from the other areas because of the number of studies conducted concerning that variable. The results of research on other behaviors must be considered still tentative, as sufficient replications have yet to be attempted. Nevertheless, these studies do hint at the wide-ranging effects a variety of musics may have on a variety of behaviors. The specific relationships remain to be defined.

Musical Factors that Affect Emotional Response

When we consider music as a signal with meaning, its form and structural content should contribute to the emotional meaning of the message. Researchers have recently focused on the idea that emotional response is strongly related to the structural factors of a given musical stimuli and examined how these factors affect listeners' emotion.

Kate Henver (1936) underlined the necessity of investigating structural elements in the function of music as a whole. In her study, she used a parallel version of a piece of music where she changed one element at a time. In this way, she studied the impact of rhythm, harmony, tonality, and the structure of the melodic line. Minor and major tonalities gave the most clear-cut results. Major tonality was connected with adjectives describing a happy mood by the subjects, and minor tonality was described with adjectives that were sad and dreamy. Firm rhythm evoked feelings of dignified and vigorous character and flowing rhythm happy feelings. Simple versus complex harmony gave a more mixed picture, where happy and serene feelings were evoked by simple harmony and complex harmony was experienced as exciting, vigorous, or sad. Ascending and descending melody gave no clear-cut results.

Melvin Rigg (1937) experimentally studied the effect of structural elements in music on 80 psychology students. Joy was considered to arise from accelerated tempo, ascending fourths in the melody, major mode, simple harmony, staccato notes, *forte* dynamics, and iambic or anapaestic rhythm. Lamentation was considered to arise from the following features: descending minor seconds in the melody, minor mode, legato phrasing, dissonance, trochaic rhythms, low register, or slow tempo. Similar constellations for sorrowful and hopeful longing and other feelings were tested. Rigg concluded that the features that were proposed to evoke joy and lamentation were statistically significant while those of longing and love were less certain.

Wedin (1972) used a check list and sorting procedure to obtain judgments in terms of the emotional qualities of the experience of 40 musical excerpts. Three dimensions were extracted: intensity-softness, pleasantness-unpleasantness, and solemnity-triviality. These dimensions were then related to such stimulus qualities as tempo, pitch, modality, and so on. *Forte* and staccato were associated with intensity (through adjectives such as lively, energetic, or agitated), *piano* and legato were related with softness (through adjectives such as soft, peaceful, gentle, or dreamy). Consonant, fluent and fast rhythm, major modality, and high pitch were connected with pleasantness (glad, playful, or light), and dissonant, firm, slow rhythm, minor mode, and low pitch were related to unpleasantness (dramatic, ominous, fateful, or dark). The existence of major modality, high pitch, and staccato in the structure of music was associated with solemnity (majestic, solemn, or dignified), while melody and intensity produced the experience of triviality (relaxed, popular, merry, or commonplace).

Nielzen and Cesarec (1982) conducted a study that was based on the assumption that the emotional experience of music depends on a constellation of structural elements rather than on separate, single elements. Ratings of single elements were factor analyzed in order to isolate coherent groups of experience. Classical and newly composed samples were collected and analyzed according to harmony (dissonant-consonant), modality (major-minor), melody (melodious-amelodious), intensity (*pp-ff*), pitch (bass-treble), rhythm (marked-vague), continuity (legato-staccato), and tempo (fast-slow). Based upon these musical categories, musical stimuli were again analyzed and labeled simple-sophisticated (harmony, melody, modality, and rhythm articulation), vivid-placid (intensity, rhythm, continuity, and tempo), dark-light (modality and pitch). Then they collected emotional responses to these musical stimuli from 25 students with little music background. Three factors of emotional responses were collected. Factor 1, which is called tension-relaxation, is measured by the scales tense-relaxed, violent-peaceful, hard-soft, and threatening-enticing. Scales happy-sad, humorous-serious, impulsive-controlled, and active-passive measure factor 2, called gaiety-gloom. Factor 3, labeled attraction-repulsion, is measured by the scales rich-poor, beautiful-disgusting, profound-superficial, and clear-diffuse. The results showed that the structural factor of simple-sophisticated was negatively correlated with the experiential factor of tension-relaxation. A positive correlation existed between the structural factor of simple-sophisticated and the experiential factor of attraction-repulsion. The structural factor labeled vivid-placid correlated strongly with the experiential factor of gaiety-gloom.

Structural factors of music appear to affect listeners' emotional experience within limits. These researchers stressed that individual characteristics such as cultural background, musical training, life experience, personality, and so on also contribute to these responses.

Preference Responses to Music

In the affective domain as described by Krathwohl and others, preference behavior, as defined here, seems to be about midway in an individual's hierarchy of possible affective involvement with an object. It represents more than simply being willing to be subjected to music (or a type of music), but less than a full commitment to that of music value. The term *preference* in studies of the affective response to music has been used in several ways, representing a variety of intersections along the continuum that Krathwohl describes. It has been employed to represent long-term commitments to styles of music as well as momentary affections for short melodic excerpts. In this section, studies that focus primarily on low to intermediate level valuing responses to music will be examined. Longer term commitments are reported in the section dealing with musical taste.

Other commonalties of the studies to be reviewed here are the measurement techniques employed. Most of the investigators whose work will be reported have chosen to employ some type of musical stimulus from which their respondents are asked to indicate their preference in some manner, while the studies reported in the section on musical taste rely primarily on questionnaire data, seldom providing musical examples for their respondents. The studies reported in this section will be organized into three major areas: (1) the effects of listener attributes on music preference, (2) factors that affect listeners' preferences, and (3) characteristics of music that affect preference.

The Effects of Listener Attributes on Musical Preference

Personality

Of the various characteristics of listeners that may affect their musical preference, one area that seems to have generated research interest is the effect of personality on preference. Some studies have examined musical preferences as predictors of personality characteristics (e.g., Cattell and Anderson 1953). Other researchers have examined the relationship from the other direction, employing personality traits to predict musical preferences (e.g., Butler 1968). The results of the studies to be reviewed suggest that moderate relationships exist between musical preference and certain personality factors (as well as shorter term emotional states.) The specific nature of these relationships has yet to be determined and needs further exploration.

An early effort indicative of the relationships that researchers have hypothesized between personality and musical preference is the *IPAT Music Preference Test of Personality* developed by Cattell and Anderson (1953). The test was designed to measure personality traits by the preferences indicated on a three-option "like" scale made by subjects to 100 brief musical selections. The test was based on the assumption that personality types should prefer a definite type of music, although the authors suggested that other environmental factors (e.g., social status) may affect the results. One reviewer (Steenberg 1959) commented that the test appeared to discriminate between normal and abnormal subjects as well as among various types of abnormalities. The test produces scores on 11 factors and is designed primarily as a clinical instrument, although it can be administered to groups. An initial question raised about the test was concerned with the test's reliability (stability over time). Do the scores represent relatively transient moods or more stable personal characteristics? To examine this question, Shutz and Lang (1963) examined the reliability of the test with normal college-age subjects under different mood conditions (relaxation/anxiety). The authors concluded that the *IPAT Music Preference Test of Personality* does reliably measure the music preference of normal subjects, and the test results seem to reflect the more enduring aspects of personality.

Butler (1968) also focused on personality factors as measured by another Cattell test when examining taste (receptivity) for electronic music. Butler measured liking for electronic music by employing a seven-point scale. Personality characteristics were measured employing the *Cattell 16 Factor Personality Test*. The results produced significant positive relationships between the unconventionality ($r = .20$) and the radicalism ($r = .48$) subscales of the Cattell test and Butler's measure of receptivity. Correlation coefficients between other factors (e.g., music achievement) included in the study and receptivity tended to be in the same range.

Researchers who have examined the relationship of music preference and personality factors have generally examined single personal traits. Brim (1977) examined the relationship of two personality factors, dogmatism and repression-sensitization, to musical preference. He reported that dogmatism was related in a curvilinear fashion ($r = .54$) with decreased individual variation in musical preference, while repression was positively related ($r = .31$) to increased preferences. The author concluded that the degree of open-endedness (dogmatism) did affect the evaluative responses of music listeners.

Koh and Hedlund (1969) examined music preference behavior on paired-comparison music preference tasks with normal subjects and schizophrenic patients. The subjects were played 20 pairs of short piano excerpts that had been previously rated. The results of a first experiment indicated that, while the range of preferences indicated tended to be narrower, the schizophrenics tended to choose the second of the paired excerpts, similar to the results observed with normal subjects. In a second experiment, a pleasant or unpleasant excerpt was interpolated between the paired excerpts. The results of this investigation indicated only a small interpolation effect with the schizophrenic subjects, which contrasted with a large effect on the intervening excerpt observed with normal subjects. The authors concluded that schizophrenics may have problems in the temporal processing of affective stimuli.

Cantor and Zillman (1973) investigated the effects of shorter term emotional states on musical preference. College-age subjects were exposed to one of four film segments designed to affect their hedonic tone (positive-negative) and their excitatory potential (low-high). They then heard three songs and rated them on several semantic differential scales, the first song immediately after viewing the segments, the second approximately two minutes later, and the third approximately five minutes after seeing the film. The results indicated that the evaluation of the first selection tended to be in a direction opposite to that of the film segment used (hedonic contrast effect). While the excitatory potential of the film segment did not effect the rating of the first song, it had a transfer effect that was identifiable on the ratings of the second song. The ratings of song three were not effected by either of the two manipulated variables. It was concluded that prior stimulation can effect music preferences and that such effects may not be limited to responses to music.

Several investigators have studied the effects on musical preferences of personality variables in social pressure or conformity settings. In one such project, Fisher and Fisher (1951) examined the effects of two personality variables, insecurity and internal anxiety, on musical preferences for unfamiliar, dramatic music. The personality variables were measured by two separate techniques: (1) demonstrated disturbance by subjects when asked to describe pictures with themes that were potentially disturbing, and (2) insecurity demonstrated in a projective human-figure drawing test. Results showed that subjects with marked personal insecurity responded to the unfamiliar, dramatic music excerpts either unusually favorably or unfavorably, while other subjects tended to choose more moderate preferences. According to the authors, they demonstrated that personal insecurity has a significant influence upon reaction to dramatic, unfamiliar music and concluded that "the reaction of the individuals to music in situations where he or she does not have the usual social cues for guiding his preference expression" reveals insecurities, anxieties, and fears that may influence their responses to music (Fisher and Fisher 1951, 272).

In a study exploring a similar question, Inglefield (1968) examined the relationship of personality variables and conformity behavior with musical preferences. He selected subjects based on their extreme scores on personality tests of inner- or other-directedness, independence, and the need for social approval. The subjects were divided into two groups, with the experimental group taking a preference inventory a total of three times, twice under different social pressure situations similar to the Asch (1956) conformity experiments, while the control group was administered the scale under more natural circumstances. Results indicated that, regardless of personality type, conformity behavior was observed. Further analysis, though, indicated differences in the scores of the "independent" and "dependent" subjects, suggesting that measures of independence may serve as predictors of musical preference conformity. Dependent subjects tended to conform more than did those identified as independent.

Lewis and Schmidt (1991) considered more diverse personality variables in their study. Personality variables were measured by the *Meyer-Briggs Type Indicator* (MBTI), which yielded four main combinations of variables: extraversion-introversion (EI), sensing-intuition (SN), thinking-feeling (TF), and judgment-perception (JP). The *Music Listener Response Scale* (MLRS) contained statements that focused on responses to music that were classified as associative, cognitive, physical, involvement, or enjoyment by means of a seven-point scale anchored by "all of the time" and "none of the time." Scores on each test were compared and analyzed. Among MBTI variables of EI, SN, TF, and JP, only SN was significantly correlated with the MLRS score, which suggests that intuitive people respond to music more deeply and sensitively. Among 16 subgroups, the ISTP (introversion, sensing, thinking, perceptual) subgroup had the lowest MLRS mean, while ENTJ (extroversion, intuition, thinking, judgment) subjects had the highest mean. The results confirm that listeners responded to music in different ways, and their response patterns bear some systematic relationship to personality variables. However, more research is needed to identify the extent to which these personality variables interact with responses to music.

Gender Effects

The gender of the listener is an easily observed and recorded characteristic, thus many studies of music preferences have included gender as an analytical variable. While few studies have focused exclusively on gender, a considerable amount of data exists that provides information on the gender–music preference relationship. Several studies will be reviewed that specifically designed gender into their data-collection strategy, although the studies reviewed here may only be considered representative of the research in this area.

A majority of the evidence reported suggests that differences in musical preference are not likely to be due to the gender of the listener. Although the results of some studies tentatively contradict this conclusion, the weight of the evidence seems to be heavily on the "no difference due to gender" end of the scale.

An exception to most of the studies is one undertaken by Johnson and Knapp (1963) that focused specifically on the gender of the subjects and its relationship with musical preferences. An analysis of the data produced correlation coefficients between the four groups (e.g., high school females to adult males) ranging between $r = .69$ and $r = .93$, which demonstrated considerable agreement. In addition, no differences were observed between males and females on preferences across the music style categories.

Several other researchers reported similar results. Long (1971), while establishing standards for the *Indiana-Oregon Music Discrimination Test* (described earlier), reported no gender differences—although girls consistently outscored boys, other factors, for example, piano experience, probably contributed to these results. He employed junior and senior high school students in geographically diverse areas of the United States and the British Isles. In a study focusing on the effects of a listening program on preference for contemporary art music, Bradley (1972) examined the data for gender effects. Although training group differences were observed, no differences due to gender were produced. Additional support came from Breger (1970), who found a strong relationship between male and female responses in a study of preferences for 12 different sounds (e.g., running water).

Amen (1977), while examining the effects of training, ensemble experience, and gender on the preference for a familiarity of classical and nonclassical musical selections with seventh grade students in the German Democratic Republic, reported some gender effects. While males in her study were more familiar with classical selections than females, females indicated a stronger preference for those excerpts. Amen reported that this result may have been confounded with ensemble participation (all the choir members in both classes happened to be females) and thus suggested further investigations be conducted before firm conclusions regarding gender differences be made.

Other Factors
In contrast to the information reported on the relationship between gender and musical preferences, the relationship between socioeconomic measures and music preference is more mixed. Problems arise when attempting to integrate and summarize the studies relating to socioeconomic status and music preference. Each of the studies employ different procedures for assessing musical preferences (discussed in the first section of this chapter). In addition, no standardized means of assessing socioeconomic data are employed, thus essentially making it impossible to integrate the results. When results are parallel, the diversity of procedures often lends strength to the conclusions. When results conflict, the studies can only be viewed in isolation.

Long (1971), while standardizing the *Indiana-Oregon Music Discrimination Test*, found a weak (r = .18–.29) but significant relationship between his measure of "musical appropriateness" and socioeconomic status. Parker (1961), using the procedure of partial correlations, examined the relationships between music aptitude, general intelligence, socioeconomic status, and preference, this time measured by the Wing *Test of Appreciation*. His results indicated a negligible relationship between socioeconomic status and musical preference (his study labels this variable aesthetic sensitivity) when the contributions of musical ability and intelligence are held constant.

In two studies, the effects of training and socioeconomic status on musical preferences were examined with different results reported. Williams (1972), while investigating the effects of instruction, musical aptitude, social status, and musical preferences (attitudes towards music), collected data from college-age subjects. Listeners rated excerpts employing semantic differential ratings. Reliability (test-retest) coefficients of the measure ranged from .49 to .86. While his results indicated some effect of instruction for certain styles of music, no socioeconomic effects were observed on music preference ratings.

In an investigation of the effects of a program designed to develop the perception of musical expressiveness on musical preference (aesthetic sensitivity), Standifer (1970) employed one verbal measure of general attitude toward music (*Hevner-Oregon Test of Attitude Toward Music*). On this measure, significant effects of socioeconomic status were observed. Low socioeconomic status subjects showed a greater gain on the Hevner test than did subjects from other socioeconomic categories.

A majority of the studies reported here employ college-age listeners. The investigation of changes in musical preference and age, save for the single study reported in the next paragraph, has generally been neglected. Yet it would seem to be of considerable importance to those interested in the affective response to music, and additional studies in this area are warranted.

The relationship of age and music preference has been investigated by Greer, Dorow, and Randall in a 1974 study. The purpose of the study was to determine the music preferences of children from nursery school and grades one through six. The study assessed preference for rock and nonrock (i.e., symphonic, classical piano, or Broadway show tunes) music and white noise employing the Operant Music Listening Recorder (OMLR). The children were tested for ten minutes with the number of seconds listening to each type of music recorded. The results indicated that while nursery and first-grade listeners equally prefer rock and nonrock selections, second through sixth graders preferred the rock examples. Results also showed an increase in rock listening time with the increase in grade level. The authors concluded that "the time between third and fourth grades appears to be a pivotal time in terms of musical taste" (Greer, Dorow, and Randall 1974, 289).

Again a problem arises when attempting to make generalizations regarding the relationships between music aptitude and music preference. Several researchers have employed different measures of aptitude and had different concepts of the preference response (aesthetic sensitivity, preference, or receptivity). Perhaps it is only possible to conclude that this relationship has yet to be determined.

Williams (1972), in an investigation of the effects of musical aptitude, instruction, and socioeconomic status on preferences for both popular and serious music of college-age students, concluded that music aptitude, measured by the Gordon *Musical Aptitude Profile* subtests of musical sensitivity, tonal imagery, and rhythmic imagery, is not strongly related to music preferences. Preferences in this investigation were measured by semantic differential scales. Parker (1961), while examining the relationship of aesthetic sensitivity (measured by the Wing *Test of Appreciation*) and musical ability (measured by the Gaston *Test of Musicality)* reported a moderate relationship ($r = .42$) between these two variables among high school students when intelligence and socioeconomic status were controlled.

In an investigation of receptivity to electronic music, Butler (1968) reported that, with college-age subjects, significant relationships were obtained between scores on the scale for receptivity to electronic music (SREM) constructed by Butler, and scores on the pitch (positive correlation) and loudness (negative correlation) subtests of the Seashore *Measures of Musical Talents.*

Music achievement is an additional characteristic of the listener whose effect on music preference has been of some interest to a few music researchers. Butler (1968) reported a positive relationship between scores on the harmonic section of the Aliferis *Music Achievement Test* and scores on his test of receptivity to electronic music.

While measuring a different type of preference, Long (1971) operationalized achievement in several ways (e.g., playing an instrument). The relationships between Long's tests of music discrimination and years of piano lessons and of other instrument lessons tend to be moderate ($r = .15-.56$) and positive.

The diverse definitions of music achievement reported in these studies again lead only to the conclusion that more work is needed to identify what relationship may exist between music achievement and music preference.

Factors that Affect Listeners' Preference

Several researchers have attempted to examine the effects of variables that may be used to manipulate the preferences of listeners. Several items fall into this category, including training (both long and short term), familiarity, repetition, expectation, and adult approval. Studies examining long-term training effects on preference are defined for our purposes here as studies that have typically classified respondents as either being musically involved on a long-term basis (e.g., music majors) or having little formal training in music. Most investigators have not examined long-term training directly but have included it as a variable of interest.

Long-Term Training
The results of studies on long-term training and affective response tend to suggest that relationships do exist, particularly with classical (concert) music, but the data on which to base such generalizations are scant. Long (1971), in a study described earlier, examined the ability of respondents to discriminate between original and altered performances. He concluded that this ability is related ($r = .15-.56$) to such training as having taken piano lessons or lessons on other instruments. In addition, moderate relationships were reported between expressed preference for concert music and experience in either a choral or instrumental group.

Duerksen (1968), in a comprehensive study of the effects of repetition and alterations on affective responses, reported significant differences between music majors and other respondents in the preferences indicated on a "like" scale with the music majors expressing more positive affect for all types of music combined than the other respondents. When the different styles of music (e.g., pop or classical) were examined individually, only classical pieces yielded a difference in preference between the groups.

Hargreaves, Messerschumidt, and Rubert (1982) examined the interacting effects of musical content, familiarity of the listener with the piece, and musical training. Pieces were selected to represent classical or popular and familiar or unfamiliar by the unanimous decision of three authors. Subjects were asked to rate the pieces on two, seven-point scales, poor quality (1) to good quality (7) and dislike (1) to like (7), and subjects were asked to describe their musical training as trained or untrained. The results showed that there were significant main effects for musical training: trained subjects gave significantly higher ratings than untrained subjects, and familiar excerpts were given significantly higher ratings than unfamiliar ones. Classical excerpts were always rated higher in quality by all subjects, but no such effect was present for the ratings of liking.

Burke and Gridley's (1990) study was designed to assess the relationship between preference for four piano pieces, the subjective complexity of those pieces, and the relationship between listeners' sophistication and liking for the same pieces. Musically trained and untrained college students rated their preference for piano recordings of J. S. Bach's Prelude and Fugue in C major, Debussy's "The Girl With the Flaxen Hair," Grieg's "Wedding Day of Troldhaugen," and Boulez's Piano Sonata no. 1, second movement. Each piece had been ranked according to perceived complexity by seven music professors. When personal preference was plotted against complexity, an inverted U-curve was obtained. Average liking was significantly higher among musically sophisticated subjects. The difference was very large in the case of the Debussy and Boulez examples. This suggests that musical sophistication might increase preference, particularly for modern pieces in which complexity is great.

Geringer (1982) conducted a study to determine the agreement among three groups of subjects regarding verbal preferences and operant preferences (time spent listening) for music and the relationship between verbal and behavioral measures. Subjects were randomly selected fifth- and sixth-grade elementary students ($n = 40$), college education majors ($n = 40$), and music majors enrolled in an undergraduate or graduate music major course ($n = 40$). Data were consistent with musical training: college music students showed marked preferences for composers in the formal tradition, while nonmusic college students and

the elementary students predominantly chose current popular composers. The verbal and operant measures of composer preference were highly
correlated among music majors. The verbal preferences of the nonmusic
students were not consistent, nor were those of elementary subjects.

Short-Term Training

While there exists a limited number of studies on long-term training
effects, several authors have been interested in the effects of different
types of short-term training on preference responses. The effects of
shorter term training on preference are not clear from the research completed thus far. While certain types of training seem effective with some
subjects (low socioeconomic status, see Standifer 1970), other training
has been shown to be no better than merely repeating passages. These
results, if substantiated by further research, may have major implications for music education program objectives.

Some investigators have focused on teaching extramusical information, while others have focused on increasing students' musical discrimination skills. By means of semantic differential scales, Williams
(1972) studied the effects of musical aptitude, social status, and instruction on attitudes toward music. Two college music appreciation class
instructors employed in the investigation had no constraints on what to
teach during the two-month period that separated the pretest and
posttest. Differences due to instruction were observed with two types of
music, current popular and serious vocal. While an increased positive
affective change was observed for serious vocal selections, a decline was
noted for current popular selections.

Larson (1971) attempted to examine the different effects of musical
and extramusical information upon music preference for a classical work.
The results, as measured on a five-option preference scale, showed that,
while those who received instruction on musical aspects showed an increase in preference, those who received extramusical information and
others stayed about the same.

Some authors have attempted to distinguish the effects of variables
such as familiarity, repetition, and training. In an attempt to distinguish
between long-term environmental effects (familiarity) and training effects, Edmunston (1969) investigated preferences for Indian music. Subjects were divided into three groups: one group received training in
Western music, one in Indian music, while the third received no training. Edmunston observed that the group trained in Indian music evaluated the excerpt of Indian music differently than the other two groups.

Amen (1977), while examining the same two variables (training and
familiarity) with both classical and popular selections and employing

seventh-grade West German students, observed that training effected respondents' familiarity ratings but not their preference responses. In fact, there was some indication that a negative relationship existed between the two variables.

Bradley (1971) was interested in the effects of special analytical training versus mere repetition on the musical preferences of seventh graders for serious contemporary music (including tonal, polytonal, atonal, and electronic music). Preference posttests were administered to measure choices in preference both for the pieces studied analytically (or just repeated) as well as other contemporary works not included in the training. The results indicated that the group that received the analytical training demonstrated significant preference gains on both study and transfer pieces, the repetition group showed gains only on the pieces they heard, while the control group, which did not receive any exposure other than the pretest, showed little change in preference.

Clarke (1970) employed two behavioral measures of affective responses to a symphony concert, information seeking and social interaction, when assessing the effects of preconcert instruction. Although the study was limited by the different methods of instruction employed by different teachers, the results indicated no relationship between these preconcert experiences and the behavioral measures of affective response.

Colwell, Greer, and Standifer have all examined the effects of training in music perception on music preferences. Colwell (1965) attempted a long-term development of musical skill and knowledge with fifth graders. His objectives were to enable students to participate in the musical experience as described by Meyer. Colwell reported that one year was too short a period to develop these skills and knowledge, even with an above-average learning situation, although he identified a population from 10 percent to 20 percent of the students who were both intellectually and musically ready to have "real listening experiences" (Colwell 1965, 250).

In a project over a similar time span, Standifer (1970) examined the effects of the perception of musical expressiveness on aesthetic sensitivity with junior and senior high school students. The objectives of the instruction centered around perceiving musical elements. Standifer employed the Hevner *Oregon Test of Attitude Toward Music* as one of several measures. The results indicated that the changes in attitudes toward music of the students who received instruction, when compared with those in the control groups, did not differ, but that, when examined for socioeconomic class differences, lower socioeconomic students were affected by the instruction in a positive manner.

Greer and associates employed operant psychology techniques in efforts to manipulate children's preferences. In the first investigation reported, Greer, Dorow, and Hanser (1973) examined the effect of music discrimination training on the music selection behavior of young children. Students in the training group were taught, employing successive approximation techniques, to match pictures of instruments with musical excerpts featuring that instrument. Experimenters employed positive verbal reinforcement to encourage the acquisition of the matching behavior. The results indicated no differences between the training groups and a nonmusic activity group, although the authors suggest some possible confounding effects, such as the number of positive verbal reinforcements received by each subject. A second experiment was designed to control for such effects. Procedures similar to the first study were used, but careful accounting of the dispensing of reinforcement was made. The results of this study showed that both groups had more preference for symphonic music than they initially had, and that the positive verbal reinforcement (adult approval) associated with a type of music with or without discrimination training was an effective procedure for changing music preference.

In a similar investigation, Greer, Dorow, Wachhaus, and White (1973) examined both the effects of approval rate and the presentation of music lessons or repetition of excerpts on the music selection behavior of fifth-grade students. The authors concluded that while no differences were apparent between clinician-artist lessons and mere repeat listening, students receiving music lessons with considerable adult positive reinforcement selected more of the music taught than students taught under low reinforcement conditions.

Repetition

Several authors have chosen to focus on the effects of repetition on musical preferences. While the strategies that different investigators have adopted are varied, the results produced have been surprisingly consistent. The effects of repetition of music compositions on affective reaction to those compositions is one of the more well documented areas reported. Additional data are needed, though, to determine how the specific characteristics of a composition (style or complexity) may interact with repetition to produce affective shifts.

Getz (1966) investigated changes in seventh-grade children's preferences for unfamiliar serious musical selections. Five selections, chosen to represent a range of preference previously determined, were repeated ten times during a ten-week period. Other compositions were also listened to as decoys. The results obtained suggested that familiarity through repetition has a distinct effect on preferences, and that maximum effect on preference seemed to occur between the sixth and eighth repetition.

A study that supports these findings was reported by Heingartner and Hall (1974). They examined the effect of repetition on musical preference for excerpts of Pakistani folk music. The excerpts were played eight times, and data from college-age students and fourth graders indicated that a strong positive relationship existed between exposure frequency and liking.

Bradley (1971 and 1972) tested the effect of repetition on structural discrimination as well as affective response to classical and previously determined best-liked popular selections. The study employed three groups of college-age subjects. One group heard each selection 17 times and rated it 9 times over a three-week period. A second group heard and rated the repeated pieces, but also responded with verbal descriptions regarding structural elements of the selections. A third group served as a control. The results of the study showed that both groups who heard repetitions of the pieces increased their liking of classical pieces while decreasing their preference for best-liked selections. Additional data indicated a somewhat unclear relationship between structural awareness, as measured by the listeners' verbal reports, and preference.

Heyduk (1975) was concerned with the effects of certain characteristics of a composition, specifically complexity, and repetition on rated preference. Four piano compositions were constructed, each representing different degrees of complexity determined by their chordal and rhythmic characteristics and subjects' complexity ratings. After each composition was rated on a "like" scale, one of the four compositions was presented and rated an additional 16 times. It was found that the affective consequences of repetition were dependent upon the subjects' preferred complexity level. Heyduk suggested "that repeated exposure effects are a function of both situational and individual factors" (1975, 84).

Hargreaves (1982) conducted two experiments that examined the effects of repetition on liking for music of different styles chosen to represent contrasting levels of objective complexity. In the first experiment, two pieces of music (easy listening and avant-garde jazz) were presented three times (with approximately one hour between hearings) during a single session. In the second experiment, three pieces (pop, classic, and avant-garde jazz) were presented four times in sessions over three weeks. Results confirmed an inverted U theory except for avant-garde jazz (liking level did not rise over repetitions), and there was no recovery effect of "week by piece." However, a significant finding was that, although repetition can change level of liking within different musical styles, the rank order of preference among styles apparently cannot be changed.

Characteristics of Music that Affect Preference

Heyduk's study introduces another aspect of the listening environment that may affect preference responses—specific characteristics of the music. A few researchers have focused on preferences for nonmusical and musical stimuli, different music scales, and noncontextual musical stimuli. Breger (1970) reported a study in which the affective responses of 60 male and 75 female subjects to meaningful sound stimuli were examined. The subjects rated 12 sounds on a pleasantness scale. The stimuli included recordings of weeping, humming, and music. Differences were observed in the ratings between the stimuli, with the male and female ratings being quite similar ($r = .84$).

In a study examining preference for single tone stimuli, Hedden (1974) manipulated frequency, intensity, and waveform. Both music major and nonmusic major college-age subjects served as raters. Hedden reported that different effects were observed for the two samples. The results with music majors indicated preferences were affected by waveform, loudness, and the different combinations of waveform and loudness, but not by frequency. The nonmusic majors showed the same effects plus an effect due to the unique combinations of loudness and frequencies. Hedden concluded by suggesting that music majors and nonmusic majors may not have similar preferences for isolated tone stimuli.

Madsen and Geringer (1976) focused on preferences for trumpet tone quality and intonation. Music majors were instructed to indicate preferences for eight sets of three trumpet performances that varied in tone quality and intonation. The results indicated that intonation was the critical preference factor, with subjects actually responding to intonation variables when indicating a preference for tone quality. Interestingly, the respondents preferred performances that were either sharp or in tune over performances that were flat.

There has been some interest in preferences for different tunings. O'Keefe (1975) examined the preferences of junior and senior high school students for pairs of melodies tuned in just intonation or the equal-tempered system. The results indicated a slight preference (56 percent) for melodies tuned in just intonation. While boys favored just intonation more than girls, no differences in preference were observed between musicians and nonmusicians.

Branning (1967) chose to investigate both melodic and harmonic intervals tuned in just or Pythagorean ratios. Branning's examples were recorded employing either simple or complex tones. Results indicated that just intonation seems to be preferred for less complex intervals (e.g., major third) and that Pythagorean tuning was generally preferred for melodic and just intonation for harmonic intervals, at least with complex tones. The data were not examined statistically, however, thus restricting its generalizability.

Leblanc (1987) examined the effect of tempo (slow, moderately slow, moderately fast, and fast) on the preference of six different age groups for jazz. Subjects were 926 students from grade three to college level. Twenty-four instrumental jazz examples representing each tempo were presented, students' behavior was observed during the test session, and free-response feedback was accumulated from students after the test. The results showed a strong and statistically significant preference for fast tempo regardless of age group. However, the listener's age had a strong effect on overall preference scores, which were highest with the youngest listeners (third grade), declined steadily to a low point at seventh grade, then rose again as age increased to college level.

Musical Taste

We suggested earlier in this chapter that musical taste and musical preference would be distinguished on two continua: the durational aspects of the behavior and the amount of commitment to the musical selection evidenced. Here, taste is considered a relatively stable, long-term valuing, while preference is characterized by a shorter term commitment. It should be pointed out that, because this relationship is viewed as a continuum and not a dichotomy, some studies may fall in areas on the continuum that make it difficult to place them.

Taste and preference will also be distinguished according to the Krawthowal taxonomy of the affective domain. Preference behaviors are thought to fall in the middle of the taxonomy (e.g., valuing), while taste behavior is thought to be classified best at either the organization or characterization levels.

The terms *preference* and *taste,* unfortunately, seem to have been used by several authors as synonyms. The distinguishing mode we have adopted, although at times seemingly artificial, does help in organizing the research in these areas. Operationalized, preferences as dependent variables are measured most often by the selection or rating of an excerpt or piece heard immediately before the response. In contrast, taste is most often operationalized by questionnaire surveys or by observing evidence of such long-term behaviors as record collecting. Interacting variables on which researchers of musical taste have focused also tend to be more stable or longer term (e.g., socioeconomic class or political orientation) than the variables focused upon by researchers of musical preference.

Although musical taste is described as a more long term and stable behavior than preference, there is no intent to suggest that individual as well as societal tastes are invariant over time. Roeckle (1968), while summarizing writings on musical taste, noted that several authors (e.g., Mueller and Hevner 1942) have provided evidence that musical tastes are never static and that what was once popular is soon replaced. Mueller and Hevner also suggested that the time a style of music takes to become popular may be positively related to the speed of its decline. Thus, the picture of changing musical taste is one of a wind-blown, undulating branch, continually moving in a consistent direction but changing with environmental conditions within clearly defined limits.

As in previous sections, this section contains a subdivision entitled Characteristics of the Listener. As noted previously, all of the factors discussed here tend to be long-term considerations. Although some of the characteristics, such as gender, age, or aptitude of the listener, were also included in the section on music preference, these studies are distinguished by the manner in which the valuing of music behavior is measured. A second division dealing with factors that affect listeners' long-term musical values concludes this section.

Long-Term Characteristics of Listeners

General Aptitude
One study has been conducted that examined musical tastes and general aptitude. Few generalizations can be based on one study, yet the results of this study appear to support a relationship between mental ability and musical taste that would likely be hypothesized by many music researchers. Mental ability may have some secondary effects on musical taste, but only as it interacts with other, more predictive variables, some of which will be examined later. Erneston (1961) examined the relationship of mental ability and past musical experiences on the formulation of musical taste among students at a college in North Carolina. He developed a musical taste score that was a composite comprised of a measure of attitude toward music, musical preference, and musical discrimination. The students first completed a musical experience questionnaire and then were administered a mental ability test. An analysis of the relationships between mental ability, past musical experience, and musical taste showed that mental ability alone did not account for significant differences in musical taste, but, when considered along with past music experience, the results yielded a significant interaction

between these two predictors of taste. Specifically, those with a variety of musical experience and high mental ability scored significantly differently on the measures of musical taste than did other students in the study.

Wells and Hakanen (1991) undertook an interesting survey of adolescent musical taste. From their study of the relationship between musical taste and the social, academic, and racial factors of the respondents, it was found that students with A grades liked heavy metal least and D and F students like it the most. They also reported that classic and jazz were liked more by A students.

Gender

Few studies have focused on gender as the primary variable in investigations of musical taste although some do include the variable in their analysis (see Appleton 1970; Baumann 1960; Birch 1962; Skipper 1975). Most of these studies show significant differences in the musical tastes of male and female subjects for a variety of types of music (e.g., jazz or classical). All of the studies sample students in the age range from high school to college. The literature generally suggests that women in this age bracket prefer classical music more than men, while men prefer jazz or rock more than women do. Birch suggested the women in his sample had broader musical tastes than the men. Gender has also been shown to interact with such variables as nationality (Skipper 1975) and race (Appleton 1970).

Christenson and Peterson (1988) examined the relationship between taste for popular music and gender, and the extent of gender-specific effects. Among 239 undergraduate students, several gender differences emerged in the appeal of the music forms. The ones liked more by female than by male students include mainstream pop, contemporary rhythm and blues, soul, black gospel, and disco. In contrast, the types liked more by males than female were 1970s rock, southern rock, psychedelic rock, and blues.

The results of these studies strongly suggest that gender may be used as a predictor of taste with students in high school and college. This relationship may likely be due to the socialization process of students of this age. As the socialization process for males and females becomes more similar in the future, gender may lose its predictive power as other factors likely gain predictive power.

Age

Age is another variable that has not received much recent attention by researchers of musical taste. As evidenced by the research reported in other sections of this chapter, most of the investigations have been conducted with subjects between the ages of 15 and 25. Earlier studies by Schuessler (1948) and Farnsworth (1969) have included samples comprised of subjects of different ages. While Farnsworth reported considerable agreement among fifth graders through adults on musical tastes for classical composers (using eminence ranks), Schuessler found age effects in musical taste responses for a variety of musics. The results do not really conflict considering the different musics being evaluated in each study. Meadows (1970) also found school level (junior high, senior high, or college) to be a significant determinant of musical preference for musical styles similar to those employed by Schuessler. More systematic research needs to be undertaken both for the relationships between age, type of music, and musical taste to be fully understood and to demonstrate how age may interact with other variables to establish an individual's or group's musical taste.

Personality
The interaction of personality and musical taste has been of interest to few recent investigators. The results of an exploratory study suggested that some aspects of personality may serve as viable predictors of musical taste. The evidence collected thus far does not allow a firm generalization to be made, but it does provide directions that can guide future research in this area. Payne (1967) conjectured that people with different temperaments will prefer different types of music. Specifically, she hypothesized that people with stable (as opposed to neurotic) temperaments will more likely prefer classical (i.e., music focusing on form) music than romantic (i.e., music focusing on feeling) music. To examine her hypothesis, Payne administered a personality inventory and a questionnaire that examined the subjects' preferences for composer to both adults and college-age subjects. The list of composers produced by the questionnaire was then categorized on a five-option scale by the classical (form) or romantic (feeling) characteristics of the composers' music. The results were then correlated with the stability/neurotic scores from the personality inventory producing a coefficient of .36. Payne suggested that the results lend some support to her hypothesis as, although the relationship reported is not strong, it was in the direction predicted. Payne commented that such other factors as age, familiarity, and music performance experience may have tended to modify the impact of personality on taste.

Wheeler was also interested in a similar question. In Wheeler's experiment (1985), the relationship between personality and musical taste was examined. The personality research form (PRF) was used for measuring personality and musical taste was surveyed by questionnaire. The scales of the PRF were significantly correlated with the taste for rock, disco, and country, but not with four other types of music (classic, folk, jazz, and soul). It appears that liking rock music is correlated with not being humble, interested in achievement, autonomous, precise, dominant, and fearful. In contrast to this, liking disco is correlated with being aggressive, defensive, orderly, playful, and seeking social recognition.

Race

The influence of race on preferences for folk and popular musical styles has been explored. The two studies reported suggest that race may be used as a factor for predicting musical taste, although the interaction of race with cultural and socioeconomic factors in predicting both tastes for popular and specific classical styles needs to be investigated before conclusions can be drawn. Appleton (1970) surveyed samples of students from two colleges in North Carolina, one predominantly black and the other predominantly white. The instruments employed to collect the data surveyed the students' preferences for popular musical styles (e.g., soul, gospel, or rock) as well as their record-buying preferences. The results of Appleton's survey suggested that there are some overlaps as well as differences in popular music taste by race. Black students tended to prefer soul, jazz, and gospel, while the results for the sample of white students indicated that they prefer rock and soul. Appleton also reported considerable homogeneity of responses within race groups and small effects of gender and geographic home.

Meadows, in a 1970 dissertation, included race as a variable while examining the musical preferences for popular and classical music styles of junior high, senior high, and college students from across the United States. His results indicated race, as well as other factors reported elsewhere, was a significant determinant of musical preferences.

Dixon (1982) conducted a survey of musical taste for 16 different genres of music (one of which was classical music) among 396 undergraduate students using a Likert scale. To find evidence of existing differences in musical tastes between black and white subjects, he controlled for education and age factors of the subjects. The results showed that there were profound taste-rank differences between the white and black students. The result may be of some importance owing to the possibility that differential exposure to musical forms may dispose individuals to evaluate musical genres more upon the basis of familiarity than upon the more intrinsic quality of the forms themselves.

Social Factors

Several researchers have focused primarily on, or included in their analysis, socioeconomic, sociopolitical, and other class stratification measures when examining determinants of musical taste (see Baumann 1960; Mashkiv and Volgy 1975; Meadows 1970; Schuessler 1948; Skipper 1975). Although they have employed various means of stratification and a variety of means of measuring musical taste, their results have been consistent—socioclass factors do affect musical taste.

Schuessler (1948) concluded that socioeconomic background likely interacts with such other variables as the probability of receiving musical training or being exposed to certain types of music to produce the observed differences in musical tastes by class. Meadows's (1970) study supported the effect of socioeconomic status on the musical tastes of junior high, senior high, and college-age students.

Baumann (1960) also investigated socioeconomic status as a determinate of teenage music preferences during the middle 1950s. His results suggested that teenagers from high socioeconomic groups (based on the Gough *Home Index Measure*) prefer classical music more than teenagers from lower socioeconomic groups.

In a 1975 study, Skipper examined the musical tastes of U.S. and Canadian college students. Musical tastes and social class membership were assessed by a questionnaire administered to students at one university in the mideastern section of each country. Skipper reported in relation to the effects of socioeconomic class on musical taste. He found that definite class differences were apparent in the data on U.S. students, with classical and folk music being the predominant choices of students with upper class backgrounds and hard rock and rhythm and blues the predominant choices of lower socioeconomic students. In addition, Skipper reported that, with Canadian students, little class effect was observed.

Political Orientation

Mashkiv and Volgy's (1975) work on the relationship of sociopolitical attitudes and musical preferences served to bring into clearer focus the two often intertwined factors of socioeconomic class and political orientation as determinants of musical taste. Specifically, the researchers focused on political alienation, social alienation, and female sex stereotyping as factors affecting preferences for rock music, folk music, and country and western music. More than 250 college-age students were stratified by their preference for the three categories of music examined. Significant differences in the groups were observed on political orientation, sex-stereotyping behaviors, and postbourgeois ideology. The authors concluded that these sociopolitical differences observed among students with different musical tastes were not due solely to the music's lyrics and not simply a symbolic attachment to some types of music, but suggested that an attachment for a particular type of music may likely affect social and political orientations.

In another study, Fox and Williams (1974) focused exclusively on the relationship between political orientation and musical taste. Music involvement was measured by questions on rock concert attendance and record purchases, while music preferences for different musical styles were measured in a rating-scale format. Their results generally indicated that a weak association ($r = .20–.28$) exists between political orientation and musical involvement and preferences for particular musical styles. Liberal students tended to be more involved with music than conservative students. Conservatives showed a greater preference for current popular hits, while liberals tended to like folk music. The authors also examined other demographic data—including sex, class year, site of hometown, father's education and family—and, although some interactions were observed, no major interaction effects were uncovered.

Christenson and Peterson (1988) conducted a study that examined the relationship between political and musical orientation. The subjects were 259 undergraduate students enrolled in an introductory public speaking course. Respondents provided a variety of background information on a questionnaire, including sex, age, parents' education level, size of hometown, and others. Political orientation was assessed through an item that asked students to place themselves in one of these categories: radical left, liberal, moderate, conservative, radical right, or don't know/don't care. Music preferences were measured through a series of 26 items, each referring to a different genre of music. The result showed that political orientation is related to music attitudes. First, there was a clear tendency for those students on the liberal side of the scale to indicate more affinity for music with black origins: liberalism was positively associated with a taste for soul, 1960s Motown, black gospel, reggae, and jazz, all performed primarily by black artists. There was an association between conservatism and preferences for recent and current generic rock music. Taste for both 1970s and 1980s rock were significantly associated with more conservative political orientations. Another interesting finding was the positive relationship between heavy metal and political alienation. These results strongly suggest that there is a relationship between taste for popular music and political orientation.

It appears from the studies reviewed that social class and political views do interact with the musical taste, at least for college-age and, to some extent, younger students. The cause-and-effect relationships of these variables and musical taste have only been preliminarily explored in the Mashkiv and Volgy study (1975). Future investigations should attempt to define more clearly the relationship, particularly exploring the association of these variables with samples of older subjects.

Factors Affecting Listeners' Musical Taste

In addition to the characteristics of listeners already reviewed, there are environmental factors that may have an effect on musical taste. These include experiences such as formal training, peer influences, the effects of mass media, and other factors. Of these factors, training has received the most attention by recent researchers.

Training

Several authors (Birch 1962; Erneston 1961; Geringer and McManus 1979; Meadows 1970) have examined the effects of formal musical experiences on musical taste and concluded that a relationship exists between these variables. Erneston (1961) examined the relationship between a composite measure of musical taste and musical experience (e.g., participation in musical organizations or private lessons) as assessed through a questionnaire. The results indicated significantly different musical tastes between those who had some type of participatory experience in music and those who did not. The type of music experience did not seem to effect taste, but the length of time spent in musical participation did, with those having spent long periods in musical activities having significantly different music tastes than others. Erneston also examined mental ability as a factor effecting taste and found an interaction of mental ability with variety and amount of musical experience. Those students with the highest mental ability who had participated in a variety of music activities for a long period consistently differed from other students in terms of musical tastes.

Birch (1962) examined a similar problem employing college students at a small midwestern college. Both musical experience and musical taste were measured through checklists completed in a personal interview. The primary measure of taste in this study was the amount and type of phonograph records owned. Birch's results indicated that more students with at least three years of high school musical experience owned records of serious music than other students, with few differences being observed as a result of the type of musical experience (e. g., vocal, instrumental, or private lesson). Meadows (1970) also observed effects due to musical experience on the musical tastes of junior high school through college students.

Geringer and McManus's (1979) survey attempted to investigate musical taste among musically trained secondary school students and trained and untrained college students with frequency of mention, ranking, concert attendance, and number of recordings owned of subjects' ten favorite composers from any musical style and period. The subjects were 116 junior and senior high school students enrolled in music performance class, 115 college education majors, and 167 undergraduate and graduate college music majors. Results showed that college music students indicated marked preference for composers in the formal tradition (96 percent), while the young and nonmusic students preferred current popular composers (79 percent). Music majors' record collections and concert attendance showed a high degree of concurrence with ranking and frequency of mention. But nonmusic major college students' and secondary school music students' record collections, concerts, ranking, and frequency data did not show a significant association. This may indicate that increased training in music leads to increased preference for composers in the formal tradition as well as stability of preference.

Although the results of these studies appear to confirm a positive relationship between musical experience and musical taste, each study tended to focus on a limited population, each defined musical experience in different ways, and musical tastes were not measured in similar ways. In an early, less-controlled study by Rubin (1951), very weak relationships between these variables were reported. Additional research in this area that focuses, in depth, on specific types of musical experiences and their relationship to the formation of musical taste is warranted.

Mass Media and Peer Group Influence
Fathi and Heath (1974) and Skipper (1975) suggested that factors other than personal characteristics or musical experience may affect taste. While the Fathi and Heath article suggested that mass media may effect the musical taste of some listeners, the Skipper article, approaching the question from a different direction, came to a different conclusion. The sparse amount of recent work in this area suggests a fertile field for systematic investigation.

Fathi and Heath (1974) explored the effects of both group influence and mass media on the musical tastes of Canadian university students. Students were interviewed to gather data on their music listening habits as well as sociodemographic information. On the basis of the interviews, listeners were divided into three groups: (1) high culture listeners (those who listened primarily to the music of composers found in college music appreciation texts), (2) mass culture listeners (those who listened primarily to music not found in music appreciation texts), and (3) mixed listeners. The authors found that, with regard to the effect of group influence, relatives appear to be most influential for high culture listeners, with attending live performances and playing instruments also of some importance. In contrast, mass culture listeners were most influenced by radio and friends. The data for mixed listeners tended to be inconsistent. A social characteristic also associated with high culture listeners was "European orientation," that is, being either a first- or second-generation Canadian or studying an academic discipline with a large amount of European influence (e.g., philosophy). The effect of religious preference on musical taste was unclear.

In a study by Skipper (1975), additional factors that may effect musical tastes are explored. Skipper focused on massification (e.g., the effects of mass media) and the influence of the United States on the musical tastes of Canadian university students. He posed several hypotheses dealing with the diversity of musical tastes of both Canadian and U.S. college students. Students at one university in the mideastern United States and/or a university in mideastern Canada were administered a questionnaire that contained items related to their orientation toward music, musical preferences, and sociodemographic characteristics. The results of the study do not support a massification theoretical position. Both Canadian and U.S. students demonstrated a diversification of musical tastes, suggesting that mass media are not producing a standardized mass taste. To some extent, the Americanization of the Canadian students' musical tastes was not supported, as the Canadian sample tended to prefer Canadian music and musicians (composers, performers, and producers).

An examination of the empirical literature on the mood/emotional, preference, and taste responses to music yields only a few variables whose relationship with these affective/aesthetic responses to music has been established. The more frequent conclusion must be that there is insufficient evidence to clearly identify interactions. Although music preferences appear to have generated more research interest than have the other responses reviewed, few of the interacting variables examined have been sufficiently explored to be certain of their effects on preference judgments.

REFERENCES

Abeles, H. F. 1974. Value judgments and construction of rating instruments to measure affective behavior. Paper presented at the National Council on Measurement in Education, April, Chicago.

Allen, W. R., and W. F. White. 1966. Psychodramatic effects of music as a psychotherapeutic agent. *Journal of Music Therapy* 3:69–71.

Amen, B. 1977. The effects of instruction in musical form on the musical attitudes of West German general music students. Paper presented at Music Educators National Conference, North Central/Southwestern Division, March, Kansas City.

Appleton, C. R. 1970. The comparative preferential response of black and white college students to black and white folk and popular musical styles. Ph.D. diss., New York University.

Asch, S. E. 1956. Studies of independence and conformity: I. A minority of one against a unanimous majority. *Psychological Monographs* 70:1–70.

Baumann, V. H. 1960. Teen-age music preferences. *Journal of Research in Music Education* 8:75–84.

Berlyne, D. E., ed. 1974. *Studies in the new experimental aesthetics: Steps toward an objective psychology of aesthetic appreciation.* New York: Halsted Press.

Biller, J. D., P. J. Olson, and T. Breen. 1974. The effect of "happy" versus "sad" music and participation on anxiety. *Journal of Music Therapy* 11:68–72.

Birch, T. E. 1962. Musical taste as indicated by records owned by college students with varying high school music experiences. Ed.D. diss., University of Missouri.

Bradley, I. L. 1971. Repetition as a factor in the development of musical preferences. *Journal of Research in Music Education* 19:295–98.

Bradley, I. L. 1972. Effect on student musical preference of a listening program in contemporary art music. *Journal of Research in Music Education* 20:344–53.

Branning, H. P. 1967. Audition preferences of trained and untrained ears on hearing melodic and harmonic intervals when tuned in just intonation or Pythagorean ratios. Ph.D. diss., University of Texas.

Breger, I. 1970. Affective response to meaningful sound stimuli. *Perceptual and Motor Skills* 30:842.

Brennis, N. C. 1970. Mood differential responses to music as reported by secondary music and non-music students from different socioeconomic groups. Ph.D. diss., University of Miami.

Brim, R. M. 1977. The effect of personality variables, dogmatism, and repression-sensitization upon response to music. Ph.D. diss., Rosemead Graduate School of Psychology.

Burke, M. J. and M. C. Gridley. 1990. Musical preferences as a function of stimulus complexity and listeners' sophistication. *Perceptual and Motor Skills* 71, no. 2: 687–90.

Butler, J. H. 1968. Personality factors as correlates of receptivity to electronic music. Ph.D. diss., University of Georgia.

Cantor, J. R., and D. Zillman. 1973. The effect of affective state and emotional arousal on music appreciation. *Journal of General Psychology* 89:97–108.

Cattell, R. B., and J. C. Anderson. 1953. The measurement of personality and behavior disorders by the IPAT Music Preference Test. *Journal of Applied Psychology* 37:446–54.

Christenson, P. G., and J. B. Peterson. 1988. Genre and gender in the structure of music preferences. *Communication Research* 15, no. 3:282–301.

Clarke, P. 1970. Children's information seeking about the symphony. *Council for Research in Music Education Bulletin* 19:1–15.

Colwell, R. 1965. *The theory of expectancy applied to musical listening.* Washington, DC: U.S. Department of Health, Education and Welfare, Office of Education, Bureau of Research.

Cotter, V. W., and S. Toombs. 1966. A procedure for determining the musical preferences of mental retardates. *Journal of Music Therapy* 2:57–64.

Crickmore, L. 1968a. An approach to the measurement of music appreciation. *Journal of Research in Music Education* 16:239–53.

Crickmore, L. 1968b. An approach to the measurement of music appreciation. *Journal of Research in Music Education* 16:291–301.

Crozier, J. B. 1973. Verbal and exploratory responses to sound sequences of varying complexity. Ph.D. diss., University of Toronto.

Dainow, E. 1977. Physical effects and motor responses to music. *Journal of Research in Music Education* 25:211–21.

Diserens, C. M. 1923. *The influence of music on behavior.* Princeton: Princeton University Press.

Dixon, R. 1982. Musical taste cultures and taste publics revisited: A research note of new evidence. *Popular Music and Society* 8:2–9.

Duerksen, G. 1968. A study of the relationship between the perception of musical processes and the enjoyment of music. *Council for Research in Music Education* 16:1–8.

Eagle, C. T., Jr. 1971. Effects of existing mood and order of presentation of vocal and instrumental music on rated mood responses to that music. Ph.D. diss., University of Kansas.

Edmunston, W. E., Jr. 1969. Familiarity and musical training in the aesthetic evaluation of music. *Journal of Social Psychology* 79:109–11.

Edwards, J. S., and M. C. Edwards. 1971. A scale to measure attitudes toward music. *Journal of Research in Music Education* 19:222–23.

Elam, R. W. 1971. Mechanism of music as an emotional intensification stimulus. Ph.D. diss., University of Cincinnati.

Erneston, N. 1961. A study to determine the effect of musical experience and mental ability on the formulation of musical taste. Ph.D. diss., Florida State University.

Farnsworth, P. R. 1954. A study of the Hevner Adjective List. *Journal of Aesthetics* 13:592–93.

Farnsworth, P. R. 1969. *The social psychology of music.* 2d ed. Ames, IA: Iowa State University Press.

Fathi, A., and C. L. Heath. 1974. Group influence, mass media and musical taste among Canadian students. *Journalism Quarterly* (Winter): 705–9.

Fishbein, M. 1967. Attitude and the prediction of behavior. In *Readings in attitude theory and measurement,* ed. M. Fishbein, 474–91. New York: Wiley.

Fisher, S., and R. L. Fisher. 1951. The effects of personal insecurity on reactions to unfamiliar music. *Journal of Social Psychology* 34:265–73.

Fisher, S., and R. P. Greenberg. 1972. Selective effects upon women of exciting and calm music. *Perceptual and Motor Skills* 34:987–90.

Forsythe, J. L. 1974. Learning music as a language. ESEA Title III Report. Columbus, GA: Muscogee County School District.

Fox, W. S., and J. D. Williams. 1974. Political orientation and music preferences among college students. *Public Opinion Quarterly* 38:352–71.

Geringer, J. M. 1982. Verbal and operant music listening preferences in relationship to age and musical training. *Psychology of Music, Special Issue: Proceedings of the Ninth International Seminar on Research in Music Education*, 47–50.

Geringer, J., and D. McManus. 1979. A survey of musical taste in relationship to age and musical training. *College Music Symposium* 19:69–76.

Getz, R. P. 1966. The influence of familiarity through repetition in determining optimum response of seventh grade children to certain types of serious music. *Journal of Research in Music Education* 14:178–92.

Greenberg, R. P., and S. Fisher. 1966. Some differential effects of music on projective and structured psychological tests. *Psychological Reports* 28:817–20.

Greer, R. D., and L. G. Dorow. 1973. Operant music preference as a dependent measure for music therapists and music educators. Typescript.

Greer, R. D., L. G. Dorow, and S. Hanser. 1973. Music discrimination training and the music selection behavior of nursery and primary level children. *Bulletin of the Council for Research in Music Education*, 35:30–43.

Greer, R. D., L. G. Dorow, and L. N. Harrison. 1975. Aural discrimination instruction and the preference of sixth-graders for music listening, story listening, and candy. In *Research in music behavior: Modifying music behavior in the classroom*, ed. C. K. Madsen, R. Greer, and C. H. Madsen, 97–108. New York: Teachers College Press.

Greer, R. D., L. G. Dorow, and A. Randall. 1974. Music listening preferences of elementary school children. *Journal of Research in Music Education* 22:284–91.

Greer, R., L. G. Dorow, G. Wachhaus, and E. R. White. 1973. Adult approval and student's music selection behavior. *Journal of Research in Music Education* 21:345–54.

Hanslick, E. 1891. *The beautiful in music*. London: Novello.

Hargreaves, D. 1982. Preference and prejudice in music: A psychological approach. *Popular Music and Society* 8:13–18.

Hargreaves, D., and M. Colman. 1982. The dimension of aesthetic reaction to music. *Psychology of Music* 9:15–20.

Hargreaves, D., P. Messerschumidt, and C. Rubert. 1982. Musical preference and evaluation. *Psychology of Music* 8:13–18.

Hart, J. H., and R. Cogan. 1976. Sex and emotional responses to classical music. *Perceptual and Motor Skills* 36:170–76.

Hedden, S. K. 1974. Preferences for single tone stimuli. *Journal of Research in Music Education* 22:136–42.

Heingartner, A., and F. Hall. 1974. Affective consequences in adults and children of repeated exposure to auditory stimuli. *Journal of Personality and Social Psychology* 29:719–23.

Hevner, K. 1935. The affective character of the major and minor modes in music. *American Journal of Psychology* 47:103–18.

Hevner, K. 1936. Experimental studies of the elements of expression in music. *American Journal of Psychology* 48:246–68.

Hevner, K. 1937. The affective value of pitch and tempo in music. *American Journal of Psychology* 49:621–30.

Heyduk, R. G. 1975. Rated preference for musical compositions as it relates to complexity and exposure frequency. *Perception and Psychophysics* 17:84–91.

Hodges, D. 1980. Physiological responses to music. In *Handbook of music psychology*, ed. D. Hodges, 392–400. Lawrence, KS: National Association for Music Therapy.

Hooper, P. P., and E. R. Powell. 1970. Influences of musical variables on pictorial connotations. *Journal of Psychology* 36:170–76.

Inglefield, H. G. 1968. The relationship of selected personality variables to conformity behavior reflected in the musical preferences of adolescents when exposed to peer group influences. Ph.D. diss., Ohio State University.

Jellison, J. A. 1975. Analyzing the effect of music and white noise on physiographic measurements. In *Research in music behavior: Modifying music behavior in the classroom*, ed. C. K. Madsen, R. Greer, and C. H. Madsen, 206–19. New York: Teachers College Press.

Johnson, O., and R. H. Knapp. 1963. Sex differences in aesthetic preferences. *Journal of Social Psychology* 61:279–301.

Klemish, J. J. 1970. A comparative study of two methods of teaching music reading to first-grade children. *Journal of Research in Music Education* 18:355–64.

Koh, S. D. 1967. Time-error in comparisons of preferences for musical excerpts. *American Journal of Psychology* 80, no. 2:171–85.

Koh, S. D., and C. W. Hedlund. 1969. Paired comparisons of musical excerpts. *Archives of General Psychiatry* 21:717–21.

Krathwohl, D. R., M. S. Bloom, and B. B. Masia. 1964. *Taxonomy of education objectives, handbook II: Affective domain*. New York: David McKay.

Krevelen, A. 1963. The influence of music on reactions to frustration. *Journal of General Psychology* 43:338–50.

Kuhn, T. L. 1976. Reliability of a technique for assessing musical preference in young children. Paper presented at Music Educators National Conference, March, Atlantic City.

Kyme, G. 1967. A study of the development of musicality in the junior high school and the contribution of musical compositions to this development. Cooperative Research Project No. OEC–6–10–164, July.

Larson, P. 1971. The effect of musical and extramusical information upon musical preference. *Journal of Research in Music Education* 19:350–54.

Leblanc, A. 1987. The development of music preference in children. In *Music and child development*, eds. J. C. Peery, I. W. Peery, T. W. Draper, 137–57. New York: Springer-Verlag.

Lewis and Schmidt. 1991. Listeners' response to music as a function of personality type. *Journal of Research in Music Education* 39, no. 4, 311–321.

Lewy, A. 1971. Affective outcomes of musical education. *Journal of Research in Music Education* 19:361–65.

Lifton, W. M. 1961. The development of a music reaction test to measure affective and aesthetic sensitivity. *Journal of Research in Music Education* 9:156–66.

Long, N. H. 1971. Establishment of standards for the Indiana-Oregon Music Discrimination Test based on a cross-section of elementary and secondary students with an analysis of elements of environment, intelligence and musical experience and training in relation to musical discrimination. *Council for Research in Music Education Bulletin* 25:26–32.

Long, N. H. 1972. Music discrimination tests—their construction, assumptions and uses. *Australian Journal of Music Education,* 11:21–25.

Ludin, R. W. 1967. *An objective psychology of music.* 2d ed. New York: Ronald Press.

Madsen, C. K., and J. M. Geringer. 1976. Preferences for trumpet tone quality versus intonation. *Council for Research in Music Education Bulletin* 46:13–22.

Martin, D. F. 1967. The power of music and Whitehead's theory of perception. *Journal of Aesthetics and Art Criticism* 25:313–22.

Mashkiv, K., and T. Volgy. 1975. Socio-political attitudes and musical preferences. *Social Science Quarterly* 56:450–56.

McMullen, P. T. 1974a. The influence of complexity in pitch sequences on preference responses of college-age subjects. *Journal of Music Therapy* 11:226–33.

McMullen, P. T. 1974b. Influence of number of different pitches and melodic redundancy on preference responses. *Journal of Research in Music Education* 22:198–204.

Meadows, W. S. 1970. The relationship of music preference to certain cultural determiners. Ph.D. diss., Michigan State University.

Meyer, L. B. 1956. *Emotion and meaning in music.* Chicago: University of Chicago Press.

Meyer, L. B. 1967. *Music, the arts, and ideas.* Chicago: University of Chicago Press.

Mueller, J. H., and K. Hevner. 1942. *Trends in musical taste.* Humanity Series, no. 8. Bloomington: Indiana University.

National Assessment of Educational Progress. 1974. *An assessment of attitudes toward music,* Report No. 03–MU–03. Washington, DC: U.S. Government Printing Office.

Neher, A. 1962. A physiological explanation of unusual behavior in ceremonies involving drums. *Human Biology* 34:151–60.

Nielzen, S., and Z. Cesarec. 1982. Emotional experience of music as a function of musical structure. *Psychology of Music* 10, no. 2: 7–17.

Noy, P. 1966. The psychodynamic meaning of music—part 1. *Journal of Music Therapy* 3:126–34.

Noy, P. 1967a. The psychodynamic meaning of music—part 2. *Journal of Music Therapy* 4:7–23.

Noy, P. 1967b. The psychodynamic meaning of music—part 3. *Journal of Music Therapy* 4:45–51.

Noy, P. 1967c. The psychodynamic meaning of music—part 4. *Journal of Music Therapy* 4:81–94.

Noy, P. 1967d. The psychodynamic meaning of music—part 5. *Journal of Music Therapy* 4:117–25.

O'Keefe, V. 1975. Psychophysical preference for harmonized musical passages in the just and equal-tempered systems. *Perceptual and Motor Skills* 40:192–98.

Palmquist, J. E. 1990. Apparent time passage and music preference by music and nonmusic majors. *Journal of Research in Music Education* 38, no. 3:206–14.

Parker, O. G. 1961. A study of the relationship of aesthetic sensitivity to musical ability, intelligence and socioeconomic status. Ph.D. diss., University of Kansas.

Payne, E. 1967. Musical taste and personality. *British Journal of Psychology* 58:133–38.

Pike, A. 1972. A phenomenological analysis of emotional experience in music. *Journal of Research in Music Education* 20:262–68.

Price, H. 1986. A proposed glossary for use in affective response literature in music. *Journal of Research in Music Education* 34, no. 3: 151–59.

Reimer, B. 1962. Leonard Meyer's theory of value and greatness in music. *Journal of Research in Music Education* 10:87–99.

Reimer, B. 1989. *A philosophy of music education.* Englewood Cliffs, NJ: Prentice-Hall.

Ridgeway, C. L. 1976. Affective interaction as a determinant of musical involvement. *Sociological Quarterly* 17:414–28.

Rigg, M. G. 1937. Musical expression: an investigation of the theories of Erich Sorantin. *Journal of Experimental Psychology* 21:223–29.

Roeckle, C. A. 1968. Notes on musical taste. *Missouri Journal of Research in Music Education* 2:5–13.

Roederer, J. G. 1974. The psychophysics of musical perception. *Music Educators Journal* 60:20–30.

Rubin, L. 1951. The effects of musical experience on musical discrimination and musical preferences. Ph.D. diss., University of California.

Schoen, M. 1940. *The psychology of music.* New York: Ronald Press.

Schuessler, K. F. 1948. Social background and musical taste. *American Sociological Review* 13:330–35.

Schutz, C., and G. Lang. 1963. The reliability of music preferences under varying mood conditions. *Journal of Clinical Psychology* 19:506.

Seashore, C. E. 1938. *Psychology of music.* New York: McGraw-Hill.

Shatin, L. 1970. Alteration of mood via music: A study of the vectoring effect. *Journal of Psychology* 75:81–86.

Simon, C. R., and J. F. Wohlwill. 1968. An experimental study of the role of expectation and variation in music. *Journal of Research in Music Education* 16:227–38.

Skipper, J. K. 1975. Musical tastes of Canadian and American college students: An examination of the massification and Americanization theses. *Canadian Journal of Sociology* 1:49–59.

Sloboda, J. 1991. Music structure and emotional response: Some empirical findings. *Psychology of Music* 19:110–20.

Smith, C. A., and D. Morris. 1976. Effects of stimulative and sedative music on cognitive and emotional components of anxiety. *Psychological Reports* 38:1187.

Sopchak, A. L. 1955. Individual differences in responses to music. *Psychology Monograph* 69, no. 11:1–20.

Standifer, J. A. 1970. Effects on aesthetic sensitivity of developing perception of musical expressiveness. *Journal of Research in Music Education* 18:112–25.

Steck, L., and P. Machotka. 1975. Preference for musical complexity: Effects of context. *Journal of Experimental Psychology: Human Perception and Performance* 104:170–74.

Steenberg, N. J. 1959. IPAT music preference test of personality. In *The Fifth Mental Measurements Yearbook,* ed. O. Buros, 143–45. Highland, NJ: Gryphon.

Stratton, V. N., and A. H. Zalanowski. 1989. The effects of music and paintings on mood. *Journal of Music Therapy* 26, no. 1:30–41.

Trolio, M. F. 1975. Affective response to distorted melodies. Ph.D. diss., Case Western Reserve University, Cleveland.

Vermazen, B. 1971. Information theory and musical value. *Journal of Aesthetics and Art Criticism* 29:367–70.

Vitz, P. C. 1966. Affect as a function of stimulus variation. *Journal of Experimental Psychology* 71:74–79.

Wallach, M. A., and C. Greenberg. 1960. Personality functions of symbolic sexual arousal to music. *Psychology Monograph* 74:1–18.

Wedin, L. 1972. A multidimensional study of perceptual-emotional qualities in music. *Scandinavian Journal of Psychology* 13:241–57.

Weld, H. P. 1912. An experimental study of musical enjoyment. *American Journal of Psychology* 23:245–308.

Wells, A. and Hakanen, E. A. 1991. The emotional use of popular music by adolescents. *Journalism Quarterly* 68, no. 3:445–54.

Wheeler, B. 1985. Relationship of personal characteristics to mood and enjoyment after hearing live and recorded music and to musical taste. *Psychology of Music* 13:81–92.

Williams, R. O. 1972. Effects of musical aptitude, instruction, and social status on attitudes toward music. *Journal of Research in Music Education* 20:362–69.

Winold, C. A. 1963. The effects of changes in harmonic tension upon listener response. Ph.D. diss., Indiana University.

Zimny, G. H., and E. W. Weidenfeller. 1962. Effects of music upon GSR of children. *Child Development* 33:891–96.

9

Physiological Responses to Music and Sound Stimuli

Dale L. Bartlett

One of the most traditional research areas associated with the experimental study of musical behavior is that categorized as physiological response. Broadly speaking, the study of physiological response draws from the fields of physiology, anatomy, neurology, and biochemistry and measures quantifiable bodily reactions that are visceral, motor, muscular, chemical, or centered in the brain. Such reactions are produced as a result, primarily, of external stimuli. Reactions are then measured in an effort to determine the corresponding qualities of observed or reported affective or somatic states.

Some of the questions researchers of physiological response seek to answer are whether music has a measurable, thus observable, effect on the human organism and whether such effects can be evaluated in terms that help our understanding of music's "power" to activate and alter the human condition. One term commonly associated with activation of the human condition is *affect*, a term that describes the feeling state derived from a bodily response to a stimulus. Music is a stimulus that can elicit such a response, and, throughout the history of experimentation, reference to affective states, whether emotional, mood, or aesthetic in nature, has provided researchers "grist" for attempting to discover links between physiological and psychological behaviors. In this case, the psychological state of affect experienced is linked to the physiologically altered state and, subsequently, to the music stimulus purportedly causing the altered state. Inferences are then made, or attempted, that the stimulus music can be manipulated into causing specific affective behavior. The discipline that investigates the interrelationships between psychological and physiological conditions is psychophysiology; and a number of the studies reviewed in this chapter appear to fall within this discipline.

Research studies that may be appropriately categorized as measuring physiological response within the general study of psychophysiology are reportedly those beginning with Couty and Charpentier (cited in Diserens 1923, 174), who used whistles, among other nonauditory stimuli, in producing increased cardiac tension and pulse acceleration in dogs. Diserens credited this study and others during the late 1800s as "the earliest well controlled experiments" (1923, 126); however, he makes brief reference to Gretry, a French musician born in 1741, as publishing perhaps even earlier observations on the physiological effects of music by feeling with the fingers of one hand the pulse pressure variations in the artery of the other hand while singing. Diserens has provided an excellent review of the studies between 1874 and 1918, the majority of these studies being European (Diserens 1923), and, although not specifically investigating psychological effects, these early experiments provide historical perspective regarding observations of the influences of music on the human organism.[1]

A perusal of these early studies illustrates the variety of research interests that emerged early in the study of physiological response. Included in Diserens's review, aside from those mentioned above, are studies by Dogiel (cited in Diserens 1923, 174), who found that both animals and humans responded to auditory and musical stimuli, respectively, with changes in blood circulation, blood pressure, respiration, and cardiac contractions. Interestingly, Dogiel tested his use of auditory stimulation on animals under the influence of strychnine. Also included are the studies of Fere and Londe (cited in Diserens 1923, 176), who used vibrating forks to demonstrate an increase in muscular force with one human subject, and Lombard (cited in Diserens 1923, 177), who claimed to show an increase in the number of knee jerks under the influence of symphonic music. Other early researches of interest reported in Diserens's review include Tanzi (cited in Diserens 1923, 179), who noted

---

1. Other reviews of selected periods and topics should be noted. See Diserens 1926 for a re-edition of the review of experimental research found in his 1923 article. See Dainow 1977; Maranto and Bruscia 1988; Soibelman 1948 for master's theses abstracts; Standley and Madsen 1990 for infants; Maranto and Scartelli 1992 for music in psychoneuroimmunology. Also see such psychology of music texts as Farnsworth 1969; Hodges 1980; Lundin 1967; Radocy and Boyle 1988; Schoen 1927 and 1940. Thorough and interesting discussions of the use of psychogalvanic measures in relation to emotion may be found in Bartlett 1925 and Wechsler 1925, both dated works but, interestingly, commentaries that are not out of date in their relevance to current issues related to physiological measurement of affective concomitants. Useful miscellaneous reviews include a review of high-intensity intermittent sound on performance, feeling, and physiology by Plutchik (1959); a review of heart-rate change and the orienting response by Graham and Clifton (1966); and a concise discussion of orienting response in Grings and Dawson 1978. Though the writings of Clynes (1977) and Clynes and Nettheim (1982) may not fit easily into the category of physiological response as defined here, Clynes's work in measurement of inner pulse shapes of music should be consulted.

an increase in reaction time to minor chords over major chords; Tarchanoff (1894, cited in Diserens 1923, 180), who demonstrated the influence of music on activity of the cutaneous glands; Warthin (1894, cited in Diserens 1923, 186), who reported an increase in heart rate while listening to piano music under hypnosis; Mentz (1895, cited in Diserens 1923, 181), who showed there was systematic variation in circulation and respiration to both simple sounds and musical selections; Binet and Courtier (1895, cited in Diserens 1923, 181), who found a relationship between the sound of a gong and reduced capillary circulation of the hand; and Darlington and Talbot (1897–98, cited in Diserens 1923, 185), who found no relationship between weight lifting and pitch.

Corning (1899) investigated the use of chromatoscope images and "musical vibrations" on various sleep conditions, and Fere (cited in Weschler 1925, 21) was the first to report on electrical variation of the human body in response to a mental stimulus during the passage of an exsomatic current (forerunner of the term *psychogalvanic reflex* proposed by Otto Veraguth in 1906).

Obviously, these early studies can be considered little more than preliminary investigations, setting the stage for more extensive experimentation that, from the early 1900s through 1994, has included more than 130 research studies incorporating music or sound sources as stimulus events, a variety of research topics, and, as might be expected, improvements in instrumentation, methodology, and statistical application according to the advancement of empirical science in general. Beginning in 1985, research capabilities extended into the study of music's influence on biochemical factors related to the immune system. This relatively new research protocol grew out of what has become a significant development in the health sciences initiated in the early 1980s, a development that could be considered a latent response by medical researchers who are looking more closely into the study of the relationships between immune systems and psychological processes, which is called psychoneuroimmunology.

Of the research reviewed here, the following physiologically related behaviors are included along with standard measurement techniques of these behaviors as described by Grings and Dawson (1978; also see Greenfield and Sternbach 1972 for an extensive and thorough discussion of physiological measurement methodology and technique).

Heart and pulse rate: expressed in units of beats per minute measured by a cardiotachometer;

Electrodermal response—commonly known as galvanic skin response (GSR): expressed as skin conductance measured by applying a very small electrical voltage across two metal electrodes placed on the skin;

Respiration rate: expressed in number of breaths per minute and measured by a pneumograph, a flexible rubber tube placed around the chest;

Blood pressure: expressed as systolic pressure (the maximum pressure during heart contraction), diastolic pressure (the minimum pressure during heart relaxation), and pulse pressure (the difference between the two and measured by an inflatable cuff or sphygmomanometer wrapped around the upper arm);

Muscular tension and tone: expressed as an electrical potential measured by an electromyograph (EMG) attached to the skin surface above the muscle to be measured;

Blood volume: expressed as a redistribution of the blood through vasoconstriction or vasodilation of the blood vessels and measured by a plethysmograph, which acts as a light device sensitive to density changes of the blood;

Skin temperature: expressed as a change in resistance measured by a thermister attached to specific parts of the body surface;

Gastric motility: expressed as the rate and contractions in the stomach and measured by a small device that is swallowed and transmits radio signals to the outside of the body or a balloon that, when inflated inside the stomach, responds to stomach contractions;

Pupillary reflex: expressed in the diameter of a constricted or dilated pupil measured in millimeters and obtained by a photograph of the eye;

Blood oxygen: expressed as arterial oxygen saturation and measured by the technique of spectroscopic oximetry;

Hormone secretion: expressed in level changes of such hormones as cortisol and measured through saliva, urine, or blood serum analysis.

In some cases, measurement techniques are less standardized and are designed by the author to accommodate a particular hypothesis. For example, the study of muscular response may be measured in a variety of ways according to the response task as described in the number of deviations in line drawing ascribed to poor muscle tonus of the arm. Pilomotor response (expressed as a "gooseflesh" feeling) may be measured merely by raising the hand to indicate the experience.

In an effort to limit this discussion, only studies that have used music or sound stimuli to effect measurable bodily changes are included. Studies investigating such topics as the effect of music on pain reduction determined through self-reporting methods are not included (for a review of such studies up to the middle 1980s, see Standley 1986), nor are studies that attempt to induce physiological changes through internal thoughts. Some seemingly relevant studies found in other bibliographies are not included because they were not available for review or because they used stimulus events other than music or sound, nor are those few studies from non-English journals included. Brain wave studies (EEG), though appropriately categorized under physiological response, are reviewed in chapter 7.

The inclusion of unpublished works may raise concern that the conclusions reported do not contribute in the most scientific manner to this body of knowledge; however, the act of publication alone—especially in early studies—may not always promise the best experimental control, which provides the greatest assurance that what we think we find is, in fact, what is true. It is apparent, when reviewing published as well as unpublished studies, that there is a disparity in the establishment of controls appropriate for the best possible generalizations to be made; nevertheless, both historical and contemporary perspective is enhanced when the greatest breadth of information is provided.

Interest in measuring physiological response for analysis of affective states has historical roots in Greek philosophy, especially the philosophy of Aristotle, whose use of "passion" to denote affective states in relation to bodily experience is contrasted with experiences of the soul. Young points out that "passions were roughly equivalent to what psychologists today call affective processes" (Young 1973, 750). Bindra (1970) notes that this attempt to characterize bodily experience as fundamental to affective states finds a historical niche, also, in the writings of Descartes, who distinguished between passions of the soul and bodily (visceral) reactions, and Darwin, who believed that emotions were causally linked to stimulus events. Bindra suggests these "affective roots" helped set the stage for William James's theory of emotion in the late nineteenth century that, according to Boring (1950), was perhaps James's most famous psychological theory. In his theory, James, who was teaching physiological psychology by 1875 at Harvard, purported "there are certain innate or reflex adjustments of the nervous system to emotional stimuli, . . . which lead automatically to bodily changes, mostly in the viscera and the skeletal muscles, that some of these changes can be felt . . . and that the perception of them is the emotion" (quoted in Boring 1950, 516). Bindra suggests James's theory is a "significant landmark because it clearly proposed certain relations among three sets of events: emotional stimulus, emotional behavior (both visceral reactions and overt actions), and emotional experience" (Bindra 1970, 5).

Suggesting that research in physiological response is, in essence, research into affective or emotional states exaggerates the relationships between the somewhat simple measurement of, for example, respiration and the apparent complexity of these states in general (see Young 1973 for a discussion of classes of affects). While it is evident that changes in affective states may be accompanied by, and even fundamental to, changes in bodily systems, it is also evident that a specific physiological response may be associated with more than one affective or emotional behavior, conditions that Meyer (1956) appropriately describes as undifferentiated response. Simply stated, crying behavior, certainly a strong and observable affect, may illustrate happiness or sadness, two quite disparate psychological states. Yet the physiological concomitants are likely quite similar for both, and the inability to link the specific bodily response to the specific affective behavior underlies the principle of undifferentiation. Meyer further adds: "The conclusion that affect itself is undifferentiated does not mean that affective experience is a kind of disembodied generality. For the affective experience, as distinguished from affect per se, includes an awareness and cognition of a stimulus situation which always involves particular responding individuals and specific stimuli" (Meyer 1956, 19).

Thus, the establishment of direct relationships between a physiological response and the psychological manifestation of that response may appear to be an elusive one, especially if too much emphasis is accorded the majority of the types of physiological behaviors discussed here that are generally the result of the autonomic nervous system acting reflexively to induce what often may be considered relatively simple onset stimulus events. At the same time, psychological behaviors that entail memory and associative experiences are generated and these can only be considered relatively complex human reactions. It is safe to say that not every bodily response leads to an emotional state, that is, an "acutely disturbed state of psychological origin" (Young 1973, 750). It is likely that most of the types of bodily responses categorized as physiological response probably include, at least, fundamental responses of feeling or simple affects. If this premise is accepted, it can also be said that to reach farther, for a more substantial link between music and affect, is, perhaps, to expect much more from this research than may be reasonable or possible.

As with the measurement of all physiological responses, it is a matter of observing whether there is a change effected by the sound or music stimulus and whether such change can be expressed as an increase or decrease in physical activity. Often the findings, as presented in the literature, are based on the manipulation of music classified as stimulative (percussive, fast tempo, highly rhythmic, loud dynamic, etc.), neutral, or sedative (melodic, slow tempo, legato style, soft dynamic, etc.). Findings also represent various and specific variables of the music stimulus: for example, rhythm, pitch, loudness, white noise, or such stimulus dimensions as pure tones of different frequencies. Dating from the beginning studies (not including those using animals), sample sizes have included 1 subject to more than 100 subjects; subject types include, among others, comparisons of males and females, musicians and nonmusicians, normal and disabled, and incorporate various age levels—even the fetus. Analysis that includes tests for statistical significance between group means did not appear in the literature until about 1942 (Lovell and Morgan, using recurring sound stimuli) and 1952 in relation to music stimuli (Ellis and Brighouse). Studies prior to these relied on descriptive statistics in support of experimental hypotheses. Practically all studies since the mid-1960s have incorporated tests for statistical significance.

In general, many of the findings of the studies presented here appear naturally to fall into such categories as an increase or decrease in response (heart rate, for example); some seem better reported as merely changes in response or as a decrease in resistance (skin conductivity, for example). To avoid repetition of studies mentioned previously, only studies beginning with 1906 will be reviewed.

Summary of Heart- or Pulse-Rate Studies

The study of heart and pulse rate is by far the most popularly investigated physiological response. The heart attracts both scientist and poet, after all. Generally speaking, listening to music causes the heart or pulse rate to increase, to decrease, or causes no change (see table 1).

TABLE 1.   The Effects of Music on Heart Rate or Pulse Rate

Study	Experimental Variables or Results
	Significant or Meaningful Increase in Heart Rate or Pulse Rate
Shepard 1906	"Agreeably exciting" music
Hyde and Scalapino 1918	During minor tones, stirring notes of the "Toreador" song, and a rhythmic march
Hyde 1927	Using gay, rhythmical melodies (such as "Toreador" and "National Emblem") with musical persons

(continued)

TABLE 1—*Continued*

Study	Experimental Variables or Results
Treves 1927[a]	Popular music; less noticeable variation with classical music
Misbach 1932	Slight increase using pure tones of varied frequencies under high loudness conditions
Washco 1933	Using such music as "Stars and Stripes"; variance in pulse rate depends on music type
Darner 1966	Prolonged exposure to pulses with a repetition rate higher than the normal heart-beat
Graham and Clifton 1966	Associated with stimulus "rejection"
Segall 1970[b]	Demonstrated by quiet, premature infants with white noise after being conditioned to mother's voice
Grimwade et al. 1971	Fetal heart rate increased with pure-tones of 500–1,000 Hz at 80 dB
DeJong, van Mourik, and Schellekiens 1973	During "beautiful music" for conservatory musicians; fast over medium or slow tempos
Landreth and Landreth 1974	In stable segments of test music with driving and insistent rhythm, mounting sequential interplay, and progressive dynamic intensity; linked to learning and repetitive exposure
Malcom 1981	Increased musical training and decreased preference during minute 2 of sedative rhythm; males greater than females during stimulative rhythm
Pignatiello et al. 1989	Approached significance in elated group condition in comparison with depressed group condition
Standley 1991	Immediate acceleration but rapid decline at initiation stage of auditory onset (an orienting response [OR]); music in combination with vibrotactile device
Shepard 1906	"Agreeably depressing" music

(continued)

[a] Reported in Soibelman 1948, 53.
[b] Reported in Standley and Madsen 1990, 60.

TABLE 1—*Continued*

Study	Experimental Variables or Results
	Significant or Meaningful Decrease in Heart Rate or Pulse Rate
Hyde 1927	Musical persons listening to Tschaikovsky's 6th Symphony ("Pathetique")
Washco 1933	Greatest decrease under "Serenade" (*Madame Butterfly*)
Shatin 1957	During silent condition in comparison to rhythm
Kagan and Lewis 1965	Infant boys to intermittent tone; infant girls to modern jazz music
Brackbill et al. 1966	Infants during no sound over other lullaby and sound conditions
Darner 1966	Listening to pulses at rates lower than the heart rate
Meyers and Gullickson 1967	College students showed reliable deceleration to the first of 30 two-frequency component stimuli and similarly when stimuli presentations were reversed
Segall 1970[c]	Female voice in crying infants
Lewis 1971	Infants attending to C-chord stimulus, which is considered relatively complex and interesting and does not startle
De Jong, van Mourik, and Schellekens 1973	During "beautiful music" for undergraduates who are not instrumental performers
Landreth and Landreth 1974	Alternating segments of Beethoven's 5th Symphony, 1st movement with changes in rhythm, texture, and dynamics
Wilson and Aiken 1977	For main effect of time under hard rock music and white noise conditions
Barger 1979	In interaction between experimental condition groups and arousal/treatment conditions
Friedman 1979[d]	Under conditions of imagery scene and imagery scene plus music
Loscin 1981	Female patients during the second half of a 48-hour postsurgery period listening to preferred music

(continued)

[c] Reported in Standley and Madsen 1990, 60.
[d] Reported in Maranto and Bruscia 1988, 37.

TABLE 1—*Continued*

Study	Experimental Variables or Results
Bonny 1983	Sedative classical/light classical music with intensive coronary care patients
Updike and Charles 1987	Patients awaiting plastic surgery listening to classical or contemporary music
Ward 1987[e]	In comparison to heart rate increase after debridement (surgical removal of unhealthy tissue with burn patients); use of music significantly influenced the maintenance of heart rate as before debridement
Zimmerman, Pierson, and Marker 1988	Combining all CCU (coronary care unit) patients in three different music/control relaxation conditions
Geden et al. 1989	Pairwise comparisons over trials for both undergraduates and nulliparous (not having borne offspring) women
Guzzetta 1989	CCU patients during music therapy/relaxation condition
Barker 1991	In comparison to significant heart-rate increase after debridement; combination of music and progressive muscle relaxation technique maintained heart rate
Standley 1991	When music followed the dental drill
Miluk-Kolasa 1993	In patients after receiving anxiety-laden surgery information using preferred music listening
Lorch et al. 1994	Contrasted with baseline conditions for premature infants using sedative music ("Moonlight" Sonata)
	No Significant or Meaningful Increase or Decrease in Heart Rate or Pulse Rate
Weld 1912	Correlation with tempo of music
Hyde 1927	Nonmusicians regardless of music

(continued)

[e] Reported in Maranto and Bruscia 1988, 122.

TABLE 1—*Continued*

Study	Experimental Variables or Results
Washco 1933	Correlation with sensitivity to elements of melody, harmony, and rhythm
Lovell and Morgan 1942	Pure-tone oscillator sounding monotonously
Ellis and Brighouse 1952	Using jazz, soothing classical, and dynamic classical music
Shatin 1957	Significant change regardless of direction or rates of rhythmic stimuli
Bierbaum 1958	Sedative or stimulative music
Zimny and Weidenfeller 1963	Exciting, neutral, and calming music
Armatas 1964	Recovery during postoperation process
Wilson and Aiken 1977	Intensity variable with specific music instances and subjective measures
Barger 1979	Varied conditions of relaxation, music, and silence
Ruiz 1979	Music programmed to gradually stimulate
Lisco 1980[f]	Stimulative and sedative music and silence
Clarke 1981	Varied frequency range conditions
Malcom 1981	Comparing sedative and stimulative rhythms
Stadum 1981	Visual biofeedback and visual biofeedback with music
O'Connell 1984[g]	Sedative music, muscle relaxation, and imagery
Davis-Rollans and Cunningham 1987	Differences between music and noise conditions for coronary care unit (CCU) patients could not be attributed to the music
Edwards 1987[h]	Comparison of music and noise conditions
Zimmerman, Pierson, and Marker 1988	Between baseline and testing for CCU patients in conditions of instrumental tapes using relaxing music, noise, and silence
Geden et al. 1989	In conditions of easy music listening, rock music listening, self-selected

(continued)

[f] Reported in Maranto and Bruscia 1988, 75.
[g] Reported in Maranto and Bruscia 1988, 88–89.
[h] Reported in Maranto and Bruscia 1988, 32–33.

TABLE 1—*Continued*

Study	Experimental Variables or Results
	music listening, placebo-attention, and no treatment
Davis and Thaut 1989	Comparing baseline and preferred, relaxing music listening conditions
Haack 1991	Infants after music therapy training of expectant mothers
Madsen, Standley, and Gregory 1991	Two music conditions and conditions of gradual tempo alterations while lying on a vibrotactile couch
Menegazzi 1991	Between self-selected music listening and no listening conditions in control and experimental subjects while experiencing laceration repair
Standley 1991	Neither music nor the dental drill alone or in combination with vibrotactile stimulation
Davis 1992	During a medical procedure under conditions of music choice and no music
Pujol 1994	Profoundly retarded children and adults during vibrotactile stimulation, with comparisons of flute vs. bells and pentatonic vs. major precomposed melodies
	Miscellaneous Studies on Heart Rate or Pulse Rate
Coleman 1920	Correspondence with walking, singing, or attention to metronome
Johnson and Trawick 1938	No correspondence with rate of external stimulus (cf. Coleman 1920)
Sternbach 1964	Differences in response to shock and noise conditions related to three levels of subject instructional set
Coutts 1965	Music had no effect on pulse rate associated with speed of bicycle riding
Keller and Seraganian 1984	In recovery from psychosocial stress as part of an aerobics program
Beckett 1990	Heart recovery rate higher and greater distance walked after aerobic walking during music listening

It is apparent from the heart-rate studies that there is much diversity in relation to the number of different independent or experimental variables used to test heart-rate response. Yet one may conclude that some degree of expected outcome under different music and sound conditions is warranted when looking at the number of studies (9 of 17 reviewed) that used test stimuli (either music or sound sources) that may be categorized as stimulative (e.g., march-style music, rhythmic melodies, high loudness conditions, white noise, fast tempos, stimulative rhythm, and auditory onset) or the number of studies (15 of 25 reviewed) that used test stimuli (e.g., "depressing" music, slow tempo or relaxation-type music, sedative classical music, chordal harmony, etc.) that may be categorized as sedative and produced increased rates and decreased rates, respectively.

However, if one is interested in the effects of music, per se, on heart-rate behavior, it should be noted that, of the 9 studies using stimulative stimuli in the increased heart-rate category, only 7 (Shepard, Hyde and Scalapino, Hyde, Washco, De Jong et al., Landreth and Landreth, and Malcom) used music. Of the 15 studies showing a decrease in heart rate, all 15 (Shepard; Hyde; Washco; Brackbill et al.; De Jong et al.; Barger; Loscin; Bonny; Updike and Charles; Ward; Zimmerman, Pierson, and Marker; Geden; Guzzetta; Barker; and Lorch et al.) used music that can be characterized as "sedative." The studies of Ward and Barker, though not showing decreased rates per se, did maintain heart-rate behavior under conditions of debridement, in which heart rate increased without the music stimulus.

In contrast, of the studies reviewed here, 16 of 28 studies showed no substantive change in variables related to heart rate regardless of the use of specific stimulative or sedative stimuli. Of the 62 different heart-rate studies included here, and given the fact that some studies tested more than one hypothesis, 15 studies produced results showing increased rates, 25 showed decreased rates, and 28 studies produced findings of neither increased nor decreased rates as the result of music or sound stimuli. Not included in these statistics are the findings from the five miscellaneous studies, which do not fall neatly into the increase/decrease categories. In this grouping, Sternbach's study focused on the influence of instructional set on physiological responsivity differences and not on whether heart rate increased or decreased.

Summary of Skin Conductivity Studies

A number of studies have focused on changes in the electrical conductivity of the skin (see table 2).

TABLE 2.   The Effects of Music on Skin Conductivity

Study	Experimental Variables or Results
	Significant or Meaningful Relationship between Changes in Resistance of Skin Conductivity and Subject Report
Davis 1934	Related to subject report of liking and excitement with increased reactions upon repetition of stimulus (Beethoven's *Missa Solemnis*)
Phares 1934	Amount of change corresponded positively with degree of affective tone experienced
Dreher 1948	High correlation with mood descriptions for musically trained
Ries 1969	Positive correlation in relation to report of music's effect on "extroverted" subjects; negative correlation in report of music's effect on "introverted" subjects
	No Significant or Meaningful Relationship between Changes in Resistance of Skin Conductivity and Subject Report
Davis 1934	Stimuli reported to be neither liked nor disliked, that is, indifferent to the subject
Ries 1969	Extroverted and introverted subjects taken together in relation to music like/dislike or music effect reports
De Jong, van Mourik, and Schellekens 1973	Comparing subjects with various levels of musical training in rating classical music as "beautiful" or "ugly"
Parmentier 1990	Comparing pretest and posttest for conditions of new-age music and new-age music plus verbal material in relation to state anxiety of female students
	Significant or Meaningful Changes in Resistance of Skin Conductivity Unrelated to Subject Report
Misbach 1932	Tonal stimuli at various frequency levels, especially above 512 Hz

(continued)

TABLE 2—*Continued*

Study	Experimental Variables or Results
Henkin 1957	Classical music loaded as to melodic and rhythmic factors and level of music experience
Shrift 1957	Stimulative and sedative music; greater amount of change associated with stimulative music
Winold 1959	Isolated chords used as increasing and decreasing harmonic tension
Weidenfeller and Zimny 1962	Exciting music produced decreased resistance, and calming music produced increased resistance in depressed and schizophrenic patients
Zimny and Weidenfeller 1962	Exciting music, in comparison to calming music, producing decreased resistance in children in kindergarten, third grade and sixth grade collectively; no difference shown between groups
Zimny and Weidenfeller 1963	Exciting music compared with neutral and calming music; college-age subjects
Sternbach 1964	Noise and shock conditions related to three levels of subject instructional set
Peretti and Swenson 1974	Decrease in resistance for musicians over nonmusicians and females over males while working a pencil maze blindfolded to create anxiety in a pretest (no music)/ posttest (music) design
Wilson and Aiken 1977	Decreased skin resistance between music and noise, over duration of listening time, and interaction of intensity, type, and time

No Significant or Meaningful Changes
in Resistance of Skin Conductivity
Unrelated to Subject Report

Study	Experimental Variables or Results
Lovell and Morgan 1942	Pure-tone oscillator with increasing and decreasing intensity
Armatas 1964	During a one-hour segment of postoperative recovery
Jellison 1975	Measuring systolic pressure under conditions of exciting music, calming music,

(continued)

TABLE 2—*Continued*

Study	Experimental Variables or Results
	white noise, or silence with stress conditions incorporating different levels of electric shock
Keller and Seraganian 1984	Recovery from psychosocial stress as part of an aerobics program

Changes in skin conductivity in relation to subject reports include four studies in which positive relationships were found between conductivity change and a liking or excitement for the music, in terms of mood descriptions for musically trained subjects, and in effect of music on extroverted subjects. A negative relationship was found in one of these studies (Ries) between the reported effect of the music and introverted subjects. In four studies related to subject reports, no relationships were found between conductivity changes and conditions in which subjects were indifferent to the music, in self-reports of mood, enjoyment, relaxation/tension, and pleasure level, in the extent of liking the music or its effects on both extroverted and introverted subjects taken together, or in various levels of musical training and ratings of classical music as "beautiful" or "ugly."

In other skin conductivity studies in which there was no attempt to correlate changes with subject reports, changes were found in 10 studies under the following conditions: at frequency levels above 512 Hz, during classical music loaded by melodic and rhythmic factors, by level of music experience, during both stimulative and sedative music (with greater change occurring during stimulative music), when hearing isolated chords of increasing and decreasing harmonic tension, in depressed and schizophrenic patients when listening to exciting music (producing a decrease in resistance) and calming music (producing an increase in resistance), in grade-school children when listening to exciting music (producing a decrease in resistance), in college-age subjects when listening to exciting music, during combinations of white noise and shock, in musicians and females after creating anxiety states, and over duration of listening time and through interaction of listening time, intensity, and type of music. Four studies reported no skin conductivity changes that could be attributed to the music or sound stimulus under the following conditions: intensity increase or decrease of a pure tone, during a one-hour period of postoperative recovery, music treatment/shock, and during recovery from psychosocial stress induced by aerobics activity.

Not unlike studies of heart and pulse rate, the measurement of skin conductivity (galvanic skin response) has produced a variety of results in relation to music and sound stimuli. Several attempts were made to demonstrate positive relationships between the music experience and GSR response; a small majority of findings did not support such a relationship. Phares (1934), although finding positive relationships between verbal reports of "affective tone" through mood scaling, concluded that GSR measurement provided little value in the analysis of music appreciation as measured through the subject's recognition of such musical factors as melody, harmony, and rhythm; she based this conclusion on the impossibility of controlling conditions, the variability of subjective phenomena, and insufficient knowledge of the true significance of the GSR response. It is likely this evaluation, though made 60 years ago, includes appropriate concerns even for today's researchers. Looking at the studies not attempting to establish a relationship between GSR response and subject reports, it appears that the majority of such studies were able to demonstrate changes in skin conductivity as compared to those that did not (10 and 4, respectively); this finding may suggest a certain degree of success in showing this particular physiological response is fairly sensitive to music and sound stimuli in experimental settings.

Summary of Respiration Studies

Table 3 presents results of studies on the effects of music on respiration.

TABLE 3.   The Effects of Music on Respiration

Study	Experimental Variables or Results
	Significant or Meaningful Increase in Respiration
Foster and Gamble 1906	Loud or soft music or major or minor; greater increase when loud or major
Lovell and Morgan 1942	When approximating intermittent and regular rate of 60 Hz tone oscillator
Ellis and Brighouse 1952	Vivid and dynamic classical music; some increase evident during subdued jazz and soothing classical pieces

(continued)

TABLE 3—*Continued*

Study	Experimental Variables or Results
Ries 1969	Breathing amplitude/deepness correlated with greater like and effect reports
De Jong, van Mourik, and Schellekens 1973	Fast music
Wilson and Aiken 1977	Faster breathing rate for music over noise; increases for both over time, for soft input over time, and adjectives checked corresponded to loud or soft music
Lorch et al. 1994	Contrasted with baseline conditions for premature infants using both stimulative music *(Saber Dance)* and sedative music ("Moonlight" Sonata)
	Significant or Meaningful Decrease in Respiration
Lovell and Morgan 1942	When approximating intermittent and regular rate of 60 Hz tone oscillator
Pignatiello et al. 1989	Velten mood conduction (Velten's statements include a series of 60 self-referent statements designed to induce mood states) over music mood conduction
	No Significant or Meaningful Change in Respiration
Foster and Gamble 1906	No marked tendency to regulate breathing or difference between loud/soft or major/minor
Weld 1912	Rate tended to increase over normal, but too irregular
Miles and Tilly 1935[a]	Some effects provided subject was interested in the music; tempo change somewhat effective, but data too fragmentary
Armatas 1964	Patients in general hospital postoperative recovery
Davis-Rollans and Cunningham 1987	CCU patients listening to classical music or noise conditions

(continued)

[a] Reviewed in Soibelman 1948, 57.

TABLE 3—*Continued*

Study	Experimental Variables or Results
Davis 1992	Higher respiration rates for control subjects during subject-selected music listening during medical procedures
	Miscellaneous Studies on Respiration Rate
Kneutgen 1970	Lullaby reproduced repeatedly by wire recorded effected synchronization of breathing with musical rhythm; jazz had no effect
Haas, Distenfeld, and Axen 1986	Successful entrainment through auditory rhythmic cues

Studies demonstrating an effective increase in respiration as a result of music and sound stimuli total seven, with one of those showing a correlation between breathing amplitude and subject reports of liking and effect (Ries), one (Wilson and Aiken) demonstrating a significant relationship between adjectives checked and loud/soft music, and one (Lorch et al.) showing similar results with both stimulative and sedative music. Those that showed a decrease in respiration include two studies. Six studies found no respiration changes; and two miscellaneous studies found respiration synchronization with a lullaby and entrainment of respiration through auditory rhythmic cues.

Summary of Blood Pressure Studies

Results of studies on the effects of music on blood pressure are presented in table 4.

TABLE 4.   The Effects of Music on Blood Pressure

Study	Experimental Variables or Results
	Significant or Meaningful Increase in Blood Pressure
Hyde and Scalapino 1918	"Stirring notes" of the "Toreador" song and a rhythmical march

(continued)

TABLE 4—*Continued*

Study	Experimental Variables or Results
Hyde 1927	Gay, rhythmic melodies such as the "Toreador" song and "National Emblem" march
Wascho 1933	During such music as "Stars and Stripes"
Pignatiello et al. 1989	Main effect for mood for systolic blood pressure with elated group over neutral or depressed groups

	Significant or Meaningful Decrease in Blood Pressure
Hyde and Scalapino 1918	Systolic and diastolic pressures during minor tones of music; diastolic pressure during "Toreador" song
Washco 1933	During such music as the Overture to *Der Freischutz,* in which melodic factors were dominant, or "Serenade" from *Madame Butterfly*
Hoffman 1980	Significant for both systolic and diastolic pressures for hypertension subjects after relaxation/awareness training with music and the sound of ocean waves
Schuster 1985	Lower systolic pressure for experimental group at onset of dialysis and during second dialysis treatment; significant difference between all succeeding pressure readings from onset to termination of treatment using self-selected music of various types
Oyama et al. 1987b	Mean arterial blood pressure for 50 dental patients under conditions of self-selected music listening and no listening
Updike and Charles 1987	Systolic and diastolic pressures resulting from self-selected music listening to classical or contemporary periods prior to surgery; corresponding subject reports of "feeling more relaxed, calm, and soothed by music"
Geden et al. 1989	Pairwise comparisons in both systolic and diastolic pressures in reported

(continued)

TABLE 4—*Continued*

Study	Experimental Variables or Results
Lorch et al. 1994	direction of pain decrease under music conditions of easy listening, self-selected, rock, and a no-music imagery condition Contrasted with baseline conditions for premature infants using sedative music ("Moonlight" Sonata)

	No Significant or Meaningful Change in Blood Pressure
Misbach 1932	Brief pure-tone stimuli of various frequencies and moderate loudness
Miles and Tilly 1935[a]	Some evidence of a steady rise as a result of increased listener appreciation of unfamiliar music; data too fragmentary
Sunderman 1946	Comparing musicians and nonmusicians in terms of their possible organic or physiological differences
Armatas 1964	Patients in general hospital postoperative recovery
Jellison 1975	Measuring systolic pressure under conditions of exciting music, calming music, white noise, or silence with stress conditions incorporating different levels of electric shock
Bonny 1983	Though an observed trend in decrease of both systolic and diastolic pressures, no significant effects of sedative classical/light classical music for ICCU patients over 50 years of age
Schuster 1985	Comparing experimental and control group conditions differing in music listening with dialysis patients selecting from a variety of musical styles
Martin 1986[b]	Music listening and no music listening during minor dental procedures
Zimmerman, Pierson, and Marker 1988	Comparing self-selected music listening, white noise, and silence

(continued)

[a] Reviewed in Soibelman 1948, 57.
[b] Reviewed in Maranto and Bruscia 1988, 79.

TABLE 4—*Continued*

Study	Experimental Variables or Results
Geden et al. 1989	Main effects of easy listening, self-selected, and rock music
Pignatiello et al. 1989	Measuring diastolic pressure under both conditions of mood induction techniques—Velten's statements or music

Of the 23 studies reviewed, 4 showed increased blood pressure, with 3 of those using stimulative music. Eight studies produced decreased blood pressure; 4 of these used sedative music, and 4 used "self-selected" music, an experimental variable incorporated to a greater extent in the past 15 years in response to increasing evidence that music that is preferred is more fitting for measuring the types of individualized responses related to physiological response. One study demonstrated a correspondence between a decrease in blood pressure and subject reports of feeling relaxed and soothed by the music. Eleven studies found no differences in blood pressure due to the experimental variables.

Summary of Muscular Tension and Motor Activity Studies

Table 5 presents the results of studies on the effects of music on muscular tension and motor activity.

TABLE 5.   The Effects of Music on Muscular Tension (EMG)

Study	Experimental Variables or Results
	Significant or Meaningful Changes in Muscular Tension (EMG)
Sears 1960	Sedative music produces tension reduction more easily and quickly than stimulative music produces tension increase; females and nonmusicians show greater response in both extent and direction than males and musicians
Holdsworth 1974	High school trumpet students produced covert neuromuscular activity to both

(continued)

TABLE 5—*Continued*

Study	Experimental Variables or Results
	visual and aural musical stimuli for which they possessed performance skills
Scartelli 1982	Greater percentage decrease in tension of the finger extensor muscles of the arm in spastic cerebral palsied adults while listening to sedative instrumental music
Scartelli 1984	Decrease in microvolts between pretest and posttest using normal adult subjects tested for relaxation of the frontalis muscle under conditions of biofeedback paired with music and sedative music only
Rider 1985	Spinal pain subjects during entrainment condition in which mood shifted from tension to relaxation
Scartelli and Borling 1986	Greatest reduction with "quiet" music using psychology students with low level of music training in the condition of biofeedback training followed by music; biofeedback training preceded by music also showed reduced EMG readings
Martin 1987[a]	Comparing pretest and posttest using combinations of preferred music, progressive relaxation, and biofeedback
Davis and Thaut 1989	Significant between subjects over time while listening to preferred, relaxing music
Thaut, Schleiffers, and Davis 1991	Significant influence of auditory rhythm on biceps and triceps muscles of female students in relation to target contact and on duration of muscular activity
	No Meaningful or Significant Changes in Muscular Tension (EMG)
Sapian 1981	During dental treatment under music, lights, and analog tone feedback

(continued)

[a] Reviewed in Maranto and Bruscia 1988, 78.

TABLE 5—*Continued*

Study	Experimental Variables or Results
Scartelli 1984	Testing normal adults for frontalis relaxation between pretest and posttest using biofeedback only in comparison with biofeedback paired with music, or sedative music alone, and between different conditions of biofeedback and sedative music
Davis and Thaut 1989	Comparing baseline and preferred music listening conditions
	Meaningful or Significant Changes in Muscle Activity or Motor Activity
Safranek, Koshland, and Raymond 1982	EMG patterns of two antagonist muscles under an auditory rhythm compared to a nonauditory rhythm condition; variation of EMG activity decreased during an even rhythm
Thaut, Schleiffers, and Davis 1991	Significant effects in EMG patterns of two antagonist muscles under different conditions of auditory rhythms

EMG studies, generally, attempt to promote relaxation states through music in conjunction with biofeedback experiences. Of the nine studies showing significant changes in muscular tension, the majority were successful with sedative or relaxing music. A unique study by Holdsworth used EMG techniques to demonstrate how muscular sets in the embouchures of trumpet students are influenced by purely visual and aural stimuli related to their performance practices. Few studies showed no changes in muscular tension. Two studies, representing an emerging field of study in the late 1980s, demonstrated influences of rhythmic stimuli in mediating muscular/motor activity and provide important clinical applications related to improved synchronization of muscular effort.

Summary of Motor/Postural Response Studies

Several researchers have investigated the effects of music on motor or postural responses (see table 6).

TABLE 6.   The Effects of Music on Motor/Postural Responses

Study	Experimental Variables or Results
	Significant or Meaningful Changes in Motor/Postural Responses
Davis 1948a	A-response (onset) muscular action potentials in both forearms under loud sound stimulation using a variety of pure-tone stimuli at various high intensities; the stimulus enhances tension that previously exists
Davis 1948b	Findings similar to Davis 1948a
Fultz 1953	Measuring dominant-hand line drawing after hearing recordings of various styles of orchestral music
Stevens 1971	Tempo of rocking behavior of severely and profoundly retarded men and women under conditions of fast, medium, and slow piano music
Anshel and Marisi 1978	Bicycle-riding endurance increased when riding in synchrony with popular rock music
	No Significant or Meaningful Changes in Motor/Postural Responses
Nelson 1963	Bicycle-riding endurance under conditions of fast music, slow music, white noise, no sound, or pure tones in various tempos

Of six studies reported in the literature, five found significant or meaningful changes in motor or postural responses. Two of these five studies did not use music as a sound stimulus.

Summary of Finger or Peripheral Skin Temperature Studies

The results of research on the effects of finger or peripheral skin temperature are presented in table 7.

TABLE 7. The Effects of Music on Finger or Peripheral
Skin Temperature

Study	Experimental Variables or Results
	Significant or Meaningful Changes in Finger or Peripheral Skin Temperature
Stadum 1981	Increased finger temperature using biofeedback through visual temperature measures and sedative music
Kibler and Rider 1983	Significant increases in finger temperature under conditions of sedative music, progressive muscle relaxation, or both together
Peach 1984	Larger skin temperature increase depending on the age group and for those not taking drugs in comparison to other types of medication; temperature increases correlated with perceived relaxation for 107 short-term psychiatric inpatients, students, and staff using GMI technique
Zimmerman, Pierson, and Marker 1988	Increase over time when combining all Cardiac Care Unit (CCU) patients over all experimental conditions of listening to self-selected music, white noise, and no music/noise
Davis and Thaut 1989	Significant difference between subjects during listening to preferred, relaxing music, and in comparing baseline and music-listening conditions
Guzzetta 1989	Increased finger temperature between control group of no music therapy intervention and other conditions of relaxation induction and music listening for 80 CCU patients
Standley 1991	Increased finger temperature among auditory stimulation groups and by gender at midtest and posttest temperatures and for conditions in which music listening was either accompanied or unaccompanied by vibrotactile stimulation, and the dental drill with vibrotactile stimulation

(continued)

TABLE 7—*Continued*

Study	Experimental Variables or Results
	No Significant or Meaningful Changes in Finger or Peripheral Skin Temperature
Kibler and Rider 1983	Conditions of sedative music, progressive muscle relaxation, and a combination of music and relaxation
Zimmerman, Pierson, and Marker 1988	Conditions of self-selected music listening, white noise, and silence
Guzzetta 1989	Over time for any of the relaxation and music-listening conditions

Of seven different studies, significant increases in skin temperature were reported in all and three also reported no changes in various other hypotheses tested.

Summary of Blood Volume Studies

Table 8 presents studies on the effects of music on blood volume.

TABLE 8.   The Effects of Music on Blood Volume

Study	Experimental Variables or Results
	Significant or Meaningful Changes in Blood Volume
Sternbach 1964	Differences due to instructional sets—subjects' expectations about the experiment—under conditions of white noise and electric shock
Falb 1982[a]	Profoundly mentally retarded adults when listening to "Air on the G-string" through systematic treatment of contingent music
Davis and Thaut 1989	Significant changes between subjects over time while listening to preferred, relaxing music

(continued)

[a] Reviewed in Maranto and Bruscia 1988, 34.

TABLE 8—*Continued*

Study	Experimental Variables or Results
	No Significant or Meaningful Changes in Blood Volume
Sears 1954	Considerable variation but no definite similarities
Jellison 1975	Under conditions of exciting music, calming music, white noise, or silence with stress conditions incorporating different levels of electric shock
Pignatiello et al. 1989	Regardless of mood induction technique of elated, neutral, and depressed groups

Research on the effects of music or sound stimuli on blood volume are evenly divided: half found significant or meaningful changes and half did not. The variety of subjects, stimuli, and tasks employed make definitive conclusions difficult to reach.

Summary of Stomach Contraction Studies

The effects of music on stomach contractions are presented in table 9.

TABLE 9.   The Effects of Music on Stomach Contractions

Study	Experimental Variables or Results
Smith and Laird 1930–31	"Profound" decrease with noises of 60 dB or greater
Wilson 1957	Male nonmusicians increased gastric activity with sedative music and diminished gastric activity with stimulative music; female nonmusicians increased gastric activity with both stimulative and sedative music, and irritating music caused gastric activity to stop
Demling, Tzschoppe, and Classen 1970	Reduction of gastric activity during popular music and symphonic music by Mozart and Beethoven

All three studies found significant or meaningful changes in stomach contractions in response to music or sound stimuli.

Summary of Miscellaneous Studies

There are several physiological responses that have received little attention; the results of these four miscellaneous studies are presented in table 10.

TABLE 10.   Miscellaneous Studies

Study	Experimental Variables or Results
Lovett Doust and Schneider 1952	Blood-oxygen saturation levels of both healthy control subjects and psychiatric patients varied according to stimulation rates and intensity of stimulation under conditions of intermittent visual, auditory, and tactile stimulation; no differences between stimulation techniques
Slaughter 1954	Significant pupil dilation during stimulative music and a trend toward constriction during sedative music
Gray 1955	Hospital patients had significantly greater pilomotor response over nonhospital subjects and between musicians and nonmusicians; no difference between men and women
Dittemore 1974	No significant differences in pupillary reflex under various conditions of frequency and amplitude tasks

In one study each, significant or meaningful changes were found in blood-oxygen saturation, pilomotor response, and pupil dilation response to music or sound stimuli. No significant difference was found in pupillary reflex.

Summary of Biochemical Response Studies

The newest line of research is that of biochemical responses to music. Results of these studies are presented in table 11.

TABLE 11.   The Effects of Music on Biochemical Responses

Study	Experimental Variables or Results
	Significant or Meaningful Changes in Biochemical Responses
Oyama et al. 1987b	Decrease in ACTH (adrenocorticotropic hormone) as analyzed from blood samples taken at specified times from 50 patients during dental procedure and music listening
Tanioka et al. 1987	30 surgical patients listening through headphones under conditions of music and anaesthesia or anaesthesia alone all increased ACTH levels one hour after start of operation but no differences between groups; expected cortisol level inhibited by music listening
Rider et al. 1988	Using both music and imagery conditions, higher levels of secretory IgA were produced than in a control group; in later trials, imagery was more effective than music
Rider and Achterberg 1989	With music and imagery, neutrophils and lymphocytes decreased according to imagery focus on these blood cells
Lane 1991	Increased IgA using a music therapy treatment intervention that included a variety of activities
Tsao et al. 1991	In 99 college subjects in conditions of music, directed imagery, combined imagery and music, and no treatment, increased secretory IgA for both the music and imagery groups; control showed a significant decrease
Bartlett, Kaufman, and Smeltekop 1993	Under conditions of music listening and perceived sensory experiences in comparison to control conditions, university students with very little musical training showed increased levels of interleukin-1 and decreased levels of cortisol; no correlation between perceived sensory experiences and level changes of IL-1 or cortisol

(continued)

TABLE 11—*Continued*

Study	Experimental Variables or Results
McKinney et al. 1994	Significant pretest-posttest decline in beta-endorphin during music imaging in comparison to silent imaging, music listening, and assessment-only
	No Meaningful or Significant Changes in Biochemical Responses
Rider, Floyd, and Kirkpatrick 1985	Nonsignificant decrease of adrenal corticosteroid levels during listening to "relaxing" music by Debussy and McLaughlin
Oyama et al. 1987a	Using 60 surgical patients and measuring blood samples (taken at various times) for cortisol, B-endorphin, and ACTH related to surgery
Miller 1992	Effects on IgA or cortisol using music therapy with 12 adult cancer patients

Studies in music and biochemistry have focused on the effects of music, often in conjunction with imagery, on the immune system by measuring hormone levels found in saliva, urine, or blood serum. This relatively new research format grew out of the field of psychoneuroimmunology that emerged in the early 1980s. Two primary immune markers that most of the studies have measured are cortisol and immunoglobulin A (IgA), hormones associated with the body's attack on stress from various health-related factors. Because research in music/imagery and psychoneuroimmunology has produced only 10 studies (at least known at this time) in its short history, it is with caution that any major conclusions are drawn. However, there seems to be evidence that stress-related hormones—cortisol and IgA—can be affected in a positive way through music and imagery conditions (Bartlett, Kaufman, and Smeltekop; Lane; Rider et al.; Tanioka et al.; Tsao et al.). Three studies (Miller; Oyama et al.; and Rider et al.) produced no significant changes in stress-related hormones. One study (Bartlett, Kaufman, and Smeltekop) tested, also, for interleukin-1 (IL-1), a hormone that is important in immune effectiveness and is likely decreased in the presence of cortisol. In this case, IL-1 was increased at the same time cortisol was decreased. One study (McKinney et al.) found beta-endorphin could be lowered through a music imaging technique over other music/imaging conditions.

Discussion

The field of study that comprises the effect of music or sound stimuli on physiological response is, obviously, a field that is broad in context and long in effort. In the early stages of this research, the context of study focused on specific bodily reactions related to stimuli that have direct evoking potential for initiating changes in such endocrine-related events as heart rate and blood pressure or a variety of other "knee jerk–like" outcomes. Throughout these 120 years, the same basic endocrine-related events have been and are, to some extent, still being researched and this may suggest little change in the context of study since the first publications.

The focus of the research has seen changes, however, especially in the last 10–15 years in the following areas: (1) there is more attention given to music stimuli serving as experimental variables that are preferred by the subject (signifying greater understanding of the idiosyncratic nature of musical experience), (2) there is greater understanding of the significant contribution of imagery experience in conjunction with the music stimulus in altering subject response, (3) the field of psychoneuroimmunology has emerged, prompting relatively innovative research protocols in relation to the immune system, and (4) there has been increased interest in research on early infants. Of these factors, the last three are directly related to the growing collaboration between the disciplines of music and health sciences, a collaboration of significant value, especially, to a field such as music therapy. Much of the research in physiological response has come from individuals in that field. All of these factors, apparently, represent research interests that have helped sustain the study of physiological response up to the current time. Another major research focus has come out of the fact that several of these types of endocrine-related bodily actions are basic ingredients in emotional reactions of both humans and animals. Thus, it was more-or-less natural to accept a possible connection between the measurements of neurological and glandular systems and psychological states of affect.

What have been the outcomes of 120 years of research effort as represented here, a research effort in which many different types of physiological responses to music or sound stimuli have been investigated and a multitude of different research hypotheses have been tested? First, music and sound stimuli have been found to influence bodily systems.

Of the nearly 190 major hypotheses tested (considering those variables that are both endocrine related and those that are not) as reported in this review, 62 percent demonstrated results that seemed to correspond with intended outcomes: for example, increased heart rate when the stimulus was stimulative, decreased heart rate when the stimulus was sedative, decreased tension of muscles when relaxing music was the stimulus, decreased resistance of the skin surface when the stimulus was stimulative, increased skin temperature when the stimulus was sedative or relaxing, and decreased cortisol when the music was relaxing. Looking at heart rate specifically, a variable that comprises 39 percent of the total hypotheses tested, 41 percent were found to show no difference regardless of the type of stimuli incorporated; thus, in this case, heart-rate research generally seems not a particularly fruitful endeavor for attempting to establish a causal relationship between the stimulus and the physical reaction. In contrast, all of the skin temperature studies established positive results, based on the particular hypothesis, a variable which seems to be linked successfully to stimulus events. Considering all studies in the heart-rate/skin temperature categories (heart rate, GSR, respiration, blood pressure, skin temperature, blood volume, gastric motility, pupillary reflex, pilomotor response, and blood-oxygen saturation), 93 tested hypotheses of 153 appeared to correspond with apparent projected changes (61 percent), and 60 tested hypotheses did not correspond with apparent projected changes (39 percent). Thus, viewing all such studies, it can be concluded that the majority demonstrate physiological responses in reaction to experimental settings of music and sound stimuli. As stated in Radocy and Boyle 1988: "Few musicians or psychologists deny that music can evoke changes in the rates of bodily processes" (204). So, if future researchers choose to continue this line of research and desire only to confirm the general findings of physiological response over 120 years of study, it seems there is at least a 61 percent chance of success, with success rates ranging from 39 percent to 100 percent (depending on the variable).

But analysis of quantities and rates of behavior is only one major evaluation to be made in relation to research on physiological response. It is important to note that in very few of these studies have the independent variables been duplicated from one study to another within a response category in an effort to substantiate selected behavioral patterns. For example, though a single type or piece of stimulative music may be the experimental variable in one study, generally that specific piece was not used in a subsequent study; yet it is through replication that behavioral patterns are best established. In this case, the argument may be made that there are likely many other musics that could serve to represent stimulative music as effectively. However, even slow, legato styles may be stimulative to some individuals, given their unique histories that may include strong, conditioned responses to that music. Taylor (1973) concluded that music precategorized as stimulative or sedative did not necessarily elicit those same responses, and, as suggested by Hodges (1980), the terms *stimulative* and *sedative* as descriptors of music types may be too general to provide valid stimulus categories.

Davis and Thaut (1989) found that subjects who listened to preferred music reported responses of relaxation and anxiety reduction, even though their physiological parameters showed arousal and excitation. Their interpretation of this apparent contradiction between psychological and physiological measures was explained by referring to Berlyne (1971) and his discussion of hedonic value and arousal. He proposes that pleasure can result from a decrease from an extremely high arousal level to a lower arousal level as well as an increase from a low arousal level to a higher, but limited, level. In addition, music classified as preferred provides important qualities in one's music listening experience: preferred music is likely that which will induce heightened interest and, perhaps, stimulation whether it is of typically stimulative or sedative types.

Although a number of the studies reviewed here have demonstrated positive results, nearly as many have not. For example, the testing of major hypotheses in heart-rate studies produced the following: 16 showed increased rates, 25 showed decreased rates, and 28 showed neither increased nor decreased rates. To account for the obvious lack of evidence from the studies of heart rate (and other physiological categories) that would provide a clear picture of the influence of musical or sound stimuli on bodily response, Dainow (1977), Grings and Dawson (1978), Harrer and Harrer (1977), and Hodges (1980) suggest possible design control issues that may act as contaminating variables. These include instructions to, and verbal response requirements of, subjects; cognitive activity unrelated to the experiment; stimulus intensity; subject attention span; subject attitude and set; anxiety from instrumentation "hook-up"; and musical education and training of the subject. Dainow suggests, also, that the act of music listening as a related issue to the research process involves not only a "purely sensory input . . . but a whole range of sensory and ideational or cognitive modes . . . including intellectual analysis or criticism" (Dainow 1977, 217; see Schachter 1957 for a discussion of effects of cognitive factors on the appraisal of bodily states). If one asks a research subject to listen to music for the purpose of securing a rate change in some bodily response, one must also try to provide some control over experimental conditions that can assure types of music-listening response modes pertinent to those conditions. The assurance of such control is highly improbable.

Second, the years of research have revealed some attempt to deal with the possible affective concomitants that may help explain the ways in which music enhances or alters our psychological states. The theory of emotion proposed by James, and later James-Lange, in the late 1800s (see the previous discussion in this chapter) "set up" researchers in psychophysiology to the possibilities of isolating specific musical/sound stimuli as possible links to the nature of emotional, thus psychological, behaviors. And it is in this area of study that most disappointments may be directed, if, in fact, one is looking for connections of this type.

Making a determination of the nature of one's psychological state relies heavily on various methods of self report. Generally, analysis of such reporting is of the subjective and nonverifiable types (such as is experienced in introspective techniques) or the more objective and verifiable types (such as is experienced in various scaling techniques). Researchers of physiological response have relied on the more objective types of analysis, incorporating such measures as mood scales, adjective checklists, like/dislike scales, and perceived anxiety states. It is generally through these types of measures that insights into the possible connections between physical responses and psychological states have been addressed.

One of the several studies (though relatively few in comparison to the whole body of research) that serves as an example of the attempt to "connect" the psychological and the physiological is by Dreher (1948), who found that musically trained subjects were better able to describe the mood characteristics of piano music and that these descriptions, which were obtained using the Hevner Adjective Checklist, were highly correlated with lower resistance measured by the GSR technique. In his paper, it is not clear whether the subjects were to indicate only the "intended" mood of the music or whether the music actually "induced" their mood conditions and descriptions. It is likely that the task in this case was to discern the mood character of the music, a task that garners little information toward our understanding of the nature of the response. Literature surveys of mood effects of music from both Dreher as reported in Lundin 1967 and Eagle 1971 concluded there to be little difference in the ability of persons to describe the mood effects of music on the basis of intelligence, musical training, or age. These factors likely are not significantly related to mood description because the measurement question itself provides a relatively superficial insight into mood as a psychological entity, and the acculturation of people within a broad segment of society is, perhaps, sufficient to condition those within the society to respond to general impressions of the mood language of music. In conclusion, Dreher's study contributes little substance about the connection between GSR response and states of mood.

As a closing thought, experience tells us that music is capable of enhancing and/or altering our psychological state and of causing us to feel and to emote. In theory, however, we may never completely be able to demonstrate, through experimental research, an understanding of why music has that capability. Yet we continue to try.

REFERENCES

Anshel, M. H., and D. Q. Marisi. 1978. Effect of music and rhythm on physical performance. *Research Quarterly* 49, no. 2:109–13.

Armatas, C. 1964. A study of the effect of music on postoperative patients in the recovery room. Master's thesis, University of Kansas.

Barger, D. A. 1979. The effects of music and verbal suggestion on heart rate and self-reports. *Journal of Music Therapy* 16, no. 4:158–71.

Barker, L. W. 1991. The use of music and relaxation techniques to reduce pain of burn patients during daily debridement. In *Applications of music in medicine*, ed. C. D. Maranto, 124–40. Washington, DC: National Association for Music Therapy.

Bartlett, D., D. Kaufman, and R. Smeltekop. 1993. The effects of music listening and perceived sensory experiences on the immune system as measured by interleukin-1 and cortisol. *Journal of Music Therapy* 30, no. 4:194–209.

Bartlett, R. J. 1925. Does the psychogalvanic phenomenon indicate emotion? *British Journal of Psychology* (July), pt. 1, no. 18:30–50.

Beckett, A. 1990. The effects of music on exercise as determined by physiological recovery heart rates and distance. *Journal of Music Therapy* 27, no. 3:126–36.

Berlyne, D. E. 1971. *Aesthetics and psychobiology.* New York: Appleton-Century-Crofts.

Bierbaum, M. A. 1958. Variations in heart action under the influence of musical stimuli. Master's thesis, University of Kansas.

Bindra, D. 1970. Emotion and behavior theory: Current research in historical perspective. In *Physiological correlates of emotion*, ed. P. Black, 3–18. New York: Academic Press.

Bonny, H. L. 1983. Music listening for intensive coronary care units: A pilot project. *Music Therapy* 3, no. 1:4–16.

Boring, G. B. 1950. *A history of experimental psychology.* 2d ed. New York: Appleton-Century-Crofts.

Brackbill, Y., G. Adams, D. H. Crowell, and M. L. Gray. 1966. Arousal level in neonates and preschool children under continuous auditory stimulation. *Journal of Experimental Child Psychology* 4:178–88.

Clarke, G. L. 1981. The influence of frequencies equated for subjective loudness on heart rate. Master's thesis, University of Kansas.

Clynes, M. 1977. *Sentics: The touch of emotions.* New York: Anchor Press.

Clynes, M., and N. Nettheim. 1982. The living quality of music: Neurobiologic basis of communicating feeling. In *Music, mind, and brain*, ed. M. Clynes, 47–82. New York: Plenum Press.

Coleman, W. M. 1920. On the correlation of the rate of heart beat, breathing, bodily movement, and sensory stimuli. *Journal of Physiology* 54:213–17.

Corning, J. L. 1899. The use of musical vibrations before and during sleep. *Medical Record* 55:79–86.

Coutts, C. A. 1965. Effects of music on pulse rates and work output of short duration. *Research Quarterly* 36:17–21.

Dainow E. 1977. Physical effects and motor responses to music. *Journal of Research in Music Education* 25:211–21.

Darner, C. L. 1966. Sound pulses and the heart. *Journal of the Acoustical Society of America* 39:414–16.

Davis, C. A. 1992. The effects of music and basic relaxation instruction on pain and anxiety of women undergoing in-office gynecological procedures. *Journal of Music Therapy* 29, no. 4:202–16.

Davis, R. C. 1934. Modification of the galvanic reflex by daily repetition of a stimulus. *Journal of Experimental Psychology* 17:504–35.

Davis, R. C. 1948a. Motor effects of strong auditory stimuli. *Journal of Experimental Psychology* 38:257–75.

Davis, R. C. 1948b. Responses to "meaningful" and "meaningless" sounds. *Journal of Experimental Psychology* 38:744–56.

Davis, W. B., and M. H. Thaut. 1989. The influence of preferred relaxing music on measures of state anxiety, relaxation, and physiological responses. *Journal of Music Therapy* 26, no. 4:168–87.

Davis-Rollans, C., and S. Cunningham. 1987. Physiologic responses of coronary care patients to selected music. *Heart-Lung* 16:370–78.

De Jong, M. A., K. R. van Mourik, and H. M. Schellekens. 1973. A physiological approach to aesthetic preference—music. *Psychotherapy and Psychosomatics* 22:46–51.

Demling, L., M. Tzschoppe, and M. Classen. 1970. The effects of various types of music on the secretory functions of the stomach. *American Journal of Digestive Diseases* 15:15–20.

Diserens, C. M. 1923. Reactions to musical stimuli. *Psychological Bulletin* 20:173–99.

Diserens, C. M. 1926. *The Influence of music on behavior*. Princeton, NJ: Princeton University Press.

Dittemore, D. C. 1974. Pupillary responses in frequency and amplitude discrimination tasks. Master's thesis, University of Kansas.

Dreher, R. E. 1948. The relationship between verbal reports and galvanic skin responses to music. *American Psychologist* 3:275–76.

Eagle, C. T. 1971. Effects of existing mood and order presentation of vocal and instrumental music on rated mood responses to that music. Ph.D. diss., University of Kansas.

Ellis, D. S., and G. Brighouse. 1952. Effects of music on respiration and heart rate. *American Journal of Psychology* 65:39–47.

Farnsworth, P. R. 1969. *The social psychology of music*. 2d ed. Ames: Iowa State University Press.

Foster, E., and E. A. M. Gamble. 1906. The effect of music on thoracic breathing. *American Journal of Psychology* 17:406–14.

Fultz, A. F. 1953. Music impressional effects on automatograph line-drawing. In *Music therapy*, ed. E. G. Gilliland, 273–76. Lawrence, KS: Allen Press.

Geden, E. A., M. Lower, S. Beattie, and N. Beck. 1989. Effects of music and imagery on physiologic and self-report of analogued labor pain. *Nursing Research* 38, no. 1:37–41.

Graham, R. K., and R. K. Clifton. 1966. Heart-rate change as a component of the orienting response. *Psychological Bulletin* 65, no. 5:305–20.

Gray, R. M. 1955. The pilomotor reflex in response to music. Master's thesis, University of Kansas.

Greenfield, N. S., and R. A. Sternbach. 1972. *Handbook of psychophysiology*. New York: Holt, Rinehart and Winston.

Grimwade, J. C., D. W. Walker, M. Bartlett, S. Gordon, and C. Wood. 1971. Human fetal heart rate change and movement in response to sound and vibration. *American Journal of Obstetrics and Gynecology* 109, no. 1:86–90.

Grings, W. W., and M. E. Dawson. 1978. *Emotions and bodily responses: A psychophysiological approach*. New York: Academic Press.

Guzzetta, C. 1989. Effects of relaxation and music therapy on patients in a coronary care unit with presumptive acute myocardial infarction. *Heart Lung* 18:609–16.

Haack, J. S. 1991. Music therapy-assisted childbirth and its effects on duration of labor, medication dosage, and fetal heart rate. Master's thesis, University of Kansas.

Haas, F., S. Distenfeld, and K. Axen. 1986. Effects of perceived musical rhythm on respiratory patterns. *Journal of Applied Physiology* 61, nos. 1–3:1185–91.

Harrer, G., and H. Harrer. 1977. Music, emotion, and autonomic function. In *Music and the brain*, eds. M. Critchley and R. A. Henson, 202–16. London: William Heinemann Medical Books.

Henkin, R. I. 1957. The prediction of behavior response patterns to music. *Journal of Psychology* 44:111–27.

Hodges, D. A., ed. 1980. *Handbook of music psychology*. Lawrence, KS: National Association for Music Therapy.

Hoffman, J. 1980. Management of essential hypertension through relaxation training with sound. Master's thesis, University of Kansas.

Holdsworth, E. 1974. Neuromuscular activity and covert musical psychomotor behavior: An electromyographic study. Ph.D. diss., University of Kansas.

Hyde, I. M. 1927. Effects of music upon electrocardiograms and blood pressure. In *The effects of music*, ed. M. Schoen, 184–98. New York: Harcourt, Brace.

Hyde, I., and W. Scalapino. 1918. Influence of music upon electrocardiograms and blood pressure. *American Journal of Physiology* 46:35–38.

Jellison, J. A. 1975. The effect of music on autonomic stress responses and verbal reports. In *Research in music behavior: Modifying music behavior in the classroom*, eds. C. K. Madsen, R. D. Greer, and C. H. Madsen, 206–19. New York: Teachers College Press.

Johnson, D. M., and M. Trawick. 1938. Influence of rhythmic sensory stimuli upon the heart rate. *Journal of Psychology* 6:303–10.

Kagan, J., and M. Lewis. 1965. Studies of attention in the human infant. *Merrill-Palmer Quarterly* 11:95–127.

Keller, S., and P. Seraganian. 1984. Physical fitness level and autonomic reactivity to psychosocial stress. *Journal of Psychosomatic Research* 28, no. 4:279–87.

Kibler, V. E., and M. S. Rider. 1983. The effect of progressive muscle relaxation and music on stress as measured by finger temperature response. *Journal of Clinical Psychology* 39:213–15.

Kneutgen, J. 1970. Eine Musikform und ihre biologische Funktion: Uber die Wirkungsweise der Weigenlieder. *Zeitschrift für Experimentelle und Angewandte Psychologie* 17:245–65.

Landreth, J. E., and H. F. Landreth. 1974. Effects of music on physiological response. *Journal of Research in Music Education* 22, no. 1:4–12.

Lane, D. L. 1991. The effect of a single music therapy session on hospitalized children as measured by salivary immunoglobulin A, speech pause time, and a patient opinion Likert scale. *Pediatric Research* 29, no. 4, pt. 2:11A.

Lewis, M. 1971. A developmental study of the cardiac response to stimulus onset and offset during the first year of life. *Psychophysiology* 8, no. 6:689–98.

Lorch, C. A., V. Lorch, A. O. Diefendorf, and P. W. Earl. 1994. Effect of stimulative and sedative music on systolic blood pressure, heart rate, and respiratory rate in premature infants. *Journal of Music Therapy* 31, no. 2:105–18.

Loscin, R. G. 1981. The effect of music on the pain of selected postoperative patients. *Journal of Advanced Nursing* 6:19–25.

Lovell, G. D., and J. J. B. Morgan. 1942. Physiological and motor responses to a regularly recurring sound: A study in monotony. *Journal of Experimental Psychology* 30:435–51.

Lovett Doust, J. W., and R. A. Schneider. 1952. Studies on the physiology of awareness: The effect of rhythmic sensory bombardment on emotions, blood oxygen saturation, and the levels of consciousness. *Journal of Mental Science* 98:640–53.

Lundin, R. W. 1967. *An objective psychology of music.* 2d ed. New York: Ronald Press.

Madsen, C. K., J. M. Standley, and D. Gregory. 1991. The effect of a vibrotactile device, somatron, on physiological and psychological responses: Musicians versus nonmusicians. *Journal of Music Therapy* 28, no. 1:14–22.

Malcom, G. L. 1981. Effect of rhythm on heart rate of musicians. Master's thesis, University of Kansas.

Maranto, C. D., and K. Bruscia, eds. 1988. *Master's theses in music therapy: Index and abstracts.* Vol. 3. Philadelphia: Temple University.

Maranto, C. D., and J. Scartelli. 1992. Music in the treatment of immune-related disorders. In *MusicMedicine*, eds. R. Spintge and R. Droh, 142–54. MMB Music.

McKinney, C. H., F. C. Tims, A. Kumar, and M. Kumar. 1994. Music, imagery, and plasma beta-endorphin. Paper presented at the 45th Annual Conference of the National Association for Music Therapy, 17–21 November, Orlando, Florida.

Menegazzi, J. J. 1991. A randomized, controlled trial of the use of music during laceration repair. *Emergency Medical Abstracts* 20, no. 4: 348.

Meyer, L. 1956. *Emotion and meaning in music.* Chicago: University of Chicago Press.

Meyers, W. J., and G. R. Gullickson. 1967. The evoked heart rate response: The influence of auditory stimulus repetition, pattern reversal, and autonomic arousal level. *Psychophysiology* 4, no. 1:56–66.

Miller, D. M. 1992. The effect of music therapy on the immune and adrenocortical systems of cancer patients. Master's thesis, University of Kansas.

Miluk-Kolasa, B. Z. 1993. Effects of listening to music on selected physiological variables and anxiety level in presurgical patients. Ph.D. diss., Institute of Surgery, Medical University at Lodz, Warsaw.

Misbach, L. E. 1932. Effect of pitch of tone-stimuli upon body resistance and cardiovascular phenomena. *Journal of Experimental Psychology* 15:167–83.

Nelson, D. O. 1963. Effects of selected rhythms and sound intensity on human performance as measured by the bicycle ergometer. *Research Quarterly* 34:484–88.

Oyama, T., Y. Sato, M. Judo, R. Spintge, and R. Droh. 1987a. Effect of anxiolytic music on endocrine function in surgical patients. In *Music in medicine*, eds. R. Spintge and R. Droh, 169–74. Berlin: Springer-Verlag.

Oyama, T., K. Hatano, Y. Sato, M. Kudo, R. Spintge, and R. Droh. 1987b. Endocrine effect of anxiolytic music in dental patients. In *Music in Medicine*, eds. R. Spintge and R. Droh, 223–26. Berlin: Springer-Verlag.

Parmentier, J. C. 1990. The effects of verbal suggestion with music to reduce state anxiety levels on female college students. Master's thesis, Texas Women's University.

Peach, S. C. 1984. Some implications for the clinical use of music facilitated imagery. *Journal of Music Therapy* 21, no. 1:27–34.

Peretti, P. O., and K. Swenson. 1974. Effects of music on anxiety as determined by physiological skin responses. *Journal of Research in Music Education* 22, no. 4:278–83.

Phares, M. L. 1934. Analysis of music appreciation by means of psychogalvanic reflex technique. *Journal of Experimental Psychology* 17:119–40.

Pignatiello, M., C. J. Camp, S. T. Elder, and L. A. Rasar. 1989. A psychophysiological comparison of the Velten and musical mood induction techniques. *Journal of Music Therapy* 26, no. 3:140–54.

Plutchik, R. 1959. The effects of high intensity intermittent sound on performance, feeling, and physiology. *Psychology Bulletin* 56, no. 2:133–51.

Pujol, K. K. 1994. The effect of vibrotactile stimulation, instrumentation, and precomposed melodies on physiological and behavioral responses of profoundly retarded children and adults. *Journal of Music Therapy* 31, no. 3:186–205.

Radocy, R. E., and J. D. Boyle. 1988. *Psychological foundations of musical behavior*. Springfield, IL: Charles C. Thomas.

Rider, M. S. 1985. Entrainment mechanisms are involved in pain reduction, muscle relaxation, and music-mediated imagery. *Journal of Music Therapy* 22, no. 4:183–92.

Rider, M. S., and J. Achterberg. 1989. Effect of music-assisted imagery on neutrophils and lymphocytes. *Biofeedback and Self-Regulation* 14, no. 3:247–57.

Rider, M. S., J. Achterberg, G. F. Lawlis, A. Goven, R. Toledo, and J. R. Butler. 1988. Effect of biological imagery on antibody production and health. Typescript.

Rider, M. S., J. W. Floyd, and J. Kirkpatrick. 1985. The effect of music, imagery, and relaxation on adrenal corticosteroids and the re-entrainment of circadian rhythms. *Journal of Music Therapy* 22, no. 1:46–58.

Ries, H. A. 1969. GSR and breathing amplitude related to emotional reactions to music. *Psychonomic Science* 14, no. 2:62.

Ruiz, O. M. 1979. Effect of music on heart rate. Master's thesis, University of Kansas.

Safranek, M., G. Koshland, and G. Raymond. 1982. Effect of auditory rhythm on muscle activity. *Physical Therapy* 62:161–68.

Sapian, A. 1981. The comparison of music, lights, and analog tone as feedback in reducing muscle tension and anxiety levels in dental hygiene patients. Master's thesis, Texas Women's University.

Scartelli, J. P. 1982. The effect of sedative music on electromyographic biofeedback-assisted relaxation training of spastic cerebral palsied adults. *Journal of Music Therapy* 19, no. 4:210–18.

Scartelli, J. P. 1984. The effect of EMG biofeedback and sedative music, EMG biofeedback only, and sedative music only on frontalis muscle relaxation ability. *Journal of Music Therapy* 21, no. 2:67–78.

Scartelli, J. P., and J. E. Borling. 1986. The effects of sequenced versus simultaneous EMG biofeedback and sedative music on frontalis relaxation training. *Journal of Music Therapy* 23, no. 3:157–65.

Schachter, S. 1964. The interaction of cognitive and physiological determinants of emotional state. *Advances in Experimental Psychology* 1:49–80.

Schoen, M., ed. 1927. *The effects of music.* New York: Harcourt, Brace.

Schoen, M. 1940. *The psychology of music.* New York: Ronald Press.

Schuster, B. L. 1985. The effect of music listening on blood pressure fluctuations in adult hemodialysis patients. *Journal of Music Therapy* 22, no. 3:146–53.

Sears, M. A. 1954. Study of the vascular changes in the capillaries as effected by music. Master's thesis, University of Kansas.

Sears, W. W. 1960. A study of some effects of music upon muscle tension as evidenced by electromyographic recordings. Ph.D. diss., University of Kansas.

Shatin, L. 1957. The influence of rhythmic drumbeat stimuli upon the pulse rate and general activity of long-term schizophrenics. *Journal of Mental Science* 103:172–88.

Shepard, J. P. 1906. Organic changes and feeling. *American Journal of Psychology* 17:521–84.

Shrift, D. C. 1957. The Galvanic skin response to two contrasting types of music. In *Music Therapy*, ed. E. T. Gaston, 235–39. Lawrence, KS: Allen Press.

Slaughter, F. 1954. The effect of stimulative and sedative types of music on normal and abnormal subjects as indicated by pupillary reflexes. In *Music Therapy*, ed. M. Bing, 246–48. Lawrence, KS: Allen Press.

Smith, E. L., and D. A. Laird. 1930–31. The loudness of auditory stimuli which affect stomach contractions in healthy human beings. *Journal of the Acoustical Society of America* 2:94–98.

Soibelman, D. 1948. *Therapeutic and industrial uses of music.* New York: Columbia University Press.

Stadum, K. 1981. Music as an adjunct to temperature biofeedback in the reduction of music performance anxiety. Master's thesis, Texas Women's University.

Standley, J. M. 1986. Music research in medical/dental treatment: Meta-analysis and clinical applications. *Journal of Music Therapy* 23, no. 2:56–122.

Standley, J. M. 1991. The effect of vibrotactile and auditory stimuli on perception of comfort, heart rate, and peripheral finger temperature. *Journal of Music Therapy* 28, no 3:120–34.

Standley, J. M., and C. K. Madsen. 1990. Comparison of infant preferences and responses to auditory stimuli: Music, mother, and other female voice. *Journal of Music Therapy* 27, no. 2:54–97.

Sternbach, R. A. 1964. The effects of instructional sets on autonomic responsivity. *Psychophysiology* 1:67–72.

Stevens, E. A. 1971. Some effects of tempo changes on stereotyped rocking movements of low-level mentally retarded subjects. *American Journal of Mental Deficiency* 76:76–81.

Sunderman, L. F. 1946. A study of some physiological differences between musicians and nonmusicians, 1: Blood pressure. *Journal of Social Psychology* 23:205–15.

Tanioka, F., T. Takazawa, S. Kamata, M. Kudo, A. Matsuki, and T. Oyama. 1987. Hormonal effect of anxiolytic music in patients during surgical operations under epidural anesthesia. In *Music in Medicine*, eds. R. Spintge and R. Droh, 199–204. Berlin: Springer-Verlag.

Taylor, D. B. 1973. Subject responses to precategorized stimulative and sedative music. *Journal of Music Therapy* 10, no. 2: 86–94.

Thaut, M., S. Schleiffers, and W. Davis. 1991. Analysis of EMG activity in biceps and triceps muscle in an upper extremity gross motor task under the influence of auditory rhythm. *Journal of Music Therapy* 28, no. 2:64–88.

Tsao, C. C., T. F. Gordon, C. D. Maranto, C. Lerman, and D. Murasko. 1991. The effects of music and directed biological imagery on immune response S-IgA. In *Applications of Music in Medicine*, ed. C. D. Maranto, 85–121. Washington, DC: National Association for Music Therapy.

Updike, P. A., and D. M. Charles. 1987. Music Rx: Physiological and emotional responses to taped music programs of preoperative patients awaiting plastic surgery. *Annals of Plastic Surgery* 19, no. 1:29–33.

Washco, Jr., A. 1933. *The effects of music upon pulse rate, blood pressure, and mental imagery*. Philadelphia: n.p.

Wechsler, D. 1925. The measurement of emotional reactions: Researches on the psychogalvanic reflex. *Archives of Psychology* 76:1–181.

Weidenfeller, E. W., and G. H. Zimny. 1962. Effects of music upon GSR of depressives and schizophrenics. *Journal of Abnormal and Social Psychology* 64, no. 4:307–12.

Weld, H. P. 1912. An experimental study of musical enjoyment. *American Journal of Psychology* 23:245–308.

Wilson, V. M. 1957. Variations in gastric motility due to musical stimuli. In *Music therapy*, ed. E. T. Gaston, 243–49. Lawrence, KS: Allen Press.

Wilson, C. V., and L. S. Aiken. 1977. The effect of intensity levels upon physiological and subjective affective response to rock music. *Journal of Music Therapy* 14, no. 2:60–76.

Winold, A. 1959. The effect of changes in harmonic tension on the galvanic skin responses. In *Music therapy*, ed. E. Schneider, 188–92. Lawrence, KS: Allen Press.

Young, P. T. 1973. Feeling and emotion. In *Handbook of general psychology*, ed. B. B. Wolman, 749–71. Englewood Cliffs, NJ: Prentice-Hall.

Zimmerman, L. M., M. A. Pierson, and J. Marker. 1988. Effects of music on patient anxiety in coronary care units. *Heart-Lung* 17:560–66.

Zimny, G. H., and E. W. Weidenfeller. 1962. Effects of music upon gsr of children. *Child Development* 33:891–96.

Zimny, G. H., and E. W. Weidenfeller. 1963. Effects of music on GSR and heart rate. *American Journal of Psychology* 76:311–14.

10

The Musical Experience and Affective/Aesthetic Responses: A Theoretical Framework for Empirical Research

Patrick T. McMullen

Researchers have long maintained an interest in the relationship between music and affective/aesthetic behavior, but, unfortunately, most work has not resulted in a clear understanding of this behavior. When I attempted to explore this relationship in the first edition of the *Handbook of Music Psychology* by summarizing the available research into some type of meaningful whole, I met with frustration. As stated in the first edition, "the initial intent . . . was to synthesize the available research examining a relationship between music as a stimulus object and affective responses. After extensive study and repeated drafts, no clear pattern could be deduced from the results of the various studies" (McMullen 1980, 183). In the same publication, Abeles stated the need for a theoretical perspective by stating "the problem limiting the progress in establishing such relationships [i.e., between affective/aesthetic responses to music] appears to be related to the lack of a theory which states the expected relationships between relevant constructs and a theory which is easily operationalized." He goes on to say, "current popular theoretical explanations of affective/aesthetic responses to music do not provide researchers with an effective guide with which to organize their work" (Abeles 1980, 134). Since these concerns were expressed in the 1980 edition of the *Handbook*, little progress is evident in resolving the issue.

A critical examination of this situation suggests that the philosophical paradigm on which such research is based still needs to be reconsidered by the field. Second, a theoretical framework needs to be adopted that incorporates a reconsidered paradigm and includes literature from fields outside what is traditional to music psychology. Although it is beyond the scope of this *Handbook* and the available space to examine fully all the philosophical and theoretical considerations, it is my intent to present a brief framework that takes some of these factors into consideration.

Researchers are often unaware that they work within philosophical frameworks that not only influence the methodologies used in empirical study, but also condition the kinds of questions asked and the research modes employed. Kuhn (1970) and Masterman (1970) call these unexamined assumptions, paradigms. Until now, most affective/aesthetic research has been conducted within what might be called a psychoacoustical paradigm. Since there does not seem to be any clear framework resulting from the work that has been undertaken within this paradigm, it can be questioned whether it is appropriate for such research. I maintain that researchers must consider adopting an alternative paradigm in order to explore any relationships between music and affective/aesthetic behavior more fully.

Brewster Smith, former president of the American Psychological Association, has outlined two approaches or paradigms for psychology that should be considered for research on this topic.

> The contrast . . . is that between the perspective of causal understanding, traditionally from a standpoint external to the behaving person, and that of interpretative understanding, traditionally from one internal to the person's perspective, a realm of feelings, meanings and values.
>
> The causal perspective, as applied to human beings, finds continuity with the natural sciences of the physical and biological world. The interpretative perspective emphasizes the uniqueness of human beings as symbolizing, culture-bearing, historical creatures who act in a frame of past and future, who can make sense or nonsense to themselves. (Smith 1978, 33)

Much of the research exploring the relationship between music and affective/aesthetic behaviors has been undertaken within the causal perspective (or paradigm) when the answer might lie within an alternative interpretative framework.

To understand the relationship between music and aesthetic/affective behavior several assumptions need to be examined. Given the limitations of this publication, only a few will be noted here. First, is the concept of music as it relates to affective/aesthetic behavior a construct internal to the human perceptual system or should it be something that is an external concept that can easily be quantified? Second, a parallel question should be whether using components of music (such as intervals, pitch, or tempo) in the research framework provide any insight into this relationship between music and affective/aesthetic behavior? Third, is the assumption of causality essential to understanding the relationship between music and affective/aesthetic behavior, or is the nature of the relationship quite different? Fourth, what is affective behavior and how does it relate to whatever is defined as music?

Key to this difference of paradigms is the assumption, in the predominant psychoacoustical paradigm, of music being external and independent of human subjectivity. Such research regards musical stimuli as if they are physical objects that can be quantified and manipulated in much the same manner as rocks or other material objects. The interpretative paradigm, and the one being proposed for affective/aesthetic research, would approach the musical experience as an internal event.

To illustrate this difference, consider the ink spots shown in figure 1. Many would perceive this as a triangle. But is the triangle external to human consciousness? It can be argued that only the ink spots are external to human consciousness (and quantum physics would even debate that; see d'Espagnat 1979), and that the concept of triangle is being created by the human mind as a result of interpreting the arrangement of spots. The same process applies to music. All that physically exists external to human consciousness is the arrangement of acoustical properties. When the human mind interprets these properties as meaningful, only then can an affective response be considered.

Fig. 1. Ink spots or triangle?

The adoption of the interpretative paradigm does not eliminate a functional connection between the arrangement of physical properties and what is interpreted as meaningful. Rather, the adoption of an interpretative paradigm only eliminates the assumption that an arrangement of properties in "physical" reality is interpreted by human beings in exactly the same manner as presented in the physical world. While the ink spots shown in figure 1 might be seen as a certain placement in space, to interpret them as a triangle or any other meaningful configuration is based on the perspective and experiences of the interpreter. (See the discussions of the Gestalt law of *Prägnanz* in chaps. 5 and 11.)

In addition to the philosophical framework within which such research is conceived, scholars and researchers must also develop and refine theoretical frameworks to guide research studies. Any particular study will be nothing more than an individual exercise in how to quantify variables and compute statistics outside a theoretical position. The common statement that "more research is necessary" is often an admission of not knowing the next step, rather than a desire to gain further knowledge about a topic. A theoretical framework should provide a road map of where to consider undertaking the next study, and it should provide a larger picture into which information from previous studies can be placed. Researchers must constantly be developing, critically examining, and modifying theoretical frameworks on which to base research, at all times taking into consideration the philosophical underpinning on which these theoretical positions are based. Abeles (chap. 8) has commented on the lack of a theory as the problem limiting the progress in establishing such relationships between affective/aesthetic responses to music.

The theoretical position proposed here is shaped within that described by Smith as an interpretative paradigm. He states that the interpretative perspective "emphasizes the uniqueness of human beings as symbolizing, culture-bearing, historical creatures who act in a frame of past and future, who can make sense or nonsense to themselves" (1978, 33). Although the theory hypothesized in this chapter has implications for cultural interpretation, at the level proposed, the intention is to be precultural or what might be referred to as the nature level. It is theorized that the dimensions proposed are common to all human beings (and possibly many living creatures) prior to any modification by human culture, education, or other variables. How each dimension is ultimately interpreted, modified, or quantified would be a function of a level of specificity above this most basic level and would change according to cultural differences.

It is hypothesized that understanding the relationships between musical stimuli and affective/aesthetic behavior is predicated on a two-dimensional framework (activation and some form of acceptance-rejection/evaluation). This framework can be found in the literature from a number of authors who have attempted to define the nature of emotions from the dimensional perspective. The basic elements of such a theory suggests that, first, the musical experience includes some form of activation or arousal. Second, human beings, in turn, make judgments about this perceived activation. The most basic judgment of these perceptions have the characteristic of being either accepted or rejected (an evaluation or assessment process). Eventually this would become the basis for preference and taste judgments in more sophisticated forms. Third, there is some evidence to suggest that these two concepts (activation and evaluation) are related to each other in the form of an inverted U-shaped curve.

The Musical Experience and Activation

The concept of activation (or arousal) can be found throughout the psychological literature. Although defined in various manners, activation is often referred to as a heightened state of arousal, either psychological, physiological, or behavioral (Fantino 1973). Lynn (1972) has stated that activation is commonly used synonymously with arousal. Some authors have used it as a basis for developing a dimensional framework for emotions. The theoretical work of D. E. Berlyne made a major contribution to understanding the relationship between activation/arousal and affective/aesthetic behavior, although much of it appears to be conceived within the causal rather than interpretative paradigm. From the more interpretative perspective, the work of Osgood, Suci, and Tannenbaum (1957) in developing the semantic differential has shown that one of the key factors in describing connotative meaning is an activity dimension.

Applying the concept of activation to musical stimuli (within the interpretative paradigm) suggests that researchers seeking to understand the relationship between music and affective/aesthetic behavior may be asking the wrong questions. The problem is not what is the relationship between music and affective/aesthetic behavior, but rather what is the relationship between what is perceived as a result of the musical experience and affective/aesthetic behavior. In other words, researchers usually seek to quantify musical stimuli by type (e.g., march or opera aria), historical period, or components of the stimuli (e.g., fast or slow tempo) rather than quantifying something resulting from the musical experience. In 1979, I used an analogy involving beef and protein to clarify this point. The human body does not need beef to maintain itself—it needs protein, which is contained within the beef. The same is true for this framework. While I am not prepared to state that activation is contained within the music, human beings do appear to encounter activation within the musical experience, and it is the activation that becomes the foundation for a possible explanation of a relationship to affective/aesthetic behavior. For too long researchers may have been seeking to quantify the wrong variable—music. A more productive approach might be to define and quantify the activation involved in the musical experience.

There appear to be two forms (or subdimensions) of activation—which I have labeled structure and energy (McMullen 1977a, 1977b, and 1978). The principles of simultaneous (energy) and successive or sequential (structure) mental processing has been suggested by Das, Kirby, and Jarman (1979). A review of the education literature will reveal that such differences in processing are common. It is theorized that, throughout the musical experience, both of these forms of processing (related to the subdimensions of activation) are present, although one may be dominant depending upon a variety of background and immediate variables. For example, informal analysis would suggest that some teenage individuals experiencing rock and roll would tend to be more involved in the energy subdimensions. More experienced listeners might focus on the structure aspects, especially when listening to more complex music such as Mozart or Beethoven (vs. rock and roll).

The first subdimension or form of activation is structure, which involves some type of comparison process between events at different points in the time continuum. Quite possibly this subdimension is a function of successive, sequential, or linear processing. Labels such as simplicity or complexity (since each of these dimensions are bipolar in nature), order, clarity, and degree of comprehensibility often are used to describe the structure dimension.

The concept of collative variables suggested by Berlyne (1971 and 1973) would be closely related—possibly even identical—to the structure subdimension of activation. Berlyne has included as collative variables such continua as familiar-novel, simple-complex, expected-surprising, ambiguous-clear, and stable-variable. Meyer (1956) has explored the concept of expectation for musical stimuli, which would also fall within the framework of the structure dimension. In essence, Berlyne has included an expectation concept within his collative variables with the inclusion of the expected-surprising continuum.

The energy subdimension or form of activation seems to represent the results of simultaneous or holistic processing of the stimulus material. As with the structure subdimension, this is possibly related to a type of mental processing. Using verbal scaling techniques, labels associated with this dimension are terms such as *excitement, energy, intensity,* and *stimulation.* Initially, I suggested that tempo and physical intensity contained in the stimulus represented the energy dimension (McMullen 1978). Berlyne had proposed psychophysical variables for aural stimuli that included such acoustical properties as intensity and waveform. In a later publication, he seems to expand this type of variable to include a tempo concept. He states that psychophysical variables include "intensity, color, and rate of change, which are a matter of spatial and temporal distribution of energy" (Berlyne 1973, 14). But such suggestions imply a causal paradigm. With the adoption of an interpretative paradigm, the physical or temporal configurations labeled as intensity and tempo are likely to be explained as more easily processed in a holistic manner, thereby appearing to be dominant factors.

The Musical Experience and Acceptance-Rejection/Evaluation

Humans (and probably other living creatures) use an acceptance-rejection evaluation process as a means of responding to their environment. The most basic judgment of these perceptions has the characteristic of valuing, which probably becomes the basis for preference and taste judgments in more sophisticated forms. Research suggests that hedonic tone/ preference responses are related to activation (or some aspect of it, such as perceived complexity) in the form of an inverted U-shaped curve (see Burke and Gridley 1990; Crozier 1974; Davies 1978; Hargreaves 1984; Heyduk 1975; Vitz 1966). If perceived activation is too high or too low, the perceiver rejects (or values it less), but it is accepted (or valued) to a greater degree within a middle range (see fig. 2).

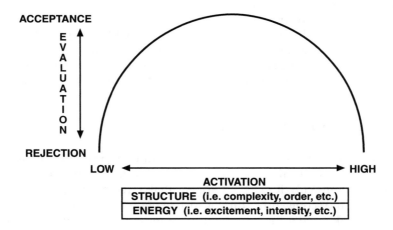

Fig. 2. **Two-dimensional framework of affective/aesthetic responses. The perceived level of activation (comprised of the perceived structure and energy elements) is related to the level of acceptance or rejection. An optimum positive response is obtained at an intermediate level, while too little or too much perceived activation results in a less positive response.**

In interpreting figure 2, imagine that we have a number of musical experiences arranged in increasing complexity, increasing excitement, or increasing intensity. Taking the activation element of complexity as an example, when a musical experience is perceived to be too simple the experience is evaluated less positively or nearer the rejection end. As complexity increases, an optimum level will be reached, and the musical experience will achieve greatest acceptance. If complexity is increased beyond the optimum level, the musical experience moves back toward the rejection end of the continuum. For a musically trained adult, "Twinkle, Twinkle, Little Star" may be too simple to elicit much acceptance. Mozart's variations on "Ah, vous dirai-je, maman" (using the tune we know as "Twinkle, Twinkle") may have a complexity level closer to optimum and bring about greater acceptance. Suppose we now create a highly complicated, computer-generated, atonal set of variations on the same tune. For many listeners, the complexity level may be such that the musical experience is less desirable.

The optimum acceptance level will vary for each individual according to such long-term variables as experience, training, personality, and so on (see chap. 8). Optimum acceptance (such as pleasure, valuing) may also vary according to immediate circumstances (e.g., the quality of a given performance or the listener's mood). Constructing a matrix of all the relevant activation elements along with all the personal variables of the person undergoing the musical experience would be horrendously complex. While this would present grave difficulties for researchers, it may more accurately reflect the real-life situation of musical experiences.

Affective/Aesthetic Behavior

Affective/aesthetic responses are as difficult to approach from an empirical and theoretical perspective as are music and the musical experience. To begin with, it does not appear that agreement can be reached on exactly the scope and nature of such experiences, although it would be highly likely that the vast majority of individuals would agree that they exist. Researchers have often ignored the fundamental theoretical concerns and attempted to resolve the issue by measuring the degree of preference or mood responses for given aural/musical stimuli, such as interval or tempo.

Two basic approaches have been used to examine and classify emotions (for a historical summary of the literature on affect and emotion, see Izard 1977). The first approach lists basic categories of emotion or affective responses. Examples are found in the work of Watson (1924), McDougall (1908), and Plutchik (1962). The second approach, which is based on the work of Spencer (1890), seems to provide greater potential for understanding any relationship between the musical experience and the affective domain. This view differentiates affects or emotions as bipolar dimensions or groupings of affective qualities. Although a number of dimensions have been suggested by various authors (see Arnold 1960; Block 1957; Burt 1950; Davitz 1969; Duffy 1962; Nowlis and Nowlis 1956; Schachter and Singer 1962; Schlosberg 1954; Wundt 1905; Young 1967), a close examination of the work of these authors suggests that two dimensions are common—some form of activation/excitement and acceptance-rejection/evaluation. More recent work, such as that by Mayer et al. (1991), has incorporated the two-dimensional concept into research on emotional states. The literature examining the concept of emotions does, however, provide insight into a proposed relationship between perceived activation and affective/aesthetic behavior.

If the position is taken that human existence can be classified into three "basic" categories—cognitive, physiological, and affective—included in the affective framework would be terms such as *emotions, affect, preference, feeling tone, mood,* and *aesthetic response*. Some of these variables are essentially the same and do not represent fundamentally different types of affective/aesthetic behavior. For the theoretical position outlined here, three basic subcategories of the affective domain can be classified—preference/hedonic tone, mood/feeling tone, and aesthetic response. (Note that emotion would be part of the mood/feeling tone classification, only more intense and with more physiological involvement. It should also be noted that this mood/feeling tone subcategory is not concerned with whether the mood/feeling tone is that of the person, a cultural descriptor of the music, or how the musical experience modifies the mood/feeling tone of the individual).

The theoretical framework outlined here suggests that two dimensions (activation and acceptance-rejection/evaluation) form the foundation for affective/aesthetic responses. The basis of the preference/hedonic tone response common to much research in this area is based on the second dimension, acceptance-rejection/evaluation. The mood/feeling tone response or subcategory of affect has been hypothesized as being grounded in some combination of activation and the acceptance-rejection dimensions. Finally, it is hypothesized that an aesthetic response is the direct experience of perceived activation, without involvement by the acceptance-rejection dimension. These hypotheses are examined in more detail subsequently.

The mood/feeling tone response is the second sub-classification of the affective domain. The work of Hevner, who developed the *Adjective Checklist* (Hevner 1935, 1936, and 1937), is probably the best known music research associated with mood responses. This listing includes such connotative terms as *happy, sad, majestic, and cheerful*. Other studies employing this checklist with music include Shimp 1940; Odbert, Karwoski, and Eckerson 1942; Rogge 1952; and Winold 1963. In a study examining the dimensions of the Hevner *Adjective Checklist,* I concluded that two subdimensions of evaluation formed the axis for the checklist (McMullen 1976). Later, I theorized that such connotative responses are not subdimensions of the evaluative dimension, but rather a combination of the two dimensions of activation and evaluation (acceptance-rejection) (McMullen 1982a). As both dimensions are bipolar, both the direction and relative weighting of each dimension within the experience contribute to both an internal experience and a possible external response referred to as mood/feeling tone. This hypothesis is in basic agreement with the authors cited above for the two-dimensional concept of emotion. Within this context, mood/feeling tone responses are considered a more psychological and milder form of emotion.

Although the aesthetic response is one that has been discussed widely, from a research perspective to date there is no clear suggestion as to the nature of the experience. In a paper presented in 1982, I presented the following hypothesis.

> Going back to the original meaning of the word *aesthetic,* which is "to perceive," it would seem logical to suggest that the aesthetic response basically is a direct perception of the incoming stimuli and a perceptual experience in which the incoming stimuli and the "self" of the perceiver are considered to be one. This suggests that, although the common usage of the term *aesthetic* implies involvement with beauty and, in turn, an evaluative aspect, it is the hypothesis of this writer . . . that the nature of the aesthetic response is pre-evaluative. Only after the experience has been completed does the individual "look back upon" the experience and place an evaluative judgment upon it. (McMullen 1982b, 12)

This position would only be modified now by adding that the "direct perception of the incoming stimuli and a perceptual experience" could be changed to activation.

The opening paragraphs of this chapter indicated the difficulties I experienced in attempting to synthesize the research concerning affective/aesthetic responses in relation to music as a stimulus object for the first edition of this *Handbook.* During the intervening years, this frustration has not been fully resolved. While considerable time and effort are being expended in research projects, it seems that too often such projects are just fragments or worlds unto themselves. They seem to be self-contained rather than a part of a more inclusive theory. This results, in part, from the unexamined philosophical positions of researchers, but it also is related to a basic lack of theoretical frameworks from which to choose research projects. It is difficult to tell which aspect of the problem is dominant, but it is clear that some solution still must be found. The continuing lack of basic or unifying theories or models will result in additional bits and pieces of unrelated data. Regardless of how promising such fragments may be, they will remain but fragments and the profession will remain at a standstill, spinning its wheels with much apparent activity, but with no real progress.

In addition to the difficulties for the research community itself, this lack of theory supported by research also makes it difficult for the applied areas of music education and music therapy to develop useful materials and approaches based on theoretical frameworks. Thus, theories and models must be developed, research must be undertaken based on these theories and models, and means must be developed for drawing from these frameworks for use in applied situations, in order for music psychology to make a more positive contribution to the applied areas of education and therapy.

Furthermore, many individuals view music psychology as though it were a self-contained discipline, independent of such broader fields as psychology or sociology, and this suggests a quality of "reinventing the wheel." Researchers and theorists in music psychology must learn to draw from the knowledge currently available in all areas of related disciplines and should seek to integrate their work with that body of information. At the same time the work of those in philosophy must be considered part of the research framework in order to more fully examine the foundations on which such research is conceived.

Within this context, the ideas proposed in this chapter are initial attempts to make a contribution to the process of resolving these major concerns at two levels. First, there is a need to consider strongly a change in the philosophical paradigm in which affective/aesthetic theory and research is undertaken. It has been suggested here that an interpretative, rather than a causal, paradigm can provide a more profitable avenue to understand relationships between the musical experience and affective/aesthetic responses.

The hypothesized two-dimensional framework—the concept of perceived stimulus activation and acceptance-rejection/evaluation as they relate to affective/aesthetic behavior—is based on the interpretative paradigm. Whether these concepts will be supported in the future is not as important here as the attempt to initiate a theoretical framework that can be integrated with philosophy, psychology, and related disciplines. With such a development, creative energies can be used more effectively by building on a common or unified structure. The efforts put forth in music psychology can thus serve to make a more positive contribution to the understanding of human beings and their musical world.

REFERENCES

Abeles, H. F. 1980. Responses to music. In *Handbook of music psychology*, ed. D. A. Hodges, 105–40. Lawrence, KS: National Association of Music Therapy.

Arnold, M. 1960. *Emotion and personality.* New York: Columbia University Press.

Berlyne, D. E. 1971. *Aesthetics and psychobiology.* New York: Appleton-Century-Crofts.

Berlyne, D. E. 1973. The vicissitudes of aplopathematic and thelematoscopic pneumatology or the hydrography of hedonism. In *Pleasure, reward and preference*, ed. D. E. Berlyne and K. B. Madsen, 1–33. New York: Academic Press.

Block, J. 1957. Studies in the phenomenology of emotion. *Journal of Abnormal and Social Psychology* 54:358–63.

Burke, M. J., and M. C. Gridley. 1990. Musical preference as a function of stimulus complexity and listeners' sophistication. *Perceptual and Motor Skills* 71:687–90.

Burt, C. 1950. The factorial study of emotions. In *Feelings and Emotions*, ed. M. L. Reymert, 531–51. New York: McGraw-Hill.

Crozier, J. 1974. Verbal and exploratory responses to sound sequences varying in uncertainty level. In *The New Experimental Aesthetics*, ed. D. E. Berlyne, 27–90. New York: John Wiley and Sons.

Das, J. P., J. R. Kirby, and R. F. Jarman. 1979. *Simultaneous and successive cognitive processes.* New York: Academic Press.

Davies, J. 1978. *The psychology of music.* Stanford, CA: Stanford University Press.

Davitz, J. R. 1969. *The language of emotion.* New York: Academic Press.

d'Espagnat, B. 1979. The quantum theory and reality. *Scientific American* 241, no. 5:158–67, 171–81.

Duffy, E. 1962. *Activation and behavior.* New York: John Wiley.

Fantino, E. 1973. Emotion. In *The study of behavior: Learning, motivation, emotion and instinct*, ed. J. A. Nevin, 280–320. Glenview, IL: Scott, Foresman.

Hargreaves, D. J. 1984. The effects of repetition on liking for music. *Journal of Research in Music Education* 32, no. 1:35–47.

Hevner, K. 1935. The affective character of the major and minor modes on music. *American Journal of Psychology* 47:103–18.

Hevner, K. 1936. Experimental studies of the elements of expression in music. *American Journal of Psychology* 48:246–68.

Hevner, K. 1937. The affective value of pitch and tempo in music. *American Journal of Psychology* 49:621–30.

Heyduk, R. 1975. Rated preference for musical composition as it relates to complexity and exposure frequency. *Perception and Psychophysics* 17:84–91.

Izard, C. E. 1977. *Human emotions.* New York: Plenum Press.

Kuhn, T. S. 1970. *The structure of scientific revolutions.* 2d ed. Chicago: University of Chicago Press.

Lynn, R. 1972. Arousal. In *Encyclopedia of psychology,* vol. 1, ed. H. J. Ensenck, W. Arnold, and R. Meili, 80–81. New York: Herder and Herder.

Masterman, M. 1970. The nature of a paradigm. In *Criticism and the growth of knowledge,* ed. I. Lakatos and A. Musgrave, 59–89. London: Cambridge University Press.

Mayer, J. D., P. Salovey, S. Gomberg-Kaufman, and K. Blainey. 1991. A broader conception of mood experience. *Journal of Personality and Social Psychology* 60:100–11.

McDougall, W. 1908. *An introduction to social psychology.* London: Methuen.

McMullen, Patrick T. 1976. Integration of the Hevner adjective checklist with dimension of the semantic differential. Paper presented at Music Educators National Conference, Atlantic City, NJ.

McMullen, P. T. 1977a. Descriptive models of verbal responses to musical stimuli. Paper presented at Music Educators National Conference, North Central— Southwestern Division Convention, Kansas City, MO.

McMullen, P. T. 1977b. Organizational and technical dimensions in musical stimuli. Paper presented at Music Educators National Conference, Eastern Division Convention, Washington. DC.

McMullen, P. T. 1978. Dimensions of meaning for musical stimuli: A non-verbal methodology. Paper presented at American Psychological Association, National Conference, Toronto.

McMullen, P. T. 1980. Music as a perceived stimulus object and affective responses: An alternative theoretical framework. In *Handbook of music psychology,* ed. D. A. Hodges, 183–93. Lawrence, KS: National Association for Music Therapy.

McMullen, P. T. 1982a. Connotative responses to musical stimuli: A theoretical explanation. *Bulletin of the Council for Research in Music Education* 71:45–57.

McMullen, P. T. 1982b. Empirical aesthetics: An overview. Paper presented at Research Symposium on Psychology and Acoustics of Music, University of Kansas, Lawrence, KS.

Meyer, L. B. 1956. *Emotion and meaning in music.* Chicago: University of Chicago Press.

Nowlis, V., and H. H. Nowlis. 1956. The description and analysis of moods. *Annals of the New York Academy of Science* 65:345–55.

Odbert, H. S., T. Karwoski, and A. B. Eckerson. 1942. Musical and verbal associations of color and mood. *Journal of General Psychology* 26:153–73.

Osgood, C. E., G. J. Suci, and P. H. Tannenbaum. 1957. *The measurement of meaning.* Urbana, IL: University of Illinois Press.

Plutchik, R. 1962. *The emotions: Facts, theories and a new model.* New York: Random House.

Rogge, G. O. 1952. Music as communication, with special reference to its role as content. Ph.D. diss., University of Southern California.

Schachter, S., and J. E. Singer. 1962. Cognitive, social and psychological determinants of emotional states. *Psychological Review* 69:379–99.

Schlosberg, H. S. 1954. Three dimensions of emotion. *Psychological Review* 61:81–88.

Shimp, B. 1940. Reliability of associations of known and unknown melodic phrases with words denoting states of feeling. *Journal of Musicology* 1:22–35.

Smith, B. 1978. Humanism and behaviorism in psychology: Theory and practice. *Journal of Humanistic Psychology* 18:27–36.

Spencer, H. 1890. *Principles of psychology*. New York: Appleton.

Vitz, P. 1966. Affect as a function of stimulus variation. *Journal of Experimental Psychology* 71:74–79.

Watson, J. B. 1924. *Behaviorism*. New York: Norton.

Winold, C. A. 1963. The effects of changes in harmonic tension upon listener response. Ph.D. diss., Indiana University.

Wundt, W. 1905. *Grundriss der psychologie*. 7th rev. ed. Leipzig: Engelmann.

Young, P. T. 1967. Affective arousal: Some implications. *American Psychologist* 22:32–40.

11

Learning Theory and Related Developments: Overview and Applications in Music Education and Music Therapy

Joe B. Buttram

The reader should be aware of some changes that have been made in this chapter in comparison to the first edition of the *Handbook*. Formerly, this chapter was devoted primarily to a description of traditional learning theory and related developments. In this edition, emphasis has been increased on applications of the concepts discussed. One reason for this change is to compensate for the loss of chapter thirteen from the earlier edition (Tunks 1980), which dealt specifically with applications. Also, readers over the past few years have indicated a preference for applications made concurrently with the presentation of theory and attempts have been made to comply. In some cases, it has been possible to make applications to music learning concurrently with the presentation of general theoretical positions; in cases merited by a significant amount of theory-based research in music learning, applications are deferred to the latter half of the chapter. Also, in some instances it has been possible to base applications on available research; in other situations, application to music learning is based on logical speculation. Further, applications have been considered for both music education and music therapy, in that this book is intended primarily for students and researchers in these two categories. The title of the chapter has been altered to reflect these changes.

Also significant since the first edition has been increased research and writing about music learning by music scholars. Some have sought to develop theories dealing with music perception, processing of musical information, or music cognition. Some of these efforts are based on traditional learning theory or aspects thereof; others cannot be classified in this manner and are concerned, simply, with various problems in music learning. In addition, an increasing number of psychologists have turned to research on music learning, some interacting with music researchers, resulting in increasing numbers of books and journal articles in the area of music psychology. Many of these theories and other articles merit attention and have been included in the latter part of the chapter dealing specifically with applications.

Other changes include an updating of the more current developments in learning theory and other research and applications in learning, along with supporting references. Inasmuch as these expansions have required additional space, it has been necessary to reduce the amount of discussion devoted to some of the more dated theories. Despite being dated, however, these older views contain much food for thought, and the more prominent learning theories remain represented, although edited for brevity. For information that has been deleted, refer to the first edition.

Organization of the Chapter

It should be noted that learning theorists often employ basic concepts and approaches that differ markedly. Terminology used is often different from one theorist to another, and the precise definitions of the terms used also vary. The definition of learning is itself a good example; some theorists define learning as observed changes in behavior not attributable to fatigue, drugs, or physiological growth; others may include numerous mediating processes and concepts such as purposefulness or insight. Similar difficulties are encountered with the acceptance and use of terms and concepts such as *sensation, perception, conditioning, reinforcement, retention, forgetting, motivation, transfer of training, thinking,* and *insight.* Thus, the reader is advised to consider the context and exact meanings of such terms.

Learning theory may be defined as "system building," or "constructing a body of theory which is cohesive and internally consistent and within which all elements, even minor ones, harmonize with the central premises" (Bigge 1976, 288). Such a description is particularly appropriate for the more formal and fully developed theoretical positions, such as those developed in the first half of the twentieth century, when theory construction was in its heyday (Amsel 1989). Other theorists are less concerned with theory and even question the importance and applicability of learning theory as a practical approach to solving educational problems (see Skinner 1950; Snygg 1954; Spence 1959). Research published since 1950 tends to reflect this view, with much less emphasis on system building and refining and increased attention to more specific learning concerns and immediately applicable research.

Such areas of interest include perception, thinking, memory, cognitive development, and problem solving, as well as such major areas of study as developmental psychology, social psychology, personality theory, and psychotherapy.

Similarly, educational research is becoming interdisciplinary, expanding into a great number of related but separate areas including psycholinguistics, anthropology, neurophysiology, artificial intelligence, and information theory (Gardner 1985). It may be that formal learning theory is declining in importance as educators turn to other sources for answers to their needs. Or, learning theory may be becoming eclectic or expanding and attempting to incorporate contributions from other disciplines. In any case, an understanding of learning theory, both historically and currently, is important for both music educators and music therapists and for research purposes as well as a means for improving classroom and clinical practices.

Theoretical views have been organized for presentation in a way that appears to be most basic and simple. The majority of theories can be classified as either associationist or cognitive. Categorization in this manner is usually based on theorists' views concerning the fundamental nature of the relationship of humans to the environment. A contrast of associationist and cognitive positions with regard to learning is illustrative.

For the associationist, learning is viewed as a formation of connections, habits, or behavioral tendencies. Terms employed reflect this orientation—*organism, S-R bond, conditioning,* and *reinforcement.* Learning is perceived as beginning with elements and combining elements in an additive or associative manner, beginning with a trial-and-error process and building in a mechanical way toward complex behavior.

For the cognitive theorist, learning is viewed as a process of gaining insights or thinking. Terms employed include *person, environment, interaction, motivation, goal, thought pattern,* and *information processing.* For the cognitive theorist, learning is a process of reorganization of perceptual or cognitive fields and involves the purposeful behavior of the individual toward a goal.

Other views selected for discussion do not fit neatly into these two categories. Some may fit in either category, and some may not qualify strictly as learning theory at all. However, these views are believed to be important to the understanding of learning and have been included in a third category, related developments. For a quick acquaintance with the discussion to be presented in the first major section of the chapter, then, the organizational plan of the work is as follows.

Associationism

Pavlov	Classical conditioning
Watson	Behaviorism
Guthrie	Contiguous conditioning
Thorndike	Connectionism
Skinner	Operant conditioning
Hull	Hypothetic-deductive S-R
Spence	Quantitative S-R
Miller and Dollard	Drive reduction
Tolman	Purposive behaviorism
Mower	Two-factor theory

Cognitivism

Wertheimer	Gestalt, perception
Köhler	Gestalt, insight
Koffka	Gestalt, laws of perception
Lewin	Field theory
Piaget	Developmental theory
Bruner	Spiral curriculum
Gagne	Task analysis
Maslow	Human potential facilitation
Rogers	Personal growth facilitation
Gardner	Cognitive Science

Related Developments

Functionalism
Psychoanalytic theory
Mathematical models
Information processing
Neurophysiology

The second section of the chapter is devoted to discussions of theories or ideas concerning music learning as proposed by music scholars, as well as findings by music researchers, with emphasis on applications of learning theory to music learning. The organizational plan for this portion of the chapter is as follows.

Applications to Music Learning
    Background
    Theories of music learning
    Areas of theory-based research in music learning

Associationism

The early history of associationism, as psychology generally, dates back to the earliest of recorded times and was originally a part of philosophy. However, the rise of "scientific psychology" in the last quarter of the nineteenth century provides more immediate roots and is to be found in the work of late nineteenth-century physiological psychologists David Hartley and Francis Galton (see Misiak and Sexton 1966). These, and a large number of other scholars, had as their focus observable behavior and its explanation in scientific, quantifiable terms. During the ensuing years, numerous scholars of the associationist tradition conducted research and developed theories that have had a significant impact on educational practices, particularly in the first half of the twentieth century. A review of the work of the most notable of these individuals follows.

Pavlov (1849–1936)

It seems necessary to consider first the work of Ivan P. Pavlov for an understanding of classical conditioning, a concept that became a most basic point of departure for a great number of theories in the associationist tradition. Pavlov, a Russian physiologist, made what has been described as a serendipitous finding while studying the digestive system of animals (Snelbecker 1974). While studying the nature of reflex mechanisms, Pavlov noted the phenomenon of stimulus substitution. He observed that a variety of stimuli, when paired with an original or reflexive stimulus, could come to elicit the original or reflexive response. For example, if an animal were repeatedly presented with food and a sounding bell simultaneously, salivation (or the reflexive response) would eventually come to be elicited by the bell alone.

These behaviors were identified by terminology that became traditional in learning theory and are usually diagrammed as shown in figure 1.

Reflexive Behavior

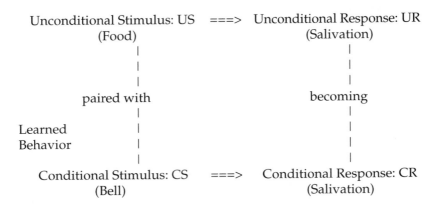

Fig. 1. Association of reflexive and learned behaviors

The bell (CS), by association over time with food (US), came to elicit salivation (originally UR), which under these new conditions became a conditioned response (CR). Thus, the gradual buildup of conditioned stimuli and conditioned responses by means of association over time with what was originally reflexive behavior provided a basis for describing how learning occurs. This process, which came to be known as classical conditioning, provided support of the law of association (Bugelski 1975) and the stimulus-response paradigm for learning.

Pavlov continued to discover numerous factors that influenced the conditioning process. These included reinforcement, extinction, spontaneous recovery, generalization and discrimination, the orienting response, and individual differences (Bower and Hilgard 1981), all of which subsequently received attention by theorists and researchers.

Watson (1878–1958)

McDonald states that J. B. Watson "achieved the final separation of psychology from the vestiges of traditional philosophical thought. . . . From this point on, one had learning theories from which to choose" (1964, 1–2). Watson's views were in opposition to earlier sensationalism and introspection and were among the initial views that gave rise to the school of behaviorism. Being a strong environmentalist, Watson held that, in addition to the body and numerous inherited reflexes, the total of an individual was what he or she had learned.

Watson relied heavily on the work of Pavlov (Bigge 1976) and became convinced that classical conditioning was how learning occurred. Learning, then, consisted of a gradual buildup of a number of stimulus-response connections or neuromuscular behaviors that allowed the individual to complete an act more complex than simple instinctual or reflexive behavior. Building on this premise, Watson postulated additional principles about how one could account for the more complex aspects of learning. Primary in this regard were the principles of frequency and recency (Hill 1971). Frequency refers to the number of times a stimulus is followed by a specific response. The greater the frequency of this stimulus-response association, the greater the probability that the same responses to that stimulus will occur under the same conditions. Recency refers to the passage of time following an S-R behavior; the more recent the behavior, the more likely this behavior will recur in a like manner under the same conditions. The response that is made most frequently is more likely to be learned, and the most recent response results in learning (or the tendency to be repeated) as well. Relying on principles of classical conditioning and the added principles of frequency and recency, Watson attempted to account for how complex human behaviors are learned. Possible applications of both concepts appear in the work of later theorists.

Guthrie (1886–1959)

Edwin R. Guthrie's theory of learning is thought to be most similar to Watson's (Hill 1964), but it is also dependent on the work of Pavlov and Thorndike (Bower and Hilgard 1981). However, Guthrie postulated only one law of learning, which came to be known as the theory of contiguity. For Guthrie, learning was an all-or-nothing affair, occurring immediately and as a result of simultaneous association of stimulus and response. That response which is likely to be repeated, or learned, is that one occurring closest in time to the eliciting stimuli. Obviously, in a one-trial learning system such as this, the response learned is the last response made (similar to Watson's principle of recency). When the last response occurs, the organism is removed from the stimulus situation and further learning under these particular conditions is not possible. Learning does not occur as a result of repetition, motivation, reward, or other factors, but simply by doing. The reader should be reminded, however, that this seemingly simplistic explanation does not deny the complexity or continuous nature of the learning process.

One immediate problem with this view is the explanation of improvement by repetition or practice. If learning is, indeed, a one-trial affair, practice would be unnecessary. However, performance appears to improve with repetition and it might seem that the associative connection of stimulus and response would be strengthened. In response to this observation, Guthrie postulates a stimulus pattern (Snelbecker 1974) or a variety of stimuli that may be noted by the learner and associated with the response. Practice results in improvement because, during repetition, the individual is provided the opportunity to associate a greater number of stimuli or cues with an act of skill; the greater the difficulty of the skill, the more cues are needed for optimum performance. Especially significant in this regard is the importance of context. To perform efficiently and with the proper stimuli and cues available, the individual should practice in context—in the situation where the skilled behavior is expected to occur. As a result, more and more proper stimuli are available so that the response may be learned and eventually repeated under the desired conditions. Guthrie's seemingly simplistic statement, that we "learn by doing," is expanded to include the qualification that we learn but by doing under those conditions that provide a greater number of appropriate stimuli that elicit the desired behavior.

Related to efficient practice are Guthrie's views on the breaking of habits. To break a habit, note the stimuli eliciting the undesirable response and, then, find a way to associate a proper response with these same stimuli. Guthrie suggests several methods including the threshold method, fatigue, and the presentation of incompatible stimuli (Snelbecker 1974). The basic idea of eliminating an undesirable response is to seek ways to associate a desired response with the stimuli present.

Although Guthrie's ideas were established primarily by research with animals, they would appear to be particularly important to humans involved in learning music. Some speculation follows. The concept of contiguity seems applicable. For best effect, the "first response" should be free from error; learning would be facilitated by allowing as few errors to occur, initially, as possible. The learning of the most "recent response" is equally interesting. The learning of a musical item and exercise should be concluded with a correct response, in that the last response is the one likely to persist. Improvement of performance by practice deserves consideration. Practice cannot be simple repetition; errors in music-learning or other behaviors are learned just as easily as correct responses; practice must systematically provide additional information (e.g., stimuli or cues) so that skill acquisition may improve and not be simple repetition. And, practice must occur "in context" so that the proper stimuli or information bearing on performance will be associated by contiguity. With regard to breaking habits, mere repetition will not eliminate errors, and the teacher needs to find ways to bring about the desired response in the situation in which it should occur. Finally, much of the above may appear to be quite logical to music researchers, teachers, and therapists, but considerable research is needed to determine the real extent of applicability.

Thorndike (1874–1949)

The theory of learning as conceived and researched by Edward L. Thorndike is recognized by authorities as being not only "one of the first recognizable and influential systems that dealt with this topic" (Snelbecker 1974, 209), but the one learning theory dominating all others in America for nearly half a century (Bower and Hilgard 1981). Thorndike's theory is referred to as connectionism and is devoted to the connection of stimulus and response as the basic learning unit and to the factors that influence the making, retaining, and use of these connections.

Thorndike's theory was derived primarily from his extensive and controlled study of animal behavior, the results of which appear in his monograph, *Animal Intelligence* (1911). In his experiments, Thorndike observed that behavior, originally random or trial and error, came to be repeated and appeared to become purposeful or learned. A typical example of such an experiment involved placing a cat (or other animal) in a puzzle box and observing the behaviors exhibited to escape the box to obtain food. Behaviors at first might involve scratching, biting, clawing, or moving about. Eventually, some one behavior would result in touching or moving an escape mechanism allowing the cat to free itself and obtain the food. On repeated trials, it was observed that the time required to repeat the freeing behavior decreased and the animal apparently "learned" to make the appropriate response. This process of learning was referred to as stamping in, or the gradual strengthening of the connection or bond between stimulus (food or hunger) and response (releasing behavior). Thorndike's observations and continued research led to the formulation and refinement of numerous principles or laws to explain animal learning systematically. Eventually, these laws were extended to account for human learning as well.

Three of these principles were designated as primary laws and included readiness, exercise, and effect (Bigge 1976). The law of readiness postulates that a "conduction unit" (the neuron and synapse involved in establishing a bond) that is more predisposed to conduct in a particular situation will do so more readily than conduction units less predisposed. Also, conduction results in greater satisfaction, while not to conduct results in annoyance. Bower and Hilgard (1981) interpret the law of readiness to indicate that, when an action tendency is aroused through preparatory adjustments, sets, and attitudes, fulfillment of the tendency in action is satisfying; nonfulfillment is annoying. Readiness, thus, means a preparation for action. Note that this idea of readiness relates to use in experimental conditions and does not refer to the typical idea of "readiness" as usually conceived by educators.

The law of exercise (or repetition) postulates that the more times a stimulus-response connection is repeated, the more likely it is to be repeated when the situation recurs. Principles of use and disuse are subsumed under this law (Snelbecker 1974). When a connection is used, such as in practice, the more likely that response will be made again. With the principle of disuse, it follows logically that, if a connection is not used, it is weakened and likely will not recur. Exercise (or practice), then, strengthens the connection between stimulus and response and increases the likelihood that this relationship will be maintained. According to Hill 1971, in the law of exercise, Thorndike incorporates Watson's laws of frequency and recency to some extent and Guthrie's law of contiguity. The law of exercise later underwent revision, and a position was adopted recognizing the importance of other factors in bringing about improvement, such as practicing in context and obtaining knowledge of results.

The law of effect is based on a pleasure-pain principle in that, if a connection results in a satisfying state of affairs, that connection will be strengthened. However, should the response result in a state of annoyance, the connection will be weakened. Stated more simply, reward results in repetition and learning of behavior, whereas punishment or displeasure tend to reduce the likelihood of repetition and consequent learning. During later refinement of this law, much greater emphasis was placed on the effect of reward and less on the effect of punishment, although this aspect was not eliminated. The principle of belongingness was also adopted, supporting the idea that a response is more easily learned if it "belongs" in a particular situation; under this condition, reward is more effective in bringing about learning. The continuing concern and research regarding the influence of reward on learning of all sorts support Bugelski's (1971) observation that the law of effect was, by far, Thorndike's most important contribution to learning theory. Certainly, this law, as developed further by Skinner and others, is prominent in contemporary research in music education.

The reader should be aware that numerous secondary laws or principles were also postulated in order to account for aspects of learning not readily or clearly explained by the three primary laws. Such laws attempted to account for variation, flexibility, and complexity in the learning process and illustrate Thorndike's concern with what is referred to as "normal learning" as well as development of laws and principles under experimental conditions using animals (Bower and Hilgard 1981). Thorndike was concerned with the application of his views to the teaching situation, including the identification of connections to be made, the proper application of reward, the order of practice, and the importance of motivation and the active role of the learner. Thorndike also recognized the importance of transfer of training and proposed a theory of identical elements to account for how past learning may apply to a new situation. Although original learning always consists of specific connections, it appears to generalize because of the presence of sufficient elements in the new situation common to the situation in which they were learned. A similar view of intelligence was also proposed, with intelligence in this case being defined as the ability to transfer effectively. If transfer depends on common elements, then, logically, intelligence (or the lack of it) would depend solely on the number of connections available to facilitate transfer. The greater the number of usable connections available, the more intelligent the individual.

These and other concepts represent major contributions by Thorndike, and most have undergone research and development by later researchers. The influence of many of the concepts are readily apparent in research about music. The law of effect is clearly evident in the use of reward to bring about learning and other changes in behavior. The principle of readiness forecasts developmental psychology and the considerable body of research in that area. Transfer of training has also been a primary topic for discussion and research in music learning. More specific discussion of applications of these concepts appears later in this chapter.

Skinner (1904–90)

The work of B. F. Skinner is considered by some to be an outgrowth of the theories of Pavlov, Watson, Guthrie, and Thorndike, particularly Thorndike's law of effect (Bugelski 1971; Snelbecker 1974). As will be seen, however, Skinner's theory of operant conditioning is somewhat different in that it is Skinner's premise that learning is controlled primarily by its consequences, rather than merely as a result of association.

Skinner believed that behavior is lawful and predictable, and it was his hope to achieve the degree of control, predictability, and precision in his approach to learning as has been the case with the physical sciences. Notably, Skinner rejected conventional theory building as well as such internal or mentalistic concepts as bonds, intervening variables, motivation, and insight. Instead, he preferred an empirical-inductive approach to research and to theory construction. Much of his research was with animals and was based on the study of observable behavior of the learner and the conditions under which this behavior might be modified.

Skinner's theory of operant conditioning is based on the premise that, if behavior is reinforced, the probability of recurrence of that behavior is increased. Skinner recognized two types of behaviors, respondent and operant. Respondent behaviors are those elicited by known stimuli and are reflexive. An organism is born with certain reflexive behaviors and acquires others by means of classical conditioning, similar to the S-R connectionism postulated by Pavlov.

Operant behavior, in contrast, is representative of most types of human behavior and learning. Operant behavior is behavior emitted by the organism, behavior which is said to operate on the environment (Hill 1971). Such behavior obviously is prompted by a stimulus or set of stimuli, but Skinner considers the presence of these stimuli not to be of primary importance. What is important is that when an operant response occurs, opportunity for reinforcement and learning is available.

It is this emphasis on the reinforcement of the operant response that differentiates Skinner's views from earlier S-R theorists. In Thorndike's view, learning occurred by association of stimuli and response and what caused the association was the effect of the response. For Skinner, learning occurs because of consequences that follow the response. Thus, in contrast to an S-R model, Skinner might postulate an R-C model. A response or operant occurs for whatever reason, and the consequence or reinforcement following the response influences the probability of repeating that response. It is in this way that Thorndike's law of effect has been revised (Hill 1971).

In a given situation, a learner is free to make any number of responses, some respondent but most operant, and these occurring for a variety of reasons. Operant behavior under these conditions is described as free operant (Snelbecker 1974) and makes available to the teacher or therapist a number of responses from which one or more can be selected and reinforced. Skinner identifies two types of reinforcement, positive and negative, either of which may strengthen the probability of repetition.

Positive reinforcement is the addition of something pleasant and would include reinforcers that fulfill biological needs, such as food and water, and secondary reinforcers, eventually acquired through a learning process, such as praise, approval, or money. In music teaching, praise for any correct response in music making would be an example. Negative reinforcement occurs as a result of the removal of the individual from an aversive situation. An example typically given is the opening of an umbrella to avoid rain. An example in music might involve the student learning to seek feedback in rehearsal concerning information needed or errors to be corrected in an effort to deal with a difficult situation. Ways that assist the student in overcoming difficulties (or removing the student from a difficult or aversive situation) are reinforcing and repeated.

Negative reinforcement is often confused with punishment. This confusion apparently results from Skinner's use of electric shock or other painful stimuli in animal studies. In controlling human behavior, reactions of disapproval, disdain, and rejection used in this manner would be comparable. If interpreted as similar to punishment and used in this manner, reinforcement would result in an accompanying emotional state preventing more appropriate responses and, consequently, desirable learning. As a result of this apparent misconception, negative reinforcement has come to be considered an undesirable and unreliable technique (Hill 1971). Properly understood and applied, however, negative reinforcement, as opposed to punishment, can be an effective technique to promote desired learning.

The opposite to reinforcement of responses is found in the concept of extinction. If one does not wish to increase the probability of response recurrence, one deliberately withholds reinforcement. Without reinforcement, the undesirable response is extinguished. The response either does not become a part of the subject's fixed repertoire of responses, or it is eventually dropped because it no longer results in reward. Thus, rather than continue to concentrate excessively on music or behavior errors, it may be advisable to ignore these responses and allow extinction to occur. It should be noted that, after extinction, spontaneous recovery may occur, and the subject may repeat the supposedly extinguished behavior at an even greater rate and intensity. The extinction process may then be repeated. Because of the possible negative effects of punishment mentioned earlier, extinction is considered the preferred method of eliminating unwanted behavior.

As has been noted, positive reinforcement is the primary and preferred method of increasing the probability of response recurrence or learning. There are a variety of ways reinforcement may be utilized, here referred to as schedules of reinforcement. Reinforcement may be continuous, that is, made available each time the desired response occurs. Continuous reinforcement is considered a proper technique for establishing a desired response initially, but, following that, intermittent reinforcement has been found to be more efficient. Intermittent reinforcement involves reinforcement of only some of the appropriate responses emitted. Intermittent reinforcement may be based on an interval schedule, that is, on specified intervals of time, or on a ratio schedule, that is, based on the number of responses emitted. Both interval and ratio scheduling may be fixed or variable with reference to both the passage of time or numbers of responses made.

The reader should be aware that Skinner's theory contains a vast number of refinements that allow him to account for the more complex aspects of the learning process. Two of these concepts are shaping and chaining (Kazdin 1975). Shaping refers to a method of reaching a long-range, desired behavior by means of successive approximations. Certain responses, although not the ultimately desired response, may be recognized as responses that may lead eventually to the ultimate response. By selecting and reinforcing responses that are increasingly similar to the long-range goal, behavior is shaped in that direction and other responses, those not moving toward the final goal, are not reinforced (extinguished) and eventually disappear. Shaping, then, refers to the reinforcement of behaviors already present in a carefully selected manner that leads to a long-range learning goal.

Chaining is a similar concept. A chain is a series of separate, finite behaviors that come to function as a unit. Chains are developed from the sequential arrangement of already existing separate behaviors as a result of a process of one discrete behavior coming to serve as a stimulus for another. This process continues until the chain is completed. Chaining is not building by successive approximation, but it is a means of explaining established sequential relationships that comprise a larger unit of behavior.

In recent years, Skinner's work has been the subject of severe criticism from several cognitive theorists as well as some within the associationist tradition (Amsel 1989). Such criticism may or may not be merited. Sparzo (1992) accounts for much of this criticism based on (1) Skinner's rejection of mentalistic concepts, (2) much misinformation on the part of his critics, and (3) Skinner's deceptively simple writing style. Sparzo also notes Skinner's enormous contributions and their implications for education. Perhaps most important is the emphasis on the consequences of action and the opportunity to reward those actions leading to the accomplishment of some desired goal.

Bower and Hilgard (1981) note a variety of applications that may be based on this behaviorist tradition. The learning process may become very sequential and systematic. Task analysis may be used, followed by devising a series of behavioral objectives to accomplish the task. Important is much active responding, such as recitation and other forms of practice, and the shaping of behavior by means of reinforcement to achieve a long-range goal. This approach may be applied not only to specific learning goals but to classroom management and other varied individual and social behaviors. And, this very systematic and quantifiable approach is readily applicable to accountability systems, including planning, curriculum construction, and evaluation. Finally, Skinner's concern for individual needs and his attempt to meet those needs through programmed instruction, involving reinforcement concepts, should be mentioned.

Applications of Skinner's views by music scholars and researchers have been extensive. Certainly, a striking application of Skinner's views has occurred in the teaching of so-called abnormal populations using operant procedures to establish, sustain, and shape desirable behavior and to extinguish undesirable behavior. These and similar procedures have been used not only in therapeutic settings but also in traditional teaching and learning situations as well (see Greer 1981; Madsen, Greer, and Madsen 1975; Madsen and Prickett 1987). For additional information, consult the applications section of this chapter.

Hull (1884–1952)

Clark L. Hull is considered to have been the most outstanding learning theorist in the United States during the 1940s and 1950s. Hull was a behaviorist in the tradition of Watson, Guthrie, Thorndike, and Skinner. However, in contrast to Skinner's inductive approach, Hull attempted to develop a hypothetic-deductive theory of learning, an approach in which general observations about behavior are made and a series of experiments are then conducted to determine the validity of the observations. Further, Hull was a Darwinian and saw learning as a major means of adaption. Hull's primary writings are set forth in two major works, *Principles of Behavior* (1943; consisting of the presentation of his system) and *A Behavior System* (1952; describing the application of the system in a variety of ways).

One of the most striking aspects of Hull's system is its formality, and, as Snelbecker states, "Hull was convinced that psychology could be a true natural science, that quantitative laws could be delineated and quite rigorous research procedures and sound empirical theory could be delineated" (1974, 255). As a result, Hull's work may be characterized as relying heavily on rigorous and controlled research procedures as developed by the natural and physical sciences and employing extensive quantifying descriptions and carefully written accounts of his findings.

Hull's theory is described as being S-R and hypothetic-deductive. His concept of behavior consists of three essential parts—the stimulus, activity within the organism designated as the intervening process, and the response. The purpose of Hull's theory, then, was to provide a comprehensive and systematic explanation of this behavior. His approach was to select and designate certain ideas about behavior or certain characteristics of behavior as postulates, or general statements about behavior, that would serve as points of departure for research. Numerous postulates and theorems were identified and stated in precise mathematical form and, if found to be experimentally verifiable, would represent laws of behavior. Hull's system is most significant not only for the resultant findings about learning but for the models and procedures developed for the study of learning. As Hill (1971) notes, "learning theory" and "Hullian theory" have become practically synonymous.

As will be recalled, much from earlier theorists was incorporated into Hull's theory, notably the S-R paradigm for learning, in which internal or external stimuli become associated with a response and learning occurs. Hull was not satisfied with this seemingly mechanical, additive, and molecular view of behavioral development. Instead, he preferred what has been described as a "molar behavioristic view" (Snelbecker 1974). As a result, several important additions were made to the learning paradigm. One of these is the concept of drive (DeCecco and Crawford 1974).

Drive, simply stated, is a hypothesized state of arousal of the organism as a result of the presence of stimuli. Primary drive would result from deprivation or from unsatisfied physiological needs, such as hunger, thirst, or pain avoidance. Secondary drives would result from the presence of stimuli that have acquired drive strength through the learning process and might include praise or material rewards. Drive, then, is an activated state of the organism, and if a response results in a reduction of drive or is associated in time with drive reduction, that response will likely be repeated and learned. Drive, then, serves two functions—an energizing or activating function and a source of reward when reduced.

Hull viewed the stimulus as the independent variable and the response as the dependent variable (Hill 1971). Connecting these two, Hull postulated one or more intervening variables. The number and strength of intervening variables must be inferred and are difficult to assess. The strength of drive may be an intervening variable but also may be closely associated with the stimulus itself. Another intervening variable postulated by Hull is habit strength, which is defined as the strength of the learned connection between stimulus and response, a connection acquired and strengthened through reinforced practice. A refinement relating to habit strength is incentive motivation, which is dependent upon strength of reward. As the size of the reward increases, so does the level of incentive motivation and so does the likelihood of responding in such a way as to bring about the larger reward. The interaction of the components of drive, habit strength, and incentive motivation may result in an additional intervening variable, excitatory potential, or the cumulative tendency for a subject to respond in one way rather than another.

For Hull, many answers regarding learning are to be found in the varying strengths of intervening variables and their interactions. The introduction of concepts of drive, intervening variables, habit strength, incentive motivation, excitatory potential, and a host of other possible intervening variables provide both recognition of, and account for, traditional and flexible modes of response (Bugelski 1971). Continued research and application of Hull's views are to be found in the work of several of his colleagues and followers, including Spence, Mower, N. E. Miller, Amsel, and Logan (Bower and Hilgard 1981).

Spence (1907–67)

Kenneth W. Spence, a student and colleague of Hull's, is regarded as the chief exponent and developer of Hullian theory (Bigge 1976). Spence's primary work was *Behavior Theory and Condition* (1956), and this text along with other writings resulted in the refinement and elaboration of several concepts that reveal both similarities and differences between the views of Spence and Hull.

Spence's theory has come to be known as quantitative S-R, and his ultimate goal was the exact quantification of behavior theory. For Spence, the task of the psychologist was to determine precisely which factors and conditions of the learner and its environment account for the response. Concepts similar to Hull include excitatory potential, habit strength, and drive and incentive motivation. The development of the concept of incentive motivation is considered to be the primary contribution by Spence (Bower and Hilgard 1981). For Spence, incentive motivation was viewed as an incentive to react to certain stimuli, these stimuli indicating that a response for which a reward may be expected will occur. Reaction to these stimuli depends not so much on the reward itself but on anticipation of a reward. This accommodation of anticipation of a reward, according to Hill 1971, indicates a significant move toward a more cognitive theory of learning.

It is Bigge's (1971) view that Spence's theory might be called an S-R expectancy theory, in which learning occurs partially through drive reinforcement and partially through incentive motivation. In Spence's later work, reinforcement by drive reduction remains, but more emphasis was placed on motivation as a contribution to excitatory potential. As a result, in addition to drive reduction, attention is given to the importance of incentive, or the more positive aspects of behavior, in bringing about learning. With Spence, then, occurs an early tendency to move the associationist and cognitive positions closer together.

Miller (1909–) and Dollard (1900–)

Neal E. Miller is considered a neo-Hullian, but one who has greatly simplified and more widely applied this position (Bower and Hilgard 1981). Miller's position is one of reinforcement by drive reduction. However, in addition to primary drives, the concept of acquired drives is developed. Also important are cues, or stimuli (both external and internal), that guide behavior. Miller's learning paradigm becomes, then, drive-cue-response-reward and is paraphrased in the statement: "in order for learning to take place, the learner must want something, notice something, do something, and get something he wants" (Hill 1964, 276).

Also credited to Miller is the development of conflict theory, a view similar to Lewin's, in which situations occur combining drive tendencies toward two or more possible rewards and requiring a forced choice (Bower and Hilgard 1981). Such conflicts are resolved on the basis of the strength or relative potential reward of possible choices. Two possibly rewarding choices would be described as an approach-approach situation, and the choice made would depend on the relative strength of the two rewards. The presence of a single goal both tempting and repelling would result in an approach-avoidance situation, with the response being oscillation and representing a true conflict situation involving considerable frustration.

Along with colleague John Dollard, Miller applied these views concerning learning and behavior to a wide variety of concerns, including thinking and verbal behavior, imitation and social behavior, personality, and psychotherapy. These and other concerns are set forth in Miller and Dollard's works, *Social Learning and Behavior* (Miller and Dollard 1941) and *Personality and Psychotherapy* (Dollard and Miller 1950).

With regard to thinking, the presence of internally produced cues is used to guide responses (Bergan and Dunn 1976). During such behavior, the individual may be said to emit responses (thoughts) that serve as cues that provide internal control. In this way, the individual may be viewed as possessing self-direction by observing self-produced cues or by thinking. Similar would be the use of verbal behavior in preparation for making a response. The individual may verbally rehearse a particular act to himself or herself, preparing emotionally and with pre-prepared cues for a more adequate performance. For the musician, this verbal preparation may be quite comparable with aural mental rehearsal for performance.

Miller and Dollard were among the earliest to emphasize the importance of imitation in learning theory, and the use of imitation was found to be particularly adaptable to social learning (Lefrancois 1975). The basic premise is that the behavior of others provides cues about how to behave and that, with sufficient experience and reinforcement, a child learns to imitate observed behavior. In early childhood, such social learning occurs as a result of interactions with parents. Drive elicits initial behavior, and, as this behavior is reinforced by approval or praise, these reinforcers become acquired drives. Particularly important in this regard is the initial approval to imitate sounds or behaviors of the adult. This procedure continues and eventually transfers to a larger social context, and the individual continues to imitate and judge the adequacy of his or her behavior based on the reactions of others.

In a similar manner, Miller and Dollard's views may be applied to personality theory and psychotherapy. Personality characteristics are acquired by learning, and this learning is based on primary and secondary drive reduction. Unacceptable social behaviors and neuroses also are learned in this manner. More important is that in psychotherapy, these same observations and procedures can be used to unlearn unwanted behaviors, to learn to respond appropriately, and to do so under originally fearful conditions. Thus, Miller and Dollard have gone a "long way toward convincing psychologists that a liberalized version of the stimulus-response-reinforcement approach was a viable and healthy alternative for learning theory" (Hilgard and Bower 1975, 177).

Tolman (1886–1959)

Edward C. Tolman is credited with developing a view known as purposive behavior, which is regarded as a combination of behaviorism and cognitive theory. Like behaviorists, Tolman considered learning in terms of stimulus and response, rejected introspection as a method, and sought to verify his theories objectively under controlled experimental conditions. However, Tolman was also concerned with cognition—with the knowing, thinking, planning, and purposefulness of behavior. Tolman was impressed with the behaviorist's objectivity in research but considered behaviorism too limiting, especially with regard to cognitive concepts. Tolman's effort is regarded as "an attempt to give cognition theory as close a connection with external stimuli and with learning as connectionist theory has" (Hill 1971, 117).

Tolman regarded behavior as molar, as an integrated action or movement that is purposeful and goal directed. Behavior is not viewed as a simple response to a specific stimuli, but as a response guided by numerous intervening variables and resulting not in a simple connection but cognition. Learning results from the formation or change in cognition; experiences with external stimuli result not so much in drive reduction as in a cognition or awareness that making the response will lead to reward.

Tolman's theory of purposive behavior is also referred to as expectancy theory (Bower and Hilgard 1981). It is the apparent learning of signs leading to a goal that is the most unique aspect of the system. The learner is said to learn meanings, not movements, and to learn numerous relationships of the behavior situation. The learner learns reward expectancy, or the knowledge that a goal exists, and place learning, or an awareness of where the goal is situated. Such learning may be demonstrated by supposed insightful behavior to obtain the reward. Learning about the spacial characteristics of the behavior situation results in a cognitive map, or an awareness of the contextual and organizational aspects of the situation.

Another term used as a composite description of Tolman's theory is *sign-gestalt-expectation* (Hill 1971). The learner comes to expect certain types of organization and that certain signs, discriminated in context, will lead to the reward. Obviously, such behavior involving intervening variables could be described as expectant, purposeful, and involving cognition.

In an expectancy system, confirmation of expectancy comes to be used as a substitute for the concept of reinforcement and an increase in the probability of repetition of a behavior. Motivation also requires additional consideration because it is important in the acquisition of cognitive structures (Bower and Hilgard 1981). Motivation determines those aspects of the environment to which the subject will attend in order to reach the goal. The role of reinforcement, then, is not a condition necessary for learning, but it serves to control motivation so that learned behavior will be emitted (Bergan and Dunn 1976). Clearly, many of these ideas appear in cognitive theory, although Tolman strove to maintain the objectivity and systematic treatment typical of behaviorists of his time.

Mowrer (1907–82)

O. Hobart Mowrer is most prominently known for the advancement of the so-called two-factor theory of learning, and his primary work is *Learning Theory and Behavior* (1960). The two-factor categorization resulted primarily because of Mowrer's earlier writings, in which he proposed two distinct kinds of learning; in a later position, the two factors became quite similar and all learning is regarded as being of one type. For Mowrer, "responses that are learned or conditioned are strictly emotional and primarily of two general categories: hope and fear" (Bugelski 1971, 118).

Responses that result in fear will lead to avoidance learning; responses that result in hope will result in approach learning. Hypothetically, the learner scans possible responses and selects those that appear to facilitate hope, inhibiting those that are fearful (Hilgard and Bower 1975).

The roles of stimulation and reinforcement are conceived in a different way in the conditioning process. Learning results from the presence of stimuli producing disequilibrium in the form of fear or hope, followed by changes in approach or avoidance on the part of the learner, the resolution of which is reinforcing. Learning viewed in this manner can be considered emotional conditioning. Mowrer's attention extended to several additional areas including the role of imagery, the importance of imitation, and the concept of habit. These views are set forth in Mowrer's primary work (1960), which is also recommended for those wanting to learn more about the derivation of learning theory and comparative views. However, the contribution that appears to be of most importance to musicians is the role of emotion in learning. From practical experience in music teaching, it is not difficult to observe the influence of emotion in inhibiting and limiting participation and achievement as well as being an incentive for persistent and enthusiastic effort and accomplishment.

Cognitivism

Cognitivism has a long and fascinating history equal to that of associationism. Philosophically, cognitivism may be traced to Plato, Descartes, and Kant and American psychologist William James (Anderson 1990). In contrast to associationism, however, early cognitive views placed emphasis not on the acquisition of behavior in an additive manner but on the perception and understanding of relationships within an organized whole. Gestalt psychology began to make an impact on the educational system of the United States in the early 1900s with the writings and research of Wertheimer, Köhler, and Koffka, all of whom, along with Lewin, came to be known as the Berlin school (Hill 1971). The following is an introduction to this position on learning and a brief discussion of the individual contributions of these theorists.

Wertheimer (1880–1943)

"The position of Gestalt psychology was formally stated first by the German philosopher-psychologist Max Wertheimer in 1912" (Bigge 1976, 61). Gestalt, means "whole" and, as used here, refers to an organized configuration or pattern, the parts of which are subordinate to the existence of the whole and which are perceived in relation to the whole. Perception, then, was the area of study that led to the formulation of Gestalt learning theory.

Wertheimer objected to the breaking of consciousness, or thought, into its parts and insisted that thinking consisted of whole, meaningful perceptions and not a collection of associated images. This belief was supported by observation of the phi phenomenon, or the phenomenon of apparent movement (Hill 1971). This concept evolved as a result of observing the rapid alteration of adjacent lights being turned off and on periodically. The perception of alternately blinking lights, when timed properly, created the illusion of light moving back and forth from point to point. This phenomenon was considered convincing evidence of the inadvisability of attempting to analyze an occurrence by the constituent parts, and that perception was really more a matter of becoming aware of interrelationships existing in a total situation. Additional examples of the organizational nature of perception were three dots perceived and identified as a triangle; water in a whirlpool perceived not as individual drops but as an intact circular movement of water; and a melody, when transposed into another key or altered slightly otherwise, still perceived as a unit. Such observations resulted in the conclusion that "the whole is more than the sum of its parts" and in concern with the unitary aspects of perception.

As study by Wertheimer, Köhler, Koffka, and their followers continued, numerous observations about perception came to be recognized as consistent characteristics of perception and were established as laws. Before undertaking a discussion of these laws, however, it seems advisable to consider briefly the contributions of Köhler and Koffka.

Köhler (1887–1967)

Wolfgang Köhler is best known for his work with insightful problem solving, the results of which appear in his primary work, *The Mentality of Apes* (1925). The following is a description of a typical experiment resulting in the identification of insightful behavior. An ape is placed in a cage with bananas hanging from the top of the cage well out of reach of the ape. The cage also contains several boxes and a stick. Several varied attempts such as climbing and leaping about by the ape fail to obtain the bananas. After a pause in activity by the ape and a period of apparent thought and contemplation, the ape stacks the boxes, climbs onto the boxes, and uses the stick to obtain the bananas. Such behavior was described as insightful behavior or "the sudden appearance of a solution for a problem" (Lefrancois 1975, 355). Insightful behavior, then, appears to be intelligent, problem-solving behavior, and, conversely, learning of problem solving in this manner is regarded as insightful learning (Bower and Hilgard 1981).

Koffka (1886–1941)

As with Wertheimer and Köhler, Kurt Koffka eventually moved from Germany to the United States. Koffka's most notable contributions appear in his text, *Principles of Gestalt Psychology* (1935), and this work is considered to be "the fullest and most systematic treatment of the problems of learning from the Gestaltist viewpoint . . ." (Hilgard and Bower 1975, 225). As indicated in the earlier discussion of Wertheimer and Köhler, learning was viewed as really a secondary consideration. Learning was considered to be a product of perception, and what was learned was determined by the hypothesized laws of perceptual organization.

The most basic or primary law of organization is the law of *Prägnanz* that states that psychological organization will always be as "good" as the prevailing conditions allow. In other words, if a disorganized perceptual situation is encountered, the individual will impose order on that field and will do so in a predictable manner. Such organization is predictable because it normally follows a series of subsidiary laws—the laws of proximity, closure, similarity, common direction, and simplicity.

The law of proximity states that stimuli grouped together tend to be perceived as a unit. The law of closure refers to the tendency of incomplete figures, such as unconnected geometric shapes, to be perceived as connected and complete wholes. The law of similarity refers to the tendency of items similar in some respect to be perceived as grouped together. The law of common direction refers to the tendency of items to be perceived as grouped if they somehow exhibit a similar direction or an orderly series of events. The law of simplicity refers to the tendency of objects to be perceived in the most regular, symmetrical, or simple manner. Visual examples of these laws are available in most psychology textbooks. Of particular interest to the musician, Franklin (1972) has provided musical examples of these laws (also see chap. 5).

Another important aspect of perception is figure-ground relationships. Figure is that shape or aspect of the perceptual experience that stands out predominantly as the "thing" perceived. Ground is the background or relatively undifferentiated portion of the perceptual experience.

The physiological representation of perception is described as a memory trace, a hypothesized neural and cerebral structure, the various components of which occur simultaneously and in an organized manner. Learning, then, consists of acquiring or restructuring memory traces that are "good" or "better" gestalts. Other considerations, such as forgetting, understanding, insight, problem solving, and thinking, are interpreted in terms of perceptual organization or reorganization and the use of previously acquired memory traces.

The result of such theoretical thinking was in direct opposition to associationist views and resulted in a view of behavior that could accommodate the more dynamic, holistic theories to follow. Hilgard and Bower say of Wertheimer, Köhler, and Koffka, that "they were, in fact, the intellectual forerunners of much of what is today called cognitive psychology, which is indeed a dominant viewpoint currently in American experimental psychology" (1975, 280).

For musicians, the implications and possible applications of these views are many. Music learning is obviously dependent on aural perception. Much, if not most, of the existing research on aural perception does not appear to be emanating from Gestalt theory but could well be interpreted in this context. The potential for theoretically based research is readily apparent—perception of tone, melody, harmony, rhythm, form, and so on. Immediate application of some of these views may well be in order—organization of the teaching-learning situation in ways to facilitate the perception of music as wholes or larger units, emphasis on the musical components, emphasis on a problem-solving approach, and procedures to bring about insightful learning being notable examples.

Lewin (1890–1947)

With the work of Kurt Lewin, a decided shift occurred in the development of learning theory. Whereas his German contemporaries were concerned with "perception, learning, and thinking, Lewin was interested in motivation, personality, and social psychology" (Hill 1971, 106).

Lewin's system was called field theory and made use of the concept of life space. Life space was defined as the individual and all aspects of his or her environment that influence his or her behavior at a given time. In describing life space and the dynamics therein, Lewin employed terminology and concepts previously developed in geometry and physics. A topological description was employed, and life space was depicted as a type of flexible and changing map; this map contained the factors determining behavior (numerous texts contain illustrations of such a topological map).

Goals exist within this space that are attractive to the individual and that the individual tends to approach while other factors may repel the individual. Thus, attractive aspects possess a positive valence, while repelling aspects provide a negative valence. The direction of the individual's behavior in such a situation is described in terms of vectors, indicating direction in tendencies to move toward a positive valence or away from a negative valence. Barriers may also exist that serve to impede the movement of the individual toward a goal.

Situations may be quite simple or very complex within the life space containing any number of combinations of positive and negative valences of varying strength. Thus, the individual may encounter an approach-approach situation in which the behavioral decision is a clear one, an avoidance-approach situation in which a difficult decision will be necessary, or an avoidance-avoidance situation in which no truly acceptable behavior is possible. The result of conflicting or competing valences along with the presence of possible barriers may result in a state of tension, anxiety, or conflict within the individual. It is under these conditions that the person may exhibit hesitant, oscillating, and uncertain behavior.

Lewin's system provided a theory by which behavior might be explained or even predicted, based on purposefulness of the individual in response to aspects of his environment found attractive or repelling to him. It was Lewin's intent that this complicated theoretical system be quantified and experimentally verified, but this was not accomplished because of his early death (Hilgard 1964). Nevertheless, Lewin's contribution is significant and, as Bigge states, "Cognitive-field theory or psychology is based on the thinking of the late Kurt Lewin" (1976, 175).

During the first half of the twentieth century, learning theory in the United States was dominated, for the most part, by associationism. For various reasons, however, cognitive theory and other areas of study amenable to cognitive theory emerged during the second half of the century and research and writing in the cognitive tradition flourished. Cited as influential in this emergence is the work of Donald Broadbent in information theory, Noam Chomsky in linguistics, Ulric Neisser's studies in perception (Anderson 1990), and writings by George Miller, Jerome Bruner, and Jean Piaget (Gardner 1985). Consequent developments have been many and varied. In some cases, theorists have chosen to broaden the concept of what may be included in learning theory; others have attempted to combine associationist and cognitive traditions under one model of how learning might occur. The following views have been selected for discussion based both on general importance in cognitive thinking as well as relevance to music education and music therapy.

Piaget (1896–1980)

Jean Piaget, a developmental psychologist, postulated a series of stages of intellectual development beginning at birth and progressing through adolescence; these stages correspond roughly to various age periods of the child. Development through these stages was considered invariant; that is, progress at a higher level is difficult without first achieving the desired level of development at a lower level (Hilgard and Bower 1975). Piaget believed that intelligence (for Piaget, a process of adapting rather than a level of ability) was based on two biological attributes found in all organisms, organization and adaptation (Biehler 1971).

Organization is the tendency of individuals to integrate experiences into some sort of coherent system. An example of early organization would be the child's ability to see, touch, grasp, and taste some object, such as a rattle. These early experiences are said to result in schema, or generalized responses, which can be repeated. Through such experiences, a variety of schema are constructed and serve as structures on which future development can build through the process of adaptation (DeCecco and Crawford 1974). Adaptation is the tendency to interact with the environment. Development does not occur by learning in response to stimuli alone, but by curious and investigative activity and adaptation by the child.

This interaction with the environment results in progressive and orderly mental development. This may be accomplished in two ways, by assimilation and by accommodation. Experiences that may fit into existing mental structures or schema are assimilated. Experiences that are sufficiently new or different, so that they cannot fit into existing structures, require accommodation or a change or modification of response and a consequently new or changed structure.

Piaget hypothesized that development occurs at discrete levels, although "new learning in the form of assimilations and accommodations takes place continuously within a given level" (Bergan and Dunn 1976, 80). When the child appears to be functioning appropriately at a given level, a state of equilibrium is said to exist. When experience or some aspect of experience requires a response that is not appropriate to the functioning level of the child, the state is one of disequilibrium. Disequilibrium is characteristic of an approaching change to a higher level of functioning, and the presence of disequilibrium "directs" the child to develop abilities appropriate to that level.

After extensive observations of the behavior of children over a long time, Piaget developed a structure describing intellectual development. This structure contains periods of development, approximate corresponding ages, and descriptions of typical behaviors. Each period is divided into several subsections and periods of age-time and are described in great detail in numerous sources (see Anderson 1990; Flavell 1963; Inhelder and Piaget 1959; Piaget and Inhelder 1969).

Stage one is described as sensorimotor and spans the time from birth to approximately two years of age. Learning is acquired principally through motor activity and the manipulation of objects. Recognition of objects, as distinguished from the environment and from other objects, is an important intellectual accomplishment. The reality of the existence of objects must be accomplished—reality not only in terms of objective existence apart from imagination, but reality of existence regardless of perspective or the visual presence of the object. A sense of causality develops in that the child gains awareness and begins to perceive the relationship between actions and their consequences. Again, numerous substages exit within this one period of development.

The second stage of development is referred to as preoperational and represents the ages of two to seven years. Of primary concern here is the transformation of sensorimotor learning into symbolic learning (primarily language acquisition), or the ability to distinguish the actual objects or events from symbols used to represent objects or events. Again, such learning is acquired through accommodating and assimilating experiences. The child learns that one object may represent a class of objects and, eventually, that language symbols may be used to represent that object or class of objects. They learn that concepts of opening or closing may refer to doors, fists, or a playbox. However, operations at this level tend to remain intuitive or egocentric, relating closely to the interest and experience of the child and lacking the characteristics bringing objectivity and utility of thought, as occur in later stages.

Stage three is the period of concrete operations and spans the period of about 7 to 11 years of age. This stage is characterized by increasing ability to classify objects and events and the relationships existing therein. Evident also is growth in language skills and in quantitative ability. Of particular interest in this period is the concept of conservation. This concept refers to the child's ability to recognize that objects originally perceived as wholes remain essentially unaltered in spite of the fact that the shape of the whole or parts of the whole may be rearranged. The usual examples are a lump of clay, when reshaped, still remains a lump of clay with the same weight and occupies the same space, and liquid, when placed in different containers, remains the same amount of liquid.

Conservation requires that the child also acquire the concept of reversibility. An object, when changed, does not lose its identity but may be reshaped or returned to its original state. The concepts of conservation, reversibility, and identity may be applied not only to objects but to other operations involving numbers, length, area, and verbal reasoning.

The fourth and final stage is the period of formal operations, which is essentially characterized by those thought processes typical of the adult. Most prominent in this regard is the capacity for abstract thought. At this stage, the adolescent departs the world of concreteness and enters the world of theoretical speculation. Young adults become problem solvers using theory (inductive or deductive), propositional thinking, and scientific reasoning to answer questions. They make assumptions, test these assumptions, make inferences, and weigh possible outcomes in terms of possible consequences.

Application of Piaget's thinking to music learning has been extensive, and further discussion appears later in the chapter.

Bruner (1915–)

Jerome Bruner's work is presented in numerous writings, the earliest definitive work being *The Process of Education* (1960). In this work, his views are centered around four main ideas—the importance or role of structure in learning, readiness for learning, the nature of intuition, and the importance of the desire to learn.

The importance of structure is illustrated by postulating two types of transfer of training. The first, specific transfer of training, refers to the ability to use specific skills in quite similar situations encountered later. More important is the second type of transfer, or the transfer of principles and attitudes. This type of transfer refers to an initial grasp and gradual broadening and deepening of ideas, both general and basic to the subject matter. It requires not only the grasp of general principles but the development of an attitude toward learning, a "sense of discovery" of relationships existing within the overall context of a field of knowledge and, with success, the increasing confidence in one's abilities and the desire to know more. In this regard, Brubaker (1976, 101) credits Bruner with correcting the "supposed perversion" of Dewey's ideas on transfer by placing renewed emphasis on the structural aspects of content and the excitement of the learner in the knowledge itself.

Several factors contribute to the formation of mental structures facilitating transfer. The grasp of fundamentals that serve to make the subject comprehensible is important. However, the retention and usability of these fundamentals are dependent on structure or an awareness of general or fundamental principles within which fundamentals acquire meaning and may be more readily retained. The emphasis on principles or concepts also makes more likely the development of a model for learning, a model that may be used when other learning opportunities are encountered.

The appropriateness of any learning at whatever level has clear implications for developmental psychology or readiness for learning. As described earlier, Piaget hypothesizes that the ability of the child varies with stages relating most closely with age-levels. It is Bruner's contention, however, that segmenting training based on hypothesized states of developmental growth may not be advisable. He further suggests that the curriculum be so arranged as to have the student encounter this material in a manner suitable to age level and interest. The teacher should build on these initial experiences as the student matures. Thus, it is considered proper and preferable that the student be introduced to basic principles of any subject in an appropriate manner at any developmental level, and that the expansion and elaboration of the subject matter be geared to levels of readiness and development, thus the concept of the spiral curriculum (Bruner 1960).

Music educators will recognize this thinking as the basis of the Manhattanville Music Curriculum Project (1970), in which the spiral curriculum is central. It should be noted that this concept is similar to an earlier theory attributed to James Mursell (1948) that is usually called a cyclical sequence. In both cases, what is referred to is the repeated presentation of materials to be learned in a variety of settings and complexities, the complexity determined by various age levels and experience of the learner.

Bruner also places great importance on the development of intuitive thinking. Intuitive thinking is contrasted with analytical thinking and characterized as proceeding by an immediate apprehension or grasp of the significance and structure of a situation or problem rather than in a well-organized and preplanned manner. Intuitive capability is highly valued among scholars, but little in the way of research is available to explain its nature or how it may be developed. Bruner suggests possibilities, these dependent on the flexibility and ingenuity of the teacher to allow risk taking on the part of the student. A grasp of fundamentals, experience, and the acquisition of cognitive structures may well facilitate intuitive behavior; however, what is suggested is that the student be encouraged to guess, to take risks, and to develop self-confidence in problem solving.

Another important concern of Bruner's is motivation. Several familiar possibilities are suggested, such as increasing student interest in the material to be learned, adjusting the material to be presented into forms appropriate to the child, development of the interests of the child, and promoting appropriate attitudes and values contributing to accomplishment. All of these suggestions focus on Bruner's primary concerns, the intrinsic value of the material to be learned and the importance of developing, within the individual, a desire or attitude to promote future learning.

Finally, Bruner's theory of instruction, which he calls prescriptive (rather than descriptive), has four major features (Bower and Hilgard 1981; Bruner 1966).

1. Predispositions: experiences that make the child willing and able to learn.
2. Structure and form of knowledge: structure of the body of knowledge so that it may be easily grasped. Any domain of knowledge can be represented in the enactive mode through action, the iconic mode through visual or other sensory images, or the symbolic mode through language.
3. Sequence and its uses: the sequence or order in which material is presented. Bruner devised a spiral curriculum that allowed for the revisiting of fundamental aspects of subject matter at increasingly sophisticated levels.
4. Form and pacing of reinforcement: nature and pacing of reward from immediate to delayed and from extrinsic to intrinsic.

Bruner also emphasizes that intellectual growth is dependent on the use of words or symbols that allow not only orderly or responsive thought but also logical or analytical thinking. Language learning is the primary medium for engaging the child with the environment and a prerequisite for cognitive development. Growth in intellectual activity is described in terms of both capacity and flexibility—the student learns to deal with a great number of simultaneously presented alternatives, to allocate time effectively, and the attention appropriate to these demands.

Bruner's thinking has been highly influential in research and practice in music education. The reader is referred particularly to the discussions of musical development and transfer of training that appear in a later section.

Gagne (1916–   )

Robert M. Gagne is a contributor to educational thought who has had considerable influence on music education (Gordon 1971; Sidnell 1973). Gagne approaches learning by first identifying different tasks or kinds of learning and the conditions under which they are likely to be encountered. On this basis, he establishes a hierarchy of learning, moving from simple to complex and employing concepts from both associationist and cognitive traditions to illustrate and support the levels or types of learning comprising the hierarchy. Eight types or varieties of learning were adopted to form the hierarchy. Gagne recognized that selecting and using only eight conditions might be arbitrary and that "it will possibly become necessary to make new formulations of these conditions, to separate some or, what appears less likely, to collapse some" (Gagne 1970, 63). The eight varieties of learning are as follows.

1. Signal learning. Similar to the classical conditioning of Pavlov, the availability of unconditioned responses and stimuli within the learner provides the basis for a variety of conditioned stimuli and conditioned responses to be developed. This is the simplest form of learning, learning to make a general and undiffused response to a signal.
2. Stimulus-Response Learning. Similar to the connectionism of Thorndike, this type of learning results in a specific S-R connection. Utilizing the concepts of reinforcement, contiguity, repetition, discrimination, and generalization, many types of motor learning, lower level tasks, and initial verbal learning may occur.
3. Chaining. Chaining involves the joining together of one or more stimulus-response connections to make possible a coordinated and more complex act of behavior. Conditions that make chaining possible include sufficient stimulus-response learning, so that chaining is possible and can result in more complex physical actions.
4. Verbal Association. This type of learning is essentially verbal chaining, the linking up of a previously learned verbal repertoire. The learning procedure may proceed from simple association of terms to longer, more meaningful verbal sequences or sentences.
5. Discrimination Learning. Discrimination learning refers to the learning of the individual to discriminate between various characteristics of objects that distinguish them from one another—shapes, sizes, colors, sounds, and so on. Of great significance at this level of learning is the possibility of interference, that is, confusion that results from the close similarity of characteristics.
6. Concept Learning. Here, the learner is required to make a common response to a group of stimuli that are in some way similar and may be grouped together to form a class of objects that result in a concept or generalization. In this way, the learner is freed from response to individual stimuli and learns on a conceptual basis, by verbal instruction, or on the basis of existing knowledge.
7. Rule Learning. Rule learning is chaining of two or more concepts that results in the ability to deal with relationships and

with rules that govern such relationships. Perhaps most important is that what is learned is a set of rules providing the student with the ability to order and understand the topic under consideration.

8. Problem Solving. The final type of learning may be referred to as thinking. Herein is the application of all previous learning in addition to "new learning," and the student engages in a thinking process, exploring and testing new hypotheses and applicability. This process is similar to the scientific method, although, at this point in the hierarchy, it is considered simply a higher form of learning.

Musicians should be aware that Gagne applies this final type of learning not only to the exploration of science but to creative efforts as well. In this case, the artist has immersed himself in the creative problem for long periods of time, resulting in a "sudden insight" that transforms the problem situation into a solution situation (Gagne 1970, 228).

The reader should be reminded that this is a generalization and, for each type of learning, Gagne carefully specifies the necessary pre-existent conditions for learning and accounts for the variables that may influence learning—contiguity, repetition, reinforcement, extinction, discrimination, retention, forgetting, and generalization. The work of Gagne has been influential, perhaps, because it has been amenable to sequencing of instruction. "In this sense he has made hierarchy the basis for his approach to a theory of instruction" (Hilgard and Bower 1975, 618).

With regard to the application of sequencing in music education, an article by Walters (1992) discusses the use of Gagne's hierarchy as well as the ideas of Bruner and Piaget, with reference to the earlier theories of Thorndike and Skinner. Sequencing is closely related to the concept of readiness and the idea that the best way to avoid difficulty with learning is by having learning experiences well sequenced. In addition to the use of hierarchies, Walters considers a variety of other characteristics, including types of concepts to be learned, content and skill involved, and whole versus part learning.

Maslow (1908–70)

The work of Abraham H. Maslow has been of particular interest to music educators as a result of Maslow's participation in the Tanglewood Symposium in 1967 (Choate 1968). Maslow is credited with the initial development of third force psychology, also sometimes referred to as humanistic psychology (Milholland and Forisha 1972). Third force psychology was a concept developed to provide a common identity for psychologists espousing views in opposition to the associationist tradition and desiring a broader concept of the study of man, a concept that would incorporate aspects of human behavior previously not emphasized—motivation, affect, creativity, and general fulfillment of human potentiality—views very similar to the cognitive tradition.

Maslow's primary contribution is to be found in a theory of motivation as presented in two major works, *Motivation and Personality* (1970) and *Toward a Psychology of Being* (1968b). Maslow postulated a hierarchy of human needs, the successful completion of which is dependent on the satisfaction of lower order needs and eventually resulting in the achievement of self-actualization or the fully accomplished individual. The hierarchy, as commonly described, is as follows.

Physiological and Organizational
1. Lower order or survival needs: needs of immediate existence, nourishment, and so on.
2. Security needs: assurance of regularity and predictability for self, family group, confidence in future.

Affiliation, Social
3. Belonging needs: acceptance within a group, knowledge that others are aware of you and that you wish to be a member of the group.
4. Esteem needs: recognition of self as a unique person with special abilities and characteristics.

Achievement, Intellectual
5. Need for knowledge: knowing how to do things and about the meaning of things, symbols, and events.
6. Need for understanding: knowledge of relationships, understanding of systems and processes that may be integrated into theory.

Self-actualization, Aesthetic Needs
7. Aesthetic needs: appreciation for beauty, a sense of order and balance.
8. Self-actualization: need to become a fully functioning human, to become fully the "self" that one truly is.

Self-actualization, then, is the highest level of functioning and can occur only when the other needs in the hierarchy are met. The self-actualized individual is one who is motivated by needs to be open and not defensive in relationships, loves and accepts self and others, avoids aggressive and manipulative behavior, acts in ways ethically good for society, displays autonomy and creativity, and is curious and spontaneous in interaction with the environment (Gage and Berliner 1975). Closely related is the fulfillment of aesthetic needs.

Maslow classifies learning as extrinisic (that which can be shared from one individual to another) and intrinsic (that which is is internal and private). Certain intrinsic experiences of the self-actualized individual are described as peak experiences or "the cognition of being" (Maslow 1968a, 72). Other descriptions would include joy, ecstasy, mystical or religious experience, and insightful experience. Peak experiences may be achieved in a variety of ways, but especially important to note is the fact that music is one of the most common vehicles through which human beings have peak experiences (Maslow 1968a).

Maslow does not provide a theory of learning in the traditional sense but offers some general guidelines as to the desired characteristics of the learning situation (Gage and Berliner 1975). Learning conceived in this manner would be self-directed, and the learner would be encouraged to achieve without threat of failure. Emphasis would be on encouraging the desire to learn, on learning how to learn, on adaptability to changing situations, and on self-evaluation. The role of feelings and the freedom to express and accept feelings would be important. The role of the arts and music is most important in this regard, and it is this rationale that prompts Maslow to regard music education as intrinsic, basic, and as belonging at the core of educational experience.

Rogers (1902–)

Carl Rogers is another prominent member of third force or humanistic psychology. Rogers is best known for the development of client-centered or nondirective therapy, the principles of which are set forth in several major works, notably *Client-Centered Therapy* (1951) and *On Becoming A Person* (1961). Basic to Rogers's therapeutic approach is the belief that individuals have the ability to work out their own problems, and that it is preferable that they do so. The role of the therapist is one of facilitation, assisting in subtle and nondirective ways. Initially, the therapist strives to establish a warm and friendly relationship, indicating complete acceptance. An atmosphere of permissiveness is sought within which individuals are encouraged to express feelings and opinions freely. By listening and responding, the therapist assists individuals in clarifying, understanding, and working out problems. The therapist does not attempt to hurry the process or provide solutions but relies on individuals to gain insight eventually into difficulties and to strive for possible solutions.

Rogers's thinking has also been applied to education and learning and closely parallels his therapeutic procedures, resulting in the concept of learning and teaching as being primarily a matter of facilitation. Discussions of applications appear in several sources. Milholland and Forisha (1972) discuss Rogers's 19 formal principles of human behavior and implications for learning, while, in *Freedom to Learn* (1969), Rogers cites ten principles that summarize his approach. Based on these two sources, the following is a summary of Rogers's views.

Individuals are the center of their own private worlds of constantly changing experience. This world of experience is depicted as a phenomenological or perceptual field to which individuals react in an organized manner, demonstrating a basic tendency to maintain and actualize self. Thus, all behavior is seen as purposeful and goal oriented. Behavior is interpreted as reflecting attempts of individuals to meet their needs and enhance themselves within the world of experience as they perceive it. Logically, then, understanding behavior is accomplished best from the perspective of the individual, by viewing behavior from this personal frame of reference.

Learning and teaching are approached within this conceptual context. Humans are believed to have a natural potential for learning and, as a result of the tendency toward self-actualization, are eager to do so. Numerous conditions within the situation influence the learning process. In a goal-oriented system, it is logical that learning will be facilitated if the subject matter to be learned is relevant to the purposes of the learner. Such functional learning is not only acquired more easily but much more rapidly.

Learning also involves a change in perception of self. Through repeated interaction with the environment, self is gradually differentiated from the perceptual field and concepts concerning self are developed. Behavior patterns become consistent with self-concept, and new experiences will be accepted or resisted to the extent that these experiences are consistent with self-concept. With regard to learning, situations threatening to self-concept are resisted, while less threatening situations provide opportunities within which learning can be more readily achieved. Threat influences perceptual capabilities; when threat is low, experience is perceived more clearly or in a more differentiated manner and is more readily assimilated with already present knowledge. Therefore, a learning situation is to be sought that is free from threat, free from humiliation, scorn, ridicule, and other human devaluation potential.

Much learning is acquired though doing, through placing the student in direct confrontation with actual problems—practical, social, ethical, philosophical, personal, research endeavors, or activities of the project sort. Learning is also facilitated by involving the student as a responsible participant in the learning process. Choice of direction, determination of resources, formulation of the problem, determination of the course of action, and realization of the possible consequences of action to be taken are all opportunities for significant learning.

Similarly, learning that is self-initiated and involves the whole person—both intellect and feelings—results in learning that is most lasting and pervasive. Learning under these conditions is highly personal and creative and results in the interaction of both cognitive and affective components. Self-evaluation is an important facilitator, not only of learning but of such characteristics as independence, creativity, and self-reliance. Individuals learn to make their own judgments and to evaluate the consequences of actions based on self-adopted standards or criteria. Finally, social learning is most important in that individuals come to recognize and adapt to changing situations.

Rogers (1969) has much to say about the role of the teacher as a facilitator in the learning process. He offers advice to the teacher that, if implemented, would provide the proper conditions for learning to occur. As was the case with Maslow, Rogers does not offer a formal learning theory. But suggestions derived from his experience in counseling as well as from his basic humanistic philosophy provide significant implications for music educators and music therapists.

Gardner (1943–   )

Howard Gardner's (1985) concept of cognitive science offers what is perhaps the most comprehensive of current views in cognitive thinking. Gardner bases his position, first, on a rejection of behaviorism as an inadequate approach to deal successfully with the varied nature of human thinking and learning. Further, he specifies, as central to his thinking, the concept of mental representations as the proper and fundamental concern of cognitive science. Mental representation refers to the many and varied features of being human—cognitive, affective, contextual, and those culturally determined. However, Gardner's views are concerned primarily with cognitive functions and consist of ways in which mental representations of these functions may best be studied and understood.

Several other features are key to his thinking. First, the development of the computer has been crucial, both as a model of how human thought might occur as well as a tool for related research. Second, he chooses to de-emphasize, for the time being, affective, contextual, cultural, and historical aspects of being in order to concentrate on cognitive aspects. Third, he adopts a highly interdisciplinary approach, seeking support from numerous fields of study that appear to be effective in studying or describing the nature of mental representations. Fourth, his work is rooted firmly in philosophy and his thinking reflects early views of Gestalt psychology.

Several major areas or methods of inquiry have been chosen by Gardner to support his views. As I have said, philosophy provides a valid contribution to cognitive science. The role of philosophy may seem, to some, separate or primarily historical; however, Gardner regards philosophy as serving to define fundamental questions and to integrate the work from various areas. Views important to Gardner include the thinking of Descartes, Kant, and the later cognitivist, Jerry Fodor. From psychology, a variety of contributions have been selected and include the thinking of Karl Lashley, Edward Tolman, Ulric Neisser (cognitive psychology), J. J. Gibson (perception), Jean Piaget (developmental psychology), Donald Broadbent and George Miller (information processing), and the views of Jerome Bruner.

Artificial intelligence involves using the computer to simulate the kind of thinking in which humans engage and, by doing so, learn more about how the mind works. Gardner regards the computer as an "aid in conceptualizing and testing theories of human intelligence" as well as helpful in the study of language and perception (Gardner 1985, 177). Notable individuals cited in the field are Allen Newell and Herbert Simon, Marvin Minsky, and David Marr. Linguistics is yet another area included, and relies on the work of Noam Chomsky. Particularly important is the characterization of mental representation as being derived from an inherent "structure of the mind," a concept at odds with the views of behaviorism. The study of language is regarded by Gardner as, perhaps, the best testing ground for the study of cognitive science. Two additional areas regarded as fruitful are anthropology and neuroscience. Anthropology is regarded as an "upper boundary" for cognitive science and deals with a wide range of global issues, including general cultural, historical, and contextual concerns. Neuroscience is regarded as a "lower boundary" and is concerned with the physiological basis for perception, cognition, and language development. The influence of a variety of individuals in this regard is noted, including K. Lashley, Donald Hebb, and Karl Pribram. Finally, it is clear that a high degree of interaction and interdisciplinary work among these separate but supportive areas is required and just what role each area plays and will continue to play is still developing.

Related to these ideas is Gardner's concept of intelligence (Gardner 1983). Rather than a single intelligence, a theory of multiple intelligences is hypothesized. These include linguistic, musical, logical-mathematical, spatial, bodily-kinesthetic, and inter- and intrapersonal intelligences. This theory of multiple intelligences parallels Gardner's general ideas on cognition in many ways. His views on both cognition and intelligence are still in the formative stage and caution is urged relative to application. Some of Gardner's most recent writing has been in human development and learning (1991). Notably, children are regarded as having distinctive ways of learning that require that different disciplines be both presented and evaluated in different ways. Gardner's thinking has already been most influential in the work of several researchers and writers in music, several of which are discussed in the application section toward the end of the chapter (also see chap. 12).

Related Developments

Included in this section are a number of disciplines that have not been classified as distinctly associationist or cognitive in character, but that have had a considerable impact on psychology and education, if not directly on learning theory itself. The areas selected include functionalism, psychoanalytic theory, mathematical models, information processing, and neurophysiology. Only a brief mention of these developments is possible here, but music scholars and researchers should be aware of the potential for the study and understanding of learning and other behaviors.

Functionalism

Functionalism, according to Hilgard and Bower 1975, represents a category that includes psychologists who are not aligned with any particular school of learning theory, but who are pursuing research in an eclectic and less formal manner. The concept of functionalism apparently stemmed from the educational views of John Dewey (1859–1952), with efforts being focused on applied research or on basic research concerned with particular aspects of mental function.

Classification of individuals and their work in this category is problematic; some indicate a strong leaning toward an associationist view, others are decidedly cognitive in orientation, while still others do indeed seem to occupy the middle-of-the-road position that functionalism implies. However, it seems fair to state that, from the period of the mid-twentieth century onward, interest has declined in the construction of formal learning theory, and attention has been given to more specific concerns, whatever the theoretical influence or position of the researcher.

Researchers who might be classified as functionalists reflect concern with all aspects of learning—conditioning, learning and forgetting, practice, perception, motivation, transfer of training, insight and problem solving, cognitive development, creativity, attitudes, social development, personality, curriculum, method, measurement and evaluation, and so on. The following texts are recommended: McGeach and Irion 1952; Underwood 1966; Woodworth 1958; Osgood 1953; DeCecco and Crawford 1974; Snelbecker 1974; Gage and Berliner 1975; Bergan and Dunn 1976; Houston 1976; Cronbach 1977; and more recently, Howard 1983; Mayer 1983; Solso 1990; and Anderson 1990. These texts contain discussions and reports of research relating not only to functionalism but to most, if not all, traditional learning theories. In particular, Snelbecker (1974, 83–113) is recommended for a discussion of the evolution of research that was theory based to the variety of types of research described as having a "fact-finding" emphasis and representative of functionalism. Noted also is the possibility that the practice of formal theory building may have undergone only a temporary decline and that the study of learning based on formal theory may emerge again in the near future.

It appears that a large portion of music research falls in this category. Research and writings until the latter part of this century are not associated with a particular learning theory but are concerned with the investigation of some aspect of music learning and some ideas about what methods or techniques might influence learning. Subjects are extremely varied and include basic perception and cognition, music listening, reading, developmental issues, performance, conducting, practice, and so on. Some of this work appears as other research in the applications section that follows.

Psychoanalytic Theory

Psychoanalytic theory and its consequent influence on learning theory began with Sigmund Freud (1856–1939). It was not Freud's intent to develop a theory of learning but rather a theory or approach for the treatment of mental illness. However, the impact of psychoanalytic thinking on psychology and education in general is important, and for this reason brief consideration will be given to this topic.

Freud's view is described as hedonistic, that is, based on the principle that people seek pleasure and avoid pain (Hilgard and Bower 1975). This position is congruent with the law of effect or the control of behavior by reward and punishment. However, rather than the seemingly mechanical posture of the associationist, psychoanalytic theory is described as dynamic in that there are forces and energies within individuals that influence their behavior.

The source of energy is the libido which is a form of life force or mental or psychic energy derived from the sexual urge, although manifested in several ways. The manner in which the libido moves may determine a variety of personality characteristics—narcissism, introversion, or regression, among other possibilities. Libido, then, appears to be an innate and somewhat undefined source of motivational energy.

Mental life is viewed as consisting of three levels, the conscious, preconscious, and unconscious. Consciousness is the mental state of which the individual is aware and preconsciousness consists of mental content that can be brought easily to a conscious level. The unconscious, however, is unknown to the individual, comprises the larger portion of the mind, and greatly influences the behavior of the individual.

Other mental structures include the id, the ego, and the superego. The id represents the instinctual energy of the individual and is guided completely by the pleasure principle. The ego is partially conscious and partially unconscious and, at birth, is small and weak. With growth by means of identification, the ego gains strength and comes to represent the rational aspects of the individual. The superego represents conscience and serves to control the activities of the id, the rationality of the ego being the conscious site of such interpersonal struggles.

Development is also divided into stages which include the infantile period, from birth to five or six; the latent period, from about six until puberty, and adolescence, from puberty until the late teens. Each stage is further divided with development proceeding through a variety of possibilities toward the mature adult. Any number of terms were added (or reinforced) to the vocabulary of psychological terms—*sublimation, identification, fixation, reaction formation, rationalization, displacement, transference,* and so on. Extended discussion is not possible here, but, for an initial orientation to Freud's views, the reader is referred to Hall's *Primer of Freudian Psychology* (1954). Other notable contributors to the development of psychoanalytic theory include Alfred Adler, Carl Jung, Erich Fromm, Karen Horney, and Harry S. Sullivan. For extended discussion of these views, the reader is referred to Munroe's *Schools of Psychoanalytic Thought* (1955).

Erick Erickson is, "among contemporary humanistic psychologists, one of the most eminent" (Cronbach 1977, 23). Erickson (1968) describes personal development as growing out of certain crises in psychosocial experience that result in progress or regression in personality growth. Healthy growth is characterized by an ability to control one's environment, to perceive oneself and the world accurately, and to function

effectively. "These are the qualities of the self-actualized, fully functioning person as described by humanistic psychologists Carl Rogers and
Abraham Maslow" (Gage and Berliner 1975, 382–83). Erickson postulates eight stages of growth based on the positive resolution of certain
crises encountered during the development of the personality. Crises
include such opposing possibilities as trust-mistrust during infancy,
autonomy-shame during early childhood, initiative-guilt in middle childhood, accomplishment-inferiority during the period of kindergarten
through puberty, identity-confusion occurring during adolescence, inti-
macy-isolation resolution of more mature life, generativity-stagnation
possibilities of adulthood, and the final crisis of integrity-despair occurring in old age. The various stages obviously overlap in time and are
developmentally dependent on the nature of the experiences individuals have with people from whom they learn and model their personalities. Thus, Erickson offers a structure depicting how self-actualization
may occur.

Mathematical Models

The use of mathematical models as a means to bring about precise quantification of learning is a recent development. Learning theorists, particularly of the associationist tradition, were always interested in quantification and the resultant high degree of objectivity, but techniques
making possible rapid and exact quantification were not always available. With the development of the computer and mathematical models
for gathering and interpreting data, this potential has been increased
enormously and employed by numerous theorists of various traditions
to conduct research in a more expeditious and scientific manner.

According to Hilgard and Bower (1975), mathematical models do
not offer a new or distinct learning theory but a means to theory construction, a form of approach, or a technique for a more precise statement of
theory and the confirmation of research findings. Others contend that
certain underlying assumptions characterize research undertaken in this
manner and that "special substance, or psychologically meaningful, descriptions of learning processes result from mathematical learning theories" (Snelbecker 1974, 359). The latter position appears to be based on the
view that a mathematical approach can result in the acquisition of data,
and the prediction and description of behavior in a quantitative manner
that is not possible by more traditional theories.

A study of the literature reveals a great number of models that have
been developed for a variety of reasons. Estes (1954) developed models
for the purpose of more precisely describing scanning or the selective

response to the number of stimuli available. This technique is referred to as a continuous linear model. Another type of model is referred to as a Markov model, developed for the purpose of studying behavior of more limited scope (Hilgard and Bower 1975). Extended discussion of these and the hundreds of other models is not possible here. Snelbecker (1974, 371) offers considerable organizational assistance by describing general characteristics that include:

1. The use of theoretical mathematical models to describe and to interpret data,
2. Probabilistic (stochastic) models rather than deterministic ones,
3. Concern with sequential effects, involving some examination of trial-to-trial changes,
4. Comparatively few outside assumptions, with parameters primarily derived directly from the data, and
5. Some preference for linear transformation in accounting for trial-to-trial changes.

Mathematical models have been applied to practically every area of concern to learning—stimulus analysis, reaction time, response possibilities, operant condition and extinction, discrimination learning, learning curves and the influence of practice, short-term memory and forgetting, incentive motivation, changing of attitudes or impressions, imitation, memory search, and, most important, the compounding of variables in a complex situation that otherwise might defy analysis. Mathematical models, then, offer the researcher an approach to research and a means of analyzing the results of research that might otherwise be unmanageable. The huge number of variables possible in music learning, musical analysis, and music listening are readily apparent and researchers may well profit by use of this approach.

Information Processing

Information processing is a recent approach to understanding learning that compares mental functions with the operation of the computer (Snelbecker 1974). Stated most simply, the computer is a complex mechanism capable of processing information in a variety of ways. Involved in this process would be receiving the information (programming), sorting the information into categories for storage in various forms, and retrieving the information on demand. A more mentalistic description of the computer operation would be that, after programming, the computer receives a command (stimulus) and proceeds to process this input through a complex of analysis (problem solving) sequences including encoding, assimilation with existing stored information (interpretation involving comparison, contrast, and evaluation), and eventual decoding resulting in an output of the results (response). A direct comparison to the operation of the mind is not intended, but the analogy does provide a basic idea of how the information-processing theorist might conceptualize and approach mental functions.

Human information-processing theories or approaches are abundant and are concerned with all aspects of human behavior—perception, cognition, learning and forgetting, motivation, development, motor response, problem solving, linguistics, and so on. Recently, information processing has become closely identified with cognitive psychology (Anderson 1990; Mayer 1983), although neoassociationists also employ these concepts (Anderson and Bower 1980; Berlyne 1965). Thus, information processing might be considered more like a tool for analyzing cognition than a theory of cognition (Mayer 1983). The purpose here is not to debate this issue nor to present a review of these developments; rather, comments on selected contributions will be made and the reader will be referred to several sources.

An article entitled "The Magical Number Seven, Plus or Minus Two" by George Miller (1956) represents seminal thinking on the subject. Miller was concerned with the limitations on human ability to process information. Limits on human capacity to receive and retain information of a discreet sort or information requiring absolute judgments is determined to some extent by the number of judgments to be made, this number being seven. To extend the amount of information to be retained, humans apparently resort to categorizing and organizing the information received into chunks, thus greatly increasing the number of discreet items that may be retained by such classification.

Application of information theory to music learning is promising. For example, Broadbent (1958) proposed a theory of attention that is concerned with selective attention to competing or simultaneously presented stimuli. It is hypothesized that perceptual limits allow reception of only a portion of the sensory information that is available, and that the brain contains a selective filter system that can be tuned to accept some stimuli and reject others, with many factors influencing which sensory elements are selected. Given that the vast majority of music learning involves the processing of huge numbers of stimuli presented simultaneously, consideration of a filter model or similar concept seems appropriate. The music researcher will also be interested in Norman's chapter on practice and skilled performance (1969, 199–212). Several pages are devoted specifically to music learning—practice, performance, and memorization. The reader will find few answers to questions but, certainly, many possible avenues for research.

Finally, information processing has become extremely useful as a means of representing and studying practically all aspects of human thought and behavior and appears to hold great potential for the study and understanding of musical information. For further general study, the reader is referred to sources cited previously, in addition to Ellis and Hunt 1989; Klatzky 1980 and 1984; Bower and Hilgard 1981; Massaro 1975; and Anderson and Bower 1973.

Neurophysiology

A final development merely to be mentioned is that of the neurophysiology of learning. Earlier learning theories, for the most part, have been concerned with behavior and those variables that could be observed or inferred to influence behavior. Neurophysiologists, however, have become concerned with understanding the actual physical machinery of the human being and, primarily, the physiological explanation of the brain and its various mental functions.

A review of neurophysiology will not be undertaken here in deference to the extended discussion in chapter 7. For further study, the reader is referred to early articles on the subject by Pribram (1964), *Education and the Brain* (Chall and Mirsky 1978), *The Oxford Companion to The Mind* (Gregory 1987), as well as a recent overview of research, including neurological studies relating to music performance, by Wilson and Roehmann (1992).

As mentioned earlier, Gardner (1985) includes neurophysiology as one of the major fields comprising his version of cognitive science. Further, he notes the rapid development of this area of study and speculates that neurophysiology may become a dominant view and, perhaps, encompass cognitive science. This statement certainly indicates its high potential and importance to the music scholar and researcher.

Applications

The purpose of this section is to provide an overview of research and writing in music education and music therapy that is theory based in some way or other. In only a few instances is any particular learning theory fully embraced; often, only some aspect of learning theory is considered. Considerable research and writing is focused on some specific aspect of music learning without reference to theory. And, this presentation is in no way intended to be other than an overview; for full understanding and interpretation, the reader is referred to the references cited.

Background

It seems safe to say that not until recent years have music scholars and researchers utilized learning theory in a systematic way. Certainly, aspects of music learning appear in philosophical writings throughout history. Work of the "sensationalists" (Fechner 1966; Helmholtz 1954; Stumpf 1883) during the late nineteenth and early twentieth centuries as well several other early researchers in music (Bingham 1910; Ortmann 1934; Pratt 1928) paved the way for research in music learning. To be mentioned also is the work of pioneers in music aptitude and achievement that reflected traditional positions with regard to learning. The well-known debate between the atomistic approach of Seashore and the omnibus approach of psychologist Mursell (see Abeles, Hoffer, and Klotman 1984) reflects existing associationist and cognitive traditions of the time. Notably, in music education, one chapter on music learning theory by Thorpe did appear in *Basic Concepts In Music Education* (1958).

In more recent times, interest and writing as related to learning theory appears to date from the Ann Arbor Symposium of 1981. Originally intended to be *Application of Learning Theory to the Teaching and Learning of Music*, the title of the documentary publication came to be *Application of Psychology to the Teaching and Learning of Music* (MENC 1981), indicating to this participant at least the lack of understanding by music scholars about what learning theory was and the current state of disarray with regard to learning theory at that time, generally. Nevertheless, some excellent papers were presented both by music scholars and psychologists that documented the situation at that time, and the interest of musicians in the use of learning theory in a systematic way received a strong impetus. Since this time, considerable research and publication has occurred in music education and music therapy related to learning theory, some of which is discussed subsequently.

Music-Learning Theories

The purpose of the discussion that follows is to examine theories or similar constructs as developed or adopted by music scholars. Some of these views are based on formal learning theory or aspects thereof, some on the elements or structure of music, and some on procedures observed by musicians in their experience with music teaching. A brief discussion of selected views follows.

Edwin Gordon has developed a music-learning theory that has received considerable attention in recent years. Gordon's views appear in two primary publications, *The Psychology of Music Teaching* (1971) and

Learning Sequences in Music: Skill, Content, and Patterns (1989). According to Beall 1991, Gordon's music-learning theory is synonymous with his learning sequences. These sequences consist of a skills taxonomy in two categories, discrimination and inference learning. The purpose of the taxonomy is to facilitate the achievement of musical understanding by means of the development of audiation, a concept central to Gordon's views. Audiation refers to silent hearing, or the ability to hear sounds not physically present at the moment.

The two types of learning, discrimination and inference learning, are organized in a hierarchy that is similar in many ways to Gagne's conditions of learning. Thus, discrimination learning includes a variety of skills that are perceptual in nature (corresponding roughly to Gagne's first four types of learning), and inference learning involves greater generalization, application, and theoretical understanding by the student, reflecting Gagne's higher conditions of learning (Beall 1991). A full issue of the *Quarterly Journal of Music Teaching and Learning* (1991) is devoted to Gordon's music-learning theory.

Heller and Campbell (Campbell and Heller 1981, Heller and Campbell 1982) advanced a model of cognition that might be described as a problem-solving approach, characterizing the learning process as active, ongoing, and hypothesis testing. Music learning is compared to language learning and follows comparable rules. Thus, the process is regarded as culture bound and dependent on the context of musical experience. The nature of cognition is considered not to be inherent in acoustical phenomena but in the perceptual process involving detection, identification, discrimination, and generalization. A model describing this process is heavily dependent on the thinking of Meyer (1956) and involves the establishment and refinement of expectations in the listening experience. Some research has been done by the authors in support of this position.

Serafine (1988) has developed a similar theory of musical cognition that also attempts to account for musical thought and understanding. In this view, musical cognition is conceived as an active and constructive process that is believed to be common to listeners, composers, and performers. The music itself is regarded merely as materials that are, then, encoded by the listener into corresponding cognitive units. Two types of processes exist: (1) temporal processes, referring to the relationship among musical elements in time, and (2) nontemporal, referring to the more general, formal structures of music. Much about the process is regarded as generic and universal. Processing is developmental in nature, varying with ages of children and with adults. The theory is clearly controversial, but it is thought to be promising, particularly in the area of child development in music (Hargreaves and Zimmerman 1992).

Lerdahl and Jackendoff (1983) propose a generative theory of musical grammar that compares music learning and cognition to language learning. Music is regarded as a mentally constructed entity and a product of acculturation. Music is learned in the form of patterns or representations of music experienced. Various considerations relating to the music itself influence the ways in which patterns are formed—thematic, formal, metric, temporal, melodic, and harmonic. Rules of well-formedness, similar to Gestalt characteristics of perception, and individual listener preferences influence the result. The interaction of these two sets of rules functions to form the basis for musical experience and understanding.

Fiske (1992) builds on the views of Heller and Campbell, Serafine, and Lerdahl and Jackendoff to propose a three-component theory. Stage one is the initial processing stage that results in a representation of the experience. Stage two consists of description, involving recall, recognition, and discrimination. The third stage (added by Fiske) involves realizing the musical structure and relationships and hypotheses-testing activity. The three stages, then, represent a hierarchy of difficulty according to the time required for processing. Fiske provides considerable research in support of his views and offers this concept of the music cognitive environment as an approach to understanding and nurturing the listening experience.

Davidson and Scripp (1992) propose a comprehensive view of cognitive skills needed in music. A matrix is provided that incorporates three distinct ways of music knowing, including production (performance or composition), perception (discrimination or monitoring), and reflection (critical thinking or reenvisioning). Modeling and metaphor are discussed as guides to learning, instruction, and increased understanding of music. The view is somewhat in response to Gardner's postulation of multiple intelligences and related to Piaget's ideas on the origin of skills. The cognitive matrix provided is believed to integrate psychological models with concepts and terminology familiar to musicians. The position does incorporate supporting research by the authors as well as by others.

Swanwick (1988) and Swanwick and Tillman (1986) propose a general model of musical development based on an analysis of children's compositions and analogies to children's play. Categories of child play include mastery (simple or sensory responses), imitation (representation or illustration), imaginative play (creative), and metacognition (awareness of thinking and experience). These categories are related to musical materials, expression, form, and valuing. The model draws support from Piaget and also resembles Bruner's spiral curriculum and the curriculum model of the Manhattanville Music Curriculum Project (Hargreaves and Zimmerman 1992).

Areas of Research in Music Learning

In addition to the development of theoretical positions such as those discussed previously, there is considerable research by scholars in music and psychology that concentrates on certain areas in an attempt to verify or build on theoretical concepts. Areas that are theory based and that have received considerable attention include music perception and cognition, musical development of the child, use of reinforcement in music learning, music therapy and students with disabilities, transfer of training in music, and motor learning. Additional areas of study include a variety of research efforts in learning that are not classified in one of the above categories and included in a final category entitled Other Research. Excellent reviews of such research appear elsewhere and will not be attempted here. Rather, a brief overview of these categories will be provided, concentrating on the relationship to theory and resources recommended for further study.

Perception and Cognition

As mentioned earlier, the study of perception was in many ways the forerunner of cognitive psychology. And, as the first component of the process of cognition, perception has continued to be basic to the study of cognition. For this reason, many writers deal with perception separately from cognition, with perception representing the earlier part of the process associated with awareness of sensation and the early stages of recognition. Cognition, on the other hand, refers to the more complex and later stages of information processing or thinking. Clearly, perception and cognition are closely associated and part of the same continuum or hierarchy of mental activity; for this reason the two will be considered here simultaneously.

As is the case with perception generally, music perception may be defined very narrowly—as sensation, detection, or the early identification of musical stimuli (see chap. 4)—with music cognition referring to recall, discrimination, and evaluative judgments (see chap. 5). Also, research may be concerned with the nature of music itself—rhythm, pitch, melody, and so on—or with the many complex factors that influence perception and cognition in activities such as listening to, reading, and understanding music. It may be noted from one comprehensive review of research in music learning (Sample 1992) that a large proportion of research studies in music is concerned with perception and cognition.

Given the central importance of perception and cognition to cognitive psychology, one might expect researchers and theorists in the cognitive tradition to be the most active and influential. However, it should be remembered that perception and cognition do not represent theory themselves, but types of mental activity or behavior about which theories are posited in order to facilitate an understanding of these activities. Thus, research and other writing concerning perception and cognition have incorporated or relied on a variety of learning theories and similar constructs. Reinforcement theory has been applied to practically all aspects of music learning, and much about perception and cognition is regarded as developmental in nature. To a lesser extent, this is true of motor learning and learning by students with disabilities. Since these areas are discussed under separate headings, discussion here will be limited to selected reports of research dealing specifically with perception and cognition and indicating reliance on theory to some extent.

Formal learning theory or related concepts are used by some researchers. Landmark contributions of individuals such as Fechner, Helmholtz, and Seashore, as well as a variety of contemporary scholars, as discussed above, are noted by Fiske (1992). Campbell (1991) cites the influence of several theorists concerned more specifically with perception, including Neisser (1966) and Gibson (1969), as well as the developmental theory of Piaget (1954). Butler (1992) indicates a Gestalt orientation and cites cognitivists Anderson (1990) and Sloboda (1985) as well as information and developmental theory. In a discussion of listening, Haack (1992) relies on the thinking of Piaget, but also notes ideas developed from social learning; also cited are extensive literature reviews on the subject by Hedden (1980). Hodges (1992), in discussing music reading, relies to some extent on information processing theory but bemoans the lack of theoretical underpinning in this important area of music learning.

Other writers tend to be more research based. For example, Cuddy and Upitis (1992) provide a comprehensive view of the perception-cognitive process, discussing how elements are perceived in combination, hierarchial relationships that may exist, how elements are grouped or sequenced, and the influence of context. Davidson and Scripp (1992) cite considerable research involving perception and cognition in support of their cognitive skills matrix. Cutietta (1993) utilizes varied research to support a cognitive view of musical perception based on perceptual characteristics of the brain.

Work by psychologists in music reflects this tendency and, for additional information concerning these views and actual research studies on perception and cognition, the reader is referred to the work of Deutsch (1982), Lerdahl and Jackendoff (1983), Sloboda (1985), Dowling and Harwood (1986), Frances (1988), and Krumhansl (1990). In addition are selected articles from two notable collections, *Musical Structure and Cognition* (Howell, Cross, and West 1985) and *Cognitive Bases of Musical Communication* (Jones and Holleran 1990).

Recent texts by music scholars Davies (1978), Radocy and Boyle (1979), Serafine (1988), and Butler (1992) contain sections dealing with learning theory, generally, and perception and cognition, particularly. For complete studies, the reader is referred to articles by these and other researchers appearing in the *Journal of Research in Music Education, Psychomusicology, Bulletin of the Council for Research in Music Education, The Quarterly, Music Perception,* and general journals of cognition and experimental psychology.

Application of findings of research in perception and cognition have been made to almost all aspects of music learning and teaching. Several articles appear in the recent *Handbook of Research on Music Teaching and Learning* (Colwell 1992), some of which appear in the discussion of other research later in the chapter. Three additional useful references in this regard are *Applications of Research in Music Behavior* (Madsen and Prickett 1987), *What Works: Instructional Strategies for Music Education* (Merrion 1989), and the journal *Update: Applications of Research in Music Education.* Research studies therein indicate a wide variety of strategies concerned with perception and cognition and, just as important, the bibliographies provided will acquaint the reader very quickly and in a most practical way with the work of currently active researchers.

Developmental Theory

The subject of child development in music is one of the most thoroughly and systematically researched of general learning theories. Several recent reviews of research exist, including Simons 1978; Tunks 1980; Hargreaves and Zimmerman 1992; Scott-Kassner 1992; and Zimmerman 1993; in addition to Hargreaves's text, *The Developmental Psychology of Music* (1986). These sources will serve to acquaint the reader with the background and current status of research; remarks here will be confined to the theoretical views employed.

The most influential of general theories has been that of Piaget. Aspects of Piaget's theory that have been applied to music research include the stages of development (as discussed earlier), symbolic development (mental structure, representation, and schema), and conservation (maintaining identity of properties with change). The influence of Piaget is readily evident in the work of other theorists, as most recently chronicled in Hargreaves and Zimmerman 1992. Bruner's concept of the early development of representational systems has also been influential; these systems are described as enactive (derived from motor actions), iconic (images and perceptual experience), and symbolic (language symbols). In addition, the work of Gardner (1973 and 1983) and Ausubel and Sullivan (1970) has been cited as influential. Theoretical positions and other developments by musicians regarded as promising include the work of Davidson and Scripp, the "spiral model" of Swanwick and Tillman, as well as Serafine's research and thinking on musical cognition, all discussed above. Scott-Kassner (1992) notes also the contributions of Webster with regard to creativity and Bentley and Gordon in music aptitude.

Research based on views such as these has resulted in descriptions of the developmental process as pertaining to a wide variety of musical concepts and skills. These include the development of auditory perception and discrimination, musical representations of experience, rhythmic awareness, singing ability, melodic and harmonic awareness, awareness of form and phrase, listening preferences and abilities, readiness for music learning, and the influence of factors such as loudness, timbre, tempo, and patterns on these abilities. Most important, of course, the research indicates relative abilities at different age levels and those levels at which improvement is most likely to occur and at which instruction will be most effective. These findings offer to the music teacher a wealth of opportunities for application to teaching and the development of materials and methods appropriate to various age levels.

The following guidelines for application of developmental views relative to perception and cognition are based on summaries by Campbell (1991) and Zimmerman (1986).

1. The musical event and response to it are central to musical activity.
2. All perceptual and cognitive processes are developmental.
3. Sequencing of activities should move from recognizing to discriminating and categorizing, from identifying to characterizing and defining, and from extracting to comparing and organizing.
4. Conceptual growth is hierarchical and should move from experience to problem solving and analysis with ever-increasing detail.
5. Curricula should be broadly constructed, flexible, and approached from the viewpoint of the child's developing perceptual and intellectual abilities.

6. Certain aspects of learning are more appropriately assigned to elementary school and others to middle school, taking into account the home environment and the influence of peer pressure.

7. Curricula should be designed with an understanding of the child's developmental processes and include all of the various elements, patterns, and interrelational aspects of music, first in a global way and then with increasing complexity.

Reinforcement

Reinforcement is a concept arising from learning theory that has received, perhaps, the greatest amount of attention by researchers in music learning in recent years (Sample 1992). The term *reinforcement* is used in a variety of ways in learning theory, from the use of food as a reward to bring about the repetition of animal behavior to very elaborate behavior modification and contingency management procedures with human subjects. Much research in music or music-related behavior is closely associated with the views of Skinner and operant learning, although other research may be less formal and concerned, simply, with the use of positive reinforcement to bring about some musical learning or other behavior desired.

Several reviews of research involving reinforcement techniques (often referred to as operant research) in music education and music therapy exist. Literature reviews by Tunks (1980), Greer (1981), and texts by Madsen, Greer, and Madsen (1975) and Madsen and Prickett (1987) provide excellent and comprehensive surveys as well as examples of research.

The use of operant learning procedures to influence all aspects of learning and behavior clearly illustrates the practical nature and versatility of this approach. Operant learning in music education and music therapy has been applied extensively to both the most basic of perceptual tasks as well as to the most complex of cognitive and behavioral activities. Research in operant learning has produced quantifiable results in the majority of these instances, indicating the efficacy of operant research procedures.

According to Greer, most operant research has been concerned with motivation and the use of reinforcement to maintain or decrease the occurrence of emitted behaviors. Music itself has been found to provide a reinforcer "for a variety of academic skills, concepts, and social behaviors" (Greer 1981, 106) and, used in this manner, music participation may be a positive influence on success in school generally. In a similar manner, reinforcement may be used deliberately to influence the learning of all music skills and attitudes including most (if not all) aspects of music behavior or learning—perceptual, performance, cognitive, and affective. Madsen and Prickett (1987) indicate the application of such research to (1) varied student responses to musical stimuli, (2) preference and perception, and (3) teacher training; potential for similar research in creativity is noted, as well as other new directions. A brief review of research studies included in *What Works: Instructional Strategies for Music Education* (Merrion 1989) confirms both the widespread application and effectiveness of this approach in music education. The application of operant learning to influence the learning of a wide variety of personal and social skills in music therapy is also well established, as discussed subsequently.

Finally, although a review of research indicates that operant learning is one of the best researched of procedures and in many ways most effective, it may be that, from the standpoint of theoretical writing and the current rise of cognitive theory, the use of operant learning may be falling into disfavor. However, one cannot deny the applicability of many of the research findings, and this approach may find great practical utility regardless of the theoretical position one chooses to adopt. One also needs to remember that theorizing tends to be pendular and much basic research is far from complete. Given the past success of operant learning as well as its amenability to quantifiable research, discounting this approach on the basis of theoretical incompatibility seems most questionable.

Music Therapy and Students With Disabilities

The reader is reminded from the outset that the discussion that follows is confined to the influence or presence of learning theory or similar constructs in music therapy and in educational efforts with students with various disabilities. In particular, it is recognized that music therapy is based on a variety of other theoretical constructs—psychoanalytic, psychotherapeutic, or clinically-based—which will not be considered here. General education efforts with students having various disabilities may not be closely associated with such views; however, music therapy and the education of students do share a common base of research findings and learning theory, and grouping these two areas seems reasonable.

The following generalizations are based on surveys of several sources. First, a keyword search was provided by CAIRSS (Computer-Assisted Information Retrieval Service System) for Music (Eagle and Hodges 1992). Also used were the *Music Therapy* and *Music Psychology Indexes*, volumes 1–3 (Eagle 1976 and 1978; Eagle and Minter 1984) as well as several journals, including the *Journal of Music Therapy* and *Music Therapy Perspectives* (NAMT), *Music Therapy* (AAMT), the *British Journal of Music Therapy,* and *The International Journal of Arts Medicine.* Additional references included Gaston 1968; Graham 1975; Madsen, Greer, and Madsen 1975; Graham and Beer 1980; Lathom and Eagle 1982; Michel 1985; Hardesty 1985; Maranto and Bruscia 1987; Bruscia 1987; Unkefer 1991; and Standley 1991; literature reviews include Tunks 1980; Greer 1981; Thaut 1991a; and Gfeller 1992.

Learning theories and constructs encountered are those already discussed and represent the associationist or cognitive traditions, in addition to neurophysiology, mathematical theory, transfer of training, and other, varied research. Reinforcement theory is the most prevalent application to both music therapy and learning for students with disabilities. Application of reinforcement, conditioning, and contingency management have been demonstrated as effective in bringing about a wide variety of musical, behavioral, and social learning, including the influence of music study or activity on academic learning in other areas. Applications of cognitive views include developmental theory, information processing, and various studies in perception and cognition. Neurophysiological approaches appear to be most promising and have been the basis for considerable research in music perception and cognition as well as general learning tasks in both music therapy and special education. Research based on mathematical theory is less well represented, but it appears as an approach to perception and cognition. Also, some research exists concerning transfer of training as related to these special populations. As was the case with learning, generally, a variety of research studies and other writings of a functional nature exist.

Some theoretical concepts and structures have arisen from such study and deserve to be mentioned. Gaston (1968) provides much of the theoretical base in support of the functional use of music in therapy and education, noting that music is human behavior and a human need with structural, social, psychological, and aesthetic characteristics that provide unique therapeutic and educational experiences. Sears (1968; see also Cole 1981) focuses on the role of music in bringing about synchronization as a therapeutic goal, citing experience within the structure provided by music, consequent self-organization, and relating to others as steps in the therapeutic process. Braswell (1968) focuses on "social facility" as a primary goal and socialization as one of the most important and beneficial outcomes of experience with music. Thaut (1991a) develops theoretical thinking and provides a construct of emotional and affective response to music based on musical perception and cognition as well as expectancy theories of Meyer and others. These and other views and refinements provide a valuable, disciplined-based theoretical structure for the use of music in therapy and education.

Transfer of Training

Transfer of training refers to the influence of any aspect of learning on future learning, including skills, knowledge, or attitudes. Clearly, this concept pervades almost every aspect of the educational process. For the most part, however, it is simply assumed that transfer occurs. For example, it is assumed that the learning of technical studies will transfer to the performance of actual music; it is assumed that analysis studied in music theory will transfer to score reading when conducting. Tunks (1992) provides the most recent and thorough discussion of transfer and cites several additional erroneous assumptions regarding transfer—that it is automatic, that it occurs with both general and specific skills, that it is positive rather than negative, and that the influence is always on future rather than on past learning.

The concept of transfer has its roots in the associationist tradition with Thorndike's identical elements account and has remained a most important consideration in the research and writing of scholars in that tradition. Also, scholars in the cognitive tradition have attempted to incorporate this idea in some way or other; Tunks cites the thinking of Bruner and Ausubel as well as general usage in information and schema theory. A variety of general research indicates some of the general aspects of transfer—general versus specific transfer as well as other conditions influencing transfer. The paucity of research in music in this area is noted. However, based on Tunks (1992), Edwards (1988), and Schuell (1988), a summary of applications of research that seem immediately meaningful and applicable to music learning follows.

1. Transfer is highly sensitive to context; teaching in varied or similar contextual situations appears to facilitate transfer.
2. Informing the learner about how transfer is to occur is beneficial.
3. The similarity of new learning to situations of future use facilitates transfer.
4. Practice—mental practice and distributed practices—appears to facilitate transfer; the amount of practice may not be a single factor; and structured practice facilitates transfer.
5. Aural models may be beneficial; cross-sensory cues may be helpful.
6. Music to nonmusic learning should be specifically designed to facilitate transfer.
7. The extent and efficiency of initial learning is influential.

It should be noted that this list suffers considerably from generalization as well as a lack of systematic research support. It is clear and striking that much research is needed in this vital and pervasive area of learning.

Motor Learning

The learning of an array of physical skills for performance and conducting purposes is a requirement of the vast majority of musicians. Thus, motor learning is a basic area of consideration. However, systematic concern with motor learning appears to be a relatively recent development, receiving impetus from the Ann Arbor Symposium and the work of Sidnell (1981). Sidnell notes a limited reliance on formal learning theory as well as the paucity of research on the subject by musicians. He does pose numerous questions concerning motor learning as applied to music learning; questions posed pertained to: the relationship to general motor learning and motor learning theory, applications of models of motor learning, proprioception in small muscle responses, the timing sequence of motor responses, efficient motor practice, the transfer of motor skills, the relationship of motor learning to other learning, memory for motor skills, developmental considerations, and possible assistance from neurophysiology.

Sidnell's influence appears in several additional articles on the subject. For example, Hedden (1987) reflects on Sidnell's contributions and reviews possible answers to the questions posed. Again, the lack of systematic research dedicated to these concerns and the conclusions that may be made is regarded as astounding. Wilson and Roehmann (1992) provide the most recent review in this area that supports the same conclusion. However, this review does indicate possible directions for research by citing some studies in muscle and brain research as applied to music performance, as well listing possible topics appropriate for future study. Thaut (1991b) provides a similar review pertaining to music therapy. As witnessed by this literature, the lack of research in this most basic area of interest to the musician continues to be striking and the need and potential for ongoing, systematic research is readily evident.

Other Theory-Based Research in Music Learning

The following consists of a variety of other topics in music learning that do not otherwise appear in the preceding categories. These areas are theory based to a greater or lesser degree and can only be mentioned here. For extended discussion of each area, the reader is referred to the *Handbook of Research in Music Teaching and Learning* (Colwell 1992). In this book, Miller cites theoretical views of a variety of thinkers, including Mandler (1988), Hebb (1949), Meyer (1956), and Dowling and Harwood (1986) and provides the background and current status of thinking with regard to the affective response to music. Tait cites theories of Bandura (1986) and Gardner (1973) in his discussion of modeling, among other teaching strategies. Rideout relies on information processing as a way to approach skill acquisition and the use of modeling and imagery to guide practice and performance. Richardson and Whitaker discuss critical thinking, indicating its philosophical origin as well as seeking a theoretical base for exploring higher order thinking or problem solving in music study.

In addition, there are specific applications of research to instructional settings, including Phillips (singing), Weerts (instrumental music), Uszler (keyboard), Atterbury (elementary general music), Sink (junior high and middle school general music), and Humphreys, May, and Nelson (music ensembles). Most of the topics above are applied in nature and relate to actual teaching and learning situations. However, the linkage to learning theory, when made, provides both a supportive structure for individual research efforts as well as an opportunity for a systematic approach to seeking results that will generalize to like and similar applied situations.

Taxonomy of Educational Objectives

The *Taxonomy of Educational Objectives*, as proposed by Bloom et al. (1956) and developed by others, has been the subject of considerable attention and writing by musicians. Although not a learning theory, the taxonomy does provide a structure within which the various types of music-learning activities could be considered and studied systematically. The taxonomy consists of three domains that are described briefly as follows.

The cognitive domain refers to knowledge and its organization in a hierarchial manner. Advantages include systematic and complete coverage of subject matter, sequencing of study from simple to complex for various levels of student development, and the evaluation of outcomes. The first level is knowledge, and includes recognizing and remembering terminology (or other specifics), the function or use of specifics, as well as generalization and abstraction. Comprehension is the second level and refers to the use of such specifics as communication, requiring translation, interpretation, and extrapolation. Application refers to the use of knowledge in a problem-solving manner. At the level of analysis, the student deals with relationships and organizational principles. The fifth step is synthesis, or the making of inferences and abstractions, with evaluation, the highest level, referring to the making of value judgments relevant not only to outcomes but all stages of the process.

The development of the psychomotor domain is credited primarily to Simpson (1966) and is devoted to the development of psychomotor skills or behaviors. This taxonomy is also organized in a hierarchial manner, ranging from simple and easier skills or behaviors to those more complex and difficult. The first level is that of perception and refers to the awareness of sensation, discrimination among stimuli, and determining the meaning of stimuli. Set refers to the preparation to complete some motor act and involves mental, physical, and emotional readiness. Guided response involves the instructor in the process in which the student may respond by imitation as well as by trial and error. At the level of mechanism, the response has been learned and becomes habitual. The finalization of the complex overt response involves the resolution of any uncertainty and the achievement of an automatic and finely tuned response. The highest stages include adaptation, or changing an established response, and origination, or the ability to develop new skills.

The affective domain is credited to Krathwohl, Bloom, and Masia (1964) and consists of a hierarchy of feelings as reflected in objectives relating to attitudes, values, interests, and appreciation. Levels of the taxonomy include receiving, or willingness to attend to stimuli; responding, or willingness to participate in some way; valuing, adopting, or demonstrating commitment to some value; organization, forming concepts and abstractions of experience; and characterization of a value or value system, or internalizing a value system guiding activity.

The *Taxonomy of Educational Objectives* is one of the most widely applied structures in education and provides a structure in which all aspects of learning may be included. Certainly this has been true in music education. A large number of music education methods and other texts include the taxonomy, and many provide excellent examples of how both traditional and research-based practices may be incorporated (see Abeles, Hoffer, and Klotman 1984; Bessom, Tatarunis, and Forcucci 1974; Hoffer 1991; Peters and Miller 1982; Tait and Haack 1984). Notably, the taxonomy is most comprehensive, its three domains including the immensely varied content in music as well as the interaction of these domains. The taxonomy provides a usable construct for curriculum construction and is particularly well suited to use in systems employing behavioral objectives or other accountability approaches. In addition, with regard to learning theory, the domain offers a context within which theory, related research, and application may be combined in a mutually supportive manner.

As revision of this chapter ends, I cannot help but be impressed at the progress made in music education and music therapy in incorporating learning theory and becoming more research based, generally. Many aspects of teaching and clinical practice have been at least addressed from a theoretical perspective, and theory has been used to guide research and application to practice. However, noted throughout the reading in preparation for this revision was the expressed need for continuous, systematic, theory-based research.

For example, Hargreaves and Zimmerman (1992) note the need for research that is theory driven if any real progress is to be made in understanding children's music learning. Hodges (1992) notes the lack of theory-based research in music reading and recommends increased efforts in this regard. Hedden (1987) makes similar observations with regard to motor learning. Meske (1985) also recommends increased theory-based research and makes a strong case for the wedding of theory and practice as a systematic means of program improvement. Jorgensen (1993) calls for the development of theories of greater substance to guide empirical research. And, finally, one can see in the literature the results of prolonged and systematic research that is theory based, such as is the case in reinforcement theory and in developmental learning.

Also, in reading the literature, many studies may be noted that deal with various aspects of learning, apparently undertaken without consideration of already existing theoretical bases and considerable supporting research. It seems most advisable that such studies take advantage of this support and the opportunity to have efforts contribute in a directional and systematic manner to advancing or confirming what is known about learning music. Finally, students in music education and music therapy have a vast history of theory and supporting research available to them that can be used to support and make more valuable their thinking and research efforts, and they are urged to take advantage of this heritage.

REFERENCES

Abeles, H. F., C. R. Hoffer, and R. H. Klotman. 1984. *Foundations of music education.* New York: Schirmer.
Amsel, A. 1989. *Behaviorism, neobehaviorism, and cognitivism in learning theory.* Hillsdale, NJ: Lawrence Erlbaum Associates.
Anderson, J. R. 1990. *Cognitive psychology and its implications.* 3d ed. New York: Freeman.
Anderson, J. R., and G. H. Bower. 1973. *Human associative memory.* Washington, DC: Winston.

Anderson, J. R., and G. H. Bower. 1980. *Human associative memory: A brief edition.* Hillsdale, NJ: Lawrence Erlbaum Associates.

Atterbury, B. W. 1992. Research on the teaching of elementary general music. In *Handbook of research on music teaching and learning,* ed. R. Colwell, 594–602. New York: Schirmer.

Ausubel, D. P., and E. V. Sullivan. 1970. *Theory and problems of child development.* 2d ed. New York: Grune and Stratton.

Bandura, A. 1986. *Social foundations of thought and action: A social cognitive theory.* Englewood Cliffs, NJ: Prentice-Hall.

Beall, G. 1991. Learning Sequences and Music Learning. *Quarterly* 2, nos. 1 and 2:87–96.

Bergan, J. R., and J. A. Dunn. 1976. *Psychology and education: A science of instruction.* New York: Wiley.

Berlyne, D. E. 1965. *Structure and direction in thinking.* New York: Wiley.

Bessom, M. E., A. M. Tatarunis, and S. L. Forcucci. 1974. *Teaching music in today's secondary schools.* New York: Holt, Rinehart and Winston.

Biehler, R. F. 1971. *Psychology applied to teaching.* Boston: Houghton Mifflin.

Bigge, M. L. 1976. *Learning theories for teachers.* 3d ed. New York: Harper and Row.

Bingham, W. van D. 1910. Studies in melody. *Psychological monographs* 12, no. 50.

Bloom, B. S., M. D. Engelhart, E. J. Furst, W. H. Hill, and D. R. Krathwohl. 1956. *Taxonomy of educational objectives, handbook 1: Cognitive domain.* New York: McKay.

Bower, G. H., and E. Hilgard. 1981. *Theories of learning.* 5th ed. Englewood Cliffs, NJ: Prentice-Hall.

Braswell, C. E. 1968. Social facility and mental illness. In *Music in therapy,* ed. E. T. Gaston, 364–71. New York: Macmillan.

Broadbent, D. E. 1958. *Perception and communication.* London: Pergamon Press.

Bruner, J. S. 1960. *The process of education.* New York: Vintage Books.

Bruner, J. S. 1966. *Toward a theory of instruction.* Cambridge, MA: Belknap Press.

Bruscia, K. E. 1987. *Improvisational models of music therapy.* Springfield, IL: Charles C. Thomas.

Bugelski, B. R. 1971. *The psychology of learning applied to teaching.* 2d ed. New York: Bobbs-Merrill.

Bugelski, B. R. 1975. *Empirical studies in the psychology of learning.* Indianapolis, IN: Hackett Publishing.

Butler, D. 1992. *The musician's guide to perception and cognition.* New York: Schirmer.

Campbell, M. R. 1991. Musical learning and the development of psychological processes in perception and cognition. *Bulletin of the Council for Research in Music Education* 107:37–48.

Campbell, W., and J. Heller. 1981. Psychomusicology and psycholinguistics: Parallel paths or separate ways? *Psychomusicology* 1, no. 2:3–14.

Chall, J. S., and A. F. Mirsky, eds. 1978. *Education and the brain.* Chicago: University of Chicago Press.

Choate, R. A., ed. 1968. *Documentary report of the Tanglewood symposium.* Washington, DC: Music Educators National Conference.

Cole, C. F. 1981. Synchronistic time in music: A theoretical model of music therapy based on the work of William Sears. Ph.D. diss., Southern Methodist University.

Colwell, R., ed. 1992. *Handbook of research in music teaching and learning.* New York: Schirmer.

Cronbach, L. J. 1977. *Educational psychology.* 3d ed. New York: Harcourt Brace Jovanovich.

Cuddy, L. L., and R. Upitis. 1992. Aural perception. In *Handbook of research on music teaching and learning,* ed. R. Colwell, 333–43. New York: Schirmer.

Cutietta, R. A. 1993. The musical elements: Who said they're right? *Music Educators Journal* 79, no. 9:48–53.

Davidson, L., and L. Scripp. 1992. Surveying the coordinates of cognitive skills in music. In *Handbook of research on music teaching and learning,* ed. R. Colwell, 392–413. New York: Schirmer.

Davies, J. 1978. *The psychology of music.* London: Hutchinson.

DeCecco, J. P., and W. R. Crawford. 1974. *The psychology of learning and instruction: Educational psychology.* 2d ed. Englewood Cliffs, NJ: Prentice-Hall.

Deutsch, D. 1982. *The psychology of music.* New York: Academic Press.

Dollard, J. C., and N. E. Miller. 1950. *Personality and psychotherapy.* New York: McGraw-Hill.

Dowling, W. J., and D. L. Harwood. 1986. *Music cognition.* Orlando: Academic Press.

Eagle, C. T. 1976. *Music therapy index.* Vol. 1. Lawrence, Kansas: National Association for Music Therapy.

Eagle, C. T. 1978. *Music psychology index.* Vol. 2. Lawrence, Kansas: National Association for Music Therapy.

Eagle, C. T., and D. A. Hodges. 1992. CAIRSS for music in arts medicine. *International Journal for Arts Medicine* 1, no. 2:21–25.

Eagle, C. T., and J. J. Minter, eds. 1984. *Music psychology index.* Vol. 3. Phoenix: Oryx Press.

Edwards, R. H. 1988. Transfer and performance instruction. *The Crane symposium: Toward an understanding of the teaching and learning of music performance.* Potsdam: Potsdam College of SUNY.

Ellis, H. C., and R. R. Hunt. 1989. *Fundamentals of human memory and cognition.* 4th ed. Dubuque: W. C. Brown.

Erickson, E. H. 1968. *Identity: Youth and crises.* New York: Norton.

Estes, W. K. 1954. *Modern learning theory.* New York: Appleton-Century-Crofts.

Fechner, G. T. [1860] 1966. *Elements of psychophysics.* Trans. D. H. Howes, E. B. Boring, and R. West. New York: Holt, Rinehart and Winston.

Fiske, H. 1992. Structure of cognition and music decision-making. In *Handbook of research on music teaching and learning,* ed. R. Colwell, 360–376. New York: Schirmer.

Flavell, J. F. 1963. *The developmental psychology of Jean Piaget.* Princeton, NJ: Van Nostrand.

Frances, R. 1988. *The perception of music.* Trans. W. Jay Dowling. Hillsdale, NJ: Lawrence Erlbaum Associates.

Franklin, E. 1972. *Music education: Psychology and method.* London: Harrap.

Gage, N. L., and D. C. Berliner. 1975. *Educational psychology.* Chicago: Rand McNally.

Gagne, R. M. 1970. *The conditions of learning.* 2d ed. New York: Holt, Rinehart and Winston.

Gardner, H. 1973. *The arts and human development.* New York: Wiley.

Gardner, H. 1983. *Frames of mind: The theory of multiple intelligences.* New York: Basic Books.

Gardner, H. 1985. *The mind's new science: A history of the cognitive revolution.* New York: Basic Books.

Gardner, H. 1991. *The unschooled mind: How children think and how schools should teach.* New York: Basic Books.

Gaston, E. T., ed. 1968. *Music in therapy.* New York: Macmillan.

Gfeller, K. 1992. Research regarding students with disabilities. In *Handbook of research on music teaching and learning,* ed. R. Colwell, 615–32. New York: Schirmer.

Gibson, E. J. 1969. *Principles of perceptual learning and development.* New York: Appleton-Century-Crofts.

Gordon, E. 1971. *The psychology of music teaching.* Englewood Cliffs, NJ: Prentice-Hall.

Gordon, E. 1989. *Learning sequences in music: Skill, content, and patterns.* Chicago: GIA Publications.

Graham, R. M., ed. 1975. *Music for the exceptional child.* Reston, VA: Music Educators National Conference.

Graham, R. M., and A. S. Beer. 1980. *Teaching music to the exceptional child.* Englewood Cliffs, NJ: Prentice-Hall.

Greer, R. D. 1981. An operant approach to motivation and affect: Ten years of research in music learning. In *Documentary report of the Ann Arbor symposium: Applications of psychology to the teaching and learning of music,* 102–121. Reston, VA: Music Educators National Conference.

Gregory, R. L., ed. 1987. *The Oxford companion to the mind.* New York: Oxford University Press.

Haack, P. 1992. The acquisition of music listening skills. In *Handbook of research on music teaching and learning,* ed. R. Colwell, 451–65. New York: Schirmer.

Haber, F. 1974. *An introduction to information and communication theory.* Reading, MA: Addison-Wesley.

Hall, C. S. 1954. *A primer of Freudian psychology.* New York: Mentor Books.

Hardesty, K. W. 1985. *Music for special education.* Morristown, NJ: Silver-Burdett.

Hargreaves, D. J. 1986. *The developmental psychology of music.* Cambridge: Cambridge University Press.

Hargreaves, D. J., and M. P. Zimmerman. 1992. Developmental theories of music learning. In *Handbook of research on music teaching and learning,* ed. R. Colwell, 377–91. New York: Schirmer.

Hedden, S. K. 1980. Development of music listening skills. *Bulletin of the Council of Research in Music Education* 64:12–22.

Hedden, S. K. 1987. Recent research pertaining to psychomotor skills in music. *Bulletin of the Council for Research in Music Education* 90:25–29.

Hebb, D. F. 1949. *The organization of behavior.* New York: Wiley.

Heller, J., and W. Campbell. 1982. Music communication and cognition. *Bulletin of the Council for Research in Music Education* 72:1–15.

Helmholtz, H. [1863] 1954. *On the sensations of tone.* 4th ed. Trans. A. Ellis. New York: Dover Publications.

Hilgard, E. L., ed. 1964. *Theories of learning and instruction.* Chicago: University of Chicago Press.

Hilgard, E. L., and G. H. Bower. 1975. *Theories of learning.* 4th ed. Englewood Cliffs, NJ: Prentice-Hall.

Hill, W. F. 1964. Contemporary developments within stimulus-response learning theory. In *Theories of learning and instruction,* ed. E. Hilgard, 27–53. Chicago: University of Chicago Press.

Hill, W. F. 1971. *Learning, a survey of psychological interpretations.* Rev. ed. Scranton: Chandler Publishing.

Hodges, D. 1992. The acquisition of music reading skills. In *Handbook of research on music teaching and learning,* ed. R. Colwell, 466–71. New York: Schirmer.

Hoffer, C. R. 1991. *Teaching music in the secondary schools.* Belmont, CA: Wadsworth.

Houston, J. T. 1976. *Fundamentals of learning.* New York: Academic Press.

Howard, D. V. 1983. *Cognitive psychology: Memory, language, and thought.* New York: Macmillan.

Howell, P., I. Cross, and R. West. 1985. *Musical structure and cognition.* New York: Academic Press.

Hull, C. L. 1943. *Principles of behavior.* New York: Appleton-Century-Crofts.

Hull, C. L. 1952. *A behavior system: An introduction to behavior theory concerning the individual organism.* New Haven, CT: Yale University Press.

Humphreys, J. T., W. V. May, and D. J. Nelson. 1992. Research on music ensembles. In *Handbook of research on music teaching and learning,* ed. R. Colwell, 651–68. New York: Schirmer.

Inhelder, B., and J. Piaget. 1959. *The growth of logical thinking from childhood to adolescence.* New York: Basic Books.

Jones, M. R., and S. Holleran. 1992. *Cognitive bases of musical communication.* Washington, DC: American Psychological Association.

Jorgensen, Estelle R. 1993. On building social theories of music education. *Bulletin of the Council for Research in Music Education* 116:33–50.

Kazdin, A. E. 1975. *Behavior modification in applied settings.* Homewood, IL: Dorsey Press.

Klatzky, Roberta L. 1980. *Human memory, structure, and process.* 2d ed. San Francisco: Freeman.

Klatzky, Roberta L. 1984. *Memory and awareness: An information processing perspective.* 2d ed. San Francisco: Freeman.

Koffka, K. 1935. *Principles of gestalt psychology.* New York: Harcourt, Brace and World.

Köhler, W. 1925. *The mentality of apes.* Trans. from 2d ed. by E. Winter. New York: Harcourt.

Krathwohl, D. R., B. S. Bloom, and B. B. Masia. 1964. *Taxonomy of educational objectives, handbook 2: Affective domain.* New York: McKay.

Krumhansl, C. L. 1990. *Cognitive foundations of musical pitch.* New York: Oxford University Press.

Lathom, W. B., and C. T. Eagle, eds. 1982. *Music therapy for handicapped children.* Denton, TX: Institute for Therapeutic Research.

Lefrancois, G. R. 1975. *Psychology for teaching.* 2d ed. Belmont, CA: Wadsworth.

Lerdahl, F., and R. Jackendoff. 1983. *A generative theory of tonal music.* Cambridge, MA: MIT Press.

Madsen, C. K., R. D. Greer, and C. H. Madsen, eds. 1975. *Research in music behavior: Modifying music behavior in the classroom.* New York: Teachers College Press.

Madsen, C. K., and C. A. Prickett, eds. 1987. *Applications of research in music behavior.* Tuscaloosa: University of Alabama Press.

Mandler, G. 1988. Emotion. In *Oxford companion to the mind*, ed. R. L. Gregory, 219–20. London: Oxford University Press.

Manhattanville Music Curriculum Project. 1970. *Manhattanville music curriculum program.* Bardonia, NY: Media Materials.

Maranto, C. D., and K. Bruscia, eds. 1987. *Perspectives on music therapy education and training.* Philadelphia: Temple University.

Maslow, A. 1968a. Music, eduction, and peak experiences. In *Documentary report of the Tanglewood Symposium*, ed. R. Choate, 68–75. Washington, DC: Music Educators National Conference.

Maslow, A. H. 1968b. *Toward a psychology of being.* 2d ed. New York: Van Nostrand Reinhold.

Maslow, A. H. 1970. *Motivation and personality.* 2d ed. New York: Harper and Row.

Massaro, D. W. 1975. *Experimental psychology and information processing.* Chicago: Rand McNally.

Mayer, R. E. 1983. *Thinking, problem solving, cognition.* New York: Freeman.

McDonald, F. J. 1964. The influence of learning theories on education (1900–1950). In *Theories of learning and instruction*, ed. E. Hilgard, 1–26. Chicago: University of Chicago Press.

McGeach, J. A., and A. L. Irion. 1952. *The psychology of human learning.* New York: David McKay.

Merrion, M., ed. 1989. *What works: Instructional strategies for music education.* Reston, VA: Music Educators National Conference.

Meske, E. B. 1985. Teacher education: A wedding of theory and practice. *Bulletin of the Council for Research in Music Education* 81:65–73.

Meyer, L. 1956. *Emotion and meaning in music.* Chicago: University of Chicago Press.

Michel, D. E. 1985. *Music therapy: An introduction, including music in special education.* 2d ed. Springfield, IL: Charles C. Thomas.

Milholland, F., and B. E. Forisha. 1972. *From Skinner to Rogers.* Lincoln, NE: Professional Educators Publications.

Miller, G. A. 1956. The magic number seven, plus or minus two: Some limits on our capacity for processing information. *Psychological Review* 53:81–97.

Miller, N. E., and J. Dollard. 1941. *Social learning and imitation.* New Haven, CT: Yale University Press.

Miller, R. F. 1992. Affective response. In *Handbook of research on music teaching and learning*, ed. R. Colwell, 414–24. New York: Schirmer.

Misiak, H., and V. S. Sexton. 1966. *History of psychology, an overview.* New York: Grune and Stratton.

Mowrer, O. H. 1960. *Learning theory and behavior.* New York: Wiley.

Munroe, R. L. 1955. *Schools of psychoanalytic thought.* New York: Holt, Rinehart and Winston.

Mursell, J. L. 1948. *Education for musical growth.* New York: Ginn.

Music Educators National Conference. 1981. *Applications of psychology to teaching and learning of music: Documentary report of the Ann Arbor symposium.* 1981. Reston, VA: Music Educators National Conference.

Neisser, U. 1966. *Cognitive psychology.* New York: Appleton-Century-Crofts.

Norman, D. A. 1969. *Memory and attention: An introduction to human information processing.* New York: Wiley.

Ortmann, O. 1934. Problems in the elements of ear dictation. In *Research studies in music,* ed. O. Ortmann. Baltimore: Peabody Conservatory of Music.

Osgood, C. E. 1953. *Method and theory in experimental psychology.* New York: Oxford University Press.

Peters, G. D., and R. F. Miller. 1982. *Music teaching and learning.* New York: Longman.

Phillips, K. H. 1992. Research on the teaching of singing. In *Handbook of research on music teaching and learning,* ed. R. Colwell, 568–76. New York: Schirmer.

Piaget, J. 1954. *Construction of reality in the child.* New York: Basic Books.

Piaget, J., and B. Inhelder. 1969. *The psychology of the child.* New York: Basic Books.

Pratt, C. C. 1928. Bisection of tonal intervals larger than an octave, and comparison of tonal distances. *Journal of Experimental Psychology* 11:17–26.

Pribram, K. H. 1964. Neurological notes on the art of educating. In *Theories of learning and instruction,* ed. E. Hilgard, 78–100. Chicago: University of Chicago Press.

Radocy, R. E., and J. D. Boyle. 1979. *Psychological foundations of musical behavior.* Springfield, IL: Charles C. Thomas.

Richardson, C. P. and N. L. Whitaker. 1992. Critical thinking and music education. In *Handbook of research on music teaching and learning,* ed. R. Colwell, 546–57. New York: Schirmer.

Rideout, R. R. 1992. The role of mental presets in skill acquisition. In *Handbook of research on music teaching and learning,* ed. R. Colwell, 472–79. New York: Schirmer.

Rogers, C. R. 1951. *Client-centered therapy: Its current practice, implications, and theory.* Boston: Houghton Mifflin.

Rogers, C. R. 1961. *On becoming a person.* Boston: Houghton Mifflin Co.

Rogers, C. R. 1969. *Freedom to learn.* Columbus, OH: Charles E. Merrill.

Sample, D. 1992. Frequently cited studies as indicators of music education research interests. *Journal of Research in Music Education* 40, no. 2:153–57.

Schuell, T. J. 1988. The role of transfer in the learning and teaching of music: A cognitive perspective. In *The Crane symposium: Toward an understanding of the teaching and learning of music performance,* ed. C. Fowler, 143–67. Potsdam: College of the State University of New York.

Scott-Kassner, C. 1992. Research on music in early childhood. In *Handbook of research on music teaching and learning,* ed. R. Colwell, 633–50. New York: Schirmer.

Sears, W. W. 1968. Processes in music therapy. In *Music in therapy,* ed. E. T. Gaston, 30–44. New York: Macmillan.

Serafine, M. L. 1988. *Music as cognition: The development of thought in sound.* New York: Columbia University Press.

Sidnell, R. T. 1973. *Building instructional programs in music education.* Englewood Cliffs, NJ: Prentice-Hall.

Simons, G. M. 1978. *Early childhood musical development: A bibliography of research abstracts. 1960–75.* Reston, VA: Music Educators National Conference.

Simpson, E. 1966. *The classification of educational objectives, psychomotor domain.* Washington, DC: United States Office of Education.

Sink, P. E. 1992. Research on teaching junior high and middle school general music. In *Handbook of research on music teaching and learning*, ed. R. Colwell, 602–12. New York: Schirmer.

Skinner, B. F. 1950. Are theories of learning necessary? *Psychological Review* 58:193–216.

Sloboda, J. A. 1985. *The musical mind: The cognitive psychology of music*. Oxford: Clarendon Press.

Snelbecker, G. E. 1974. *Learning theory, instructional theory, and psychoeducational design*. New York: McGraw-Hill.

Snygg, D. 1954. Learning: An aspect of personality development. In *Learning theory and clinical research*, ed. the Symposium Committee, 129–137. New York: Wiley.

Solso, R. L. 1990. *Cognitive psychology*. 3d ed. Boston: Allyn and Bacon.

Sparzo, Frank J. 1992. B. F. Skinner's contributions to education: A retrospective appreciation. *Contemporary Education* 63, no. 3:225–33.

Spence, K. W. 1956. *Behavior theory and conditioning*. New Haven, CT: Yale University Press.

Spence, K. W. 1959. The relation of learning theory to the technology of education. *Harvard Educational Review*, 29:84–95.

Standley, J. 1991. *Music techniques in therapy, counseling, and special education*. St Louis: MMB Music.

Stumpf, K. 1883. *Tonpsychologie*. Leipzig: S. Hirzel.

Swanwick, K. 1988. *Music, mind, and education*. London: Routledge.

Swanwick, K., and J. Tillman. 1986. The sequence of musical development. *British Journal of Educational Psychology* 3, no. 3:305–39.

Tait, M. J. 1992. Teaching strategies and styles. In *Handbook of research on music teaching and learning*, ed. R. Colwell, 525–34. New York: Schirmer.

Tait, M., and P. Haack. 1984. *Principles and process of music education: New perspectives*. New York: Teachers College Press.

Thaut, M. H. 1991a. Neuropsychological processes in music perception and their relevance in music therapy. In *Music therapy in the treatment of adults with mental disorders*, ed. R. K. Unkefer, 3–32. New York: Schirmer.

Thaut, M. H. 1991b. Physiological and motor responses to music stimuli. In *Music therapy in the treatment of adults with mental disorders*, ed. R. K. Unkefer, 33–49. New York: Schirmer.

Thorndike, E. L. [1898] 1911. *Animal intelligence*. New York: Macmillan.

Thorpe, L. P. 1958. Learning theory and music teaching. In *Basic concepts in music education*, ed. N. B. Henry, 163–94. Chicago: University of Chicago Press.

Tunks, T. 1980. Applications of psychological positions on learning and development to musical behavior. In *Handbook of music psychology*, ed. D. A. Hodges, 275–290. Lawrence, KS: National Association for Music Therapy.

Tunks, T. 1992. The transfer of music learning. In *Handbook of research on music teaching and learning*, ed. R. Colwell, 437–47. New York: Schirmer.

Underwood, B. J. 1966. *Experimental psychology*. 2d ed. New York: Appleton-Century-Crofts.

Unkefer, R. F., ed. 1991. *Music therapy in the treatment of adults with mental disorders*. New York: Schirmer.

Uszler, M. 1992. Research on the teaching of keyboard music. In *Handbook of research on music teaching and learning*, ed. R. Colwell, 584–93. New York: Schirmer.

Walters, D. L. 1992. Sequencing for efficient learning. In *Handbook of research on music teaching and learning*, ed. R. Colwell, 535–45. New York: Schirmer.

Weerts, R. 1992. Research on the teaching of instrumental music. In *Handbook of research on music teaching and learning*, ed. R. Colwell, 577–83. New York: Schirmer.

Wilson, F. R., and F. L. Roehmann. 1992. The study of biomechanical and physiological processes in relation to musical performance. In *Handbook of research on music teaching and learning*, ed. R. Colwell, 509–24. New York: Schirmer.

Woodworth, R. S. 1958. *Dynamics of behavior*. New York: Holt, Rinehart and Winston.

Zimmerman, M. P. 1993. An overview of developmental research in music. *Bulletin of the Council for Research in Music Education* 116:1–21.

Zimmerman, M. P. 1986. Musical development in middle childhood: A summary of selected research studies. *Bulletin of the Council for Research in Music Education* 86:18–35.

12

The Influence of Music on Human Behavior

Donald A. Hodges

and

Paul A. Haack

Human beings are musical creatures and the music we create, in turn, shapes and influences us. Some of the effects of music are obvious, such as when we tap our toes to an energizing rhythm, others are less so. Taking stock of the ways music influences human behavior requires the assistance of behavioral and other scientists. Because music is, after all, a form of human behavior, it is logical to look to those whose work is the study of human behavior. Accordingly, this chapter is organized around sections on biological, anthrophological, sociological, and psychological perspectives on the influences of music on human behavior. Because many biological and psychological issues are covered more extensively in other chapters of this book, these sections are additive and, thus, more attention is paid to anthropological and sociological perspectives.

Biological Perspectives

Previous chapters have provided extensive coverage of such biological topics as hearing, the brain, and physiological responses. The extensive literature cited in those chapters provides ample evidence of a significant body of research from which to derive biological perspectives of musical behavior. This section includes several additional topics bearing on biological issues, including freedom from instinctive behaviors, extended infant dependency, the influence of human biology on music, the influence of music on human biology, and the biological necessity of music.

Freedom from Instinctive Behaviors

Although much of animal behavior is instinctive, human beings are relatively free from instinctive behaviors (assuming instinctive behaviors to be "complex, species-specific, relatively unmodifiable behavior patterns" [Lefrancois 1979, 292]). Because of this freedom, we are able to make conscious decisions that enormously expand our repertoire of behaviors. One of the conscious decisions human beings have always made is to create music. Birds "sing" (i.e., they emit vocalizations that we humans call birdsong) and it is possible that they derive pleasure from it. However, the sounds they make and the manner in which they produce them are, except for a few rare species, primarily the results of genetically programmed instructions. We sing and we derive great pleasure from it. But we do not sing certain songs that have been genetically prewired into our systems. Our songs are conscious creations, with a bewildering and seemingly infinite set of variations. Freedom from the tyranny of instinctive responses is a human trait of vast importance to our music and to creativity in general.

Extended Infant Dependency

In the course of evolutionary history, the human brain grew so large that, if infants were now born at full term (in terms of brain development), the braincase or skull would be too large to pass through the birth canal. As a result, we are born with our brains incompletely developed—it takes the first six years of life for the brain to reach 90 percent of its adult size—and we must spend an inordinate amount of time, compared to other animal species, dependent on others for survival (Cowan 1979; White and Brown 1973).

One of the most important things that occurs during this period of infant dependency is the communication of love and affection. Music plays an important role in sharing and expressing these feelings to babies. Rhythmic behaviors (such as rocking, stroking, and patting), pitch patterns (such as speaking with varied tone and inflection), and especially singing lullabies are all musical ways of communicating love. The term *motherese* has been coined in reference to the particular kind of speech patterns mothers use with their infants (Birdsong 1984). The musical aspects of motherese are critically important, not only as an aid to language acquisition, but especially in the communication of emotions. Long before youngsters begin to talk, they are adept at deciphering the emotional content of speech, largely due to the musical characteristics of motherese. Add to these music from crib mobiles and musical toys, and the near omnipresence of music during the extended time of infant dependency becomes apparent.

The Influence of Human Biology on Music

Beyond the brain, there are other physical attributes that contribute to the enormous variety of human musical behaviors. Our hearing mechanism is, of course, critically important to our music making. The limits of hearing for pitch and loudness and discrimination sensitivity for small changes are all factors that influence the kind of music we produce. In terms of the musician as small-muscle athlete (Wilson 1986), the body parts we use most often in music-making—fingers, hands, lips, and vocal tract—are precisely those parts most strongly represented in the sensory-motor cortex of the brain.

Another physical attribute important to music is a vocal tract that allows us to attach emotional connotations to our vocalizations at will. The vocal utterances of our nearest animal neighbors, the primates, have an emotional content of a somewhat limited, prescribed nature, while we are free to express a much wider range of feelings in myriad vocal styles (Farb 1978; Malmo 1975; Williams 1980).

The rhythmic nature of our bodies also has implications for our music. We live in a rhythmic environment and our body clocks work in a rhythmic fashion. Disruptions in body rhythms are often indications of illness, such as depression (Wehr 1982). Our music has a strong rhythmic element to it precisely because of biological and environmental rhythms.

The Influence of Music on Human Biology

While human biology influences music, it is equally true that music exerts a powerful influence on human biology. A six-month-old fetus can respond to sounds it hears inside the mother's womb (Restak 1983; Verny with Kelly 1981). A condition known as marasmus refers to the fact that babies less than a year old will die if they do not receive enough love and affection (Farb 1978; Montagu 1977 and 1978; Montagu and Matson 1979) and, as previously discussed, music plays an important role in the expression of love to infants.

Music has an effect on motor systems. Many common listening experiences elicit physical responses, as in tapping a toe to the beat. The energizing effect of music allows for the coordination of many work behaviors, as when fishermen haul in nets. This connection between music and physical response is seen in many exercise activities, such as aerobics and jazzercise, and certainly in dance. Many children's games are coordinated to singing or chanting. Finally, the rhythmic energy of music is often used to effect coordinated motor movements in stroke and Parkinson's patients (Thaut, McIntosh, and Rice 1995), and pitch aspects are useful as melodic intonation therapy with speech-impaired individuals (Naeser and Helms-Estabrooks 1985).

Many physiological processes are affected by music, including changes in heart rate, blood pressure, breathing rate, muscle tension, pupil dilation, peristaltic contractions (digestion), brain waves, and brain chemistry (see chap. 9). The International Society for Music in Medicine has been founded by physicians who use music in a variety of medical settings (Spintge and Droh 1992; Spintge and Pratt 1995). Music has been effective as a painkiller in such diverse ills as terminal cancer, chronic back pain and crippling spinal injuries, severe burns, psychiatric disorders, dental problems, labor, and such stress-related problems as migraine headaches, high blood pressure, and ulcers. Loud music can have a deleterious effect on hearing. At particular risk are those who listen to certain styles of popular music (especially heavy metal) via headphones (Barrett and Hodges 1995).

Summary

Biological perspectives of musical behavior promote a synergistic relationship between music and the body. Human body systems (e.g., auditory, visual, motor, and central nervous systems) are called into play to create the ordered experience of sounds that we call music. In turn, musical experiences influence the body. This two-way relationship is not an inconsequential one. In *Programs of the Brain*, Young states:

> Proper study of the organization of the brain shows that belief and creative art are essential and universal features of all human life. They are not mere peripheral luxury activities. They are literally the most important of all the functional features that ensure human homeostasis. (Young 1978, 231)

All human beings are born to be linguistic, but the language used is determined by the culture in which one is raised. In the same way, all human beings are born to be musical, without having the specific musical styles predetermined. Music is, thus, an essential part of our biological makeup. It is not something artificially added to our behavioral repertoire, nor is it something we do in a genetically prescribed way. Music is a necessary result of our biology and a vital ingredient in that which makes us human. Furthermore, music has broad and pervasive influences on biological aspects of our behavior.

Anthropological Perspectives

Anthropologists have a message for us that can be stated rather simply but is profound in its impact on our understanding of the significance of music. The message is this: *All people in all times and in all places have engaged in musical behaviors.* There is much to be said to elaborate on this statement, of course, and that is the purpose of this section.

In the field of anthropology, music can be studied along with the many other products and processes of various cultural groups. In addition, there are specialists, known as ethnomusicologists, who study world musics specifically. The following brief list gives a sample of the literature in this field of study: *The Anthropology of Music* (Merriam 1964), *Becoming Human Through Music* (MENC 1985), *The Ethnomusicologist* (Hood 1971), *Folk Song Style and Culture* (Lomax 1968), *40,000 Years of Music* (Chailley 1964), *How Musical is Man?* (Blacking 1973), *The Music of Man* (Menuhin and Davis 1979), *Music of the Whole Earth* (Reck 1977), and *The Study of Ethnomusicology* (Nettl 1983). In addition to these books, there are many articles in such journals as *Ethnomusicology, Ethnomusicology Newsletter,* and *World of Music.* The October 1972 issue of *Music Educators Journal* was entitled "Music in World Cultures" and contained 24 articles devoted to this subject. There are still many cultural groups whose music has not been fully studied, but the research that has been compiled provides much useful information about the anthropological significance of music.

Time Line of Early Artistic Behaviors

One of the more fascinating relationships between anthropology and art is the inquiry into art's beginnings. This is an important topic because the individuals who created the earliest known art are essentially the same as we are, biologically and psychologically. For human beings, it appears that biological evolution stopped (or at least greatly slowed down) approximately 35,000 years ago (Dubos 1974). From that time to this, humanity has adapted to the environment through cultural evolution, not biological evolution. Thus, being essentially the same creatures as our ancient forebears, we are able to respond to the expressions inherent in their art. Furthermore, we can learn a great deal about our own creative impulses by studying humankind's first efforts at art.

The time line that follows is in no way meant to be exhaustive. Rather, it is simply to give some hint of how long art has been with us and the extent to which we have engaged in it.

500,000 years ago. Shiny quartz crystals have been found in caves in China. Homo erectus may have collected objects of beauty as early as this time (Prideaux 1973).

200,000 years ago. Hand axes and other tools and utensils were shaped far more beautifully than required for utilitarian purposes (Boorstein 1992; Pfeiffer 1969).

70,000 years ago. Cave paintings from this time include a depiction of a bow (Kendig and Levitt 1982). Many anthropologists believe that, initially, the bow may have been as much a musical instrument as it was a weapon (Mumford 1966).

60,000 years ago. Artifacts found in a cave in Lebanon—including ocher-colored spearpoints, daggers, and hand axes buried with fossilized remains of deer and other animals—indicate ceremonies accompanied by dancing and singing (Constable 1973).

40,000 years ago. Remains, such as human skeletons buried with flowers, show spiritual concerns with death around 40,000 years ago. Burial rituals apparently included both music and dance. There are also indications that Neanderthals used pigments for cosmetics (Pfeiffer 1980b; Rensberger 1981; Wilford 1986).

35,000 years ago. Cro-Magnons fashioned and wore jewelry. "Ice-age art" flourished in caves from 10,000–35,000 years ago (Farb 1978; Menuhin and Davis 1979). The vast amount of art found and the continuity for over 35,000 years speaks to its importance.

30,000 years ago. Flutes and bull roarers or thundersticks have been found in southern France, the Pyrenees, and Russia (Pfeiffer 1980a). Although it is impossible to reconstruct the music that would have been heard that long ago, the positioning of the tone holes on the flutes indicates that these were no mere duck calls. Early humans were probably creating music of artistic significance (Wilford 1986).

25,000 years ago. The first appearance of a pipe held by a Pan-like figure occurs in a Magdelenian cave painting (Prideaux 1973). A hollow bone flute with two or three holes was found in Czechoslo-vakia, dated around 25,000 years ago (Putman 1988).

20,000 years ago. Flutes, rattles, and bone-and-rock percussion instruments indicate that Cro-Magnons engaged in festival and ritual events around 20,000 years ago (Farb 1978). Musical instruments have also been found in Africa and western Asia going back 15,000–20,000 years. These include boomerangs, bull roarers, whistles, flutes, and trumpets.

16,000 years ago. Rock engravings show dancers, which indicates the presence of music.

10,000 years ago. Flutes and whistles dating back to 10,000 years ago have been found in Colorado (Stanford 1979). Decorated pottery and rock carvings have also been found in caves in Brazil (von Puttkamer 1979).

6,000 years ago. Rock carvings in Utah may be 6,000 years old (Smith and Long 1980). Many of the figures shown are musicians and dancers. Literary references to musical behavior and fragments of instruments attest to a rich musical life in Mesopotamia and India.

5,000 years ago. Egyptian bas-reliefs allow us to describe an entire orchestra, including wind, string, and percussion instruments, harps, and singers (Farmer 1969; Jenkins 1970). From the details provided, such as hand positions, some speculations can be made about the sounds produced. In addition, some of the actual instruments have survived. Diggings in South America show the Mayan civilization to be more than 4,000 years old (Hammond 1982). Artifacts include art, architecture, jewelry, pottery, weapons, tools, and musical instruments (such as clay occarinas with five tone holes). Rock paintings of musicians were found in Tanzania (Leakey 1983). During this period, the Chinese selected their rulers by means of formal examinations in the "six arts," which included music, archery, horsemanship, writing, arithmetic, and the rites and ceremonies of public and private life (Ellison 1984).

3,800 years ago. The oldest known example of musical notation was a cult song inscribed in cuneiform (Claiborne 1974). Since it was discovered in Syria, the Near East has been identified as the birthplace of Western music.

2,500 years ago. Ancient Chinese civilizations equated each season of the year with a musical tone or musical instrument. A huge set of bells has been found made out of cast bronze (Shen 1987; Stickney 1982).

1,200 years ago. Remote caves in Guatemala were covered with paintings of musicians (Stuart and Garrett 1981).

Prehistoric art is connected to modern times by the earliest examples of writing. Most of the early writing samples are business records, historical accounts, and the like; however, many contain creative efforts, including hymns, that corroborate the ideas about humanity's artistic nature gained from a study of prehistoric art (Claiborne 1974). Clay tablets from Sumeria and Asia Minor (2,000 B.C.) contain writings that discuss the place of music in ritual, the organizations of cult musicians, and so on. The *Bible* contains, of course, many references to the use of music in worship, war, healing, and so forth (Kraeling and Mowry 1969).

The records we have of humankind's earliest artistic behaviors must represent only a tiny fraction of all our ancestors' creative output. But enough remains to establish clearly that human beings have always and everywhere been artistic creatures.

Prehistoric Cave and Rock Art

One of the most glorious examples of artistic creativity of any epoch is the magnificent cave art of 10,000–35,000 years ago (Collins 1976; Leroi-Gourhan 1982; Marshack 1975; Pericot-Garcia, Galloway, and Lommel 1967; Pfeiffer 1969 and 1980b; Prideaux 1973). In the late nineteenth century, a series of caves in Spain and France were discovered containing hundreds of paintings, drawings, engravings, and smaller carvings in bone, stone, and clay. The Cro-Magnons who occupied these caves had obviously invested a great deal of time and energy in these art works. Taking a detailed look at these works can bring us much information about early music.

Many of the paintings are on the ceilings and walls of remote cave rooms and not easily accessible. Artists worked there with the aid of crude stone lamps (Leroi-Gourhan 1982). Rocks with natural, cuplike indentations were filled with animal fat and fitted with wicks of moss or twigs. Modern experiments using the same abundant materials have demonstrated that these ancient lamps burn without smoking and give off as much light as an ordinary candle. Scaffolds were also built to allow the artists to reach the ceilings.

The bulk of these paintings depict animals. Bison, deer, wild cattle, ibexes, horses, wolves, cats, boars, birds, and rhinoceros are all represented. Occasionally human figures are shown. Though some of the figures are etched into the cave walls, many are painted with red, black, brown, yellow, and white pigments. Many of the paintings take advantage of the natural contours of the rock to produce rounded, more natural images.

Although not all of them are as old as the cave art just described, similar art works have been found in remote caves all over the world (Pericot-Garcia, Galloway, and Lommel 1967). Rock carvings have been found in Norway, Sweden, Ireland, Great Britain, France, Belgium, Germany, and Italy. Worldwide, rock carvings have been discovered in Russia, China, Turkey, Afghanistan, Asia Minor, Southeast Asia, Indonesia, New Guinea, Australia, the Fiji Islands and other Pacific islands, all over the continent of Africa, and throughout North and South America. To gain some idea of how many rock carvings have been discovered so far, consider that over 40,000 have been found in Northern Italy alone, that there are more engraved rocks in Scandanavia than in the rest of Europe put together, and there are many more rock carvings in Africa than in all of Europe.

Perhaps the most startling aspect of these art works is that they are no mere crude scratchings made by unintelligent, uncreative creatures. These are works of art in the fullest sense of the term; they possess vision, craftsmanship, subtlety, insight, ingenuity, and, above all, great beauty. There can be no question that these artists possessed a high degree of aesthetic sensitivity.

In what ways does the existence of cave art relate to the importance of music? Not only does the sheer beauty of these paintings demonstrate that early human beings were capable of creating expressive works, but the tremendous amount of it indicates that art was an important part of their lives. If these hundreds of thousands of paintings and carvings have been preserved in the deep recesses of remote caves where they were protected from the elements, how much more art must have been produced in the open air and subsequently destroyed? If early humans were this adept and active in the visual arts, could one not suppose, by inference, that they were equally involved in other expressive, artistic modes, such as music?

In support of this contention, there are several important points to consider. The presence of musical instruments and the depiction of musicians and dancers provide the strongest support. Another point is that there are various indicators that religious ceremonies were often held in the same rooms as the paintings. Given the strong connection that music and religion have had throughout human history, it is likely that music was heard in these caves during Cro-Magnon times. Further support comes from a film of a present-day Australian aborigine executing a cave painting (Mumford 1966). He is perhaps more a priest than artist, as each gesture of the painting is accompanied by songs and ritual dances, which appear to take a much more important place in the ceremony than the decoration itself.

We can never know, of course, exactly when or where the first music was made. What is important is to note the evidence we do have. Human beings are artistic creatures by nature. Art does not occur only when a certain amount of leisure time is available; art does not occur after the "important business" of life is taken care of or after a certain level of technology has been reached. Art occurs as part and parcel of human life.

Art and Technology

Another way of documenting the artistic nature of humanity is through an examination of the development of technology. A popular misconception of the chronology of art and technology is that, as our skill in making tools improved, we were able to do more work at a faster pace and thus gain leisure time that could then be spent on creative or artistic activities. Nothing could be further from the truth.

Anthropologists agree that solving artistic and creative problems often led to inventions that later were found to have utilitarian uses. An excellent example can be seen in the historical development of ceramics. The first example of pottery is thought to be a shard found in Japan, determined to be 12,000 years old (Prideaux 1973). However, the first kilns existed more than 15,000 years earlier. If the early kiln was not used to fire pottery, what was its use? Many examples of modeled clay figures have been found—bison, bears, foxes, lions, and human figures. These are not childlike "mudpies" dried in a fire, but mixtures of earth and powdered bone calculated to make the heat spread evenly to produce a new, rock-hard material. Whether these figures were created as art objects or used in some ancient ritual, clearly an artistic use of a technological invention predates the utilitarian use by thousands of years.

Another example of technology dating from Cro-Magnon times involves stone blades. One particular example, called the "laurel leaf" blade because of its shape, is a finely chipped stone blade that appears to have served no utilitarian purpose. It is eleven inches long and only four-tenths of an inch thick, too thin and too fragile to be used for hunting. It must have been used for ceremonial purposes or at least as an object of admiration. Perhaps a master craftsman turned it out just to show his great skill. Other similar objects, such as knives, have been found showing no signs of wear; some of these are richly decorated. Speaking specifically of the laurel leaf blade, Prideaux says:

> Clearly, to produce an object of such daring proportions required craftsmanship bordering on art, and many archeologists think this masterpiece and others like it may have been just that—works of art that served an esthetic or ritual function rather than a utilitarian one and may even have been passed, as highly prized items, from one man or group to another. (Prideaux 1973, 61)

Contemporary Bushmen have been observed putting the tip of a hunting bow on a dry melon shell and tapping on the string with a reed to make music (Mumford 1966). Australian aborigine spear throwers, long wooden poles with an "elbow" joint, are also used for beating out rhythms for dancing. The first attempts at metallurgy, some 8,000 years ago, were originally for making beads and ornaments (Farb 1978). Metallurgical techniques were not used to make tools for another 2,000 years. Welding was first used to join parts of statues together. The wheel was initially used for religious objects and toys; only much later was it used for locomotion. Without trying to create an exhaustive list, the point surely has been made that artistic and technological problem solving are part of the same process. Human beings are as much artists as toolmakers.

All musical instruments may be viewed as tools to produce sounds. These musical tools allow us to extend our sound production capabilities beyond what we can accomplish with our voices, whistling, or body percussion. Just as cars, planes, and boats extend our locomotion capabilities, so do the hundreds of musical instruments extend our music-making skills in terms of range, volume, timbre, dynamics, technique, and so on.

Generally, musical instruments may be divided into four major categories: idiophones (struck instruments, such as xylophones, gongs, and bells, and shaken instruments, such as rattles), membranophones (drums), aerophones (wind instruments), and cordophones (stringed instruments). Some musical instruments are relatively simple from a modern technological standpoint. Other instruments represent major technological achievements and state-of-the-art engineering. A modern grand piano, for example, supports a string tension of 30 tons (Backus 1977). Compared to the grand piano, the African thumb piano (mbira) is true simplicity. The issue, however, is not one of greater technology creating better instruments, but simply different ones. If one asks whether humanity has made progress in music over the past several thousand years, the answer would be yes in terms of technological developments but no in terms of what music does for its listeners. Each culture's music does, and has always done, just what its users want it to. Music written for the piano does not necessarily do a "better" job of pleasing listeners today than harpsichord music did in the seventeenth century or than music played on the mbira does for its people.

Electronic music instruments (perhaps a fifth category), such as the synthesizer, computer, and MIDI (musical instrument digital interface) devices, provide an excellent illustration of the connection between art and technology. Here are instruments of incredible sophistication, instruments that are being improved at a tremendously rapid pace, and instruments that are dramatically changing our experiences with music. Musical uses of electronic technology did not wait until such engineering was perfected. Composers and performers have, in fact, been at the cutting edge, pushing technology to provide them with ever more advanced tools for creating and manipulating sounds.

The new technology of the compact disc (CD) provides an excellent example of the interrelationships between art and technology, how it is not technology and then art, but both simultaneously. CD players produce their amazing quality of sound by means of an incredible sampling rate of 44,100 times per second. This means that each second of sound is sliced into 44,100 pieces. Each "slice" is then given a number that represents the sound characteristics of that portion of the music. The disc on which this information is stored can hold up to 2 billion bits of information. During playback, the newest CD players sample the information stored on the disc at up to four times the original sampling rate, thus making certain that none of the bits of information is lost and that all are used in the reproduction of the musical message. This technology, first used for musical applications, is now being linked with computers for the storage of other kinds of information. Currently, each CD-ROM can hold up to 250,000 pages of text—along with accompanying graphics, sound tracks, and movies—making encyclopedias, dictionaries, and other reference works instantaneously available to the computer screen. In talking about the role of music in these space-age advancements, Elmer-Dewitt said: "Without the CD music market, data CDs would not exist. . . . Every time Bruce Springsteen and Stevie Wonder sell a compact disc, it's good news for the data side" (1987, 71).

Bronowski believes that art and technology arise out of a common capacity to draw conclusions from past experiences and visualize the future. Both art and technology enable us to move our minds through time and space. "Man is unique not because he does science, and he is unique not because he does art, but because science and art equally are expressions of his marvellous plasticity of mind" (Bronowski 1973, 412).

Invariants

As used in Dubos 1981, the term *invariants* applies to particular aspects of human behavior that are universal but whose actual realizations vary widely from group to group. Invariants occur because of the biological and psychological unity of humanity. All people have the same invariant needs, but the expressions of those needs are culturally determined. There are at least four invariants that bear a special relationship to music: religion, celebrations and rites, altered states of consciousness, and dance.

Religion

All human groups engage in some type of religious worship (Ember and Ember 1973). Furthermore, music, along with such other practices as prayer and exhortation (preaching), is used the world over in such spiritual exercises as chanting, hymn singing, and meditation with the accompaniment of suitable background music. Perhaps music and religion are so inextricably intertwined because both are concerned with the ineffable. Music helps us to experience and express spiritual concerns in a way that words cannot. "It is not the business of a composer to preach over the dead, but his requiem mass may help make death vivid and significant as no verbal account can" (Broudy 1968, 13).

Celebrations

Human beings seem to feel the need periodically to set aside mundane tasks and worries and so people celebrate all over the world (Turner 1982). At these times they congregate to participate in holidays, festivals, ceremonies, spectacles, pageants, rites of passage, fairs, carnivals, parades, extravaganzas, jubilees, commemorations, coronations, and other rites and observances. These occasions provide for a heightened focus as well as a release of the human spirit, a means of transcending daily routines. "Probably it is through their monuments, their ceremonies, and their rites that societies best express their ideals and reveal what they would like to become" (Dubos 1974, 201–2).

Nearly as common as celebrations themselves is the presence of music in celebrations. While we cannot say that there are no celebrations without music, it would be a difficult task to name very many. Conversely, it is a simple task to provide many, many examples of the ways in which music is used in celebrations, ranging from marching bands on parade to aborigine fertility dances. Music, especially when accompanied by dancing, seems to be a powerful way of expressing joy, thanksgiving, and all the other feelings connected with the idea of celebrating.

Altered States of Consciousness

Music also has a special connection with a human invariant that is some-times a part of celebrations, sometimes a part of religious worship, but can also be a private affair. In many different ways, human beings every-where seek altered states of consciousness. A survey of 4,000 cultures in-dicated that more than 90 percent of these groups practiced some kind of institutionalized altered-state ritual (Hooper 1981 and 1982). To this in-ventory must be added the individual journeys many take via such means as prayer, meditation, daydreaming, or drugs. Music has an important role to play in both group and private activities designed to bring persons to altered states of consciousness (List 1984). Chanting to a mantra or whirling to the feverish pounding of drums are examples of ways to reach altered states with the aid of music (Farb 1978). This serves a very practical purpose for adolescent males in central African tribal societies who follow their bush schooling with several days of continuous dancing to drum rhythms that results in an altered state of consciousness; this allows them to undergo circumcision without benefit of anesthesia. More generally, often in the name of "dance" and accompanied by music, virtually all of the world's children will spin themselves to the point of dizziness and collapse in their experimentation with altered states of consciousness.

Dance

Dance, another human invariant (Hanna 1984), is closely related to the three previously mentioned invariants and rarely exists, if at all, without music. In fact, music and dance may be the original and still most closely "related arts." Dance has a special character in that it seems to grow out of the exhilaration of movement; it is a vibrant, exultant glorification of hu-man locomotion through space and time, with music providing the au-dible time framework and referent. Dance is a means of giving physical reality to music. Performing musicians realize just what physical effort is involved in music making. Dancers take those physical gestures beyond the constraints of keyboard, bow, or baton and transform them into unfet-tered, whole-body-oriented, physical expressions of the sound.

    The invariant of dance is culturally expressed in thousands of folk dance styles. The polka, Scottish fling, square dance, and Amerindian rain dance are but a few of many familiar examples; each of these is as notable for the accompanying music as for the actual dance steps.

Music: A Human Invariant

Music is also a human invariant and, as with the previously discussed invariants, is quite diverse. One way of sensing the diversity of worldwide styles is through an examination of the cantometrics project (Lomax 1968). *Cantometrics* is a term that describes the efforts of Lomax and his colleagues to use song—specifically folk songs—as a tool of measurement (canto = song, metrics = measurement). The goals of the project were to devise a descriptive technique for categorizing folk-song styles from cultures around the world and to relate these folk-song styles to specific patterns of social behavior.

To accomplish these tasks, a cantometrics coding book was developed. Over a period of years, this measurement tool was refined to the point that, with it, one can "broadly characterize song performance style in such a way that the main families of song performance may be recognized, their geographical distribution mapped, and their relationship to cultural continuity, acculturation, and the expressive arts perceived" (Lomax 1968, 35). Various aspects of song performances—such as range, interval width, rhythmic organization, melodic shape, and vocal quality—were mapped onto a grid. Only unaccompanied and accompanied song performances were evaluated. Certain aspects of instrumental accompaniments were rated, but purely instrumental performances were not.

Matched ethnographic (i.e., socioeconomic information and cultural origins, growth, and change) and cantometric data from 233 cultures were analyzed. These 233 cultures were grouped into nine major geographical regions as follows.

I. South America
Pategonia, Andes, Interior Amazonia, Mato Grosso, Eastern Brazil, Guiana, Caribbean, Central America

II. North America
Mexico, Southwest Hunters, Pueblo, Eastern Woodlands, Plains, Great Basin, California, Northwest Coast, Arctic America

III. Oceania
Proto-Malay, New Guinea, Micronesia, Melanesia, Eastern Polynesia, Western Polynesia

IV. Old High Culture
Central Asia, East Asia, Himalayas, Tribal Southeast Asia, Urban Southeast Asia, Malay, Urban Indonesia, North Africa, Sahara, Near East, Middle East, Village India

V. Africa
Western Sudan, Eastern Sudan, Upper Nile, African Hunters, South African Bantu, Central Bantu, Northeastern Bantu, Madagascar, Equatorial Bantu, Guinea Coast, Afro-American, Moslem Sudan, Ethiopia

VI. Europe
   Old European, Western Europe, Western Europe Overseas,
   Mediterranean Europe, Latin America
VII. Tribal India
VIII. Arctic Asia
 IX. Australia

Two of the major conclusions to be drawn from the Cantometrics Project provide major anthropological documentation for the significance of music.

1. Music is a universal form of human behavior. "No branch of the human family, no matter how well- or ill-equipped technologically, fails to symbolize its social norms in a suitable song style" (Lomax 1968, 7). "So far as we know, every branch of the human species has its songs. Indeed, singing is a universal human trait found in all known cultures as a specialized and easily identifiable kind of vocal behavior" (3). "Singing is a universal trait of culture" (xi).

2. Song is an integral part of culture. This is indicated through high correlations between norms of song performance and patterns of social interaction. "Song style symbolizes and reinforces certain important aspects of social structure in all cultures" (Lomax 1968, vii). "In general, a culture's song performance style seemed to represent generalized aspects of its social and communication systems" (ix). "Apparently, as people live so do they sing" (4). "If song performance and lifestyle vary together, one is the reflexion and reinforcement of the other" (6). "Song can no longer be treated as a wayward, extra, belated, though pleasant afterthought upon the serious business of living" (6).

Evidence from the cantometrics project and from hundreds of ethnomusicological studies gives ample evidence to the universality of music. But this fact gives rise to an important question. If music is a universal phenomenon of humankind, what is universal about it? Asked another way, are there aspects of all music (the product) and all music making (the process) that are common to all peoples? Ethnomusicologists have debated this issue to a considerable extent (see Boiles 1984; List 1984; Merriam 1964; Nettl 1977 and 1983; Nketia 1984).

One of the first difficulties is that of defining terms. Most societies have a word for music as well as for a variety of musical activities. Other groups, such as the Hausa of Nigeria or the Southern Paiute of Nevada, engage in many musical activities but have no single word that refers specifically to music. Societies that do have a word for music often mean different things by it. Even in the Greek roots of western civilization, music meant not just the sound/time art of today but the various arts under the guidance of their various muses. If there is no agreement on what exactly music is or is named, there does seem to be agreement that the intent to make music is universal and that one can generally recognize when music is being made.

Other universals include structural elements, such as the fact that music has a beginning and an end. It consists of manipulating one or more of the elements of pitch, rhythm, timbre, and form in some organized fashion that is recognized by the societal group as music and is generally pleasing. Singing is universal. So is the use of repeated beat patterns. Other universals include the use of pitches separated by discrete intervals, musical scales of 5–7 pitches, and the octave (Monmaney 1987).

Another way of looking at universals in music is to look at what roles music plays in various societies. In his landmark text, *The Anthropology of Music*, Merriam (1964) makes it clear that, while music is a universal trait of humankind, the role of music is not the same for all people. Accordingly, he differentiates between uses and functions of music. Uses of music refer to the relatively specific ways in which music is employed, for example, as an expression of love or an invocation to the gods. The functions of music are the more basic reasons or purposes for those uses of music. There are many uses of music, too many to be ennumerated here. However, Merriam lists ten functions of music that help to explain what role music might play for any given society.

There may actually be more functions than ten or fewer; no one really knows for certain, because the functions are not mutually exclusive or discrete. One of the difficulties is the extreme variation among human societies. The !Kung culture, for example, consists primarily of songs, dances, and stories (Leakey 1981). They have few possessions apart from musical instruments. Other cultures do not emphasize music nearly to that degree. Thus, the role that music plays varies greatly and many of these functions may overlap and occur simultaneously within the same musical experience. The point of the review of functions that follows is to give some idea of what music does for most human societies.

As an added dimension, a pedagogical aspect will be incorporated into this section for those concerned with music curriculum development. In this respect, it should be noted that the four invariants discussed in the previous section could, in and of themselves, form the thematic framework for a general music course of study at any educational level. In addition, they are excellent bases for related arts courses, or basic themes for integrated curricula. The functions of music that follow provide an equally powerful and even more specific curricular framework for music education, one that may become a most essential aspect of music schooling for life in the twenty-first century.

Given the multitude of ways that music is being used in today's sound-saturated society, youth truly need "functional literacy" in music. They need to understand and be aware of the functions and influences of music that surround their lives, and they need the ability to choose and use music wisely and well—to program their own sound environment to meet their own needs rather than constantly be subject to the whims and dictates of the media and others. Thus, following a brief review of each of Merriam's functions, an example will be derived from the realm of world cultures, followed by further examples directly relevant to the daily lives of U.S. students. In using such examples in curricular settings, the latter examples could lead to the former, giving the class a cross-cultural entrée to the study of world musics.

The Function of Emotional Expression

One function of music that seems to be fairly widespread among different cultural groups is that of emotional expression. Music is a common way of expressing a wide variety of feelings. This function can be experienced singly, as one person hums while working, in small groups, as young children chant and sing while playing, or in the largest gatherings, as in the celebrations that involve every member of the group. Emotions can be expressed and shared during quiet times or in times of great excitement. Musically expressed emotions include a full range of feelings, from the more crystallized forms of hate, fear, or joy to the more subtle and refined feelings of loneliness, contentment, or daydreaming. The overwhelming point is that music allows for the expression of sentiments that cannot be otherwise verbalized.

The Kaingana of Brazil mourn with a series of death chants (Sullivan 1984). These are sung not only at funerals but at anytime one might think about death. Song provides a way of ritual remembering, so that the departed are not forgotten. Other purposes include keeping the cremated bones intact and frightening away ghosts. These songs are so powerful and have such an effect on the singers that they later wash their mouths out with muddy water as a means of ridding themselves of such potent medicine.

Young people in the United States often experience the emotional expression of chanting a cheer at an athletic event, or of singing a fight song or alma mater in victory or in loyalty to a school. Sometimes young men and women share a "special" song, "their song," that speaks to and for them, one to the other, in ways that they might otherwise feel too embarrassed or inadequate to attempt to verbalize. And while death tends to be almost a taboo topic in the United States, here, too, there is a considerable body of music, ranging from the ballad recounting Billie Jo's jump off the Tallahatchi Bridge to Penderecki's *Threnody to the Victims of Hiroshima*.

The Function of Aesthetic Enjoyment

This is a difficult function to assess owing to the lack of a consistent or universal definition of "aesthetic." A first step is not so difficult, in that many cultures around the world share aesthetic views similiar to our own Western views that art (or specifically music) can be viewed or contemplated apart from a more utilitarian function ("art for art's sake"), that a concept of beauty is integrally bound up with the notion of art, and so on. However, Merriam goes to some lengths to illustrate that there are cultures that do not share similar views, at least in so much as we are able to translate complex and abstract concepts cross-culturally. It may be, however, if we are willing to grant the broadest possible definition to the aesthetic function, or even perhaps more appropriately, to grant culturally defined definitions, that peoples all over the world do share some common traits with regard to the contemplation, appreciation, and/or evaluation of both art products and processes. Precisely what these traits are, or how they might be verbalized, is still in need of further scholarly attention.

One example of the aesthetic function of music may be found in India, where there are a number of musical traditions known as *gharana* (Deshpande 1973). Each *gharana* has a unique artistic discipline that follows certain laws (*kaydas*). The origin of each *gharana* is in the vocal quality (*swara*) of its founder. The *swara* and *laya* (musical time) are two of the most important aesthetic principles in these musical traditions. While one style might emphasize *swara* to the neglect of *laya*, or vice versa, aesthetic judgments are made on a proper balance being maintained between the two. For example, the *gharana* known as "Alladiya Khan" or Jaipur style is prized because of the near-perfect integration of the two facets.

Young people in U.S. schools may have experienced the fruits of the "music education as aesthetic education" philosophy that espouses focusing perception on the properties of the music, with the expectation that students thus will become more aware of and more apt to experience its expressive qualities. Pieces may be used that offer good examples of formal properties relating to repetition/contrast, excitement/relaxation, various types of thematic development incorporating tension and release, and so on. Students employ the aesthetic attitude when they follow the formal and/or expressive flow of a piece to gain the satisfaction that comes with recognition and the "feelingful" experiences and insights it may yield.

The Function of Entertainment

By comparison to the function of aesthetic enjoyment, the function of entertainment seems much easier to document and to accept as clearly universal. Musical behaviors are fun; they bring pleasure. People enjoy making music, listening to others make it, or doing things, such as dancing, to music. The function of entertainment most often coexists with other functions and it is clearly one that pervades many musical behaviors. For example, the most common form of entertainment among the Kassena-Nankani of northern Ghana is the *jongo*, a dance suite that is also performed on many social occasions (Robertson 1985). *Jongo* is frequently performed with a set of four cylindrical drums (*gulu*), an hourglass drum (*gunguna*), and a set of seven flutes (*wia*). *Jongo* is danced only by adults, but it is widely imitated by children. Before the children are allowed to play instruments, they practice imitating the sounds using various body parts. A common sight is the drumming of a rhythm pattern on another's buttocks, which often elicits peals of laughter. Adults take great delight in ending a dance performance with a gesture that challenges another to outdo their performance.

For young people in the United States, listening to pop CDs and attending rock concerts are common uses of music that relate to the function of entertainment. Such uses tend to be more passively oriented than the more concentrated perceptual focus on the music associated with the aesthetic function. However, here may be a good example of overlapping functions because a person may listen to the same piece of music with varying degrees and types of attention and purpose. And in the more active sense of performance, people frequently hum, sing, or play an instrument to amuse themselves and to pass time for themselves and others.

The Function of Communication

Music communicates. What, how, and to whom it communicates are culturally determined issues. Within each musical language, a variety of communications is possible. Persons who are conversant with not only the musical language, but with the cultural language as well, are better able to share in the communication processes of that culture. Persons who are not fully a part of the cultural exerience may extract some of the "messages" being communicated but are likely to be more or less limited in their ability to receive the full communication. Music may suffer, by comparison to verbal language, from the lack of specific external referents, but it has a precisely corresponding advantage of ambiguity (i.e., each person is free to derive personal meanings from a musical experience).

A religious brotherhood in Morocco known as *Gnawa* uses music in very specific forms of communication (Schuyler 1981). For example, in the game *txabia* (a form of hide-and-seek), the *m'allem* (master) plays musical clues on the *ginbri*, a three-stringed lute. These musical clues tell the seeker where to find a hidden object or how to perform a secret task, such as carrying out all the necessary preparations for a tea ceremony. Although it looks completely mystifying to an outsider, the process relies on using two basic melodies in a fashion similar to the Western game of "hot and cold." One melody translates as "it's not there" and the other as "there it is"; however, the words are not sung during the game. The musical code is further complicated by any number of possible variations that give specific refinements to the message.

Young Americans in the armed services are particularly familiar with the musical communications called "reveille" and "taps." The former communicates energy and the urgency to "get up!" The latter communicates with a languid theme that it is time to rest—for the night or permanently. The use of music to communicate (and to make permanent in the memory) commercial messages has become particularly widespread and sophisticated, to the degree that, whether it is Pepsi or a foreign automobile, the musical style is tailored to the presumed musical taste of the targeted socioeconomic subculture. Of course, communication is rarely a discrete function and frequently deals with the communication of such other functions as emotional expression.

The Function of Symbolic Representation

All societies use music as a means of symbolizing many aspects of their culture. On one level, song texts may be used symbolically, in the way that pre–Civil War slaves expressed their longings for freedom in symbolically laced spirituals. On different levels, music may symbolize other cultural values and behaviors.

Initiation rites of boys of the Barasana (Columbia) require a great deal of musical accompaniment (Sullivan 1984). Life-giving breath of ancient ancestors is symbolized by the air blown from the long flutes that are played during the ceremony. The air blown over the initiates turns them into strong adults. Moreover, the length and shape of the instruments represent the body of a mythical ancestor, Manioc-stick Anaconda, whose dismembered limbs are said to have formed the original Barasana people.

Young people in the United States use music to symbolize their social values through their preferences and allegiances to popular styles ranging from heavy metal, through rap, medim rock, hybrids such as jazz rock and country rock, to homespun family values–type country. Music is also associated with and used to symbolize nations, states, schools, and a great variety of industries and commercial products. Also, in the United States as in most of the world, musical instruments and their sounds are associated with and symbolize masculine and feminine qualities. For all the concerns about, and attempts to neutralize, gender stereotyping in the United States, it is still as dangerous for a boy to play a flute in band as it is for a woman in remote New Guinea to look at or touch one.

The Function of Physical Response
Dance has already been listed as a human invariant. The very nature of music's rhythmic structure elicits a ready physical response from all groups. Physical activities other than dance are often accompanied by music, such as walking or marching, working, games or sports, and children's play.

Among the Hawaiians, music and dance are inseparable (Keali'-inohomoku 1985). Formal dance, the hula, requires training at the hands of a master. Candidates are selected on the basis of talent and dedication, but are not discriminated against by virtue of gender or age. In opposition to Western custom, Hawaiian dance accompanies the music in a way that will express the all-important text. Texts are expressed through "enhanced speech" or recitative by a chanter. Chanters undergo rigorous training and can achieve an exalted position within the society. The poetry that serves as the basis for the chant covers a wide variety of subject matters, including recollections of past heroes and events, sacred prayers and incantations, and personal expressions of love, humor, or grief.

In the United States, the stimulating sounds of rock or the polka also elicit physical responses in more or less formal ways. The bugle calls mentioned with regard to communication have musical qualities that prompt movement or relaxation. Meredith Wilson's *Music Man* gives us a wonderful example of the role of tempo in sedative and stimulative music when he uses virtually the same melodies and harmonies but slows the tempo markedly to transform the energetic "Seventy-six Trombones" to the lullabyelike "Goodnight My Someone." Music therapists are particularly versed in the uses of music to help stimulate clients to exercise and socialize, or to help sedate them. And, of course, could we have the sustained activity of exercise like aerobics without music?

The Function of Enforcing Conformity to Social Norms
Children in every society need to learn the appropriate (that is, socially approved) behaviors. Music is one of the most common and most effective

means of helping to shape these behaviors. Through the use of music, young children learn right and wrong behaviors, through music they are initiated into adulthood, and even adults express disapproval of inappropriate behaviors through protest songs.

Among the Venda of South Africa there is an initiation school (*domba*) that prepares young women for marriage, childbirth, and motherhood (Blacking 1973). Through the music and dance of the *domba,* the girls learn much of what they need to know to carry out these adult roles. In a series of songs and stylized dance steps, such as the *khulo* where the girls sing in imitation of a pattern played on the reed pipes (*mutavha*) by the men, they enact various stages of the reproductive cycle.

Aspects of the reproductive cycle are also popular subjects of certain types of U.S. commercial music. Such songs may make sexual activity outside of marriage, for example, appear to be a highly desirable and legitimate social norm, or an illicit activity detrimental to the individual and society at large. Heavy metal rock music promoting drug use as the norm has been met with the DARE song and other antidrug music. Younger children feel the stings of their peers' "Nya-Nya" chants when they don't conform, and Billy hears "Billy's Got a Girlfriend" chants when he mingles with the opposite sex too soon. Children are also subject to the social conformity musics of institutions such as "Sesame Street" and "Mister Rogers." And, of course, young people as well as adults hear about the norms of friendship, true love, and patriotism through music. Interestingly, probably one of the greatest social conformance pressures is to like and listen to the music of one's group.

The Function of Validation of Social Institutions
and Religious Rituals
Public ceremonies, military campaigns, such significant family events as birthdays, initiation ceremonies and rites of passage, marriages, and funerals are all validated through music. A great deal of the social fabric of many societies receives strength and support through music. Indeed, many social institutions would be woefully incomplete, and thus invalidated, if the music were missing. This is also true for religious rituals and observances.

Music in Buddhist temple ceremonies invites the congregation to enter a state of peaceful contemplation (Khe 1984). In the Vietnamese tradition, music accompanies many parts of the service, including the chanting of verbal formulas (*mantras*), chanting prayers or teachings of Buddha (*xuong*), chanting highly elaborate melismas (*tan*) accompanied by a small gong (*tang*) and a wooden drum (*mo gia tri*), and chanting for the purification of the souls of the dead (*khai xa hac*). Other instruments may be used during funeral ceremonies; these may be played by lay musicians and may include the oboe (*ken*), flute (*sao*), and lute (*dannguyet* or *dan nhi*).

In the United States, the birthdays of children of all ages are not properly validated without the singing of "Happy Birthday." Likewise, the president's inauguration is not properly done without the playing of "Hail to the Chief" and "Ruffles and Flourishes," which serve to validate his role as Commander in Chief of all the nation's armed services. Songs like the "Star-Spangled Banner," "America," and "America the Beautiful" all serve to validate our nation's ideals, with state and school songs serving a similar purpose. Actually, the "Star-Spangled Banner" may be the greatest validator of all, because most athletic rituals could not begin without it! America's rites of passage are marked with a fairly specific body of wedding and funeral music. And, religious rituals in different denominations often employ different bodies of music that serve to validate their own denomination. It is notable that "Protestant" hymns, including Luther's own, have become valid for use in Catholic churches in conjunction with Christianity's recent quest for ecumenicism.

The Function of the Contribution to the Continuity and Stability of Culture

Music is a major vehicle for education and for maintaining a social history. This is true for all societies, but most especially for those that rely on an oral tradition. Learning songs and dances of the group is a major way of enabling youngsters to learn who they are and where they have come from. Myths, legends, folktales, records of important battles and conquests, are all passed from one generation to the next via song and dance.

With painstaking care over the past thirty years, Chinese musicologists have collected more than 180,000 folksongs and estimate that there may be as many as 120,000 more still to be gathered (Ling 1984). These songs represent a people scattered over 30 provinces, encompassing remote mountain ranges and offshore islands. An important facet of these songs is that many of them provide direct links to the ancient Chinese cultures of 2,000 years ago or more. Many of these are field songs, sung by peasants at work in the rice paddies. A recently unearthed pottery sculpture, dated from the first or second century A.D., depicts farmers in a rice field, one of whom plays a drum. During times of political disruption, such as the Cultural Revolution of 1966–76, these songs provided an important means of preserving ancient traditions and values. In fact, the continuity and stability of Chinese culture over several thousand years is due, in no insignificant way, to these songs.

Likewise, young Americans learn the folk songs of their heritage. Songs such as "Sweet Betsy from Pike" tell of the frontier spirit of our nation, and newer musics relate the same tradition with regard to newer frontiers of outer space, human equality, environmentalism, and social justice. Of course, the musics used in the function of validation generally apply and often are used for the purpose of enhancing the continuity and stability of culture as well. It is important to note also that, in a multicultural society such as the United States's, not only is the macroculture sustained through music, but subcultures also have their sustaining traditions, such as the mariachi sounds of Mexican-Americans and the spirituals of African-Americans.

The Function of Contribution to the Integration of Society
Although music can be experienced individually, it is first and foremost a group activity. Drawing a picture or reciting a poem are solo activities. Singing and dancing invite group participation. Individuals are integrated into the group as they join in the corporate activities of music making. Music provides a rallying point that focuses on social unity. For an outsider to become accepted as a full member of the group, it will be necessary for him or her to partake of the social acts of singing and dancing. An ethnomusicologist describes the experiences of her daughter in northern Ghana and in Washington, DC: "In both of these settings, Vanessa's inclusion into a new peer group was partly dependent on her mastery of certain song and dance formulae that identified her as an insider, even though she was a newcomer to these cultural traditions" (Robertson 1985, 95).

As a result of the Diaspora, the Jewish world has historically been divided into Ashkenazic (Occidental) and Sephardic (Oriental) communities (Bahat 1980). Jews exiled into primarily northern European locations are identified as Ashkenazim (after the Old Hebrew name for Germany). Jews who were displaced into Persia, India, Spain, and the Mediterranean Basin are known as Sephardim (Old Hebrew for Spain). During their centuries of exile, the Jews faced the problem of retaining their cultural identity while living in foreign lands. This has resulted in a pluralism of Jewish musical styles. Within the more European-influenced Ashkenazic styles there is considerable diversity, as between Russian and German Jews, for example. Likewise, there is the variety of North African and Bablyonian Jewish music within Sephardic styles.

The inclusive and exclusive aspects of the power of music to integrate members of a society may be seen in this situation. On the one hand, the common thread of Jewish music enabled a scattered people to maintain their cultural identity over vast distances of time and space.

On the other hand, modern Israel is having a difficult time integrating all the subcultures into one ethnic whole. "If we start with the assumption that the aim in Israel is to achieve a unified national culture, the questions that inevitably arise are how far should one attempt to blend the unique and deeply rooted musical heritages of the many and varied ethnic communities, and what are the means whereby this is to be achieved?" (Hofman 1982, 148).

As noted earlier, one of the most important things a young person in the United States needs to do to be integrated into "the group" is to like and use the same music as the others in the group. Having the ability to perform in the school band not only makes one an integral part of that group, but of the entire school that the band represents and whose activities it supports. Similarly, singing in one's church choir makes a person a more integral part of the entire congregation. The uses of patriotic, state, and school songs for the integration of society again points up some overlap, particularly among the last several functions. And again, the national anthem is a particularly potent force for integration as all rise for it, and many join in its singing. "We Shall Overcome" and "Bridge Over Troubled Waters" were used to spur on integration of isolated segments of Americans; and this very day at the Rotary Club noon meeting, rival merchants are integrating via a couple of songs prior to lunch for the larger good of their community welfare projects.

Even if these are not the exact ten functions of music that are universal to all human societies, they are certainly representative of most of the world's music. The biological and psychological unity of humankind assures that music will be a human invariant, and its functions also approach invariant status. Yet, the built-in power of individuality assures that the music of one group may be markedly different from the music of another group as specific uses and sounds of music vary around the world.

A quote from Merriam serves to conclude this section. "Music is clearly indispensable to the proper promulgation of the activities that constitute a society; it is a universal [invariant] human behavior—without it, it is questionable that man could truly be called man, with all that implies" (Merriam 1964, 227).

Summary

Anthropological perspectives on musical behaviors indicate that the relationship between music and human societies is a symbiotic one. Blacking describes this eloquently in a pair of opposing chapters: "Humanly Organized Sound" and "Soundly Organized Humanity"

(Blacking 1973). In his first chapter, Blacking states that music is a product of human behavior due to biological processes and cultural agreement. Aural perceptions and the brain's ability to create and perceive patterns of sounds combine with cultural agreement to give us music. Music, then, is "sound that is organized into socially accepted patterns" (1973, 25). Above all, music exists because human beings have imposed a sonic order rather than passively accepting the sounds that nature provides.

Having stressed that music is humanly organized sound, Blacking then writes about "Soundly Organized Humanity." We have already seen how music affects physiological processes. Blacking acknowledges these bodily changes but concentrates more on the effects of music on social behaviors. Basing his comments on a thorough study and analysis of music from many different cultures, he asserts that one of the main functions of music is to help organize human social behaviors. In particular, music helps in the age-old problem of learning how to be human. Music does not change societies in the same way as developments in technology or changes in political organizations, but it serves an equally important role as it reinforces, enhances, and clarifies common human experiences and feelings.

The anthropological significance of music can be presented rather simply. All people in all times and in all places have engaged in musical behaviors. The documentation for this statement began with an examination of prehistoric art. Through inferences from the visual arts, depictions of musicians and dancers, and through actual musical instruments, we know that music was part of our behavioral repertoire from the earliest times. This evidence is corroborated and extended throughout the study of the history of technology and earliest examples of writing.

The study of cultures worldwide provides scientific evidence that musical behaviors are a human invariant. The intent to be musical is one of certainty. Though the particular musical styles found around the world vary widely, the functions of music are rather uniform. The overriding role of music is a symbiotic one, with cultural patterns shaping music and music influencing social behaviors.

Reck attempted a massive undertaking when he wrote about *Music of the Whole Earth*. One of his opening remarks eloquently expresses the anthropological signficance of music.

> The earth is also full of a variety of musics, musics that can be as different as men are from men, or societies from societies, or the frozen ice lands of the north from the steaming tropical jungles, yet that are somehow tied together by that wonderful common

denominator, the human being. Men and women everywhere have eyes, noses, ears, voices, and hands, inventive and inquisitive brains, and (perhaps most important) a capacity for feeling. For art, and music is an art, concerns a depth of expression which somehow reaches beneath the surface of our being and touches on mysteries essential to the core of what we are; and all the scientific inquiry and philosophizing of recent and distant centuries (even the superrationalism of our computers) has not been able to put "that," the feeling, its mysteries and importance, into words or equations. (Reck 1977, 1)

Sociological Perspectives

Human beings are social creatures. We gather together in informal and formal groups, ranging from two friends spending time together to global institutions such as the United Nations. While we can exist alone, and sometimes have a need for solitude, interaction with other human beings is clearly our course. Those rare individuals who prefer to live apart from human society are usually considered exceptions to the nearly universal rule. Likewise, musical behaviors are primarily group behaviors. Musicians may spend many hours in isolation composing or practicing, but almost always these are means toward an end of sharing with a group. The purpose of this section, then, is to examine the role music plays in social behaviors. Particular attention will be paid to music in contemporary U.S. society—as was the case with the last paragraph of each "functions" discussion in the preceeding section. In fact, "anthropological perspectives" and "sociological perspectives" are far from discrete topics, and the former has already said much about the latter and present topic. Thus, the emphasis here on contemporary American society.

The sociology of music is represented by such books as the following: *Images of American Society in Pop Music* (Cooper 1982), *Introduction to the Sociology of Music* (Adorno 1976), *Music and Its Social Meanings* (Ballantine 1984), *Music—Society—Education* (Small 1977), *One for the Money: Politics and Popular Song* (Harker 1980), *Sing a Song of Social Significance* (Denisoff 1983), and *The Sociology of Music* (Dasilva, Blasi, and Dees 1984). In addition to more than 300 journals specifically related to music, articles and research on the sociology of music can be found in many current periodicals such as *Time, Newsweek,* or the daily newspaper. Because music is so prevalent in our society and because it is always changing, there is always fresh material to report on the sociological significance of music.

Music in U.S. Society

Music is such a pervasive form of human experience that anyone in our society can have some sort of meaningful experience with music. One way of expressing how music touches us all is by means of three continua.

Birth<————————————————>Death
Least<————————————————>Highest Cognitive Functioning
One<————————————————->Thousands

Age is not a criterion for a meaningful musical experience. Newborns respond actively to sounds, especially to lullabies and the musical aspects of speech (e.g., pitch, timbre, rhythm, and loudness). At the other end of the continuum, elderly people find music to be one of the pleasures of life still available to them. No one is excluded from a musical experience by virtue of age. Some might even extend this continuum to prebirth (some research indicates that during the last trimester in the womb the fetus responds to sounds and music) and postdeath (one of the common aspects of reports of near-death syndrome is the presence of music).

Likewise, the presence or absence of cognitive abilities does not preclude a meaningful musical experience. Though lack of cognitive functioning may somewhat limit certain kinds of musical involvement, even severely and profoundly retarded persons can benefit significantly from musical experiences. At the upper end of the scale we have only to look at the musical activities of such mental giants as Thomas Jefferson and Albert Einstein, both of whom were avid violinists, to be reminded that highly intelligent people find pleasure in music.

Musical pleasure is not bounded by how many people are involved. Each one of us, by ourselves, can find pleasure in such solitary musical activities as listening, playing an instrument, or singing. At the other end, there are no clear limits on how many people can participate at one time. Outdoor concerts reguarly draw crowds well into the thousands; over 300,000 people were in attendance at the Woodstock Festival concerts in 1969, and over 400,000 heard the Boston Pops Orchestra on 4 July 1977 (Dearding and Dearding 1981). Also, 400,000 school children participated in the World's Largest Concert sponsored by the Music Educators National Conference (Soundposts 1986). At this televised concert, school music groups all over the country performed the same half-hour program simultaneously.

To these three may be added such other criteria as gender, race, ethnic background, and socioeconomic status, none of which can prohibit a person from having a meaningful musical experience. Music may not be the only human behavior that can fit all of these criteria, but it is surely one of the most common of human experiences. In fact, there is so much music in U.S. society that to detail its every usage would be nearly impossible. What follows is an attempt to give some general sense of how often and in what ways music appears in our midst. Almost every item on this list will be familiar, but many of them have come to be such common parts of the scene that we hardly take notice of them.

1. Music at Home. In many homes it is possible to hear music from the first moment of the day until the last. Radio music alarms wake us up and help us go to sleep; televisions, radios, stereos, and children practicing help keep the sounds going all day. More than 62 million people in our country say they sing or play a musical instrument (Derloshon 1994) and 97 percent feel that children benefit from arts education by becoming more creative and imaginative (Washington International Arts Letter 1992). With the presence of radios, televisions, and/or stereos in nearly every home, almost any kind of music from "hard" rock to grand opera is available to every citizen of our country. According to Steinel 1984, 98.5 percent of the teenagers surveyed said they listened to music. Music is even finding new ways to enter our lives; music software is among the most popular programs being sold for home computers.

2. Music at School. Music is generally a part of the educational scheme from preschools to universities. Nearly every elementary school in our country offers some type of music instruction. For secondary schools, the second-highest school related activity is music, with 20.7 percent of the students involved in band or orchestra and 17.6 percent in choral groups; over 6.5 million high school students are active participants in some form of musical activity (Steinel 1984). The nation's colleges spend some $500 million per year on campus concerts and entertainment (Baskerville 1979). Also notable is the fact that for the first time (fiscal 1995), the federal government has a dedicated allotment for music and art in the schools. It is only $75 million, or about 5/1000th of one percent of the budget, but it is a first (McCullough 1995).

3. Music in the Community. Every community has musical performing groups, ranging from church choirs, school groups, community bands, to guest artist series. In 1984, people spent more time attending arts events than sports events (MEJ 1985).

In that year alone, 103 million people heard live popular music concerts and another 58 million heard classical concerts.

4. Music in the Marketplace. Music and the business world have an enormous reciprocal impact. The business community has long been a strong supporter of symphony orchestras and ballet companies. In return, cultural opportunities are an increasing factor in enticing new businesses to locate in a community. For many years, some of the larger corporations have sponsored employee-related activities, such as a company choir or a series of lunch-time concerts. Music is also used, of course, in many factories and offices as an effective means of improving production and in many retail stores to affect buying behavior.

Music is a multi–billion dollar per year business. In fact, some have placed music among the top economic generators (Jones 1986; Koepp 1985). The arts generate $314 billion dollars annually (Music Educators National Conference 1995); this is nearly equal to the construction industry and represents about 6 percent of the gross national product. Other dollar figures, such as $10.04 billion in U.S. recording sales in 1993 (Scherer 1995) and $4.5 billion in retail value of 1993 music industry shipments (Derloshon 1994), should be enough to document that the music industry is not an insignificant part of the nation's economy.

5. Music in Religion. Although there may be a few religious sects that restrict the use of music, it is far more common for music to be an integral part of the worship experience. Music is often a common thread that runs throughout and connects the various parts of a service.

6. Music for Special Occasions. A marching band struts down the street, a group of Christmas carolers makes its way merrily from door to door, a dance band strikes up a lively tune at a party— these are just three examples of the ways music is used in celebrations. As a nation, Americans are hard working, but we also like to party. The calendar is punctuated with such wild, extravagant celebrations as Mardi Gras or New Year's Eve and with quieter times, such as campfire cookouts and wedding anniversaries. The removal of all music from festivities such as these would vastly change their nature.

7. Music in Politics. In the political arena, music has the power to help rally a crowd behind a candidate at a nominating convention or to help dramatize the visit of an important foreign dignitary. In a sense broader than party politics, the national anthem

and other patriotic songs help us to symbolize and express what it means to be an American.

8. Music in the Military. Music has always been an important part of a war experience. Young men have marched off to battle to the sounds of drums and bugles. Music has helped those who stay at home to symbolize their support for or opposition to a war effort and, more important, their hope that once again "Johnny will come marching home." Even during peacetime, soldiers are paced through the day with bugle calls, they "count cadence" (or chant "jodies") as they march along, and military ceremonies of all kinds are accompanied by music. Music is important enough to the military that each branch of the military supports a wide variety of performing organizations, and there are several schools of music for the training of military musicians.

9. Music in Health Care Systems. Music therapists use music as a therapeutic agent for a wide variety of handicapping conditions and health-related concerns. Goals may vary from the alleviation of physical pain to the enhancement of self-esteem. The International Society for Music in Medicine has been founded to provide support for physicians, nurses, and other health-care professionals who use music in clinical settings. Performing arts clinics provide medical treatment for musicians and other artists who sustain career-related injuries or health problems.

10. Music and Physical Activities. Music has always had a close association with physical activities. The difference in active crowd participation between those sporting events with a musical support group—football and basketball—and those without—tennis and swimming—is readily apparent. Exercising to music—jogging with radio headsets, aerobic dancing, or jazzercise—has become very popular in recent years. One company even markets a "no hands" harmonica that can be played while hiking or jogging.

11. Music in the Commercial Media. Music can clearly influence a viewer's assessment of a television commercial message. In one experiment, the emotional impact of a television commercial was increased when appropriate background music was added and decreased when music of an opposite character was used (Wintle 1983). Radio and television as we know them now would be unthinkable without music. There were 9,317 radio stations and 1,194 television stations with broadcasting licenses in 1985 (Shemel and Krasilovsky 1985). Ninety-eight percent of U.S. households have at least one television set (85 million house-

holds), and 99 percent own a radio. The average American is exposed to over 1,600 commercial messages in each 24-hour period by one medium or another (Parker 1984). The vast majority of those commercials on radio and television are accompanied by music.

Music serves many purposes in film productions. From the earliest days of film, music has been used to mask or neutralize unwanted sounds emanating from the viewing environment or the viewers themselves. Further, it "masks" uncomfortable silence that causes tension or otherwise disturbs audiences. Film is a very disjunct medium with "shots" often changing every few seconds; music provides continuity. It also provides dramatic support to reinforce the film's emotional and dramatic dimensions: recurring themes that refer to specific characters, places, or times; underscoring dominant moods of love, conflict, and so on; reflecting action or "Mickey-Mousing"; undergirding the dramatic buildup or resolution of a scene; providing naturalistic sounds, imitating or suggesting real sounds; and providing counterpoint or ironic juxtaposition to the action. The economic aspects of film music is another dimension involving theme songs to promote a film before it is even released, with sound track tapes and CDs, as well as sheet music after. Interlocking promotions for food, clothing, toys, and other mementos also involve music.

12. Music in Professional and Social Organizations. There are more than 300 musical organizations that provide people with nearly any musical interest the opportunity to meet with like-minded people (Marquis 1983). These groups vary from the Accordion Federation of America to the Piano Technicians Guild.

13. Musical Occupations. More than 57 musical occupations have been identified, ranging from church choir director to military band member and night club entertainer (MEJ 1982). Almost 1 percent of the workforce are employed in arts-related occupations (Teaching Music Today 1995).

14. Music in Places to Go. Nearly every place we go has music as part of the environment, including such places as grocery stores, restaurants, and doctor's offices.

15. Miscellaneous. Throughout our society there are numerous ways we encounter music. Some of the unexpected places we encounter music come from being placed on hold on the telephone, from crib mobiles, from ice cream trucks, and from musical greeting cards.

The preceding list is not exhaustive, but it certainly should suffice to indicate the omnipresence of music in our society. An interesting experiment to conduct would be to try to go through a 24-hour period without hearing any music, noting the disruptions from the normal routine. The radio alarm could not be used to get up by; in fact, no radio or television could be turned on all day. The places one went and the activites one engaged in would all have to be monitored very carefully. Such an experiment should prove to any disbeliever the ubiquity of music in our midst.

Reflections of Society in Music

While artists sometimes function as visionaries, trying to lead a society toward a loftier goal (e.g., Beethoven's vision of all humanity living in peace and harmony as expressed in the Ninth Symphony), they also serve by holding up a mirror to society, reflecting how people live, what they think, and how they feel. Musical behaviors are social behaviors, and, as such, they influence and reflect the mores of the surrounding social structure. Thus, music is at times a headlight and at other times a taillight. The musical world is a microcosm of the larger world, operating on similar social principles. By examining the sociality of musical behaviors, a greater understanding of the significance music has for our lives can be obtained.

In every community there are a variety of music performance settings. In a small town, these may be somewhat limited, while in a huge city, such as New York, the number and variety of performance settings would be nearly incalculable. Typical performance settings that may or may not occur in any given community include church choirs, symphony orchestras (amateur and professional), municipal bands, jazz combos, rock groups, school music ensembles, and private piano studios. For each of these performance settings there are, perhaps, two levels of social behaviors occurring simultaneously: the social behaviors of performing musicians and the social behaviors of music listeners. Implied, also, are the social interactions between performers and listeners.

Social Behaviors among Performing Musicians

One level of social behavior occurs among the performers themselves. If the musicians have rehearsed and performed together over some period of time, they will have developed relationships and particular social bonds with one another. A new member of the group will need some time to feel totally comfortable and to be accepted as a part of the group. In larger groups, smaller cliques may form based on a variety of factors, such as age, gender, or membership in a particular section of the musical ensemble (e.g., altos in a choir or trombones in a band).

Often these social bonds are so strong that members of a musical group are like members of an extended family. This may be due, in part, to the amount of time spent together, and may be especially true of those groups that travel frequently or who even live together. A feeling of "family" may also derive from the fact that so much time is spent in working together as a coordinated unit. Furthermore, the "project" they are working on is something that involves an expression of feelings. This expression does not require that all members feel or experience the same emotion simultaneously, but it does require that the musical elements be coordinated in such a way as to convey the desired expression. This, in combination with the tremendous physical and mental energy required for public performance, makes for a powerful social bonding force.

A feeling of family does not mean, of course, that all the social interactions are pleasant. As with any family, there may be rivalries, arguments, or even long-term feuds as well as strong bonds of affection. No matter how much internal strife there may be, however, something larger continues to hold the bonds in place.

School music teachers experience this phenomenon of "family" frequently. In fact, social values are often given as important reasons for including music in the public school curriculum. Teamwork, cooperation, discipline, and a feeling of esprit de corps are all virtues that can result from participation in a musical ensemble. As surrogate parents, music teachers watch their students go through many trials and tribulations. Students tend to congregate and loiter in rehearsal rooms to be near each other and their music teachers. Private teachers also form strong bonds with their students. While the students may rebel against the teachers' (parents') authority from time to time, they often turn to one or the other for guidance and commiseration.

The social network operating within a musical organization may evidence itself in dress, mannerisms, and speech. Often the performance attire serves not only to separate the group from the audience but also to reinforce the social behaviors within the group. Standing, sitting, or moving about the stage are all controlled by the conventions suited to particular circumstances. A symphony orchestra in formal black rises as a unit to acknowledge applause. A robed choir processes to their station in an appropriately decorous manner. A marching band in uniform maneuvers down the street or on the field in an exaggerated form of controlled precision. The jargon used by any group also acts as a means of unification and, at the same time, as a means of separating the group from the audience. The musical language spoken by performers at the Metropolitan Opera and the Grand Old Opry is likely to be different.

These group social behaviors can be applicable to individual performers as well. For example, a budding pianist may learn at the first recital appearance to bow in polite acknowledgment of applause. Even for those who appear as soloists within a larger performing context (e.g., a rock singer), there may be the added element of a stage personality that influences the performing deportment. Behaviors scarcely acceptable in normal social settings may be adopted as attention-getting devices. Sometimes the stage personality is completely different from the private persona; at other times it may take over and dominate a person's behavior both on and off stage.

Generally, musicians are permitted more unusual or deviant behaviors than most other people in a society, probably because such behaviors are thought to go with their creative or artistic personalities. The nature and degree of the permitted deviations vary among different types of musicians. "Classical artists" may be accepted and even expected to be somewhat aloof, have arrested social development, or be mechanical and technological imbeciles. "Rock stars" are allowed and even expected to be libertines, lechers, drunks, and/or drug users. Even high school band directors frequently have license to leave school during the day to have coffee and hang around the music store, while other teachers are expected to remain in school.

Within any group of performers, there is a social hierarchy. This is clearly in place in an opera house, where a prima donna is accorded special privileges, in jazz, where the name of the group is often the name of the main star (e.g., the Count Basie Orchestra), and in commercial music, where acts are often built around an individual performer (e.g., Diana Ross was the focal point of the Supremes). Even different instruments or ensembles have a social hierarchy. The accordion, for example, suffers from a social stigma in some circles, but would reign supreme in others. A string quartet is a recognized ensemble with a great deal of social prestige, while a tuba quartet might not rank as highly.

For members of an ensemble that requires a conductor, there is an extra social dynamic to consider. The conductor must create a unified whole out of many disparate individuals. No ensemble can perform successfully as a pluralistic society; imagine what would happen if each member of a 40-voice choir decided to sing at a different tempo. The manner in which a conductor bends individual wills to his or her own is what creates such an interesting and potentially charged social atmosphere. On the performers' part there may be a love-hate relationship with the conductor.

Even within smaller groups that do not require a conductor, there is a social hierarchy of leader and followers. Sometimes this may be abundantly clear, at other times it may be a shifting leadership role or even a focal point for disagreement. Sometimes the music itself will designate who is to be the leader. Music making involves following a set of social guidelines and structure, just as any human activity does. Cooperation and teamwork are essential ingredients in nearly every music-making situation.

Performers need cooperation and support from their audiences, too. Although composer Milton Babbit took an extreme position when he wrote an article entitled "Who Cares If You Listen?" (1958), the majority of musical experiences are aimed at eliciting some type of response from the listeners.

Social Behaviors among Music Listeners
Just as the musicians in different performance settings exhibit a variety of social behaviors, so do the audiences. Compare the audiences at an opera, a Friday night barn dance, and a heavy metal rock concert. The variations in socioeconomic status, age, dress, speech patterns, and mode of physical movement is likely to be considerable. Even if the same person went to all three types of performances on successive nights, the dress, speech, and mannerisms would vary in order to provide social acceptability.

For more formal performances, there is an extended social ritual that involves placing the event on a calendar long in advance, purchasing tickets, planning a meal before or after the concert, leaving early to obtain a good parking space, being seated by an usher, perusing the program, growing quiet as the house lights dim, and so on. Even during the performance a social etiquette is in place, as patrons of classical concerts learn not to applaud between the movements of a symphony. Teenagers at rock concerts learn that a somewhat different style of behavior is acceptable. In fact, crowd control in the form of monitoring for smoking dope, destruction of property, rape, and muggings, has become a major issue in many cities. Some cities have passed ordinances restricting attendance at rock concerts to a minimum age; other cities have sought ways to ban certain rock groups from performing in civic facilities.

The type of music one listens to can often reveal a considerable amount of information. For example, imagine walking down the corridors of a large apartment building. Pausing briefly outside each door we can hear music coming from inside each apartment. Using only this musical information, what could we know about who was inside? Certainly there would be limitations on what we could know. Yet, if we heard nursery songs outside one door, would we not suspect that a young child lived there? If we heard mariachi music coming from another apartment, might we not guess the presence of a Hispanic family? As with the larger network of human families where races, nationalities, and tribes are identifiable through their music, so it is within a given society, especially a pluralistic one such as ours. There are a number of ways different subgroups might be identifiable through their music, such as age, gender, race, and socioeconomic status (see chap. 8).

As much as music listening habits might be a means of identifying and thus potentially separating one group from another, music also has a powerful capacity to bring people together. Through their common participation in or enjoyment of a shared musical experience, people of various and disparate backgrounds are brought together. Barriers of age, gender, economic status, race, and nationality can all be transcended through music. The power of music to unify millions of people all around the globe at one time was demonstrated in the opening ceremonies of the 1984 Olympics. More than 2.2 billion people worldwide watched the three hour and twenty minute spectacular on television, along with the 80,000 people in the stadium. The program was nearly nonstop music, as indicated by this schedule of activities (San Antonio Light 1984).

Opening Ceremonies 1984 Olympics

6:30 P.M. Musical overture, ringing of church bells and a fanfare of 120 trumpets and 20 timpani; entrance of the colors

6:45 P.M. Introduction of All-American Olympic Marching Band

6:50 P.M. "Music of America"—American Suite, Pioneer Spirit, Dixieland Jubilee, Urban Rhapsody, The World is a Stage, Big Band Bash, and Dance Medley

7:35 P.M. Stadium card stunt; Antwerp flag ceremony; John Williams' *Olympic Theme*

7:50 P.M. Parade of the athletes

9:10 P.M. Speeches

9:25 P.M. Olympic Hymn, the lighting of the flame, parade of flags, taking of oaths

9:40 P.M. *Ode to Joy* and "Reach Out"

9:50 P.M. Exit of athletes and musicians

While different age groups might generally prefer "their own" type of music, that barrier can be easily crossed, as was demonstrated in a project involving the combining of an elementary school choir with residents of a nursing home (Smiley 1986). Both the young and the old remarked positively about the experience. Socioeconomic, political, and perhaps even philosophical barriers were crossed in the Farm-Aid and Aid-to-Africa concerts (San Antonio Light 1985). The United States is a pluralistic society, yet members of all the various subgroups can be unified through the "Star-Spangled Banner." Gaston stated that "the potency of music is greatest in the group" (1968, 27). By that he was referring to the socialness of the musical experience. "Music provides a gestalt of sensory, motor, emotional, and social components in which, for the most part, the participants concur. It unifies the group for common action, and it is this setting that elicits or changes many extramusial behaviors" (Gaston 1968, 27).

The Influence of Music on Social Behaviors

"Argument over loud music leads to death" screams a newspaper headline (San Antonio Light 1986). The article, which details how one man was shot and killed as a result of another man being kept awake by his loud music, provides an extreme illustration of how music can influence social or, in this case, antisocial behaviors. In another, less violent example, imagine several married couples at a dance. During one dance the couples all exchange partners. This is perfectly acceptable behavior, as long as the music is playing. If, however, the new partners stay intertwined in each other's arms after the music stops, this is not acceptable behavior at most social gatherings. These are but two examples of the many ways that music influences social behaviors. The purpose of this section is to examine some of the ways music shapes social behaviors in American society.

Music as a Socializing Agent
Human behavior is not instinctive and thus we must learn how to behave as human beings. We learn these behaviors through a process of socialization, and it is important to note that the behaviors we learn are those that are appropriate to the society in which we are raised. The agents of socialization are many, but, in the United States, they would include at the very least home, school, church or synagogue, peers, and the media (radio, television, and the movies).

A comprehensive review of the socialization process might appear to give music only a small role to play. Without exaggerating its contributions, however, there are some aspects about the role of music (and its constituent elements, such as rhythm, pitch patterns, and timbre) that bear detailed examination.

The process begins at birth with the onset of rhythmic breathing and continues as the baby gradually adapts himself or herself to the rhythmic cycles of the world into which he or she has been born. Over the next months, the patterns of family life, particularly the parent's cycle of activity and rest, will condition and shape the baby's social rhythms. This is highly important, since nearly all social interactions are rhythmically based.

Further musical influences occur during infancy with the singing of lullabies, the playing of "musical" games (e.g., pat-a-cake and peek-a-boo), and the presence of crib mobiles and musical toys (e.g., Jack-in-the-box). Many of these musical activities enable parents and babies to establish critical bonds of communication. Moreover, first lessons are being learned in the most important subject of all—how to love and to be loved. A good example of this is the "I'm gonna gitcha" game (Stern 1982). The parent chants: "I'm gonna gitcha . . . I'm gonna gitcha . . . I'm gonna gitcha . . . Gotcha!" At each repetition, the pitch and volume increase, while the amount of time between each repetition is progressively prolonged. Activities such as this are so important that they form the basis for acquiring cognitive expectancies and for interrelating cognition and affect (Beebe et al. 1982).

Speech is an extremely important social tool and, once again, musical elements (especially rhythm) play a crucial role in language acquisition (Stern 1982). Newborns move their limbs in rhythm to the speech they hear around them (Bohannan 1983; Restak 1983). If they hear a different language, their rhythms will change subtly. Just as social messages have been received by the infant via the musical elements of speech, so he or she must learn to control pitch, timbre, loudness, and rhythm in his or her own speech in order to convey desired and appropriate messages.

Music continues to play an important role throughout childhood. There are singing games to be played over and over, the alphabet is frequently learned via song, and nursery rhymes are chanted in a sing-song fashion. Children's television programming is full of music, and the musical background to cartoons often eliminates the need for dialogue. Children at play are characterized by their singing and chanting. Early religious instruction is often highly musical. Certainly, children learn a great deal about how to act in socially appropriate ways through musical means.

Several research studies have tested the effects of music on the socialization of elementary school children. In general, the results indicate that "regular, frequent classroom music instruction appears to have a significant positive effect on self-reliance and total social adjustment of elementary school children" (Hanshumaker 1980, 23). This effect is even more pronounced for mentally retarded youngsters who exhibit antisocial behaviors.

Music may actually increase in importance in the teen-age years. During a time when establishing self- and group identity are so critical, music seems to have the power to help teenagers deal with both. A shy, awkward, lonely youngster can find solace in music. Seeking to create their own group awareness, teenagers sometimes use music as a tool to drive a wedge between themselves and their parents. And what an effective tool it is, too, for nothing more clearly characterizes teenage rebellion than new styles of music. In one study, teenagers ranked stereos as their most important possessions and explained the extraordinary importance music has in their lives with such comments as "Because when I'm not real happy and gay, I turn it on and it makes me happy again"; "[Not to have music] would mean that all my good days would turn into bad days . . . 'cause it helps me recover good, recover from the bad days" (Csikszentmihalyi and Rochberg-Halton 1981, 80).

The connection of music with teenager's moods was clearly documented in case studies of two teenagers (the complete study involved 75 teenagers; see Fischman 1987). Kathy was a directed student, while Greg was a disaffected, rebellious student. They each wore an electronic pager for three days. Each time they were beeped they recorded what they were doing and how they felt. It is interesting to note that Greg was listening to music at times when he was experiencing extremely negative feelings, while Kathy was playing her violin at times when she indicated her most positive feelings.

Music is part of the socializing force that influences how teenagers talk, dress, and act; how they feel; and what they think. It even influences how they spend money. Music was a primary agent in the creation of a new economic and social demographic group in the mid-1950s. Music worked in tandem with movies, which incorporated the new musical style. Previously, the under-24 demographic group was almost entirely subordinate to the socioeconomic power of adults. Since 1955, the under-24 demographic group has come to be an increasingly powerful force in the marketplace. In the 1960s, this group further divided into two distinct groups: teenagers and the 18–24-year-old market. In the 1980s another group was created, with preteens forming another powerful buying public.

Music continues to be important to college-age students. A number of them participated in a survey in which they identified the most common stimulus that gave them a "thrill" (Goldstein 1980). Music was in first place, with 96 percent of the subjects indicating it was their most common thrill-causing experience. Music also plays an important role in the courtship of young adults; it is a part of their environment whether they are in the car, at the movies, dancing, or spending a quiet evening together. As noted earlier, many couples have identified a song as "our song" that represents an important moment in their courtship and often symbolizes their love in first bloom for the remainder of their lives. Music may be an important part of the ambiance at the time of a marriage proposal. Certainly music is an important part of most wedding ceremonies.

Because the socialization process is more nearly complete during adulthood, music may not function in quite the same way for adults. However, the social aspects are still important in that musical tastes can be a part of one's social identity. Whether singing hymns at an "old-time" revival or being "seen" at the opera, adult social lives are often marked by particular musical experiences. Moreover, each kind of musical experience is accompanied by the appropriate dress, appropriate behaviors, and appropriate expectations. Even the way one walks and talks may vary with different musical experiences.

In an interesting sidelight to the main discussion of social and musical behaviors, researchers have discovered that "persons involved in social interactions unconsciously move 'in space' with one another through a rhythmic coordination of gestures and movements which exhibit all the characteristics of a dance" (Montagu and Matson 1979, 150). Using sophisticated film equipment that allows projection at very slow or very fast speeds, these researchers have filmed such diverse social interactions as two people in conversation and family gatherings. Often the synchronous movements of the participants are so rhythmic they can be coordinated with music as if they had been choreographed. In fact, another researcher did exactly that (Hall 1976). First, he filmed children on a playground. After extensive study of the four-and-a-half-minute film, he began to see how synchronized the children's movements were. When he later found some music to accompany the film clip, the synchronization between the children's movements and the music was so exact that people could not believe it had not been previously choreographed.

The rhythmic aspects of human behavior are so powerful that entrainment is possible. Entrainment occurs when two or more persons become attuned to the same rhythm. Nonhuman examples of entrainment include a school of fish or a flying V of migrating birds changing directions suddenly (Bohannan 1983). Human entrainment has been demonstrated experimentally when two people in conversation produced brain wave tracings so identical as to appear to have emanated from the same person (Davis 1982; Montagu and Matson 1979). Entrainment may also be operating in riots and other large crowd behaviors. Musical entrainment probably occurs at nearly any concert, but is particularly evident in overt audience behaviors, such as at rock concerts and dances.

The richness of this literature can be illustrated by a brief consideration of two books—*Rhythmic Aspects of Behavior* (Brown and Graeber

1982) and *Interaction Rhythms: Periodicity in Communication Behavior* (Davis 1982). Both books deal with rhythm, albeit from different perspectives. Table 1 provides brief annotations of a few selected chapters from Brown and Graeber 1982.

TABLE 1.   Annotations of Selected Chapters from *Rhythmic Aspects of Behavior* (Brown and Graeber 1982)

Chapter Title	Author	Annotation
Rhythmicity as an Emerging Variable for Psychology	F. Brown	"The image of the totality of life as an orchestral beating, throbbing, surging polyrhythm is scientifically more accurate than that of rhythmicity being a barely perceptible undulation upon the placid sea of life" (4).
Chronobiologic Approach for Optimizing Human Performance	P. Naitoh	Chronobiologists study the ways in which circadian rhythms influence human performance. "Chrono-psychologists then can attempt to match the hours of work demanded by society with the hours of peak performance of its workers. In other words, they may attempt to schedule the temporal dimension of the lifestyle of workers for them to be on the job at their chronobiologically best time" (54).
Behavioral Aspects of Circadian Rhythmicity	R. Weaver	Just as circadian rhythms influence human behavior, they, in turn, are influenced or modified by certain behaviors. "There is not only a dependency of behavior on circadian rhythmicity, or a rhythmic fluctuation in behavior with the period of circadian rhythms, but there is also the opposite relation (i.e., a dependency of circadian rhythmicity on the behavior of the subjects)" (156).

(continued)

TABLE 1—*Continued*

Chapter Title	Author	Annotation
Circadian Rhythms and Human Memory	S. Folklard	Circadian rhythms affect human memory processes. Immediate memory tends to be strongest in the morning and decreases during the day, while delayed retention is better following presentation in the afternoon. "Although no chronobiologist will find this surprising, 'mainstream' experimental psychologists typically are totally ignorant of the fact that their measures may be subject to regular circadian fluctuations" (268).
Ultradian Rhythms in Behavior and Physiology	D. Kripke	Biological rhythms with shorter cycles than circadian rhythms influence bodily processes and human behavior. These might include horomonal secretions, REM (rapid eye movement) sleep, fantasy, hemispheric dominance, and perceptual processing. "The significance of these cycles in both normal and pathologic functioning deserves our attention" (336). "Careful experimental observations are certainly demonstrating that when we are awake, there is multiform cyclic regulation of our bodies, our behavior, and our minds" (337).
Circadian Rhythm Disturbances in Depression and Mania	T. Wehr	"There are many different rhythms in human biology and behavior. The periods of these rhythms range from less than 1 second to more than 1 year. Nearly every aspect of human biology and behavior exhibits a circadian rhythm" (400). Strong evidence is accumulating that disturbances in these rhythms may be related

(continued)

TABLE 1—*Continued*

Chapter Title	Author	Annotation
		to a variety of affective disorders, such as depression and manic-depression.

Interaction Rhythms (see table 2) is based on papers from a conference on interaction rhythms, which are those dynamic rhythm patterns that occur between two or more individuals. These rhythm patterns may vary from microbits, which are studied by means of slow motion film, to macrobits, covering days and weeks of interactions between individuals.

TABLE 2.   Annotations of Selected Chapters from *Interaction Rhythms: Periodicity in Communication Behavior* (Davis 1982)

Chapter Title	Author	Annotation
Preface: Comments on the Significance of Interaction Rhythms	A. Scheflen	"Any dancer or musician could have told us that we must share a common rhythm to sing or play or dance together. . . . But why didn't we realize earlier that interaction rhythms were essential in every human interaction?" (14).
Movement and Sound: The Musical Language of Body Rhythms in Interaction	E. Chapple	"We hear with our bodies, we make music with our bodies, and we use our bodies as instruments through which we intensify the meanings of which it is capable, and by which we set in motion similar patterns in the bodies of others" (37–38).
Cultural Microrhythms	W. Condon	"A person moves in the rhythm and timing of his or her culture, and this rhythm is in the whole body" (66).
Rhythmic Communication in the Mother-Infant Dyad	Beebe et al.	". . . repetition and rhythm are chief means by which the infant acquires cognitive expectancies

(continued)

TABLE 2—*Continued*

Chapter Title	Author	Annotation
		and affective involvement; . . . within the structure that rhythm provides, aspects of both affect and cognition are simultaneously organized" (93–94).
Some Interaction Functions of Rhythm Changes between Mother and Infant	D. Stern	The control of tempo and rhythm, in terms of regularity and irregularity, are important in both cognition and affect. In the "I'm gonna gitcha" game, the mother varies the rhythm of tickling movements to create both a cognitive awareness and emotional response on the part of the infant.
The Cross-Cultural Variation of Rhythmic Style	A. Lomax	"My central thesis is that rhythmicity in communication is largely a function of social and cultural contexts, and that its effects on behavior are best understood if a broad view of these facts is taken into consideration. There are tidal rhythms and biological rhythms; there are subliminal rhythms that knit the species; the animals organize their behavior in loose and engaging rhythmic style. But only human beings have created and adapted a variety of multileveled rhythmic systems in species development. Only human beings control and tune their behaviors in precise multimodal rhythmic coordination. Only human beings can self-consciously design and elaborate new schemes of rhythmic behavior out of the old. All these rhythmic skills have contributed centrally to the development of human culture" (173).

(continued)

TABLE 2—*Continued*

Chapter Title	Author	Annotation
On Operationalizing the Notion of Rhythm in Social Behavior	M. Mathiot and E. Carlock	"We propose, therefore, that the traditional conception of musical rhythm as interface between beat and tempo can be applied to rhythm in social behavior" (176–77).

The Influence of Music in the Workplace

We used to sing while we worked as cowboys, fishermen, railroaders, or field hands. Talking was forbidden to slaves working in the fields, so they sang. The singing not only made the labor seem more endurable, but also became a primary means of communication. Now we do not often sing while we work, but music still influences how we work—even more than it used to.

Perhaps the most specific and controlled use of music to influence human behavior is to be found in Muzak. Actually the name of a company, Muzak has become synonymous with a certain kind of "wallpaper" music, so-called because, like wallpaper, it is not so much to be noticed directly but becomes a part of the environment. This type of music is often found in grocery stores, elevators, banks, hotel lobbies, airports, offices, and factories. To most people, all of this music is pretty much the same; however, there can be significant differences.

On its 60th anniversary in 1994, Muzak claimed to be serving/affecting 80 million people daily. However, the oceans of strings playing wordless Beatles tunes is no longer the prime model. While extremes are still avoided, more contemporary and lively musics can be had on "Hitline," the company's Top 40 channel, or its FM One channel, FM standing for foreground music. Muzak has several commercial competitors in addition to those businesses that simply pipe in radio music.

Little experimental research has been done to determine the effects of this music on specific behaviors. The effects of much of this music in such places as grocery stores or restaurants is generally unknown. Music marketed by Muzak, however, is, according to their publicity, carefully selected, arranged, and packaged in order to achieve specific results. Ascending programs have a series of pieces that gradually increase in tempo, volume, and other stimulative aspects; descending programs do the opposite. Some tapes are programmed to fit ascending-descending curves relating to workers' presumed energy level fluctuations during the day. This format is what Muzak calls its "Stimulus Progression" programming.

Although it must be remembered that they are a business out to promote their own cause, as any good company does, Muzak has made available some of the data from their research. In general, these data indicate that workers perform better with improved attitudes and communication, increased efficiency and concentration, and reduction in errors (Boyd 1985). Muzak can cause shoppers to slow down and buy more or diners to eat faster, the better to increase customer turnover. One experiment, conducted in grocery stores, compared the effects of Muzak with contemporary, upbeat music, FM "easy listening," and no music at all (Dorfman 1984). Muzak caused customers to walk as much as 30 percent slower and to buy as much as 12 percent more than the other conditions. According to one of their own publications, here are some examples of the benefits derived from using Muzak (Muzak 1974 and 1991).

- A 29 percent decrease in nonessential conversation or activities among telephone company employees,
- A 32 percent decrease in lateness and absenteeism among the employees of a giant corporation,
- A 39 percent decrease in errors in the accounts payable section of a business office,
- An 8 percent increase in productivity, even after a bonus system had been installed, in a publishing company,
- A 19 percent increase in key punch productivity at an electric utility company with a corresponding decrease of 32 percent in errors,
- A 53 percent decrease in airline agent turnover,
- an $8.4 million increase over expectations in bank earnings,
- A 25.5 percent better accuracy rate in editing,
- A 25 percent increase in enjoyment of the workplace, and
- A 16 percent increase in problem solving abilities.

If these figures are the result of rigorous, controlled experimentation, as Muzak claims they are, they give a clear indication of the powerful influence music can have on working behaviors.

The Influence of Music on Thought, Attitude, and Social Behavior

Music is an extremely powerful way of expressing the shared beliefs, attitudes, mores, and values of a society or its subgroups. In fact, a particular kind of music or a specific piece of music is normally associated with a group precisely because it communicates something important to that group. Singing "We Shall Overcome" was one of the most effective means of expressing what the civil rights movement was about during the 1960s. People who shared in Martin Luther King's dream were brought together in a powerful, emotional way when they linked arms and sang that song. During this same time, "protest" songs by such folk singers as Bob Dylan and Joan Baez helped many express their feelings of revulsion toward U.S. involvement in the Vietnam War. Music can, of course, cross national borders and reflect a more global sense of the human condition. In 1960, Krystoff Penderecki wrote *Threnody to the Victims of Hiroshima*. Here, a Polish composer expressed feelings about an event involving the people of Japan and the United States. Yet it goes beyond the United States, Japan, and Poland and speaks to all human beings who will listen to the message.

Scholars have long been interested not only in the ways music reflects how people feel but also in the ways it influences what people think and how they behave. The ancient Chinese philosopher Confucius and Greek philosophers such as Damon, Plato, and Aristotle were all proponents of the idea that music could, as Damon put it, "not only arouse or allay different emotions, but also inculcate all the virtues—courage, self-restraint, and even justice" (Strunk 1965, xi). Music was highly prized for its ability to create model citizens for the ideal state.

Many scholars since the Greeks have advanced the same idea. Martin Luther included music in his formal educational scheme because of his belief that "music is one of the greatest gifts that God has given us; it is divine and therefore Satan is its enemy. For with its aid many dire temptations are overcome; the devil does not stay where music is" (Lewis 1963, 15). Closer to home, Lowell Mason called upon similar ideas as part of his petition to include music in the public schools of Boston. After his first year of teaching music as part of the school curriculum, the Boston School Board reaffirmed this portion of his argument when they stated: "Of the great moral effect of vocal music, there can be no question" (Birge 1966, 51).

On the other hand, Haack (1995) adopts the attittude that music per se is essentially morally neutral. If it does have a moral "spin," that is determined by the user and the use to which it is put. Of course, music does have a "halo" effect due to its common and frequent association with such positive forces as love and religion. However, this presumed innocence can make music an even more insidious tool in the hands of someone wanting to use it for socially negative purposes.

In the twentieth century we have had many examples of the connection between music and political or religious thought. Hitler used the music of Wagner for his own malevolent purposes (Moller 1980).

The Chamber of Culture, a committee of the Nazi Ministry of Propaganda, carefully screened and selected music appropriate for creating the desired emotional atmosphere at rallies, in factories, on radio broadcasts, and in all aspects of German life. Shostakovitch was censured by the Soviet government for writing music that was not deemed appropriate by the state. In China during the Cultural Revolution, Western music was denounced as decadent and forbidden (Cheng 1987). State-approved music was blasted over loud speakers as a massive propaganda device, and much of this music was used for such mundane purposes as the dedication of a new hydroelectric facility. In Iran, while the Ayatollah Khomeini was in power, tight restrictions were placed on the types of music that could be broadcast.

In the United States, music has been connected with political movements from colonial days until now (Denisoff 1983). Preceding and during the Revolutionary War, groups such as the Freemasons and Sons of Liberty fanned the flames of rebellion through their songs. The Civil War, World Wars I and II, and all the other conflicts before and since have been fought to musical accompaniment. Most recent were the previously mentioned protest songs of the 1960s and 1970s that were directed toward involvement in Vietnam.

Of course, music has been used as a means of influence for much more than military campaigns. "Songs of persuasion," as Denisoff calls them, can be used in any social or political situation. He lists six primary goals.

1. The song attempts to solicit and arouse outside support and sympathy for a social or political movement.
2. The song reinforces the value structure of individuals who are active supporters of the social movement or ideology.
3. The song creates and promotes cohesion, solidarity, and high morale in an organization or movement supporting its worldview.
4. The song is an attempt to recruit individuals for a specific social movement.
5. The song invokes solutions to real or imagined social phenomena in terms of action to achieve a desired goal.
6. The song points to some problem or discontent in the society, usually in emotional terms. (Denisoff 1983, 2–3)

In an interesting glimpse into the future, Haack (1982), using Orwell's famous *1984* as a basis, has shown us what the influence of music might become. There are more than 25 distinct references to music in Orwell's book, and nearly all of them represent what Haack calls the "malpractice of music." "The most striking feature of these references is the constant, blatant propagandizing and mind-controlling function that the music serves" (1982, 26). Although we are safely past the year 1984 and are not yet at the totalitarian state prophesied by Orwell, there are many examples of an increasing malpractice of music in the past 50 years.

One segment of the musical community that has been accused of musical malpracice is heavy metal music. At least five basic themes of concern have been identified in heavy metal music (Stuessy 1990): (1) extreme rebellion, (2) extreme violence, (3) substance abuse, (4) sexual promiscuity and perversion, and (5) Satanism. By their very names—Metallica or Nine-Inch Nails—some rock groups create controversy. The on- and offstage behavior of many rock stars adds fuel to the flame of those who believe that "hard" rock is antisocial.

Many teachers, ministers, youth workers, community leaders, and parents across the country have grown increasingly concerned about the possible negative effects of heavy metal music and rap on teenagers and preteens. A group of U.S. Senators' wives led by Tipper Gore was concerned enough to organize the Parents Music Resource Center in Washington, D.C. The U.S. Senate itself held hearings as a prelude to the possibility of legislative controls on the heavy metal industry. As a result of these kinds of activities, several record companies voluntarily began to print the lyrics on record album covers, so that they can be screened before purchase. Some cities have enacted ordinances that prohibit children below certain ages from attending heavy metal concerts. Other cities have tried, often without success, to find a legal means of barring certain rock groups from performing in city-owned facilities.

As a specific example of musical malpractice, some have accused the producers of certain rock records of implanting Satanic messages through a technique known as "backmasking" (Arar 1982; Martinez 1986; Peters and Peters with Merrill 1985). When these records are played backwards, the messages are alleged to be clear; played in a normal manner, they are supposed to produce subliminal effects. Though there is a great deal of controversy about how often this technique is used and exactly what the effects are when it is used, apparently there is enough concern for both the National Association of Broadcasters and the Federal Communications Commission to outlaw its use. In an experiment to study the effects of subliminal suggestions on the perception of tempo in music, it was demonstrated that musical skill level was influential, not subliminal spoken messages (Walls, Taylor, and Falzone 1992). Even if backmasking or subliminal messages are not used, however, heavy metal music is still thought by some to be a major means of promoting Satanism among young people.

MTV (Music Television) represents another major area of concern, or another type of possible musical malpractice. MTV reaches nearly 30 million homes via cable television. Concern arises out of the fact that more than half the rock videos on MTV feature violence or strongly suggested violence; furthermore, there are an average of 18 instances of violent or hostile action each hour on MTV (Jones 1986; Silverman 1983). In rock videos, as in live performances, the powerful message communicated by the music is greatly magnified by the visual image.

Does heavy metal music, MTV, and the like influence teenagers' social behaviors? The answers to this question are yes, probably, and perhaps. Yes, many teenage behaviors are clearly influenced by the music they listen to. Styles of clothing, hair, makeup, jewelry, speech, dance, and mannerisms are all intertwined with musical styles. Buying habits are also influenced, as money is spent on stereos, jamboxes, and Walkmans, albums, concert tickets, and tour T-shirts.

The probably answer comes in recognition of the fact that increases in teenage converts to Satanic cults, rape, vandalism, and involvement with drugs have risen sharply in recent years. It is difficult to separate cause from effect, but clearly the opposite—that heavy metal music has nothing whatsoever to do with the behaviors of those who listen to it—is not palpable.

The perhaps answer is in response to questions of whether there are any direct links between heavy metal rock and specific acts, such as a particular teenager's suicide. Several instances have been reported where a teenager has commited suicide with a heavy metal album nearby, such as "Shoot to Thrill" by AC/DC (which promotes suicide as a positive solution to life's problems). A particularly notable account of a teenage triple suicide can be found in a case study by Storm (1993) titled "The Role of Music in the Life and Death of a Teenager." To take either extreme—that the music by itself caused the incident or that the music had no connection—does not make sense. Certainly one can see, however, how the music may have interacted with drugs or alcohol, depression, relationship problems (breakup with girl/boyfriend, problems with parents or school) and reinforced a gathering notion.

A special committee of the American Medical Association reported on its study of "Adolescents and Their Music" in the *Journal of the American Medical Association* (Brown and Hendee 1989). The committee cited evidence associating immersion in the rock culture, and especially an affinity to heavy metal styles, with low school achievement, premarital sex, drug use, and/or Satanic activities. The report notes that association does not mean causation and that the study was not designed to establish cause and effect, which would be a more challenging task. However, another research report prepared for the Carnegie Council on Adolescent Development, titled "Popular Music in Early Adolescence" (Christensen and Roberts 1989), does suggest a cause and effect relationship between violence in music and a heightened disposition toward violence in listeners, at least over short time spans. What may well be happening, regardless of what causes what, is that the musical behaviors and the socially negative behaviors mentioned in the studies feed upon and reinforce one another, with the danger of moving to extremes together. The AMA study states that the average high school student hears 10,500 hours of rock music between grades 7 and 12—well over 30 hours per week. The AMA report concludes that doctors should attempt to be aware of the listening habits of their young patients as a clue to their emotional health and well-being, especially if problems are suspected.

The extent of the influence of rock music on teenage behavior was revealed in a study in which 90 percent of nearly 1,000 teenagers who were surveyed expressed a positive attitude toward disc jockeys; moreover, they felt disc jockeys understood them better than their parents or ministers and said that they were the strongest influence on their choice of music (Booker 1968). For their part, the disc jockeys stated their major purpose was to entertain listeners, thus to retain high ratings and promote sponsor's products, rather than to educate or enlighten. One disc jockey, whose managers objected to the music he played because it was laced with radical politics and profanity, stated in defense of his right to free speech: "I make no judgment on whether this is good stuff" (Silverman 1983).

Peer relationships, influences, and pressures have long been thought to affect adolescents' behaviors in a variety of ways and this appears to include musical behaviors as well. Being able to discuss the same music is important for peer acceptance and belonging to the peer group. In fact, the heaviest music listeners were found to spend more time with friends and less with family (Larson, Kubey, and Colletti 1989). Such listeners also spent less time attending their school classes.

In an extensive research review titled "Adolescents and Media Music," Thompson (1994) concluded that it would be foolhardy to ignore the degree to which music permeates the lives of adolescents. His review confirms the magnitude of exposure, the variety and potency of the sources of musical influence, and the high level of gratification that adolescents receive from their music. The various studies he cites, and his conclusions concerning them, tend to reaffirm the preceding discussion in this section of the *Handbook*.

College-age students with the highest total sensation-seeking scores prefer rock music more than other styles, such as country and western, jazz, or classical (McCarthy 1987). According to a newspaper account, a Soviet researcher also contends that rock music is addictive (San Antonio Light 1987). Some rock fans who tried to see how long they could go without listening to rock music lasted less than three days. They experienced many of the same withdrawal symptoms as drug addicts.

Music used in commercials may be an even more pervasive influence than rock music (Hodges 1982). One of the most successful advertising techniques is to pair a catchy jingle with a product in consumers' minds. The music for such products as soft drinks ("Coke adds life!" or "I'm a Pepper"), rice ("Rice-A-Roni, the San Francisco treat"), and cars ("See the USA in your Chevrolet") has become firmly implanted in the public's mind. In fact, they are so firmly implanted that 99 percent of subjects in all age groups successfully recognized the music to selected brand-name commercials. When that statistic is paired with the fact that the average American encounters 1,600 commercial messages in 24 hours, most of which have a musical accompaniment, the potential influence is enormous (Parker 1984).

Does it really work? Apparently major companies, such as Coca-Cola and Pepsi-Cola, believe in the power of music and the image of the musician when they sign figures like Michael Jackson and Madonna to multi–million dollar contracts. At least three reasons have been advanced for the effectiveness of music in advertising. "First, because it is one of the most powerful aids to memorability in the human experience. Second, because it can create a mood or feeling about something in a way that almost nothing else can. And third, because it acts as a triggering mechanism influencing the sale at the point of purchase" (Woodward 1982, 13).

Summary

Sociological perspectives of musical behavior indicate that never before in the history of humanity have so many different kinds of music been available to so many different kinds of people. Of course, it is the electronic media that have been responsible for this profusion of sounds. The amount and diversity of music and the multiple roles it plays in society give sociologists a very wide territory to cover. In discussing the scope of the sociology of music, one writer sees "the overall musical process, involving the interaction and interdependence of artist, work, and public, as constituting the frame of reference for all the different aspects of musico-sociological thought and activity" (Silbermann 1982, 578).

So what important messages do sociologists have to give us about the significance of music? The first, and perhaps most important, message is that no member of a given society can be automatically kept from a meaningful experience by virtue of any generic criteria, such as age, intelligence, or race. American society is characterized by enormous diversity, yet all can share in the experience of interacting with music. In fact, there is so much music in our society, and it occurs in so many different settings, that it would be nearly impossible to live in the United States and not encounter music in some way. Music can be heard in the home, at school, at work, in worship, on holidays and special occasions, in politics, in the military, in health-care systems, in conjunction with physical activities, in the media, in professional and social organizations, in many occupations, in many of the places we go, and in numerous miscellaneous situations.

One of music's social functions is to reflect the society of which it is a part. One sociologist states that "social structures crystallize in musical structures; that in various ways and with varying degrees of critical awareness, the musical microcosm replicates the social macrocosm" (Ballantine 1984, 5). One way society is reflected in music is through the behaviors of the musicians themselves. Social rules and structures govern musicians' behaviors just as they do members of any group. In many ways, musical groups create their own social unit, often with a unique set of strictures.

Society is also reflected in the behaviors of music listeners. Music can either serve as a means of identifying certain groups, and thus potentially as a divider, or as a unifier, bringing people of different backgrounds together. Listeners can sometimes be identified or categorized on the basis of age, race, or socioeconomic status. Sometimes, as is often the case with youth music, the type of music listened to can serve as a barrier to separate the listeners from the rest of society. On many other occasions, exactly the opposite occurs—barriers of age, race, and socioeconomic status are transcended by a common listening experience.

Music not only reflects the way a society lives, it often influences how it lives. Music plays a significant role in the socialization process, for example. From cradle to grave we learn many important messages about what it means to be human and how to behave in certain situations through the music we hear. Music is one of the many factors that helps to shape each individual to be the unique person he or she is. At each stage of development we may gain important insights about who we are through reflection on our musical experiences and musical values.

Music influences us in our working behaviors. This is most noticeable in the use of Muzak or similar music services in certain factories and work areas. Muzak data indicate increased production, improved attitudes, and reduced absenteeism and errors. Also common is the type of unobtrusive, "wallpaper" music that is sometimes confused with Muzak. The effects of this type of music generally have not been researched to the extent that Muzak's have, but there is ample reason to believe that it does create a pleasant ambience for diners at a restaurant, calm the nerves of patients waiting in doctors' and dentists' offices, and slow down the walking pace of grocery shoppers, the better to increase their time in the store (and sales as well).

Historically, music has exerted a significant influence on people's thoughts, attitudes, and social behaviors. Songs of persuasion have been used as tools of propoganda for numerous social issues. Music always plays an important role during wartime; it is used to elicit support for a cause and to protest unwanted involvement. Music is particularly influential in the lives of teenagers. Many of their attitudes and behaviors are highly influenced by the music they listen to. Music exerts a powerful influence on our buying habits and is a major ingredient in radio and television advertising.

Though we are often unaware of the musical influences in our lives, its impact is highly significant. As Merriam has noted,

> The importance of music, as judged by the sheer ubiquity of its presence, is enormous. . . . There is probably no other human cultural activity which is so all-pervasive and which reaches into, shapes, and often controls so much of human behavior. (Merriam 1964, 218)

Psychological Perspectives

Psychology is, generally speaking, the study of human behavior. Because this generalized definition covers such a vast array of topics, the field of psychology is one of enormous diversity. Perhaps it is due to such diversity that the situation in psychology is somewhat different from that found in biology, anthropology, or sociology. Psychologists are much more divided in their opinions and are more likely to belong to a "camp" with a particular orientation toward human behavior. Many of these disparate views have formed into major ideologies that tend to focus on certain aspects of human behavior to the exclusion of others. Some psychological theories have had a long enough history that their proponents may be relatively typecast as to their particular orientation. Thus, a Freudian psychologist and a behaviorist would view human behavior in distinctly different and somewhat predictable ways. Other major approaches would include Gestalt psychology, developmental psychology, cognitive psychology, and humanistic psychology. Many psychologists, however, do not align themselves along these more traditional lines and are working on such developing areas as information theory, mathematical models, or artificial intelligence. Sometimes a psychologist's work is organized around a topic, such as language acquisition or perception.

Psychologists have included music as one of their research interests for a long time. Indeed, far more books in music psychology have been written by psychologists who are interested in music than by musicians who are interested in psychology (see chap. 1). The connection between psychology and music was made even stronger in a series of cooperative efforts called the Ann Arbor Symposium. Held in 1978–79, these meetings provided an opportunity for scholars from both disciplines to share and discuss topics of mutual fascination.

Several topics in psychology are covered thoroughly in other chapters, including psychoacoustics, perception, cognition, tonal and musical memory, and learning theories. The remaining topics in this section include discussions of musical intelligence, the musical personality, and music as therapy.

Musical Intelligence

In studying human behavior, one of the topics psychologists inevitably deal with is intelligence. At a superficial level, it is easy to understand that human beings are intelligent creatures and that some human beings are more intelligent than others. However, specifying exactly what intelligence is or in what ways one person is more intelligent than another is quite a different matter. For example, one might ask whether a nuclear physicist is necessarily more intelligent than a poet. When a baseball player at bat adjusts his swing to the rotation and movement of a ball moving toward him at 90 miles per hour so that the bat and ball intersect at a precise moment in time and space—is that a form of intelligence?

Traditional definitions of intelligence normally involve such various mental abilities as the ability to think and reason, to learn, or to solve problems. The most prevalent means of evaluating a person's intelligence is through the use of a test that yields an intelligence quotient (IQ). Although there are more than 200 different IQ tests available, the average IQ is commonly around 100, with persons scoring above 130 considered to be of superior intelligence and persons scoring below 70 considered to be mentally deficient. Closely related, and even more frequently used in academic settings, are standardized tests of academic achievement, such as the *Scholastic Aptitude Test* (SAT), the *Iowa Tests of*

Basic Skills (ITBS), or the *Graduate Record Examination* (GRE). There is such a high correlation between IQ tests and academic achievement tests that they are often considered nearly synonymous measures of intelligence. For example, there is a 95 percent overlap between the *Otis Quick-Scoring Test of Mental Ability, Beta* and the *Stanford Achievement Tests* (Gage and Berliner 1975).

Quite understandably, the connection between a person's IQ score and his or her value as a person has been unavoidable. This is particularly true in school, where many gifted and talented programs use specific cut-off scores on mental ability tests as the primary criterion for selection. Likewise, in school, recognition is given to those with high SAT scores. The notion that a person's worth should be determined by a score on a test is anathema to many, of course, and they have found many faults with their usage. In addition to the philosophical disagreements, critics have contended that IQ tests are culture bound, discriminating against minorities, and that they are not good predictors of adult success (Goleman 1986). In fact, the data show only a moderate correlation between IQ and later success in adult life.

One of the major criticisms of these tests is that they are too narrow in their concept of intelligence. Skills exhibited by the poet and baseball player are clearly excluded by most of these tests. Because the direction of intelligence testing was highly influenced by the original interest in predicting success in school and the obvious intent of academic achievement testing, these tests do not measure human intelligence in a broad sense. Other societies in other times and places would not place as high a premium on linguistic and mathematic skills as we do. Even in our own society, social skills, artistic gifts, and many other types of intelligence are not measured by these tests.

In opposition to the notion of measuring intelligence with a single-score IQ, several theories of multiple intelligences have been proposed. For example, Gall hypothesized the existence of 37 mental faculties and Guilford created a cube containing 120 vectors of the mind. One of the more recent theories of multiple intelligences is that proposed by Gardner (1983). He suggests seven types of intellectual competence.

1. Linguistic intelligence,
2. Musical intelligence,
3. Logical-mathematical intelligence,
4. Spatial intelligence,
5. Bodily-kinesthetic intelligence,
6. Interpersonal intelligence, and
7. Intrapersonal intelligence.

He stresses the idea that each of these forms of intelligence is an equally valuable and important way of knowing.

In support of his theory of multiple intelligences, Gardner lists eight criteria of an intelligence, or signs by which a type of intelligence might be identified. These criteria will be reviewed with specific attention to a rationale for including musical intelligence on Gardner's list.

Potential Isolation by Brain Damage

The literature on amusia (loss of musical skills) was reviewed in chapter 7. Since the literature reports cases of amusia without aphasia (loss of language skills) and cases of aphasia without amusia, the contention of music being represented by separate neural mechanisms seems warranted. This idea is also supported by a wide variety of neuromusical research.

The Existence of Prodigies, Idiot Savants, and Other Exceptional Individuals

The existence of prodigies and savants (again, covered in chap. 7) serves to support the contention that music is an autonomous form of intelligence. It also lends credence to the notion that there are musical neuromechanisms in the same or similar way that there are for language. Training and/or experience can be identified in most instances of prodigies and savants, but can hardly account completely for such unusual skills.

An Identifiable Core Operation or Set of Operations

Any musical performance is more than the sum of its constituent parts. Nevertheless, music theorists have for hundreds of years recognized various elements of music, such as rhythm and pitch. After all, many familiar tunes can be identified by their rhythm patterns alone (think of "Happy Birthday" or "Jingle Bells"). According to Gardner, the manner in which these elements of music are processed represents a set of operations or basic information-processing mechanisms that deal with specific kinds of input. In music, a set of operations might include such concepts as rhythm and pitch-pattern processing, timbre perception, awareness of structure or form, and affective responses.

A Distinctive Developmental History, along with a Definable Set of Expert "End-State" Performances

How does one get from the babbling stage of infancy to an appearance at Carnegie Hall? Aside from the well-known humorous answer—practice, man, practice—it is clear that we progress through a number of developmental stages. Three of the most difficult barriers to a definitive developmental scheme are the tremendous variety of musical behaviors among cultural groups, the variety of behaviors within a given cultural group, and the lack of standards regarding expected musical skills among the general populace. Standards for the nonacademic use of language (including reading, writing, and speech) are fairly well understood and that is that most persons become proficient users of their parent language. The same may not be said for music in some cultural groups, however. What do we expect, for example, of U.S. citizens in the way of musical competence? It is perfectly acceptable in our society to be musically illiterate, while illiteracy in languge creates a tremendous social barrier. This is most evident in our educational system, where students are expected to demonstrate mastery of language skills at progressive levels of difficulty. While one might argue whether students are, in fact, achieving this mastery, the standards are nevertheless in place and much attention and energy have been focused in recent years on the maintenance and/or upgrading of these standards. There are no such equivalent competency standards for music. Individual schools or school districts may, of course, have a more-or-less rigorous set of musical competency expectations, but there is no national norm. (The voluntary national standards that are a part of the *Goals 2000: Educate America* act provide a start.)

A lack of developmental standards in music is not the same thing as a lack of a developmental history for musical skills. While we may not know what normal musical behavior should be at all stages, we do know that persons with advanced musical skills have undergone a considerable period of development. Although prodigies provide puzzling exceptions to the rule, most musicians have spent years making what is sometimes painstakingly slow progress.

The "end-state" performances that Gardner includes in this criterion are easy to observe in the behaviors of accomplished composers, performers, conductors, teachers, therapists, and others. The developmental history, including both genetic and environmental influences, leads to final flowering in extraordinary levels of excellence. The roll call of musical "giants" is a long and distinguished one and gives ample proof that music has a distinctive developmental history that results in expert end-state performances.

An Evolutionary History and Evolutionary Plausibility
Speculations on the evolutionary plausibility of musical behaviors were provided in chapter 2. It is possible that musical capacities developed in human beings in connection with mother-infant bonding, the acquisition of language, the development of unique modes of knowing, and by playing important roles in social organization.

Support from Experimental Psychological Tasks

A significant amount of data has been gathered with respect to psychological aspects of musical behavior. In fact, because this entire book is replete with the results of just such experiments, only one example will be given here. Gardner cites a study by Deutsch as the kind of support he deems necessary to support music as an autonomous form of intelligence. In a study of tonal memory, Deutsch (Deutsch and Deutsch 1975) presented subjects with a series of tones that were competing with interfering material to remember. When the interfering material was other tones, recall for the trial pattern was seriously impaired, with as much as 40 percent error. When the interfering sounds were verbal, however, the effects were very slight and only 2 percent error occured. This provides some indication that verbal and tonal processing occurs in separate neural networks.

Support from Psychometric Findings

Many pencil-and-paper tests of music have been developed over the past 70 years, beginning with the *Seashore Measures of Musical Talents* in 1919. These tests have been divided into two general types: tests of musical aptitude and tests of musical achievement. Musical aptitude is concerned with determining potential for achievement in music; its value is predictive.

The major tests of musical aptitude, along with their dates of publication and revision, are (Boyle and Radocy 1987; George 1980): *Seashore Measures of Musical Talents* (1919, 1925, 1939, 1956, and 1960), *Kwalwasser-Dykema Music Tests* (1930 and 1954), *Drake Musical Aptitude Tests* (1934 and 1954), *Wing Standardized Tests of Musical Intelligence* (1939, 1948, 1957, 1960, and 1961), *The Gretsch-Tilson Musical Aptitude Test* (1941), [Gaston] *Test of Musicality* (1942, 1950, 1956, and 1957), *Kwalwasser Music Talent Test* (1953), [Gordon] *Musical Aptitude Profile* (1965), [Bentley] *Measures of Musical Abilities* (1966), [Gordon] *Primary Measures of Audiation* (1979), and [Gordon] *Intermediate Measures of Audiation* (1982).

Obviously much time and energy has been expended in attempts to measure musical aptitude. The primary focus of most of these tests has been on measuring sensory capacities. Sensitivity to minimal differences in pitch, loudness, rhythm, and timbre are common features. Another common feature is measurement of tonal or musical memory. Some of the test authors have attempted to eliminate environmental influences by using nonmusical sound sources, such as electronic tone generators, while others have used such musical instruments as the piano or violin in an attempt to increase external validity. Unfortunately, the results have not been very satisfactory, as the general predictive ability of these tests is relatively low. One of the major difficulties is that different musical behaviors (e.g., conducting a band or singing in a rock group) may require different aptitudes. Progress is being made, however, and it may be that one day it will be possible to predict an individual's future success in musical endeavors with much greater accuracy.

Musical achievement is concerned with measuring what has been learned to date; its value is diagnostic. Major tests of musical achievement are: *Beach Music Test* (1920, 1930, and 1938), *Kwalwasser-Ruch Test of Musical Accomplishment* (1924 and 1927), *Kwalwasser Test of Music Information and Appreciation* (1927), *Knuth Achievement Tests in Music* (1937 and 1967–68), *Aliferis-Stecklein Music Achievement Tests* (1947, 1949, and 1950), *Snyder Knuth Music Achievement Test* (1968), [Colwell] *Music Achievement Tests* (1969 and 1970), *Iowa Tests of Music Literacy* (1970), *Simons Measurement of Music Listening Skills* (1974), and *Silver Burdett Music Competency Tests* (1979).

Tests of music achievement have an advantage over music aptitude tests in that they are more easily geared toward specific musical tasks. For example, a test of music notation reading skills is quite different from a test of identifying instrumental timbres. When specific achievement tests have been matched appropriately with the desired skills, the results have been quite satisfactory. In fact, because the results from a signficant body of research literature suggest that the best predictor of future success is past success, achievement tests are increasingly used for predictive, as well as diagnostic, purposes.

Of particular interest to Gardner's criterion that psychometric findings should support the contention that musical intelligence is a separate form of intelligence are the research studies correlating "musical intelligence," as measured by these tests, and general IQ. Although wide variations have been reported in the literature, a generalized conclusion may be that there is a positive correlation of a low to moderate degree between musical intelligence and general intelligence. While the two are most often paired to some degree, it is certainly possible for a person of high IQ to have minimal musical skills (see chap. 2), and, as the case of musical savants indicates (see chap. 7), the opposite is equally possible. The final conclusion is one of support for the uniqueness of musical intelligence apart from general IQ.

Three research studies have been reported that contend that music can cause an increase in spatial intelligence. In one experiment (Rauscher, Shaw, and Ky 1993), college students who listened to a Mozart piano sonata for ten minutes demonstrated a short-term spatial reasoning increase. This study was replicated and extended using minimalist music (Philip Glass) and trance-style dance music; these musical styles did not enhance spatial intelligence scores (Rauscher et al. 1994). Finally, spatial reasoning scores of 19 three-year-olds were increased significantly by participating in eight months of music lessons (Rauscher et al. 1993); scores on four other intelligence measures did not change.

Susceptibility to Encoding in a Symbol System
Just as linguistic intelligence is encoded in the written word, logical-mathematical intelligence in mathematic symbols and computer languages, and spatial intelligence in graphic designs (e.g., a blueprint), so is musical intelligence encoded in its own notational symbol system.

Evidence of the autonomy of musical intelligence by virtue of a unique encoding system was obtained with the observation of a successful composer who suffered from alexia, the loss of the ability to read words (Gardner 1983). While this person could barely read a single word, he could still decipher musical notation with ease. This is significant evidence that musical and linguistic symbols are processed by the brain in different ways.

Through these eight criteria Gardner makes a strong case for considering musical intelligence as an autonomous form of human intelligence. Clearly, human beings are just as equipped to function musically as they are linguistically, mathematically, or in any other way. Each form of intelligence provides us with a unique way of knowing. To the extent that we fully engage in exploring all the possibilities of each mode of knowing, we realize our fullest human potential. To the extent that we devalue or limit our use of any particular form of intelligence, we are less than we have been created to be.

Music as a Way of Knowing

Another way to characterize this notion is to think of music as a human knowledge system. A knowledge system is a mode of sharing, expressing, understanding, and knowing information about our inner and outer worlds and for understanding relationships within and between the two. All animals rely on knowledge systems to function in the environment; the term *human* applied to knowledge systems simply designates the particular ways of knowing that humans have. Although there is no commonly agreed upon list of human knowledge systems, the labels Gardner used for his seven types of intelligence will be adopted for use because they have already been discussed in some detail. Other knowledge systems might be identified and labeled.

The musical knowledge system arises from innate brain structures and represents a unique means of functioning in the environment that is no better or worse than that provided by other knowledge systems. The concept of musical intelligence, then, may relate to the degree of efficiency with which one is able to operate within the musical knowledge system. All human beings are endowed with a musical knowledge system, but individuals have different levels of facility to operate within the system. Another distinction between the concepts of a musical knowledge system and musical intelligence may be that the term *knowledge system* has a broader connotation in usage, since it might also accommodate such aspects as talent, ability, aptitude, achievement, and musicality that may not always be associated with the idea of intelligence.

Although it is convenient to discuss each knowledge system separately, in reality there are many interconnections. For example, in thinking of performing musicians as "small muscle athletes," there are connections between musical and bodily knowledge systems. Or consider that the connections between musical and logical-mathematical knowledge sytems extend back at least to the ancient Greeks, if not long before, and the placement of music in the upper quadrivium along with mathematics, geometry, and astronomy. This interrelationship extends to the current use of computers and synthesizers in MIDI technology. Music, in fact, has rich connections with all the other knowledge systems; multiple connections among many of the knowledge systems can be seen in an experience such as opera, which involves a combination of music, words, costumes and staging, movement and dance, and an exploration of inter- and intrapersonal relationships.

Knowledge Gained through a Musical Knowledge System

Each human being, then, has built-in systems for knowing his or her inner and outer worlds. Through these systems one can discover, understand, share, and express an infinite variety of thoughts and feelings. Each knowledge system may be more or less appropriate for dealing with a particular thought or feeling. For example, joy can be known in a variety of ways through the linguistic, musical, spatial, bodily, and personal knowledge systems but perhaps less so through the mathematical knowledge system. One might experience joy at solving a difficult mathematical problem, but the notion of logically deducing the constituents of joy or of representing joy by a mathematical formula seems inappropriate. Mathematics takes center stage, however, when the central issue is space and time as they relate to an understanding of the universe.

If one assumes agreement on the foregoing, that music does indeed represent a knowledge system, it then becomes legitimate to ask, what does one know, understand, share, or express through music? Our society recognizes and understands what is to be gained through the language and mathematics knowledge systems; the generally accepted notion that a "basic" education consists of reading, writing, and arithmetic is but one example. But what is gained through music?

Before presenting a partial list of possibilities, two brief caveats must be stated: (1) the given list is not meant to be exhaustive; such an exercise would be tedious, if not unnecessary; and (2) as with the earlier list of knowledge systems, while it is convenient to discuss each item separately, there is, of course, a significant amount of intertwining. Nine items are presented here merely for the purposes of stimulating thinking; these represent only a few of the things we know, discover, understand, experience, share, or express through music.

1. Feelings. Central to any discussion of music as a knowledge system must be the idea of feelings. From one end of the continuum dealing with vague, unlabeled moods to the other end dealing with such crystallized emotions as grief or joy, music is intrinsically connected with feelings.

2. Aesthetic experiences. All human beings have a need for beauty and to activate their innate responsiveness to the organized sounds that we call music.

3. The Ineffable. Precisely because music is a nonverbal form of expression, it is a powerful means to express or to know that which is difficult or impossible to put into words. Two of the most common human experiences that are frequently known through music are love and spiritual awareness.

4. Thinking. Musical thought is just as viable as linguistic, mathematical, or visual thought. It can be a potent means of expressing ideas and of knowing truth. For example, Ives's "thoughts" on the meaning of life in the universe are expressed potently and eloquently in "The Unanswered Question."

5. Structure. Closely allied to the idea of thinking is structure. The human mind seeks patterns, structure, order, and logic. Music provides a unique way of structuring sounds across time, as well as providing a means of structuring thoughts, feelings, and human experience.

6. Time and Space. Time and space are the "stuff" of the universe. All human knowledge systems provide ways of dealing with time and space. As indicated in point 5, music is a means of

organizing sounds across time. Although music occurs in real time, it deals more with felt time. Music, in connection with dance (bodily-kinesthetic knowledge system) is a primary means of experiencing space in time.

7. Self-knowledge. Maslow's description of the role of music in intrinsic, and especially peak, learning experiences provides an excellent model for how music allows for insights into our private, inner worlds (see chap. 11).

8. Group Knowledge. Group knowledge through music can be divided into two types of experiences: (a) music helps cement the bonding of those members of a group who share common ideas, beliefs, and behaviors; and (b) music helps isolate and separate one group from another. Group identity through music is both inclusive and exclusive.

9. Healing and Wholeness. From more specific applications of music in therapy and medicine to more general interactions, music has profound effects on human beings. Music provides a vehicle for the integration of body, mind, and spirit.

All nine of these, and the many others that could be listed, can be subsumed under the idea that music provides knowledge of the human condition (i.e., the condition of being human).

Tait and Haack (1984) use a simpler framework when they characterize the human experience as one of thinking, feeling, and sharing. One aspect of being human is that, while all human beings experience common thoughts and feelings, no one else can share in another individual's particular thoughts and feelings. Thus, while all may experience loneliness, exultation, anger, or grief, each person's experience is unique. The power of music, and the other arts as well, is that it allows us to share, to express, to discover, to understand, in short, to know grief in a way that encompasses the general notion of human grief, while speaking directly to our own personal, private sense of grief. Reimer (1989) characterizes this way of knowing by saying that music provides knowledge *of*, not knowledge *about*, grief.

Implications of Music as a Human Knowledge System

Imagine that the case for the influence of music on human behavior has been made so persuasively that our society accepted music as a human knowledge system. Furthermore, it is accepted that all human knowledge systems are equally important, as each allows us to deal with our inner and outer worlds in its own unique manner. The implications these views have for potential social changes are considerable. The role of music in business, government, religious organizations, and so on might be changed considerably. As important as these changes might be, the discussion here will focus on education and health care.

Although music represents a built-in knowledge system that allows human beings to know aspects of their inner and outer worlds in a unique mode, such knowledge does not come automatically. All the knowledge systems represent potential learning modes. More than any other animal species, for whom many specific behaviors are prewired, human beings rely heavily on learning for built-in potential to be realized. Human knowledge systems will not simply come to full fruition through a natural growth process; a series of environmental interventions in the form of learning experiences are necessary to activate the knowledge system. Full development of any knowledge system will only come as innate potential is realized in environmental circumstances. We must learn how to use language, how to think logically, use mathematical symbols, and so on through the list.

Many aspects of a knowledge system can be learned informally, by observation and imitation. However, formal learning experiences, primarily in the form of an education, are the real keys to unlocking and realizing full human potential. Thus, education might be defined as the systematic development of human knowledge systems. One of the most important implications to come out of this discussion is that human beings need to be educated in all knowledge systems in order to achieve maximum human potential.

One can learn how to speak, to count, to run and jump, to draw, and to sing through informal means. But it takes systematic development to become a novelist, a mathematician, a ballerina, an artist, or a composer. In the U.S. educational system, great emphasis is placed on linguistic and logical-mathematical knowledge systems and very little on the musical, spatial, and bodily knowledge systems. One might well ask whether the lack of attention paid to the personal knowledge systems in the educational process is in any way connected to our high suicide, crime, drug, and divorce rates.

In terms of formal education as schooling, adoption of the notion of a variety of equally valuable knowledge systems carries with it the implication that the curriculum will reflect these knowledge systems. All students should have an opportunity to experience and develop their capabilities in all knowledge systems. Clearly, this is counter to the prevailing back-to-basics emphasis on language and mathematics skills, but it is far more consistent with the current understanding of the human mind from a behavioral sciences perspective. It would be the final realization of the

Tanglewood declaration: "We now call for music to be placed in the core of the school curriculum" (Choate 1968, 139).

Similar implications would hold for music in health-care systems (considering music therapy, music medicine, and performing arts medicine as three parts of a whole). Rather than being relegated to the fringes, as is often now the case, music could be brought into the mainstream of a holistic treatment of human health. As the U.S. health-care system moves gradually more toward prevention than intervention, music should occupy a greater role. The influence of music on human behavior seen from the broadest perspective (or rather from multiple perspectives) serves, again, as a model for integrating body, mind, and spirit.

Bruner (1969) writes about art as a mode of knowing, and, perhaps, the most important thing we can learn through music is about ourselves and about all of human nature. Imagine, if you will, that we were to communicate with alien space beings and our first task was to tell them what we humans are like. Thomas speculated that we might do it like this.

> Perhaps the safest thing to do at the outset, if technology permits, is to send music. This language may be the best we have for explaining what we are like to others in space, with least ambiguity. I would vote for Bach, all of Bach, streamed out into space, over and over again. We would be bragging, of course, but it is surely excusable for us to put the best possible face on at the beginning of such an aquaintance. (Thomas 1974, 53)

While this was a hypothetical suggestion, something very much like Thomas's suggestion was, in fact, carried out. When NASA was preparing to launch Voyagers 1 and 2 into space, they engaged Carl Sagan (1978) to head up a special team. It was the job of this team to devise a means of communicating with extraterrestrials, should the spacecrafts ever be captured or discovered. After much debate, they decided that music would be the most effective means of telling aliens what human beings are all about. The scientific-technological side of human beings would be evident from the spacecrafts themselves. But music would provide some indications of our emotional nature. Thus, music from all around the world was recorded and sent aboard the Voyagers to tell alien beings in outer space what we are like as human beings. Clearly, music is an important way of knowing.

The Musical Personality

One of the topics that has engaged psychologists for many years is the study of personality. Personality encompasses all of human behavior and includes such personal traits as one's abilities, character, opinions and beliefs, attitudes, emotional responses, temperament, and cognitive style. Often psychologists use adjectival descriptors in paired antonyms to identify specific traits—introverted-extroverted, relaxed-tense, and practical-imaginative are common examples.

Various psychologists have developed measuring devices to determine a person's personality characteristics. Examples include the *Gordon Personal Inventory, Minnesota Multiphasic Personality Inventory, Edwards Personal Inventory, California Personality Inventory,* and *Cattell's 16 Personality Factor Inventory* (Gage and Berliner 1975; Lefrancois 1979). Persons with relatively stable personality traits are said to be of a certain personality type. However, with something as complicated as human personality, it is understandable that there are limitations inherent in a pencil-and-paper test. Personality traits may change over time and often depend on subtle interactions with other human beings. For example, a person may be quite shy and retiring in one social setting and very outgoing and garrulous in another.

These difficulties, the complexity and diversity of musical behaviors, and the paucity of research on musical personalities are perhaps the main reasons there is no clear profile of what personality traits might characterize musicians. So many different personality traits have been identified in musicians that many have said that musicians have a heterogeneous personality. Schleuter (1971) and Thayer (1972) found that personality factors were not systematically related to either musical achievement or aptitude. Kemp (1982), however, felt that these studies were in error and that musicians instead have a polymorphous personality. He contended that all musicians share a common core of traits that might be considered musicianship linked. The core of traits Kemp identified in musicians includes introversion, pathemia, and intelligence. By introversion he does not mean timid withdrawal but inner strength and richly diversified thought processes. Pathemia deals with sensitivity and imaginativeness. Within the rather large sample of musicians he studied, there were many differences. But when these musicians were compared with naive musician groups, there was a clear demonstration of a stable core of these musicianship-linked traits.

Another personality trait that has been identified in musicians is psychological androgyny (Kemp 1985). This term refers to the fact that male musicians are more sensitive than naive musician males, often assumed to be a feminine trait, and that female musicians are more aloof and self-sufficient than female naive musicans, a trait more often found in males.

More detailed investigations have been made between different types of performing musicians. In one study, Kemp (1981) obtained data about the personality traits of members of 16 major symphony orchestras. Often string players were at opposite ends of a continuum from brass players. String players tended to perceive themselves and to be perceived by others as unathletic, insecure, and introverted, while brass players have more of an athletic, self-confident, and extroverted image and self-image. The remaining orchestra members were in the middle, with woodwind players nearer to string players in personality and percussionists nearer to brass players.

In another study, singers were found to be more extroverted than instrumentalists, perhaps because they are required to project themselves more directly rather than through an instrument (Lipton and Builione n.d.). Keyboard musicians were characterized by extroversion and, paradoxically, by conservatism and submissiveness. One possible explanation, though pure speculation, is that the former trait might be more pronounced in solo performers, while the latter two are more appropriate for accompanists and chamber musicians. Music educators tend to be intelligent, assertive, less interested in social approval, and somewhat defensive. It must be remembered that these differences are all within the relative constraints of the overall polymorphous profile of introversion, pathemia, and intelligence.

Another personality trait that characterizes musicians is anxiety. Trait anxiety is a long-term personality characteristic, while state anxiety has to do with nervousness in an immediate situation. Stage fright or the stress of performing publicly is perhaps the major form of state anxiety among musicians. It is reasonable to assume that a certain amount of stage fright "comes with the territory" and that many musicians are able to overcome it and, in fact, may be aided by it. However, there are also many performers who experience a more severe form of stage fright, and most would seek to reduce performance anxieties if possible.

There are at least three components to anxiety (Lehrer 1978): (1) physiological responses, (2) cognitive activity, and (3) behavioral responses. Physiological responses to performance anxiety may include increases in heart rate, perspiration, and blood pressure, "weak knees," "butterflies in the stomach," sweaty palms, dry mouth, and general muscle tension. The primary cognitive activity in connection with performance anxiety is worrying. Some individuals may report a general feeling of disorientation or inability to think clearly and withdrawal symptoms such as lethargy or avoidance behaviors. Behavioral responses might include nervous mannerisms and superstitious or ritual behaviors. Each individual has a different tolerance level for these symptoms and may find them only mildly annoying or completely debilitating. Musicians who are placed in chronic, stressful situations may suffer more harmful effects, such as ulcers, high blood pressure, or nervous breakdowns.

In a study of stress among symphony musicians (Haider and Groll-Knapp 1981), representative members of the Vienna Symphony were monitored during rehearsals and public performances for heart rate and brain wave activity. Maximum pulse rate averages were 110–120 beats per minute. However, certain individuals peaked at more than 150 beats per minute over short periods. The mean pulse rate was 85.2 during rehearsals and 93.5 during concerts. Even more critical was the difference between resting pulse rate and maximum pulse rate, or the exertional rate. The mean exertional rate was 27.3, with individuals peaking as high as 83 beats above their resting rate. This is surely one significant indicator of stress.

Electroencephalogram (EEG) readings of brainwave activity are more difficult to interpret. However, one indicator of stress is the overriding predominance of beta wave activity over long periods of time. Alpha waves (8–12 cycles per second) are present during periods of relaxed awareness. These are replaced by beta waves (13–30 cycles per second) during periods of concentration or intense mental activity. In normal circumstances, beta waves are produced for only short periods of time, interrupted frequently by alpha waves. However, in this study of the Vienna Symphony, EEG readings of the musicians during rehearsals and performances showed a significant preponderance of beta wave activity over relatively long periods of time. Particularly during concerts, interruptions by alpha waves were very rare.

These findings were corroborated by another report of these same symphony musicians (Piperek 1981). A psychologist who interviewed these musicians remarked on the fact that most psychologists say that intense concentration cannot be maintained for more than 20–30 minutes (Schulz 1981). However, concerts typically last for as long as two hours, during which time each individual must be able to be integrated with the whole at intervals as small as 1/100th of a second. The result, of course, is considerable stress. When this pattern is repeated several times a week throughout many years of a performing career, it is not difficult to imagine what some of the long-term effects might be. Other sources of strain in the orchestra included consistent loudness levels above 100 dB, eye strain due to poor lighting, general working conditions, and various social frictions between and among the musicians and management.

Another method of measuring performance anxiety is self-report. Salewski (1982) used three techniques: a behavioral checklist, an Anxiety Scale Questionnaire, and a structured interview. She found that performance anxiety could be measured with these devices and that their use could be useful to both teachers and students.

There is some research that indicates that anxiety may actually enhance performance for some individuals. This is especially true for those who have achieved a high level of task mastery. In one experiment, singers experienced an increase in anxiety from voice lessons to jury performances, but the jury performances were judged signficantly better. These results have been corroborated by several researchers (Hamann 1982 and 1983; Hamann and Sobaje 1982; Weisblatt 1986).

In one study, anxiety was found to be greater just prior to performance than during performance (Hamann 1983). This, in combination with the research findings discussion in the preceding paragraph, may indicate that worrying about a performance is more stressful than the actual performance. In spite of the evidence that performances are enhanced by anxiety, many performers would like to find a way to reduce their nervousness. Several techniques that have been tried are briefly described here. Students at the Eastman School of Music underwent biofeedback training in which tension in muscles in the forehead was monitored (Nideffer and Hessler 1978). Students used a variety of techniques, such as meditation or mental imaging, to decrease the muscle tension. These procedures were applied to mental imaging of performance situations, with the result that the students reported better musical performances.

Systematic desensitization is another technique that has been successfully applied to performance anxiety (Nagel 1984; Wardle 1975). This technique involves deep muscle relaxation, the construction of anxiety hierarchies (a list of various aspects of an anxiety-producing situation), and emotive imagery. A similar relaxation therapy is known as the Alexander Technique (Ben-Or 1978; Brandfonbrenner 1986; Murray 1986; Reubart 1985). This approach is based on three stages: inhibition (cessation of one's habitual responses), direction (conscious direction of certain muscle or motor patterns), and activity (allowing an activity to occur without interfering with the "directions"). Many musicians have found this technique to be helpful.

Perhaps the most controversial approach to dealing with performance anxiety is the use of drugs (Nies 1986; Wilson 1986). The most commonly used drug in this regard is Inderal, whose generic chemical name is propranolol. Inderal is also known as a beta blocker because it interferes with the body's natural response to fight-or-flight situations. Interestingly, only small amounts of the drug are needed and there are apparently few side effects. While nervous symptoms are controlled, ability to concentrate, alertness, and memory are seemingly unaffected.

No drug is risk free, however, and Inderal cannot be prescribed legally for stage fright. As more and more musicians seemingly are using Inderal, the debate about the appropriateness of such an approach to conquering performance fears is intensifying.

The most recent and current work in music performance anxiety is being carried on by Leblanc (1995). He has developed "A Theory of Performance Anxiety" and formatted it in terms of "Sources of Variation in Music Performance Anxiety." LeBlanc has identified 39 variables that he believes to be factors in the development and treatment of performance anxiety, and he has arranged them in a hierarchy that implies a progression of time between its 11 stages. His model outlines actions and decisions a performer must take and make in preparing for and presenting a performance. The model begins with the performer's characteristics and learning history (stage 11), moves to preparation for performance (stages 10–7, including such factors as difficulty of music, adequacy of instrument, physical health, and affective state), progresses to the performing environment (6), the performer's self-perceptions (5), the act of performance itself (4–3), concluding with evaluation of the performance (2–1). This theory, which has been developed over a period of seven years, should provide a rich new perspective and pool of variables to guide researchers in this area of concern.

Music as Therapy

Because psychologists are engaged in the process of understanding human behavior, it is understandable that the knowledge they have gained has been used to help individuals with various behavioral problems. Most often the therapeutic approach taken stems from one of the orientations that was outlined at the beginning of this chapter (Kovel 1976). Both the techniques used and the results sought will be consistent with the prevailing philosophical tone. Thus, a Freudian psychologist seeks to resolve repressed inner conflicts through the process of psychoanalysis. A Gestalt psychologist concentrates more on feelings than thoughts and may foster an intense emotional experience in a group setting to promote healing. A humanistic therapist, in what is often called client-centered or nondirective therapy, invites clients to discover for themselves the solutions that are best for them by getting in touch with their truest, inner selves. A behavioral therapist seeks to change undesired or inappropriate behaviors by using techniques of reinforcement in a program of behavior modification. These one-sentence, generalized descriptions certainly do not do justice either to the therapeutic approaches mentioned or to those many approaches left out. However, their main objective is simply to illustrate the application of psychological viewpoints to therapeutic treatments.

Music can also be used therapeutically. In ancient times or even today in certain nontechnological societies, the songs and chants of the medicine man or shaman play an important role in the healing process. In contemporary societies such as our own, music therapy is more scientifically oriented, as is evidenced by this brief definition. "Music therapy is the scientific application of music or music activities to attain therapeutic goals. Music therapy can also be defined as the structured use of music to bring about desired changes in behavior" (Carter 1982, 5).

Music therapists work with an extremely wide range of clients with handicapping conditions. They work with clients who are mentally retarded, mentally ill, physically disabled (including people with impaired vision, hearing, or speech, and people who are orthopedically handicapped or who suffer from such diseases as cerebral palsy or muscular distrophy), and emotionally or behaviorally disturbed (such as those with autism or schizophrenia). Music therapists also work in a wide variety of settings, including hospitals, institutions, public schools, day-treatment centers, community health-care facilities, geriatric centers, private clinics or studios, and penal institutions. More recently, music therapists have begun to work with nonhandicapped individuals in wellness programs.

With such a wide diversity of client populations and clinical settings, the specific objectives of treatment will vary tremendously. However, the general goals are rather uniform. In the foreword to his landmark text of 1968, Gaston states three principles of music therapy: (1) the establishment or reestablishment of interpersonal relationships, (2) the bringing about of self-esteem through self-actualization, and (3) the utilization of the unique potential of rhythm to energize and bring order.

Among the most important areas in the treatment of handicapped persons are communication, academic, motor, and social skills (Eagle 1982). Music therapists are not primarily interested in the development of musicianship per se. Music is a means, not an end, and nonmusical behaviors take precedence over musical skills. However, it is important to realize that all persons, handicapped or not, have a need for aesthetic experiences, and moments of musical beauty and truth are important ingredients in the healing process.

Perhaps the greatest power of music as a healing agent comes from the fact that it is a form of nonverbal communication. For those who are unable to communicate via language or for those for whom verbal communication is threatening, music provides a vehicle for interchange. Too, the nonverbal aspect of music often allows a music therapist to establish a personal relationship with a client who resists personal contacts. In this way, music therapy can be used to establish bonds of communication so that other therapists can become involved in the healing process. Another important aspect of music as nonverbal communication is the ambiguity of that communication. While words are often discrete and limiting, music can express the ineffable and can support individual feelings.

Trying to descibe what music therapists do and the results they achieve is somewhat difficult because of the wide diversity of clinical situations in which they operate. However, a few case studies might serve to illustrate some of the possibilities. S was an autistic child of nine who had been working with a music therapist for two years (Romerhaus 1968). At the beginning of the instructional period, S used speech on a minimal basis and much of his behavior was ritualistic and compulsive. During the next two years, S had learned all the letter names on the piano, learned to read music, and had progressed into a second piano instruction book. He moved from a hospital back to his home and attended a special education first grade class. Here is an example of music therapy providing an avenue for the focusing of attention and for making direct progress in skill development that appears to have transferred into other academic areas.

Three teenagers, Julie, Sharon, and Eric, were all diagnosed as having spastic cerebral palsy (Miller 1982). They were nonverbal, with their only communication being a nodded yes or shaken no. Although they were experiencing many of the same emotional upheavals as most teenagers undergo, they were unable to express their feelings due to their lack of verbal communication skills. They were referred for treatment to a music therapist who engaged them in a variety of musical activities. They played the organ using a head stick and experimented with different kinds of expressive sounds. They had "discussions" in which the students would indicate what emotion certain sounds were expressing ("Does this sound happy or sad?"). Eventually they wrote a story and added musical accompaniment. "The primary value of music therapy with Julie, Eric, and Sharon was to enhance their emotional expression. Since their communicative abilities were quite limited, music therapy provided an outlet for feelings the children ordinarily had no way to express" (Miller 1982, 30–31).

Jo was brought to an adolescent psychiatric unit by his parents because of a history of stealing, lying, running away, and threatening physical harm to his family (Paul 1982). Music therapy sessions were designed to help with poor social skills, disruptive behavior, and low self-esteem. Singing and guitar lessons were made contingent upon controlling negative behaviors. Over a period of time, Jo increased the amount of time he spent practicing guitar and singing and therefore made significant progress. He made significant progress, too, in controlling his negative behaviors. Music became an acceptable outlet for him, and, as his self-esteem increased, he became a group leader on his unit.

These three examples indicate some of the activities and results of music therapy treatment sessions. Singing, playing instruments, listening, creating or improvising, and moving to music are all a regular part of the program. Sometimes these activities are couched within a particular therapeutic framework, such as behavior modification. Sometimes particular approaches are characterized by certain activities, such as in guided imagery sessions or psychodrama. Often, however, the therapeutic approach is eclectic and based on a careful, on-going assessment of the individual client's needs. Whatever the approach, music therapists are proving more and more to be accepted and valuable members of treatment teams.

In recent years, two related areas have developed: music medicine and performing arts medicine. Music medicine refers to the use of music to affect health directly, normally as administered by a doctor, nurse, or other health-care practitioner. The International Society for Music in Medicine has sponsored five symposia on music medicine and two related publications, *MusicMedicine* (Spintge and Droh 1992) and *MusicMedicine 2* (Spintge and Pratt 1995); IJAM, the *International Journal of Arts Medicine,* is the official journal for the field. Examples of music medicine include the use of music to control pain (anxiolytic music); to reduce blood pressure, heart rate, or muscle tension; or to effect changes in the endocrine system (psychoneuroimmunology). Music may be used effectively in a wide variety of clinical settings, such as in surgery, anesthesia, pain therapy, obstetrics, and dentistry. The research literature is published in widely divergent disciplines and is found under well over 2,000 different journal titles (Eagle and Hodges 1995). (More specific discussions of related research can be found in chaps. 7 and 8.)

Performing arts medicine refers to a specialty treating the medical problems of musicians, dancers, and other performing artists. Currently, there are 18 performing arts clinics in the United States. The journal *Medical Problems of Performing Artists* is devoted to this topic, and a search on the CAIRSS music research database under PAM (performing arts medicine) elicits more than 1,000 articles. Frequently mentioned injuries include overuse syndrome, carpal tunnel syndrome, nerve entrapment, and vocal nodules.

Triangular relationships among music therapy, music medicine, and performing arts medicine are in a process of being established.

Definitions, distinctions, research strategies, and persons involved (both as healers and as patients) are evolving. There is a strong sense among those interested that, while much growth is necessary, there is enormous potential for using music effectively as a healing agent.

Summary

Psychological perspectives of musical behavior indicate that music is significant in a number of important ways. First, they tell us that their main job is to understand and explain human behavior. Because music is a form of human behavior, the ways in which psychologists account for other forms of behavior can often be used to account for musical behavior as well. Thus, if behavioral psychologists provide a means for understanding how we learn and modify certain behaviors, they can also provide an explanation for how we learn and modify certain musical behaviors. If developmental psychologists seek to document the paths we travel from infancy to adulthood, those same techniques may be used to describe the development of musicality. If cognitive psychologists discover certain principles that govern sensory perception and organization, these same principles can be applied to the perception and organization of music.

Psychologists tell us that musical intelligence is a unique way of knowing that is supported as a viable member of the human intelligences by rigorous criteria. Considerable evidence has been gathered that indicates music to be a universally innate phenomenon of human beings. We are all musical in the same sense that we are all linguistic and mathematical. Music can also be viewed as a symbol system. Music has the power to symbolize and express a wide range of feelings. Because this expression is nonverbal, it is difficult to describe or discuss, but this fact does not make it less real or less valuable. In fact, the very ambiguity of musical expression gives it much of its potency and permits it to operate in the wider realm beyond words, unlimited by the relative specificity and exclusivity of words.

Musical personalities have been explored by psychologists. Although there is wide variation among musicians, there appears to be some consistency when musicians are compared with other groups. A relatively stable core of traits seems to include introversion (in terms of inner strength and richly diversified thought processes), pathemia (sensitivity and imaginativeness), intelligence, and psychological androgyny (sensitivity in males and self-sufficiency in females).

Just as psychologists use their knowledge and skills in helping those with behavioral problems, so do music therapists use music as a means for aiding those with a wide variety of handicapping conditions. Music is generally nonthreatening and can be used to build bridges of communication between the therapist and client. Music can increase self-esteem and help improve relationships with others. Music can also be used as a tool for learning and for bringing about desired changes in various behaviors.

Psychologists and musicians working together in the field of music psychology have increased our understanding of music, and thus its significance, in many ways over the past fifty years. Perhaps Carl Seashore, the preeminent music psychologist of the early twentieth century, best expressed the connection between psychology and music when he said,

> Considering what music meant to me then (as a young man) and what it means to me now after a life career in the science of music, there comes to me an analogy from astronomy. Then I was a stargazer; now I am an astronomer. Then the youth felt the power of music and gave expression to this feeling in the way he loved and wondered at the stars before he had studied astronomy. Now the old man feels the same "power of music," but thinks of it in the manner that the astronomer thinks of the starry heavens. Astronomy has revealed a macrocosm, the order of the universe in the large; the science of music has revealed a microcosm, the operation of law and order in the structure and operation of the musical mind. It is a wonderful thing that science makes it possible to discover, measure, and explain the operations of the musical mind in the same attitude that the astronomer explains the operation of the stars. (Seashore 1967, xi)

The multiple perspectives presented in this chapter leave no room for doubt about the influence of music on human behavior. Biologists tell us that all human beings are musical by nature; we are designed to be musical creatures. Anthropologists tell us that all human beings in all times and in all places have been musical; music is an integral part of the way we live. Sociologists tell us that just as we shape our music, it shapes us; many social interactions are shaped and modified by music. Psychologists tell us that any explanation of the mind and how it works can account for musical behavior along with all other forms of human behavior; furthermore, music provides unique access to our affective world.

Taken collectively, biological, anthropological, sociological, and psychological perspectives clearly document that music is a potent influence on human behavior. Although each area has been considered separately, the reality is that all these perspectives merge into a unified human experience. The musical experience is one that integrates body, mind, and spirit; it is both personal and corporate and operates within the context of a given time and space, yet transcends time and space. Any view of humanity consistent with the data must place music at the core of the human experience.

Everyone concerned with the uses of music in society—music educators, music therapists, music performers, music programers, composers, and others—needs to be aware of this body of research. Beyond knowing the literature, they must integrate this broad view (or these multiple views) into the fabric of their disciplines. Music education, music therapy, music performance and composition, as well as music theory and musicology, must be informed and shaped by these data. Finally, this information needs to be shared with society at large. When all of us have been made aware of the tremendous influence of music on human behavior and its influential role as a uniquely human knowledge system, music will be more accurately acknowledged for the significant role it plays in human society.

REFERENCES

Adorno, T. 1976. *Introduction to the sociology of music*. Trans. E. Ashton. New York: Seabury Press.
Arar, Y. Fighting Satan's evil in rock 'n' roll. 1982. *San Antonio Light*, 25 May.
Babbitt, M. 1958. Who cares if you listen? *High Fidelity* 8, no. 2:38–40, 126–27.
Backus, J. 1977. *The acoustical foundations of music*. 2d ed. New York: Norton.
Bahat, A. 1980. The musical traditions of the oriental Jews.*World of Music* 22, no. 2:46–55.
Ballantine, C. 1984. *Music and its social meanings*. New York: Gordon and Breach.
Barrett, D., and D. Hodges. 1995. Music loudness preferences among middle school and college students. *Texas Research Reports*. In press.
Baskerville, D. 1979. *Music business handbook and career guide*. Los Angeles: Sherwood.
Beebe, B., L. Gerstman, B. Carson, M. Dolinas, A. Zigman, H. Rosensweig, K. Faughey, and M. Korma. 1982. Rhythmic communication in the mother-infant dyad. In *Interaction rhythms: Periodicity in communication behavior*, ed. M. Davis, 79–100. New York: Human Sciences Press.
Ben-Or, N. 1978. The Alexander technique. In *Tensions in the performance of music*, ed. C. Grindea, 84–95. New York: Alexander Broude.
Birdsong, B. 1984. Motherese. In *Science yearbook 1985: New illustrated encyclopedia*, 56–66. New York: Funk and Wagnalls.
Birge, E. 1966. *History of public school music in the United States*. Washington, DC: Music Educators National Conference.
Blacking, J. 1973. *How musical is man?* Seattle: University of Washington Press.
Bohannan, P. [1981] 1983. That sync'ing feeling. Reprint. *Update* 2, no. 1:23–24.

Boiles, C. 1984. Universals of musical behavior: A taxonomic approach. *World of Music* 26, no. 2:50–64.

Booker, G. 1968. The disc jockey and his impact on teenage musical taste as reflected through a study in three north Florida cities. Ph.D. diss., Florida State University.

Boorstein, J. 1992. *The creators.* New York: Random House.

Boyd, E. 1985. Now hear this: Just don't listen. *San Antonio Today* 2:30–36.

Boyle, J., and R. Radocy. 1987. *Measurement and evaluation of musical experiences.* New York: Schirmer.

Brandfonbrener, A. 1986. Coping with stress. *Medical Problems of Performing Musicians* 1, no. 1:12–16.

Bronowski, J. 1973. *The ascent of man.* Boston: Little, Brown.

Broudy, H. 1968. The case for aesthetic education. In *Documentary report of the Tanglewood symposium,* ed. R. Choate, 9–13. Washington, DC: Music Educators National Conference.

Brown, E., and W. Hendee. 1989. Adolescents and their music. *Journal of the American Medical Association* 262, no. 12:1659–63.

Brown, F. 1982. Rhythmicity as an emerging variable for psychology. In *Rhythmic aspects of behavior,* ed. F. Brown, and R. Graeber, 3–38. Hillsdale, NJ: Lawrence Erlbaum Associates.

Brown, F., and R. Graeber, eds. 1982. *Rhythmic aspects of behavior.* Hillsdale, NJ: Lawrence Erlbaum Associates.

Bruner, J. 1969. *On knowing: Essays for the left hand.* New York: Athenuem.

Carter, S. 1982. *Music therapy for handicapped children: Mentally retarded.* Project Music Monograph Series, ed. W. Lathom and C. Eagle. Washington, DC: National Association for Music Therapy.

Chailley, J. 1964. *40,000 years of music.* New York: Farrar, Straus, and Giroux.

Chapple, E. 1982. Movement and sound: The musical language of body rhythms in interaction. In *Interaction rhythms: Periodicity in communication behavior,* ed. M. Davis, 31–51. New York: Human Sciences Press.

Cheng, N. 1987. Life and death in Shanghai. *Time Magazine,* 8 June, 42–56.

Choate, R. ed. 1968. *Documentary report of the Tanglewood symposium.* Washington, DC: Music Educators National Conference.

Christensen, P., and D. Roberts. 1989. Popular music in early adolescence. Report prepared for the Carnegie Council on Adolescent Development.

Claiborne, R. 1974. *The birth of writing.* New York: Time-Life Books.

Collins, D. 1976. *The human revolution: From ape to artist.* New York: Dutton.

Condon, W. 1982. Cultural microrhythms. In *Interaction rhythms: Periodicity in communication behavior,* ed. M. Davis, 53–77. New York: Human Sciences Press.

Constable, G. 1973. *The Neanderthals.* New York: Time-Life Books.

Cooper, B. 1982. *Images of American society in pop music.* Chicago: Nelson-Hall.

Cowan, W. 1979. The development of the brain. *Scientific American* 241, no. 3:113–33.

Csikszentmihalyi, M., and E. Rochberg-Halton. 1981. Object lessons. *Psychology Today* 15, no. 12:78–85.

Dasilva, F., A. Blasi, and D. Dees. 1984. *The sociology of music.* Notre Dame, IN: University of Notre Dame Press.

Davis, M., ed. 1982. *Interaction rhythms: Periodicity in communication behavior*. New York: Human Sciences Press.

Dearding, R., and C. Dearding. 1981. *The Guinness book of music*. Guinness Speculations Ltd.

Denisoff, R. 1983. *Sing a song of social significance*. Bowling Green, OH: Bowling Green State University Popular Press.

Derloshon, J. 1994. *Music USA 1994*. Carlsbad, CA: National Association for Music Merchants.

Deshpande, V. 1973. *Indian musical traditions: An aesthetic study of the Gharanas in Hindustani music*. Trans. S. Deshpande. Bombay, India: R. G. Bhatkal.

Deutsch, D., and J. Deutsch, eds. 1975. *Short-term memory*. New York: Academic Press.

Dorfman, A. 1984. How Muzak manipulates you. *Science Digest* 92, no. 5: 26.

Dubos, R. 1974. *Beast or angel? Choices that make us human*. New York: Scribner.

Dubos, R. 1981. *Celebrations of life*. New York: McGraw-Hill.

Eagle, C. 1982. *Music therapy for handicapped individuals: An annotated and indexed bibliography*. Washington, DC: National Association for Music Therapy.

Eagle, C., and D. Hodges. 1995. CAIRSS for music: Accessing music medicine research. In *MusicMedicine 2*, ed. R. Spintge and R. Droh. St. Louis: MMB Music. In press.

Ellison, J. 1984. Gifted and talented. *Psychology Today* 18, no. 6:19.

Elmer-DeWitt, P. 1987. From Mozart to megabytes. *Time Magazine*, 16 March, 71.

Ember, C., and M. Ember. 1973. *Cultural anthropology*. Englewood Cliffs, NJ: Prentice-Hall.

Farb, P. 1978. *Humankind*. New York: Bantam Books.

Farmer, H. 1969. The music of ancient Egypt. In *Ancient and Oriental music*, ed. E. Wellesz, 255–82. London: Oxford University Press.

Fischman, J. 1987. The ups and downs of teenage life. *Psychology Today* 21, no. 5:56–57.

Folkard, S. 1982. Circadian rhythms and human memory. In *Rhythmic aspects of behavior*, ed. F. Brown, and R. Graeber, 241–272. Hillsdale, NJ: Lawrence Erlbaum Associates.

Gage, N., and D. Berliner. 1975. *Educational psychology*. Chicago: Rand McNally.

Gardner, H. 1983. *Frames of mind: The theory of multiple intelligences*. New York: Basic Books.

Gaston, E., ed. 1968. *Music in therapy*. New York: Macmillan.

George, W. 1980. Measurement and evaluation of musical behavior. In *Handbook of music psychology*, ed. D. Hodges, 291–391. Lawrence, KS: National Association for Music Therapy.

Goleman, D. 1986. Rethinking the value of intelligence tests. *New York Times*, 9 November.

Goldstein, A. 1980. Thrills in response to music and other stimuli. *Physiological Psychology* 8, no. 1:126–29.

Haack, P. 1982. Is big brother watching? *Music Educators Journal* 68, no. 9:25–27.

Haack, P. 1995. Music, violence, and music behavior. Typescript.

Haider, M., and E. Groll-Knapp. 1981. Psychophysiological investigation into the stress experienced by musicians in a symphony orchestra. In *Stress and music*, ed. M. Piperek, 15–34. Vienna: Wilhelm Braumuller.

Hall, E. 1976. *Beyond culture*. New York: Anchor Press.

Hamann, D. 1982. An assessment of anxiety in instrumental and vocal performances. *Journal of Research in Music Education* 30, no. 2:77–90.

Hamann, D. 1983. Anxiety and musical performance. How will it affect your students? *Update* 2, no. 1: 7–9.

Hamann, D., and M. Sobaje. 1982. Anxiety and music: A study of musical performance and its relation to anxiety theories. Typescript.

Hammond, M. 1982. Unearthing the oldest known Maya. *National Geographic* 162, no. 1:126–40.

Hanna, J. 1984. Towards discovering the universals of dance. *World of Music* 26, no. 2:88–101.

Hanshumaker, J. 1980. The effects of arts education on intellectual and social development: A review of selected research. *Bulletin of the Council for Research in Music Education* 61:10–28.

Harker, D. 1980. *One for the money: Politics and popular song*. London: Hutchinson.

Hodges, D. 1982. Musical identification and lyric recall of selected brand name commercials. Typescript.

Hofmann, D. 1982. Music educators in Israel: Challenge to a multi-cultural society. In *International society for music education yearbook*, ed. J. Dobbs, 9:148–51.

Hood, M. 1971. *The Ethnomusicologist*. New York: McGraw-Hill.

Hooper, J. 1981. Releasing the mystic in your brain. *Science Digest 89* 4:78–81, 120–22.

Hooper, J. 1982. Mind tripping. *Omni* , October, 154–60.

Jenkins, J. 1970. *Musical instruments*. London: County Hall.

Jones, B. 1986. Saturday morning wasteland. *Kansas Alumni*, June, 21–27.

Keali'inohomoku, J. 1985. Music and dance of the Hawaiian and Hopi peoples. In *Becoming human through music*, 5–22. Reston, VA: Music Educators National Conference.

Kemp, A. 1981. Personality differences between the players of string, woodwind, brass, and keyboard instruments, and singers. *Bulletin of the Council for Research in Music Education* 66–67:33–38.

Kemp, A. 1982. The personality structure of the musician. *Psychology of Music* 10, no. 2:3–6.

Kemp, A. 1985. Psychological androgyny in musicians. *Bulletin of the Council for Research in Music Education* 85:102–08.

Kendig, F., and G. Levitt. 1982. Overture: Sex, math and music. *Science Digest* 90, no. 1:72–73.

Khe, T. V. 1984. Buddhist music in eastern Asia. *The World of Music* 26, no. 3:22–30.

Koepp, S. 1985. Little labels. *Time Magazine*, 11 March, 51.

Kovel, J. 1976. *A complete guide to therapy*. New York: Pantheon Books.

Kraeling, C., and L. Mowry. 1969. Music in the Bible. In *Ancient and Oriental music*, ed. E. Wellesz, 283–312. London: Oxford University Press.

Kripke, D. 1982. Ultradian rhythms in behavior and physiology. In *Rhythmic aspects of behavior*, ed. F. Brown, and R. Graeber, 313–343. Hillsdale, NJ: Lawrence Erlbaum Associates.

Larson, R., R. Kubey, and J. Colletti. 1989. Changing channels: Early adolescent media choices and shifting investments in family and friends. *Journal of Youth and Adolescence* 18, no. 6:583–99.

Leakey, M. 1983. Tanzania's stone age art. *National Geographic* 164, no. 1:84–99.

Leakey, R. 1981. *The making of mankind.* New York: Dutton.

LeBlanc, A. 1995. *A theory of music performance anxiety.* East Lansing, MI: Michigan State University. Typescript.

Lefrancois, G. 1979. *Psychology for teaching.* 3d ed. Belmont, CA: Wadsworth.

Lehrer, P. 1978. Performance anxiety and how to control it: A psychologist's perspective. In *Tensions in the performance of music,* ed. C. Grindea, 134–154. New York: Alexander Broude.

Leroi-Gourhan, A. 1982. The archeology of the Lascaux cave. *Scientific American* 246, no. 6:104–12.

Lewis, R., ed. 1963. *In praise of music.* New York: Orion Press.

Ling, Y. 1984. China recovers her past in folk songs—a report. *World of Music* 24, no. 1:44–49.

Lipton, J., and R. Builione. N.d. Is it true what they say about classical musicians? Stereotypes and personality traits. Typescript.

List, G. 1984. Concerning the concept of the universal and music. *World Music* 26, no. 2:40–47.

Lomax, A. 1968. *Folk song style and culture.* New Brunswick, NJ: Transaction Books.

Lomax, A. 1982. The cross-cultural variation of rhythmic style. In *Interaction rhythms: Periodicity in communicative behavior,* ed. M. Davis, 149–74. New York: Human Sciences Press.

Malmo, R. 1975. *On emotions, needs, and our archaic brain.* New York: Holt, Rinehart and Winston.

Marquis. 1983. *Music industry directory.* New York: Marquis Professional Publications.

Marshack, A. 1975. Exploring the mind of ice age man. *National Geographic* 147, no. 1:62–89.

Martinez, J. 1986. Former Satanist warns of danger to youth. *San Antonio Light,* 28 September.

Mathiot, M, and E. Carlock. 1982. On operationalizing the notion of rhythm in social behavior. In *Interaction rhythms: Periodicity in communicative behavior,* ed. M. Davis, 175–94. New York: Human Sciences Press.

McCarthy, P. 1987. Rock fans: A thrill-seeking bunch. *Psychology Today* 21:19.

McCullough, D. 1995. A sense of proportion. *American Educator* 19, no. 1:38–44.

Menuhin, Y., and C. Davis. 1979. *The music of man.* New York: Methuen.

Merriam, A. 1964. *The anthropology of music.* Chicago: Northwestern University Press.

Miller, S. 1982. *Music therapy for handicapped children: Speech impaired.* Project Music Monograph Series, ed. W. Lathom and C. Eagle. Washington, DC: National Association for Music Therapy.

Moller, L. 1980. Music in Germany during the Third Reich: The use of music for propaganda. *Music Educators Journal* 67, no. 3:40–44.

Monmaney, T. 1987. Key notes on the mind. *Omni* 9, no. 4:45–46, 67.

Montagu, A. 1977. *Life before birth.* New York: New American Library.

Montagu, A. 1978. *Touching: The human significance of the skin.* 2d ed. New York: Harper and Row.

Montagu, A., and F. Matson. 1979. *The human connection*. New York: McGraw-Hill.

Mumford, L. 1966. *The myth of the machine: Technics and human development*. New York: Harcourt Brace Jovanovich.

Murray, A. 1986. The Alexander technique. *Medical Problems of Performing Musicians* 1, no. 4:131–32.

Music Educators Journal. 1982. Careers and music. *Music Educators Journal* 69:2.

Music Educators Journal. 1985. Arts beat sports at attendance game. *Music Educators Journal* 71:6–11.

Music Educators National Conference. 1985. *Becoming human through music*. Reston, VA: Music Educators National Conference.

Muzak. 1974. *Muzak: Digest of selected Muzak studies and attitude surveys*. New York: Muzak.

Muzak. 1991. *Muzak research review*. Seattle: Muzak.

Naeser, M., and N. Helm-Estabrooks. 1985. CT scan lesion localization and response to melodic intonation therapy with nonfluent aphasia cases. *Cortex* 21, no. 2:203–23.

Nagel, J. 1984. Reducing students' stagefright: Can music teachers be psychologists? *Update* 2, no. 3:16–18.

Naitoh, P. 1982. Chronobiologic approach for optimizing human performance. In *Rhythmic aspects of behavior*, ed. F. Brown, and R. Graeber, 41–103. Hillsdale, NJ: Lawrence Erlbaum Associates.

Nies, A. 1986. Clinical pharmacology of beta-adrenergic blockers. *Medical Problems of Performing Musicians* 1, no. 1:25–29.

Nettl, B. 1977. On the question of universals. *The World of Music* 19:2–13.

Nettl, B. 1983. *The study of ethnomusicology*. Urbana: University of Illinois Press.

Nideffer, R., and N. Hessler. 1978. Controlling performance anxiety. *College Music Symposium* 18, no. 1:146–53.

Nketia, J. 1984. Universal perspectives in ethnomusicology. *The World of Music* 26, no. 2:3–20.

Parker, T. 1984. *In one day*. Boston: Houghton Mifflin.

Paul, D. 1982. *Music therapy for handicapped children: Emotionally disturbed*. Project Music Monograph Series, ed. W. Lathom and C. Eagle. Washington, DC: National Association for Music Therapy.

Periot-Garcia, L., J. Galloway, and A. Lommel. 1967. *Prehistoric and primitive art*. New York: Abrams.

Peters, D., and S. Peters, with C. Merrill. 1985. *Hidden persuader: The truth about backmasking*. Minneapolis: Bethany House.

Pfeiffer, J. 1969. *The emergence of man*. New York: Harper and Row.

Pfeiffer, J. 1980a. Icons in the shadows. *Science80* 1, no. 4:72–77.

Pfeiffer, J. 1980b. Religious roots. *Science80* 1, no. 8:14–16.

Piperek, M. 1981. Psychological stress and strain factors in the work of a symphony orchestra musician. In *Stress and music*, ed. M. Piperek, 3–14. Vienna: Wilhelm Braumuller.

Prideaux, T. 1973. *Cro-Magnon man*. New York: Time-Life Books.

Putman, J. 1988. The search for modern humans. *National Geographic* 174, no. 4:438–77.

Rauscher, F., G. Shaw, and K. Ky. 1993. Music and spatial task performance. *Nature* 365:611.

Rauscher, F., G. Shaw, L. Levine, and E. Wright. 1993. Pilot study indicates music training of three-year-olds enhances specific spatial reasoning skills. Paper presented at the Economic Summit of the National Association of Music Merchants, Newport Beach, CA.

Rauscher, F., G. Shaw, L. Levine, K. Ky, and E. Wright. 1994. Music and spatial task performance: A causal relationship. Paper presented at the American Psychological Association Annual Convention, Los Angeles, CA.

Reck, D. 1977. *Music of the whole earth.* New York: Scribner.

Reimer, B. 1989. *A philosophy of music education,* 2d ed. Englewood Cliffs, NJ: Prentice-Hall.

Rensberger, B. 1981. Facing the past. *Science81* 2, no. 8:41–50.

Restak, R. 1983. Newborn knowledge. In *Science yearbook 1984: New illustrated encyclopedia,* 48–52. New York: Funk and Wagnalls.

Reubart, D. 1985. *Anxiety and musical performance: On playing the piano from memory.* New York: Da Capo Press.

Robertson, C. 1985. Process of transmission: Music education and social inclusion. In *Becoming human through music,* 95–113. Reston, VA: Music Educators National Conference.

Romerhaus, B. 1968. Clinical experiences with hospitalized early childhood schizophrenic children. In *Music in therapy,* ed. E. Gaston, 193–195. New York: Macmillan.

Sagan, C. 1978. *Murmurs of earth: The voyager interstellar record.* New York: Random House.

Salewski, B. 1982. An application of observation and self-report methods to the measurement of music performance anxiety. Typescript.

San Antonio Light. 1984. Games on verge of day in the sun. *San Antonio Light,* 28 July.

San Antonio Light. 1985. 160,000 rock for African famine relief. *San Antonio Light,* 14 July.

San Antonio Light. 1986. Argument over loud music leads to death. *San Antonio Light,* 10 June.

San Antonio Light. 1987. Rock fans need music "fix." *San Antonio Light,* 11 June.

Scheflen, A. 1982. Preface: Comments on the significance of interaction rhythms. In *Interaction rhythms: Periodicity in communicative behavior,* ed. M. Davis, 13–22. New York: Human Sciences Press.

Scherer, B. 1995. Can we save our audiences? *BBC Music Magazine,* March: 25–26.

Schleuter, S. L. 1971. An investigation of the interrelation of personality traits, musical aptitude, and musical achievement. *Experimental research in the psychology of music: 8. Studies in the psychology of music,* 90–102.

Schulz, W. 1981. Analysis of a symphony orchestra: Sociological and sociopsychological aspects. In *Stress and music,* ed. M. Piperek, 35–56. Vienna: Wilhelm Braumuller.

Schuyler, P. 1981. Music and meaning among the Gnawa religious brotherhood of Morocco. *World of Music* 23, no. 1:3–10.

Schwadron, A. 1967. *Aesthetics: Dimensions for music education*. Washington, DC: Music Educators National Conference.

Seashore, C. [1938] 1967. *Psychology of music*. Reprint. New York: Dover.

Shen, S. 1987. Acoustics of ancient Chinese bells. *Scientific American* 256:104–10.

Shemel, S., and M. Krasilovsky. 1985. *This business of music*. New York: Billboard Publications.

Silbermann, A. 1982. What questions does the empirical sociology of music attempt to answer? *International Social Science Journal* 94, no. 34:571–81.

Silverman, D. 1983. Music rocks cablevision [the] wrong way. *San Antonio Light*, 20 July.

Small, Christopher. 1977. *Music—society—education*. New York: Schirmer.

Smiley, J. 1986. Let's start a rhythm band. M. Mus. project, University of Texas at San Antonio.

Smith, G., and M. Long. 1980. Wilderness art: Utah's rock art. *National Geographic* 157, no. 1:94–117.

Soundposts. 1986. 400,000 Participate in WLC '86. *Soundposts* 2, no. 4:2–4.

Spintge, R., and R. Droh. eds. 1992. *MusicMedicine*. St. Louis: MMB Music.

Spintge, R., and R. Pratt. eds. 1995. *MusicMedicine 2* St. Louis: MMB Music. In press.

Springer, S., and G. Deutsch. 1989. *Left brain, right brain*. 3d ed. New York: Freeman.

Stanford, D. 1979. Bison kill by ice age hunters. *National Geographic* 155, no. 1:114–21.

Steinel, D. 1984. *Music and music education: Data and information*. Reston, VA: Music Educators National Conference.

Stern, D. 1982. Some interactive functions of rhythm changes between mother and infant. In *Interaction rhythms: Periodicity in communicative behavior*, ed. M. Davis, 101–17. New York: Human Sciences Press.

Stickney, J. 1982. The sound of music from a lost world. *Discover*, May, 57–59.

Storm, B. 1993. The role of music in the life and death of a teenager. M.A. music research project, University of Minnesota.

Strunk, O. 1965. *Source readings in music history: Antiquity and the middle ages*. New York: Norton.

Stuart, G., and W. Garrett. 1981. Maya art treasures discovered in a cave. *National Geographic* 160, no. 2:220–35.

Stuessy, C. 1990. *Rock and roll: Its history and stylistic development*. Englewood Cliffs, NJ: Prentice-Hall.

Sullivan, L. 1984. Sacred music and sacred time. *World of Music* 26, no. 3:33–51.

Tait, M., and P. Haack. 1984. *Principles and processes of music education: New perspectives*. New York: Teachers College Press.

Taylor, J. 1986. Poll shows music matters. *San Antonio Light*, 5 July.

Teaching Music Today. 1995. Fact Sheet. *Teaching Music Today*, p. 47.

Thaut, M., G. McIntosh, and R. Rice. 1995. Rhythmic auditory stimulation as an entrainment and therapy technique in gait of stroke and Parkinson's patients. In *MusicMedicine*, 2, eds. R. Pratt and R. Spintge. St. Louis: MMB Music. In press.

Thayer, R. 1972. The interrelation of personality traits, musical achievement, and different measures of musical aptitude. In *Research in the psychology of music*, vol. 8, ed. E. Gordon, 103–18. Iowa City: University of Iowa Press.

Thomas, L. 1974. *The lives of a cell: Notes of a biology watcher.* New York: Bantam Books.

Thompson, P. 1994. Adolescents and media music. *Update* 12, no. 2:9–15.

Turner, V. 1982. *Celebration: Studies in festivity and ritual.* Washington, DC: Smithsonian Institution Press.

Verny, T., with J. Kelly. 1981. *The secret life of the unborn child.* New York: Summit Books.

von Puttkamer, W. 1979. Man in the Amazon: Stone age present meets stone age past. *National Geographic* 155, no. 1:60–83.

Walls, K., J. Taylor, and J. Falzone. 1992. The effects of subliminal suggestions and music experience on the perception of tempo in music. *Journal of Music Therapy* 29, no. 3:186–97.

Wardle, A. 1975. Behavior modification by reciprocal inhibition of instrumental music performance anxiety. In *Research in music behavior: Modifying music behavior in the classroom,* ed. C. Madsen, R. Greer, and C. Madsen, 191–205. New York: Teachers College Press.

Washington International Arts Letter. 1992. *Washington International Arts Letter* 31, nos. 6 and 7:1.

Weaver, R. 1982. Behavioral aspects of circadian rhythmicity. In *Rhythmic aspects of behavior,* ed. F. Brown, and R. Graeber, 105–71. Hillsdale, NJ: Lawrence Erlbaum Associates.

Wehr, T. 1982. Circadian rhythm disturbances in depression and mania. In *Rhythmic aspects of behavior,* ed. F. Brown, and R. Graeber, 399–428. Hillsdale, NJ: Lawrence Erlbaum Associates.

Weisblatt, S. 1986. A psychoanalytic view of performance anxiety. *Medical Problems of Performing Musicians* 1, no. 2:64–67.

White, E., and D. Brown. 1973. *The first man.* New York:Time-Life Books.

Wilford, J. 1986. Artistry of the ice age. *New York Times Magazine,* 2 October, 46–60.

Williams, L. 1980. *The dancing chimpanzee.* New York: Allison and Busby.

Wilson, F. 1986. Music and medicine: Inderal for stage fright? *Piano Quarterly* 134:30–35.

Wintle, R. 1983. The emotional impact of music on television commercials. Rev. E. Ostleitner. *Bulletin of the Council for Research in Music Education* 74:88–90.

Woodward, W. 1982. *Insider's guide to advertising music.* New York: Art Direction Book Co.

Young, J. 1978. *Programs of the brain.* New York: Oxford University Press.

Contributors

Harold F. Abeles is Professor of Music and Education at Teachers College, Columbia University.

Dale L. Bartlett is Professor of Music Education and Music Therapy at Michigan State University.

Joe B. Buttram is Professor of Music Education at Ball State University.

Jin Won Chung is Adjunct Professor of Music at Ewha Women's University in Seoul, Korea.

Charles T. Eagle is Professor Emeritus of Music Therapy at Southern Methodist University.

Paul A. Haack is Professor of Music Education at the University of Minnesota.

Donald A. Hodges is Professor of Music Education at the University of Texas at San Antonio.

Wanda B. Lathom-Radocy is Professor Emerita of Music Therapy at the University of Missouri at Kansas City.

Scott D. Lipscomb is Assistant Professor of Music at the University of Texas at San Antonio.

Patrick T. McMullen is Professor of Music Education at the State University of New York at Fredonia.

Rudolf E. Radocy is Professor of Music Education at the University of Kansas.

Author Index

Subject Index